Bill Loesch

Human Resources Management

Human Resources Management

Perspectives and Issues

Gerald R. Ferris
Texas A&M University

Kendrith M. Rowland
University of Illinois at Urbana-Champaign

Allyn and Bacon, Inc.
Boston • London • Sydney • Toronto

A Division of Simon & Schuster
160 Gould Street
Needham Heights, Massachusetts 02194–2310

A previous edition was published under the title *Current Issues in Personnel Management,* by Kendrith M. Rowland and Gerald R. Ferris, copyright © 1986, 1983, and 1980 by Allyn and Bacon, Inc.

Series Editor: Jack Peters
Senior Editorial Assistant: Dottie Bibbo
Production Administrator: Annette Joseph
Production Coordinator: Susan Freese
Editorial-Production Service: Kailyard Associates
Cover Administrator: Linda K. Dickinson
Cover Designer: Lynda Fishbourne

Library of Congress Cataloging-in-Publication Data

Human resources management.

Includes index.
1. Personnel management. I. Ferris, Gerald R. II. Rowland, Kendrith Martin.
HF5549.H8735 1988 658.3 87–35067
ISBN 0–205–11381–8

Printed in the United States of America

10 9 8 7 6 5 4 3 2 1 93 92 91 90 89 88

Contents

Preface

About ten years ago, we decided that a book of current readings with an applied orientation was needed in the field of personnel management. At the time, few readings books existed in the field, and most of those were aimed at a reasonably high level, focusing on articles from the more scholarly journals. This was also a time when the field of personnel management was undergoing change, and people were beginning to look upon it and its potential role within organizations with more respect. So, along with a couple of colleagues, we published the first edition of *Current Issues in Personnel Management* in 1980.

Three years later we published the second edition of *Current Issues,* continuing the emphasis on applied articles and adding evidence of the shifts in personnel management attitudes. The third edition was published in 1986 with a similar focus as the two previous editions but also contained some notable changes. It addressed the rapidly emerging theme of strategic human resources management, a concept that was and continues to be met with skepticism concerning both its value and viability. Our position has been more sympathetic and supportive. Rather than dismiss it as a passing fad, we prefer to regard strategic human resources management as a concept that is at a preliminary point in its evolution, with much need for development but also with much opportunity and potential for contribution.

Historically, this brings us to the present volume. As a result of our own thinking and rethinking over the years, the present book carries a different title. In the interest of being current with perspectives, issues, and ideas, as well as terminology, we simply adopted the more contemporary title of *Human Resources Management: Perspectives and Issues.* In many respects, our mission has not changed. We continue to focus on the needs of undergraduate, professional, and master's-level courses in personnel and human resources management. In the process, we have attempted to conceptualize, identify, and articulate what we consider the important contemporary perspectives and issues in the field and then to organize a set of current readings that addresses these perspectives and issues with a decidedly applied rather than scholarly orientation.

This volume consists of fifty-eight readings organized into nine chapters. In a field as dynamic as personnel and human resources management, there is particular need for up-to-date material. Of the fifty-eight readings, twenty-five were published since 1985 and eight were written especially for this volume (comprising 57 percent of the book), and all but one of the remaining twenty-five pieces were published since 1982. We have always felt that original papers are particularly important because they offer the latest in current thinking. Thus, eight original papers, developed specifically for this book, are included on the topics of strategic human resources management, career planning, recruitment, interviewing, affirmative action, feedback, work stress, and employee assistance programs.

Acknowledgments

We would like to gratefully acknowledge the assistance and support provided by the many people who helped make *HRM* possible. First, we extend a personal expression of appreciation to our friend and editor at Allyn and Bacon, Jack Peters. Jack has been with us a long time, a consistently patient and supportive key player.

Second, we would like to thank our colleagues who gave unselfishly of their time to contribute original papers for this book. They are Terry Beehr (Central Michigan), Pat Fandt (Central Florida), Don Fedor (Washington State), Kristofer Fenlason (Central Michigan), Dave Gilmore (North Carolina—Charlotte), Micki Kacmar (Texas A&M), Tom Kolenko (Wake Forest), Ed Marlow (Eastern Illinois), Nancy Marlow (Eastern Illinois), Nancy Napier (Boise State), and Chathapuram Ramanathan (Southern Illinois).

Third, we would like to thank three graduate students who assisted in the search for articles and the final preparation of the manuscript: Mark Crisp, Micki Kacmar, and Valerie Yates, all of Texas A&M University. We also extend a special thank-you to Argie Butler and Debby Simpson for their clerical help.

G. R. F.
K. M. R.

Human Resources Management

CHAPTER 1

Strategic Human Resources Management

Although the field of personnel and human resources management (PHRM) has existed for nearly seventy years, only recently has there been some major redirection in thought concerning its importance to the effectiveness of organizations. For many years, PHRM was viewed as a maintenance function, a repository of files and information, but nothing that had any noticeable impact on the "bottom line."

During the mid to late 1960s and 1970s, a different perspective developed, elevating the status of PHRM. A number of factors contributed to this change and to the practice of PHRM in organizations. Perhaps most critical was the enactment of a considerable amount of federal legislation, particularly with respect to fair employment practices. As a result, the personnel function gained more visibility and influence as it acquired responsibility for a variety of critical interactions with powerful federal regulatory agencies, such as the Equal Employment Opportunity Commission (EEOC), the Occupational Safety and Health Administration (OSHA), and the Internal Revenue Service (IRS), which carefully monitored—and continue to monitor—the employment practices of organizations with respect to fairness, health and safety, and retirement income security. Other factors that led to the increased importance of PHRM include the focus on productivity and the changing nature and demographics of the United States work force.

All these factors, when placed in the context of significant economic and political change in the rest of the world, have created the need for a new, more business-focused perspective on the field, that of strategic human resources management (HRM). It essentially takes a broader, more integrated view of the personnel function, seeks to link it to the long-term strategies of the organization, and asks how the personnel function can help accomplish those strategies. In this environment, the importance of

PHRM will continue to increase as the field proactively and creatively responds to changing requirements and expectations.

The readings in this chapter discuss both future directions and challenges for personnel management, as well as the nature of strategic human resources management. In the first article, Tichy, Fombrun, and Devanna present a framework for conceptualizing strategic human resources management. They then describe, with illustrative examples from many companies, how human resources management can be effectively linked to the strategic management of the firm.

In the second article, Napier focuses on the integration of strategic management, human resources management, and organizational effectiveness and discusses the relevant issues and research evidence available to date. She then proposes a framework that illustrates how the three foregoing components influence each other as a basis for potential integrative actions.

In the final article of Chapter 1, Ferris and Curtin discuss the special roles of the personnel function in organizational effectiveness. In this regard, they examine organizational entry and exit, work redesign, and planning and evaluation.

Suggestions for Further Reading

Baird, L., & Meshoulom, I. (1984). Strategic human resource management: Implications for training human resource professionals. *Training and Development Journal, 38,* 76–78.

Butler, J. E., Ferris, G. R., & Smith, D. A. (1988). Exploring some critical dimensions of strategic human resources management. In R. S. Schuler, S. A. Youngblood, & V. Huber (Eds.), *Readings in personnel and human resource management* (3rd ed.). St. Paul: West.

Fombrun, C. J. (1982). Environmental trends create new pressures on human resources. *Journal of Business Strategy, 3,* 61–69.

Golden, K. A., & Ramanujam, V. (1985). Between a dream and a nightmare: On the integration of the human resource management and strategic business planning process. *Human Resource Management, 24,* 429–454.

Kandel, W. L. (1984). Preventive law and personnel policies. *Employee Relations Law Journal, 10,* 120–128.

Magnus, M. (1983). Trends and issues in personnel management. *Personnel Journal, 62,* 238–242.

Miles, R. E., & Snow, C. C. (1984). Designing strategic human resources systems. *Organizational Dynamics, 12,* 36–52.

Miller, E. L., Beechler, S., Bhatt, B., & Nath, R. (1986). The relationship between the global strategic planning process, and the human resource management function. *Human Resource Planning, 9,* 9–23.

Napier, N. H., & Peterson, R. B. (1984). Putting human resource management at the line manager level. *Business Horizons, 27,* 72–81.

O'Toole, J. (1985). Employee practices at the best managed companies. *California Management Review, 28,* 35–66.

Strategic Human Resource Management

Noel M. Tichy
Charles J. Fombrun
Mary Anne Devanna

Technological, economic, and demographic changes are pressuring organizations to use more effective human resource management. While sagging productivity and worker alienation have popularized management tools such as quality circles and profit sharing plans, the long-run competitiveness of American industry will require considerably more sophisticated approaches to the human resource input that deal with its strategic role in organizational performance.

Recent attacks on American business have stressed the short-run financial outlook of its management and its distinctly callous treatment of workers. The Japanese organization, on the other hand, is seen as the prototype of the future, as its planning systems center on worker loyalty.

This article, however, argues that we should not evaluate the Japanese organization per se. Rather, we should focus on human resource management in terms of its strategic role in both the formulation and the implementation of long-run plans. The strategic human resource concepts and tools needed are fundamentally different from the stock in trade of traditional personnel administration. This article, therefore, stresses the strategic level of human resource management at the expense of some of the operational concerns of the standard personnel organization. Several companies are described as examples of sophisticated American organizations that have instituted strategic human resource management as an integral component of their management process. Specifically, this article presents a framework for conceptualizing human resource management; links human resource management to general strategic management; and describes some current applications of human resource management as a strategic tool in achieving corporate objectives.

STRATEGIC MANAGEMENT

Three core elements are necessary for firms to function effectively:

1. *Mission and Strategy.* The organization has to have a reason for being, a means for using money, material, information, and people to carry out the mission;

2. *Organization Structure.* People are organized to carry out the mission of the organization and to do the necessary tasks;

3. *Human Resource Management.* People are recruited into the organization to do the jobs defined by the division of labor. Performance must be monitored, and rewards must be given to keep individuals productive.

Figure 1 presents these basic elements as interrelated systems that are embedded in the work environment. In the past, human resource management has been largely missing from the general strategic management process. Thus, our aim here is to help make human resource manage-

Reprinted from "Strategic Human Resource Management" by N. M. Tichy, C. J. Fombrun, and M. A. Devanna, *Sloan Management Review,* Winter 1982, pp. 47–61, by permission of the publisher.

Figure 1
Strategic Management and Environmental Pressures

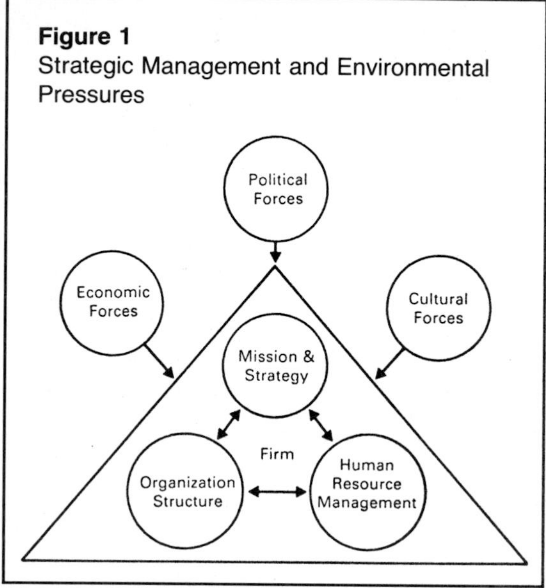

ment an integral part of the strategic arena in organizations.

Strategy is defined as a process through which the basic mission and objectives of the organization are set and a process through which the organization uses its resources to achieve its objectives. In turn, structure reflects "the organization of work into roles such as production, finance, marketing, and so on; the recombining of the roles into departments or divisions around functions, products, regions, or markets and the distribution of power across this role structure."[1] The structure of the organization embodies the fundamental division of labor, describes the basic nature of the jobs to be done, and aggregates them into groups, functions, or businesses. It also defines the degree of centralized control that top management holds over the operating units.

Structure Follows Strategy

In his historical study of American industry, Chandler provided a convincing argument that the structure of an organization follows from its strategy.[2] He identified four major strategies that resulted in structural or organizational design changes. They are: (1) expansion of volume; (2) geographic dispersion; (3) vertical integration; and (4) product diversification. Each of these strategies is followed by a structural transformation from function through to product forms. But while Chandler's work focused attention on the structural supports needed to drive a strategy and on the use of the organization's formal design in the implementation of a strategy, he did not discuss the role of the human resource systems in the implementation process.

STRATEGY, STRUCTURE, AND HUMAN RESOURCE MANAGEMENT

The addition of human resource management to the strategic arena was presented by Galbraith and Nathanson who expanded on Chandler's analysis.[3] They focused on such issues as fitting performance measures to the strategy and structure as well as to rewards, career paths, and leadership styles. Table 1 modifies and expands upon their work to illustrate how strategy, structure, and human resource management systems fit together. The fundamental strategic management problem is to keep the strategy, structure, and human resource dimensions of the organization in direct alignment. In the rest of this article, we will discuss some of the human resource management concepts and tools that are needed to describe completely the strategic management role.

Human Resource Policies: A Context

A number of fundamental organizational policies provide the context for considering human resource management. These policies vary from organization to organization and tend to limit or constrain the actual design of a human resource system. While they are not the focus of this article, they are identified as important contextual issues that organizations must consider along the way. These policies are:

1. *Management Philosophy.* A basic policy that influences the overall design of a human resource system is the organization's management philosophy, i.e., its "psychological contract" with employees. An organization typically specifies the

Table 1
Human Resource Management Links to Strategy and Structure

		Human Resource Management			
Strategy	*Structure*	*Selection*	*Appraisal*	*Rewards*	*Development*
1. Single product	Functional	Functionally oriented: subjective criteria used	Subjective: measure via personal contact	Unsystematic and allocated in a paternalistic manner	Unsystematic largely through job experiences: single function focus
2. Single product (vertically integrated)	Functional	Functionally oriented: standardized criteria used	Impersonal: based on cost and productivity data	Related to performance and productivity	Functional specialists with some generalists: largely through job rotation
3. Growth by Acquisition (holding company) of Unrelated Businesses	Separate, Self-contained Businesses	Functionally oriented, but varies from business to business in terms of how systematic	Impersonal: based on return on investment and profitability	Formula-based and includes return on investment and profitability	Cross-functional but not cross-business
4. Related Diversification of Product Lines through Internal Growth and Acquisition	Multidivisional	Functionally and generalist oriented: systematic criteria used	Impersonal: based on return on investment, productivity and subjective assessment of contribution to overall company	Large bonuses: based on profitability and subjective assessment of contribution to overall company	Cross-functional, cross-divisional, and cross-corporate/divisional: formal
5. Multiple Products in Multiple Countries	Global Organization (geographic center and world-wide)	Functionally and generalist oriented: systematic criteria used	Impersonal: based on multiple goals such as return on investment, profit tailored to product and country	Bonuses: based on multiple planned goals with moderate top management discretion	Cross-divisional and cross-subsidiary to corporate: formal and systematic

Adapted from J. Galbraith and D. Nathanson, Strategy Implementation: The Role of Structure and Process *(St. Paul, MN: West, 1978).*

nature of the exchange with its employees. On one end of the spectrum is "a fair day's work for a fair day's pay," a purely extrinsic *quid pro quo* contract. Many U.S. blue-collar jobs fit this description. At the other extreme is the contract that stresses "challenging, meaningful work in return for a loyal, committed, and self-motivated employee," an intrinsically oriented contract. Some of the Scandinavian companies committed to quality of work life are positioned at this end of the spectrum. Such organizations typically develop people from within and seldom go to the external labor market to fill job openings.

2. *Reliance on Development or Selection.* Organizations vary in the degree to which they weigh the impact of these two factors of performance. Some companies do almost no training or development. Other companies, such as AT&T, invest heavily in development. A company such as GE ascribes to a management philosophy that stresses both careful selection and development.

3. *Group versus Individual Performance.* The human resource systems can be geared toward collective, group-based performance or individual performance, or toward some mixture of the two. When the emphasis is on group performance, the selection must take into account social compatibility; the appraisal system must be group focused; and rewards must provide incentives for the work group.

THE HUMAN RESOURCE CYCLE

In light of these policies, we may now focus on four generic processes or functions that are performed by a human resource system in all organizations—selection, appraisal, rewards, and development. These four processes reflect sequential managerial tasks. Figure 2 represents them in terms of a human resource cycle. Clearly the dependent variable in Figure 2 is performance; the human resource elements are designed to impact performance at both the individual and the organizational levels.

Performance, in other words, is a function of all the human resource components: selecting people who are best able to perform the jobs defined by the structure; motivating employees by rewarding them judiciously; training and developing employees for future performance; and appraising employees in order to justify the rewards. In addition performance is a function of the organizational context and resources surrounding the individual. Thus, strategy and structure also impact performance through the ways jobs are designed, through how the organization is structured, and through how well services or products are planned to meet environmental threats and opportunities.

Figure 2
The Human Resource Cycle

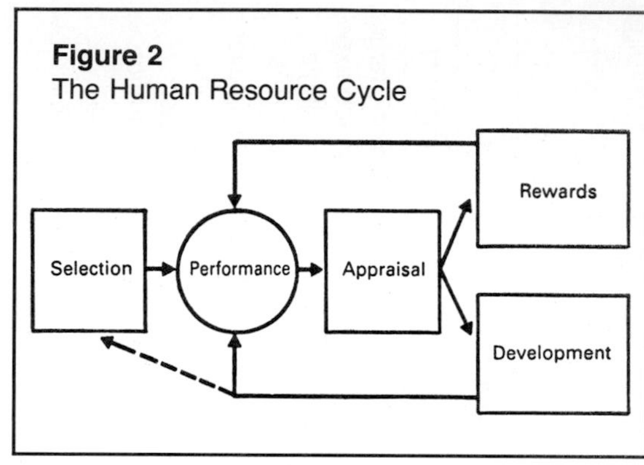

In order to put these functions in the various contexts of the organization, we rely upon Robert Anthony's distinction among the three levels of managerial work: the strategic level, the managerial level, and the operational level.[4]

The strategic level deals with policy formulation and overall goal setting: its objective is to position effectively the organization in its environment. The managerial level is concerned with the availability and allocation of resources to carry out the strategic plan. To be in the business(es) specified by the strategic plan, the company must decide what its capital, informational, and human resource needs are. At the operational level, the day-to-day management of the organization is carried out. (Operational activities are ideally carried out under the umbrella of the managerial plan.)

Table 2 illustrates the kinds of activities associated with these three levels for each generic component of the human resource cycle. For example, in the selection/placement area, operational level activities include the annual staffing and recruitment plans. Managerial selection is

Table 2
Human Resource Activities

Management Level	*Selection*	*Appraisal*	*Rewards (Compensation and Fringe Benefits)*	*Development*
Strategic	Specify characteristics of people needed to run business in long term Alter internal and external systems to reflect future	In long term, what should be valued? Develop means to appraise future dimensions Early identification of potential	In world as it might be in long term, how will work force be rewarded? Link to the long-term business strategy	Plan developmental experiences for people running business of the future Systems with flexibility to adjust to change Develop long-term career paths
Managerial	Longitudinal validation of selection criteria Development of recruitment marketing plan New markets	Validated systems linking current and future potential Assessment centers for development	Five-year compensation plans for individuals Cafeteria-style fringe packages	General management development programs Organization development Foster self-development
Operational	Staffing plans Recruitment plans Day-to-day monitoring systems	Annual or more frequent appraisal system(s) Day-to-day control systems	Wage and salary administration Benefit packages	Specific job skill training On-the-job training

more concerned with manpower planning for the intermediate future. For instance, a company that is about to open two plants in different parts of the country would want to know the kinds of people the company will need and how it should go about finding the people to run the plants. Strategic selection is concerned with identifying who can best run the business(es) in the long run.

SELECTION, PROMOTION, AND PLACEMENT PROCESS

The selection, promotion, and placement process includes all those activities related to the internal movement of people across positions and to the external hiring into the organization. The essential process is one of matching available human resources to jobs in the organization. It entails defining the organization's human needs for particular positions and assessing the available pool of people to determine the best fit.

Three strategic selection concerns are particularly salient. The first involves devising an organization-wide selection and promotion system that supports the organization's business strategy. For example, if a company will be diversifying over a ten-year period, it is most likely that the types of people needed to run the new business will be different than they had been in the past. Thus, a redesign in the selection process will be required. This process is taking place in the oil industry as it launches its twenty-year diversification effort.

The second strategic concern requires creating internal flows of people that match the business strategy. Companies that diversify or change their strategic direction need to alter traditional promotional patterns in order to move new types of people into key positions. AT&T's move into the competitive electronic communication and knowledge business has necessitated their developing internal promotion systems for profit-driven people who are able to innovate and deal with competitive markets. This is a major change from the regulated telephone monopoly that was service oriented, that was low on innovation, and that was not managed competitively where profit was regulated.

The third strategic concern is matching key executives to the business's strategy. There is a growing interest in meshing strategic planning with executive skills. This is especially true in companies that are using a product portfolio analysis approach to strategic management. The Boston Consulting Group's (BCG's) portfolio matrix is the most common and simplest formulation. Using the BCG approach, there is a set of prescribed business practices for managing each type of business. Several examples of companies already committed to using senior executive selection as a strategic management tool are presented below.

General Electric. GE uses a more complex portfolio matrix with nine cells. Yet the underlying concepts are based on the same product life cycle notions represented in the BCG matrix. GE defines its products in terms of the kinds of management practices required for success. Thus, its products are defined as "growers" for wildcats, "defenders" for stars, "harvesters" for cash cows, and "undertakers" for dogs:

> *Its [GE] general managers are being classified by personal style or orientation as "growers," "caretakers," and "undertakers." . . . They [GE] have a shortage of growers but they are making a great effort to remove the undertaker types who are heading up growth businesses. The lighting business is mainly mature but we [GE] just designated international operations as a growth area to our five year forecast. . . . John D. Hamilton, the manager responsible for manpower planning, says he and the executive manpower staff at corporate headquarters looked at the whole pool of corporate talent. They decided to move in a manager who had an industrial rather than a lighting background, but who seemed to show entrepreneurial flair.*[5]

Corning Glass Company. At Corning, an extensive effort is underway to assess the company's top 100 executives for such qualities as entrepreneurial flair. The goal is to have a clearer profile of the organization's pool of executive talent specified in terms of capabilities for managing different parts of the BCG matrix. An example of this process occurred in December 1979:

> *Corning reshaped its electronic strategy deciding that the market was starting to expand again, and that it needed a growth oriented manager. It placed a manufacturing specialist who had shown a great deal of flair in working with customers in the top marketing slot for electronics, and says Shafer, "It looks like he's turning it around."*[6]

Chase Manhatten Bank. During the period between 1975 and 1980, the bank underwent major managerial changes. A key to the bank's successful turnaround from a troubled bank in the mid-seventies was its careful strategic level selection and placement of executives. Historically, at Chase, as is the case in banking in general, senior level positions were filled based on the historical precedent: the old boy networks played a major role. Furthermore, the tradition was to reward those with banker skills and not those with managerial skills, which were implicitly considered to be of less importance. But under the stress of serious performance problems, Chase Manhatten Bank had to reexamine these practices. As a result, a very systematic effort was launched to strategically manage senior selection and placement decisions. For example, "When the trust manager retired, corporate management decided that the department, whose operation had been essentially stable, should focus on a more aggressive growth strategy." Instead of seeking a veteran banker, Chase hired a man whose experience had been with IBM "because it was felt that he would bring a strong marketing orientation to the trust department, which the new strategy required."[7]

Texas Instruments. At TI, there is an explicit attempt to match management style to product life cycles. "As a product moves through different phases of its life cycle, different kinds of management skills become dominant."[8] The mismatch of managerial style to the product life cycle can be quite serious. For example, a risk-taking entrepreneurial manager who is in charge of a cash cow business is likely to reduce the profitability of the business by trying to "grow" the business and take risks. On the other hand, putting a cost-cutting, efficiency-oriented manager in charge of a growth business can stifle innovation and prevent the business from acquiring market share. TI feels that, in the past, it did not pay adequate attention to the match between product life cycle and managerial style. As a result, TI feels it lost its early lead in integrated circuits. During the growth stage, TI had a "cash cow manager in charge rather than a grower or entrepreneurial type."[9] The result was that "tighter controls were introduced, but TI failed to recognize that a research orientation was really what the Integrated Division needed at the growth stage. TI has since redoubled its efforts to match management orientation with job needs. Bucy, now president, personally reviews the records of the top TI managers."[10]

REWARD PROCESSES

Performance follows the selection process. Once people are in their jobs, they need to be rewarded for good performance. The list of rewards that exist in organizational settings is surprisingly long. The following is a partial list of potential rewards:

- Pay in its various forms: salary, bonuses, stock options, benefits, and perquisites;
- Promotion: both upward mobility and lateral transfers into desirable positions;
- Management praise;
- Career opportunities: a long-term chance for growth and development;
- Appreciation from customers and/or clients of the organization;
- Personal sense of well-being: feeling good about oneself for accomplishing objectives;
- Opportunity to learn: a chance to expand one's skills and knowledge base;
- Security: a sense of job and financial security;
- Responsibility: providing individuals with a sense of organizational responsibility;
- Respect from coworkers;
- Friendship from coworkers.

Most organizations, however, do not do a very good job of managing these rewards to produce desired organizational behaviors. As a result, the reward system is one of the most underutilized and mishandled managerial tools for driving organizational performance. As can be seen from the human resource cycle in Figure 2, rewards are a major factor in influencing performance. Assuming that the organization can appraise performance, which is not always a good assumption, the organization then has a rationale for allocating rewards based on how well people perform: many times organizations think of rewards only in terms of managing pay.

Thus, a major strategic issue concerning the reward system is how to use it to overcome the tendency toward shortsighted management. The rewards for this year's profits generally turn out to be both financial incentives and promotions. Motivation of senior executives toward long-term strategic goals is difficult, given that the reward system often encourages short-term achievement at the expense of long-term goals. The following excerpt is a statement made in the *New York Times:*

> *Though bonuses based on achieving sales or earnings goals have long been common, the emphasis on long term is a new element. Top corporate executives, under pressure from Wall Street and Stockholders have been rewarded with bonuses and stock options when immediate profits spurt. The auto industry, for example, is notable for its short term rewards.*[11]

It is unreasonable and unwise to recommend that managers be rewarded only for long-term strategic goals, as businesses must perform in the present to succeed in the future. Thus, the reward system should provide balanced support to short-term and long-term strategic goals.

BALANCING LONG- AND SHORT-TERM GOALS

Texas Instruments. TI has thought long and hard about the use of its reward system for driving the company's short- and long-term goals.

One major part of TI's strategy since the early 1960s has been to adhere rigidly to the "learning curve theory." Simply put, it states that "manufacturing costs can be brought down by a fixed percentage, depending on the product, each time cumulative volume is doubled."[12] The strategy involves constant redesign improvement of the product and of the processes of production so that prices can drop as fast as possible. This strategy was implemented by organizing Product Customer Centers (PCCs), which are decentralized profit centers that could be closely monitored for cost performance. The reward system was closely tied to the PCCs so that managers worked hard to make the learning curve theory operative. However, there were some problems.

The Product Customer Centers and associated reward systems worked against another organizational strategy—the development of innovations for future products. The rewards were structured to drive managers to be overly concerned with short-run efficiencies and not with long-term strategic goals.

The solution to this dilemma was to design a new organization and to drape it over the existing PCC structure. The new organization, which was called Objectives, Strategies, and Tactics (OST), was created to supplement the PCCs, which remained intact. The OST structure was used for the formulation and implementation of strategic long-range plans, and it consisted of the same managers as that of the PCC organization.

Thus, the top managers at TI wear two hats. Wearing one hat, they are bottom line, efficiency-focused managers who work to drive the PCC system and who are rewarded and evaluated for accomplishing the efficiency objectives. Wearing the other hat, the OST one, the managers are involved in working toward a strategic objective that may have a ten- to twenty-year time horizon. Separate monitoring and appraisal systems tied to the OST organization are used to drive performance in the long-term strategic area. For example, a manager may be responsible for PCC efficiency, while, at the same time, he may work in the OST structure toward a strategic objective in the development of products in the computerized auto industry of the future. If 60 percent of his time was allocated to the PCCs and 40 percent of his time to OST, then his compensation would be split to reflect the short- and long-term aspects of the job.

TI also used the reward system to encourage another set of desired strategic behaviors when it discovered that managers tend to set low-risk objectives in order to enhance their chances of receiving a bigger bonus, and thereby stifling their creativity and innovativeness. TI altered the reward system through a "wild hare" program that provided funding for more speculative programs. Under this program, managers were asked to rank speculative projects on a separate basis. The bonus system was then tied into this process.

Another strategic reward mechanism for fostering organizational innovation is to provide any organization member(s) with a chance to obtain a grant from a pool containing several million dollars to fund innovative projects. The result has been the emergence of informal groups who apply for grants from the innovation pool, called IDEA; these groups then attempt to turn these ideas into viable products.

MANAGEMENT DEVELOPMENT

Activities designed to insure that individuals are properly equipped with skills and knowledge to carry out their jobs fall into the management development category. These activities range from simple job training for lower-level employees to long-term development of senior executives. The three major areas of the developmental process are: (1) job improvement: the development of specific job skills and competencies; (2) career planning: a longitudinal focus on individual growth and development in relation to organizational opportunities; and (3) succession planning: the organizational focus on insuring an adequate supply of human resource talent for projected needs in the future based on strategic plans.

At the long-term strategic level, the developmental process includes such activities as management education, job assignments, and the use of mentor relationships. Some of the strategic level developmental concerns are discussed briefly.

Insuring that the organization has an adequate supply of human resource talent at all levels is no easy task, especially when the organization is undergoing rapid strategic changes. The key to this concern is to have a human resource planning system that makes accurate forecasts of needs and of resources available to meet those needs. Such systems, however, are not easily built, and even though most large companies have manpower planning systems, they are often very inadequate as a result of two basic flaws.

The first flaw is that data about people that are fed into the system are very unreliable because managers generally do not appraise employees well. As it now stands, the appraisal process that provides this data is the weakest link in the human resource cycle. Thus, planning systems that are built on these data are also inadequate. In order to plan for the future, it is necessary to have an inventory of current human resources that include both an assessment of current performance and of the future potential of key individuals.

The second basic flaw is that there is a missing link between human resource planning systems and business strategy. Although many organizations have given lip service to the missing link, the reality is that it has been treated as an afterthought that has usually been delegated to the human resource staff without any line management involvement. As a result, the human resource plan is a paper exercise that is not utilized by the strategic decision makers.

There is a handful of U.S. companies that have strategically managed the development of senior executive talent. Among these companies are General Motors, Exxon, General Electric, Texas Instruments, IBM, and Proctor & Gamble. The emphasis has been on carefully developing managers by following such principles as:

1. Sustained interest in and support for management development and succession planning on the part of top management;

2. Efforts to identify young professionals deemed to have potential for top-level management positions;

3. Comprehensive and systematic rewards used for managerial performance;

4. The appraisal includes data from multiple sources and is used in making decisions about management development;

5. Special recruiting efforts to provide appropriate raw materials for general managers of the future;

6. Opportunities for capable young professionals to develop managerial skills early in their careers;

7. Compensation policies and salary administration to help stimulate management development and retain key personnel;

8. Clear developmental objectives and career plans for managers at all levels;

9. Effective coaching from personnel's superiors;

10. Stressing results in the performance appraisal process.

Some companies have been very strategic in developing managers. For example:

Exxon. The Compensation and Executive Development (COED) system at Exxon is designed to insure a disciplined approach to the development of managerial talent for the company. The system is directed from the top, where the COED committee is headed by the CEO, Clifford Garvin, and is made up of members of Exxon's Board. The committee is in charge of reviewing the development and placement of the top 250 Exxon executives. Meeting nearly every Monday, the COED committee carefully reviews the performance of executives and examines their developmental needs. To insure that there is a continual flow of managerial talent for the company and that all positions have back-up candidates, the committee then compares the performances of all the executives and makes decisions according to their future developmental needs.

There is also a COED system within each of the Exxon subsidiaries, where the president of each subsidiary has his or her own COED committee, which is similar to the one Mr. Garvin heads. Each subsidiary also has a senior level staff for the COED committee: this enables the COED system to reach the top 2,000 or so managers at Exxon.

In discussions with senior Exxon managers, it is rather striking to hear the universal acclaim given the system. Most agree that the system accounts for Exxon's overall success and that it is an excellent system for developing managers.

General Motors. General Motors is another company with an equally strong tradition of management development that dates back to Alfred Sloan.

> *At General Motors, the supreme court of executive review in recent years included the top six executives in the company. . . . During the week-long sessions in the Board room of Detroit headquarters each February and July, they spend long days and nights listening to analysis of more than 600 managers from each of GM's ten vice presidents and group executives. . . . A variety of questions are covered to get an accurate picture of where the individual stands in his career development. . . . We don't have jobs at GM, we have careers. Along with performance, the probing is centered on just what kind of potential the executive may have. Here are some examples. Does the executive seem to be developing at the rate expected? What is the job contributing to the person's ability? Is it rounding out the person as we intended? What should be the next job for this executive? Should it be in another division or involve greater responsibility? If so, who would we put in this executive's place?*[13]

Chase Manhatten Bank. A more targeted use of management development took place at Chase Manhatten Bank. A management development program was designed to support the company's first formal strategic planning process. The two-week program for the top officers of the bank focused on awareness and frameworks needed to support the new strategic planning process. The program had the involvement of the then chairman, David Rockefeller, and the then president, Willard Butcher. Both symbolically and substantively, the program strongly reinforced the importance of the new strategic planning process.

APPRAISAL PROCESS

Perhaps the least liked managerial activity is doing the annual performance appraisal. The activity is often only a perfunctory paper exercise. Performance appraisals are like seat belts: everyone agrees that they are important and that they save lives, yet no one uses them. Similarly, the problem with appraisal systems includes poorly designed procedures, a psychological resistance of managers to give negative evaluations, and a perceived invalidity. The appraisal system, nonetheless, is central to the human resource cycle. It contributes to three essential processes:

1. Rewards can be allocated in relation to performance only through the use of an appraisal system by which performance can be measured. Such appraisal systems range from subjective personal evaluations to impersonal criteria based on profitability, return on investment, market share, and other quantitative measures.

2. Human resource planning relies on valid appraisals. A current inventory of talent can be made only through a valid appraisal process that shows those who have been performing well and those who have not. In addition, future human resource projections must be based on an assessment of the potential of the employees, which is indicated by the appraisal process. Without the data provided by a valid appraisal, such forecasting is impossible, as there is no basis for making predictions.

3. The development process is also built on the appraisal process. Based on an assessment of an individual's performance and potential, both the individual and the organization can plan for future training and development. A weak data base leads to a hit or miss training program and retards the development process.

Relationship to Strategy

A strategic concern for companies is to develop appraisal processes that are supportive of the business strategy. A study by Lorsch and Allen indicated that such a link influences total performance.[14] In this study, the authors compared the appraisal systems in diversified companies to those in integrated companies. They found that the diversified companies placed more emphasis on objective and result measures such as productivity, profit, volume, etc. The integrated firms, however, tended to rely more on operating and intermediate measures, as well as on more subjective evaluation of abilities such as "planning," "controlling," "organizing," and "leadership." The diversified appraisal system worked better because the divisions were more self-contained, having little interdivisional or corporate contact. The integrated companies, on the other hand, had greater interdivisional contact and greater sharing of resources, which made it hard for them to decide who exactly was responsible for how much of the end results. These two simple examples underscore some of the strategic issues involved in matching an appraisal process to the business strategy.

The key to an effective appraisal system at the strategic level is the commitment of quality managerial time to systematic examination and evaluation of executive talent. The descriptions of the Exxon and GM development systems, which were discussed earlier, are in part descriptions of their appraisal systems as the two systems are interrelated. But perhaps the company with the best strategic appraisal system is General Electric, where much time and staff work go into appraising the top 600 executives.

General Electric. The diversification of GE makes the appraisal of managers more complex than that of most other companies. Unlike GM or Exxon who have one major line of business, GE has more than 240 businesses. As a result, GE has developed elaborate approaches to handling the appraisal of key managers.

An example of this is the slate system. The top 600 positions at GE are carefully managed and monitored by the chairman. A special human resource staff that is under the direction of a senior vice president reviews these key executives. This staff works with line managers to develop slates of acceptable candidates for key managerial positions in the company. Positions must be filled from among those on the approved slate; that is, a business head cannot select his own vice president of marketing unless the individual is among those on the official slate list for the position. Although a manager may select an individual who is not on the slate, the decision must ultimately be kicked up the hierarchy at GE to the chairman. However, this kind of selection is frowned upon and thus very few people who are not on the slate are selected for key managerial positions.

One of the services that the human resource staff provides in developing the data base for the slate system is an in-depth executive review of key managers. Highly trained personnel spend several weeks preparing a report on a single executive. The process involves interviews with subordinates, peers, bosses, and even customers of GE to get a composite picture of the individual's strengths, weaknesses, accomplishments, failures, and potentials. These reviews estimate the expected future progress of the individual at GE and give extensive suggestions for further development. The completed report is then reviewed by the individual who can voice disagreement. It then becomes part of the individual's file. (Only forty of these reviews are conducted in a year.)

IMPLEMENTING STRATEGIC HUMAN RESOURCE MANAGEMENT

In another article, we discussed a methodology for moving a human resource function into the strategic arena.[15] The approach is based on a human resource audit that provides the organization with data on the internal capacity of the human resource function and data from the line concerning the kind of services the organization needs at the operational, managerial, and strategic levels. As a result of our conducting these audits in several large companies, we developed the following suggestions for making the human resource function more strategic:

The Internal Organization of the Human Resource Function. The first area of focus is on how to properly organize, staff, and manage the human resource function. This involves:

- Step 1. Identify the portfolio of human resource tasks at the strategic, managerial, and operational level for each human resource element.

- Step 2. Reorganize the human resource function to reflect the operational, managerial, and strategic needs of the business. The operational level is best served by a traditional functional personnel department where there are separate units carrying out recruitment, compensation, development, etc. The managerial level must be organized to cut across the subfunctions identified at the operational level (recruitment, development, compensation, etc.) by using such design tools as liaison managers, teams, or, under limited conditions, a matrix organizational design. The strategic level activities require an elite senior human resource management (individual or team, depending on the size of the organization) that is supported by strong managerial human resource services.
- Step 3. The human resource staff must be trained in the more strategically focused organization. At the operational level, the function must be staffed with technically focused professional personnel and/or with MBAs who are starting out in their careers and who need to learn the nuts and bolts of personnel. At the managerial level, individuals, who possess a more general managerial orientation and background either through actual work experience or through an MBA degree, should be selected from the operational level. Finally, at the strategic level, staffing should be based on selecting human resource executives who have political skills, a broad business orientation, and a broad human resource management background. A proactive stance toward the strategic future of the organization is also required.
- Step 4. The reward and control systems must be altered to support the strategic human resource function. The rewards and controls should reflect specific tasks at each of the three levels. Most personnel reward and control systems are geared toward operational level activities: these should be expanded to reward and control people in terms of the new strategic and managerial level activities.

Linking the Human Resource Function to the Line Organization. Major changes are also required to link the human resource function to the user organization. Most personnel functions are linked to the operational business activities. With the addition of new managerial and strategic activities, new linking mechanisms will be required:

- Step 1. Provide the business with good human resource data bases. These include environmental scanning of labor markets and social and economic issues that impact the long-term human resource context of the organization. In addition, data on the internal labor pool are required in both a present and a future context. Internal marketing data on the human resource needs of various user groups in the organization are especially helpful.
- Step 2. Alter the senior management role when it comes to human resource management issues so that these concerns receive quality attention. The managers need to be committed to weighing human resource issues with the same level of attention as that of other functions, such as finance, marketing, and production.
- Step 3. The line organization must alter its incentive and control systems so that the overall human resource function is managed. It will also be necessary for the organization to have ways of measuring the overall performance of the human resource function at the strategic, managerial, and operational levels. This will entail ongoing audits of the human resource function to determine how well it is doing in providing services to its clients. Also, adjustments must be made in budgeting for human resource services, as some of these adjustments will require new sources of corporate funding.

These steps are illustrative of what is involved in developing a more strategic human resource function. Obviously, every organization must develop its own answers and a tailored strategic stance in terms of its human resources.

SUMMARY AND CONCLUSIONS

Human resource management is a major force in driving organizational performance. Thus, when business is castigated and when American industry is unfavorably compared to that of Japan or West Germany, two major factors are underscored: (1) our lack of a long-term perspective in management; and (2) our lack of skill in managing people. Both of these factors can be changed only with a concomitant change in the human resource activities inside our organizations; that is, it requires changes in the way people think and behave. In the final analysis, three concluding points should be made about human resource management:

1. Human resource activities have a major impact on individual performance and hence on productivity and organizational performance.

2. The cycle of human resource activities is highly interdependent. The human resource system is therefore only as strong as its weakest link.

3. Effective strategic management requires effective human resource management.

ENDNOTES

1. See A. Chandler, *Strategy and Structure: Chapters in the History of American Industrial Enterprise* (Cambridge, MA: MIT Press, 1962).

2. Ibid.

3. See J. Galbraith and D. Nathanson, *Strategy Implementation: The Role of Structure and Process* (St. Paul, MN: West Publishing, 1978).

4. See R. Anthony, *Planning and Control Systems: A Framework for Analysis* (Boston, MA: Division of Research, Graduate School of Business Administration, Harvard University, 1965).

5. See *Business Week,* 25 February 1980, p. 173.

6. Ibid., p. 166.

7. Ibid., p. 166.

8. Ibid., p. 168.

9. Ibid., p. 168.

10. Ibid., p. 168.

11. See *New York Times,* 24 April 1980.

12. See *Business Week,* 18 September 1978, p. 68.

13. See *New York Times,* 4 September 1980.

14. See J. Lorsch and S. Allen, *Managing Diversity and Interdependence* (Boston, MA: Division of Research, Harvard Business School, 1973).

15. See M. Haire, "A New Look at Human Resources," *Industrial Management Review* (now *Sloan Management Review*), Winter 1970, pp. 17–23.

Strategy, Human Resources Management, and Organizational Outcomes: Coming Out from Between the Cracks

Nancy K. Napier

For many years, researchers and managers have examined and discussed specific aspects of strategic management (e.g., strategy types, planning, implementation, and evaluation), human resources management (e.g., employee selection, appraisal, and training), and organizational outcomes (e.g., company performance and effectiveness). Attempts to link these areas of concern, however, have been limited in research and practice. Because research that tries to investigate relationships among these elements does not fit neatly into a single discipline, it may tend to "fall between the cracks."

There are several reasons why researchers and managers should want to integrate these three areas. First, to increase our understanding of the way organizations do (and perhaps should) operate, we must examine a more comprehensive set of issues. Second, because top managers are often forced to think "outside of a single discipline," research should help them decide what types of human resources practices "fit" their firms' chosen strategies. Finally, managers are seeking guidance and creative thinking on how to integrate strategy, human resources issues, and organizational outcomes. We see evidence of this from the number of "business best-sellers" in recent years.

Integrating strategy, human resources management (HRM), and organizational outcomes should help guide and contribute to the more effective use of—and decisions about—human resources (Foulkes, 1986). If managers understand the links between strategy and compensation, for instance, they can better design programs that will motivate and reward employees as firms alter or change their strategies over time.

A model linking these elements should be useful for understanding how each element affects the others. Figure 1 exhibits how managers and researchers can study pairs of elements (i.e., strategy-HRM; HRM-outcomes), or all three together. Managers must realize that human resources practices can be either influenced (by strategy) or influencers (of organizational outcomes). For example, a firm pursuing a growth strategy may design a compensation system to reward managers who bring in *new* business, rather than those who maintain existing accounts. In this case, the human resources practices are influenced by strategy. Such a compensation practice

Figure 1
Role of HRM in Linkages

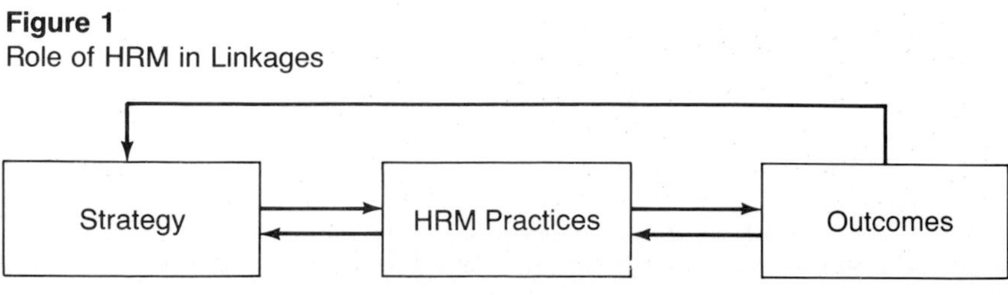

could be an "influencer" if it in some way affects firm performance.

In addition, of course, it is also possible that human resources practices can act as an influence on strategy selection and planning (Butler, Ferris, & Smith Cook, 1988). For example, the types of employees (i.e., their skills and abilities) in an organization may affect the decision to pursue different kinds of strategies, such as whether to grow by developing internally or by acquiring other firms. Likewise, it may be that human resources practices could be affected by outcomes; an organization that performs better may be more likely to increase its emphasis or spending on HRM activities. This whole area of examining links between strategy, human resources management, and organizational outcomes, is in an early stage of research development. There is much speculation, but few firm conclusions. We simply do not yet know what causes what.

WHAT WE DO KNOW ABOUT THE LINKS

The next section reviews some of the information about links between business strategy, human resources management practices, and outcomes.

Strategy-HRM Links

At present, the information about the link between strategy and human resources practices is both conceptual (more theory-oriented) and empirical (data-based). This link is the one we know most about in terms of what effect strategy seems to have on human resources activities. Even so, much of the writing about it has been based on speculation of what should occur, rather than on what actually occurs.

The theory-oriented writings have been useful for human resources researchers and managers. First, the writings show that people *outside* personnel and human resources, such as senior managers, think that HRM issues are indeed important and contribute to effective implementation of an organization's strategy (Leontiades, 1982). If *others* believe this, then it is easier for the human resources manager to convince all managers of the importance of "people issues." Second, some of the researchers who think about these issues keep raising the same elements as being particularly important, such as performance and reward systems (Galbraith & Nathanson, 1978; Miles & Snow, 1978). As more information on these frequently mentioned issues becomes available, we will have greater confidence in whether—and how—they are related to strategy. Finally, more and more researchers are suggesting *how* to go about discovering or examining those potential links. In other words, rather than just saying that strategy *should* relate to human resources practices, we are gathering facts about the actual relationships, as well as ideas about how to study those links in greater depth. In particular, researchers are developing ways to measure important variables like strategy and human resources practices. In addition, there is more guidance about how to conduct research to answer questions about the links (Dyer, 1984; Olian & Rynes, 1984).

The existing empirical knowledge, or that based on collecting and analyzing data from firms, has focused on links between strategy and such human resources functions as compensation, management transfer patterns, and career patterns. The general conclusion is that there are differences in certain compensation components (e.g., bonus size and the way it is decided) in firms pursuing different strategies. Firms with different growth strategies vary in how they pay managers (e.g., salary vs. bonus), the type of performance criteria used, and what comparison groups they use for manager performance (Napier & Smith, 1987; Pitts, 1974, 1975, 1977). For instance, a firm that wants to grow by acquiring new firms may evaluate a manager's performance on the ease with which a new firm is integrated into the existing one, taking into account the expectation that neither firm may perform as well financially as before the merger. Another example concerns firms that pursue different diversification strategies. When firms diversify, or grow by getting into new product areas, they tend to reward managers with bonuses. The greater the diversification (i.e., the more unrelated the products), the higher the bonus (Napier & Smith, 1987). In other words, firms pursuing different strategies are likely to structure human resources practices, such as pay or performance evaluation, to support their strategies.

There are several problems with the existing research on strategy and HRM. First, we still have little information about what happens in a number of different strategies. Most of the data-based knowledge has come from research on generic strategies or growth strategies. Thus, as firms become more sophisticated in formulating strategy, the existing research may be too general to help managers.

A second problem is that we have little sense of how strategy affects the full range of HRM activities (e.g., training, staffing, recruiting). Since most of the research has focused on compensation, performance criteria, and transfer patterns, other human resources areas have been neglected. In addition, we know very little about how organizations design HRM practices to be consistent with each other while supporting a given strategy. For example, in a high growth strategy firm, a major human resources practice may be to reward managers who develop new product markets. In addition to a reward practice to support the strategy, the firm may also need to provide training to managers who need it and to those who are newly hired. The training must help managers gain the ability to develop new markets and thus be consistent with the reward practices.

Another limitation of existing research is that it has focused on HRM practices for very specific and thus limited groups of employees, usually the middle manager or the manager at the strategic business unit (SBU) level. One reason for the focus on these managers is that computer data bases exist on financial and market information for certain units (e.g., SBUs) within firms. The strategic business unit level has been a popular one for researchers to investigate because it is both discrete and possible to identify managers at that level. There is less information about managers at levels where no readily available data bases exist.

Finally, a difficulty with current knowledge about strategy-HRM issues is that we still believe that integrating strategy and HRM will lead to good outcomes (e.g., financial performance). Unfortunately, that belief has yet to be confirmed. A number of popular books, such as *In Search of Excellence* (Peters & Waterman, 1982), present anecdotal evidence to support such links, but as yet we have little firm empirical data in that regard.

HRM-Outcomes Links

Our knowledge about HRM-outcomes links seems to follow at least two streams: (1) how effective are the human resources functions and the department, and (2) what is the overall contribution of HRM activities to the organization?

In the first stream, researchers and managers have assessed the effectiveness, costs, and benefits of specific human resources management activities. The focus has been on three general areas: (1) ways to assess the *costs* of specific human resources activities, such as selection, training, or benefits (Cascio, 1982), (2) methods to evaluate the *effectiveness* of human resources activities, such as the pre-post evaluation of training programs (Hall, 1984; Wexley & Latham, 1981), and (3) general approaches to the *audit* of the strengths and weaknesses of the overall human resources activities (Devanna, Fombrun, & Tichy, 1981). Each of the three categories is relatively well developed. For instance, Cascio (1982) proposes models, some of them very complex, for assessing the costs of human resources activities. For example, in assessing the cost of selecting a bank teller, a firm would consider the costs of a newspaper ad, time spent screening and interviewing candidates, training time, and lost productivity while the new employee is learning the job. Unfortunately, these costs typically are not tied to firm performance. Also, the models do not often address ways to attach monetary values to benefits.

The methods to assess the effectiveness of programs (e.g., training) usually involve evaluating employee attitudes about the program. For example, training programs are often evaluated by how trainees react to the program right after its completion. Less frequent is an assessment of employee performance. Napier and Deller (1984) evaluated bank teller mistakes made before and after a training program and suggested that tellers of highly trained and untrained supervisors performed better than tellers of moderately trained supervisors. As with the cost assessment literature, though, there is rarely any link of program effectiveness to firm performance. This is partly because of the difficulty of separating out the impact of a single factor like a training program on the performance of a large unit, such as a bank branch or firm.

Finally, personnel department audits are often used to justify departmental activities and determine areas for future focus. Again, our knowledge in this area is limited.

The second stream of research in this area has examined differences in high- and low-performing organizations, and the nature of the human resources practices in each (Kanter, 1983). So far, again, we have no firm conclusions about whether good HRM practices are related to high performance. The research of the topic seems to suggest that it does, but we are still gathering information.

Putting It All Together: Strategy-HRM-Outcomes

There has been limited examination of all three elements together. There are several case descriptions of organizations' attempts to link strategic planning with HRM issues, such as planning, compensation, development, and firm performance. For example, Misa and Stein (1983) examined whether and how HRM concerns were included in strategic decisions in high-performing and low-performing firms. They found that high-performing firms had more human resources department participation in business decisions and strategic planning than did poorer performers. Also, Horovitz and Thiebault (1982) found that high-performing firms pursuing the same strategy had similar management systems.

Others have argued that a better "match" between strategy and HRM issues is associated with better firm performance or effectiveness. For example, Tichy, Fombrun, and Devanna (1982) have discussed how firms that appear to match strategic business unit level strategy, type of manager, and human resource practices seem to have better firm performance.

Our knowledge about how to integrate strategy, HRM, and organizational outcomes is clearly limited. A major problem for learning about the integration is that there are few organizations that actually have successfully linked the three elements, thus making it more difficult to find firms to examine.

Although our knowledge about the integration of strategy, HRM, and organizational outcomes is not extensive, it is encouraging that there is increasing interest in examining these relationships. While there is currently much interest in the strategy-HRM links, it is critical for managers to consider how all three elements are tied together, and how beneficial it can be to integrate them.

AN ILLUSTRATIVE FRAMEWORK

The three elements (i.e., strategy, HRM, outcomes) can be viewed on a three dimensional matrix (Figure 2) to help managers consider how each may affect the others. In addition to these three main elements, a fourth is critical. That element is the type or level of employee affected by the other three factors. For example, many firms find that the approaches to selection or pay will vary depending upon the level of employee (e.g., line worker, middle manager, etc.).

The vertical axis of the matrix identifies overall strategy classification. Any given firm might employ a single strategy within one classification. There are several strategy classification schemes proposed in the literature (Galbraith & Nathanson, 1978; Miles & Snow, 1978; Pitts, 1974; Porter, 1981; Rumelt, 1974). For example, the Miles and Snow (1978) typology refers to four general stances a firm may take in its industry: defender, prospector, reactor, analyzer. A defender firm seeks to protect its current market share and concentrates on maintaining the status quo. A prospector, on the other hand, aggressively pursues new markets, new product ideas, and the like. A reactor responds to what happens in the market and takes advantage of such occurrences where possible. An analyzer combines strategies, acting as a prospector in some markets and a defender in others.

Rumelt (1974) describes a strategy classification based on the extent of product diversity in a firm. Product diversity refers to the range of products a firm offers and the degree to which those products are related to each other. They can be related through using similar technology or market

Figure 2
A Working Matrix

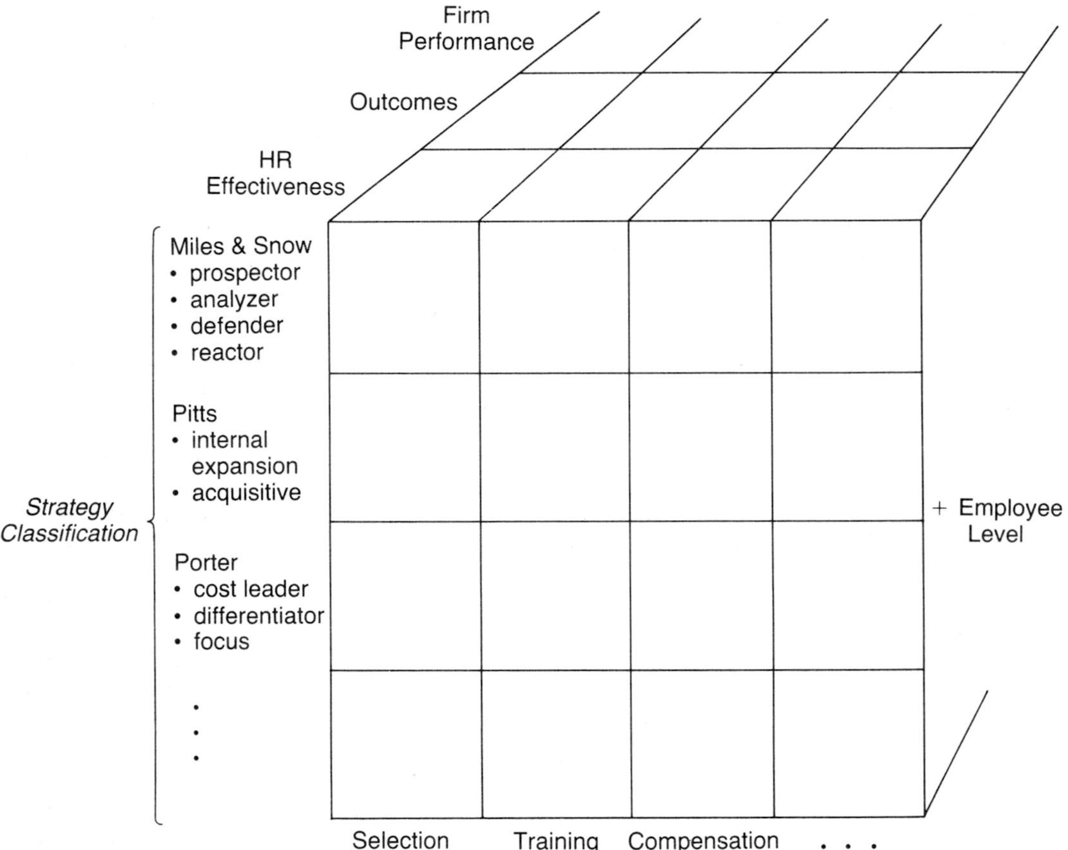

channels, for instance. According to Rumelt's (1974) classification, firms that produce only one product, that is, generate all revenues from a single product, are called single business firms. Firms that rely on a few similar products, that is, receive 70% of revenue from those products, are called dominant product firms. Firms producing many widely diverse products are unrelated firms.

Porter (1981) classifies firms into three groups: cost leadership (firms that pursue a strategy of having relatively lower costs than competitors), differentiators (firms providing a product or service that distinguishes the firm from competitors in some way, e.g., offering more luxury, better service), and focus firms (those concentrating on selling to a specific market group).

The HRM dimension of the matrix, shown on the horizontal axis, emphasizes the set of personnel activities related to managing employees: acquiring (human resource planning, recruitment, selection), allocating (placement, orientation, socialization), developing (training, development, career management), managing performance of (performance appraisal, compensation, discipline), and maintaining (benefits, health/safety). Within each activity are specific types of actions or stages that would apply to each kind of employee. For example, acquiring practices vary widely for different levels of employees and organizations. For firms with a policy of promoting from within, the selection process would likely focus more on past employee performance within the firm rather than education or other types of experience. Likewise, some firms may seek new hires for certain types of jobs, (e.g., research and development, marketing) to acquire new ideas. Thus, some of the factors to consider under the selection activity might include *source* of new employee (i.e., inside/outside the firm), *criteria used* (e.g., within firm performance, evaluation), and *goal* of selecting a new employee (e.g., gain new ideas, learn about a competitor, reward employee).

The third matrix element, organizational outcomes, refers to ways we tell how well a firm is doing in terms of meeting goals (effectiveness) or achieving financial, marketing, or other types of performance standards.

The fourth element, level of employee, includes common categories of top, middle, and first-line levels of management and non-management employees. The level of employee is important because HRM functions differ significantly by level. For example, most firms typically have much more specific job descriptions or responsibility lists for non-management and lower-level managers than for top managers. Similarly, the recruitment techniques may vary markedly. Executive search firms or "the old boy network" are more common at top levels; at lower levels, media advertisements (newspaper, newsletter) or other methods, such as walk-ins, are more common.

The matrix can help managers consider what types of human resources activities relate to different strategy classifications. The following example shows how a firm pursuing different growth strategies might design its human resources selection function for top management.

In this example, a strategy of growth is pursued either by internal expansion or by acquisition of other firms. From earlier research, we know that there are indeed links between growth strategy and incentive compensation, manager transfer patterns, and the size of the corporate-level technological staff (Pitts, 1974, 1975, 1977). It follows, then, that selection of top managers may also vary, given the emphasis on different criteria or talents needed in managers responsible for different approaches to growth (Gerstein & Reisman, 1983). In particular, firms that expand internally tend to use mainly subjective (non-quantifiable) performance criteria, with fewer objective, quantifiable ways to assess performance (Pitts, 1974). Therefore, we would expect that these firms might also be likely to use more subjective selection criteria in choosing candidates for top management positions. In firms that grow by expanding internally (e.g., developing and marketing their own new products), the existing management pool is well known to the evaluators selecting candidates. Thus, in addition to specific objective criteria (e.g., how the manager's unit performed in a previous time period), the criteria may also focus on how the promoted manager would fit in with top management, suggesting more emphasis on a subjective assessment of personality traits.

In firms that grow by acquiring other firms, however, the candidate pool in the new firm will be less well known, since the firm is buying new units. In this case, top management may use more objective criteria in selection decisions. Those criteria could be, for example, years of experience or examples of achievement in previous organizations.

It also seems reasonable that firms that grow through internal expansion will use transfers to promote managers to top management positions whereas firms that acquire others to grow will tend to draw upon managers from units being purchased ("new" insiders) or from other organizations altogether ("outsiders").

In addition, we would expect internal growth firms to use more subjective methods of selection (e.g., "gut feel" of evaluators through interviews), while acquiring firms will tend to use more objective methods. For instance, acquiring firms may use such methods as external assessment by a psychologist or some type of assessment center, in addition to interviews.

SUMMARY AND CONCLUSION

Managers need to understand the importance of integrating strategy, human resources management, and organizational outcomes. It is an area to bring out from "between the cracks." During the 1980s there has been increasing interest in understanding the links between these elements as well as developing evidence in research and practice that should further clarify the links.

Even with the limitations mentioned here, managers can—and should—use what we do know in linking the elements together. This means that human resources as well as other functional areas and top managers must recognize the importance of links and how to use them. It is critical that human resources managers understand their firms' strategies and be involved in forming and implementing the strategies. For too long human resources departments and managers have focused on specific personnel activities without understanding their role in the firm at large. It is up to these managers to show top management the importance human resources issues play in setting and achieving the firm's strategy and in contributing to organizational outcomes. On the other hand, top managers also need to learn more about how human resources issues may contribute to strategy implementation and firm performance.

The matrix discussed here should help human resource and top managers to see how strategy, HRM, and outcomes are related and how to begin to fit the pieces together.

REFERENCES

Butler, J. E., Ferris, G. R., & Smith Cook, D. A. (1988). Exploring some critical dimensions of strategic human resources management. In R. S. Schuler, S. A. Youngblood, & V. Huber (Eds.), *Readings in personnel and human resource management* (3rd ed.). St. Paul, MN: West.

Cascio, W. F. (1982). *Costing human resources: The financial impact of behavior in organizations.* Boston: Kent.

Devanna, M. A., Fombrun, C. J., & Tichy, N. M. (1981, Winter). Human resource management: A strategic perspective. *Organizational Dynamics,* pp. 51–67.

Dyer, L. (1984). Studying human resources strategy: An approach and an agenda. *Industrial Relations, 23,* 156–169.

Foulkes, F. K. (Ed.) (1986). *Strategic human resources management: A guide for effective practice.* Englewood Cliffs, NJ: Prentice-Hall.

Galbraith, J. R. & Nathanson, D. A. (1978). *Strategy implementation: The role of structure and process.* St. Paul, MN: West.

Gerstein, M. & Reisman, H. (1983, Winter). Strategic selection: Matching executives to business conditions. *Sloan Management Review,* pp. 33–49.

Hall, D. T. (1984). Human resource development and organizational effectiveness. In C. J. Fombrun, N. M. Tichy, & M. Devanna (Eds.), *Strategic human resource management* (pp. 159–182). New York: Wiley.

Horovitz, J. H. & Thiebault, R. A. (1982). Strategy, management design, and firm performance. *Strategic Management Journal, 3,* 67–76.

Kanter, R. M. (1983). *The change masters.* New York: Simon and Schuster.

Leontiades, M. (1982). Choosing the right manager to fit the strategy. *Journal of Business Strategy, 3,* 58–69.

Miles, R. E. & Snow, C. C. (1978). *Organizational strategy, structure, and process.* New York: McGraw-Hill.

Misa, K. F. & Stein, T. (1983). Strategic HRM and the bottom line. *Personnel Administrator, 28,* 27–30.

Napier, N. K. & Deller, J. (1984, February). Train right or don't train. *Training and Development Journal,* pp. 90–94.

Napier, N. K. & Smith, M. (1987). Product diversification, performance criteria, and compensation at the corporate manager level. *Strategic Management Journal, 8,* 195–201.

Olian, J. D. & Rynes, S. L. (1984). Organizational staffing: Integrating practice with strategy. *Industrial Relations, 23,* 170–183.

Peters, T. J. & Waterman, R. W. (1982). *In search of excellence.* New York: Harper & Row.

Pitts, R. A. (1974). Incentive compensation and organization design. *Personnel Journal, 53,* 338–348.

Pitts, R. A. (1975). *Interdivisional rotation of middle managers in large diversified firms.* Paper presented at the Annual Meeting of the Academy of Management, New Orleans.

Pitts, R. A. (1977). Strategies and structures for diversification. *Academy of Management Journal, 20,* 197–208.

Porter, M. E. (1981). *Competitive strategy: Techniques for analyzing industries and competitors.* New York: Free Press.

Rumelt, R. (1974). *Strategy, structure, and economic performance.* Boston: Division of Research, Harvard Business School.

Tichy, N. M., Fombrun, C. J., & Devanna, M. (1982). Strategic human resource management. *Sloan Management Review, 23,* 47–61.

Wexley, K. N. & Latham, G. P. (1981). *Developing and training human resources in organizations.* Glenview, IL: Scott, Foresman.

Shaping Strategy: Tie Personnel Functions to Company Goals

Gerald R. Ferris and Dan Curtin

Productivity through people.

Few phrases have come to be so widely applied to business strategy today as this one. Managers at all levels are becoming aware of the contributions that their people make to organizational success.

It is important, though, to state more specifically how personnel management affects organizations. What do effective companies do in personnel management that ineffective companies fail to do?

The following represent the important and special roles of the personnel function which contribute to organizational effectiveness.

ENTRY AND EXIT

The effective management of hiring, flow-through, and exit from organizations is extremely important in companies during good times and bad. Bringing better people into the organization, whose skills better match the demands of the job, is crucial. Recent studies have demonstrated the cost savings to organizations due to using particular selection devices (such as testing) over and above the quality of decisions made without using such devices. One study estimates that the labor savings across U.S. Federal Government jobs from improved selection procedures could be approximately $15 billion per year!

The number and types of new employees sought must fit into a broader personnel-management strategy which is integrated with the strategic plan of the firm. Effective forecasting and planning for environmental changes, growth, cutback, or diversification provide necessary information to develop an appropriate staffing strategy. Organizations that conduct such analyses will fare better when staff reductions may be required.

One procedure is layoffs. However, the recent focus by the courts on the nature of layoffs places increasing demands to have qualified professionals handling this process. Seniority-based layoffs have recently been challenged under fair-employment practices legislation as potentially discriminatory.

Another alternative procedure for managing exit is to encourage early retirements. This practice, if well planned and part of an overall strategy of increasing effectiveness, can be useful in cutting costs and reducing the size of the workforce. However, if not well integrated, the practice may result in more serious consequences for the organization. Pension-plan rules and tax laws place some restrictions on encouraging early retirement. They typically require the organization to offer early retirement to everyone in a particular category for a certain period of time.

Within certain limits, then, the organization has virtually no control over who accepts early retirement. This can be detrimental if good people that you want to stay on end up leaving, or if too many people accept the invitation to retire. To take action on the exit process can be dangerous if it has not managed as part of an integrated human resources plan.

Another aspect of the exit process which has become prominent in recent years is outplacement. Some firms have recently stripped off entire levels of management, but they often assist these people in locating comparable employment elsewhere. Outplacement is an activity that needs to be managed by people who possess skills or ex-

Reprinted from *Management World* with permission of AMS, Willow Grove, PA 19090.

pertise in this area. Such responsibilities typically fall upon the personnel function.

Many personnel professionals, finding themselves unprepared to handle this new responsibility, have rushed to training programs on outplacement. Often, the process of middle-management reductions has already started and been bungled, and the training is taken as a reaction to the recognized need, after the fact. By then, organizational damage has already been done.

WORK REDESIGN

As a consequence of exit processes, there are fewer people in the organization. Of course, one reason for exit, such as layoffs, is because product demand is reduced. However, layoffs as a cost-cutting strategy may result in too few people to perform all of the jobs that exist. If these jobs are critical to the operation and cannot be eliminated, work redesign or job consolidation may be called for.

Such efforts begin with a systematic analysis of different positions in the company to determine the skill and ability demands. The information then serves as a basis for determining which jobs have comparable skill demands, allowing a more logical and effective job-consolidation effort. Work redesign might increase motivation if it results in job enrichment through greater responsibility and challenge, and not simply more tasks of a routine nature.

An alternative to layoffs, but one which may require redesign, is the use of worksharing or four-day workweeks. Schedules could also be arranged whereby two people could share a single job. These practices, as with layoffs, are usually handled by the personnel department.

While attractive, these alternatives also present administrative and legal barriers. Unemployment benefits are not provided for short workweeks in most states since three days of work would disqualify an applicant. However, in California, the state unemployment benefit has been redesigned to recognize job sharing and short workweeks.

Personnel managers must work to negotiate and push for legislation to make these alternatives more feasible. They can become another tool for the professional to use in human resource planning. This, however, would place even greater administrative burdens on personnel departments.

PLANNING AND EVALUATION

Personnel managers should place great emphasis on sound planning and make more extensive use of program evaluation procedures. Sound human resources forecasting and planning efforts should be integrated with systematic performance evaluation and focused career-planning systems. Through internal, long-range analysis, organizations can plan for and make effective use of existing human resources to prepare for freezes on bringing new people into the organization. The economy's better now, but we need to be ready for the next downturn. Successful organizations are proactive and plan for fluctuations in the environment during good times, rather than being forced into a crisis or reactionary posture during bad times.

In tough times, organizations should not drop all training and productivity improvement programs. In fact, during such times, there is even a greater need for such programs. If we are experiencing a hiring freeze and are cutting back the size of our workforce through layoffs, we may have to train current employees for work which they have not performed previously.

A major focus on the use of training programs will be ensuring that they produce proposed results. Program evaluation to determine the effectiveness of the training intervention should be required. This applies as well to the use of productivity improvement programs like quality circles. Researchers and practitioners alike have recently emphasized the importance of personnel management issues in organizational effectiveness. There are three important lessons for managers: be proactive, plan effectively, and take a strategic focus.

The personnel function will maintain its pivotal role in the future, whether in good times or bad. Many large firms that have had to pare their operation have no intention of ever becoming that large again. Therefore, they see the importance of more careful and focused human resource efforts, of working smarter rather than just harder, and of planning effectively.

Of critical importance is the integration of strategic planning with the personnel function. It should be the goal of every personnel professional to push for this, *before* the next recession.

CHAPTER 2

Human Resources Planning

Personnel and human resources management is often viewed as a series of activities designed to process people into, through, and out of organizations. In this view, the first activity is human resources planning, which seeks to determine the number and kinds of people the organization needs now and may need in the foreseeable future, and how to satisfy those needs—perhaps even anticipate them. With the growing interest in strategic human resources management and its linkage to strategic business planning, we will probably see attempts at more systematic human resource planning in the future.

The linkage between human resources planning and strategic business planning is important in the development of an informed forecast of the firm's human resources needs. It addresses critical issues such as the future direction of the organization—whether growth or decline is projected, what types of skills will be required, and so forth—and the current and potential availability, or supply, of human resource skills in the organization and the marketplace.

Human resources information systems are established by organizations to help keep track of such matters. Timely and accurate information may enable an organization, for example, to postpone or implement a variety of recruitment and training activities or to capitalize on the availability of a given mix of skills to pursue a new venture.

Within a broader, more integrated view of the personnel function, career planning and development activities in organizations represent a logical component of human resources planning. Making sure that the right people with the right skills are at the right place at the right time is quite consistent with helping people plan their careers in organizations, establishing paths to take and time frames to be met.

In the first article, Nkomo attempts to determine the extent to which organizations actually utilize the comprehensive human resources planning models that have been presented in the literature. Survey results suggest that nearly half of the responding firms have no formal human resources management plan. Less than 15 percent reported having a fully integrated plan.

In the second article, Dyer examines two objectives of human resources planning: future staffing needs and personnel flows (e.g., hiring, movement, losses). He presents a discussion of the rationale for and mechanics of forecasting and planning for future staffing needs. Furthermore, he demonstrates how a number of different inputs are used to arrive at human resources needs.

Gatewood and Gatewood, in the next article, stress the importance of strategic forecasting of a human resource plan. They show how current forecasting techniques can be adapted to help in this planning and how expert data (i.e., opinions of people) can be utilized in the forecasting effort.

The last two articles in this chapter concentrate on the area of career development. Milkovich and Anderson suggest that the organization, through its human resources management activities, can help employees progress through their career stages. They also suggest that it is important for individuals to take some steps to help guide their own career path. Fandt presents a conceptual framework for integrating human resource management with strategic career management decisions. The author focuses on the interrelationship between the components of career management, which are reviewed in the article, and two strategic business positions companies can assume.

Suggestions for Further Reading

Burack, E. H. (1985). Linking corporate business and human resource planning: Strategic issues and concerns. *Human Resource Planning, 8,* 133–145.

Dyer, L., Shafer, R. A., & Regan, P. J. (1982). Human resource planning at Corning Glass Works: A field study. *Human Resource Planning, 5,* 1–45.

Hoffman, W., Wyatt, L., & Gordon, G. G. (1986). Human resource planning: Shifting from concept to contemporary practice. *Human Resource Planning, 9,* 97–105.

Mills, D. Q. (1985). Planning with people in mind. *Harvard Business Review, 63,* 97–105.

Shurplin, A. D. (1985). Human resource planning: Low-cost strategies to improve workers' job security. *Journal of Business Strategy, 5,* 90–93.

Stone, T. H., & Fiorito, J. (1986). A perceived uncertainty model of human resource forecasting technique use. *Academy of Management Review, 11,* 635–642.

Stumpf, S. A., & Hanrahan, N. M. (1984). Designing organizational career management practices to fit strategic management objectives. In R. S. Schuler &

S. A. Youngblood (Eds.), *Readings in personnel and human resources management* (2nd ed.). St. Paul, MN: West.

Stybel, L. J. (1982). Linking strategic planning and management manpower planning. *California Management Review, 25,* 48–56.

Vetter, E. W. (1985). Getting human resources planning on the dean's list. *Training and Development Journal, 39,* 16–18.

Von Glinow, M. A., Driver, M. J., Brousseau, K., & Prince, J. B. (1983). The design of a career oriented human resource system. *Academy of Management Review, 8,* 23–32.

The Theory and Practice of HR Planning: The Gap Still Remains

Stella M. Nkomo

Strategic management has gained currency in the study of just about all the major functional areas of an organization. A good deal of literature can be found on strategic marketing, strategic production management, strategic research and development, and more recently strategic human resource management.[1]

Concomitantly, substantial attention has been focused on strategic human resource planning as a means of directly linking the attainment of organizational goals to human resource objectives and programs.[2,3] Proponents stress the increasingly important role of human resource management in strategy formulation and implementation. The cumulative impact of governmental, economic, sociocultural and demographic changes during the 1970s has often been cited as a major reason for the heightened interest in strategic human resource planning applications in organizations.[4] Advocates of human resource planning argue that the use of formal human resource planning models in organizations will contribute to the effective and efficient utilization of human resources.

Although many models of human resource planning have been developed and proposed, there is less empirical knowledge about the actual practices of organizations, the extent to which the prescriptive models are used, or the benefits of such planning. Jain and Murray have suggested that many of the ideas about "best practices" in personnel/human resource management have often met three fates: (1) adopted by only a small proportion of work organizations; (2) discontinued after a few years' use; or (3) adopted merely as a "paper phenomenon."[5] The objective of the present survey is to determine the degree to which organizations have adopted the formal, comprehensive models described in the literature. The major question addressed is: To what extent do firms use the comprehensive models proposed in the literature? The focus of this survey is on strategic (long-range) human resource planning practices as opposed to operational (short-range) human resource planning. (For brevity, the use of the term "human resource planning" in this paper refers to long-term or strategic human resource planning.) At the strategic level of human resource planning, the emphasis is relatively long-term (three to five years) and may be defined as the process designed to prepare the organization for the future and to ensure that decisions regarding the use of people contribute to the achievement of organizational objectives.

Previous studies of human resource planning have consisted of rather small sample sizes or have concentrated on case studies of a few individual firms.[6,7,8,9,10,11] Few of these studies have systematically investigated the extent of completeness in the human resource planning process used by firms or specified the level of human resource planning under investigation. It would appear that the opportunity and need exist to explore more closely the extent of human resource planning in organizations.

METHOD

The sample for this survey consisted of firms listed in the *Fortune 500 Directory.* Questionnaires along with a cover letter were mailed to the vice president of personnel/human resources in each of these 500 companies. A total of 287 responses were received, representing a 57 percent return rate. Of the responses received, 264 questionnaires were fully usable. Over 35 percent of the respondents were top level corporate personnel officers—senior vice presidents and vice presidents of personnel/human resources. The remainder were at the director/manager level.

Questionnaire. To measure the completeness of an organization's human resource planning process, a questionnaire was designed based on an analysis of the normative requirements for such planning as outlined in the literature.[2,3,12] This literature suggests that a complete human resource planning process should:

1. *Analyze the external environment (environmental analysis):* Systematic identification and analysis of key external trends, forces and phenomena having a potential impact on the management of an organization's human resources.

2. *Be integrated with strategic business planning.* Human resource objectives and strategies will be largely derived from overall organization strategic plans. At the same time, the strategic choices of an organization will be constrained by the quality and quantity of its current human resources or those available in the labor market. Therefore, intimate linkage with strategic business planning is essential.

3. *Analyze current human resource supply:* An analysis of the current number of employees, their work-related skills, demographic make-up, performance levels, potential performance attitudes, etc. This information is used to form a baseline of human resource abilities and capabilities available for future organizational requirements.

4. *Forecast future human resource demand:* A projection of quantitative and qualitative staffing needs (numbers and types of employees for each job category) required for future periods.

5. *Generate, analyze and develop strategies and policies to achieve human resource objectives:* Identification of possible functional area programming activities (e.g., recruitment, selection, compensation, training and development) to meet human resource needs.

6. *Review and monitor progress toward the attainment of human resource objectives:* Ongoing evaluation of the results of human resource programming activities and the correction of any deviations identified.

These major characteristics were used in the construction of a questionnaire aimed at identifying the type of human resource planning used by an organization. Respondents were asked to specify the existence and extent of human resource planning in their organization by choosing the appropriate responses. Additionally, managers were asked to make an evaluation of the contribution of human resource planning efforts to overall organization performance and the benefits derived in the areas of labor cost savings, employee satisfaction, employee productivity, management development, EEO/Affirmative Action and staffing effectiveness. Further, companies were given the option of providing copies or samples of their human resource planning manuals, forms or other documents that illustrate the human resource planning process used in their organization. Several firms forwarded such materials.

CLASSIFICATION SCHEME

Based on questionnaire responses, each respondent firm's human resource planning process was classified objectively into one of the following categories:

Category 1. No formal human resource planning.

Category 2. Partial or incomplete human resource planning.

Category 3. Fully-integrated human resource planning.

The human resource planning process of Category 3 firms included all six components described above. If a firm did not meet all of the requirements for Category 3, it was assigned to Category 2. Firms placed in Category 1 did not prepare formal human resource plans.

RESULTS

Human Resource Planning Category. Based on the categorization scheme, 121 firms (46 percent) do not prepare any formal human resource plans, 104 (39 percent) had incomplete human resource plans and only 39 (14.8 percent) prepare the fully integrated plans advocated in the literature. It is of interest to note that several Category 1 firms indicated that they expected to begin formal human resource planning in the very near future.

Industry Breakdown. Table 1 shows the respondents classified by industry and human resource planning category. Although a wide array of manufacturing industries are represented, certain groups dominate the sample. The most dominant groups are food and kindred products, chemicals and allied products, primary metal products, ma-

Table 1
Respondents By Industry Group and HRP Category (N = 264)

	Human Resource Planning Category[a]		
Industry	*1*	*2*	*3*
Mining	4	1	0
Construction	0	1	0
Food and Kindred	16	9	3
Textile Mill Products	4	2	1
Apparel & Other Finished Goods	2	0	2
Lumber & Wood Products	0	1	1
Furniture & Fixture	1	0	0
Paper & Allied Products	4	3	3
Printing/Publishing & Allied Products	4	4	1
Chemicals & Allied Products	14	19	6
Petroleum Refining & Related Industries	11	9	4
Rubber & Miscellaneous Plastic Materials	1	2	2
Stone, Clay & Glass Products	2	3	0
Primary Metal	12	7	2
Fabricated Metal Products Except Machinery and Transportation Equipment	5	3	2
Machinery Not Electrical	17	9	4
Electrical & Electronic Machinery	6	13	0
Transportation Equipment	9	10	6
Measuring, Analyzing and Controlling Instruments	4	5	2
Miscellaneous Manufacturing Industries	0	2	0
Railroads/Line Haul	1	1	0
Wholesale Trade	2	0	0
Retail Fuel	1	0	0
Services	1	0	0
Total	121	104	39

[a]*Small cell sizes limit making any strong inferences about industry differences in human resource planning practices.*

chinery (not electrical), electrical and electronic machinery, and transportation equipment. The small cell sizes limit making any strong inferences about industry differences in human resource planning practices.

Firm Size and Human Resource Planning. Table 2 contains information regarding sample characteristics in terms of total assets, sales and number of employees. An examination of Table 2 suggests that size is associated with the use of formal human resource planning in sample firms. The users of formal human resource planning as a group were larger than non-users in terms of total assets, number of employees and sales. It is of interest to note, however, that the relationship does not appear to be linear. Firms using the fully-integrated processes are smaller than Category 2 human resource planners.

Initiation of Human Resource Planning. Eighty-five percent of the respondent firms initiated human resource planning during or after 1970. The data indicate a steady growth in use over the last two decades. Prior to 1960 only four firms in the sample engaged in human resource planning. During the 1960s, 15 firms in the sample initiated planning, while during the 1970s 78 firms began formal human resource planning. From 1980 to the present, 45 additional *Fortune* 500 firms initiated human resource planning. If this trend continues during the decade, we may witness a more pervasive use of strategic human resource planning in organizations. The data lend some support to the proposition that external environmental pressures during the 1970s led to a heightened interest in human resource planning applications.[4]

Planning Responsibility. Over 90 percent of the respondents reported that the primary responsibility for human resource planning rested either with the corporate personnel department or the division personnel department or a combination thereof. Few organizations reported active line management involvement in the process. This suggests that most organizations view human resource planning as a major personnel activity. This is in stark contrast to findings reported by Geisler[13] over 15 years ago when manpower planning did not exist as a separate personnel staff activity.

External Environmental Analysis. For firms with a formal human resource planning process, the most prevalent environmental factors monitored are major trends and changes in technology, labor market conditions and economic conditions. This finding is not surprising since it is evident that technological developments can have a major impact on job skill requirements and knowledge of labor supply and demand is a prerequisite for effective forecasting. Few firms are presently analyzing changes in the more intangible social/cultural environment in preparing their human resource plans.

Functional Area Strategy. One stated purpose of human resource planning is to foster integration of the various functional areas of personnel/human resource management. Recruitment/staffing, management succession and training and devel-

Table 2
Size and Category of HRP (N = 264)

Variable	*1* *No Formal* N = *121*	*2* *Incomplete* N = *104*	*3* *Fully-Integrated* N = *39*
Average Assets (billions)	1,307	2,904	2,747
Average Sales (billions)	1,617	4,117	3,895
Average Number of Employees	19,754	54,778	33,589

opment were the major areas for which strategies and programs were developed as part of the human resource planning process. Few companies reported developing strategies or objectives to cover health safety and labor relations (see Table 3). Thus, strategy formulation issues for human resources are confined to the traditional concerns with human resource flows and allocations.

Internal Human Resource Supply Analysis. An important part of the human resource planning process is an internal analysis of the present work force to identify strengths and weaknesses. Table 4 summarizes the factors considered by respondents. The major areas emphasized are the number of employees by job categories, employee demographics (e.g., age, sex, race) and current performance levels. Less attention is focused on ascertaining qualitative information about employee potential and employee attitudes.

A majority of the firms in the sample concentrate their human resource planning on managerial and technical/professional employees. Only 20 percent of the firms reported coverage of all of their employees. This finding is not surprising because one would expect that strategic human resource planning efforts would be concentrated on those employee groups which represent a relatively large investment and a longer time frame to develop.

Table 3
Functional Areas in Which Strategies and Programs Are Developed

Function	N	*Percent*[a]
Recruitment/Staffing	130	90.0
Compensation	84	58.7
Training and Development	130	90.9
Management Succession	136	95.1
Employee Benefits	56	39.2
Affirmative Action	97	67.8
Labor Relations	50	35.0
Health and Safety	31	21.7

[a]Percentages do not total 100 percent since each firm may analyze several of these factors.

Table 4
Factors Considered in Internal Analysis of Workforce

Factor	N	*Percent*[a]
Number of Employees by Job Category	107	74.8
Skill Analysis of Work Force	83	58.0
Employee Demographics	102	71.3
Current Performance Levels	107	74.8
Employee Potential	91	63.6
Employee Attitudes	45	31.5
Other	15	10.7

[a]Percentages do not total 100 percent since each firm may analyze more than one of these factors.

Forecast of Future Human Resource Demand. Eighty-six percent of the firms who engage in human resource planning prepare a forecast of future human resource demand. A list of specific forecasting techniques used in human resource planning is presented in Table 5. It is interesting to note, however, that the vast majority of the firms do not use sophisticated forecasting techniques (e.g., regression analysis, Markov models, computer simulation, etc.), but rely heavily upon tra-

Table 5
Forecasting Techniques Used in HRP

Technique	N	*Percent*[a]
Replacement Charts	120	83.9
Skills Inventory	73	51.0
Manning Tables	77	53.8
Time Series/Regression Analysis	7	4.9
Delphi	5	3.5
Computer Simulation	14	9.8
Markov	6	4.2
Other	11	7.7

[a]Percentages do not sum to 100 since a firm may use more than one of these techniques.

ditional forecasting techniques like replacement charts. Contrary to the emphasis placed on Delphi and Markov techniques in the literature, very few firms reported use of these techniques, which would allow more what-if analyses. This finding implies that human resource forecasting efforts have been largely confined to providing a supply of employees as replacements rather than analyzing the impact of alternative business strategies on human resource demand and supply.

Integration with Strategic Business Planning. Fifty-seven percent of the responding firms reported that there is either no integration of human resource planning with strategic business plans or that human resource planning was carried out after strategic business plans are developed. This finding implies that most human resource planning is carried out either in isolation from organizational planning or in a reactive mode rather than a proactive mode. Only one-third of the firms who engage in human resource planning reported an integral relationship between human resource planning and strategic business planning. Firms who have achieved this linkage reported three ways in which this was being accomplished: (1) strategic human resource issues are studied by the personnel staff and their findings are presented to management as inputs to strategic planning; (2) planning committees comprised of line managers, personnel staff and corporate planners are formed to identify and analyze key human resource issues; and (3) line managers are asked to identify the human resource implications of proposed strategic plans and to indicate possible actions to meet strategic human resource needs.

Review and Evaluation. Seventy-four percent of the responding firms reported that their human resource planning process included procedures for reviewing progress toward the attainment of objectives and procedures for correcting any deviations identified.

Benefits of Human Resource Planning. For firms engaged in formal human resource planning, managers were asked to make an evaluation of its contribution to organization performance and the benefits derived in the areas of labor cost savings, employee satisfaction, employee productivity, management development, EEO and staffing effectiveness. An analysis was performed to test for differences in these evaluations between firms classified as Category 2 (incomplete human resource planners) and those classified as Category 3 (fully integrated human resource planners). The results of this analysis are reported in Table 6. Firms using a fully-integrated human resource planning process rated the contributions of the planning significantly higher than firms which were classified as using incomplete approaches.

CONCLUSION

Formal strategic human resource planning is still in its infancy even among *Fortune* 500 firms. Although 54 percent of the sample firms prepare formal human resource plans, only a small fraction (14.8 percent) prepare the comprehensive plans outlined in the literature. Although the trend appears to be toward greater applications of human resource planning in the future, longitudinal research will be needed to track new adoptions and also to monitor consistency and persistence of use.

Most organizations in the survey viewed the human resource planning function as a major responsibility of corporate and divisional personnel/human resource departments. Few organizations reported active line management involvement in the process. In a majority of the sample firms, human resource planning was not integrated with strategic business planning, and appeared to be carried out in isolation from strategic business planning or was treated as a derivative of strategic business planning rather than a primary function.

An important question arises: Why have so few firms developed comprehensive human resource planning systems? Although this question is not specifically addressed in this research, many possible explanations exist. First, despite the lip service given to the cliche, "people are our most important asset," in many organizations people are viewed as an operating cost and not as a major corporate resource or investment. Most well-operated companies routinely apply the "return on investment" concept to their financial and

Table 6
Perceived Benefits of Strategic Human Resource Planning

	Planning Category[a]	
Benefits	*Incomplete* N = *56*	*Fully Integrated* N = *25*
1. Contribution to Organization Performance	3.30	[b]3.92
2. Labor Cost Savings	1.93	[c]2.68
3. Employee Productivity	2.30	[c]3.00
4. Employee Satisfaction	2.80	[b]3.32
5. Management Development	4.00	[b]4.52
6. EE0/AA Goals	2.94	3.44
7. Reducing Under- and Over-Staffing	2.91	[b]3.52

[a]*Measured on a 5-point Likert scale; 1 = low and 5 = high*
[b]*Significant at the .01 level.*
[c]*Significant at the .05 level.*

production operations; yet they fail to apply this concept to the management of their own human resources.

Second, strategic planning for human resource requirements has generally lagged behind planning for capital and financial resources in many organizations. One respondent suggested that because of the unique flexibility of human resources, planning is often less critical. It is often assumed that the right number and right kind of people will be found when needed. This has often led to an emphasis on short-term operational personnel activities at the expense of long-term strategic programs.

Third, another contributing factor may be the difficulty of personnel/human resource managers in overcoming the historical lack of influence and power personnel departments have had with corporate management. Jain and Murray have noted that in many organizations the personnel specialist is an individual with neither the background nor potential to create an image of a highly qualified, confident participant in top-level strategy and decision-making.[5]

Finally, organizations may be relying more on informal planning mechanisms. Quinn has suggested that many important strategic decisions are often made outside of the formal planning structure, even in organizations with well-accepted planning cultures.[14] It is possible that firms classified as non-human resource planners in this survey have informal systems that allow them to effectively meet human resource needs. This possibility warrants further examination.

The results of this survey suggest that the literature is far ahead of actual practices in most U.S. firms. Craft in a critical review of human resource planning theory in 1980 cautioned, "Human resource planning risks becoming the current personnel fad which makes great promises and ends up as an equally great disappointment through its failure to deliver on unrealistic expectations."[15]

Perhaps the broad generalizations and recommendations found in the literature offer little practical guidance for organizations interested in developing a human resource planning system. Questions of how to better align business strategy and human resource strategy, how to assess alternative human resource strategies and the situational variables indicating the appropriateness of human resource planning for a particular organization are largely unanswered. It is time for personnel managers and researchers to take a closer look at how to effectively implement human resource planning.

REFERENCES

1. Mary Anne Devanna, Charles Fombrun and Noel Tichy, "Human Resource Management: A Strategic Perspective." *Organizational Dynamics,* Winter 1981, pp. 51–67.

2. James Walker, *Human Resource Planning.* New York, NY: McGraw-Hill, 1980.

3. Lee Dyer, "Human Resource Planning," in Kenneth Rowland and Gerald Ferris, eds. *Personnel Management,* Allyn and Bacon, Boston, MA, 1982.

4. Stella M. Nkomo, "Stage Three in Personnel Administration: Strategic Human Resource Management," *Personnel,* July-August 1980, pp. 69–77.

5. Harish Jain and Vector Murray, "Why the Human Resources Management Function Fails," *California Management Review,* 26, 1984, pp. 95–110.

6. Elmer H. Burack and Thomas G. Gutteridge, "Institutional Manpower Planning: Rhetoric or Reality," *California Management Review,* Spring 1978, pp. 13–22.

7. K. M. Rowland and S. L. Summers, "Human Resource Planning: Disregarded Assumptions and New Priorities." Paper prepared for the American Society for Personnel Administration, 1982.

8. Guvene G. Alpander, "Human Resource Planning in U.S. Corporations," *California Management Review,* 22, 1980, pp. 24–32.

9. Harvey Kahalas, Harold L. Pazer, John S. Hoagland and Amy Levitt, "Human Resource Planning Activities in U.S. Firms," *Human Resource Planning,* 3, 1980, pp. 53–66.

10. Lee Dyer, Richard Shafer and Paul J. Regan, "Human Resource Planning at Corning Glass Works: A Field Study," *Human Resource Planning,* 5, 1982, pp. 115–148.

11. Lee Dyer and Nelson D. Hyer, "Human Resource Planning at IBM," *Human Resource Planning,* 7, 1984, pp. 111–125.

12. George T. Milkovich, Lee Dyer and Thomas A. Mahoney, "HRM Planning," in Stephen J. Carroll and Randall S. Schuler, eds., *Human Resources Management in the 1980s.* Washington, DC: Bureau of National Affairs, Inc., 1983, pp. 2-1–2-28.

13. Edwin Geisler, *Manpower Planning: An Emerging Staff Function.* New York, NY: AMA Bulletin, NO. 101, 1967.

14. James B. Quinn, *Strategies For Change: Logical Incrementalism.* Homewood, IL: Richard D. Irwin, Inc., 1980.

15. James Craft, "A Critical Perspective on Human Resource Planning," *Human Resource Planning,* 3, 1980, p. 52.

Setting Human Resource Planning Objectives

Lee Dyer

Conceptual models of human resource planning (HRP) abound. A careful review of these models seems to suggest that the process is best viewed as involving three interrelated phases: (1) setting HRP objectives, (2) planning personnel programs, and (3) evaluation and control. The discussion here is limited to the first phase, setting HRP objectives.

HRP objectives are of two types. The first involves future staffing needs, or the number and

Adapted from *Personnel Management,* © 1982, Allyn and Bacon, Inc.

types of employees an organization will require to meet its goals during a planning period. The second set of HRP objectives pertains to desired personnel flows; that is, to the combination of accessions, internal moves, and losses that will result in personnel availabilities to match anticipated needs. The importance of HRP objectives lies in the fact that they serve as both targets and standards: targets for subsequent steps in the planning process and standards for judging the value of the plans made.

ESTABLISHING FUTURE STAFFING NEEDS

Business plans[1] determine future staffing needs. Through business planning, management charts an organization's future in terms of financial objectives, product mix, technologies, resource requirements, and the like (Walker, 1980). Once the direction of the business is set, the human resource planner assists in developing workable organizational structures and in determining the numbers and types of employees that will be required to meet financial and output goals.

This is no easy task. The expertise of many levels of management and several functional specialists may be required (Frantzreb, 1976; Walker, 1978). Further existing methodologies are at best crude. Research has so far failed to develop adequate means of determining whether organizations are currently under- or over-staffed, let alone techniques to establish appropriate staffing levels for new businesses or emerging technologies.

As a consequence, *managerial estimates* often are relied upon. Estimates of total staffing needs may be made by top management in the unit or employee group at issue (top-down), or initial estimates may be made by lower level managers whose figures are refined and consolidated through group discussions at successively higher levels (bottom-up). A variant is the *delphi technique* through which independent estimates of future staffing needs are elicited by means of successive iterations of questionnaires. At each iteration, estimates are sought and clarifying data may be provided. The expectation is that four or five iterations will result in a convergence of estimates.

Practices apparently vary concerning the amount of guidance and assistance managers receive when making estimates of future staffing needs. Minimal guidance may come in the form of checklists of factors to be considered or questions to be asked (Walker, 1980). Managers may also be provided the results of time study analyses or a set of predetermined staffing guides (Ettelstein, 1977; Niehaus, 1979). In certain circumstances, statistical projections may be derived. Two of these—*regression analysis* and *productivity ratios*—use such work load indicators as sales volume, production levels, value added, productivity rates, and budgets to forecast future staffing needs. The third technique—*personnel ratios*—relies on relative patterns of employment levels in various units or among selected occupational groups, while the fourth—*time series analysis*—simply extrapolates past staffing levels, giving no consideration to future business plans.

The various statistical projection techniques tend to be limited in practice. All, for example, rely on past data, which restricts their use to situations where a relevant history exists. Further, because of the heavy reliance on historical data, statistical techniques work best in relatively stable organizations that anticipate little change in product mix, productivity levels, technology, or organizational design.

ESTABLISHING FUTURE HUMAN RESOURCE FLOWS AND AVAILABILITIES

Given a set of staffing needs, how can adequate numbers of the right types of people be made available on a timely basis to meet them? As shown in Figure 1, future personnel availabilities are a function of the personnel levels in various job categories at the beginning of the planning period adjusted to reflect: (1) losses resulting from retirement, termination, resignation, and other reasons; (2) gains and losses resulting from internal moves into or out of job categories through promotions, lateral moves, or demotions; and (3) accessions through recruitment or other means.

From Figure 1 it is apparent that an organization's current work force provides the base from

Figure 1
Model of the Process Used to Establish Personnel Flows and Availabilities

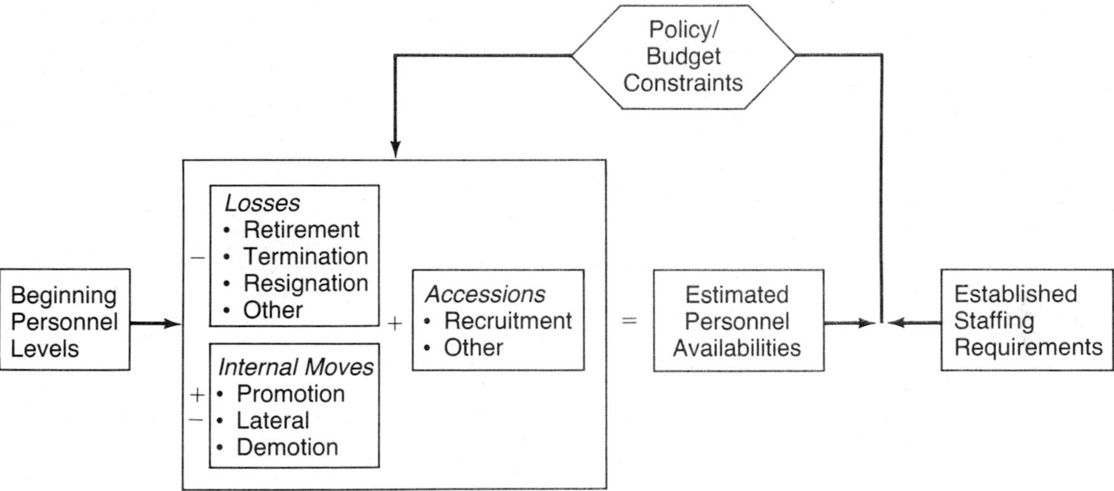

which estimates of future flows and availabilities are made. Judgmental analyses require extensive data about each employee, including name, job title, performance rating, promotability rating, years of service, years on present job, geographic location, previous jobs held, training programs attended, special skills possessed, and career interests. Some statistical analyses begin with nothing more than a simple count of people in each job category. Others additionally include a record of certain employee characteristics (e.g., age or length of service) that are expected to be related to one or more flow rates (e.g., retirements or resignations).

Judgmental analyses of flows and availabilities may be done using executive reviews, replacement analysis, or vacancy analysis. *Executive reviews* tend to focus on special groups of employees, particularly those at the very highest levels and those judged to have the potential to reach these levels. These reviews are carried out through one or more meetings at which executives thoroughly discuss each person under review to determine which are likely to (or should) leave the organization, be promoted, or be reassigned during the planning period. Determinations are made on the basis of the data previously mentioned: performance, long-term potential, career aspirations and the like. As the deliberations proceed, anticipated moves (flows) emerge and judgments can be made concerning the overall adequacy of current personnel in light of established needs.

Replacement analysis is similar to the executive review procedures except that the "technology" tends to be more formal and greater numbers of employees may be involved. It begins with the development of replacement charts showing for each job under consideration the incumbent and one or more replacements who could fill the job should it become vacant. By examining replacement charts, managers can systematically determine likely vacancies resulting from retirements, terminations, and so forth, and plan out desired internal moves.

Executive reviews and, especially, replacement analysis often are conducted with no explicit consideration given to changes in staffing needs. Further, they provide only qualitative information concerning future personnel flows. A judgmental method designed to overcome these shortcomings is *vacancy analysis.* Here, beginning staff levels are arrayed by job categories (states), and from these numbers are subtracted anticipated losses to yield what is called effective supply. Effective supply is matched against established staffing needs to yield a preliminary estimate of anticipated vacancies. Each vacancy is then considered to determine whether it is likely to be filled internally and, if so, from which job categories.

Statistical techniques for forecasting and/or analyzing future personnel flows and availabilities include Markov analysis, simulation, renewal analysis, and goal programming.

Markov analysis is used to track past patterns of personnel movements and to project these patterns into the future. The theoretical and mathematical underpinnings of Markov analysis are complex (Bartholomew and Forbes, 1979), but it is one of the more straightforward statistical techniques to use (Niehaus, 1979).

Markov analysis begins with the development of a transition matrix that models the unit or employee group under consideration, as shown in part A of Table 1. The percentages represent average rates of historical movements between job categories (states) from one period to another (often one year and the next). In this case, a five-year historical analysis revealed, for example, that in any given year about 10 percent of the middle managers moved to top management, while 80 percent stayed in middle management, 5 percent were demoted to lower management, and 5 percent left the unit. Using these data, future personnel flows can be projected by multiplying the staffing levels at the beginning of the planning period by the computed probabilities, and future availabilities determined by summing the columns.

An example involving a one-period projection is shown in part B of Table 1. Projections made in this way—here 100, 190, and 490 for top, middle, and lower management, respectively—can be compared with established staffing requirements and anticipated shortages and surpluses, and their causes noted. Assuming no growth or contraction, the present analysis shows parity at the top, and shortages of 10 and 110 people at the middle and lower levels, respectively. From these data, changes in flow rates that might help match availabilities with needs can be suggested. For example, to fill the anticipated shortage of middle managers, the organization might plan to recruit ten people from outside, or to increase slightly (to 7 percent) the proportion of lower-level managers to be promoted and to offset the effects of this by recruiting more heavily at the lower level.

Table 1
Elements of a Markov Analysis

(A)		M_1	M_2	M_3	*Exit*
Top Management (M_1)		.80			.20
Middle Management (M_2)		.10	.80	.05	.05
Lower Management (M_3)			.05	.80	.15
(B)	*Beginning Personnel Levels*	M_1	M_2	M_3	*Exit*
Top Management (M_1)	100	80			20
Middle Management (M_2)	200	20	160	10	10
Lower Management (M_3)	600		30	480	90
Forecasted Availabilities		100	190	490	

As described, Markov analysis leaves to the analyst or decision-maker the task of judgmentally generating possible alternative flows that might match personnel availabilities with established staffing needs. A straightforward extension, however, permits this to be done statistically, and for the options to be tested using computer *simulation* techniques.

By far the greatest use of simulation to date, however, has been in the specialized area of affirmative action planning. Here affirmative action goals are analogous to established staffing levels in the more general case. Various combinations of flow shares for minorities and women are modeled to determine which (if any) are likely to yield full utilization of these groups (Churchill and Shank, 1976; Ledvinka and LaForge, 1978; Chew and Justice, 1979; Milkovich and Krzystofiak, 1979).

Markov analysis, and simulations based on it, are known as supply-push models because promotions and other internal movements are estimated by applying historical transition rates in various job categories without considering whether vacancies exist in other job categories, or whether individuals are ready to move. Since these features do not reflect reality in many cases, some researchers have begun to experiment with renewal, or demand-pull, analysis.

Renewal analysis, like vacancy analysis, is driven by job vacancies. Vacancies are created by organizational growth, personnel losses, and internal movements out of various job categories. Growth (or shrinkage) is factored in by setting job category sizes equal to established staffing requirements. Then, a computer program is used to: (1) remove from each job category individuals expected to be lost, (2) fill vacancies at the top according to established rules, (3) repeat (1) and (2) for the next category down, and so forth until all vacancies are eliminated (or it becomes obvious that they cannot be). While simple conceptually, renewal analysis is theoretically and mathematically complex (Bartholomew and Forbes, 1979).

Goal programming, the fourth statistical technique, optimizes one or more goals (called objective functions) subject to a series of linear constraints. The usual goal is to meet established staffing requirements as closely as possible (i.e., to minimize the deviations between requirements and estimated personnel availabilities). Another possible goal is to minimize staffing costs. Typical constraints include upper limits on the percent of flows from each job category, upper limits on the number of new recruits permitted in each category, and total salary budgets.

Goal programming is a powerful and flexible technique. One great advantage is its ability to "look ahead" and calculate a set of flows in earlier time periods that will smooth out the effects of significant events (e.g., a steep drop in staffing requirements) in later periods. Markov and renewal analyses lack this capability. Goal programming also can be used to play "what if" games by altering goals and/or constraints in various runs.

Although goal programming is particularly complex, all statistical methods of estimating personnel flows and availabilities involve significant data manipulations that may be feasible only with the aid of computers. Fortunately, personnel departments are increasingly gaining access to, and expertise with, computers, and new software programs are appearing regularly.

Whether done judgmentally or statistically, or by using a combination of the two, analyses of future personnel flows and availabilities in the context of staffing requirements ultimately result in objectives that drive the second phase of the HRP process. Sample objectives include the following:

1. Controlling the flow rates decided upon, including retirements, terminations, layoffs, resignations, transfers, promotions, lateral movements, demotions, and inflows through recruitment

2. Controlling the flow shares of women and minorities (to meet affirmative action goals and timetables)

3. Meeting desired replacement ratios (i.e., number of ready replacements per position)

ENDNOTE

1. The term *business plans* is used here in a generic sense. It is realized that governmental and not-for-profit institutions also develop long- and short-range plans from which staffing needs are derived.

REFERENCES

Bartholomew, D. J., & Forbes, A. F. (1979). *Statistical techniques for manpower planning.* Chichester, England: Wiley.

Chew, W. B., & Justice, R. L. (1979). EEO modeling for large, complex organizations. *Human Resource Planning, 2,* 57–70.

Churchill, N. C., & Shank, J. K. (1976). Affirmative action and guilt-edged goals. *Harvard Business Review, 54,* 111–116.

Ettelstein, M. S. (1977). Staffing guides: A tool for manpower forecasting. In R. B. Frantzreb (Ed.), *Manpower planning.* Sunnyvale, CA: Advanced Personnel Systems.

Frantzreb, R. B. (1976). *Manpower planning.* Sunnyvale, CA: Advanced Personnel Systems.

Ledvinka, J., & LaForge, R. L. (1978). A staffing model for affirmative action planning. *Human Resource Planning, 1,* 135–150.

Milkovich, G. T., & Krzystofiak, F. (1979). Simulation and affirmative action planning. *Human Resource Planning, 2,* 71–80.

Niehaus, R. J. (1979). *Computer-assisted human resource planning.* New York: Wiley.

Walker, J. W. (1980). *Human resource planning.* New York: McGraw-Hill.

Walker, J. W. (1978). Human resource planning: An odyssey to 2001 and beyond. *Pittsburgh Business Review, 47,* 2–8.

The Use of Expert Data in Human Resource Planning: Guidelines from Strategic Forecasting

Robert D. Gatewood and Elizabeth J. Gatewood

Expert data (opinions of individuals) are frequently a part of forecasting activities associated with business policy and strategic management decisions. As a result, specific techniques and guidelines regarding the use of judges and the gathering of information have been developed. This article discusses the use of expert data in human resource planning (HRP) and how some of the information from the forecasting literature is relevant for HRP activities.

The basis of HRP systems is the forecasting of labor supply and labor demand. Labor demand is the number and types of jobs that will be required by the organization at some future time: labor supply is the available present employees together with potential employees now external to the organization.

The labor demand of an organization should be directly related to the projected business strategies of the organization, e.g., growth, diversification, retrenchment strategies. It is these projected strategies that ultimately lead to forecasts of the number and type of needed managerial, technical and professional staff, as well as when these will be needed. Also related to projected business strategies is the forecast of labor supply. Available in-house staff are determined by using information about such items as current staff levels, anticipated recruitment and movement rates, and training and development programs. The results of

Reprinted from *Human Resource Planning, 6,* pp. 83–94.

these two forecasts are then compared, yielding an estimate of future personnel shortages and/or surpluses.

Obviously, the compilation of these forecasts requires the gathering and processing of diverse data. Walker (1980) discusses this in some detail (Figure 1). As Walker indicates, the starting point of such forecasting is the understanding of the environmental and organizational conditions affecting future organizational personnel requirements: external labor supply, legal constraints, economic developments, technological patterns and trends, management philosophies and policies, and patterns of employee turnover and mobility. The analyses of these data lead to the steps in both demand and supply forecasting. For demand forecasting the following data become essential: present authorized positions, organization structure, occupational mix and planning criteria, and projected organizational changes in budgets, operations, and activities. Supply forecasting requires data such as the following: data about the present employees in terms of demographics, performance appraisal, interests, and previous educa-

Figure 1
The Human Resource Forecasting Process

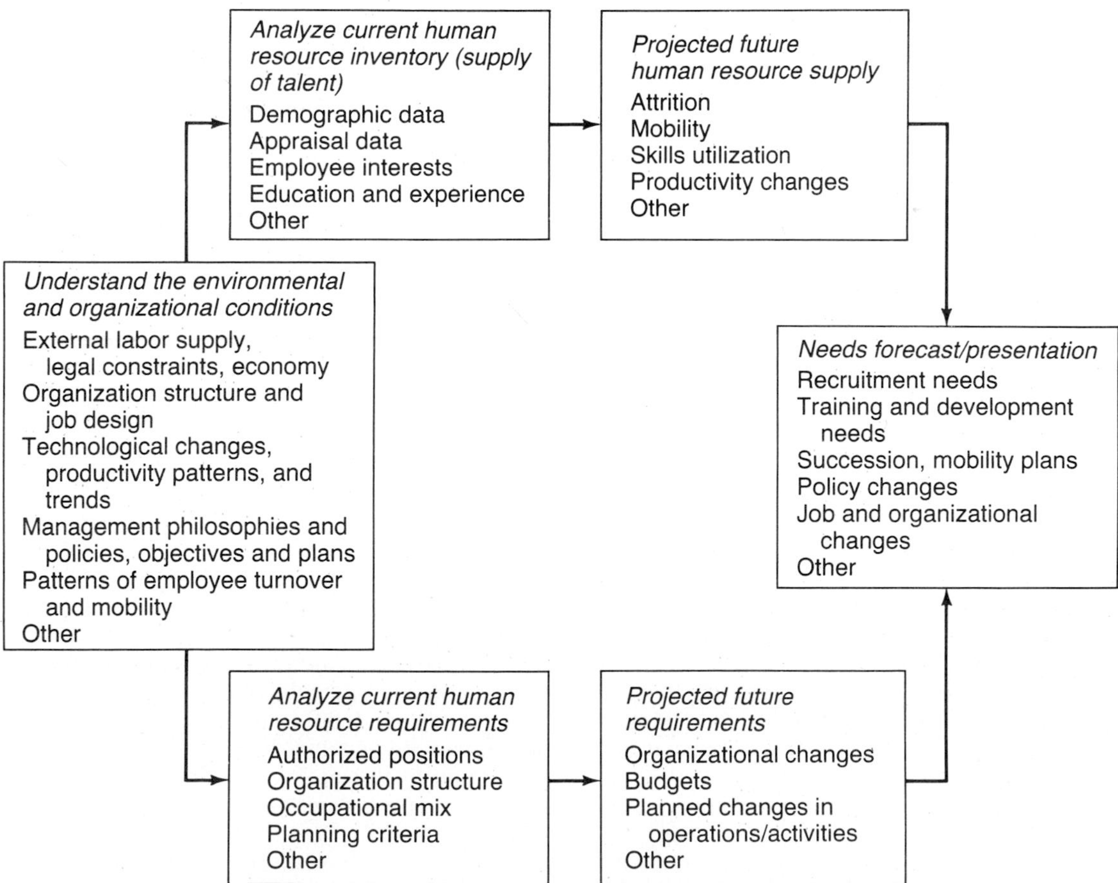

Source: Human Resource Planning, *J. W. Walker, p. 102, © 1980, McGraw-Hill. Reprinted by permission.*

tional and work experience, as well as projected data about attrition and mobility among workers, productivity levels, and skill utilization patterns. The end product of the supply and demand forecasts should be the formulation of specific statements regarding recruitment needs, training and development needs, and succession and mobility plans. Cashel (1978) discusses the difficulty in the accurate gathering of these types of data:

> *The big unknowns in human resource planning are . . . the rapidity and extent to which new technologies will be introduced; the improvements in productivity that will be realized; and the degree to which staff growth will occur to fill needs for more methods, better training, more sophisticated tariffs, and more system analysis and programming to support a more complex, computer oriented technology. These are unknown. And because predictions about them are uncertain, the predictions about people are also uncertain. (p. 65)*

Sheridan (1981) also reports the necessity and difficulty of forecasting data necessary for HRP, especially characteristics of the population and the labor force, changes in the economy, changing social values, and legislation.

Of assistance in these difficult human resource forecasting activities has been the development of techniques and models specifically intended for HRP and the adaptation of techniques and models borrowed from other areas with similar data sources and analytic needs. These forecasting models are usually categorized as either quantitative or qualitative according to their use of mathematical statements. Examples of quantitative techniques and their use in HRP are: succession analysis (replacement analysis and blockages); markov/stochastic renewal models (probability-based flow forecasts); regression analysis (correlations to projected changes); and linear and non-linear dynamic programming (future needs identified to achieve defined objectives). Given numerical inputs representing the data previously discussed, frequently under the assumption of the continuance of recent historical trends, these forecasting methods apply mathematical formulae to yield either point or range estimates of the variable in question. These forecasting models are obviously valuable to manpower planning efforts. Their development frequently forces the identification and study of variables related to manpower needs and the specification of the inter-relationship among these variables. The completed model also frequently allows the updating and reforecasting of both supply and demand at regular intervals.

However, the nature of the data required in HRP forecasting often is not appropriate for quantitative models. Walker (1980) refers to this as the "art" of human forecasting. He states, "Forecasting human resource needs is an imprecise art, depending heavily on the judgment of those involved in the process." (p. 100). Burack and Mathys (1980) also point this out in discussing forecasting the supply of manpower:

> *. . . the supply of manpower is obtained from both within and outside the organization. The forces affecting these two areas of supply and the accuracy of forecasting vary greatly. In all cases, however, none can be handled in purely quantitative terms without also involving some appropriate managerial judgments and assumptions. Although forces and activities largely within the firm are certainly more controllable and predictable than those outside the organization, even this assertion holds only in a relative sense. Our studies indicate that even in the case of internal manpower, substantial gaps in information exist. (p. 25)*

It is the use of these managerial judgments that require non-quantitative forecasting techniques. These are generally referred to as qualitative forecasting techniques and have long been used in strategic planning activities. Wheelwright and Makridakis (1980) write that in general, business forecasting qualitative models are used when little or no historical data are available and most often when two issues are being addressed: (a) predicting the time at which some technology or change will be adopted, and (b) predicting what technology and discoveries will be made in a specified area or specific time frame.

There seem to be issues in human resource planning similar to these, e.g., the prediction of trends or changes in trends such as education, social values, government regulations, mobility, and economics. Organizational changes, and productivity and technological changes in specific time frames are important for manpower forecasts. Frequently there is also a lack of historical data in these areas.

The basis of qualitative forecasting techniques is the employment of experts to help in preparing the forecasts. Various techniques simply present alternative procedures for helping these experts to express their judgments of the future. It is this dependence on the judgment of experts that makes qualitative approaches less desirable than quantitative methods to many forecasters when there is a choice between the two types. Experts vary considerably in their judgments, thus making the forecast seemingly partially dependent upon the specific expert concerned. Qualitative methods usually do not yield a detailed procedure of obtaining a forecast as do most quantitative forecasting techniques. In the qualitative approaches, the expert, rather than the mathematical model, is the processor of data. These experts arrive at the best "forecast" through human judgmental processes with all attendant strengths and limitations. Qualitative forecasting is widely used in several business forecasting activities: both Ayres (1969) and Cetron and Ralph (1971) report that approximately 50% of the organizations surveyed in their respective studies indicated the use of these forecasting methods.

HRP forecasting frequently necessitates the use of expert judgment, even in circumstances where quantitative data exist. For example, in supply forecasting educational patterns are of great importance and can partially be identified through existing educational census data. However, the National Center for Education Statistics (1978) has pointed out that future college enrollments and the degrees granted, unlike elementary and secondary school enrollments, depend upon factors other than demographics. Factors such as the status value of a degree, hiring policies of major organizations and the intrinsic value of higher education all become relevant and not necessarily dependent on long-term trends. Related to this, Kahn (1974) discusses the rapid expansion of a professional and technical class and Ginzberg (1979) has written about the professionalism of the U.S. labor force. Sheridan (1981) discusses the importance of economic forecasting in manpower planning, mentioning the differences in patterns of productivity, inflation, and technological advancement. Similarly, governmental regulations, societal values and job design patterns have frequently been non-systematic variables.

Some of the forecasting of available current personnel usually can be performed by quantitative analyses. However, the projected future human resource supply, as noted previously by Burack and Mathys (1980), also frequently necessitates judgmental analysis for variables such as mobility, productivity changes, and skills utilization. On the labor demand side of forecasting a corresponding situation occurs. The analyses of current human resource requirements can be determined in a straightforward procedure; however, the projected future requirements usually necessitate judgments about factors such as organizational changes, expenditures, and operational shifts.

There are, of course, many qualitative forecasting techniques from the general business literature that structure and utilize judgments. Sometimes these forecasting techniques are used in combination with quantitative analysis. This article addresses four of these, pointing out uses for HRP: curve-fitting, Delphi, cross-impact analysis, and a modified vector auto-regression model. Finally, relevant literature discussing the use of judges and guidelines to minimize the difficulty in gathering data from judges will be presented.

CURVE FITTING

Curve fitting is frequently used in quantitative forecasting. In such cases, a substantial amount of historical data is gathered and some form of a curve is developed to approximate the basic trend of a time series. Makridakis and Wheelwright (1978), however, discuss curve fitting as a qualitative technique in general business forecasting. In the qualitative technique the basic principle is similar—the determination of a line or curve that represents the pattern of the information under study. In this case, however, the curve is determined with considerably less historical data, more judgment, and frequently over longer periods of time. As an example the authors discuss the use of the "S-curve" that has proven to be useful in describing many technological changes and developments. This curve implies a slow start, a step growth, and then a plateau. The S-curve, for example, has been used to estimate product life cycles, population growth patterns, and the development of transportation speed. In these cases judgmental data have been used to formulate the S-curve. Frequently this is done by judgments of the similarity between the variable under study and other variables with known developmental patterns.

In HRP such curve fitting would seem to have applications in both the forecasting of supply and demand. Demand in many organizations is directly affected by life cycle of products and technological change of equipment used or equipment produced. As mentioned previously, "S-curves" have frequently been used in these areas to obtain relevant projections.

On the supply side there are many curves or distributions of scores on variables relevant to HRP that could be formed by judgments or projections from limited data. For example, learning curves characteristic of training for particular jobs within organizations have long been identified. If these could be estimated for both current and anticipated managerial and technical positions in the organization, then important data for the projection of labor supply would be available. This would provide basic information regarding expected times of movement through either a particular position or a series of positions. This information together with turnover data would assist projections of internal supply at specific times.

Normative distributions of individual skills and knowledge have frequently been generated in conjunction with ability or aptitude test development. Many testing publishers and developers provide such a normative distribution for specific tests. State employment agencies and educational institutions also have data or test score banks that could provide normative data. Data of these types could assist judgments about the availability of specific skilled individuals. For example, if it is realized that current selection requirements yield hirees who could be estimated as averaging at the 80th percentile on a given skill, this would be valuable information in estimating the availability of labor at projected higher or lower skill levels for future jobs. Similarly, normative distributions of job characteristics could be estimated and could conceivably be useful in HRP projections. There are many job analysis systems (e.g., *Position Analysis Questionnaire* [McCormick, Jeanneret, and Mecham, 1972]; *Management Position Description Questionnaire* [Tornow and Pinto, 1976] or job characteristic measurement devices [*JDS* Hackman and Oldman [1975]; *JCI* Simms, et al. 1976) that either provide normative data about task characteristics or present measurement devices to collect information that would permit the generation of such curves. Many of these task characteristics have frequently been linked to motivation-performance relationships. The location of particular jobs on such a normative curve should enhance projections about demand levels.

DELPHI TECHNIQUE

One of the most well-known qualitative forecasting techniques is the Delphi approach developed by the Rand Corporation. The objective of this approach is to obtain a reliable consensus of opinion from a group of experts, while minimizing certain negative aspects of group interaction: social persuasion, unwillingness to abandon publicly stated positions, and the bandwagon effect of majority opinion (Helmer and Rescher, 1959). The format of the technique is to utilize experts in a non-interactive manner to provide estimates and supportive information over several rounds of questions. Experts do not meet to debate the estimates but are kept physically separate, thus avoiding the social-psychological deficiencies in interactive group decision making. A narrowing of differences is achieved through the circulation of judgments and information on a round-by-round basis. The effect is to press for an individual reevaluation of judgments and a consideration of the estimates and information of others. Milkovich,

Annoi, and Mahoney (1972) report an often cited use of the Delphi technique in manpower forecasting. The study utilized seven company managers, who had some involvement in the firm's existing method of generating forecasts, to estimate the number of buyers the firm would need one year in the future. After five rounds, the median estimate and interquartile range was determined and compared to the actual number of buyers hired during the next year. Estimates of needed buyers determined from simple regression models were also generated. Thus, forecasts were obtained by both a qualitative and quantitative technique, and each could be compared against the actual number hired. The results of the comparison indicated high agreement between the Delphi estimate and actual number hired with less agreement between quantitative forecasts and number hired.

Basu and Schroeder (1977) report similar results in a general forecasting problem. They compared Delphi forecasts of five-year sales with both unstructured, subjective forecasts and quantitative forecasts that used regression analyses and exponential smoothing. The Dephi forecasting consisted of three rounds using 23 key organization members. When compared against actual sales results for the first two years, errors of .3% and less than 4% were reported for Delphi, errors of 10 to 15% were reported for the quantitative methods, and errors of approximately 20% were reported for the previously used unstructured, subjective forecasts.

Despite these results there has been criticism of the Delphi technique. Sackmann (1975) and Armstrong (1978) have written critically of its accuracy. Makridakis and Wheelwright (1978) summarize the general complaints against the Delphi technique in terms of: (a) a low level of reliability of judgments among experts and therefore the dependency of forecasts on the particular judges selected; (b) the sensitivity of results to ambiguity in the questionnaire that is used for data collection in each round; and (c) the difficulty in assessing the degree of expertise incorporated in the forecast. They also report positive features of the technique: its enthusiastic reception by many organization members, the structure and organization of subjective judgment, and its usual involvement of organization members in the forecasting technique, thereby increasing the acceptance of the resultant forecast.

If used appropriately the Delphi technique would seem to be useful for HRP. Certainly topics with limited or uncertain historical data: government policy development, specific educational patterns, skill levels necessary for new technology, productivity levels associated with changed work processes, would all seem amenable to the technique. In general, the Delphi technique is useful in answering one, specific, single dimension question. There is less support for its use to determine complex forecasts concerning multiple jobs or classes of personnel. Such complex model building generally is more appropriate for quantitative models with Delphi results serving as inputs.

CAUSAL CROSS-IMPACT ANALYSIS

Another forecasting method from the Rand Corporation, causal cross-impact analysis makes use of expert judgment as input for the development of a quantitative, interactive, simulation model. As described by Helmer (1977) causal cross-impact analysis begins with the development of two sets of data for a particular forecasting problem. One set is identified developments (events and trends) with high expected impact on the future of the variable being forecasted. For each event a probability of its occurrence is estimated; for each trend an estimate of its value (e.g., level, magnitude) is generated. These data are determined for each scene (a specific time period) in a series of scenes. The second set of data, the cross-impact matrix, estimates how the occurrence of an event or how the deviation of a trend from its expected value in a given scene would affect other event probabilities and trend values in the subsequent scene. The information for these sets of data can be obtained by use of the Delphi technique, curve fitting or any other subjective process.

Since these data matrices are frequently large and complex in terms of interactions, an attempt is made to keep the information in each cell as simple as possible. This is done so as not to overload either the experts who have to use their judgments to supply the entries or the analysts who have to make use of them. Each cell is limited to a single entry, rather than a range, even at the risk of over-simplifying the model. Other restrictions are that the impact of an event or trend is only manifested directly in the following scene rather than in several subsequent ones, and that the size of the impact is independent of the scene in which it takes place.

Using these estimated data, prescribed formulae are applied to establish upper and lower bounds for events and trends, define distributions of variable values, identify "normal" ranges of occurrence of the variables, establish carryover effects, and determine values for each scene adjusted for cross-impacts. Once this has been done, the matrices can be analyzed using a computer and the techniques of simulation.

Through application of these procedures a set of probabilities can be developed that represents the interactions among a number of different events and trends, each of which is uncertain. Once these probabilities are known the model can be used for several purposes. One is sensitivity analyses, a determination of the extent to which the outputs are affected by changes in the input estimates. A variety of scenarios can be generated, each descriptive of a particular set of events and trends. Estimated effects on these due to changes in policies can be analyzed.

Cross-impact analysis is not without criticism. One area that has been questioned has been some of the assumptions of the techniques. Among these are the following: (a) the validity of some of the data transforms and the resulting distributions, (b) defining impact as being dependent upon deviation from expected values, and (c) the consideration of impacts only among pairs of developments. In addition, Mitchell and Tyderman (1976), Kelly (1976) and Fontela (1977) have all addressed mathematical limitations of using conditional probabilities in computing "scenarios." In contrast to these criticisms, several beneficial uses of the technique have been reported for the development of complex events (Rochberg, Gordon, and Helmer, 1970).

Cross-impact analysis is more complex and costly than curve-fitting or Delphi. The extensive judgments are used as input to the formation of multi-variable, multi-sequence mathematical formulae. Probably because of this complexity, no HRP applications were identified in the literature. It would seem, however, to be a potentially useful technique for either supply or demand forecasting, especially if the close examination of a complex model of supply or demand is desired. For example, in supply forecasting, model events could be desired levels of specific labor groups, and trends could be variables such as drain from competitors, formal education patterns, and government regulations. The model could identify interactive relationships among these variables, as well as the probability of these desired levels of labor occurring within specified time frames. Similarly, HRP demand forecasting for specific jobs could be analyzed relative to technological changes, organizational plans and policies, and personnel systems. In such a case, model events could be specific numbers of certain jobs or a class of jobs (e.g., computer programmer II or entry level managers). Model trends could be company strategic decisions, training programs, wage and salary policies, or work process changes. Again assuming adequacy of data, the predicted interrelations among organization trends and job levels would become more clear.

TECHNIQUES FOR INCORPORATING EXPERT DATA DIRECTLY INTO REGRESSION ANALYSIS

Mann (1981, 1982) has developed two regression-based forecasting techniques that also use expert data as input into the development of regression equations. The first is an adaptation of Vector Auto-regression (VAR) techniques which yield a result conceptually similar to that of cross-impact matrix analyses. Vector Auto-regression yields a system of regression equations under the assumptions of an interactive model. For example, if applied to an internal labor supply forecasting problem of number of entry-level managers, variables such as previous levels of staffing, internal mobility, turnover, recruiting, and production rates might be utilized. The traditional VAR analyses require extensive historical data and yield a series of regression equations in which each of the variables under study is "predicted" separately by all other variables. The result, therefore, is the specification of an interactive model among these variables that would allow many of the same types of investigation that were discussed in regard to cross-impact analyses. Mann's (1981) modification of the VAR model allows for the direct utilization of expert data as input into the development of the system of regression equations instead of having input be only historical data. A sample of experts is used and each is asked to give a point estimate of the level of each of the variables under study for a specified number of time periods. The responses of the total sample are utilized to estimate distributions of each variable for each time period. It is from these data that the VAR system of regression equations is developed.

Mann (1982) has also developed an alternative single equation technique. In this technique experts are presented with a series of conditional statements to which each supplies a point estimate of a specified variable in each of a specified number of time periods. Again, the data of all experts is used. In contrast to the system of equations that characterizes the VAR model, the result is only one regression equation in which all variables under study are regressed on the variable of main interest. Using the previous example, internal mobility, turnover, recruiting, and production rates would be used to predict number of entry level managers. Experts would be asked to respond to questions such as "If recruiting is at ______ rate, mobility at ______ rate, and production at ______ rate, what would be the total number (or additional number) of entry level managers at the end of the period January–March?"

Neither technique has been used in HRP, although the implications for their use are apparent. Either supply or demand forecasting problems could be addressed and useful regression models developed that would allow for the testing of changes in the levels of many variables. Input data can be more easily and directly gathered than has previously been the case in such forecasting. Testing of these techniques in economic forecasting has yielded accurate prediction when compared with actual results.

ACQUISITION OF JUDGMENTAL DATA

General business forecasting specialists have focused in some depth on the problems associated with the gathering and the use of subjective judgments in forecasting. This work addresses the issues of selection of judges, procedures for eliciting useful information and precautions against overloading the judges' decision-making capabilities. Obviously these issues are of direct importance for the use of subjective data in HRP tasks.

Armstrong (1978) in his detailed treatment of forecasting methods and models discusses guidelines for the development of data in judgmental forecasts. These guidelines were formulated after an extensive review of the literature. Regarding the selection of experts or judges, he advises the following:

a. do not always use the most expensive experts (assuming all experts have at least a minimum level of competence in the area to be forecast);
b. do not use judges who are personally involved in the situation being forecast.

The first conclusion is based on studies from psychology that used various levels of trained judges to make predictions of personality constructs, studies from finance that predicted stock market success, and other studies from medicine, sports, and sociology that examined a range of predicted topics. Armstrong's conclusion is that special training and expertise are primarily useful in estimating and explaining current status. However, there appears to be an early plateau in the relationship between expertise and forecasting accuracy. The second conclusion is based on studies that indicate that the greater the judge's involvement in the forecast situation, the greater the bias in forecasts. He explicitly cautions against such activities as using sales personnel in the forecasting of sales.

Regarding posing questions to judges, Armstrong recommends the following:

a. provide only the minimum relevant information to the judge.

b. organize the information so it is easy for the judge to comprehend. Scenarios may be useful when the effects of many trends must be considered;

c. word the question in different ways, especially in cases where uncertainty is high (as in long-range forecasting);

d. use decomposition (identifying the key components of the problem) when uncertainty is high, prior theory exists or different judges have different information.

These principles all revolve around the crucial problem of information overload of judges. This is the issue of how complex a problem or question asked of experts can be and not exceed their ability to utilize relevant data in decision making. The overall effect of these points is to structure the information to judges as much as is possible, reduce non-relevant or extraneous data and rephrase and restructure ambiguous or complex questions. This problem of information overload has also been treated in management science studies of decision making. Huber (1974) summarizes relevant studies looking at alternative methods of eliciting from appropriate experts subjective probabilities (SP's) and multi-attribute utilities (MAU's). The former entails the estimate of outcome probabilities, while the latter is addressed both to aggregate utility derived from several attributes (characteristics or dimensions) and to identifying and weighting the input of each attribute in overall utility judgments. Both areas of study are analogous to decision-making tasks of experts in HRP problems (e.g., estimating organizational policy changes, various governmental regulations, specific staffing demands, etc.).

As part of this review, Huber compiled a list of guidelines for eliciting such information. Of this list, the following seem particularly relevant for HRP use:

a. to whatever extent possible, train estimators in the task of quantifying their subjective probabilities; in particular, some tutoring for those estimators who have little quantitative background is important;

b. it is necessary to realize that encoding (the actual explication of judgments) is just one step in the overall process. Earlier steps concerned with motivation and structuring of the problem must be deliberately approached;

c. if relevant historical data are economically available, these should be obtained and used as input data for the expert. These data can then be incorporated with whatever pertinent data he/she has that were not part of the historical data base;

d. in situations in which there is little prior data, more than one method to obtain information should be used if at all possible. If discrepant results occur, the judge should be utilized to resolve these discrepancies;

e. in choosing the methods to be used in obtaining judgments, the background and interests of the judges should be carefully examined;

f. whenever possible, data should be obtained from several estimators and these data combined to obtain a single estimate;

g. methods requiring complex information processing should be avoided unless there are strong arguments to the contrary.

Other studies (Pitz, Heerboth and Sachs, 1980; Fischer, 1977; Hoepfl and Huger, 1970; Huber, Daneshgar and Ford, 1971) have also addressed issues of global judgments suffering from error variance induced by information overload. Their conclusions are similar to these statements.

CONCLUSION

In HRP the use of expert data and qualitative forecasting is necessary. The determination of future supply and demand of labor requires, given the nature of the topic, human judgments. Typically, historical data are not complete or there are reasons to suspect departure from previous trends. This is especially true in matters such as economic conditions, government policies and regulations, technological changes, and organizational policies and strategy. The major concern is not whether to use subjective data, but how best to use it. The literature from the field of general business forecasting and decision making is relevant to this question.

There are several different ways expert data can be used in manpower forecasting. Some of the most directly useful seem to be curve fitting, Delphi groups, cross-impact matrices, and judgments as inputs to Auto-regression Vector analysis techniques. No matter which techniques are used, there are important principles to be addressed in collecting data from experts. Foremost is the complexity of the information processing task. The literature in business forecasting clearly points out the relatively limited ability of judges to consistently process multiple data and consistently use decision rules. Therefore, precautions in terms of limiting the task of judges, structuring the questions and problems posed to judges, and providing as much explicit supporting data as possible should be utilized. Providing historical background data, multiple methods of obtaining judgments and multiple judges have also proven useful in gathering consistent, accurate information. The total effect of these procedures is to reduce one of the major criticisms of the use of expert judgments in HRP—the unreliability and egocentricity among experts. The work in business forecasting indicates that consistency in judgments can be greatly enhanced through the use of these precautions.

REFERENCES

Armstrong, J. S., *Long-Range Forecasting,* (John Wiley & Sons: New York, 1978).

Ayres, R. V., *Technological Forecasting and Long-Range Planning,* (McGraw-Hill: New York, 1969).

Basu, S. and R. Schroeder, "Incorporating Judgments in Sales Forecasts: Application of the Delphi Method at American Hoist & Derrick." *Interfaces,* 1977, 7, 3, pp. 18–27.

Burack, E. H. and N. J. Mathys, *Human Resource Planning: A Pragmatic Approach to Manpower Staffing and Development,* (Brace-Park Press: Lake Forest, IL, 1980).

Cashel, W. S., "Human Resource Planning in the Bell System," *Human Resource Planning,* 1978, 1, 1, pp. 59–65.

Cetron, M. and C. A. Ralph, *Industrial Application of Technological Forecasting,* (John Wiley & Sons: New York, 1971).

Fisher, G., "Convergent Validation of Decomposed Multiattribute Utility Assessment Procedures for Risky and Riskless Decisions," *Organizational Behavior and Human Performance,* 1977, 18, pp. 295–315.

Fontela, E., "Scenario Generation by Cross-impact Analysis," *Futures,* February, 1977, 9, 1, pp. 87–89.

Ginzberg, E., "The Professionalism of the U.S. Labor Force," *Scientific American,* March, 1979, pp. 48–53.

Hackman, J. R. and G. R. Oldham, "Development of the Job Diagnostic Survey," *Journal of Applied Psychology,* 1975, 60, pp. 159–170.

Helmer, O., "Problems in Futures Research: Delphi and Causal Cross-impact Analysis," *Futures,* 1977, February, pp. 2–31.

Helmer, O., and N. Rescher, "On the Epitomology of the Inexact Sciences," *Management Science,* 1959, 6, 1, pp. 47–61.

Hoepfl, R. T. and G. P. Huber, "A Study of Self-explicated Utility Models," *Behavioral Science,* 1970, 15, pp. 408–414.

Huber, G. P., "Methods for Quantifying Subjective Probabilities and Multi-attribute Utilities," *Decision Sciences,* 1974, 5, 3, pp. 430–458.

Huber, G. P., R. Daneshgar, and D. L. Ford, "An Empirical Comparison of Five Utility Models for Predicting Job Preferences," *Organizational Behavior and Human Performance,* 1971, 6, pp. 267–282.

Kahn, H. (Ed.), *The Future of the Corporation,* (Mason & Lipscomb: New York, 1974).

Kelly, P., "Further Comments on Cross-impact Analysis," *Futures,* August, 1976, 8, 4, pp. 341–345.

Litterman, R., "Techniques of Forecasting Using Vector Autoregression," Ph.D. dissertation, University of Minnesota, 1979.

Makridakis, S. and S. C. Wheelwright, *Forecasting: Methods and Applications,* (John Wiley & Sons: New York, 1978).

Mann, R., "Evaluation of a Referred Technique for the Assessment of Bayesian Prior Distributions in the Vector Autoregression Model: An Experiment in Regional Economic Forecasting," *Annual Meeting of American Institute for Decision Sciences,* 1981.

Mann, R., "On the Use of Predictive Information in Mixed Estimation," *Annual Meeting of American Institute for Decision Sciences,* 1982.

McCormick, E. J., P. R. Jeanneret, and R. C. Meckam, "A Study of Job Characteristics and Job Dimensions as Based on the Position Analysis Questionnaire (PAQ)," *Journal of Applied Psychology,* 1972, 56, 4, pp. 347–368.

Milkovich, G. T., A. J. Annoni, and T. A. Mahoney, "The Use of the Delphi Procedures in Manpower Forecasting," *Management Science,* 1972, 19, 4, pp. 381–388.

Mitchell, R. B. and J. Tydeman, "A Note on SMIC 14," *Futures,* February, 1976, 8, 1, pp. 64–67.

National Center for Education Statistics, "Projects of Education Statistics to 1986–87," 1978.

Pitz, G. F., J. Heerboth, and N. J. Sacks, "Assessing the Utility of Multiattribute Utility Assessments," *Organizational Behavior and Human Performance,* 1980, 26, pp. 65–80.

Rochberg, R., T. Gordon, and O. Helmer, "The Use of Cross-impact Matrices for Forecasting and Planning," *The Institute for the Future, IFF Report R–10:* Middletown, Connecticut, 1970.

Sackman, H., "A Skeptic at the Oracle," *Futures,* 1976, 8, pp. 444–446.

Sheridan, J. A., "The Relatedness of Change: A Comprehensive Approach to Human Resource Planning for the Eighties," *Human Resource Planning,* 1981, 4, 2, pp. 11–33.

Sims, H. P., A. D. Szilagyi, and R. T. Keller, "The Measurement of Job Characteristics," *Academy of Management Journal,* 1976, 19, pp. 195–212.

Tornow, W. N. and P. R. Pinto, "The Development of a Managerial Job Taxonomy: A System for Describing, Classifying, and Evaluating Executive Positions," *Journal of Applied Psychology,* 1976, 61, 4, pp. 410–418.

Walker, J. W., *Human Resource Planning.* (McGraw-Hill: New York, 1980).

Wheelwright, S. C. and S. Makridakis, *Forecasting Methods for Management,* 3rd edition, (John Wiley & Sons: New York, 1980).

Career Planning and Management

George T. Milkovich and John C. Anderson

Career planning and management have become "big business" over the last few years. Several reasons may account for this:

1. Rising national concerns for quality of work life in America for all levels of workers among all economic, racial, and sexual groups

2. A chronic need for capable, talented personnel, particularly among individuals with technical and managerial skills

3. Continuing pressures from equal opportunity and affirmative action agencies to upgrade and promote minorities and women into managerial and "nontraditional" jobs

4. Rising aspirations and expectations of new workers coupled with a diminished rate of economic growth and advancement opportunities

The current practices within the career planning and management field can be divided into two approaches: those pertaining to organizational assistance to individuals at various career stages and those pertaining to managing one's own career. The first perspective suggests that the issues and dilemmas faced by employees over the stages of a career should drive the strategies developed by the employer for managing human resources.

MANAGING INDIVIDUAL CAREERS

One of the best developed frameworks for tailoring the personnel management system to career stages is shown in Figure 1 (Schein, 1978). The three components of the model should be noted:

Individual needs. The major developmental tasks faced by employees at various stages of their work lives

Organizational Needs. Human resource planning activities such as planning for staffing, growth, and replacement

Adapted from *Personnel Management,* © 1982, Allyn and Bacon, Inc.

Figure 1
Human Resource Planning and Career Stages

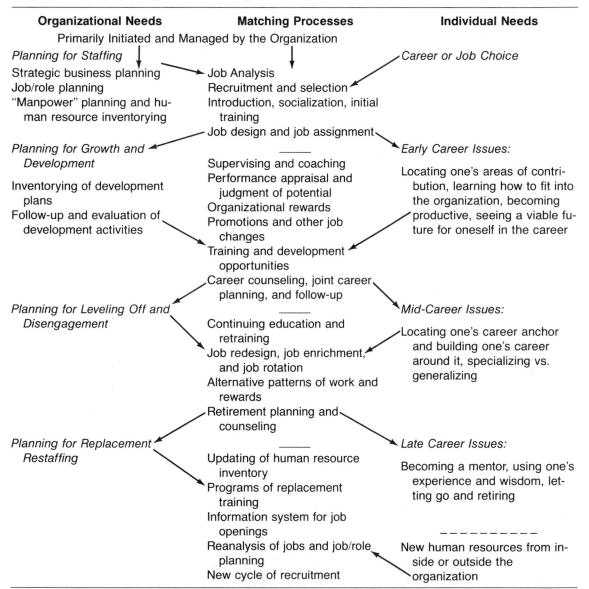

Organizational Needs	Matching Processes	Individual Needs
	Primarily Initiated and Managed by the Organization	
Planning for Staffing Strategic business planning Job/role planning "Manpower" planning and human resource inventorying	Job Analysis Recruitment and selection Introduction, socialization, initial training Job design and job assignment	*Career or Job Choice*
Planning for Growth and Development Inventorying of development plans Follow-up and evaluation of development activities	Supervising and coaching Performance appraisal and judgment of potential Organizational rewards Promotions and other job changes Training and development opportunities Career counseling, joint career planning, and follow-up	*Early Career Issues:* Locating one's areas of contribution, learning how to fit into the organization, becoming productive, seeing a viable future for oneself in the career
Planning for Leveling Off and Disengagement	Continuing education and retraining Job redesign, job enrichment, and job rotation Alternative patterns of work and rewards Retirement planning and counseling	*Mid-Career Issues:* Locating one's career anchor and building one's career around it, specializing vs. generalizing
Planning for Replacement Restaffing	Updating of human resource inventory Programs of replacement training Information system for job openings Reanalysis of jobs and job/role planning New cycle of recruitment	*Late Career Issues:* Becoming a mentor, using one's experience and wisdom, letting go and retiring — — — — — — — — — — New human resources from inside or outside the organization

Source: E. G. Schein. Career Dynamics: Matching Individual and Organizational Needs. © *1978 (Reading, Mass.: Addison-Wesley 1978), p. 201.*

Matching Process. The techniques common to most employers including job analysis, recruiting, training, and so forth.

The model illustrates how one may rethink an employer's human resource activities in light of the proposition that every employee goes through career stages. But organizational "needs" may include efficiency, productivity, cost control, performance, EEO, and control of turnover and absenteeism. Similarly, individual "needs" may include achievement, self-determination, a sense of self-worth, security—the list is long. While Schein recognizes the importance of these needs, their linkage to individual and organizational outcomes is not well developed.

The diagram in Figure 2 focuses on the consequences of matching career stages with the available personnel programs. What are the individual and organizational consequences of developing personnel programs that "match" the developmental tasks hypothesized to be inherent in an employee's work life? How will an employee's job satisfaction and work behaviors be affected, and how will these attitudes and behaviors affect organizational outcomes? The linkage between the matching process and outcomes remains to be investigated. Indeed, it is not at all clear that the major developmental issues have been adequately examined.

The second perspective focuses on programs designed for individual self-career exploration and planning. Essentially, planning one's own career is similar to any other planning process:

1. Develop a self-inventory.
2. Establish personal occupational objectives.
3. Obtain occupational, organizational information.
4. Design actions to achieve objectives.
5. Evaluate progress.

An enormous pool of references, self-help guides, and "organizational survival kits" directed toward individual and career planning exist (cf., Irish, 1973; Mardon and Hopkins, 1969; Simon and Kirschenbaum, 1972; Fitzroy, 1973; Bolles, 1972; Jennings, 1967; Hall, 1976). These approaches provide such commandments as "be an outstand-

Figure 2
Organization Careers: What Are the Consequences?

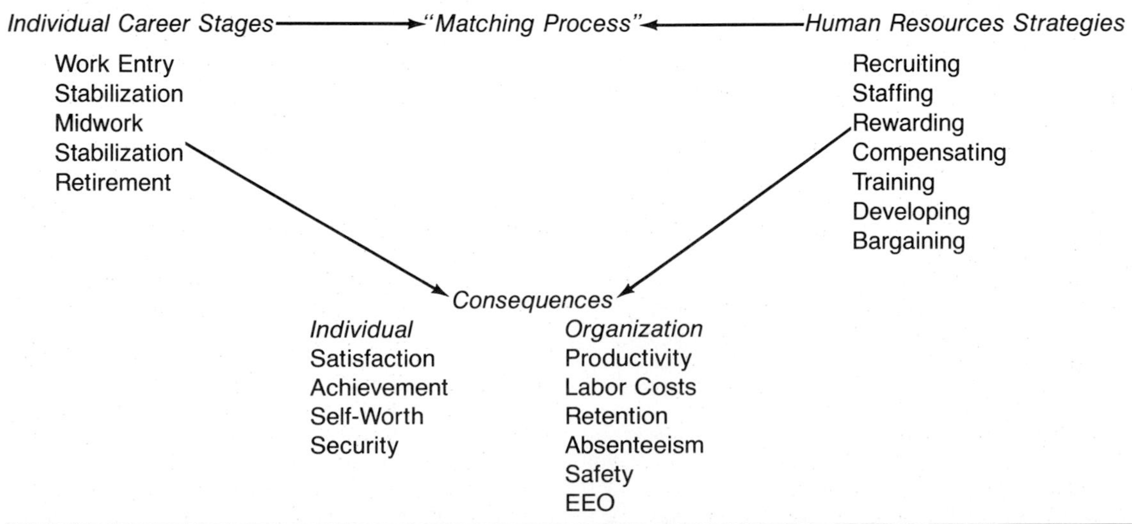

ing performer; don't be blocked by an immobile superior; always favor increased exposure and visibility; (and) practice self-nomination." These programs seem to imply that all individuals have a uniform set of aspirations and values, an assumption that is generally not supported by research.

Many organizations, through a variety of human resource programs, offer a process within which an employee may plan his or her own career. They may provide such information as career options available, forecasts of employment trends, or sources of career counseling. However, career planning is usually tailored to the individual's self-interests; while some employers may assist in that process, contracts to offer the "career" that evolves from the planning are seldom offered or implied.

MANAGING CAREER SYSTEMS

Although a substantial body of literature has developed concerning the nature of individual careers and career stages as well as organizational practices to deal with individual career issues, the opposite is true for careers from an organizational perspective. Further, little is known regarding the consequences of career planning and management from either the individual or the organizational perspective (Gutteridge, 1976). Thus, researchers and managers of human resources face several challenges in the future:

1. *Investigate the consequences of designing human resource systems to assist individuals through the development tasks.* The influence of career planning and management on productivity, employee attitudes, labor costs, concepts of self-worth, attendance, safety, EEO, and so forth, are not well researched.

2. *Identify existing career sequences.* Most organizations are not even aware of the career paths that are present in their structures. How many career lines exist? Do they have early or late ceilings? Are there dead-end jobs? What is the typical time required to traverse the career?

3. *Identify discrimination in the career system.* Current affirmative action legislation goes far beyond hiring procedures to include promotion and transfer policies. Do minorities have the same opportunities to enter and progress through all career sequences in the organization? Are minority and nonminority employees moving at the same rate? Are similar criteria applied to all employee groups?

4. *Describe and analyze organizational, workforce, and environmental factors.* It is clear that the design of career systems is tightly coupled with the structure and technology of the organization as a whole. However, the relationships are still not well investigated. How will new forms of organization structure change the nature of career systems? How do worker participation plans impact career sequences? How does transition to a no-growth economy affect career planning and development? How does the aging and professionalization of the workforce change the expectations (or requirements) for career structures and mobility rates? What is the relative impact of each of these factors on the components of the career system?

5. *Integrate career planning and management with human resource and strategic planning in the organization.* In general, career planning and development has been considered separately from other aspects of the planning function. However, it is obvious that all are concerned with the same goal—efficient allocation of resources. Career paths and projected mobility rates cannot be developed in isolation from estimates of product demand, diversification, and organizational growth, or without estimates of internal labor supply, turnover, and retirement.

6. *Consider innovative and alternate career systems.* Changes in the workforce and expectations of work require that more attention be paid to alternate career systems in the future. Will fast tracks and rotational programs successfully fill the needs of new professional employees? How does the career system take into consideration not only dual-career families, but also work-sharing arrangements between spouses? With slowed economic growth, how can career expectations be met or modified?

REFERENCES

Bolles, R. (1972). *What color is your parachute?* Berkeley, CA: Ten Speed.

Fitzroy, N. D. (1973). Career guidance for women entering engineering. *Proceedings of Engineering Foundation Conference,* Henniker, NH.

Gutteridge, T. (1976). Commentary: A comparison of perspectives. In L. Dyer (Ed.), *Careers in organizations.* Ithaca, NY: New York State School of Industrial and Labor Relations, Cornell University.

Hall, D. T. (1976). *Careers in organizations.* Palo Alto, CA: Goodyear.

Irish, R. K. (1973). *Go hire yourself an employer.* Garden City, NJ: Anchor Press/Doubleday.

Jennings, E. E. (1967). *The mobile manager: A study of the new generation of top executives.* Ann Arbor, MI: Bureau of Industrial Relations, University of Michigan.

Mardon, J., & Hopkins, R. M. (1969). The eight year career development plan. *Training and Development Journal, 23,* 10–15.

Schein, E. H. (1978). *Career dynamics: Matching individual and organizational needs.* Reading, MA: Addison-Wesley.

Simon, H. L., & Kirschenbaum, H. (1972). *Values clarification: A handbook of practical strategies for teachers and students.* New York: Hart.

Linking Business Strategy and Career Management: An Integrative Framework

Patricia M. Fandt

Driven by increasing competition, long-range and strategic business planning has taken on more importance to organizations. In addition, human resources planning has become more important as organizations begin to regard human resources as instrumental to the successful fulfillment of strategic purpose (Dyer, 1983).

Strategic human resources planning has become a magic phrase. Today there is considerable attention devoted to establishing the linkage between human resources management (HRM) and the organization's strategies to maximize employee behaviors and organizational performance (Tichy, Fombrun, & Devanna, 1984). However, there is little in HRM theory to guide this notion.

A recent review of the evolution of HRM by Mahoney and Deckop (1986) suggests possibilities for synthesizing HRM activities within the context of business-level strategy. They propose an integrative approach in which HRM activities are designed to *support* specific strategic orientations. As yet, however, no accepted conceptual framework for such an integrative approach has been developed. This paper provides a starting point for such a conceptual framework by linking career management, as a component of human resource planning, to business-level strategy.

Both strategic planning and career planning are concerned with fundamental issues that affect future organizational growth and success. Both share a common framework of (1) assessing current strengths and weaknesses, (2) charting a direction and setting goals, and (3) making the key decisions needed to achieve or implement these goals (Golden & Ramanujam, 1985).

The existence of an organizational plan, however, is not enough. What is required is a conceptual framework that will integrate career management with the planning and decision-making guidance system, which the process of strategic planning fosters. The framework presented here can fulfill this requirement by describing the interrelationship between business-level strategy and career management. A strategically linked career management (SLCM) framework provides guidelines for developing a career management system that taps the organization's full complement of human capabilities, while facilitating business-level strategies.

Career management practices that support and advance an organization's strategy are a result of the integration of HRM and strategy formulation. SLCM can propel both the individual and the organization toward a future where work performance is mutually beneficial. It suggests a close relationship with, as well as coordination among, business and organization planners and human resources planners.

BUSINESS-LEVEL STRATEGY

During the 1950s, the concept of strategy was introduced and advanced by the Harvard Business School. The Harvard view of strategy was (and is) normative, in that strategy was treated as a situational art or act of integrating complex decisions.

Chandler's (1962) research was the first to employ strategy as a descriptive concept. According to Chandler, strategy referred to "the determination of the basic long-term goals and objectives of the enterprise and the adoption of courses of action and allocation of resources necessary for carrying out these goals" (p. 13). Strategy, therefore, involves matching organizational skills and resources with constraints and opportunities in the environment.

According to Hofer and Schendel (1978), organizations can be expected to exhibit characteristics reflecting their strategic orientation on a continuum between efficiency and effectiveness. Several typologies have been proposed in the strategic management and organization theory literatures for studying various aspects of effectiveness and efficiency behavior. Mahoney and Deckop (1986) suggest that the Miles and Snow (1978) typology might be a useful vehicle for integrating HRM and strategy in future research, because it is the only one that characterizes an organization as a complete system in terms of strategic orientation.

The Miles and Snow (1978) typology classifies organizations according to four strategic orientations. These orientations predict process and the structural characteristics of the association between efficiency and effectiveness. Miles and Snow labeled these four orientations or profiles as (1) Prospector, (2) Defender, (3) Analyzer, and (4) Reactor. While the Defender strategy is efficiency oriented, the prospector strategy is effectiveness oriented. The two are essentially opposite strategies. The Analyzer has a combination of the characteristics of a Prospector and a Defender, and would be at the midpoint between efficiency and effectiveness strategies. A Reactor has no consistent or coherent strategy. The SLCM framework develops two organizational profiles linking the Prospector and Defender strategy concepts with the appropriate career management program.

CAREER MANAGEMENT

Career management is generally regarded as critical to the effective management of large organizations (Burack, 1983). From the organizational perspective, the planning and development of career management programs is an integral part of the HRM function. Careers are managed by the organization to ensure the efficient and productive allocation of human and capital resources.

Career management is not a unidimensional construct, but a set of variables whose dimensions encompass all managerial and professional employees. Broadly defined, career management is considered the activities and opportunities that organizations sponsor to help ensure that they will meet or exceed their future human resources requirements (Stumpf & Hanrahan, 1987). Career management in the SLCM framework includes three components: (1) career development, (2) career planning, and (3) training and development.

Career Development

An organization's career development policies are critical to a career management system, because they define the guidelines and procedures that establish a fit between the organization's strategy and structure, its competitive employment practices, and management's personality (Moravec, 1982). The two most essential elements of career development are (1) management succession/replacement and promotion criteria and (2) career mobility.

Management succession/replacement and promotion criteria include guidelines for staffing policies related to replacement, succession, upgrading, promoting, and transferring. This incorporates managerial and professional-level movement horizontally or vertically between divisions and across functions.

Policies involving promotion-from-within versus acquiring-from-outside are determined by promotion criteria. The organizational commitment to the development of internal candidates for position openings places strong emphasis on employee development (Hall, 1984). Promotion-from-within advances people who have a similar value orientation to that of higher-level managers. Additionally, the promotion-from-within approach maintains continuity with a sense of organizational history and a strong network of social relationships in the organization (Stumpf & Hanrahan, 1987). In contrast, a policy of bringing in "outsiders" fosters cross-fertilization of ideas and innovation.

Career mobility refers to the career ladders or paths by which employees move between jobs, positions, departments, or divisions of the organization. Career ladders identify and establish progression sequences required for advancement. For the organization, career ladders reflect efficient routes for skill development and also prescribe movement patterns (intraorganizational mobility) valued highly in the organization (Burack, 1983). The focus here is on utilization of effective management of human resources flows within the organization (Abelson, Ferris, & Urban, 1988).

There are two basic approaches to the development of career ladders in organizations: (1) functional and (2) clustered. The more traditional approach is oriented to specific functional areas and is concerned primarily with vertical movement. The clustered approach relies on lateral, diagonal, or vertical movement.

Career Planning

Career planning encompasses activities and programs specifically designed to aid the professional employee in self-assessment of skills, interest, and values, setting career objectives and goals, developing a career orientation, and/or providing guidance and evaluation. These programs include assessment centers, career counseling, and mentor-protégé relationships.

Assessment centers provide a variety of testing techniques designed to allow candidates the opportunity to demonstrate, under standardized conditions, the skills and abilities most essential for success in a given job (Joiner, 1982). They can provide an opportunity for candidates to demonstrate managerial potential and skills through a number of job-relevant situations. Assessment centers are appropriate and likely to result in better predictions when the target job requires a variety of complex skills, the requirements of the target job vary substantially from those at the next lowest level in the organization, or when applicants come from a variety of different backgrounds (Burack, 1983).

Generally, career counseling serves many different purposes. It provides sources of information, exchange of ideas regarding plans for the future (reality checking), serves as a sounding board to aid the individual in further shaping his or her own career goals and ideas, and offers important information on company opportunities, policies, and programs. Career counseling services are targeted to a wide range of personal issues. The benefits are to coach or guide individuals effectively through challenging career issues they may confront (Stumpf & Hanrahan, 1987), and help them to perform effectively and expand their own capabilities (Wolf & White,

1982). Organizations benefit by formalizing counseling processes and staying in touch with their employees; that is, learning of their abilities, needs, and desires (Dalton, Thompson, & Price, 1977).

Recent literature has focused on mentoring as a valuable relationship in which a person of expertise guides and develops a novice in an organization or profession (Kram, 1985). It can serve also as an important training and development tool for upward professional progression (Roche, 1979), an influence variable in promotion decisions (Stumpf & London, 1981), and a device for influencing commitment and self-image (Levinson, Darrow, Klein, Levinson, & McKee, 1978). Mentor-protégé relationships are recognized as crucial tools for training and promotion career success for both males and females (Hunt & Michael, 1983). The central role of mentors can provide support from "political" or career sponsorship to management coaching and role modeling (Wolf & White, 1982).

Mentor-protégé relations have traditionally been considered spontaneous with informal organizational support (Kram, 1985). Increasingly, this powerful force has been formalized in some organizations (Stumpf & London, 1981; Wolf & White, 1982). HRM programs are seeking to capture benefits from such support roles for their executive development efforts by designing and implementing programs intended to foster mentoring relationships between senior and junior managers.

The benefits of a mentor relationship accrue to both members of the pair and to the organization. Evidence of the effects of mentoring include higher levels of productivity and competence (Alleman, Cochran, Doverspike, & Newman, 1984; Dalton et al., 1977), development of leadership (Roche, 1979), greater retention of highly qualified employees (Hunt & Michael, 1983), clarification of roles and expectations, stronger professional identities (Stumpf & Hanrahan, 1987), and positive influences on organizational culture (Wolf & White, 1982).

Training and Development

The training and development component of the organization's career management program includes those activities that systematically alter the behavior, knowledge, skills and/or motivation of employees in a direction to increase organizational goal achievement. Training and development programs can range on a continuum from informal to formal and encompass the orientation of new employees, performance improvement, performance maintenance, and development of new skills (Miller, 1977).

As a result of the high costs of developing human resources, organizations need to determine which types of training programs are most effective in meeting their strategy. For example, Abelson et al. (1988) suggested the value of identifying the task-specific skills that serve to facilitate within-organization mobility and inhibit interorganizational movement.

STRATEGICALLY LINKED CAREER MANAGEMENT FRAMEWORK

The SLCM framework presents two career management programs synchronized with the organization's strategic orientation. Two organizational profiles emerge that represent opposing business-level strategies. The career management system components are designed to support the organization's strategy. The logic of this proposition rests on the assumption that different organizational strategies require different career management systems.

The Prospector and Defender orientations or profiles from Miles and Snow's (1984) typology are applied as the opposing business-level strategies for SLCM profiles. Table 1 summarizes the Defender and Prospector SLCM profiles.

Defender Profile

The Defender stresses efficiency or "doing things right" with an orientation toward problem *solving*. A strong emphasis is placed on manufacturing efficiency resulting in an organization that shows strengths in production, applied engineering, and financial management. This type of organization attempts to locate and maintain a secure niche in a relatively stable product or service area, and

TABLE 1
SLCM Profiles

Career Management Components	*Business Level Strategy*	
	Defender	*Prospector*
Career Management Emphasis		
Building:		
Internal sources	X	
Acquiring:		
External sources		X
Career Development		
Succession/Replacement:		
Promotion From Within	X	
Acquire From Outside		X
Career Mobility:		
Functional Career Ladders	X	
Clustered Career Ladders		X
Vertical Movement	X	
Lateral Movement		X
Career Planning		
Assessment Centers	X	
Career Counseling:		
Formal: Organization Oriented	X	
Informal: Individual Oriented		X
Mentoring:		
Formal: Organization Sponsored	X	
Informal: Individually Customized		X
Training and Development		
Formal: Coordinated/long term	X	
Informal: Customized/responsive		X

then successfully "defend" it through stability, efficiency, and high quality (Miles & Snow, 1984).

The Defender tends to offer a more limited range of products or services than its competitors and tries to protect its domain by offering higher quality and superior service at a lower price. Growth usually comes through market penetration.

Management control in a Defender organization is through centralization within a functional structure. In turn, a career management system that supports this strategy must be centrally controlled and specifically coordinated.

The stability of production processes in Defender organizations generally affords the time to emphasize a career management program of *building* human resources. That is, individuals are brought into the organization at entry levels through careful selection and placement.

A Defender is characterized by "growing its own" and succession/replacement planning is supported by a promotion-from-within career development approach. This type of policy relies on internally developed human resources and considerable intraorganizational mobility.

Career mobility in the Defender organization

is characterized by functional career ladders, oriented to specific department areas. Furthermore, mobility tends to be narrowly defined and advancement often is restricted to jobs with similar titles and descriptions. The primary career advancement method is vertical movement. That is, promotion to upper management progresses through either production, engineering, or finance channels.

Career planning is designed to offer employees formal channels for assessment of skills, interests, and career guidance in three ways. First, the extensive use of assessment centers provides opportunities for employees to develop and demonstrate managerial potential, while allowing the organization an equal opportunity to develop predictable, planned human resources inputs. Second, career counseling services offer formal programs to disseminate organizational policies and information. Finally, mentoring is encouraged as a strategy to maintain continuity. Spontaneous mentor-protégé relationships that are *informally* sanctioned and rewarded by peers and superiors are most appropriate in the Defender organization.

A business-level strategy of stability and efficiency emphasizes standardization of behaviors and centralized decision making, which is reflected in the lengthy tenure of the dominant coalition. Managers in the dominant coalition are encouraged to develop a base of technical support, respect, and power throughout the organization.

The Defender organization invests heavily in extensive skill building and formalized, coordinated, and long-term training programs. Once hired, employees are expected to be with the company for most of their careers. With many opportunities for intraorganizational mobility, task-specific training is a recommended course of action (Abelson et al., 1988).

Strong emphasis is placed on orientation and socialization of the new employees in the Defender organization. Formal on-the-job training experiences mean learning the product and manufacturing process from first-hand involvement. Formal off-the-job training includes university or trade association-sponsored programs.

In summary, career management in the Defender organization is characterized as *building* human resources. The Defender profile (see Table 1) includes career development programs based on internal human resources and a promotion-from-within policy following functional career ladders. Career planning involves the use of assessment centers, formal career counseling, and informal support for mentoring relationships. Formal and extensive training and development programs provide intraorganizational mobility while they advance and maintain the Defender strategy.

Prospector Profile

At the other extreme, the Prospector strategy orientation stresses effectiveness or "doing the right things" with an orientation toward problem *finding*. A Prospector will emphasize product and market effectiveness, developing an organization whose competency is product research and development, market research, and engineering. This type of organization typically operates within a broad product-market domain that undergoes periodic redefinition (Miles & Snow, 1984).

The Prospector seeks broad and changing markets and product development. As innovators and creators of change, their strategy is based on flexibility, multiple technologies, and acquisition. The organization values being "first in" in new product and market areas and is considered an innovator. Growth in a Prospector organization comes from new markets and products.

Management control in a Prospector firm is decentralized with a divisional structure. In support of this strategy, a career management program emphasizes broad flexible planning, responsiveness, decentralized control, and the *acquisition* of human resources.

Growth into new markets/products or through acquisition necessitates that skills and expertise be brought in from external sources. Since staffing needs may be unpredictable and unrelated to expertise already available in the existing organization, the Prospector organization has a succession/replacement approach to human resource acquisition. A Prospector must often *acquire* expertise from external sources or quickly identify and develop key human resources internally. Therefore, promotion to upper management is as apt to come from the outside as from within, through experience in marketing or product development.

Career mobility in a Prospector organization is broadly defined and characterized by clustered career ladders with an interrelationship of career channels. Divisional and interdivisional movement may be lateral, diagonal, as well as vertical. As technology changes or departmental personnel needs fluctuate, the clustered approach facilitates intraorganizational mobility (Burack, 1983). A strategy that requires bringing in expertise from external sources demands *individually* focused career planning. That is, career counseling is informal and relies on employees to take a proactive approach with their careers. Programs are based on encouraging employees to use skills assessment and self-management opportunities to make their own choices and commitments.

The Prospector strategy stresses flexibility and effectiveness through innovative behavior and decentralized control processes. Managers in the dominant coalition often have relatively short tenure and are encouraged to quickly develop a supportive following. The key to supporting this strategy is *formalized* mentor-protégé programs intended to foster mentoring relationships between senior and junior managers. While these programs cannot totally duplicate the interpersonal chemistry of the mentor/protégé relationship that occurs naturally in organizational life, they can provide important and productive services to an organization's effort to develop managerial talent (Kram, 1985). Mentorship is formally recognized, encouraged, and rewarded by peers and superiors in the organizations.

Training and development programs are characterized along informal lines. Because expertise is often brought in from external sources, training is decentralized and focuses on specific and customized needs of personnel. That is, the most appropriate action is providing task-specific training. Emphasis is placed primarily on on-the-job training. In addition, innovative behavior is encouraged and rewarded, decreasing the need for formalized programs. Job rotation is encouraged to develop managerial experience and accelerate promotion of highly competent individuals.

In summary, the Prospector career management program is characterized as *acquiring* human resources. The Prospector profile (see Table 1) includes career development programs based on both internal and external human resources and flexible career mobility using clustered career ladders. Career planning focuses on informal career counseling emphasizing proactive employee involvement. In addition, career planning encompasses formal mentoring programs. While training and development programs may be informal, they are task-specific, responsive, and oriented toward organizational needs that support this Prospector strategy.

CONCLUSION

This paper provides a conceptual framework for the integration of business-level strategy and career management in the organization. Previous research has called attention to the need to establish the linkage between HRM and business strategy. The integrative framework also serves as a further effort to define and lend structure to the emerging discipline of strategic HRM.

The SLCM framework outlines the components of a career management system specifically designed to support an organization's strategic orientation. The conceptual model presented here provides an integration between the organization's career management program and its business-level strategy in an attempt to articulate the relationship between these variables and the organization's strategic profile (Defender or Prospector). The strategically linked career management (SLCM) framework provides guidelines for developing a career management system that taps the organization's full complement of human capabilities, while facilitating business-level strategies.

REFERENCES

Abelson, M., Ferris, G., & Urban, T. (1988). Human resources development and employee mobility. In R. S. Schuler, S. A. Youngblood, & V. Huber (Eds.), *Readings in personnel and human resource management* (3rd ed.). St. Paul, MN: West.

Alleman, E., Cochran, J., Doverspike, J., & Newman, I. (1984). Enriching mentoring relationships. *Personnel and Guidance Journal, 21,* 329–332.

Burack, E. H. (1983). *Career planning and management.* Lake Forest, IL: Brace-Park Press.

Chandler, A. D. (1962). *Strategy and structure.* Garden City, N.J.: Doubleday.

Dalton, G. W., Thompson, P. H., & Price, R. L. (1977). The four stages of a professional career—A new look at performance by professionals. *Organizational Dynamics, 6,* 19–42.

Dyer, L. (1983). Bringing human resources into the strategy formulation process. *Human Resource Management, 22,* 257–271.

Golden, K. S., & Ramanujam, V. (1985). Between a dream and a nightmare: On the integration of the human resource management and strategic business planning processes. *Human Resource Management, 24,* 429–452.

Hall, D. T. (1984). Human resource development and organizational effectiveness. In C. J. Fombrun, N. M. Tichy, & M. A. Devanna (Eds.), *Strategic human resource management.* New York: Wiley.

Hofer, C. W., & Schendel, D. (1978). *Strategy formulation: Analytical concepts.* St. Paul, MN: West.

Hunt, M. D., & Michael, C. (1983). Mentorship: A career training and development tool. *Academy of Management Review, 8,* 475–485.

Joiner, D. A. (1982). Assessment centers in the public sector: A practical approach. *Public Personnel Management Journal, 11,* 435–439.

Kram, K. E. (1985). *Mentoring at work.* Glenview, IL: Scott Foresman.

Levinson, D. J., Darrow, C. M., Klein, E. G., Levinson, M. H., & McKee, B. (1978). *The seasons of a man's life.* New York: Knopf.

Mahoney, T. A., & Deckop, J. R. (1986). Evolution of concept and practice in personnel administration/human resource management. *Journal of Management, 12,* 223–241.

Miles, R. E., & Snow, C. C. (1978). *Organizational strategy, structure, and process.* New York: McGraw-Hill.

Miles, R. E., & Snow, C. C. (1984). Designing strategic human resource systems. *Organizational Dynamics, 12,* 36–52.

Miller, D. B. (1977). How to improve the performance and productivity of the knowledgeable worker. *Organizational Dynamics, 6,* 62–80.

Moravec, M. (1982). A cost-effective career planning program requires a strategy. *Personnel Administrator, 26,* 28–32.

Roche, G. R. (1979). Much ado about mentors. *Harvard Business Review, 57,* 17–28.

Stumpf, S. A., & Hanrahan, N. M. (1987). Designing organizational career management practices to fit strategic management objectives. In R. S. Schuler, S. A. Youngblood, & V. Huber (Eds.), *Readings in personnel and human resource management* (3rd ed.). St. Paul, MN: West.

Stumpf, S. A., & London, M. (1981). Management promotions: Individual and organization factors influencing the decision process. *Academy of Management Review, 6,* 539–549.

Tichy, N. M., Fombrun, C. J., & Devanna, M. A. (1984). The organizational context of strategic human resource management. In C. J. Fombrun, N. M. Tichy, & M. A. Devanna (Eds.), *Strategic human resource management.* New York: Wiley.

Wolf, J. F., & White, O. F. (1982). Strategies for implementing senior advisor programs. *Public Personnel Management Journal, 11,* 192–198.

CHAPTER 3

Organizational Entry

Historically, processing people into organizations has been one of the most important activities of the personnel function. This activity took on increased significance with the advent of fair employment practices legislation, which stated that people must be evaluated for employment on the basis of their potential for satisfactory job performance and not on the basis of other, unrelated personal factors.

Assuming that adequate human resources planning has taken place to determine how many people with what types of skills are needed to further the organization's strategic plans, decisions regarding recruitment and selection activities to process people into the organization, within the requirements of the law, can be considered and perhaps implemented.

Federal legislation with respect to fair employment practices has had a major influence on personnel and human resources management over the past twenty-five years. Title VII of the Civil Rights Act of 1964, in order to move toward a greater sense of fair treatment for all, made it a violation to discriminate on the basis of race, color, religion, sex, or national origin in the employment relationship. Subsequent legislation and court decisions moved the pendulum away from blatant discrimination toward equality for all. Some would argue that in recent years the pendulum has swung too far to the other side and that we are seeing evidence of "reverse discrimination," which clearly was not the intention of those working to promote civil rights. Additional legislation, such as the Age Discrimination in Employment Act of 1967 and a 1978 amendment that disallows mandatory retirement before age 70, expanded the application of fair employment practices to all activities in the processing of people *through* and *out* of organizations as well. Examples include promotion and transfer activities, training and development, compensation, and termination.

The use of personnel testing, as an aid to making employment decisions, declined after the passage of the Civil Rights Act. It has increased in subsequent years, however, as companies have begun to realize that it is not tests per se that are discriminatory, but how and in what situations they are used.

The Reagan administration, while it has not made major cuts in the budgets of federal regulatory agencies that oversee compliance with the law in regard to the employment relationship, has at least relegated these agencies to a lower level of visibility and generally deemphasized the issues they address. Counterforces to this federal posture are emerging, however. Many state and local governments are creating their own laws and ordinances to protect employee rights.

The process of entry into the organization involves both recruitment and selection. Recruitment concerns itself with attracting as large a qualified pool of candidates as possible to apply for the organization's available openings. The selection of personnel then involves making the fine distinctions necessary to better match job requirements with personal skills and abilities.

A number of different personnel screening tools aid the organizational entry process. Despite its recognized lack of objectivity and validity, nearly every organization employs the interview in some phase of the entry process. Since it is unlikely that we will see a decline in interview usage, we need new ways to make it a more effective decision-making tool. Multiple interviews, a structured interview, or using the interview only for evaluating the characteristics that it is good at measuring are ways it might be improved.

Other selection devices include personnel tests, reference checks, weighted application blanks, and simulations or work samples. The use of simulations is seen quite clearly in the assessment center technique, common in the selection of people for managerial positions.

In the first article, Feild and Gatewood discuss the strengths and weaknesses of seven commonly utilized job analysis techniques. Each of the techniques are then rated on twelve factors considered by the authors to be of importance to firms contemplating a job assessment procedure. Thompson and Thompson, in the next article, examine on a case-by-case basis the job analysis procedures that have been accepted and rejected by the courts in validating selection tests. With this information, they propose a set of standards for job analysis that they believe will withstand legal scrutiny. The term *tests,* as used here and elsewhere, typically means all devices or tools used in making selection decisions, including application forms, job-knowledge examinations, intelligence and personality tests, interviews, and so forth.

Schwab, in the third article, looks at two areas in the recruitment process: methods used to recruit employees and evaluation of potential employees. In the first section, he discusses the various methods utilized to recruit different types of employees and how managers view these techniques. The common two-step evaluation process of initial screening by the personnel department followed with an interview by the employing department is the focus of the second section. In the fourth article, Kolenko presents some existing recruitment models and frameworks that may help predict and explain both recruiter and applicant behavior. He debunks several recruiting myths and then gives suggestions for improving recruiting effectiveness. Gilmore, Ferris, and Kacmar next present the recruitment process as a two-way information exchange–decision procedure. Following a review of the issues that may influence the process, the authors offer recommendations to the recruiter and applicant for making the recruitment interview more effective for both parties. Voluck considers the impact current discrimination laws have on the recruitment process in the next article, noting questions that should not be asked during the interview as well as cautioning readers about state laws to consider.

The next three articles discuss the utilization of employment testing. Lasden presents reasons why the use of employment testing is on the rise, and then looks at some repercussions testing can cause. Madigan, Scott, Deadrick, and Stoddard discuss validity generalization, a statistical technique that has proved some employment tests valid across many job types. They also look at how the U.S. Job Service has changed the duties of its employees to become more efficient, and the service it can provide employers by using the General Aptitude Test Battery as a means of screening applicants. Yoder and Staudohar take a further look at employment testing. After discussing test reliability and validity, they describe how shifting legal and political pressures for bottomline results have in several instances overshadowed the quality of a given test or testing program. Their appeal is to preserve the application of a reliable and valid testing program in the employment selection process.

Next, Marlow and Marlow focus on five recent Supreme Court decisions regarding Affirmative Action (AA). They also look at the impact President Reagan could make on the now close votes on AA cases by continuing to appoint conservatives to the Supreme Court.

Souder and Leksich address the role of the assessment center and take a positive view of its future in training, performance evaluation, and career counseling. Finally, Gerstein and Reisman propose a strategic selection system for correcting many of the current weaknesses in the selection of executives. They believe that the selection process for senior managers should be designed to achieve the best match possible between situation and executive, because different strategic situations require different characteristics in the ideal executive candidate.

Suggestions for Further Reading

Baker, D. D., & Terpstra, D. E. (1982). Employee selection: Must every job test be validated? *Personnel Journal, 61,* 602–605.

Bloom, R., & Prien, E. P. (1983). A guide to job-related employment interviewing. *Personnel Administrator, 28,* 81–88.

Blumrosen, A. W. (1983). The bottom line after *Connecticut* v. *Teal. Employee Relations Law Journal, 8,* 572–586.

Boudreau, J., & Rynes, S. (1987). Giving it the old college try. *Personnel Administrator, 32,* 78–85.

Breaugh, J. A. (1983). Realistic job previews: A critical appraisal and future research directions. *Academy of Management Review, 8,* 612–619.

McCanna, W. F., & Comte, T. E. (1986). The CEO succession dilemma: How boards function in turnover at the top. *Business Horizons* (May–June), 17–22.

Olian, J. D., & Rynes, S. L. (1984). Organizational staffing: Integrating practice with strategy. *Industrial Relations, 23,* 170–183.

Sheibar, P. (1986). Succession planning: Senior management selection. *Personnel, 63,* 16–23.

Sonnenfeld, J. A. (1986). Heroes in collision: Chief executive retirement and the parade of future leaders. *Human Resource Management, 25,* 305–333.

Wright, P. M., & Wexley, K. N. (1985). How to choose the kind of job analysis you really need. *Personnel, 62,* 51–55.

Matching Talent with the Task

Hubert S. Feild and Robert D. Gatewood

Many human resource specialists believe job analysis is the first step in developing effective personnel selection programs. There's a historical basis for that belief. As long ago as 1908, Frenchman Par Lahy, working for the Paris Transportation Society, described the job tasks he used to select vehicle operators.[1] More recently, the EEOC *Uniform Guidelines on Employee Selection Procedures* laid out the legal reasons for using job analysis as part of the selection program.

Over the years, several methods of analyzing jobs have been developed, but aside from their purpose they have little in common. They differ in data collection, procedures and results.

Because comparing these methods is not easy, human resource managers who wish to select and use one method often find themselves in a quandry. Such a comparison is the focus of this article.

ROLE OF JOB ANALYSIS IN PERSONNEL SELECTION

Implementing a job analysis involves a sequence of activities and decision points. Even though these activities may vary, at least seven major decision points are typically involved: (a) organizing for a job analysis, (b) choosing the jobs to be studied, (c) reviewing the relevant literature, (d) selecting individuals to provide job information, (e) collecting job information, (f) identifying job or employee specifications, and (g) incorporating employee specifications in selection measures. Particularly important are the last three decision points. Figure 1 summarizes their role.

Broadly speaking, collecting information for job analysis results in either work-oriented or worker-oriented products. Work-oriented products involve defining a job in terms of work-related information, such as task activities or worker functions. Employee performance measures, such as performance appraisals or productivity assessments, are by-products of this information. In addition, from work-oriented information, job analysts' inferences of judgments can be used to develop worker-oriented products. These products involve identifying employee specifications, such as knowledge, skills, abilities or other characteristics necessary for successful job performance. Once employee specifications have been identified, predictors or selection instruments such as tests, application forms and employment interviews can be developed to measure them.

Assuming that selection instruments and performance standards are both derived from job analysis, instruments used in selecting employees will likely correlate with performance measures. A validation study tests this correlation.

What is important here is recognizing that the job analysis process has an impact on the effectiveness of any personnel selection system. Where job analysis is incomplete, inaccurate or simply not conducted, a selection system may be nothing more than a game of chance—a game that employers, employees and job applicants alike may lose.

METHODS OF JOB ANALYSIS

In this section, seven common job analysis techniques are described. No one particular technique is advocated. The overview focuses on those methods that appear most popular in personnel selection applications.

Figure 1
Role of Job Analysis in Human Resource Selection

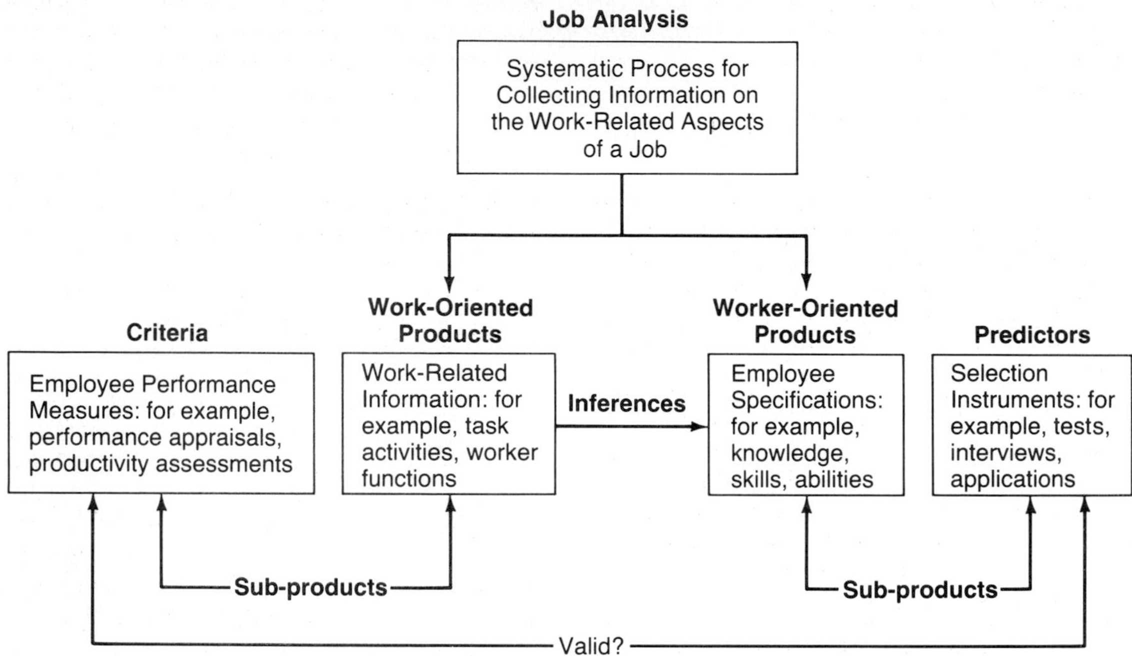

JOB ANALYSIS INTERVIEW

The interview is a method of job analysis that serves a variety of purposes. Essentially, a job analysis interview consists of a trained analyst asking supervisors and incumbents about all aspects of a job—the duties and responsibilities; knowledge, skills, and abilities required; equipment and other conditions of employment.

Job analysis data collected through interviews are typically obtained through group or individual interviews. The participants are familiar with the job being studied. Large groups of incumbents may be used if all are performing the same major activities. The method can be applied to a variety of jobs ranging from the physical to the mental.

Generally speaking, a job analysis interview should not be relied upon as the sole or even the principal method of collecting job data for personnel selection purposes. When employed as a supplementary source, however, interview data can be helpful. For example, interviews can be used to develop the content of other job analysis methods, such as task analysis inventories, or to verify responses to other methods.

TASK ANALYSIS INVENTORY

A task analysis inventory is a questionnaire listing a large number of tasks for which respondents make some form of judgment. Task statements usually emphasize "what" gets done rather than "how" or "why" a task is performed. Respondents judge these tasks on a rating scale that provides options that respondents use to express their perceptions of a task.

The prime objective of this method is to define the principal tasks that account for incumbents' performance on a given job. Since most jobs studied with a task inventory are reasonably complex, the rating scale data are used to define the most critical tasks. Subsequent statistical analysis of task ratings define the critical job content. Regardless of the statistical analyses used, the most important tasks are the basis on which inferences regarding the content of selection measures are made; that is, these tasks serve as the source of statements about necessary employee specifications and the development of selection measures.

Because any job may involve many different duties, task analysis is typically directed toward only one job or a class of very similar jobs. Most often, the inventory is intended for use by incumbents; nevertheless, supervisors and observers can use it, assuming they are knowledgeable about the job being studied.

Task inventories offer an efficient means for collecting data from a large number of incumbents. In addition, they lend themselves to quantifying job analysis data. Quantitative data are invaluable in analyzing jobs and objectively determining core job requirements. However, task inventories can be very expensive and time-consuming to develop. Moreover, motivation problems often become significant when inventories are long or complex. Ambiguities and questions that may arise during the inventory may not be addressed, whereas in a method like the job analysis interview, problems can be resolved as they come up.

POSITION ANALYSIS QUESTIONNAIRE

Of the job analysis methods cited, the Position Analysis Questionnaire (PAQ) probably has the broadest base of research and breadth of application.[2] Roughly 20 years of research has established the PAQ as one of the leading off-the-shelf or existing measures of jobs. Primarily, the PAQ was developed to analyze a wide spectrum of jobs. Because the questionnaire focuses on generalized worker behaviors, it can be used for virtually any job.

The PAQ is a standardized job analysis questionnaire containing 194 items or elements. Of this total, 187 define work activities and the rest, compensation issues. These elements are not task statements; rather, they represent general human behaviors involved in work. An analyst using the PAQ must decide which elements relate to the job under study and then use rating scales to indicate how they apply to the job. The rating scales can be completed by a job incumbent, a supervisor or an independent job analyst observing the performance of the job or interviewing a supervisor or incumbent.

There are, however, some important limitations on applying the PAQ. First, it requires the reading level of a college graduate, a requirement that will have an obvious impact on selecting an appropriate job analyst using the PAQ. Second, the PAQ assesses basic work behaviors rather than specific tasks. Consequently, behavioral similarities in jobs may mask actual task differences. Because the PAQ does not focus on task activities, it may not be suitable for content validity studies or the development of job descriptions incorporating job task information.

Despite these limitations, the method has some clear assets. It provides a standardized means for collecting quantitative job data across a wide spectrum of jobs. Standardization helps ensure that different jobs are similarly measured.

The PAQ has been found to provide reliable and valid job data and it is one of the few for which extensive reliability and validity data have been reported. Finally, an estimate of employee job aptitudes can be obtained from the PAQ. This particular capability can help to suggest the specifications necessary in establishing a viable human resource selection program.

GUIDELINES ORIENTED JOB ANALYSIS

Guidelines Oriented Job Analysis or GOJA[3] is a multi-step process designed to develop a selection plan reflecting the job being studied. Through a step-by-step process, a job incumbent identifies and characterizes the important duties of a job. After collecting preliminary job data, the incumbent lists the duties actually performed on a job, detailing what is done, how and why it is done, and what is produced.

Once associated duties have been defined, the job incumbent rates how often each duty is performed, as well as its importance to successful job performance. The listing and rating of duties represent roughly half of the GOJA process applied to a specific job. The remaining portions of the process use the identified job content to determine the employee specifications used to develop a selection measure.

An important asset of GOJA is the systematic process an analyst is taken through in analyzing a job. It is one of the few methods that takes a user step-by-step from content of the job to content of a selection plan. Documentation for the relevant decision points is accumulated as the process is applied. Given the legal significance of documentation in job analysis, particularly in content validation, the level of detailed documentation provided by GOJA is a prime advantage.

Like all methods requiring paper-and-pencil measures, GOJA has some limitations. The ability to express oneself in writing, incumbents' motivation to participate, and incumbents' training in using the method are all concerns. Apparently, little empirical research is available on the validity and reliability of the data produced. Until such information is developed, it is hard to assess the overall utility of the method objectively. Of course, the same is true for many job analysis methods. With the exception of a few techniques, empirical research studies on job analysis methods such as GOJA are limited in both quality and quantity.

IOWA MERIT EMPLOYMENT SYSTEMS

The Iowa Merit Employment Systems (IMES)[4] method is similar to GOJA: it is a systematic, multi-step process designed to lead to content valid selection devices such as tests. The objective of IMES is to produce selection measures whose contents are derived from jobs for which they are to be used. Job and selection measure content are matched in a sequence of steps from job analysis through specification of knowledge, skills and abilities.

As with GOJA, IMES was developed for users following a content validation model. Job information is collected through a questionnaire—essentially a workbook to be completed by the respondents. Those completing the questionnaire, either incumbents, supervisors or both, serve as "subject matter experts" (SMEs). In small group sessions, SMEs develop an exhaustive list of job tasks. Task statements are written to reflect what action is taken, how and why it is taken, and to whom or what the action is directed.

Once identified, the tasks are rated according to factors such as frequency of and time spent on a task, criticality or significance of error, necessity of adequate task performance upon job entry, and relationship of successful task performance to successful performance on the job. These task ratings data serve as the basis for defining the content of job selection measures.

Many of the same strengths and weaknesses that characterize GOJA also characterize IMES. In addition, the success of IMES is largely dependent upon the skills of the group leader conducting the process. Considerable time and money may be required to locate and prepare people to conduct the job analysis sessions properly. Thus, prior to the use of IMES, give careful thought to selecting such leaders.

FUNCTIONAL JOB ANALYSIS

Functional Job Analysis (FJA)[5] is probably the most thorough procedure for applying a standardized, controlled language for describing and measuring what workers do on a job. The key ingredient in analyzing a job is the development of task statements. Once identified, these tasks are rated by a job analyst using special sets of rating scales. The ratings provide a basis for inferring employee specifications required for task performances.

Judgments about jobs are based on two premises:

1. All jobs require workers to deal, in some degree, with people (clients, customers, co-workers), data (information or ideas), and things (machines or equipment).

2. The tasks a worker performs in relation to people, data and things can be measured by rating scales.

Task statements similar to those in IMES are initially developed under FJA. A job analyst rates these statements in terms of the degree to which they require involvement with people, data and things; the discretion the worker has in task performance; and the general educational development (that is, reasoning, mathematical and language development) required in task performance.

The appropriate use of FJA generally relies upon a *trained* analyst's applying the method to a job. Even though the method can be expensive, it represents a comprehensive procedure for analyzing a job and appears to provide reliable task data.

JOB ELEMENT METHOD

The Job Element Method (JEM)[6] is designed to identify directly the characteristics of superior workers on a job. Supervisors and incumbents develop a list of these characteristics and then rate them to identify those essential to superior performers. These qualities are *job elements.* Job elements include a wide variety of characteristics that describe superior performers on a job, such as a knowledge, an ability or skill, an interest or a personal characteristic. Once identified, these elements are translated into more specific characteristics called *sub-elements;* selection measures are then developed from these.

Implementing JEM calls for assembling a panel of subject matter experts to develop a list of job elements and sub-elements for a specific job. The identified elements are rated and a trained analyst subsequently isolates the most important elements and sub-elements. Finally, job tasks are developed using Functional Job Analysis and are referred to each of the sub-elements identified for a specific job.

JEM has been criticized as being unwieldy and unstructured; nevertheless, it has been useful for approximately 25 years in developing selection tests for trade and labor occupations.

COMPARISON OF JOB ANALYSIS METHODS FOR PERSONNEL SELECTION

Each of the seven job analysis methods have been used in developing selection programs. The *Uniform Guidelines* specify that any method of job analysis may be used if it provides the information required for a specific validation strategy.[7] However, a potential user may be in a quandary as to which method to choose. Unfortunately, the answer is not as straightforward as one might like. First, the research base delimiting the usefulness of various approaches is far from complete. Many of our judgments about job analysis methods rest more on opinion than on fact. Second, any overall assessment must account for a variety of considerations, such as cost, time involved and ease-of-use. Some methods are appropriate in light of some criteria while others are more useful given other considerations.

Even though an overall assessment may not be feasible, an evaluation of the seven methods can be made in terms of specific factors that are important for selection. Using a variety of criteria and drawing upon the work of Gary Brumback, Edward Levine and their colleagues,[8] we have made a summary comparison of these methods, which is shown in Table 1 and discussed below. The assessments provide some critical considerations that should be reviewed by anyone thinking of adopting a specific technique for personnel selection.

1. *Currently Operational: Has the method been tested and refined so that it is now operational and ready for use?* Each of the seven methods has been tested and can be adopted for use. However, each method has unique strengths and weaknesses that affect its applicability in various selection situations.

2. *Off-the-Shelf: Is the methodological instrument to be used ready-made or must it first be designed and constructed?* Only one method, the PAQ, is ready for application without further research. Methods such as GOJA, IMES, and FJA are ready in part, but job tasks must be developed prior to application.

3. *Occupational Versatility: To what extent can the method be applied to a wide variety of jobs?* All the various techniques can be applied to a wide variety of jobs, but those that focus principally on tasks are generally limited to jobs whose task content is simple to describe. Task-based methods may not be so versatile across occupations as methods like the PAQ that deal with broader worker functions.

Table 1
Summary Comparison of Seven Job Analysis Methods

Evaluation Factor	*Interview*	*Task Inventory*	*Guidelines Oriented Job Analysis (GOJA)*	*Iowa Merit Employment Systems Approach (IMES)*	*Functional Job Analysis (FJA)*	*Position Analysis Question-naire (PAQ)*	*Job Element Method (JEM)*
Currently Operational	Yes	Yes	Yes	Yes	Yes	Yes	Yes
Off-the-shelf?	No	No	In Part	In Part	In Part	Yes	In Part
Occupational Versatility?	High	Moderate/ High	High	Moderate/ High	High	High	High
Standardization	No	Yes	No	No	No	Yes	No
User/Respondent Acceptability?	High	Moderate/ High	High	Moderate/ High	High	Low/ Moderate	Moderate
Required Amount of Job Analyst Training?	Moderate	Low	Low/ Moderate	Moderate/ High	High	Moderate	Moderate/ High
Sample Size?	Small	Large	Moderate	Small	Small	Small	Small
Suitability for Content Validity?	Low	High	High	High	Moderate	Low	Low
Suitability for Criterion-Related Validity?	Low/ Moderate	High	High	High	High	High	High
Reliability?	Unknown	High	Unknown	Moderate/ High	High	High	Unknown
Utility in Developing Selection Measures	Low	Moderate	High	Moderate/ High	Moderate	Moderate	Moderate/ High
Cost?	Moderate/ High	Moderate/ High	Moderate/ High	Moderate/ High	Moderate/ High	Low/ Moderate	Low/ Moderate

Source: Based, in part, on Gary B. Brumback, Tania Romashko, Clifford P. Hahn, and Edwin A. Fleishman, Model Procedures for Job Analysis, Test Development and Validation *(Washington, D.C.: American Institutes for Research, 1974), pp. 102–107; Robert D. Gatewood and Hubert S. Feild,* Human Resource Selection *(Hinsdale, IL: Dryden Press, 1987), p. 218.*

4. *Standardization: Are the procedures used with the method so structured that data collected from different sources at different times can be compared?* Methods that use small groups of analysts in collecting job information may not have the capability of producing comparable data. For example, where different panels of subject matter experts are used to develop employee specifications for a job, such as with JEM, different lists of specifications may be developed by the different

panels. In contrast, because the PAQ required job analysts to use a structured procedure for rating a specified list of work behaviors, it is the most standardized of the methods reviewed.

5. *User/Respondent Acceptability: To what extent is the method, including the various aspects of its application, acceptable to respondents and users?* Most of the methods are at least minimally acceptable. In general, the longer time required for respondents to complete the measure, the less acceptable the method. Most respondents would prefer easier, briefer methods. The time required of respondents to develop or rate tasks creates problems in many of the task-based methods. Some studies have shown the PAQ as receiving some of the most unfavorable opinions by users of various methods.[9] Given its basic nature, the PAQ would probably elicit the greatest diversity of opinion of any of the seven methods.

6. *Required Amount of Job Analyst Training: How much training must a job analyst receive to apply the method correctly?* FJA places a premium on identification and correct preparation of task statements, and thus requires the highest level of training. Training is mandatory not only in task development but in applying FJA rating scales to the specified tasks.

Methods like IMES and JEM require moderate levels of job analyst preparation. Since these two methods employ a specific sequence of activities, an analyst should be familiar with the steps. Also, these methods involve group application; thus, an analyst must also be prepared to direct group meetings and conduct group job analyses.

7. *Sample Size: How many respondents or sources of information are required to produce dependable job analysis data?* The PAQ involves the fewest number of respondents, typically three or four. The JEM is also efficient in this respect, requiring approximately six to eight participants. These methods contrast with those like the task analysis inventory, which may involve hundreds of respondents. The questions facing users of methods like the PAQ and JEM are: How reliable are these few judges, and how widely applicable are the results? Unless job analysts are carefully selected, statistical and legal challenges may be difficult to meet.

8. *Suitability for Content Validity: Will the method support the requirements for establishing content validity of a selection measure?* A selection measure is supported by showing that it samples representative aspects of a job. Since the PAQ and JEM place little emphasis on specific job tasks, these methods should not be used in content validation research. Unless the job interview focuses specifically on task data, it alone should not be relied upon either.

9. *Suitability for Criterion-Related Validity: Will the method support the requirements for establishing criterion-related validity of a selection measure?* A selection procedure based on criterion-related validity is supported by establishing a statistical relationship between scores on a selection measure and measures of job performance.

Most methods are useful in identifying content of selection measures and criteria of job performance that can be used in a criterion-related validation study. An exception may be the job analysis interview. Since some job analysis interviewers follow a format that may not produce information on specific tasks performed on a job, the data collected in the interview may not meet the needs of a criterion-related validity study.

10. *Reliability: Will the method provide consistent, dependable results?* Most of the methods can yield reliable job data. For some, such as the interview and GOJA, not enough research has been conducted to verify their reliability. In contrast, IMES and the PAQ have established procedures for determining the extent to which analysts agree in their job assessments.

11. *Utility in Developing Selection Measures: How useful is a procedure in developing selection measures for a particular job?* Ideally, job analysis methods suggest content of selection measures, such as questions to be used in a test. In addition, acceptable job analysis methods should also serve as a source for content of criterion measures, such as rating scales, to be used in a validation study. Most of the methods can meet these needs.

12. *Cost: What is the estimated cost of the method? (Cost includes cost of materials, necessary training, consulting assistance, salary of job analysts and clerical support.)* In terms of total dollar expenditures, the PAQ is probably the least

expensive of the methods. JEM and IMES can be relatively inexpensive; however, panels of job experts have to be convened on several occasions. Thus, indirect costs associated with taking key personnel from their jobs for extended periods must be considered.

Task inventories can be expensive to develop, apply and analyze. Because task inventories must be tailored to a job, costs will increase accordingly. Generally speaking, the more tailored the approach, the greater the costs.

CONCLUSION

Although it would be desirable, there is not one clear, suitable, standard method for meeting *all* the technical and legal considerations of a job analysis for personnel selection applications. Situations, problems and technical issues are so varied that proper conduct of a job analysis is a complex, resource-consuming process.

There is no *one* standard way to conduct a job analysis. As Paul Sparks, former personnel research coordinator of Exxon, said, "I for one find it very difficult to find an agreed-upon professional standard in the area of job analysis. . . . We're due for a lot more research, a lot more litigation and a lot more court decisions before we have a standard."[10]

REFERENCES

1. Par Lahy, "La selection psycho-psysiologique des machinistes de la société des transports en common de la region parisienne," *L'Année Psychologique,* 1924, *25*, pp. 106–172.

2. E. J. McCormick, P. R. Jeanneret, and R. C. Mecham, "A study of characteristics and job dimensions as based on the Position Analysis Questionnaire (PAQ)," *Journal of Applied Psychology,* 1972, *56*, pp. 347–368.

3. R. E. Biddle, *Guidelines Oriented Job Analysis* (Sacramento, CA: Biddle and Associates, Inc. September 9, 1982).

4. J. W. Menne, W. McCarthy, and J. Menne, "A systems approach to the content validation of employee selection procedures," *Public Personnel Management,* 1976, *5*, pp. 387–396.

5. S. A. Fine and W. W. Wiley, *An Introduction to Functional Job Analysis* (Kalamazoo, MI: W. E. Upjohn Institute for Employment Research, 1977).

6. E. S. Primoff, *How to prepare and conduct job element examinations* (Washington, D.C.: Personnel Research and Development Center, U.S. Civil Service Commission, 1975). E. S. Primoff, C. L. Clark, and J. R. Caplan, *How to prepare and conduct job element examinations: Supplement* (Washington, D.C.: U.S. Office of Personnel Management, 1982).

7. Equal Employment Opportunity Commission, Civil Service Commission, Department of Labor, and Department of Justice, Adoption of four agencies of uniform guidelines on employee selection procedures, *Federal Register,* August 25, 1978, *43*, p. 38300.

8. G. B. Brumback, T. Romashko, C. P. Hahn, E. A. Fleishman, *Model procedures for job analysis, test development and validation* (Washington, D.C.: American Institutes for Research, 1974), pp. 102–106. E. L. Levine, R. A. Ash, and N. Bennett, "Exploratory comparative study of four job analysis methods," *Journal of Applied Psychology,* 1980, *65*, pp. 524–535. E. L. Levine, R. A. Ash, H. L. Hall, and F. Sistrunk, "Evaluation of job analysis methods by experienced job analysts," *Academy of Management Journal,* 1983, *26*, pp. 339–347.

9. See, for example, E. L. Levine, et. al., "Exploratory comparative study of four job analysis methods," *Journal of Applied Psychology,* 1980, *65,* pp. 524–535.

10. Bureau of National Affairs, "Professional, legal requirements of job analysis explored at Chicago conference," *Daily Labor Report,* May 30, 1980, pp. A-1 to A-8.

Court Standards for Job Analysis in Test Validation

Duane E. Thompson and Toni A. Thompson

Job analysis, long recognized as the foundation of many personnel practices, is receiving increased attention, particularly in relation to employee selection. Much of this attention has been stimulated by interest in alternatives to criterion-related validity which place reliance on job analysis as a means of defining job content and the ubiquitous possibility of having to justify selection procedures in court.

The landmark case of *Griggs v. Duke Power Co.* (1971) established the principle of job relatedness and, at least by implication, the legal need for job analysis in the validation of selection procedures. Although subsequent cases relying on *Griggs* did not consistently require evidence of job analysis, a trend toward insistence on some form of job analysis is evident even in early cases.[1] In 1975 the Court in *Albemarle v. Moody* reinforced the need for job analysis holding that Albemarle's validation effort was deficient because there had been "no analysis of the attributes of, or the particular skills needed in, the studied job groups." Even though *Albemarle* and other cases such as *Rogers v. International Paper* (1975) and *Wade v. Mississippi Cooperative Extension Service* (1976) disallowed the use of tests due to the lack of job analysis, they did not discuss how or by what method the analysis should have been conducted.

Other cases have dealt with the requirements for an adequate job analysis either through the rejection of inadequate analysis or through the acceptance of job analysis efforts. These cases indicate the emergence of job analysis standards accepted by courts which may be litigated. It should be noted at the outset that, since most of the recent test validation cases which have come before the courts have involved content-oriented strategies, the job analysis implications gleaned from them may be more applicable to this form of validation.

JOB ANALYSIS PROCEDURES REJECTED BY THE COURTS

The first four cases reviewed in this section were heard by the Southern District Court of New York and involved selection tests alleged to be content valid. In each instance the court did not allow unsubstantiated claims or meager efforts to stand as job analysis. The final case involves a substantial effort which was also rejected.

In *Chance v. Board of Examiners* (1971) the court rejected a cursory job analysis that consisted of gathering statements of duties and consulting with job experts.

By way of rationale for the rejection of the job analysis, the court stated:

> *In constructing an examination that will have 'content' validity the preferred course is to have an empirical analysis made of the position for which it is given, usually by experts or professionals in the field. Such an analysis requires a study to be made of the job, of the performance by those already occupying it, and of the elements, aspects and characteristics that make for successful performance.*

In 1973, the same court heard *Vulcan Society v. Civil Service Commission* (1973). The court stated that in order for a test to be content valid, "the aptitudes and skills required for successful

Reprinted from *Personnel Psychology, 35,* pp. 865–874.

examination performance must be those aptitudes and skills required for successful job performance." Further the court identified job analysis as the "starting point" in construction of a content valid test and defined job analysis as:

> *. . . a thorough survey of the relative importance of the various skills involved in the job in question and the degree of competency required in regard to each skill. It is conducted by interviewing workers, supervisors, and administrators; consulting training manuals; and closely observing the actual performance of the job.*

The witness for the defense, the Assistant Chief of the Division of the Department of Personnel, testified that he had never performed a job analysis. Rather, the procedure he followed in preparing the examination was to gather together the file on the previous examination, the former notice of the exam, the class specifications and a magazine published by the Personnel Department. The court concluded that this method was neither a legally nor a professionally acceptable job analysis for the development of a content valid examination. As with *Chance,* on appeal the Second Circuit asserted that the judge in the lower court was correct in his conclusion that the procedure followed was an inadequate substitute for the required job analysis.

Kirkland v. Department of Correctional Services (1974) went into greater depth regarding job analysis and job analysis procedures than any previous case. It is particularly instructive, therefore, to look at this case in some detail. The judge began by stating that:

> *The cornerstone in the construction of a content valid examination is the job analysis. Without such an analysis to single out the critical knowledge, skills, and abilities required by the job, their importance relative to each other, and the level of proficiency demanded as to each attribute, a test constructor is aiming in the dark and can only hope to achieve job relatedness by blind luck.*

The reasoning behind the judge's strong statement is that his reading of case law and professional publications had led him to the position that for a test to be content valid, it must adhere to three criteria:

1. The knowledge, skills and abilities tested for must be critical and not peripherally related to successful job performance.
2. . . . Portions of the exam should be accurately weighted to reflect the relative importance to the job of the attributes for which they test.
3. The level of difficulty of the exam material should match the level of difficulty of the job.

The job analysis allegedly performed by the defendants was examined against these criteria. The defendants argued that, since the term job analysis means "a series of operations or understandings, discussions by which you identify what people do and why and what can be tested and what should be tested," they did not have to produce written evidence such as a job description to prove that a job analysis had indeed been performed. The judge said that "the difficulties presented by the defendants' approach are manifold" and because the analysis had not been reduced to writing, ". . . the existence of such an analysis (had) not been proven."

Specifically, what the Civil Service Commission had used in lieu of a job analysis, and what the court took exception to, was:

1. Job audits of a different job (that of Correction Officer not Correction Sergeant) prepared for a different purpose;
2. outdated materials;
3. a one paragraph class specification that contained only cursory information;
4. so-called knowledge, skills and abilities statements which were actually descriptions of the five examination subsets rather than the knowledges, skills and abilities demanded by the job; and
5. the rule book for the job.

Finally, the judge stated that:

> *. . . the record does not establish that the knowledge and qualifications possessed by the test constructors was such that they can*

simply be deemed to have had in their heads a job analysis sufficient to satisfy legal and professional requirements.

Accordingly, the examination was disallowed.

The fourth in the set of cases heard by the Southern U.S. District Court of New York was *Jones v. Human Resources Administration* (1975). Here, the court set out four aspects of the job analysis performed by the defendants which caused it to be unacceptable:

1. the job analysis interviews did not cover the full spectrum of tasks performed by those in the position;

2. portions of the job analysis process were not included in written form by the job analyst and the analyst was not the test constructor;

3. the job analysis did not give any idea about what the position involved or what was required to perform it, the level of proficiency required for each skill was not identified and relative weights were not included; and

4. only four incumbents were included in the interview process.

In *U.S. v. City of Chicago* (1978), the Court of Appeals reversed and remanded the District Court case due to several factors. Two were related to job analysis. The lower court had accepted a particular promotional exam as content valid on the basis that the examination tested "all or nearly all of the important parts of the job," but the Court of Appeals said that:

It is not enough . . . that the various functions of a captain are tested—there must be a correlation between the importance of a job function as determined by the job analysis and the weight given to this function on the examination.

The second factor was that the criterion related validation attempt was judged not to conform to the guidelines since there had been no job analysis.

A sixty-one page district court opinion *U.S. v. State of New York,* (1979), attests to the fact that even sophisticated job analysis efforts may be rejected by the courts. Over one and a quarter million dollars had been spent on the development and administration of "the 1975 trooper examination" which had been constructed with technical assistance provided to the state by the U.S. Civil Service Commission. A job-element/job-coefficient validation effort had been undertaken where "element = a worker characteristic which influences success in a job including combinations of abilities, skills, knowledges or personal characteristics." According to the court:

. . . the job element method of job analysis followed by the NYSP in development of the 1975 trooper examination does not focus on what troopers actually do on the job, but only on the underlying traits or characteristics that troopers believe characterize successful job performance.

And,

A task-oriented analysis was not done during the development of the 1975 trooper examination. There is no documented linkage between the content domain of the examination and the actual tasks, duties, and activities of the position of New York State Trooper. To the extent that this was not done, the development of the 1975 trooper examination based on a content validity strategy was not in accordance with professional standards or in compliance with federal guidelines on employee selection.

Based on the above rationale, the court rejected content validation effort.

JOB ANALYSIS PROCEDURES ACCEPTED BY THE COURTS

In the following cases, the job analyses were accepted as adequate. In some of the decisions it appears as if the judge allowed the case to be decided on the strength of expert testimony rather than the merits of the actual job analysis. Since few details are available regarding the specific procedures used in the job analysis process and given the relative lack of judicial sophistication, these cases are discussed only briefly. *Davis v.*

Washington (1972), *Guardians Assn. of NYC Police Dept. v. Civil Service Commission of NY* (1980) and *Contreras v. City of Los Angeles* (1981) are covered in some detail.

The job analysis performed in *Davis v. Washington* (1972) was accepted because:

> *The judgmental question portrayed by the critical incidents chosen by the most informed and expert members of the Police Department and reviewed by another panel of police and testing experts without doubt comprise a suitable sample of behaviors and skills extremely relevant to the job of police sergeant.*

The job analysis was also accepted by the Supreme Court on appeal in *Washington v. Davis* (1975).

Although not a significant case, the rationale for acceptance of the job analysis in *Shield Club v. City of Cleveland* (1974) is interesting:

> *It is concluded and determined that the job analysis prepared by George W. O'Connor is not in sufficient detail to permit its employment by an educational psychologist to ascertain the content validity or job relatedness of the 1972 Sergeant's Promotional Examination. However, it is concluded and determined that, assuming O'Connor otherwise has the qualification to render an opinion as to the content validity or job relatedness of the 1972 Sergeant's Promotional Examination, his job analysis is sufficient, coupled with his wide experience in police administration and police work, to form a basis for any opinion which he may be qualified to render.*

In *Bridgeport Guardians v. Police Dept.* (1977), the court accepted the exam as content valid even though it was acknowledged that the preparation departed from APA standards. The job analysis was an interview procedure with nine of the forty-three incumbents designed to elicit duties and critical incidents.

In *Firefighters Institute for Racial Equality v. City of St. Louis* (1977), the job analysis was deemed adequate but the test was disallowed because it "did not reflect (the) findings in the job analysis." The job analysis procedure consisted of interviews with randomly selected incumbents wherein "all components of the job, critical incidents, and qualities considered to be necessary or desirable for satisfactory performance" were identified. The information was then ranked in importance and relative frequency based on analysis of the totality of the interviews.

Guardians Association of NYC Police Dept. v. Civil Service Commission of New York (1980), has been hailed as a landmark appeals decision, in part because the judge emphasized that earlier decisions tended to critique the job analysis and test construction too rigorously based on the *Guidelines.*

> *Thus, the Guidelines should always be considered, but they should not be regarded as conclusive unless reason and statutory interpretation support their conclusions. As this court has previously stated: 'If the EEOC's interpretations go beyond congressional intent, the guidelines must give way.'*

According to the court, the job analysis performed by the City, while somewhat flawed, as the District Court and the Department of Justice pointed out, was nevertheless adequate to meet *Guideline* standards. The job analysis was described in some detail.

1. The Department of Personnel identified 71 tasks that police officers generally perform, based on interviews with 49 officers and 49 supervisors.

2. A panel of seven officers and supervisors reviewed the list of tasks to add any tasks that had been omitted and to eliminate duplicated items and items that were not performed by entry-level officers.

3. A questionnaire was distributed to 5,600 police officers requesting them to rate each of the 42 tasks on the basis of frequency of occurrence, importance and the amount of time normally spent performing the task. The 2,600 responses received were analyzed by computer to yield a ranking of the 42 tasks. The ranking was confirmed by observations made by faculty members of John Jay College.

4. The Department of Personnel divided the list of 42 ranked tasks into clusters of related activities.

5. Each one of the clusters was analyzed by a separate panel of police officers to identify the

knowledge, skills and abilities (KSA's) required to perform the tasks at the entry level and to assign percentages reflecting relative importance of each of the identified KSA's for the cluster as a whole.

The final case to be discussed, *Contreras v. City of Los Angeles,* dealt, in part, with the validation of an examination for selection of auditors. In this case the Ninth Circuit Court of appeals relied heavily on a three step procedure for validation of selection examinations articulated in an earlier Ninth Circuit case, *Craig v. County of Los Angeles* (1980). As stated in *Craig:*

> *The employer must first specify the particular trait or characteristic which the selection device is being used to identify or measure. The employer must then determine that that particular trait or characteristic is an important element of work behavior. Finally, the employer must demonstrate by 'professionally acceptable methods' that the selection device is 'predictive of or significantly correlated' with the element of work behavior identified in the second step.*

The job analysis procedure was described in considerable detail. An unspecified number of auditors and auditor supervisors employed in civil service positions throughout the city were used to determine "what skill, knowledge and ability was essential to the position of auditor." This group accomplished the task-based job analysis in four meetings.

> *At the first meeting, they compiled a list of the tasks performed by City-employed auditors. At the second meeting, they determined what skills, knowledge, and ability are required to perform those tasks. At the third meeting, these skills, knowledge and ability, known as job 'elements,' were ranked by the job experts on the basis of their importance to the job of auditor. . . . By definition, these critical elements were the various skills, knowledge, or ability sufficiently essential to the job of auditor to be tested on the auditor examination. At the fourth meeting, the job experts weighted the critical elements according to their relative importance of the auditor position. . . . The final product of these meetings, a compilation of elements critical to the position of auditor, weighted according to their relative importance, was used by the City's examining division to create the 100-question auditor examination.*

The plaintiff challenged the validation study on several grounds including the claims that the job analysis "did not ensure that the questions tested essential job attributes" and that it "did not eliminate questions that tested elements obtained through a brief, on-the-job orientation." The court held that the job analysis phase of the validation study had identified the "skills, knowledge or abilities critical or essential to performance of the auditor function." The second claim was also rejected since those involved in the analysis "selected only those traits that a 'barely acceptable worker' at the 'minimum level of proficiency' would need 'on the first day of the job'."

STANDARDS

A set of standards which delineates the components and characteristics of a job analysis necessary to withstand legal scrutiny can be gleaned from the foregoing discussion of cases.

The first of these criteria is that a job analysis must be performed, and it must be on the exact job for which the selection device is to be used. In addition, the analysis must be reduced to written form, such as a job description, and the job analyst must be able to describe the procedure.

Data for the job analysis should be collected from several up-to-date sources: interviews with incumbents, supervisors and administrators; training manuals and other pertinent publications; observed on-the-job performance; and questionnaires and checklists. The data should be collected by an expert job analyst; however, the expertise of the analyst is not sufficient to prove a "good" job analysis has been performed. And, data collected from individuals should be from a large enough sample to be relevant to every position the test is intended to cover.

Tasks, duties and activities must be identified and included in the job analysis. All of the tasks must be covered, but it seems as if only the most important ones must be included on the test. The relative degree of competency necessary for entry level must be specified.

Terms used by the courts which denote types of information to be identified through job analysis are elements, aspects, characteristics, aptitudes, knowledge, skills, abilities, and critical incidents. It is not obvious which of these must also be included in the job analysis. Knowledge, skills and abilities are mentioned with the greatest frequency and they are necessary, usually, for construction of a content valid exam.

Finally it should be noted that the courts stress the identification of tasks as prerequisite to an acceptable job analysis. One might be tempted to attribute this solely to the content-based strategy employed in the cases which have recently been before the courts. Even if this is the reason, it would not be unreasonable to assume, however, that the courts might continue to view this type of information as essential to a thorough job analysis even if other descriptors were to be used for other functions such as criteria identification, job family development, component analysis, or inferences regarding constructs.

ENDNOTES

1. See for example: *Rowe v. General Motors Corp.* (1972); *Brito v. Zia* (1972); *Fowler v. Schwarzwalder* (1972); *Western Community Org. v. Alioto* (1972) (1973); *Watkins v. Scott Paper* (1976).

CASES CITED

Albemarle Paper Co. v. Moody 10 FEP 1181 (1975)
Bridgeport Guardians v. Police Dept. 16 FEP 486 (1977)
Brito v. Zia 5 FEP 1203 (1972)
Chance v. Board of Examiners, 3 FEP 673 (1971)
Chance v. Board of Examiners, 4 FEP 596 (1972)
Contreras v. City of Los Angeles, 25 FEP 867 (1981)
Craig v. County of Los Angeles, 24 FEP 1105 (1980)
Davis v. Washington, 5 FEP 293 (1972)
Firefighters Institute for Racial Equality v. City of St. Louis 14 FEP 1486 (1977)
Fowler v. Schwarzwalder 5 FEP 270 (1972)
Griggs v. Duke Power Co. 401 U.S. 424 (1971) 3 FEP 175 (1971)
Guardians Assn. v. Civil Service Comm. 23 FEP 909 (1980)
Jones v. Human Resources Administration 12 FEP 265 (1975)
Kirkland v. Department of Correctional Services, 7 FEP 694 (1974)
Rogers v. International Paper Company 10 FEP 404 (1975)
Rowe v. General Motors Corp. 4 FEP 445 (1972)
Shield Club v. City of Cleveland 13 FEP 533 (1974)
U.S. v. City of Chicago 14 FEP 882 (1978)
U.S. v. State of New York 21 FEP 1286 (1979)
Vulcan Society v. Civil Service Comm. 5 FEP 1229 (1973)
Vulcan Society v. Civil Service Comm. 6 FEP 1045 (1973)
Wade v. Mississippi Cooperative Extension Service 12 FEP 1041 (1976)
Washington v. Davis 12 FEP 1415 (1975)
Watkins v. Scott Paper, 12 FEP 1191 (1976)
Western Community Org. v. Alioto 4 FEP 772 (1972)
Western Community Org. v. Alioto 6 FEP 85 (1973)

Organizational Recruitment

Donald P. Schwab

In the literature on organizational recruitment, two general questions have been given substantial attention: What methods do organizations use to attract prospective employees? How do organizations initially evaluate individuals generated through the recruiting process?

RECRUITING METHODS

Organizations can obtain recruits through several different methods. One method is reactive, simply letting job seekers initiate the process by applying at the organization. Others are more proactive, in-

Adapted from *Personnel Management,* © 1982, Allyn and Bacon, Inc.

cluding advertising and the use of labor market intermediaries (e.g., employment services). The results of a Bureau of National Affairs (BNA, 1979) survey of recruiting methods used by a sample of organizations ($n = 188$) for five occupational groups is shown in Table 1.

As Table 1 shows, organizations tend to use multiple methods for all occupational groups. This is most descriptive of professional/technical recruiting; least so for sales. There are also substantial differences in the use of specific methods by occupation. Employee referrals, walk-ins, high schools, and the public employment service are all used more extensively for office/clerical and plant/service than sales, professional/technical, and management. However, private agencies and colleges/universities are more likely to be used to recruit the latter groups. Special publications, and especially search firms, are reserved almost exclusively for recruiting professional/technical and management employees.

Method Effectiveness

Of course, use of a method tells only a small part of the story. Which methods are most likely to yield an adequate number of applicants of high quality? The BNA (1979) asked its participating sample of personnel executives to give a judgment regarding the "most effective source for each (oc-

Table 1
Organizational Recruiting Methods by Occupation

	Occupation				
Source	*Office/ Clerical*	*Plant/ Service*	*Sales*	*Professional/ Technical*	*Management*
Employee Referrals	92	94	74	68	65
Walk-ins	87	92	46	46	40
Newspaper Advertising	68	88	75	89	82
Local High Schools or Trade Schools	66	61	6	27	7
U.S. Employment Service (USES)	63	72	34	41	27
Community Agencies	55	57	22	34	28
Private Employment Agencies	44	11	63	71	75
(company pays fee)	(31)	(5)	(49)	(48)	(65)
Career Conferences/Job Fairs	19	16	19	37	17
Colleges/Universities	17	9	48	74	50
Advertising in Special Publications	12	6	43	75	57
Professional Societies	5	19	17	52	36
Radio-TV Advertising	5	8	2	7	4
Search Firms	1	2	2	31	54
Unions	1	12	0	3	0

Note: Figures are percentages of companies providing data for each employee group.

Source: Reprinted by special permission from Personnel Policies Forum, *copyright 1979, by the Bureau of National Affairs, Inc., Washington, D.C.*

cupational) group." The responses to this question are shown in Table 2.

Except for plant/service employees, newspaper advertising was endorsed more frequently as most effective in every occupational group. Walk-ins are relatively highly endorsed for office/clerical and plant/service. Private employment agencies obtain similarly high endorsements for sales, professional/technical, and management.

Of some surprise are the relatively few endorsements obtained by employee referrals. A similar survey of roughly 600 employers by the U.S. Department of Labor (1976) found that employee referrals were viewed as most successful (32.5 percent), followed by newspaper advertisements (29.6 percent). A survey of over 1,000 employers in Great Britain found that "recruitment through personal contacts" (which would include referrals among others) was the most "satisfactory" external recruiting method (*Department of Employment Gazette,* 1975).

Surveys of this sort are potentially limited because they measure managerial *perceptions* of effectiveness. These perceptions may or may not correspond to actual effectiveness. Moreover, it is not clear how effectiveness is defined by those who provide the information. A survey of the Chicago labor market (Rees and Shultz, 1970) asked employers to elaborate on their reasoning for the reported perceptions of effectiveness. Quality of

Table 2
Organizational Judgments of Most Effective Recruiting by Occupation

	Occupation				
Source	*Office/ Clerical*	*Plant/ Service*	*Sales*	*Professional/ Technical*	*Management*
Newspaper Advertising	39	30	30	38	35
Walk-ins	24	37	5	7	2
Employee Referrals	20	5	17	7	7
Private Employment Agencies	10	2	23	25	27
U.S. Employment Service (USES)	5	6	0	1	1
Local High Schools or Trade Schools	2	2	0	0	0
Colleges/Universities	1	1	8	15	2
Community Agencies	1	3	0	1	2
Unions	0	2	0	0	0
Career Conferences/Job Fairs	0	1	2	2	1
Professional Societies	0	1	1	0	2
Search Firms	0	0	2	5	17
Radio-TV Advertising	0	1	0	0	1
Advertising in Special Publications	0	0	3	5	8

Note: Figures are percentages of companies providing data for each employee group as indicated in Table 1. Columns may add to more than 100 percent because of multiple responses or less than 100 percent because of nonresponses.

Source: Reprinted by special permission from Personnel Policies Forum, *copyright 1979, by the Bureau of National Affairs, Inc., Washington, D.C.*

applicants was the most frequently reported reason for preferring a method, although cost and convenience were also criteria reported (Ullman, 1966).

There have been few attempts to assess effectiveness against a "hard" criterion. In one exception, Hill (1970) obtained performance data on clerical employees in three insurance organizations. Although the results were not statistically significant (at $p < .05$), performance ratings on persons who were referred by other employees were higher than those who obtained employment through other methods in all three organizations.

Studies using employment survival as the criterion of effectiveness are partially summarized in Table 3. It shows one-year survival rates as a function of recruiting method. In all seven samples, survival rates are higher among persons who were referred by other employees compared to gate applications, want-ad users, or users of private employment agencies.

A number of explanations have been offered for these results. Ullman (1966), for example, suggested that employees who are referred have a more accurate perspective of the job and hence are more likely to remain on it. Stevens (1974) alternatively suggested that market intermediaries, such as employment agencies, may pressure the applicant to accept an option that might otherwise be rejected. "The result may be simply a redistribution of unemployment from the present to the future" (p. 13). Hill (1970) noted that the apparently positive effect of employee referrals may reflect criterion contamination. The same employees who recommend initial employment may influence subsequent assessments of performance and hence chances of survival.

Evaluation and Needed Research

To date, recruiting research has done little more than document the methods organizations use to attract job seekers and identify managerial perceptions of the value of these methods. A few studies have assessed performance and survival as a consequence of recruiting method. While the latter clearly represent an improvement over prior methodologies, they too have serious limitations.

Table 3
One Year Survival Rates as a Function of Recruiting Method

	*Method**			
Source	*Employee Referrals*	*Gate Applications*	*Want Ads*	*Private Agencies*
Decker and Cornelius (1979)				
Bank Employees	69%	57%	67%	52%
Insurance Agents	70	64	57	62
Abstract Service	96	90	79	94
Gannon (1971)				
Bank Employees	74	71	61	61
Reid (1972)†				
Engineering and Metal Trades	39	25	16	—
Ullman (1966)				
Clerical, Company 1	25	—	12	—
Clerical, Company 2	72	—	26	38

**Some studies reported results from additional methods not included here.*

†Value for gate applications was referred to in the study as "notice/off-chance."

A major deficiency occurs because these studies have not explained the reasons for the differential consequences of alternative method usage. Perhaps as Ullman (1966), and more recently Wanous (1980), suggest, the differential consequences stem from the information provided by alternative sources. Employee referrals, for example, may provide relatively "realistic" previews of the job. Thus employees who obtain a job through this method may be more aware (and hence presumably more tolerant) of the employment conditions they experience once in the organization. This explanation clearly emphasizes the importance of the employees' psychological adjustment. If true, it would have direct implications for designing the information content of recruiting programs.

A different explanation involves the hypothesis that job seekers recruited from alternative methods constitute samples from different applicant populations. Job seekers who use referrals may differ, not because they have acquired different information during recruiting, but because they come from a different population than job seekers recruited through other methods.

The latter hypothesis, if valid, has very different implications for recruiting practice. Specifically, it suggests that organizations should focus on identifying the method(s) that taps into the population with the most satisfactory *base rate*(s) (i.e., the percentage of applicants who would be successful if hired). Methods differ greatly in their potential for doing this. For example, employee referrals are essentially constrained to the group that constitutes current employees' existing acquaintances. Advertising, alternatively, is potentially flexible in the population it taps. Illustrative of this possibility is Martin's (1971) description of how Hughes Aircraft directed written advertisements to different populations of potential applicants. By monitoring responses to different ads (by assigning each a unique return box number), Hughes was able to determine response rates as a function of advertising content and geographical location. A simple extension of this methodology would also allow an assessment of subsequent human resource outcomes, such as survival rates.

A second limitation of available research has been its failure to account for the potential interaction between recruiting method and the labor market. Response rates to recruiting appeals vary substantially as a function of the unemployment level (e.g., Martin, 1971). Quality of applicants probably also varies in response to varying levels of unemployment. However, it is unknown whether response rates and applicant quality vary uniformly across method as the market becomes relatively loose or tight. Only if they do, can generalizations be made from studies done cross-sectionally in labor markets with specific (though usually unreported) unemployment levels.

Finally, research has not accounted for potential interactions between recruiting method and the attributes offered to induce applicant participation. Suggestive of such an interaction is Ullman's (1966) discussion of the Chicago labor market study. He reported that firms preferring applicants from newspaper advertisements (versus referrals) were generally low paying and otherwise unattractive in terms of attributes offered. Perhaps current employees of such organizations were providing accurate job previews to their acquaintances so that self-selection worked adversely among those joining through referrals. Newspaper advertisement respondents, alternatively, may not have been aware of the organization's unattractive attributes. In any event, such evidence combined with the theoretical importance of attributes clearly suggests the need to incorporate them in future studies of recruiting method effectiveness.

EVALUATION OF APPLICANTS

Once the applicant has made contact with the organization through whatever method, evaluation typically takes place in two stages. Stage one usually involves the personnel department and ordinarily consists of an initial screening only. Formal selection techniques, such as psychological tests, are administered during this stage. Candidates who successfully pass this stage are then typically sent to the employing department (second stage), which makes the final hiring decision, usually on the basis of a personal interview(s) only.

Conventional descriptions of personnel activities make a sharp distinction between recruiting and selection. The former is usually depicted as generating applicants, with only passing reference to quality (that is, quantity is emphasized). Selection, in this scheme, is viewed as the primary function to sort among those applicants.

This arbitrary distinction breaks down in practice. As already suggested, organizations are likely to attempt to identify and recruit from applicant populations with high probabilities of job success. In addition, information acquired about applicants throughout the recruiting process is often used evaluatively in the decision to make employment offers.

The independent variables that have an impact on the evaluation process are briefly discussed below. These variables are the job applicants themselves, the decision makers who evaluate the applicants, and the hiring environment.

Job Applicants

Most of the research on organizational evaluation criteria has focused on characteristics of applicants. One stream of research has focused on variables that may serve as job qualifications. These include academic qualifications, work experience, and psychological test scores. After viewing this research, Schwab and Olian (1980) concluded that "however qualifications are manipulated, they account for a large percentage of variance explained in overall suitability ratings on employment recommendations."

Research has also focused on personal characteristics of applicants, particularly those having equal employment opportunity implications. [See also a review by Arvey (1979).] Sex is the single most studied characteristic of this sort. Schwab and Olian (1980) found nine studies in which males, *ceteris paribus,* were evaluated more favorably than females, an equal number in which there were no differences, and two in which females were evaluated more favorably. Some studies have also found interactions between sex and the type of job sought. Although statistically significant results are typical, sex, acting as a main effect or in interaction with job type, has accounted for very little variance in evaluations.

Less research has been performed on race and age of applicants. Regarding race, Schwab and Olian (1980) found only five studies; none of these studies found evidence that blacks received lower evaluations than whites. Only two studies were found dealing with age, so generalizations are unwarranted.

Research has been performed also on whether or not applicant nonverbal communication (e.g., gesturing) during interviews influences organizational assessments of employment suitability. Imada and Hakel (1977), Dipboye and Wiley (1977), and McGovern and Tinsley (1978) found that employer representatives are influenced by nonverbal communication, although just which nonverbal components are most influential is yet to be established. This research is especially interesting because it suggests that job seekers may acquire such skills (in contrast, for example, to the acquisition of academic credentials) and thereby improve their employment prospects. It is also interesting since nonverbal communication is unlikely to represent an important qualification for many jobs.

Decision Makers

There is little research to suggest how variables other than applicant characteristics might influence evaluations of employment suitability. Several studies have focused on the organizational representative making the employment recommendation. Most convincing here is strong evidence that decision makers exhibit wide differences in applicant preferences (see, e.g., Rowe, 1963; Mayfield and Carlson, 1966). Unfortunately, little is known about what accounts for these differences.

Hiring Environment

There has been a noticeable absence of research on how variables that transcend both the applicant and decision maker may influence employment decisions. For example, what impact do equal employment opportunity regulations or affirmative action plans have on such decisions? Do employment decisions vary systematically as a function of the state of the labor market? How do organizational selection policies influence recruiters' assessments of suitability? These questions are of obvious significance, but Schwab and Olian (1980) were unable to find any research regarding them.

Evaluation and Needed Research

In reviewing the research on organizational evaluations of applicants, one cannot help but suspect that the methodological *tail* has wagged the substantive *dog.* Research has been almost exclusively experimental. As a consequence, it has dealt primarily with applicant variables that are easily manipulated experimentally. To a lesser extent, characteristics of the decision makers have been investigated.

What is most urgently needed is research on how environmental variables influence organizational evaluations of applicants. Organizational characteristics should be studied in much greater detail. For example, does variance in the level of organizational attributes influence its employment standards? Do high wage organizations attract and choose more highly qualified applicants, as has been suggested by some labor economists (e.g., Reynolds, 1951)? How do policies regarding the employment of women and minorities affect actual employment decisions? Only one study (Rosen and Mericle, 1979) has addressed this issue. Are the employment requirements necessary to pass through the initial screening, as conducted by the personnel department, the same as those necessary to be offered a job by the employing unit?

Until questions of this sort are addressed, one will not likely find out if the error variance component, which is so large in most studies, truly represents individual differences among decision makers or organizational differences that have simply been uncontrolled in prior research. A potentially helpful literature to suggest research strategies is available in marketing on organizational buying behavior (for a review, see Sheth, 1977). The analogies between the two types of decisions appear quite extensive.

In all probability, research accounting for organizational variance in applicant evaluations will have to move from the laboratory into the field. In the process, investigators would be well advised to study applicants other than new entrants, which have been overrepresented to date. They would also be well advised to incorporate the sequential nature of employment decisions as they actually occur in the usual employment process.

REFERENCES

Arvey, R. D. (1979). Unfair discrimination in the employment interview: Legal and psychological aspects. *Psychological Bulletin, 86,* 736–765.

Bureau of National Affairs (1979). *Personnel activities, budgets, and staffs* (ASPA–BNA Survey No. 38). Washington: Bureau of National Affairs.

Department of Employment Gazette (1975). Employers, recruitment, and the employment service. *Department of Employment Gazette, 83,* 1251–1257.

Dipboye, R. L., & Wiley, J. W. (1977). Reactions of college recruiters to interviewee sex and self-presentation style. *Journal of Vocational Behavior, 10,* 1–12.

Hill, R. E. (1970). New look at employee referrals. *Personnel Journal, 49,* 144–148.

Imada, A. S., & Hakel, M. D. (1977). Influence of nonverbal communication and rater proximity on impressions and decisions in simulated employment interviews. *Journal of Applied Psychology, 62,* 295–300.

McGovern, T. V., & Tinsley, E. A. (1978). Interviewer evaluations of interviewee nonverbal behavior. *Journal of Vocational Behavior, 13,* 163–171.

Martin, R. A. (1971). Employment advertising—Hard sell, soft sell, or what? *Personnel, 48,* 33–40.

Mayfield, E. C., & Carlson, R. E. (1966). Selection interview decisions: First results from a long-term research project. *Personnel Psychology, 19,* 41–53.

Rees, A., & Schultz, G. P. (1970). *Workers and wages in an urban labor market.* Chicago: University of Chicago Press.

Reynolds, L. G. (1951). *The structure of labor markets.* New York: Harper.

Rosen, B., & Mericle, M. F. (1979). Influence of strong versus weak fair employment policies and applicant's sex on selection decisions and salary recommendations in a management simulation. *Journal of Applied Psychology, 64,* 435–439.

Rowe, P. M. (1963). Individual differences in selection decisions. *Journal of Applied Psychology, 47,* 304–307.

Schwab, D. P., & Olian, J. D. (1980). *Gate keeping in organizations.* Unpublished paper, University of Wisconsin, Center for Personnel/Human Resource Management, Madison.

Stevens, D. W. (1974). *Assisted job search for the insured unemployed.* Kalamazoo, MI: Upjohn Institute for Employment Research.

Ullman, J. C. (1966). Employee referrals: Prime tool for recruiting workers. *Personnel, 43,* 30–35.

United States Department of Labor (1976). *Recruitment, job search, and the United States employment service* (R&D Monograph No. 43). Washington: Employment and Training Administration, Department of Labor.

Wanous, J. P. (1980). *Organizational entry: Recruitment, selection, and socialization of newcomers.* Reading, MA: Addison-Wesley.

College Recruiting: Models, Myths, and Management

Thomas A. Kolenko

Over the past fifty years, college recruitment has evolved into a formal mating ritual whereby talent seeking employers attempt to entice the best and the brightest college graduates into their corporate ranks. Most graduating students willingly participate in the process, hoping it can provide the payoff of gainful employment after years of academic preparation. Specifically, college recruitment is the process of locating, identifying, and attracting qualified graduating college students capable of and interested in filling available job vacancies (Heneman, Schwab, Fossum, & Dyer 1986). This initial contact between employers and potential employees informally provides employment information and selection opportunities for both the firm and the job seeker.

Even though today's business climate has been shaped by corporate downsizing efforts, white collar layoffs, merger and acquisition activity creating redundant talent pools, and the loss of jobs overseas, the college recruitment function remains a critically important personnel activity. However, today's graduating seniors' job aspiration levels, career preferences, and job choice criteria may or may not reflect the reality of current labor market options or conditions. The recruitment function, if managed correctly, must adjust for this complexity and potential conflict of interest between recruiter and applicant.

College recruitment remains a significant annual activity in corporate America and on college campuses for several reasons. First, it provides a centralized pool of professional, technical, and future managerial personnel so necessary in today's competitive global economy. Campus recruiting has become a widely used source of specialized entry level talent in engineering, finance, accounting, computer science, law, and supervisory management. In a recent 1985 survey of 230 organizations, Lindquist and Endicott (1986) report that nearly half (49 percent) of all managers and professionals with less than three years work experience were hired through college recruitment efforts.

Second, college recruitment efforts often provide the first formal contact between graduating students and their corporate career alternatives. While college placement offices typically provide the setting, reality testing of future employment options is left solely up to the job seeking student. The job applicant now has to learn how to participate effectively in the recruiting process (e.g., acquire interviewing skills), as well as make critical career/job choice decisions. Astute employers are equally aware that their recruitment actions and activities are closely scrutinized by students and competitors alike, and must carefully manage the students' image of the firm. Third, the relatively long time frame for campus recruiting almost universally follows the academic year. Thus, organizations have to determine their human resource requirements at least nine to eleven months in advance of knowing whether they have been successful at attracting qualified applicants or if the staffing needs still exist. The cyclical nature of the campus recruiting process makes it extremely difficult for firms to add new talent at other times, outside of the college graduation cycle. Student job search efforts are similarly constrained by academic coursework, fixed interview schedules, and out-of-town company visits.

Lastly, the costs associated with this recruitment method are considerable. Bergmann and Taylor (1984) reported costs estimates of $1,500 to $6,000 per college hire, while Rynes and Boudreau (1986) computed a median cost of $1,925 in 1985 dollars for each graduate hired. In a recent survey of college recruitment programs in firms composing the Fortune 1,000, Boudreau and Rynes (1987) reported that these activities were allocated 16 percent of the personnel staff and budget. With such high stakes and the current emphasis on accountability in human resource management, successful college recruitment necessitates the examination of all cost-effective hiring strategies.

Those participants, employers and students alike, who understand the "rules," trends, and procedures involved in the college recruitment process possess a considerable advantage. A shared understanding of respective goals and objectives has the potential for increasing the efficiency and effectiveness of each party. Graduating seniors who are aware of the goals and dynamics of the recruiting interview, corporate site visit, and job offer should be more effective in optimizing their subsequent job choices. Recruiting employers who understand student behaviors, concerns, and reactions to particular recruiting efforts can tailor and upgrade their recruiting programs to maximize corporate human resource goals. It is important to recall that in the end *both* parties have decisions to make that affect their futures.

Three recruiting issues are addressed here, which should help both parties better manage themselves throughout the recruitment process. First, existing recruitment models and conceptual frameworks that try to explain and predict the actions of both parties are reviewed. Next, numerous common myths that seem to exist on the part of students and employers are evaluated against available evidence. Lastly, management strategies and practices that should improve the effectiveness of each party are presented.

RECRUITING MODELS

Several comprehensive reviews of organizational recruitment research have duly noted the lack of any substantive theoretical orientation in researcher efforts (Schwab, 1982; Rynes, Heneman, & Schwab, 1980). Sound theoretical frameworks hold benefits for personnel researchers, employers, and job applicants alike. Such theories would be capable of explaining and predicting key relationships between critical recruiting factors and outcomes of interest to organizations and job seekers (e.g., organizational and job choice behavior, impacts of certain screening methods on work force productivity and employee satisfaction). Instead, the focus has been on narrow investigations of recruitment activities or student perceptions, with similarly narrow payoffs for employers and job seekers. (Some recent notable exceptions are Taylor & Bergmann, 1987, and Rynes & Boudreau, 1986.)

Existing recruiting models and conceptual frameworks have drawn freely from vocational counseling, motivational psychology, and decision sciences to provide partial explanations for organizational procedures and individual perceptions and behaviors. Often these efforts have been largely descriptive and rarely address organizational and individual perspectives simultaneously.

Comprehensive Matching Models

Davis, Lofquist, and Weiss's (1968) Theory of Work Adjustment (TWA) has provided the foundation for several current efforts at describing the process of organizational entry (Wanous, 1980) and structuring the examination of major personnel activities such as recruitment (Heneman et al., 1986). The richness of their model for recruitment purposes lies in its focus on optimizing the congruence or correspondence between individuals and their work environments in an effort to increase job performance, tenure, and employee satisfaction. Thus, organizational recruitment efforts that maximize the overall fit between applicant and job environment on multiple dimensions are hypothesized to influence critical personal and organizational outcomes.

Wanous (1980) has adopted the TWA logic in his Realistic Recruitment Model, which stresses that applicant needs and organizational environment matching is just as important as the efforts to fit applicant capabilities with job requirements. When inflated or unrealistic expectations of organizational life occur in first job situations, the potential for mismatch increases. Conversely, when applicants overstate their qualifications on a resume or practice extensive impression management in recruiting interviews, optimal individual-job matching is distorted (Greenhaus, 1987). Recent anecdotal evidence has also identified the need for new hires to match a prospective employer's corporate culture and value orientation.

Critical consequences of mismatch for the new hire and the organization can result in low job satisfaction and commitment levels, voluntary new hire turnover, low job performance, and even employee termination decisions. Therefore, ethical commitments to honesty in recruiting is the joint responsibility of job seeker and employer if comprehensive matching models are to prove useful.

Organizational Process Models

The organizational perspective on college recruitment has not focused on theory construction or model building, but rather on the development of processes and procedures to cull requisite talent in a reliable manner. The conceptual distinction between recruitment and selection is blurred in the eyes of many professional researchers when final organization objectives are considered (Boudreau & Rynes, 1985; Schwab, 1982). Breakdowns in an organization's recruiting program can have costly implications for other personnel functions such as training and development, compensation, and the design of the work environment. Unfortunately, the effects of ineffective recruitment may not appear for years.

A basic college recruitment procedural breakdown from the organization's perspective is presented to acquaint the novice job seeker with the extensive "unseen" efforts undertaken by corporations. Graduating students who are aware of the basic process will understand the objectives, practices, and sequencing of corporate recruiting actions and their role within these efforts. This overview is essentially descriptive, with critical comments and recommendations included later in the section on management.

Most large business organizations experience recurring and predictable needs for specialized talent from college campuses, which they centralize into a formal college recruitment program. While the number of steps or stages in the college recruitment process may vary, the sequence, goals, and methods are surprisingly similar. The college recruitment model described by Chicci and Knapp (1980) is representative of most large corporate efforts. The process typically begins with a recruiting needs analysis in late spring, which seeks to estimate specific new talent requirements based on corporate business objectives and the firm's current human resources base for the coming year. Each new position request is formalized into an employee requisition, which describes the job's responsibilities and the skills and abilities required to perform it. Campus recruiters work from these requisitions. In early summer, a formal recruiting program is developed, which covers the selection of appropriate schools and the formulation of the recruiting schedule.

The third stage consists of program implementation. Here, the typical sequence of activities includes: traditional fall and spring campus interviewing, initial screening decisions leading to site visit invitations, candidate evaluation and selection, job offer formulation and communication, and candidate follow-up. Lastly, evaluation and control efforts are undertaken to assess whether job vacancies still exist, the quality of new hires, and cost efficiencies of the program. Recall that the recruitment process is yearlong and often filled with midstream changes due to volatile business conditions or budgetary constraints. Late summer's staffing projections may not correspond at all with a spring scramble for additional candidates or a corporate-wide hiring freeze. Often, graduating seniors only acknowledge hiring freeze possibilities when they experience them firsthand, yet today's corporate management has long recognized the utility of such an option.

Job Choice Models

Two models of applicant job choice behavior have dominated the current literature. Each represents a decidedly different explanation for choice decisions due to basic differences in their underlying assumptions. The first model, expectancy theory, essentially suggests that applicants engage in a rational, systematic search for job attribute information on various prospective employers, and are motivated to choose the job with the greatest likelihood of satisfaction based on their valued attributes. In spite of less than twenty investigations of student job choice behavior to date, Wanous, Keon, and Latack (1983) provide considerable evidence supporting the expectancy theory explanation.

A rival model, known as unprogrammed decision making proposed by Soelberg (1967), has generated considerably less support or researcher interest to date. This approach assumes that applicants are not driven to seek or use extensive information about potential employers in their decision making, but rather use this data to rationalize or defend their choice *after* it has been made. Here, job seekers become attracted to firms that are acceptable on one or two critical dimensions, develop an implicit organization choice based on those factors, and then engage in perceptual distortion to confirm the favorability of their implicit choice.

A central concern to job choice decision making is the role of information. How does information overload, the kind generally experienced after campus interviews and site visits, affect the job choice decision? How do applicants acquire information on labor market conditions, and how does this affect their job choice decisions? Wanous (1980) asserts that the better the information job candidates possess, the more effective their organizational choice will be. Yet, others have reported that in general job seekers make their choices on the basis of very little information about available job opportunities (Heneman et al., 1986). Furthermore, do the three "theories" of college recruiting proposed by Behling, Labowitz, and Gainer (1968) merely address different types of information available to students: objective factors, subjective factors, and critical recruiting contacts? Why do candidates who are initially attracted to a job sometimes distort or ignore negative information and only focus on the positives of a job (Greenhaus, 1987)? What are the optimal amounts, sources, and types of information organizations need to communicate to job seekers to influence their choices? These questions remain essentially unanswered by current research evidence.

Overall, the lack of theoretical frameworks for understanding recruitment activities and their impact on the choices of both organizations and individuals has handicapped the development of an integrated body of knowledge in this area. Researchers and practitioners are then left with the task of linking the available, but often disjoint evidence into useful prescriptions for action. Theory construction efforts could do much to speed advances in our understanding of the recruitment activity and are to be encouraged.

RECRUITING MYTHS

Graduating seniors and employers approach the college recruitment process with a specific set of assumptions about what is appropriate and useful recruiting behavior. Each party tends to behave in a manner consistent with these assumptions or beliefs throughout the process, all in the hope of accomplishing its particular objectives. New studies and research findings continually question the validity of prior assumptions in an effort to improve the correspondence between myth, reality, and successful recruiting behavior. A critical evaluation of ten current recruiting assumptions or myths that handicap effective recruiting programs for students and employers was undertaken.

Student Myths

Today's graduating college students can improve their job search success if they are aware of the following recruiting myths and their behavioral implications.

Myth 1. College placement centers are the best job source for graduating college students. Prospects for securing a good job in your major area of study through college placement centers can vary widely according to current research evidence. Heneman et al. (1986) report a 50–66 percent placement rate for those students participating in on-campus recruiting. In a recent study of survey responses from more than 2,500 graduates of Maryland colleges in 1984, Bowman (1987) reported that only 11 percent of all entry-level jobs were found through college placement offices. However, those jobs were superior in terms of annual salary and showed a strong relationship to the student's academic major, when compared with jobs found through personal contacts, direct application, want ads, and employment agencies. Overall, those positions secured through placement offices had an average starting salary of $23,282 a year with nearly 75 percent of them directly related to the graduate's major. By comparison, the jobs found through the other sources had average starting salaries ranging from $16,000 to $17,000, with only 25–50 percent directly related to the student's major. The type of jobs secured using placement offices helped account for the significant salary differences.

This evidence suggests that placement centers have the potential for securing well-paying jobs in the student's major area, but only for a limited number of graduating students. What of the remaining students not employed as a result of on-campus recruiting efforts? For them, research has generally shown that informal sources (e.g., direct applications, employee referrals, contacts made by faculty, friends, and relatives) are more effective than formal sources (e.g., advertising, employment agencies) at securing gainful employment (Heneman et al., 1986). Bowman (1987) reported that nearly two out of three college graduates in his study who secured entry-level employment used informal sources. While many of these informal sources yielded jobs of nearly similar salary levels, they were more often outside of the student's academic major.

Myth 2. Applicant behaviors necessary to secure a job are predictive of future job performance levels. Often students assume that the best jobs go to those most qualified to perform those jobs. In reality, the best jobs often go to the best applicants, those who know the most about how to get hired. For example, as Henemen et al. (1986) point out, the critical key to successful on-campus recruiting is a strong performance in the on-campus interview. Understanding common recruiting procedures and focusing on each sequential step as a different but related hurdle to overcome can help. Skills at impression management (Greenhaus, 1987) and the ability to mine informal contacts for job leads are two applicant skills that may be very effective for job search, but generally do not predict on-the-job performance.

Myth 3. Applicants consider how they were treated in the recruitment process as important as the specific job offer attributes when making their job choices. While research findings on this proposition are far from definitive, existing evidence suggests that the effects of job attributes upon relations are much stronger than those of recruitment activities (Rynes & Miller, 1983; Powell, 1984). Greater clarity was given to this issue by Taylor and Bergmann (1987), who found that recruitment practices predicted applicants' reactions (i.e., probability of offer acceptance, company attractiveness rating) *only* at the initial campus interview stage of the overall recruitment process. They reasoned that recruitment activities influence applicant's reactions primarily through their impact on the individual's inferences about job attributes. However, when more detailed and direct information regarding job attributes was obtained during later recruitment stages, recruitment activities appeared to lose their informational potency. Greenhaus (1987) also reported that there is some indirect evidence that the effects of recruiting practices in general are greater when the job offer terms are average, as opposed to very good or very bad. Clearly, additional research is needed to validate these recent findings.

Myth 4. The best jobs are found several months after graduation when applicants have the time necessary to devote to a thorough job search. Few studies of new college graduates job search efforts have investigated the search duration issue. Bowman's (1987) study of Maryland college graduates found that the best jobs (i.e., highest paying, within major) were found prior to graduation day. The results of this study suggest that graduates who put off an intensive job search until after graduation will most likely find entry-level jobs paying significantly less. Those jobs are also less likely to be in their academic major. College graduates seeking entry-level positions outside of the normal college recruitment cycle would be closed out of firms that only add talent through their campus recruiting programs. More research is needed on how college graduates secure full-time employment after graduation and the timing of those events.

Myth 5. Master's degree candidates are always given preference over undergraduate applicants for entry level jobs. Approximately one third of the respondents to the 1983 Endicott college recruiting survey expressed a disenchantment with master's degree candidates, especially MBAs, according to Lindquist and Endicott (1984). A more recent study by Rynes and Boudreau (1986) reported that 18 percent of their survey respondents had lowered applicant qualification levels for certain job categories, attesting to some dissatisfaction with master's level job seekers. Explanations given for this action included the belief that master's degree students had unrealistically high expectations for a job, were too expensive, or were not much better qualified than bachelor's degree applicants. This survey-based evidence should not be construed as the identification of a major recruiting trend. Instead, it indicates that employers may be less reluctant to exercise an option they have had for years in certain jobs—that of hiring cheaper bachelor's degree candidates.

Employer Myths

Managerial personnel often have certain assumptions about the college recruitment process, which can have severe consequences for their firm's ability to attract and retain critical entry-level talent. These employer myths can influence recruiting behavior if not challenged by available evidence.

Myth 6. The best measures of a successful college recruiting program are the number of job vacancies remaining unfilled and a low cost per hire. Objective measures of college recruitment program effectiveness could permit between-organization comparisons and evaluation, yet these measures have received very little research attention to date. Recent research has reported that most organizations filled all their college graduate job vacancies, with only 4.5 percent remaining unfilled at the end of the recruiting season (Boudreau & Rynes, 1987; Rynes & Boudreau, 1986). These same researchers noted that just over 50 percent of the employers they surveyed calculate costs per hire. In general, they found that few attempts were made by employers to evaluate whether particular recruiting practices were actually associated with the on-the-job effectiveness of new employers. Wanous (1980) has also voiced concerns that recruiting effectiveness has to be assessed against more long-term outcomes such as voluntary employee turnover and job satisfaction levels, in addition to job performance measures.

Myth 7. Candidates prefer to be interviewed by a recent hire of the firm rather than an older experienced manager. Employers might believe that applicants would prefer recruiters similar to themselves in age and background, who might be better able to describe the transition to corporate life. Instead, Rynes et al. (1980) concluded that applicants prefer campus interviews with recruiters who are somewhat older than themselves, who are job incumbent rather than full-time recruiters, and who can discuss job specific issues. This knowledge of company and job attributes, in addition to strong interpersonal skills, seems to identify recruiters who can effectively influence applicant interest and behavior. In addition, Taylor and Bergmann (1987), in their investigation of a large corporate recruiting program, found that applicants interviewed by recruiters who held bachelor rather than graduate degrees tended to report a lower probability of job offer acceptance level.

Myth 8. Management should try and attract as many candidates as possible in its recruitment efforts. Wanous (1980) has noted that such recruitment objectives are typical of traditional recruitment programs that focus on trying to "sell" the organization to outsiders. These efforts were seen as: self serving for personnel departments interested in keeping their workload up, creating an appearance of good budgetary investment given the need to screen and reject a larger proportion of applicants, and retaining "gate keeping" control in the organization.

Clearly, the critical factor is not the sheer number of candidates, but the number of *qualified* applicants. Heneman et al (1986) recommend the calculation of historically based yield ratios for each step in the recruitment process to determine the optimal number of applicants needed at that stage. (Yield ratios express the relationship of applicant inputs to outputs at various decision points in the recruiting program.)

Others have focused on the specificity of the recruiting message to attract qualified applicants. For example, Mason and Belt (1986) recommend that if the firm's objective is to maximize the difference in response rates of qualified and unqualified applicants to recruitment advertising, the advertisement should contain a detailed job description and job specification. It is also evident that certain sources provide more qualified applicants than others.

Myth 9. Today's on-campus recruiters are well prepared for their roles. Given their significant role as the applicant's first contact with the firm and as a key recruiting process decision maker, it is surprising to find that most campus recruiters appear to receive little training (Rynes & Boudreau, 1986; Heneman et al., 1986). In a study of accounting student reactions to on-campus recruiting, the interviewees gave interviewer performance grades of *C, D,* and *F* to 45 percent of the CPA firms' recruiters (Scott, Pavlock & Lathan, 1985). Furthermore, organizations appear to assess campus recruiter performance on procedural grounds (e.g., keeps appointments, reports interview results) rather than by using more objective measures of recruiting success such as new hire performance levels or employee retention (Rynes & Boudreau, 1986).

Myth 10. Most job candidates typically wait until they have all offers in hand before making a final decision. While few records are kept on the number of offers received per college graduate, current labor market conditions do not parallel the 1965–66 applicant shortage reported by Behling et al. (1968) where 12.9 percent of job openings were listed for each student registered with a college placement office (at a major midwestern university).

Today's graduating seniors face a labor market where their options are severely constrained for several reasons. First, many students do not possess job offers prior to graduation (Bowman, 1987). Common sense also dictates acceptance when only one reasonable offer surfaces. Second, employers try to keep their entry level offers competitive and know few companies will break ranks to secure candidates unless they are in the "campus star" category. Third, the behavioral decision-making literature has noted that individuals select the first alternative (i.e., job offer) to meet all their minimal decision criteria levels. Thus, today's college graduate may be more likely to make job choices that are reasonably satisfactory, rather than engage in heavy bargaining for optimal job alternatives with employers. All this could change with labor market shortages in particular academic majors.

COLLEGE RECRUITING MANAGEMENT

Successful management of the college recruitment function has payoffs for employers and applicants alike. Magnus (1987) reported that a survey of *Personnel Journal* subscribers found over 57 percent engaged in on-campus recruiting efforts. Conversely, almost all college graduates have experienced the anxiety of on-campus job interviewing. With so many players, why aren't there more joint recruiting successes to report? Based on reactions from both sides of this matching process, the management of this activity can and needs to be improved. However, before any review of organizational and individual strategies for dealing with college recruiting are undertaken, some discussion of the evaluation and control of existing recruiting efforts is in order.

Evaluation and Control

Following the old business adage that it's difficult to manage what you can't measure, there is a critical need for employers and personnel researchers to assess the effectiveness and efficiency of their recruiting efforts. Only through such empirical scrutiny can targets for cost reduction or increased effectiveness be identified. Magnus (1987) argues that the new pressure for accountability in the personnel function and the increasing costs of recruiting top performers has caused many companies to reevaluate their recruitment methods.

However, several researchers have reported a reluctance by employers to objectively assess their college recruiting efforts or at least to share such information externally. Rynes and Boudreau (1986) identified several reasons for this behavior which included: 1) a nonstrategic orientation toward college recruitment held by management, 2) current labor market conditions that favor employers, 3) a lack of expertise at program evaluation, and 4) practitioner perceptions that the potential savings would be low. Wanous (1980) also argued that most organizations hold a short-sighted view of the impact recruitment activities can have on a firm's overall success.

While the motivational reservations are more difficult to resolve, the "lack of expertise" excuse can be addressed. Useful evaluation and control discussions now exist in most personnel/human resource management textbooks (see Heneman et al., 1986; Cascio, 1982). Typically, these discussions focus on the importance of evaluation against early planning objectives, specification of recruiting program time, cost, and staff requirements, analysis of recruiting source effectiveness, EEO reporting obligations, and some empirical assessment of critical outcomes (e.g., unfilled job vacancy levels, retention rates, new hire job performance ratings). Several evaluative measures have been recommended and include: cost per hire by source, the number and quality of resumes by source, acceptance/offer ratio, analysis of post-visit and offer rejection surveys, and overall cost of recruiting operations. Notably absent from these measures were efforts to tie specific recruiting practices to available posthire outcomes. For example, individual recruiter effectiveness was rarely assessed against posthire performance appraisal ratings or retention levels.

More sophisticated system-wide evaluation efforts have been proposed by Boudreau and Rynes (1985) using utility analysis as a way of assessing the incremental contributions of various personnel staffing options to overall organizational efficiency levels. For example, utility analysis could evaluate whether the cost incurred in current recruitment activities would be outweighed by the economic benefits associated with easier and improved selection procedures, better employee retention, lower training needs and costs, or higher levels of job output (Heneman et al., 1986). At present, few organizations appear to use this more complex, global evaluation technique. However, all the forementioned evaluation efforts are designed to do one thing—help improve the efficiency of future recruitment efforts.

Organizational Strategies

Human resource managers have several major tasks to accomplish through their on-campus recruiting efforts. Essentially, they must develop programs to fill existing or anticipated job vacancies through the recruitment process. They are responsible for the accurate assessment of candidates, honest communication of job-related information, and, finally, the extension of job offers to those most likely to succeed in the firm.

Several strategies have been discussed in the recruiting literature for accomplishing these related tasks. The traditional "selling" strategies have emphasized the need for employers to positively bias or "sugarcoat" information regarding the organization and the job vacancy. At one time it was felt that this was the best way to attract qualified applicants. However, this approach, sometimes dubbed the "flypaper approach," also assumed that once an offer was accepted, the individual would remain with the organization forever. This strategy was found to create an unrealistically high set of applicant expectations for the job that was rarely met—resulting in dissatisfaction and high voluntary turnover levels.

A "realistic recruitment" strategy is currently being advocated to keep applicant expectations reasonable, yet still maintain a competitive recruiting interest on campuses (Wanous, 1980). To keep job expectations in line with organizational reality is a delicate task, especially with the novice job seekers who usually participate in college recruiting programs. Thus, "reality vigilance" must be managed throughout all stages of college recruitment. While not radically innovative, this approach seems to serve candidate and long-term organizational needs much more equitably.

The following guidelines are presented to help organizations accomplish their recruiting tasks in a timely, effective, and efficient manner. Most of these recommendations are supported by research evidence.

1. *Employers should establish a "presence" on college campuses beyond just the on-campus interviewing period.* Recent efforts at establishing a corporate identity on campuses have used: scholarships, classroom speakers, equipment donations, faculty research support, technical literature, internships, and the development of faculty contacts (Magnus, 1987). These programs allow students to develop a more realistic and informed set of job expectations, while permitting organizations to raise their campus visibility and identify the best candidates early.

2. *Employers need to focus on upgrading the content and specificity of information in their recruiting brochures.* Several studies have noted applicant dissatisfaction with the overly general focus taken in most recruiting brochures. It is recommended that more detailed information be provided on the job attributes of entry level positions. Critical information should be included on those job attributes earlier identified to have had a significant positive influence on prior applicants' decisions to join the organization (Scott et al., 1985; Bergmann & Taylor, 1984). Well designed recruiting brochures would save interviewer time spent answering routine questions and generate more interest in the firm's career options.

3. *Employers must devote more time and resources to train on-campus interviewers to answer the specific job-related questions of applicants.* Very little time has been spent instructing recruiters on what to tell candidates about the company or the job vacancies (Boudreau & Rynes, 1987; Rynes et al., 1980). Students expect the information exchanged in campus interviews to possess "face validity" and for employers to use it to select site visit candidates. Using job incumbent or middle level managers does not relieve one of the training task. In most cases, these individuals have to be trained in interviewing techniques and the legality of certain interview questions. Fortunately, this training is available and has proven effective at raising interviewing skill levels. Other efforts to improve interviewing are covered in another article in this book (see Gilmore, Ferris, & Kacmar).

4. *Employers need to communicate site visit itineraries and agendas to students prior to their arrival.* Bergmann and Taylor (1984) recommend using key personnel and operating executives to determine what important information students should receive before the visit. The greatest attention should be focused on communicating detailed information about the vacant position(s) early, thus permitting the student to decline the expensive site visit if the job is clearly unacceptable. In many cases, the novice job seeker has many questions, but is reluctant to ask anyone for fear of appearing naive or immature. Questions dealing with travel arrangements, expense reimbursements, and contact personnel should routinely be answered by the employer.

During the site visit, the student should meet with potential supervisors and co-workers in an effort to assess the interpersonal relationships present in the job and organization (Bergmann & Taylor, 1984). The site visit should also provide supplemental information on job attributes that may be difficult to assess from recruiting literature, such as corporate culture or housing alternatives. (Someone should also be identified as a contact person; if additional problems or questions arise, the candidate can call that person directly.)

5. *Employers need to make certain that the attributes of their vacant positions are comparable to those of their recruiting competitors.* Since recent evidence has shown that job attributes, *not* recruitment activities, appear to exert significant influence on applicant perceptions and subsequent behaviors towards an employer, substantial information regarding job attributes should be provided by employers. Some of the key job attri-

butes that influence decisions of applicants are pay, nature of work offered, geographic location, and promotional opportunities. Few applicants seem to consider benefits, working conditions, supervision, or co-workers as important factors in their job choice. Smaller employers are often at a disadvantage since many do not have elaborate recruiting brochures to attract initial student interest or communicate job attributes (Scott et al., 1985). They have the added burden of attracting candidates and convincing students that their job attributes are comparable to those in larger companies.

Individual Strategies

Management of the college recruitment function from the applicant's perspective is often overlooked until one recalls that joint decision making has to occur for successful placement. Individuals need to understand their role within the overall process to be able to influence the final job offer decisions made by employers. For most graduating seniors, the quest for a job involves a quest for information. Information on *how* to search, *where* to search, and *what* information to search for has to be acquired. While many of these needs have been addressed in popular best-sellers, surprisingly little systematic research has been performed to validate these recommendations to the novice job seeker. It is no wonder that most candidates base their job choices on very little information. Collecting useful information takes time, energy, and resources. Thus, getting a first job is a job in information gathering.

Recall that the job seeker also functions as an information broker. The candidate must decide what information to share with prospective employers, when is the best time to reveal that knowledge, and to whom in the organization. Equally relevant is knowing what *not* to share with employers. In most cases, the status of current personal relationships or current marriage plans should not be introduced. All information you supply will be considered by prospective employers, even if it has little to do with your ability to perform the job successfully. Therefore, focus on sharing your positive qualities just as most organizations do in their recruiting literature.

Candidates also have a responsibility for the effectiveness of the overall matching process and should be willing to remove themselves from the recruitment process when it appears that the job would be unacceptable. Such self-selection decisions may be difficult to make in today's labor market, but will serve the individual and organizational needs better in the long run.

The primary goal of the individual job seeker is to obtain a job that is reasonably consistent with the preferred work environment. Managing your role in the college recruitment process can be a full-time job, yet most students have to *add* this job to their current workload. What steps can the individual take to insure the likelihood of a positive outcome upon graduation? What personal strategies have been found effective in managing the recruitment process? The five recommendations below will aid the individual job seeker in managing the task.

1. *Job applicants must understand, clarify, and define their own preferred work environment.* Research on personal goal setting has shown that the more specific the goal, the more focused the efforts to accomplish it, and the greater the likelihood of successfully achieving it. Therefore, place considerable attention on defining your goal early in the job search process. Examinations of past part-time work experiences; discussions with faculty, relatives, and friends; internship experiences; and career planning seminars can all be used as potential data. Which job attributes did you prefer in those earlier work experiences? Do you still find them important? Making a short list of the preferred job characteristics will help focus your early search. This listing should reflect your own personal values, interests, and talents. For example, the list may include: preferences for a small organization, opportunities to travel, leads to supervisory responsibilities, midwestern location, and promotion from existing employee ranks. From this list, the applicant has a ready qualifier for identifying prospective employers.

2. *Job applicants should use outside, informal job sources in addition to on-campus recruiting.* Broadening the search to include additional sources of job leads maximizes the candidate's exposure to the "hidden" job market. These "hid-

den" jobs may be due to recent vacancies, available at smaller companies that do not recruit on campus or at firms that do not recruit at your school, or they may be outside the local labor market. Common sources of such job leads include direct applications, personal contacts, newspaper or trade journal advertisements, and personnel search firms.

Research evidence supports the power of such informal job leads, especially when the percentage of applicants placed through formal sources like on-campus recruiting can be rather low. Wanous (1980) argues that these informal leads provide a more objective, credible source of information, containing both positive and negative job attribute information. However, these informal sources also require considerably more effort on the part of the applicant. Often students want to believe that they will secure a job through the placement office because the required effort is less. Many authors have commented that you should never turn your job search over to anybody else. Common sense reminds us that the person most interested in ending the job search successfully is you.

3. *Job applicants should devote considerable effort to managing first impressions in job interview situations.* As previously noted, candidate performance during job interviews, whether they be on campus or during site visits, is extremely important to employer decision making. These brief meetings amount to mutual sales presentations, where the best in both "products" is usually displayed. Studies have shown that interviewers tend to make rather quick decisions, give undue weight to negative information, and make comparisons to a stereotype of the ideal candidate.

The burden of overcoming these decision biases is left up to the job applicants, who must actively manage the situation to present themselves in the most favorable light. Some techniques include taking "practice" interviews with other firms, the "dress for success" approach, and asking "artificial questions" of the interviewer to appear very interested in the employer. Few of these behaviors will provide the honest information candidates need to make critical job decisions nor will they provide the firm with valid information upon which to base its decisions. Thus, college recruiting can evolve into a cat-and-mouse game if both parties are not vigilant.

Be aware that interpersonal skills can be developed over time. In interview situations, research has found that applicants who exhibited knowledge about the firm, had specific career goals, asked pertinent job related questions, appeared articulate and poised were more effective at influencing recruiter decisions positively. The key then to interview effectiveness is advanced preparation/knowledge and solid interpersonal skills on the part of interviewees.

4. *Job applicants must engage in a careful and systematic assessment of each potential employer to make a realistic job choice.* Greenhaus (1987) states that collecting such information is very difficult for two different reasons. First, certain organizations may be reluctant or unable to provide some important pieces of information. Second, candidates may find it difficult to focus attention on information provided or may fail to seek certain information. Simultaneous needs to impress *and* assess are often difficult to manage in job search situations.

Assessments should be targeted against the preferred work environment characteristics discussed earlier. Site visits can provide rich information in areas impossible to assess through interviews alone, such as corporate culture and co-worker relations. Direct questioning should be limited to formal issues (e.g., benefits, hours of work, job duties) if possible. Sensitive information dealing with the rate of advancement of women or company safety records may best be collected informally. Discretion, honesty, and sensitivity may be required to adequately collect critical information on a potential employer.

5. *Job applicants should select the job offer that maximizes the overall fit between their needs, skills, and preferences and the work environment capable of satisfying them.* Based on the logic and evidence supporting the comprehensive matching and expectancy models discussed earlier, candidates are encouraged to use multiple criteria (e.g., job satisfaction, career future, etc.) in their choice process. Greenhaus (1987) encourages the use of paper and pencil decision ma-

trices to keep the vast amounts of information as visible, useful inputs to the decision. Subjective, emotional elements to job choice should optimize the match for the job candidate—not for parents, friends, or professors. The responsibility for the decision should not be given away to those who will not experience the choice on a daily basis. Others have the right and should be encouraged to provide inputs; however, life on the job will be yours alone.

CONCLUSION

College recruiting remains one of the most popular methods for infusing new talent and innovative ideas into corporate America. It is an annual ritual with a well defined sequence, which neither party can effectively alter without the cooperation of the other. At present, we lack a universal theoretical framework to direct our investigations of the relationships between its various components (e.g., recruiting sources, methods, media) and the personal and organizational outcomes normally affected (e.g., job satisfaction, employee retention, job performance). This paper also challenged several of the major assumptions held by applicant and employer that can adversely impact the recruitment process and its outcomes. Hopefully, when assessed against available evidence, the case for changing our assumptions can be made stronger. However, the real test remains within the overall management process. Will employer and applicant ever focus on the exchange of vital information without the cat-and-mouse overtones of past practices? Responsible participation in the process is needed by both parties if they are to accomplish their specific objectives in today's markets.

REFERENCES

Behling, O., Labovitz, G., & Gainer, M. (1968). College recruiting: A theoretical base. *Personnel, 47,* 13–19.

Bergmann, T., & Taylor, M. S. (1984). College recruitment: What attracts students to organizations? *Personnel, 61,* 34–46.

Boudreau, J., & Rynes, S. (1987). Giving it the old college try. *Personnel Administrator, 32,* 78–85.

Boudreau, J. W., & Rynes, S. L. (1985). Role of recruitment in staffing utility analysis. *Journal of Applied Psychology, 70,* 354–366.

Bowman, W. (1987). How college graduates find good jobs. *Journal of College Planning & Employment, 47,* 32–36.

Cascio, W. F. (1982). *Applied psychology in personnel management* (2nd ed.). Reston, VA: Reston Publishing.

Chicci, D. L., & Knapp, C. L. (1980). College recruitment from start to finish. *Personnel Journal, 59,* 655–659.

Davis, R. V., Lofquist, L. H., & Weiss, D. J. (1968). A theory of work adjustment: A revision. *Minnesota Studies in Vocational Rehabilitation, 23,* Minneapolis: Industrial Relations Center, University of Minnesota.

Greenhaus, J. H. (1987). *Career management.* New York: Dryden Press.

Heneman, H. G. III, Schwab, D. P., Fossum, J. A., & Dyer, L. D. (1986). *Personnel/human resource management* (3rd ed.). Homewood, IL: Irwin.

Lindquist, V. R., & Endicott, F. (1984). *Trends in the employment of college and university graduates in business and industry (38th annual report).* Evanston, IL: Northwestern University.

Lindquist, V. R., & Endicott, F. (1986). *Trends in the employment of college and university graduates in business and industry (40th annual report).* Evanston, IL: Northwestern University.

Magnus, M. (1987). Is your recruitment all it can be? *Personnel Journal, 66,* 54–63.

Mason, N., & Belt, J. A. (1986). Effectiveness of specificity in recruitment advertising. *Journal of Management, 12,* 425–432.

Powell, G. N. (1984). Effects of job attributes and recruiting practices on applicant decisions: A comparison. *Personnel Psychology, 37,* 721–732.

Rynes, S., & Boudreau, J. (1986). College recruiting in large organizations: Practice, evaluation, and research implications. *Personnel Psychology, 39,* 729–757.

Rynes, S. L., Heneman, H. G. III, & Schwab, D. P. (1980). Individual reactions to organizational recruiting: A review. *Personnel Psychology, 33,* 529–542.

Rynes, S. L., & Miller, H. E. (1983). Recruiter and job influences on candidates for employment. *Journal of Applied Psychology, 68,* 147–154.

Schwab, D. P. (1982). Recruiting and organizational participation. In K. M. Rowland & G. R. Ferris (Eds.), *Personnel management* (pp. 103–128). Boston: Allyn & Bacon.

Scott, R. A., Pavlock, E., & Lathan, M. (1985). On-campus recruiting: The students speak up. *Journal of Accountancy, 8,* 15–39.

Soelberg, P. O. (1967). Unprogrammed decision making. *Industrial Management Review, 8,* 19–29.
Taylor, M. S., & Bergmann, T. J. (1987). Organizational recruitment activities and applicant's reactions at different stages of the recruitment. *Personnel Psychology, 40,* 261–285.
Wanous, J. P. (1980). *Organizational entry: Recruitment, selection and socialization of newcomers.* Reading, MA: Addison-Wesley.
Wanous, J. P., Keon, T. L., & Latack, J. C. (1983). Expectancy theory and occupational/organizational choices: A review and tests. *Organizational Behavior and Human Performance, 32,* 66–86.

The Nature of Employment Interview Decisions

David C. Gilmore
Gerald R. Ferris
K. Michele Kacmar

Most adults in our society spend a significant portion of their waking hours at work, and usually this work is compensated and includes an employment relationship with a formal organization. This employment relationship begins in the selection process, which involves decisions both by the individual and the employing organization. These decisions are influenced by a number of factors, but information that is exchanged during selection interviews plays a large part in the determination of who is offered employment and who decides to accept these offers. Decisions are made by both the organization and the individual in the selection interviewing process. We intend to look at decision making in the selection interviewing process from both perspectives: what factors influence selection interviewing decisions made by the organization and what influences potential employees in deciding whether to pursue employment with an organization.

In an interview, both the interviewer and the applicant form impressions of each other that are used in their subsequent decision making. The interviewer, as a representative of the organization, can be viewed as representative of the type of people in that organization and the applicant may base his or her decision about the organization on impressions formed in an interview. Mitchell (1978) has suggested that people use what could be referred to as an "implicit personality theory" when evaluating another person in such a situation. With limited information, people tend to fill in the gaps and form an overall impression, which is used to make decisions. From the standpoint of an applicant, the overall impression of the interviewer may generalize to the entire organization, and ultimately influence the applicant's decision to pursue employment possibilities with that organization.

We regularly utilize implicit personality theories in our daily lives. How many times have we seen someone on the street whom we have never met, yet within seconds form an impression of "what that person is like," simply based upon the way the person is dressed or perhaps his or her hair style? Thus, through our initial impressions, based on quite limited information in many cases, we tend to mentally create a "complete picture" of that person that is consistent with our first impression. A conservatively dressed, well-groomed young man implicitly conveys to us the image of someone who holds a certain type of job and possesses a given set of beliefs and values. Since it is human nature to maintain consistency in our thinking, our implicit personality theory would not allow us to conclude that this young man is a delinquent troublemaker. Equally inconsistent for us is the conclusion that a slovenly dressed, unshaven young man, with shoulder-length hair is in fact a virtual genius, holding a Ph.D. in nuclear physics and quite competent at what he does.

INTERVIEWER DECISION MAKING

Interviewers also appear to use implicit personality theories when evaluating an applicant for a position. Many reviews of the literature on the employment interview provide information on the variables that influence interviewers' judgments (Schmitt, 1976; Arvey, 1979; Gilmore & Ferris, 1980). A recent review by Hakel (1982) suggests that interviewers are influenced by first impressions, order and favorability of information, stereotyping, contrast effects, non-verbal behaviors, and other biases. In a typical interview, first impressions are particularly important. The applicant's appearance, social skills in the sometimes awkward greeting and introduction portion of an interview, and the applicant's first few responses to the interviewer can play a critical part in the overall evaluation of a candidate. It also appears that interviewers often search for negative information, and give it inappropriate weight when found. Information that appears early (primary effect) and information that occurs last in the interview (recency effect) appear to have more influence than information in the middle of an interview, particularly if that information is negative.

Webster's (1964) research indicates that applicants are often compared to a stereotype of the ideal applicant, and if the applicant is similar enough to this stereotype, a favorable decision is made by the interviewer. Unfortunately, in a typical interview, relatively few pieces of information can be obtained, and the interviewer must fill in the gaps based upon his or her implicit personality theory. These inferential leaps that fill in the gaps may not be justified, and even the appropriateness of the interviewer's ideal applicant stereotype is certainly open to question. Hakel (1982) also reports that the relative favorability of interviewees immediately preceding the applicant can influence evaluation. This contrast effect suggests that any given applicant is seen more positively when following a particularly poor candidate. Aside from what the applicant says in the interview, non-verbal behaviors (e.g., eye contract, handshake, posture, etc.) can also influence the interviewer's evaluation of the applicant. Some of these variables are under the control of the applicant (e.g., appearance, social skills, responses to questions), and presumably can be modified through training and experience. Other issues are either under the control of the interviewer (e.g., order of information, stereotypes, etc.) or simply are chance occurrences (contrast effects). Obviously, interviewers should be aware of these issues, and should attempt to minimize their influence in the final decision-making process.

IMPROVING THE INTERVIEW

Recent work in employment interview techniques by Janz, Hellervik, and Gilmore (1986) offers much hope for improving current practice. Instead of trying to cover the applicant's entire background in the interview, issues that appear critical to job performance and cannot be investigated easily by other means such as testing should be focused upon in the interview. In many jobs, where technical qualifications are either not terribly important or not easily evaluated and "people" skills and issues of work motivation are critical, interviewers should concentrate on the latter two areas in the relatively limited interview time. Also, instead of asking for the applicant's opinions about these issues, or how they think they might hypothetically deal with a "people" problem or a work motivation problem, Janz et al. suggest that interviewers ask how the applicant actually dealt with such a situation in the past. Applicants then relate a specific incident revealing behavioral data that can be used to draw inferences about how the applicant might behave in the future.

By using these types of behavioral description questions, by focusing on a few relevant aspects of job performance in the interview, and by being aware of the many factors that can conceivably influence an interviewer, it is possible to make the selection interview a more reliable process. We must move toward the standardized coverage of relevant content, and try to avoid irrelevant information if we intend to use the interview to make valid decisions that affect people's lives.

APPLICANT DECISION MAKING

A somewhat neglected area in recruiting interview research is the process by which applicants determine whether they are favorably disposed toward a particular organization and will continue to pursue employment possibilities with it. In making this decision, applicants must first decide whether they are qualified for the position, and would enjoy working in that type of position for that particular company.

The first decision (i.e., qualification) is normally made for the applicant. Companies rarely extend an invitation for an interview to an unqualified applicant, at least not knowingly so. The exception to the rule may be a position in which the necessary job skills cannot be easily determined from a resume and application form. Such positions might include jobs that require frequent contact with customers or clients, where verbal skills, not discernible in writing, are essential.

The second decision requires more involvement on the part of the applicant. To determine whether the type of job and company are "right," an applicant must gather specific information. The main avenue to this information is the interviewer in the employment setting, or the person sent to do campus recruiting. Research has shown that interviewers are often perceived as poorly informed, and consequently they alienate many applicants, either because they have not read the applicant's resume or because they have little specific information about the type of job for which the applicant is being considered (Rynes, Heneman, & Schwab, 1980). Some companies utilize job incumbents as interviewers because job incumbents are likely to be seen as more credible sources of information than full-time interviewers or recruiters (Fisher, Ilgen, & Hoyer, 1979).

Because job incumbents have a more thorough understanding of the specific responsibilities of the job, they are in a position to provide more realistic information about it. This more candid information could be invaluable to the applicant when making a decision, but will it hinder an organization in attracting new employees? Wanous (1980) argues that realistic job information does not reduce an organization's ability to recruit, but instead reduces subsequent turnover because employees do not have inflated expectations. In a later study, Reilly, Brown, Blood, and Malatesta (1981) found a strong relationship between realistic job recruitment procedures and a reduced turnover rate when results from eleven different studies were aggregated. These findings have been difficult for some to accept since, intuitively, it seems that telling applicants about the bad as well as the good things on the job would have an adverse impact on the total applicant pool. This issue has not been resolved and needs more research.

Interviewers are faced with making the same two decisions about an applicant that the applicant must make about the organization. That is, the interviewer must first determine if the applicant is qualified for the position and, second, if the individual would "fit" into the organization. As with the applicant, the first decision is normally made before the interview begins. If specific guidelines concerning qualifications have been established by the company, such as grade point average (GPA), major field of study, and work experience, and these guidelines were carefully followed in the screening process, all applicants interviewed should be able to adequately perform the job. So how does the interviewer determine appropriate candidates to recommend for an additional interview?

One way the interviewer has of determining how well the applicant will fit into the organization is by noting the effect the recruitment process has on him or her. The recruitment procedures utilized by the company during the interview can disseminate important but unspoken facts. For example, if the qualifications for an entry-level position are much higher than elsewhere, the company may be trying to tell the applicant a little about the organization's culture. If the applicant is not afraid of the high standards, the interviewer may feel more confident about the applicant's capacity for fitting in. This process goes further than a realistic job preview by adding information about the organization's work environment as a whole and has been referred to as early socialization of the applicant to the organization (Rynes, in press).

IMPRESSION MANAGEMENT IN THE INTERVIEW

Another avenue open to an applicant when trying to prove to a recruiter that he or she will fit into the organization is the use of impression management. Tedeschi and Reiss (1981) described impression management as behaviors of an individual aimed at influencing the impressions formed about that individual by others. Some impression management behaviors are tactical in nature in that they are undertaken with clear, rather short-term objectives in mind. Other impression management behaviors are more strategic in nature in that they are undertaken as part of an overall long-term plan. Since an interview is of short duration, it is more appropriate to consider tactical impression management behaviors.

Some specific tactical impression management behaviors have been delineated by Jones and Pittman (1982); they include self-promotion (i.e., the target perceives the self-promoter as having desirable abilities or skills), entitlements (i.e., verbal claims of responsibility for positive events), and enhancements (i.e., self-enhancing communication, other-enhancing communication, opinion conformity, and favor-doing). Many of these tactics could easily be utilized in an interview situation. However, it is less clear what types of outcomes might be expected from using them.

Enhancements or ingratiation behaviors are likely to occur in an interview setting. For example, opinion conformity might occur when an interviewer states his or her opinion about the type of employee needed for the job, and the applicant quickly agrees with the statement, even though his or her true opinion might not coincide with the statement. Self-enhancing communication, in which the applicant attempts to persuade the interviewer that he or she possesses positive qualities, motives, or intentions is also very likely to occur in an employment interview.

The determination of how well an individual will fit into an organization is not solely in the hands of the interviewer. Applicants can influence the decision made by the interviewer in an attempt to control the outcome. An interview does not just happen to an applicant; it is a process in which both the applicant and the interviewer participate. The more active the applicant becomes in the interview process, the more likely a favorable outcome will occur. That is, applicants who verbalize alot and sell themselves are more likely to favorably impress an interviewer.

One way applicants can attempt to influence an interviewer's opinion is through their appearance. Baeyer, Sherk, and Zanna (1981) measured the physical appearance of a group of female subjects when they attended an informational meeting, and again when they knew that they would be participating in an interview. The ratings clearly increased in the interview setting, and the researchers suggested that the subjects were motivated to impress the job interviewer.

Applicants can also tailor their appearance to fit if they have "done their homework" and can identify the type of image that is most advantageous to portray. One example might be how an informed applicant would dress for an interview with IBM. It would not be difficult for an applicant to learn that IBM has a well-known dress code. If an applicant arrives at an initial interview "in uniform," the interviewer will know that the applicant is familiar with IBM's culture and that he or she wants to look like a member of the team. Other firms may have similar but less well-known appearance guidelines.

There are two possible outcomes from any type of impression management attempt. First, the interviewer could perceive the applicant exactly as the applicant intended, that is, in a positive light. This type of outcome likely would lead to a favorable evaluation. The second possible outcome would be that the interviewer could feel manipulated. The applicant's attempts may be too transparent, and the interviewer might feel the applicant is simply an "operator." The most likely consequence from this reaction would be a decision not to recommend the applicant. How transparent the impression management attempts are to the interviewer may be related to the ability of the applicant: some individuals are simply better at it than others. Several personality characteristics that influence the likelihood an individual may engage in impression management includes self-monitoring (Snyder, 1974), self-attention and social anxiety (Schlenker & Leary, 1982), and Machiavellianism (Ralston, 1985).

In an employment interview setting, self-monitoring (i.e., the ability of an individual to tune into the situational cues available and to read these correctly) may be one of the most important characteristics that an applicant can possess. If an interviewer begins to feel manipulated by the applicant, the verbal and nonverbal feedback may reflect these feelings. If the applicant is high on self-monitoring, and can read these cues and react appropriately to them, perhaps by switching impression management tactics, a favorable impression may still be possible. Thus, applicants have to present themselves in a positive fashion but must take care not to oversell themselves.

RECOMMENDATIONS FOR APPLICANTS

To obtain the best possible outcome from the job search process (i.e., a good job that meets the individual's needs), the following steps are suggested *for the applicant seeking a job:*

1. The applicant should obtain as much information as possible about a prospective employer, even before the first interview. Libraries, friends, and present employees can provide facts about an organization, and these sources may be more or less objective than information obtained from interviewers.

2. The applicant should prepare for the first interview by practicing. Unless the individual is a seasoned job seeker, the first few interviews may not adequately represent the person's true abilities. Also, preparing good questions to ask an interviewer can help obtain relevant information and may favorably impress the interviewer.

3. The applicant should convey the picture of a competent rational person. Presenting one's background in an interview as a logical sequence of steps leading toward the objective of a career in an organization is much more advantageous than portraying oneself as a victim of happenstance or chance. The reasons for choosing a major, a minor, particular academic courses, and what organizations with which to interview should appear the result of rational decision making. Obviously, extracurricular activities and prior work experiences should be presented in such a way that will not discourage a prospective employer.

4. The applicant should learn as much as possible about the organization's culture—appropriate dress, work ethics, goals and its mission—to better the chances of appearing to fit into the organization.

RECOMMENDATIONS FOR INTERVIEWERS

To obtain the best possible applicants in the most efficient manner, the following points are suggested *for the interviewer:*

1. The interviewer should develop a "game plan" for the interview so that he or she knows what is going to happen. The interviewer should decide ahead of time what is to be covered in the interview (e.g., rapport building, obtaining information from the applicant, providing information about the job, answering applicant's questions); communicate this plan to the applicant so that he or she knows what is going to happen (this helps to reduce anxiety); ask questions that will elicit desired information (e.g., avoid leading questions or those that can be answered with a "yes" or "no"); and follow the same format for all applicants to insure equal treatment.

2. The interviewer should develop this game plan based upon job-relevant information. If the interviewer doesn't have first-hand knowledge of the job, he or she should seek out appropriate job analysis information. Using more behavioral description questions should help. Applicants expect the interviewer to ask job-related questions

and to be able to provide specific information about the job.

3. The interviewer should try to make the applicant feel at ease in the interview. A cordial greeting, appropriate verbal and nonverbal communication, and concern for the applicant's welfare will help applicants relax and present their best responses. The introduction of stress, whether intentional or not, makes the applicant feel uneasy, can differentially disrupt some applicants who might otherwise be good prospects, often is not job related, and can discourage some applicants who assume that stress is an enduring characteristic of the organization.

4. The interviewer should conduct the interview so that the applicant does most of the talking. Aside from the period in which the interviewer is providing job-related information to the applicant, the interviewer should be listening. Little information is obtained from an applicant who spends most of the interview nodding and smiling appropriately while the interviewer talks. A good rule of thumb is that the applicant should talk about 75 percent of the time.

5. The interviewer should develop active listening skills so that he or she can ask probing questions, and remember what the applicant said in response to them.

6. The interviewer should provide a clear description of the job and the organization to the prospective employee. This description should be specific and realistic; many applicants will quickly sense if they are being oversold. Too favorable a presentation may unduly raise expectations and lead to later dissatisfaction and/or turnover.

7. The interviewer should develop the skills to both observe and provide nonverbal communication. Applicants reveal considerable information through their nonverbal behavior, which can be helpful to an interviewer, particularly when the applicant is being considered for a job where face-to-face contact is required. Conversely, nonverbal cues given by the interviewer, such as eye contact, gestures, and posture can convey to an applicant much about the interviewer's interest in him or her.

8. The interviewer should become aware of the biases that he or she has by determining the later job success of former interview candidates and by participating in training experiences. A good interviewer will substantiate his hunches about people by seeking job-relevant information and determining if his or her stereotype of an applicant is accurate. Also, an interviewer should guard against making early (first impression) judgments in the interview, and avoid overevaluating negative information about an applicant. It would be helpful if interviewers received feedback on the actual job performance of individuals whom they interviewed, and thus were able to compare their interview impressions with actual job performance.

9. The interviewer should record observations during and/or at the conclusion of the interview, so that information about one applicant is not confused with another. These notes will be helpful when the interviewer makes later judgments. Only by careful recording can an interviewer hope to keep the information from becoming a confusing collection of impressions.

10. The interviewer should be aware of current legal and ethical issues surrounding the interview process. Careful planning of questions can avoid intrusion upon an applicant's privacy and potential legal difficulties. Interviewers who "fly by the seat of their pants" are asking for trouble and may offend applicants who are good prospective employees.

Thus, the task of interviewing, if it is done well, is not easy, and should not be taken lightly. The interviewer is one of the applicant's primary contacts with an organization, and often his or her impact upon the applicant is enduring. To attract high quality applicants, the interviewing process must be conducted in a professional manner.

CONCLUSION

During the interview, considerable information is exchanged between the interviewer, who represents an organization, and the applicant, who is seeking employment. This exchange of information, or the "sizing up" that occurs, has considerable impact upon the organization's ability to recruit new human resources, and the applicant's potential career. If organizations do not recruit new members well, their eventual survival may be hindered. For the applicant, the interview is a crucial step in his or her working life, and must be done well. Anything less than a good interview from either the organization's or the applicant's point of view is an unfortunate waste of valuable human resources.

REFERENCES

Arvey, R. D. (1979). Unfair discrimination in the employment interview: Legal and psychological effects. *Psychological Bulletin, 86,* 736–765.

Baeyer, C., Sherk, D. L., & Zanna, M. P. (1981). Impression management in job interviews: When the female applicant meets the male "chauvinist" interviewer. *Personality and Social Psychology Bulletin, 7,* 45–51.

Fisher, C., Ilgen, D., & Hoyer, W. (1979). Source credibility, information favorability, and job offer acceptance. *Academy of Management Journal, 22,* 94–103.

Gilmore, D. C., & Ferris, G. R. (1980). Problems in the employment interview. In K. M. Rowland, M. London, G. R. Ferris, J. L. Sherman (Eds.), *Current issues in personnel management.* Boston: Allyn & Bacon.

Hakel, M. D. (1982). Employment interviewing. In K. M. Rowland & G. R. Ferris (Eds.), *Personnel management.* Boston: Allyn & Bacon.

Janz, T., Hellervik, L., & Gilmore, D. C. (1986). *Behavior description interviewing.* Boston: Allyn & Bacon.

Jones, E. E., & Pittman, T. S. (1982). Toward a general theory of strategic self-presentation. in J. Suls (Ed.), *Psychological perspectives on the self.* Hillsdale, NJ: Erlbaum.

Mitchell, T. R. (1978). *People in organizations: Understanding their behavior.* New York: McGraw-Hill.

Ralston, D. A. (1985). Employee ingratiation: The role of management. *Academy of Management Review, 10,* 477–487.

Reilly, P. R., Brown, B., Blood, M., & Malatesta, C. (1981). The effects of realistic previews: A study and discussion of the literature. *Personnel Psychology, 34,* 823–834.

Rynes, S. L. (in press). Recruitment, organizational entry, and early work adjustment. In M. D. Dunnetle (Ed.), *Handbook of industrial and organizational psychology* (2nd ed). New York: Wiley.

Rynes, S. L., Heneman, H. G., & Schwab, D. P. (1980). Individual reactions to organizational recruiting: A review. *Personnel Psychology, 33,* 529–542.

Schlenker, B., & Leary, J. (1982). Social anxiety and self presentation: A conceptualization and model. *Psychological Bulletin, 92,* 641–699.

Schmitt, N. (1976). Social and situational determinants of interview decisions: Implications for the employment interview. *Personnel Psychology, 29,* 79–101.

Snyder, M. (1974). The self-monitoring of expressive behavior. *Journal of Personality and Social Psychology, 30,* 526–537.

Tedeschi, J., & Reiss, M. (1981). Predicaments and verbal tactics of impression management. In C. Antaki (Ed.), *Ordinary language explanations of social behavior.* London: Academic Press.

Wanous, J. P. (1980). *Organizational entry: Recruitment, selection, and socialization of newcomers.* Reading, MA: Addison-Wesley.

Webster, E. C. (1964). *Decision making in the employment interview.* Montreal, Canada: Eagle.

Recruiting, Interviewing, and Hiring: Staying within the Boundaries

Philip R. Voluck

Employers naturally try to recruit the *best* employees for their company. However, they often settle for merely an acceptable candidate. They hire individuals with the basic technical skills but no idea of their overall role in the company or the philosophy and goals of the company. The best employees have goals, objectives and work philosophies compatible with those of their employers.

Employers settle for less than the best because they cannot find the right path through the maze of legal restrictions that make the interviewing and hiring process so confusing. Many employers believe that if they ask the wrong question, they may well be answering a discrimination complaint. And they are right!

LEGAL RESTRICTIONS ON HIRING

Federal, state and local discrimination and employment laws regulate the recruiting and hiring of employees. These laws prohibit employers from discriminating on the basis of age, religion, handicap, race, national origin or sex. As of May 1987, it will be unlawful for employers to discriminate on the basis of citizenship. Because these prohibitions exist, employers should not question applicants regarding these "protected" areas. Unsuccessful applicants often maintain they were questioned improperly when alleging they were denied employment for discriminatory reasons. Defending an employment discrimination lawsuit, even successfully, can be very expensive, as well as demoralizing to other employees.

Many questions and interviewing techniques that seem innocent may, in fact, have an adverse impact on certain protected groups. For these reasons, employers should review their employment applications and their interview questions and procedures. All questions must be job-related. A good rule of thumb is *if the question is not job-related, do not ask it.*

The following outline of the most common forms of discrimination indicates subjects which should *not* be incorporated into the hiring process. This list serves only as a partial guide. Individual state laws also vary in their prohibitions. Carefully audit specific questions to avoid exposure to potential liability.

1. *Marital and Family Status*—Employers should not ask whether an applicant is married, single, divorced, etc. Such questions may have an adverse impact on certain protected groups. For example, an employer that imposes morality requirements combining marital status with other factors, such as pregnancy or having children out of wedlock, may violate the law.

2. *Age*—Employers should not ask applicants their age, unless the question is necessary to determine if the prospective employee meets the minimum age requirement for employment in that state. However, questions seeking information regarding the applicant's relevant work experience are proper. Recent amendments to the Age Discrimination in Employment Act made mandatory retirement ages unlawful for most employers. Interview questions should focus on ability to do the job, not on an applicant's age.

3. *Handicaps*—Employers may ask applicants whether they have any physical condition or handicap that might limit their ability to perform the job for which they applied, and to indicate what

Reprinted from the May 1987 issue of *Personnel Administrator*, copyright 1987, The American Society for Personnel Administration, 606 North Washington Street, Alexandria, Virginia 22314.

reasonable job accommodations might have to be made to enable them to perform the job. However, applicants should not be asked to characterize their general medical condition or state of health. Under the law, excluding applicants from employment because of physical or mental impairments is only permissible if the impairment substantially prevents them from successfully performing the job. In most states, refusing to hire an individual suffering from AIDS who is capable of performing a job violates the state law which otherwise protects the handicapped.

4. *Sex*—There are few jobs for which being a male or female is a bona fide occupational qualification (BFOQ). Any inquiry pertaining to sex should, therefore, be avoided, even though the question would apply to both sexes. If the job for which the applicant is being considered could not be performed by a pregnant employee, the employer should use a medical examination to screen new hires after the selection decision has been made.

5. *Race or Color*—Employers should not ask applicants how they feel about having to work with co-workers of different races. In addition, employers should not ask applicants whether having a supervisor of a different race or color would present a problem. Employers should not make any notations regarding race or color on the job application. If an applicant challenges an employment decision, an employer might have a difficult time explaining that a notation on a job application pertaining to the subject's race or color was not used in the selection procedure but only as an affirmative action or EEO measure.

6. *Citizenship or Birthplace*—Employers may ask applicants whether they are U.S. citizens or whether they have the legal right to be employed in this country. An employer should not ask applicants whether they are citizens of another country, or where they or any members of their family were born, as such questions may run afoul of laws prohibiting discrimination on the basis of national origin. As of May 1987, when the new Immigration Reform and Control Act goes into effect, employers will have to verify that *all* prospective employees are eligible for employment in the United States. The law will require employers to examine documents which establish the identity of the applicant and that the applicant is authorized to work in the United States. Note that employers will only have to determine that an applicant is authorized to work in the United States, not where an applicant was born. The Immigration Reform and Control Act will make it unlawful to hire and to continue to employ unauthorized (illegal) aliens knowingly.

7. *Criminal Convictions and Arrests*—Criminal convictions should only bar employment if they have a direct relationship to the requirements of the particular job. Refusing employment or discharging employees on the basis of arrest records is unlawful unless an employer has evidence that such actions are necessary to the operation of the employer's business. An arrest is not conclusive as to wrongdoing and is irrelevant to work qualifications. Merely asking about arrest records tends to have a "chilling" effect on minority applicants and may violate the law.

8. *Religion*—Employers should not inquire into an applicant's religious faith, denomination or affiliation. If employers are concerned about adequate staffing on Saturdays and Sundays, they may ask applicants whether they are regularly available for work on those days. However, if the employer requests work on an employee's religious holiday, the employer has a legal obligation to make reasonable accommodations for that employee's religious observances and practices.

9. *Education: Dates of Attendance*—Employers may inquire into the extent of an applicant's education and the names of schools attended, as well as degrees or diplomas received. Employers should not ask for the dates of attendance at schools, since dates of attendance may be indicative of age.

SPECIAL STATE LAWS

Employers should be aware that state laws may affect recruiting and hiring programs. For example, many states prohibit the use of polygraph tests or voice stress analyzers, except in limited situations, such as when the applicant, if hired, would have access to controlled substances. State laws may also prohibit discrimination against applicants because they have a General Education Development certificate instead of a high school diploma. Health care employers should take note that several states prohibit discrimination against anyone who refuses to participate in an abortion procedure.

PRE-EMPLOYMENT TESTING

Many employers rely on written tests to make important employment decisions. These tests involve legal risks. Administering tests to applicants is not illegal. However, the test must be shown to be job-related and should be validated before it is implemented. A test is not validated merely because an employer demonstrates that the knowledge, skills and abilities tested by the examination coincide with some of the knowledge, skills and abilities required for successful job performance. The employer must also show that the attributes selected for examination are centrally, and not merely peripherally, related to successful job performance; that the various parts of the examination are accurately weighted; and that the level of difficulty of the examination measures the level of difficulty of the job.

Rejected applicants often attack such tests as biased, regardless of their validity. Extreme care should be taken when choosing, administering or developing pre-employment tests.

THE HIRING DECISION

Once employers have accumulated as much information as lawfully possible about a prospective applicant, they must decide whether the applicant can make a meaningful contribution to the organization.

The employer should attempt to obtain additional information by conducting a thorough reference check. The employer should send a written request to an applicant's former employers on company stationery. The letter should identify the title of the person who is making the request. A written request should be supplemented with a telephone call if a response is not received within a reasonable period of time. Careful employers, however, will give only minimal responses over the telephone. If a former employer is willing to discuss the details of a former employee's tenure, the prospective employer will have a valuable insight to facilitate the selection decision.

Today many employers hesitate to provide references for former employees. They consider references dangerous because of the increasing propensity of individuals and companies to sue each other over unfavorable or misleading references. References have been the focal points of lawsuits alleging libel or slander, discrimination, and negligence.

POST-EMPLOYMENT INFORMATION

Once employers have made the selection decision, they will have to obtain information about the new employee that it could not lawfully ask job applicants. For proper personnel and employee benefits administration, new hires must answer questions concerning age, sex, marital status, number of dependents, physical condition, and even racial or ethnic origin. However, the employer may not use this information in subsequent selection decisions such as training, pay, promotions, demotions or layoffs. The answers to any of these sensitive questions should be kept separate from the employee's personnel file to avoid even the appearance that impermissible criteria figured in any later selection decision.

Some companies find that on-the-job observation during a "tryout" period is the most satisfactory test of applicants. The possibility of engaging in discriminatory hiring practices is greatly reduced if an employer makes its hiring decision on the basis of on-the-job observations. This is especially true when an application suggests that an applicant is of only borderline quality.

Employers who choose to use a tryout period must alert applicants on the application form that there will be a trial or probationary period. The application form in non-union companies should also clearly state that any employment relationship is at-will. A statement that employment is at-will avoids any implication that once the trial period is completed, employment is permanent. The application might state, for example: "I understand that, if employed, I will be required to complete a trial period of employment satisfactorily. I further understand that either the company or I can terminate my employment and compensation, with or without cause and with or without notice, at any time." In making such a statement the employer must strike a careful balance between its desire to maintain an at-will employment relationship and good personnel practices that do not alienate employees.

A HIRING PROFILE

Designing an effective, lawful recruiting and hiring program may well be the core of successful human resource planning. Proper employee selection ensures that the company will have the right employees to fulfill its mission and carry out required tasks. Improper employee selection not only results in employees who are less than the best, but also in violations of various discrimination laws. Properly implementing the recruiting and hiring program is, therefore, crucial to the success of any business organization.

A thorough recruiting and hiring system that incorporates *a profile of the type of employee to be actively recruited* is one method of avoiding legal risks and the pitfalls of improper employee selection. In developing an effective hiring profile, the organization must first define its corporate philosophy, by making a formal, written commitment to its goals, including a statement regarding its work philosophies.

After developing a work philosophy, the organization should determine the qualities which successful employees possess and which are compatible with the work philosophy. For example, some companies require individuals who are "creative," "flexible," and "assertively confrontational." Other companies may need individuals who are "respectful" and "trusting of authority." The attributes exhibited by prospective applicants during the recruiting and selection process can be examined against those attributes which the company needs.

A hiring profile could also incorporate a list of desired responses which could guide the interviewer in evaluating whether a prospective applicant would be a successful employee. All personnel with hiring authority must use the profile and its answer guidelines to ensure uniform interpretation of applicant responses.

The hiring profile might also include a post-employment audit to confirm that new hires are meeting the company's expectations. The post-employment audit may show that modifications of the hiring profile are necessary.

Developing a thorough, legally acceptable hiring profile can be a complex task. However, successful companies have proven that an investment in human resources is worthwhile. After all, a company is only as good as its people.

The Trouble with Testing

Martin Lasden

There's no telling how many of us have high psychological test scores to thank for the jobs we now hold. But it was concern over the fate of those who didn't score very well that put corporate personnel departments on the defensive throughout the 1960s and '70s. It was a two-pronged attack, led on the one hand by social critics such as William H. Whyte, Jr., author of *The Organization*

Man, who argued forcefully that corporations were using tests to select for highly malleable, unimaginative yes-men. "If the tests were rigorously applied across the board, half the most dynamic men in business would be out walking the streets looking for a job," Whyte wrote. Meanwhile, acting on behalf of groups protected by the Civil Rights Act of 1964, the Equal Employment Opportunity Commission launched its own assault, aggressively challenging employers—often in court—to prove the validity and relevancy of employment tests.

In the face of all this heat it is no wonder that by the end of the 1970s, the use of psychological screening tests had decreased precipitously from the decade before—as much as 40%, according to some estimates. But now, all of a sudden, the decline seems to be over. Test sales once again are on the rise.

There are no official industry-wide statistics to refer to, but in a business where millions of dollars are said to be at stake, strong bellwether signs indicate that we are indeed in the midst of an incipient testing boom. In Palo Alto, CA, Consulting Psychologists Press reports a 10% increase in its test sales over the last year. In Chicago, Londonhouse Inc., a major publisher of honesty tests, reports a 30% rise. Another Chicago company, Science Research Associates, a subsidiary of IBM, sold 25% to 30% more tests in 1984 than in 1983. Psychological Services Inc. reported a 43% increase in '83, and was doing even better as of late '84. In Monterey, CA, after watching the market as a spectator for some 10 years, Publishers Test Service, a division of McGraw-Hill, has finally decided to jump in with a line of employee-selection tests expected to gross the company at least $200,000 the first year, according to a spokesman.

Why now? Certainly, the economic recovery and the decrease in unemployment has something to do with it, for not only are there more new positions to fill, but more old ones, too, as stable staffers tantalized by the prospect of new opportunities decide to move on to greener pastures, thus multiplying the pressure on businesses to evaluate job applicants as quickly and efficiently as possible.

Economic recovery notwithstanding, however, the impact of a more lenient attitude among government regulators and the courts cannot be underestimated. Over the last few years, the courts, in particular, have shown a much greater willingness to accept the notion that if a test can be validated in one company for one job, it can be applied to similar jobs in other companies without having to prove its validity all over again. It is this "validity generalization" concept that works to lighten dramatically the burden of proof on companies to demonstrate the fairness of their tests.

John Hunter and Frank Schmidt are two psychologists best known for their work in support of such generalizations. They write: " . . . Our research shows that while the degree of validity might vary slightly from one job to the next, every aptitude that was valid for one job was valid for all the jobs."

NUMBERS GAME

What it boils down to, of course, is a question of numbers. Do the numbers suggest that the reliability of an already validated test varies significantly enough under real-world conditions to merit concern, or, as Schmidt and Hunter argue, are such variations often found to be the result of sampling errors and other methodological flaws? Among opposing statisticians, it's a question likely to evoke the sort of debate that test users will be unable to decipher easily. Numbers, after all, are highly malleable, especially in the hands of experts, and unless one is blessed with a good ear for minutia, confusion rather than enlightenment is the likely outcome.

This does not necessarily cast aspersions on the quality of Schmidt and Hunter's work. But in the wild and wooly world of testing—a world replete with past scandals, exaggerated claims and an insufficiency of enforced standards—validity generalization very well may be the wrong concept for the wrong time. Indeed, it may encourage the sort of complacence that gave occupational testing a bad name in the first place.

Consider, for example, the Programmer Aptitude Test (PAT) developed by IBM in the mid-1950s. IBM assured employers that PAT could accurately predict the performance of would-be programmers. And over the next 10 years, PAT did indeed become the most widely used test in the United States, with most employers accepting its validity on blind faith. If you can't trust IBM, after all, who can you trust?

But by the mid-1960s, that trust was shown to be misplaced. Flaws were found in the original validation research, and new studies came out. In one such study, published in 1967, half of the top PAT scorers in a nationwide survey of 233 turned out to be below-average programmers (as rated by their supervisors), while the bottom fourth of the PAT scorers turned out to be somewhat better than the below-average group. Eight years later, in a paper presented to the International Federation for Information Processing, another researcher, G. Penny, observed: "Year after year such tests go their random way, possibly doing no more than bolstering selectors' confidence in their own procedures without regard to any harm they may do to the career or self-image of the applicants."

Like toxic waste, the damage done by bad tests is cumulative. It increases over time. It's also insidious in the sense that, once sold on a worthless test, an employer might go for years without being aware of the unjust damage that's being done, simply because poor scorers are never hired to prove the instrument wrong. (Why should hiring managers stick their necks out if the test is assumed to be valid, and good money is being paid for the results?) Self-fulfilling prophecies are, thus, exceedingly easy to generate. And in the marketplace where tests are sold, such prophecies are perpetuated both by the vendors and the users—vendors who, in the face of stiff competition, are given to over-promoting their wares, and users who, faced with the age-old problem of hiring the right person for the right job, prove highly vulnerable to the allure of a quick and easy answer.

BLAME IT ON THE CHINESE

The use of tests to evaluate job applicants is said to date back to China's Han Dynasty (206 BC to 220 AD), where written examinations were used to select candidates for government positions. Here in this country, following the Civil War, it was also the government that first began to experiment systematically with employment tests, seeing in those tests the antidote to a civil-service spoils system fraught with corruption. It was in this same progressive spirit that other job-screening tests were first introduced into the private sector during the early 1900s. Acting on the belief that a science of vocational guidance could eliminate worker unrest, wasted potential and a whole host of other social ills, Hugo Munsterberg, H. D. Hollingsworth, Walter D. Scott and other noted psychologists threw themselves into the task of developing exams for a whole range of occupations, including sales, typing and other types of clerical work.

Two world wars followed, and with each, massive military testing programs were initiated. These, in turn, stimulated testing booms in the private sector. But in each case, the great expectations raised by testing advocates went unfulfilled, and the booms, launched with great fanfare, could not be sustained. As Matthew Hale noted in an article published in 1982 under the auspices of The National Research Council Committee on Ability Testing, the first wave had run out of steam by the mid-1920s. "Most employers had neither the patience nor the money to adopt testing programs," he wrote, "especially because psychologists so often disagreed among themselves over the proper techniques, and because careful validation programs, when instituted, often showed a low correlation between test scores and job success. . . . One psychologist estimated that about 40% of the companies that began to use tests after World War I found that they did not work."

Sparked by the much-touted success of the military in choosing pilots and spies during World War II, interest in employment testing once again peaked in the 1950s, only to run smack up against the civil rights concerns of the '60s, and charges that the very instruments once thought to promote equal opportunity were inherently biased against women, minorities, and nonconformists.

Now, prompted by the economic recovery, the Reagan-era relaxation of government restrictions and the pent-up demand of employers who know how expensive hiring mistakes can be, we are seeing once again the emergence of a testing boom. Will this third wave prove any more enduring than the previous two? If history is any guide, the answer is: probably not. Probably not, because with all the progress that's been made in the science of psychometrics over the last two decades, testers have yet to do what they need to do most: come up with an effective way to police their own profession, to discipline it and to avoid the hazards of over-promotion.

EXPECTATIONS

It's a particularly endemic problem because the buyer in search of a test is naturally attracted to the simplest of all possible solutions: "With this test you'll be able to pick out the best, weed out the worst and not have to engage in any other costly, time-consuming screening activities." However, that's precisely the sort of thing that gets testers in trouble, not only because it creates unfulfillable expectations, but also because it tends to spawn impersonal screening procedures that reduce human beings to a series of faceless, unappealable numbers. Such are the numbers that exacerbate the frustration and discontent of those who don't get hired, while reinforcing the image of the tester as an insensitive lout.

Things get especially dicey when one considers the use of tests to measure specific personality traits such as self-confidence, flexibility, expressiveness or integrity. To be sure, the appeal of gaining insights into a job applicant's personality cannot be denied, especially when looking for someone like a manager or salesperson who needs to work with people all day. But over the course of the last 30 years such tests have been the focus of much controversy.

William Whyte articulated the concerns of many when he cited these tests as a threat to individuality and the precursor to grimly homogenized corporate cultures. Here, however, advocates of personality testing can take heart that just as there are doubts about the tests doing much good, doubts are also raised as to whether they can be shown reliably to do any harm in the sense Whyte talks about. In fact, the most extensive surveys done on these instruments over the years have shown their predictive power to be exceedingly weak. Psychologist Robert Guion, who conducted one such study in 1965, writes: ". . . One cannot survey the literature on the use of personality tests in industry without becoming thoroughly disenchanted."

But again, unimpressive performance correlations do not translate into lackluster marketing campaigns. One testing company, for example, makes 11 implied promises on one piece of paper, without any elaboration: "Increase productivity. Recognize genius. Facilitate promotion and transfer decision-making. Duplicate your successful employees. Spot a potential thief. Pinpoint areas for improvement. Increase your profits. Cut on-the-job accidents. Don't hire that troublemaker. Better utilization of existing employees. Reduced employee unrest and turnover."

In an industry where literally anyone can develop a test one week and sell it the next—an industry in which, according to the 1983 edition of *Tests in Print,* there already are well over 2,600 tests from which to choose—it is hard to imagine how a reasonable set of standards could ever be enforced. And the problem is not only making sure that disreputable tests are not used, but also that reputable ones are used correctly. Take, for example, one of the most well-established personality tests on the market, the Sixteen Personality Factors Questionnaire, or 16 PF, as it's called. As of 1976, some 2,000 scholarly documents had been published in support of the test's validity in measuring 16 distinct personality characteristics. Still, as test researcher George Dudley notes, using the 16 PF—or any test for that matter—as the sole indicator of whether to hire or fire somebody, would be "unwise, unfair and unacceptable."

"Testing is a way to get at the truth sideways," says Dudley, president of Behavioral Science Research Press of Dallas, "and if you believe that the only way to get at the truth about another person is to administer a test, then you're not only fooling yourself, but you're also demonstrating a very negative view of mankind. You're saying that truth cannot be determined by asking the subject, or those who know the subject, but only by asking a testing expert."

Dudley, whose company publishes reports on occupational testing for a number of industries, is among those researchers urging much more humility upon their brethren—a view that urges testers to step back and examine what it is that's really being accounted for. Consider all that contributes to the success of an insurance salesman, for example: the state of the economy, monetary incentives, quality of training, quality of supervision, quality of the product, etc., etc. Given the complex interplay of all those variables, it's difficult to imagine how a test measuring personality alone could ever account for much more than 25% of the variance. In fact, Dudley estimates the impact of personality on performance to be more on the order of 9% to 15%. That's high enough to be of some practical use to employers, but certainly too low to justify making these tests the sole criterion for hiring.

With respect to making validity generalizations, again Dudley's research shows cause for caution. He finds that the impact of personality differs significantly not only between companies, but within the same company over time. Among insurance salesmen, dominant, hard-charging, innovative personalities don't seem to be doing as well as they did 10 years ago, Dudley notes. Rather, it's the more conservative, consultative types who are now the better bets. He does not know why this is so; he merely notes the statistical shift. "When using a test, you have to exercise the same vigilance that one exercises when driving a car," he says. "You have to look in front of you, you have to look behind you, and you have to anticipate the curves. Otherwise you're going to crash."

CAUTION

Dudley's comments, it should be noted, do not directly challenge the work of Schmidt and Hunter, who argue for validity generalization for aptitude scores. Aptitude is undoubtedly a more stable test variable. But certainly Dudley and others do challenge those who would extend the concept of generalization to the area of personality, something that many personality testers have been quite willing to do. Moreover, there is a direct challenge here to those testers who claim their instruments have the power to eliminate automatically from further consideration any candidate who falls below a certain cutoff score.

It is in this sense that cautious researchers put themselves directly at odds with one of the largest trade associations in the country, the Life Insurance Marketing and Research Association (LIMRA). For more than 50 years, LIMRA has been the major force behind the testing of prospective insurance agents. The association's Aptitude Index Battery, recently renamed Career Profile, is administered to hundreds of thousands of prospective insurance agents each year. In fact, well over 80% of the agents hired in the United States take the Career Profile, and in 1983 some 35,000 more Career Profiles were issued than the year before. Recognizing the excellent statistical work that went into its construction, critics do not accuse the Career Profile of being an inherently bad test. But they do have a problem with the way it is commonly used.

It comes down to this: On a scale of 0 to 19, how fair is it to automatically eliminate from consideration any applicant who scores below a 10? At LIMRA, psychologist William Love acknowledges that under such a cutoff policy, some potentially good candidates are rejected. But he argues that the incidence is so low (one in 10, he says) that it wouldn't be worth the time or money for employers to search for these high-performing, low-scoring applicants. "It would be like trying to catch a fish in a near-empty fishing hole," he says. In fact, to increase the usefulness of the Career Profile, LIMRA has encouraged its customers to raise the cutoff score to 15.

As a personality test, the Career Profile is a questionnaire that tries to get at such traits as flexibility, forcefulness, cooperativeness and honesty. It also includes questions that ask about the subject's background—age, education, financial status and so on. These demographic questions are not just incidental, but in fact constitute an important part of the test—because older applicants, who have been out of school longer, who have made more money and who themselves have had the opportunity to purchase life insurance, are more likely to be successful agents, according to LIMRA's research. And so, to reflect that pattern, the test is scored to penalize youth. By how much is it penalized? Not much, LIMRA's Love says.

But out in the field, managers tell a different story. One such manager, who works for an insurance company in the Southwest, attests to a huge penalty. He claims that in several cases, where favored applicants failed to score above the test's cutoff point, he invited them back to retake the test, coaching them to change their answers to any age-related questions. (In effect, he told them to lie.) Coached in this way, he says, one applicant increased his score from a seven to a 17. (The applicant may have changed his answers to other questions as well, of course.)

Such quiet subversion among field managers is not uncommon, industry sources say, because by establishing a definitive cutoff score, corporate home offices are imposing an often-resented restriction. It's the home office, attracted to the prospect of an easy answer and politically sensitive to the influences of LIMRA, pitted against the field manager whose hiring authority is being limited by the results of a single test. And with a seven, there's no opportunity for appeal. A seven is a seven is a seven.

CHEAT SHEET

"If tests are being legitimately applied to assist in the career-planning process, then it's in your interest to answer the tester's questions as honestly as you can," Dudley says. "But if tests are being used to *inflict* insights upon you, then it's in your interest to tell the tester exactly what it is he wants to hear."

Under the latter circumstances, Dudley says, there are some practical tips for taking such tests. For example, say the question asks: "If someone cuts in front of you in line, what would you do?" The question is most likely trying to gauge your dominance. Knowing what personality testers typically look for, Dudley says your best bet with such questions is to show your assertiveness: In this case, say that you'd ask the person to get back in place rather than doing nothing.

If the question seems to be addressing your self-confidence, the philosophical tone underlying your answer should be: "Every cloud has a silver lining." Another good cliche to remember is that sticks and stones will break your bones, but names will never hurt you. Keep this in mind, and your answers should reflect a favorable amount of emotional resilience.

Now that you know that, it's only fair to tell you that those are strictly broad rules of thumb. The idea of trying to "beat" a personality test sounds appealing, harkening back to the old Wall Street definition of naivete as telling the truth to the company psychologist, but it has two drawbacks. First, there are some well-constructed and thoroughly validated tests out there—the Minnesota Multiphasic Personality Inventory (MMPI), for example—and you're highly unlikely to "beat" them, even if you know a bit about them. In fact, something like the MMPI is more likely to call you a liar than to be greatly deceived by you. Secondly, depending on the job, the company and the tester, there's no guarantee that *this* tester is looking for the qualities that appeal to "typical" testers.

Altogether, it's a shame that the idea of beating a personality test is even an issue, because in conjunction with interviews, reference checks and records of past achievement, tests can be useful tools. It's not that the knowledge isn't there to construct good tests. Rather, what's really missing, it seems, is the wisdom and/or the discipline to use them well.

Employment Testing: The U.S. Job Service Is Spearheading a Revolution

Robert M. Madigan
K. Dow Scott
Diana L. Deadrick
Jil A. Stoddard

For most of the past 20 years, the use of psychological tests in selection and promotion has diminished steadily. Faced with the difficult and often expensive task of developing evidence of test validity, employers frequently have opted to discontinue or forego testing. This trend is now being reversed. Surprisingly, impetus for this resurgence in testing is partially attributable to a federal agency, the U.S. Employment Service (USES). The validity generalization (VG) testing program currently being implemented by USES through local Job Service offices in many areas of the country sharply contradicts prevailing beliefs regarding the use of employment tests. The central tenets of the program are that standardized ability tests are fair and valid predictors of performance for all jobs, and that such tests provide employers (and the nation) with a powerful tool for improving work force productivity. This article provides an overview of the VG program, its relationship to current employment testing regulations, the potential benefits to employers of using VG, and some issues associated with the program.

VALIDITY GENERALIZATION

The term "validity generalization" is drawn from an extensive and controversial stream of research launched in the 1970s by John E. Hunter (Michigan State University) and Frank L. Schmidt (then of the U.S. Office of Personnel Management). Their conclusion that standardized tests of cognitive (mental) ability are generally valid for employment selection decisions provides the basis (and the name) for the USES program. A brief overview of their research and findings as they apply to the USES program is provided here.[1]

The research by Hunter and Schmidt can be described as a reinterpretation of findings from previous investigations of the validity of employment tests. Thousands of validation studies have been conducted over the past 50 years, but the findings have been inconsistent. Similar tests for similar (or identical) jobs in different settings often yielded widely varying coefficients (correlations between test scores and job performance). This apparent inconsistency led to the generally accepted conclusion that the validity of an employment test for a particular job is specific to the situation. As a result, employers usually have been required to develop evidence of the validity of any tests used, regardless of findings elsewhere.

Hunter and Schmidt tested an alternative explanation for the historical inconsistency in test validation studies. Noting that the number of workers (sample size) in most previous studies was relatively small, and that the results of such studies are potentially influenced by a variety of technical deficiencies, they reasoned that inconsistent findings could be primarily attributable to statistical errors. Using a meta-analysis research method that provides a means to correct or adjust for such sources of error, Schmidt, Hunter and as-

Reprinted from *Personnel Administrator, 31* (1986), pp. 102–112 by permission of K. Dow Scott.

sociates developed a persuasive body of evidence that the validity of ability tests for employment screening is relatively stable across jobs and organizations. Subsequent studies also strongly indicated that the validity of ability tests is generally higher than that of other selection procedures such as interviews, reference checks, experience ratings, etc.

In one study, Hunter cumulated the results of 515 studies of the validity of the General Aptitude Test Battery (GATB) carried out over a 45-year period by the Employment Service.[2] Three general abilities (cognitive, perceptual, and psychomotor) derived from GATB scales were found to be valid predictors of job proficiency for all jobs. Moreover, although there was considerable variation in the validity of these three abilities across jobs, the differences were adequately accommodated by grouping all jobs into five broad job families reflecting a hierarchy of job complexity. Since the job sample was representative of the 12,000 jobs included in the *Dictionary of Occupational Titles*,[3] the findings in this study were generalized to all jobs.

In a series of related studies, Hunter and the Employment Service addressed the topic of the fairness of psychological tests. The issue of test fairness actually consists of two distinct questions: (1) is the test fair in the sense that it is an accurate estimate of job performance ability for all applicant sub-groups? and (2) does use of the test adversely (disproportionately) limit job opportunities for minority group members?

Research evidence pertaining to question (1) is overwhelmingly positive. Virtually all studies conducted over the past 15 years by numerous researchers have concluded that ability tests are fair to minority groups. In fact, with respect to the GATB, an analysis of 51 studies showed that use of the GATB to predict job performance was likely to overestimate, rather than underestimate, the job performance of blacks.[4]

The answer to question (2) depends upon the extent of the difference in average test scores between nonminority and minority members on the particular tests. Significant differences in ability test scores between groups are nearly universal; the GATB is no exception. Although these differences vary by minority group and type of ability, the difference in average scores between nonminorities and blacks is substantial for all three general abilities. For example, if the cutoff score on cognitive ability was set at the average of the majority group, only 23 percent of black applicants would pass. The figure for perceptual abilities and psychomotor abilities are 25 percent and 41 percent, respectively.[5] Thus, the use of the three general ability scores based on the GATB could be expected to produce a racially unbalanced work force.

In summary, the validity generalization program is based on the following research findings:

1. GATB scores are valid predictors of job proficiency although validity varies somewhat by type of job.

2. GATB scores fairly estimate job abilities for all groups.

3. Use of unadjusted GATB scores will adversely affect job opportunities for minorities.

THE GATB

The General Aptitude Test Battery was put into use in 1947 by state employment services offices after an extensive developmental research effort. It has been the focus of a continuing program of research to refine the tests and validate their use for vocational counseling and employee selection. Hence the GATB has a broad research record for many occupational classifications, and is probably the best validated multiple aptitude test battery in existence for employment applications.

The test battery consists of 12 timed tests (parts)—eight paper and pencil tests and four apparatus tests. Each part requires performance of familiar tasks such as name comparisons, arithmetic computations and reasoning, form perceptions, pegboard manipulations, etc. The 12 parts yield eight specific aptitude scores: verbal aptitude, numerical aptitude, spatial aptitude, form perception, clerical perception, motor coordination, finger dexterity, and manual dexterity. In addition, a general intelligence or learning ability score is derived from the arithmetic reasoning, vocabulary, and spatial perception test scores. These nine aptitudes measure basic abilities or capacities to learn various jobs.

Past research on the GATB had concentrated on developing norms (standards) for specific occupations and identifying patterns of aptitudes for occupational families. Norms were developed by identifying the specific aptitudes most relevant to particular occupations, and determining the degree to which these aptitudes related to proficiency in job performance or success in occupational training. A minimum or "cutting" score for each aptitude was set at the level that would effectively screen out a majority of the potentially unsuccessful workers for that occupation. The combination of aptitudes and minimum scores that comprised a norm differed for each occupation.

Use of GATB data in the VG program differs from the historical approach in three key respects. First, specific aptitude scores are combined into the three general ability scores noted above. These ability scores are then weighted and combined to produce overall aptitude scores for each of the five broad job families that Hunter had previously identified. Thus, minimum or critical scores on any specific aptitude are eliminated. Second, the overall score for each job family is converted to a percentile score to facilitate the use of a top-down hiring strategy (hire the best qualified), as opposed to use of the test scores to screen out the unqualified. Third, separate rankings (within-group percentiles) are computed for nonminorities, blacks, and hispanics. In effect, this procedure adjusts the GATB scores of minorities to eliminate adverse impact.

THE JOB SERVICE PROGRAM

Implementation of VG in local offices of the Job Service currently varies within and between states. For example, local Job Service offices in Michigan tested 73,600 applicants during 1985, and over 26,000 VG-selected applicants were referred to employers. Other states are just beginning to implement the program, but at least 25 states offer VG testing in some locations. A number of localities are following the "full implementation" model piloted in Roanoke, Virginia, and recommended by USES. In this approach, testing replaces interviews by local office personnel as the basic tool for all applicant screening and referral activities. As a consequence, significant operational changes are required, both in the nature and mode of service to applicants, and in the role of the local office staff.

To achieve maximum efficiency, the Roanoke office tailored all internal procedures around VG. Because the GATB is most efficiently administered in groups, individual applicant registration and interviewing were replaced by group registration (intake) and testing sessions. In the daily intake sessions, new applicants are given assistance in completing the necessary forms, and an orientation to program procedures and the nature of the GATB is provided. All applicants are encouraged to take the GATB, which is administered daily at a centrally located testing center.

As of January 1986, 80 percent of applicants were being tested. Results of the testing were entered into the local office records (computer files), and applicants are sent a report of their percentile rank for each of the five job families. These percentiles are interpreted as an indicator of the applicant's relative suitability (aptitude) for jobs of that type. When a job order is received, the job family to which it belongs is determined and a file search is initiated to identify and rank applicants for referral to the job. Other criteria established by the employer and preferences of the applicant also are considered in making referrals. For instance, an employer might require a specific type of training or experience, or an applicant's availability for certain hours or types of work could be restricted. Referrals would then be based on percentile ranking within these constraints.

Implementation of the VG program significantly changes the role and activities of Job Service interviewers. Much of the time formerly spent on initial assessment interviews is devoted to matching applicant's records with employer requirements. Interviewers are encouraged to become more knowledgeable of the particulars of the jobs they fill and the employers they serve. In order to facilitate this, Roanoke interviewers are designated as "account representatives" for specific employers, with responsibility for all transactions with that employer. According to officials in the Roanoke office, these changes have resulted in increases in the number and quality of candidates who are referred to employers. This improved responsiveness to employer needs has led to increased use of the job service by employers.

VG AND THE "UNIFORM GUIDELINES"

The VG program appears to challenge standards in the *Uniform Guidelines for Employee Selection Procedures* in a number of key respects. First, as noted above, the basic premise that the validity of ability tests is specific to particular situations is rejected. Employers using the VG program are informed that the VG testing program is valid and fair. Hence, they are relieved of the burdensome responsibility for conducting validation studies (of the GATB) in their organizations.

Second, because the three general abilities are believed to be valid predictors of success for all jobs, the detailed job analysis required by the guidelines is unnecessary. The analysis need only be sufficient to classify jobs into their appropriate job family. Since the worker function ratings in the occupation code of the *Dictionary of Occupational Titles* (DOT) provided the original basis for grouping jobs into five families, and the 515 jobs in the study were representative of the 12,000 jobs in the DOT, the basic job analysis for most jobs in the U.S. economy already exists.

Third, the VG program uses test scores to rank applicants. Research by USES has shown that ability test performance is directly related to job performance, i.e., as test scores increase there is a corresponding increase in average job performance. This finding appears to provide adequate justification for a "top-down" selection strategy. On the other hand, the thrust of the guidelines has been to "encourage" use of the minimum score (low cutoff) method.

Finally, the use of within-group percentile scores for non-minorities, blacks, and hispanics appears to be proscribed by the disparate treatment provision of the guidelines. Separate rankings are clearly a case of subjecting different racial groups to different standards (albeit for the purpose of eliminating adverse impact). The guidelines appear to allow use of different standards only in situations where a test is potentially unfair.

In short, the VG program is consistent with the ultimate objective of the EEOC, to increase employment opportunities for minorities. In fact, if the VG program is used to supplant less objective screening procedures, the overall selection ratio of minorities should increase over current levels. However, this is accomplished by means of a race-conscious hiring procedure based on premises that have heretofore been explicitly rejected by the EEOC. It is conceivable that the VG program, or more specifically, the procedures and findings of Hunter and Schmidt, will be defined as new, "professionally acceptable techniques" (under Sec. 14 of the guidelines). However, the silence of the EEOC to date and the continuing debate over validity generalization within the academic community suggest that this is unlikely.

BENEFITS TO EMPLOYERS

Few employers would challenge the proposition that the productivity of good workers significantly exceeds that of poor workers. The difference in productivity between top and bottom workers can vary widely by job or organization, but research findings suggest the ratio is about two to one for the typical job. Since valid ability tests increase the probability of selecting successful employees (better than other known selection devices), it follows that the use of valid tests to rank applicants provides an economic benefit to employers.

Documentation of the dollar value of productivity improvement attributable to testing has been difficult and expensive to develop in the past. Attempts to translate productivity differences among employees into dollar terms required detailed cost accounting procedures, and this approach was only applicable to a limited range of jobs. However, reasonable (conservative) estimates are now readily calculated for most jobs by means of recently developed procedures.[6] Hence, analyses of the monetary value (utility) of VG testing to individual employers will be forthcoming as the program is implemented more widely.

Application of this type of analysis to federal hiring data for 1980 indicates that optimal use of the GATB for all hiring decisions in that year would have had a value to the government of over $1 billion, or approximately 16 percent of total wages. Although an estimate of this magnitude naturally invites skepticism, it is actually based on *conservative* assumptions regarding the validity of VG test scores and variance in worker productivity. Furthermore, the figure escalates substantially if the continuing effects of improved selection (average tenure) are included in the calculation. Thus, the economic benefits of testing are likely to be much larger than was previously believed.

To some employers, a promise of increased worker productivity through better selection of qualified applicants will be viewed with misgiving or disinterest. Productivity improvement often is primarily a function of technology, and in some instances the contribution of workers to total productivity is virtually impossible to determine. However, cost reduction is of interest to all employers, and there is solid logic and evidence to support the use of VG to reduce costs. For instance, the validity of the GATB (and other ability tests) for predicting successful performance of applicants in various types of training programs is well established. Improved selection of trainees results in fewer failures, which translates directly into savings in training and employment costs. Similar reports of the effectiveness of VG have been received by the authors from Roanoke area employers, and are frequently reported in other VG pilot project areas. For example, a study by Philip Morris found a significant increase in the rate of training success for employees hired via a selection procedure incorporating VG over that of two comparison groups.[7]

The VG program offers other possible monetary and intangible benefits to employers. For example, one Roanoke area employer attributes a dramatic reduction in turnover to reduced administrative costs by using the Job Service as a sole source of job applicants. Fewer applicants are processed by the company and the quality of referrals has often increased, as evidenced by a reduction in the number of referrals per placement for many of these employers. Furthermore, the close working relationship between employer and Job Service personnel engendered by this procedure facilitates responsiveness to employer needs by the local Job Service office.

While the potential benefits appear to be significant, employers must recognize that the VG program is not a panacea. Test information is only one factor in employment decisions. The organization also must improve validity and fairness in other aspects of the selection decision process. Moreover, ability is only one component in the employee performance equation. Management practices often determine whether those abilities are properly developed, and whether the employee's energies are focused and tapped. In other words, tests might be valid predictors of job performance and training success, but the extent to which organizations capitalize on improved selection procedures depends to a large degree on how well they manage their human resources.

A standard caveat pertaining to the use of employment tests also applies to the VG program. To state that ability tests have high validity for predicting successful job performance is not to imply that they are perfect predictors. On the contrary, it merely suggests that the probability of mistakes in assessing the relative abilities of applicants is reduced. Predictions for particular applicants will sometimes be wrong, but over the long run the proportion of "correct" decisions will exceed that of decisions made without benefit of test information. Hence, organizations with a high level of employment activity will more quickly realize the benefits of VG screening.

ISSUES

Surprisingly little discussion or debate over the consequences of nationwide implementation of the VG program has surfaced in the professional or popular press (perhaps the program has not yet captured sufficient attention). Whatever the reason, VG testing is likely to renew or reinvigorate debate over some basic policy issues.

For example, the use of within-group percentiles to rank applicants appears to be at odds with the position taken by other federal agencies. Not only could separate rankings for nonminorities, blacks, and hispanics constitute disparate treatment, but this procedure also raises the more emotion-laden issue of preferential treatment. Given equivalent qualifications (in terms of test performance) for a minority and a nonminority candidate, the minority candidate will be ranked higher. This procedure is a logical and reasonable compromise between the conflicting national goals of economic efficiency (hire the best qualified) and equal economic opportunity for members of minority groups. However, by explicitly using different standards, the program also appears to be inviting charges of reverse discrimination. It is interesting to speculate how the current leadership of the EEOC and the Justice Department might view this particular form of quota in view of their adamant opposition to preferential hiring under any conditions.

A second issue pertains to the basic mission of the Job Service. The VG program very closely aligns the agency with employer perspectives and values. Obviously, job orders from employers are necessary to meet the needs of job seekers, and VG holds considerable promise for expanding the number and type of job orders placed with local offices. However, the emphasis on identifying the best qualified means some less qualified (in terms of test performance) individuals will be excluded from referral to jobs that they could perform successfully. The question boils down to one of the proper role of the public employment system. Should the Employment Service focus primarily on those most in need? (This was its function in the '70s, and it was not a marked success. Individuals most in need often are not competitive in the job market. As a result, employers found they could get better applicants elsewhere.) Or, should the Employment Service concentrate on helping employers make optimal use of the nation's human capital? An affirmative answer here raises a question of individual rights: Should a government agency be so closely identified with employer interests in decisions that affect people's life chances?

From the perspective of individual applicants, there is little doubt that widespread adoption of VG will directly affect the distribution of economic winners and losers. Some of the able, but chronically unemployed, will have opportunities that were previously denied them. (The Roanoke Job Service staff can attest to this fact.) On the other hand, top-down referral of applicants based on VG scores will exclude people who would have been considered if minimum standards were used. The consequences for the less able (and the developmentally disabled) could be severe. Moreover, extensive use of VG testing could exacerbate the "permanent underclass" problem in our society by creating a new class of stigmatized unemployed, the "low scorers" (some of whom will be erroneously labelled).

If the VG program is to be successfully implemented on a national level, problems of this genre will need to be addressed. While such problems will undoubtedly prove difficult to resolve, they must be kept in perspective. The previous approach based on interviewing was less effective and was plagued with similar and equally formidable problems. On the other hand, VG testing holds the promise of significantly contributing to productivity improvement, one of the keys to stemming the flow of jobs offshore. If this is borne out, the net effect of nationwide implementation of VG on job opportunities could be positive.

CONCLUSIONS

From the perspective of individual employers, the VG program appears to be one of those rare "no lose" opportunities. It offers a number of potential benefits with little perceptible risk or cost. As noted above, the extent to which a particular employer can realize benefits from the program depends on a number of factors.

However, from the evidence to date it appears that the majority of employers would be well advised to take two actions. First, they should carefully re-examine their beliefs and/or practices with respect to the use of ability tests in employment decisions. If employment activity is high, they could be missing an opportunity to significantly improve the quality of selection decisions.

Second, employers should re-evaluate their use of the Job Service. They might be under-utilizing a valuable resource. With the advent of the VG program, many local Job Services offices can provide a comprehensive applicant screening service at no cost.

REFERENCES

1. Readers unfamiliar with this research can find a thorough summary and extensive references in the USES Test Research Reports 45–49 available through the Job Service officials in their area. Also, *Personnel Psychology,* Winter 1985, provides an overview of many of the issues raised with respect to VG in a question-and-answer format.

2. J. E. Hunter, *The Dimensionality of the General Aptitude Test Battery and the Dominance of General Factors over Specific Factors in the Prediction of Job Performance.* Washington, DC: U.S. Employment Service, 1982.

3. U.S. Department of Labor, *Dictionary of Occupational Titles,* 1977.

4. U.S. Dept. of Labor, Employment and Training Administration, *Fairness of the General Aptitude Test Battery: Ability Differences and Their Impact on Minority Hiring Rates,* USES Test Research Report No. 46, Washington DC, 1983.

5. *Ibid.*

6. Wayne F. Cascio, *Costing Human Resources: The Financial Impact of Behavior in Organizations.* Boston: Kent Publishing Co., 1982.

7. Dennis L. Warmke, "Successful Implementation of the 'New' GATB in Entry-Level Selection," paper presented at the ASPA Region IV Conference, October 15, 1984.

Testing and EEO: Getting Down to Cases

Dale Yoder and Paul D. Staudohar

As tied to equal employment opportunity, testing has been watched closely by regulatory authorities. Court decisions and federal agency guidelines on testing practice have caused substantial revision of employer policies in recent years. A battalion of industrial psychologists have come forward to validate tests and thereby provide a rebuttal to charges of discrimination in employment.

Has this regulation of testing led to greater reliability and validity of employment decisions? Has it helped to reduce discrimination? Based on numerous research studies, the answer to both questions is an unqualified yes. But as any personnel manager is aware, the field of testing involves a host of more subtle questions for which unequivocal answers are elusive. Indeed, although much of the current focus is on EEO compliance, questions of whether or not to test, and what testing practice is appropriate and ethical, have been matters of argument for several decades.

This article brings together for critical review several recent developments in testing that answer some questions and raise others.[1] Significant among events examined are the Uniform Guidelines on Employee Selection Procedures; controversy over the PACE selection procedure used for testing prospective federal white-collar employees; extensive studies conducted by the National Research Council; and continuing efforts by the U.S. Supreme Court to evaluate testing policy in light of EEO standards.

A brief description of the tests used in selection distinguishes four principal types: achievement, aptitude, personality and interest tests.

Reprinted from the February 1984 issue of *Personnel Administrator,* copyright 1984, The American Society for Personnel Administration, 606 North Washington Street, Alexandria, Virginia 22314.

Achievement tests sample and measure the applicant's knowledge and skills. They ask applicants to demonstrate their competence. Aptitude tests measure an applicant's capacity or potential for doing well on the job. Personality tests probe for the dominant qualities of the personality as a whole, the combination of aptitudes, interests and usual mood and temperament. Interest tests seek information about an individual's job values, needs and preferences regarding various fields of endeavor such as scientific, artistic, literary, social service and business. Achievement and aptitude tests have been the primary targets of EEO regulation.

UNIFORM GUIDELINES

In the late 1960s and early 1970s, various government agencies (e.g., the Equal Employment Opportunity Commission, U.S. Department of Labor and U.S. Civil Service Commission) each developed and issued policy guidelines on the appropriate use of employee selection procedures, including testing.[2] These guidelines were used by federal agencies to evaluate the selection procedures of employers covered by Title VII of the CivilRights Act of 1964 and related legislation. The separate regulations caused competition and inconsistency among the enforcement agencies. Substantial confusion resulted among firms and public employers seeking to comply with the law. Because the jurisdictions of the various agencies coincided in certain areas, two different guidelines were sometimes applicable to the same employer. For instance, employers with government contracts subject to the regulations of the Office of Federal Contract Compliance Programs were also subject to EEOC jurisdiction under Title VII. Uniform guidelines were clearly needed for fairness, efficiency, credibility and consistency.[3]

On December 30, 1977, proposed new "Uniform Guidelines on Employee Selection Procedures" were published in the *Federal Register.* This document was based on recommendations of the EEOC, Civil Service Commission and the Departments of Justice and Labor. It was designed to eliminate problems over selection that resulted from court decisions and varied professional practice.[4] The "Uniform Guidelines" were finally adopted in 1978 by the federal EEOC agencies. Their purpose is to explain what private and public employers must do to prove that their procedures are nondiscriminatory—as evidenced by scores on written tests and selection rates for covered groups.[5] A summary of the Guidelines is shown in Figure 1. "Validity" as used in the figure refers to the ability of a test actually to measure the quality it is assumed to appraise, as evidenced by some acceptable criterion. A selection procedure is unfair if it has an "adverse impact" (as defined in Figure 1) on a particular race, sex or ethnic group. However, evidence of fairness can be provided by showing that the selection procedure predicts likelihood of job success or failure for the group in question on the job being tested; i.e., a clear relation between performance on the test and performance on the job.

Three principal concepts are cited in the Guidelines as acceptable for use in validating tests: (1) criterion-related validity; (2) content validity; and (3) construct validity.[6] These concepts are highly technical and complex, and may be interrelated in practice. Although the definitions vary somewhat, their basic characteristics are:

1. *Criterion-related validity*—a selection procedure is justified by a statistical relationship between test scores and measures of job performance.[7] This validity seeks to determine the extent to which individuals' relative standing on a test correlates with their relative standing on such criteria as sales volume, hourly output, probability of turnover and performance ratings. For example, doing well in a secretarial job might mean that a secretary remains with the organization for at least 18 months, or that the secretary has received favorable performance reviews that result in salary increases.[8]

2. *Content validity*—a selection procedure is justified by demonstrating that it representively samples significant parts of the job. An example would be an accuracy and words-per-minute test given to a typist. Studies of content validity seek to determine whether the content of a test adequately samples the universe of skill, knowledge or behavior that it was designed to assess.[9]

3. *Construct validity*—involves identifying the psychological trait (the construct) which underlies successful job performance, and then devising a

Figure 1
Uniform Guidelines on Employee Selection Procedures

Coverage: Private and public employers, federal contractors and subcontractors, unions, employment agencies, apprenticeship committees, and licensing and certification boards. Those private employers are covered who have 15 or more employees for 20 weeks or more in a calendar year; federal agencies, and state and local governments which employ 15 or more employees or receive federal funds, are covered.

Application: The Guidelines apply to all employee selection procedures used in making employment decisions, such as hiring, retention, promotion, transfer, demotion, dismissal, or referral. Employee selection procedures include job requirements (physical, educational, experiential), and evaluation on the basis of application forms, interviews, performance tests, paper and pencil tests, and performance in training programs or probationary periods.

Adverse Impact: A four-step process is used to determine adverse impact.

(1) Calculate the rate of selection or percentage selected for each race, sex, and ethnic group (divide the number of persons selected from a group by the number of applicants from that group).

(2) Observe which group has the highest selection rate.

(3) Calculate the impact ratios, by comparing the selection rate for each group with that of the highest group (divide the selection rate for a group by the selection rate for the highest group).

(4) Observe whether the selection rate for any group is substantially less (i.e., usually less than 4/5ths or 80 percent) than the selection rate for the highest group.

For example, suppose a comparison of the black selection rate (30 percent) with the white selection rate (60 percent) shows that the black rate is 30/60, or one-half of the white race. Since the one-half (50 percent) is less than 4/5th (80 percent), adverse impact would usually be indicated.

Validity Studies: When a selection procedure has adverse impact on any race, sex or ethnic group, the Guidelines generally call for a validity study or the elimination of adverse impact. Users who continue the use of a selection procedure with an adverse impact until the procedure is challenged increase the risk that they will be found to be engaged in discriminatory practices, and will be liable for such costs as back-pay awards, plaintiffs' attorneys' fees, and loss of federal contracts.

Source: Adapted from U.S. Office of Federal Contract Programs, "Adoption of Questions and Answers to Clarify and Provide a Common Interpretation of the Uniform Guidelines on Employee Selection Procedures." EEOC Office of Personnel Management, Department of Justice, Department of Labor, and Department of the Treasury, from the Federal Register, *44, no. 43 (March 2, 1979), part IV, 11996–12009.*

selection procedure to measure the presence and degree of the trait. The trait is not "observable" but is "constructed" from psychological theory about how people perform. Examples of psychological constructs are leadership ability, clerical aptitude and mechanical ability. The test must measure the trait it purports to measure, and the trait must be related to job performance.

Testing in the absence of proof of validity is obviously risky. Validation is a rigorous, expensive and time-consuming process. Organizations that use tests may be required to provide evidence of their validity.

The Guidelines note that it is not necessary to use the same method for validation of all parts of a selection process. For example, where a selection process includes both a physical performance test and an interview, the physical test might be supported on the basis of content validity, and the interview on the basis of a criterion-related study.

Although the Guidelines are helpful in providing a consistent format for all employers to follow, achieving validity remains difficult. For instance, some tests have been found to be valid for whites, but not for blacks, and vice versa.[10]

A comprehensive study of the correlation between aptitude test scores and job success has been made by Edwin Ghiselli.[11] He analyzed the results of several hundred published and unpublished reports on test validity conducted between 1919 and 1971. A key finding was that on the average, test scores accounted for a predictive validity of only .22 (r = 0.22) on job proficiency criteria. Ghiselli notes that this value is a conservative description of the predictive power of *single* occupational aptitude tests, and that judiciously selected *combinations* of tests would have higher validity. Nonetheless, his study shows that the correlation between tests scores and job proficiency has been very low. Besides using a combination of tests to improve validity, another aid may be to base the test on systematic job analysis. Tests constructed in the absence of job analysis have had lower validity.[12]

As a result of EEO pressures, much has been learned about proper validation of tests. Careful applications of approved criteria to tests provide for far higher correlations currently than those found in the Ghiselli study of an earlier period. There is significantly less abuse of tests in causing discrimination in selection procedures today.

PACE

EEO requirements appear to contemplate that what is judged to be valid currently may not be deemed proper at some time in the future. A case in point is the Professional Administrative and Career Exam (PACE). After extensive effort to determine initial validity, widespread use of PACE began in 1975 for the selection of applicants for over 100 professional, administrative and career occupations in the federal government. The written test has five parts, each of which is weighted in accordance with job requirements of the occupations covered.

In 1977 four major studies were published that corroborated the initial determination of validity of the PACE written test.[13] Participating in the studies were 922 experienced employees, including internal revenue officers, customs inspectors and two groups of social insurance claims examiners. Their job performance was evaluated and compared with their performance on PACE. The studies found that performance on PACE was highly predictive of job performance for all four groups. Because PACE measures abilities common to many jobs, this validity was applicable to all occupations covered by the examination.

Despite the elaborate validation techniques applied to the design of PACE, and studies finding positive correlation with job performance, the test was later invalidated, not by proof of invalidity, but as a result of a job bias suit brought by several civil rights groups. In 1981 an agreement was reached between these groups and the White House to phase out PACE completely by 1984. It is to be replaced by 118 separate exams for individual occupations. The cost of developing these new tests has been estimated by the Internal Revenue Service at $115 million.[14]

The demise of PACE as a consequence of legal and political pressure illustrates the tentative nature of all validity studies and verifications. The civil rights groups challenging the exam pointed, not without justification, to less than appropriate levels of selection of racial minorities for jobs screened by PACE. Thus, even though a test may be valid per se, if results over time show that it is not producing a sufficient level of minority hires, the test may lose its validity immunity. In short, a test may be valid but not legal.

This outcome raises a serious question as to whether the Uniform Guidelines provide legally defensible decision rules on which to utilize tests. Tests with high validity may nonetheless have adverse impact under the Guidelines. The PACE challenge resulted in giving up a test that was proven to be quite valid. What the Guidelines thus provide is a bottom-line approach. Notwithstanding test validity, if insufficient numbers of persons in protected groups are employed, trained or promoted under selection procedures, these procedures, including tests, are not legally acceptable. Critics have charged that this is like throwing out the baby with the bath water.

NATIONAL RESEARCH COUNCIL STUDIES

Over a four-year period, the National Research Council's 19-member Committee on Ability Testing conducted one of the most exhaustive studies ever on employment testing, culminating with two books published in 1982.[15]

Among its conclusions are the following:

- Standardized tests do not discriminate against blacks, but employers should not rely on them solely since there is ample evidence that examinations have been used for skills irrelevant to the job.
- Blacks and whites with similar test scores generally do equally well in job performance.
- Tests cannot bear the societal burden of resolving the "destructive tension" between the competing goals of selecting the most productive workers and achieving equal opportunity.
- Blacks, Hispanics and Native Americans do not, as groups, score as well as do white applicants as a group.
- Test bias should not be blamed for differences in scores between minorities and whites.
- "Social facts" such as less education and other disadvantages account for the differences.
- The Equal Employment Opportunity Commission and the courts have used testing requirements to force a dramatic shift in governmental policy from the requirement of equal treatment to that of equal outcome.
- No alternative to a standardized test has been found that is equally informative, equally adequate technically, and also economically and politically viable.

These conclusions appear to undercut portions of the conventional wisdom surrounding tests. They dispel at least some of the cynicism over testing that has arisen in recent years. Assuming that the study by the National Research Council is itself valid, the application of government policy can be viewed as based solely on "results," i.e., achieving minority group parity in labor markets.

Assuming that tests and other selection procedures are in fact designed in such a way to make them inherently nondiscriminatory and valid, a paradox arises if they are nonetheless not in compliance with bottom-line EEO objectives. Must procedures be made discriminatory in favor of protected minority groups in order to achieve legal approval? If so, they would no longer have technical validity. In the face of this conundrum, it is little wonder that many organizations have abandoned tests completely in their selection procedures.

The key conclusion may be that employment tests continue to be useful for many reasons, important among which is that they can help prevent discrimination. Yet there have been numerous abuses of testing practice in the past that have caused discrimination against minorities. Tests are thus a two-edged sword, facilitating discrimination in some cases and preventing it in others, depending on the validity of the individual testing procedure. As reviewed in the next section, decisions of the U.S. Supreme Court have sought to prevent abuse and establish standards for evaluating the impact of tests.

SUPREME COURT DECISIONS

Overriding all policy on testing is the Civil Rights Act of 1964, Title VII, which prohibits employment discrimination on grounds of race, color, sex, religion and national origin. Minority groups have raised several issues involving tests under this law. A common charge is that selection tests are not relevant to the jobs in question. For example, litigants have cited the "chairman of the board syndrome," which requires applicants to demonstrate potential for much higher level work than they are ever likely to perform.[16]

The landmark U.S. Supreme Court decision on testing is *Griggs v. Duke Power Company.*[17] In this case, the employer required a high school education or the passing of aptitude tests as a condition of employment. At issue was whether the employer's use of these requirements discriminated against blacks in violation of the Civil Rights Act of 1964. The Court noted that if the tests operated to disqualify blacks from employment at a substantially higher rate than white applicants, and did not demonstrably measure job performance, they would violate Title VII.

Satisfactory scores on the company's aptitude tests were not found to measure satisfactory performance in such jobs as handling coal, and resulted in a disproportionate number of blacks being disqualified for employment. Therefore, by an 8–0 vote, the Court held that use of the tests was unlawful. The employer failed to meet the burden of proving that the tests were "predictive of or significantly correlated with important elements of work behavior which comprise or are relevant to the job or jobs for which candidates are being evaluated."

The rationale of *Griggs* was reaffirmed by the Supreme Court in 1975 in *Albemarle Paper Co. v. Moody.*[18] In this case, employees sued the company and their union for alleged Title VII violations. They contended that the company used certain pre-employment tests which had a racially discriminatory effect and lacked a sufficient relation to job performance. The company had studied its tests in an effort to validate them properly as measuring probable job performance. However, the Court found that the company's validation study was deficient in at least four respects: (1) it failed to show a correlation between tests and performance in all jobs; (2) it failed to use explicit criteria by which supervisors were to measure job performance; (3) it was limited to top-level job groups; and (4) it was applied to job-experienced white workers, but not to new job applicants. Because of these deficiencies, the Court held in a 7–1 vote that the company violated Title VII by use of the tests. A key implication of *Albemarle* is that organizations may be required to validate a particular test for each separate job in which it is used as a screening measure.[19]

Griggs and *Albemarle* both involved an interpretation of Title VII. In a subsequent Supreme Court case, a test was challenged under the due process clause of the Fifth Amendment to the U.S. Constitution, and provisions of the U.S. Code dealing with standards of job relatedness. In *Washington v. Davis,*[20] the District of Columbia police department gave a test—designed to measure verbal ability, vocabulary, reading and comprehension—to applicants for its pre-employment police training program. Black applicants who failed the test claimed that because a greater percentage of white applicants passed the test, it was racially discriminatory and contrary to due process. However, for several years the percentage of new black recruits approximated the percentage of blacks living in the recruiting geographical area. The Court noted that the test was neutral on its face, and that it served the valid purpose of seeking to upgrade communicative abilities which are important in police work. In a 7–2 decision it held that the test did not violate either constitutional due process or the U.S. Code. It is interesting to note that had the plaintiffs brought suit under Title VII, the Court would have applied the more rigorous standards of *Griggs* and *Albemarle,* and the outcome might have been different.

The most recent Supreme Court decision on testing examines its use in promotions. Tests for promotions require candidates to demonstrate knowledge and skill required in the higher job. They have long been used in civil service, but have achieved less acceptance in private employment.

In *Connecticut v. Teal,*[21] the first step in the selection process for promotion to supervisor of state employees was a written test. Black candidates achieved a passing rate on this test that was only 68 percent of the passing rate for white candidates. Blacks who failed the test contended that it violated Title VII by requiring passage of a test that disproportionately excluded blacks and was not job related.

The employer's defense was that in choosing supervisors from the eligibility list, it promoted 22.9 percent of the black candidates and only 13.5 percent of the white candidates. Therefore, contended the employer, the bottom-line result was more favorable to blacks than to whites and precluded the finding of a Title VII violation.

By a 5–4 vote, the Court rejected this argument noting that its concern was not with overall numbers promoted, but rather with promotion requirements that create a discriminatory bar to work opportunities. Thus an employer is not allowed to discriminate against some blacks simply because it treats other blacks favorably.

Did the selection process in the *Teal* case have an adverse impact on blacks as a group? The answer seems to be "no" because blacks were promoted at a rate that was approximately 170 percent greater than the promotion rate for whites. But the Court emphasized that it is not the overall rate that should be examined. Instead, the key criterion is the denial of work opportunity through discrimination regarding each candidate. A problem with this logic is that the complainants' evidence of discrimination was itself based on group figures (lower overall black performance on the test), yet the employer's group figures showing actual disproportionate hiring in favor of blacks were disregarded as insignificant proof.

The point of reference in the *Griggs, Albemarle* and *Davis* cases, as well as the Uniform Guidelines, is whether the test has an adverse impact on a protected group. In contrast, in the *Teal* case the Court chose the individual in the protected group as the point of reference. The *Teal* case may thus seem illogical and confusing when considered in light of previous rationale for determining Title VII violations in testing cases.

CONCLUSIONS AND RECOMMENDATIONS

Decisions of the Supreme Court in *Griggs, Albemarle,* and *Davis* appear to be consistent with the Uniform Guidelines. Both take the position that a prima facie violation of Title VII may be established by policies or practices that are neutral on their face and in intent, but which nevertheless discriminate in effect against members of a protected group. What is fair in form may be discriminatory in operation.

The lack of clarity in adjusting testing practice to EEO policy suggests that the problem may not be with the Uniform Guidelines, but with their interpretation as illustrated by PACE and the *Teal* case. The unusual and perhaps unfair fate of PACE underscores the tenuous status of validated tests and undercuts the justification for their application. Indeed, the trial federal court to which the challenge of PACE was brought did not even make a determination on the validity of this test. The notion of the bottom-line, underlying the Uniform Guidelines through the principles of adverse impact, was introduced without positive result by the employer as a defense in *Teal.*

Valid tests do not alone ensure EEO compliance, but remain accurate predictors of job performance and a force against discrimination in employment. This point is substantiated by the studies of the National Research Council. Reconciling selection procedure with EEO requirements is an elusive task, in some ways the most difficult that personnel managers have to contend with. Whether testing as a part of this procedure is feasible in light of EEO requirements is an important question for individual organizations. Valid tests provide a useful function in choosing qualified employees in a nondiscriminatory manner. But they are neither infallible nor immune from legal repudiation.

Testing is a key part of the EEO mosaic. It deserves preservation and protection. Most Americans favor EEO goals in general terms, but reject the use of preferential treatment to achieve them.[22] At the same time, it is said to be difficult to move toward equality in employment and eliminate the effects of past discrimination unless some preference is shown. The question of how much preference is justified will continue to be a subject of great concern. There are no easy solutions to the problems, but valid tests have an important role to play in moving toward their resolution.

In light of the complex and at times confusing policy prescriptions of the executive and judicial enforcement branches of federal authority, managers must carefully review regulations for clues to selection practices that avoid discrimination. In support of that objective we suggest the following steps:

1. Establish a systematic job analysis program to provide accurate job descriptions and job specifications throughout the organization as an essential foundation for all selection practices, including hiring, promotion, training and appraisal.

2. Require periodic (probably annual) audits of the validity of all selection practices. Experiment with promising combinations of devices for nondiscriminatory selection. Discontinue or

revise practices that raise suspicion of EEO challenge.

3. On your own, or in cooperation with other like-minded managements, utilize a continuing research program to avoid adverse impact.

4. Maintain the use of fully validated tests to avoid discrimination and toward providing superior employee placement and productivity.

REFERENCES

1. Portions of this article are based on the authors' recent book, *Personnel Management and Industrial Relations* (Englewood Cliffs, NJ: Prentice-Hall, Inc., 1982).

2. For example, see Office of Federal Contract Compliance, U.S. Department of Labor, *Questions and Answers on the OFCC Testing and Selection Order,* (Washington, DC: OFCC 1974).

3. In 1976, uniform guidelines known as the "Federal Executive Agency Guidelines" were issued by the Departments of Labor and Justice and the Civil Service Commission. At this time, however, the EEOC reaffirmed its earlier (1970) guidelines. Thus, despite the effort at uniformity, there were two somewhat different sets of guidelines applicable to employers. See "Comments on the proposed uniform guidelines on employee selection procedures," *The Personnel Administrator,* Vol. 23, No. 6, June 1978, p. 41.

4. Winton H. Manning, "Test validation and EEOC requirements: Where we stand," *Personnel,* Vol. 55, No. 3, May–June 1978, p. 71; and Peter C. Robertson, "The Search for Alternatives—The Need for Research under the Uniform Guidelines on Employee Selection Procedures," *Proceedings of the 1979 Annual Spring Meeting,* Industrial Relations Research Association (Madison, WI: IRRA, 1979), pp. 483–489.

5. U.S. Office of Federal Contract Compliance Programs, "Uniform Guidelines on Employee Selection Procedures (1978) as Adopted by the Equal Employment Opportunity Commission, Civil Service Commission, Department of Labor, and Department of Justice," from the *Federal Register,* 43, No. 166, August 25, 1978, Part IV, pp. 38290–38315.

6. Ernest J. McCormick and Joseph Tifflin, *Industrial Psychology,* sixth edition (Englewood Cliffs, NJ: Prentice-Hall, Inc., 1974), pp. 101–108.

7. Frank L. Schmidt and John E. Hunter, "The future of criterion-related validity studies in Title VII Employment Discrimination Cases," *The Personnel Administrator,* Vol. 22, No. 7, September 1977, pp. 39–42.

8. Katherine Swartz, *Screening in the Labor Market, A Case Study,* Working paper No. 6 (Berkeley: Graduate School of Public Policy, University of California, April 1977), p. 20.

9. Robert M. Guion, "Content validity in moderation," *Personnel Psychology,* Vol. 31, No. 2, Summer 1978, pp. 205–213.

10. John E. Hunter and Frank L. Schmidt, "Differential and single-group validity of employment tests by Rade: A critical analysis of three recent studies," *Journal of Applied Psychology,* Vol. 63, No. 1, February 1978, pp. 1–11.

11. "The validity of aptitude tests in personnel selection," *Personnel Psychology,* Vol. 26, No. 4, Winter 1973, pp. 461–477.

12. Gerald A. Kesselman and Felix E. Lopez, "The impact of job analysis on employment test validation for minority and nonminority accounting personnel," *Personnel Psychology,* Vol. 32, No. 1, Spring 1979, pp. 91–108.

13. United States Civil Service Commission, *Fiscal 1977 Annual Report* (Washington, DC: U.S. Government Printing Office, 1978), p. 5.

14. Government Employee Relations Report, Bureau of National Affairs, Inc., December 15, 1980, p. 892:6.

15. *Ability Testing: Uses, Consequences and Controversies, Parts 1 and 11* (Washington, DC: National Academy Press, 1982).

16. Stephen L. Cohen, "Issues in the selection of minority group employees," *Human Resource Management,* Vol. 13, No. 1, Spring 1974, p. 16.

17. 401 U.S. 424 (1971).

18. 422 U.S. 405 (1975).

19. Thaddeus Holt, "A view from Albemarle," *Personnel Psychology,* Vol. 30, No. 1, Spring 1977, pp. 65–80; Lawrence S. Kleiman and Robert H. Faley, "Assessing content validity: standards set by the Court," *Personnel Psychology,* Vol. 31, No. 4, Winter 1978, pp. 701–713; and James Ledvinka and Lyle F. Schoenfeldt, "Legal developments in employment testing: Albemarle and beyond," *Personnel Psychology,* Vol. 31, No. 1, Spring 1978, pp. 1–13.

20. 426 U.S. 229 (1976).

21. United States Supreme Court, No. 80–2147, Slip Opinion, June 21, 1982.

22. This conclusion is confirmed by a number of public opinion polls cited in Seymour Martin Lipset and William Schneider, "The Bakke Case: How would it be decided at the Bar of public opinion?" *Public Opinion,* March–April 1978, pp. 38–44. See also George Gallup, "Preferential job hiring opposed," *San Francisco Chronicle,* May 21, 1981, p. 8.

Affirmative Action, the Reagan Administration, and Recent Supreme Court Decisions

Edward K. Marlow and Nancy D. Marlow

*In 1980, Ronald Reagan was swept into the presidency with what he considered a mandate from the people to get government off their backs. One of his main areas of concern was Affirmative Action; his feeling was that people should be selected for jobs on the basis of merit and not on the basis of any type of quota. As a result of subsequent actions, the Reagan administration has been accused of trying to dismantle Affirmative Action (AA). Many people feel that the Justice Department, in particular, has attempted to defeat AA by attacking two of AA's major tools—goals and preferential treatment.

REAGAN'S ACTIONS TOWARD AA AND OFCCP

The president has exercised his power to make changes in the policies of the Office of Federal Contract Compliance Programs (OFCCP) and to reduce its budget. These activities quite clearly threaten the heart of AA because they lessen the ability of the federal government and other interested parties to monitor hiring and other personnel polices.

In his first year in office, President Reagan proposed a 22 percent decrease in the OFCCP budget ($39.8 million for FY 1982), but Congress ultimately authorized $42.5 million. Proposed changes to Executive Order 11246 in 1981–82 would have exempted employers with fewer than 250 employees from AA requirements. (The proposed changes never took effect.) This proposal was made in the interest of "reducing the burden of compliance to small employers."

In 1983, the White House staff formulated a set of plans, which included recommendations to discontinue the OFCCP. Instead, the National Self-Monitoring Reporting System (NSMRS) was developed. Under this system, voluntary monitoring of AA plans would replace the OFCCP compliance reviews (duRivage, 1985). Since the Labor Department is currently reviewing the legality of the NSMRS, the OFCCP is still pursuing agreements with federal contractors. However, three major corporations (Hewlett Packard, General Motors, and IBM) have signed NSMRS agreements.

The Justice Department also argued the constitutionality of quotas, which is its interpretation of "goals and timetables." According to the Justice Department, it is unconstitutional to give preferential treatment *to any group.* To justify reparation for a past harm, an *individual* must show that he or she was the direct victim of discriminatory action.

In mid 1985, the Justice Department proposed a draft Executive Order, revising the AA order. This proposed order would have required affirmative recruiting—maybe. It stated, "Each government contractor . . . shall engage in affirmative recruitment . . . expand[ing] the number of qualified minorities and women who receive full consideration for hiring and promotion." However, it also contained the following section: "Nothing in this executive order shall be interpreted to require . . . a government contractor or subcontractor . . . to discriminate against, or grant any preference to, any individual or group . . . with respect to any aspect of employment" ("Affirmative Action Doomed?" 1985).

REAGAN'S SUPREME COURT APPOINTEES

As with most presidents, Ronald Reagan wanted a Supreme Court that had the "proper" judicial outlook. And as with most presidents, Reagan has made appointments to the Supreme Court that reflected his outlook. However, in this area Reagan has not had as much success as many of his predecessors. Despite the fact that several of the current members of the Court are over eighty, during the first six-plus years of his administration he had the opportunity to appoint only two justices to the Court—Sandra O'Conner and Antonin Scalia.

On July 7, 1981, Reagan made history by appointing the first woman to the Supreme Court—Sandra Day O'Conner. He characterized her as a "'person for all seasons,' possessing those unique capabilities of temperament, fairness, intellectual capacity and devotion to the public good which have characterized the 101 'brethren' who have preceded her."

A Republican not known well outside of Arizona, O'Conner was variously characterized as a "moderate" and a "conservative." However, according to those familiar with her political and judicial records, she is not a hardline conservative (Facts on File, 1981).

On June 17, 1986, Reagan named federal appeals court Judge Antonin Scalia to the Supreme Court. A legal scholar with a notable record, Scalia was a deeply rooted conservative on judicial, social, and political issues. The Court's impetus toward conservatism was expected to gain from the appointment. Attorney General Meese reported that the president had applied three basic criteria in the selection. "One is intellectual and lawyerly capability. Secondly, integrity, and thirdly, *a commitment to the interpretation of the law rather than being a lawmaker*" [emphasis added] (Facts on File, 1986).

However, several of the current members of the Court are well past retirement age. If one or more of them should retire during Reagan's last year of office, he would have the opportunity to appoint more conservatives. Since many of the decisions of the Court on AA have been 5–4 or 6–3, one or two new justices could make a considerable impact and shift the direction of the Court for many years. (*Note:* As this volume was going to press, Supreme Court nominee Robert Bork was facing inevitable defeat by the Senate.)

In 1984, many anticipated the death of AA as a result of the Stotts decision *(Memphis Firefighters* v. *Stotts).* In this case, the Supreme Court ruled that nondiscriminatory seniority systems could not be abrogated under an AA plan to save the jobs of women and minorities. Instead, remedies could be invoked only for actual victims of bias. Although the Court ruled that this decision applied only to the particulars of the case, many opponents of AA chose to interpret it very broadly. AA, however, is alive and well. In fact, several recent Supreme Court decisions have infused AA with new life and direction.

RECENT AFFIRMATIVE ACTION CASES: A REVIEW

Case 1. *Wygant* v. *Jackson Board of Education*

This case was similar to the *Stotts'* case in that it involved layoffs. In this Court decision, however, the interpretation of AA was greatly expanded by the justices in an apparent attempt to stabilize the issue.

Case Background. The Court in this case decided by a vote of 5–4 to invalidate the Jackson Board of Education plan to lay off three white teachers for every minority teacher in order to preserve racial and ethnic ratios. The five majority justices agreed that the Jackson plan violated the 14th Amendment's guarantee of equal protection under the law. This was the first time the Civil War era provision was extended to white plaintiffs.

In the plurality opinion, Justice Powell stated that the Court would "strictly scrutinize" layoff plans that discriminate by race. To be considered valid, a public employer must demonstrate "convincing evidence" of past discrimination and offer a "narrowly tailored" remedy. In such cases, consideration would be given for "adverse financial as well as psychological effects" on white workers who are personally "innocent of discrimination."

The justices also discussed the constitutionality of AA in hiring policies. Justice Powell found a distinction between hiring policies and layoff policies since "the burden to be borne by innocent individuals [in hiring policies] is diffused to a considerable extent among society generally."

Case 2. *Local 28 of New York Sheet Metal Workers International Association* v. *EEOC*

The central issue in this case was preferential hiring.

Case Background. This case started in 1963 because of alleged discrimination against minority (black and Hispanic) representation in the union. The union had been in and out of court, and twice held in contempt of court for disobeying lower court orders to increase minority representation. In the last phase of the case, the union, supported by the Justice Department, tried to overturn the lower court order of reaching a goal of 29.23 percent nonwhite membership, a figure proportional to the local nonwhite labor pool, by August 31, 1987. The deadline had been extended repeatedly since it was first set in 1975.

The arguments in this case centered around "whether the remedial provision of Title VII empowers a district court to order race-conscious relief that may benefit individuals who are not identified victims of unlawful discrimination."

The Supreme Court ruled by a 5–4 majority to uphold the lower court order. The dissenting justices argued that the 29.23 percent target was an impermissible quota, but generally agreed that federal judges have the authority to set goals and timetables under such circumstances.

Case 3. *Local 93 of the International Association of Firefighters* v. *City of Cleveland*

This case also concerned preferential hiring.

Case Background. The Cleveland case involved the voluntary AA plan agreed upon by the city of Cleveland and minority firefighters (black and Hispanic) to give minorities 25 percent of the lieutenant positions in the fire fighting force. In 1980, the minority firefighter organization, the Vanguards, filed suit in federal court, charging the city with discrimination in hiring, assigning, and promoting firefighters in violation of Title VII and the Constitution. At that time, fewer than 5 percent of the lieutenants were minorities, although nearly half of the city's population was made up of minority members. Unsuccessful in litigating similar issues for eight years, the city agreed to a court-approved settlement of a promotion ratio of one minority for every white until 25 percent of the slots were occupied by minorities. The white-dominated Local 93 challenged the settlement and asked the Supreme Court to overturn the consent decree.

The focus of the case was "whether 706 (g) of Title VII of the Civil Rights Act of 1964, as amended, . . . precludes the entry of a Consent Decree which provides relief that may benefit individuals who were not the actual victims of the defendant's discriminatory practices."

The Supreme Court ruled with a 6–3 majority that the lower-court federal judges have broad discretion to approve such consent decrees of racial relief to remedy past discrimination. The dissenting judges objected to the implication of reverse discrimination as a result of the courts approving such consent decrees. In an additional statement, Justice O'Connor wrote, "the creation of racial preferences by courts . . . must be done sparingly."

Case 4. *United States* v. *Paradise*

Early in 1987, the Supreme Court reached another decision on preferential hiring.

Case Background. Alabama created its state police patrol in 1935. Thirty-seven years later, not a single black trooper had been employed. Blacks brought suit to remedy the situation, and the case went to trial before a U.S. District Court. Judge Frank Johnson agreed with the plaintiffs: the pattern of racial discrimination was too plain to be denied. In 1972, Judge Johnson ordered Alabama to hire one black trooper for each white trooper hired until blacks constituted about 25 percent of the force. However, the state ignored the order, apparently hoping that the decree would either go away or be forgotten.

Seven years later, Judge Johnson entered another order to end the discrimination. Still, Alabama found reasons why nothing significant could be done. In 1984, Judge Johnson apparently reached the end of his patience. Almost twelve years had passed, and the effects of Alabama's racial discrimination remained "pervasive and conspicuous at all ranks above the entry-level position."

Johnson said, "Of the six majors, there is still not one black. Of the 25 captains, there is still not one black. Of the 35 lieutenants, there is still not one black. Of the 65 sergeants, there is still not one black. Of the 66 corporals, only 4 are black. . . . The preceding scenario is intolerable and must not continue."

Johnson then entered the order that became the crux of the Supreme Court decision: "for a period of time," at least 50 percent of the promotions to corporal must be awarded to black troopers if qualified black candidates were available. In February, 1984, the state promoted eight blacks and eight whites to the rank of corporal.

This decree raised questions under the 14th Amendment. Given that the state in the past had denied "equal protection of the law" to blacks, was the state now denying equal protection to whites? Were the racial quotas constitutionally permissible?

The Supreme Court, in a 5–4 split, upheld the one-for-one promotions. The majority found that the order was fashioned only to remedy an intolerable situation. The state's conduct had been pervasive and egregious. However, Justice Brennan, writing for the majority, emphasized the conditions under which such a decree might be justified. The requirement could be waived if no qualified black candidates were available. The order "applies only when the department needs to make promotions"; the order does not require gratuitous promotions.

"Most significantly, the one-for-one requirement is ephemeral; the term of its application is contingent upon the department's own conduct. The requirement endures only until the department comes up with a procedure that does not have a discriminatory impact on blacks—something the department was enjoined to do in 1972 and expressly promised to do by 1980."

In the majority's view, the one-for-one requirement did not impose an unacceptable burden on innocent third parties. "The temporary and extremely limited nature of the requirement substantially limits any potential burden on white applicants for promotion. . . . Because the one-for-one requirement is so limited in scope and duration, it only postpones the promotions of qualified whites."

Case 5. *Johnson* v. *Transportation Agency*

Shortly after the Paradise case, the Supreme Court rendered a decision that may be even more of a milestone. In this case, the Court ruled that public employers, as well as private, may *voluntarily* implement affirmative action to correct *sex* discrimination. In many ways, this was a major change in direction for the Court.

Case Background. In 1978, the Santa Clara County, California, transportation agency voluntarily adopted an AA plan. A principal goal of the plan was to correct the imbalance of men and women in the work force, particularly in skilled and managerial jobs. Among the skilled craft workers, none of the 238 jobs had ever been held by a woman.

When the job of road dispatcher opened up in 1979, the agency interviewed nine people and found seven qualified, including Diane Joyce, who was a road maintenance worker. Joyce and Paul Johnson, another road worker, had considerable experience working as road yard clerks with the transportation agency. Johnson scored two points higher than Joyce on an oral examination, and the examiners who conducted the test unanimously recommended Johnson for the promotion. Joyce, however, got the job. Johnson then sued the county.

A federal district court in San Francisco declared the plan illegal, but in 1985 a federal appeals court, also in San Francisco, upheld the plan. Mr. Johnson appealed to the Supreme Court, backed by the Reagan administration's friend-of-the-court brief.

The Supreme Court concluded that the plan did not establish a specific quota and merely set up flexible goals that did not put male workers at a disadvantage. "The agency has sought to take a moderate, gradual approach to eliminating imbalance in its work force," Justice Brennan said, "one which establishes realistic guidance for employment decisions, and which visits minimal intrusion on the legitimate expectations of other employees." The court said Johnson may have been minimally more qualified for the job, but that the ruling does not mean unqualified people will be hired or promoted.

Justice Brennan's opinion was joined without expressed reservation by four other justices. However, Justice Stevens in a separate statement explained his ambivalence. The foundation of the Court's affirmative action ruling, namely the *Webber* decision, "is at odds with my understanding of the actual intent of the authors of the legislation." However, he also said that the Court's interpretation is "now an important part of the fabric of our law" and must be obeyed. Justice O'Conner also provided a separate opinion. She preferred a much stricter standard for voluntary AA. She said voluntary AA is valid only if an employer's lack of women or minority workers would be sufficient to prove in court a case of illegal discrimination.

The dissenters accused the majority of easing the voluntary AA standards established in the 1979 ruling. Justice Scalia said, "We effectively replace the goal of a discrimination-free society with the quite incompatible goal of proportionate representation by race and by sex in the workplace." The dissenters said the ruling perverts the 1964 law "into a powerful engine of racism and sexism."

The Court supported for the first time hiring goals designed to correct discrimination based on sex rather than race. They decided by a 6–3 vote that the federal law permits an employer to decide voluntarily to correct a "manifest imbalance" in the work force through an AA plan, as long as the rights of other workers are not "unnecessarily trammeled."

This decision removes some of the uncertainty that surrounds AA plans and may put renewed pressure on private and public employers to hire and promote more women and minorities without fear of reverse discrimination lawsuits. In addition, the decision is significant since it reaffirms the 1979 *Webber* decision, which has been widely criticized by conservatives and the Reagan administration. It also extends the *Webber* decision to include public employers. (*Note:* In a charge of "reverse discrimination," Brian Webber charged that Kaiser Aluminum had unjustly denied him access to an in-house training program in favor of less qualified minorities. The Supreme Court decided against Webber.)

The three dissenting justices, however, showed how strongly feelings still run on this issue, urging that the time has come to overrule the *Webber* decision. Although the Court remains sharply divided on the legality of AA, a majority once again rebuffed the Reagan administration's position that sex (instead of race) should not be considered in hiring and promotion, except to help specific individuals who can prove personal discrimination.

EFFECTS AND IMPLICATIONS OF THE SUPREME COURT RULINGS

The Supreme Court rulings have important effects on and implications for the management of human resources.

The Supreme Court decisions reaffirm the legality of, and hence the underlying need for, the preferential treatment of nonvictim minorities to remedy the present effects of proven past "egregious discrimination." However, the Court also has established some general ground rules for AA plans:

1. They must avoid rigid quotas.
2. They must be temporary in duration.
3. They must be carefully tailored to remedy precise discrimination in each case.
4. They should not unnecessarily restrict the rights of white male workers.

These ground rules send a clear signal to employers that the preferential treatment of minorities and women is permitted only when the specified conditions and ground rules are taken into consideration.

Although the Court in the past two years has advanced the cause of AA and clarified several important questions, there are still some important unanswered questions:

1. How long should racial and sexual preferences be allowed?

2. What constitutes "egregious discrimination?"

3. Can white males, especially more senior and better qualified males, who are passed over as a result of racial preference, successfully challenge AA programs as reverse discrimination? (This may have been partially answered in the Johnson case; however, the Court did say that Johnson was only marginally better qualified than Joyce.)

All these unresolved issues in fair employment imply that the debate over AA, especially issues involving preferential treatment, is far from over. One common thread links the last four cases (*Cleveland Firefighters, Sheet Metal Workers, Paradise,* and *Johnson*); they are all "worst case scenarios." In the first three cases, the defendant had defied court orders for minority hiring for several years, and in the *Johnson* case there had never been a woman in any of the 238 skilled jobs. It is not clear what the Court would rule in situations that have less obvious discrimination.

What does the future hold for AA? It seems obvious that the use of goals, quotas, and preferential treatment can never be more than a temporary measure. A major question that no one seems to have the answer for is, "How long is temporary?"

SUMMARY

As always when dealing with AA dilemmas, the Supreme Court's rulings have not been unanimous. In fact, the decisions were reached with narrow and shifting majorities. Although the cases were quite different, the Court decisions about them shared landmark significance in two areas:

1. For the first time, the Supreme Court said that lower court federal judges had broad authority to set goals and timetables requiring employers guilty of past discrimination to hire and promote specific numbers of minorities. The Court also reaffirmed its position on voluntary AA plans and further extended it to include women. This rejects the current position of the Justice Department that federal judges do not have such power, and that the use of goals and timetables to remedy past discrimination is invalid.

2. The Supreme Court also said that upon finding persistent and egregious discrimination, preferential treatment in hiring and promotion may be awarded to women and minority workers, even though they are not direct victims of past discrimination. This repudiates the Justice Department's argument that only victim-specific remedies should be made.

REFERENCES

Affirmative action doomed? (1985, August 22). *Engineering News-Record,* p. 10.

Britt, L. P. (1984, September). Affirmative action: Is there life after Stotts? *Personnel Administrator, 29,* 96–100.

duRivage, V. (1985, June). The OFCCP under the Reagan administration: Affirmative action in retreat. *Labor Law Journal, 36,* 360–368.

Facts on File. (1981). Volume 41, p. 465.

Facts on File. (1986). Volume 47, p. 448–449.

Firefighters Local 1784 v. *Stotts,* 34 EPD, S. Ct. 2576 (1984).

Johnson v. *Transportation Agency.* (1987, March 27). *BNA Daily Labor Report,* D-1.

Local 93, Firefighters v. *City of Cleveland,* 138 U.S. 200 (1986).

Sheet Metal Workers v. *EEOC,* 478 U.S. (1986).

Steelworkers v. *Webber,* 443 U.S. 193 (1979).

United States v. *Paradise.* (1987, February 22). *BNA Daily Labor Report,* D-1.

Wygant v. *Jackson Board of Education,* 476 U.S. (1986).

Assessment Centers Are Evolving Toward a Bright Future

William E. Souder and Anna Mae Leksich

Assessment centers have become a popular format for conducting training, performance evaluations, personnel appraisals and career counseling within the U.S. Government and over 3,000 companies.[1,2,3] But what are the pros and cons of assessment centers? How effective are they? What is their future?

Conceptualized in the early 1900s by German psychologists, assessment centers were commonly used to select German military officers during the 1930s.[4,5] An awareness of the German practices encouraged the U.S. military to consider similar procedures. Thus, in 1943 the U.S. Office of Strategic Services (OSS) developed an assessment center to train espionage agents.[6,7]

After World War II, many military psychologists and officers joined private companies, where they started assessment centers as aids to personnel selection and promotion decision making.[6] However, most of these efforts were sporadic, small-scale operations. In 1956, the American Telephone and Telegraph Co. conducted a major study of managerial values.[8,9] This study soon evolved into a large-scale corporate assessment center. AT&T has since sent more than 200,000 employees through their center.[7]

AT&T's efforts attracted considerable attention and awakened a new interest in industrial assessment centers. In 1962, Standard Oil of Ohio initiated an assessment center for their managers. Shortly thereafter, IBM, Sears, GE and J. C. Penny developed AT&T-type assessment centers. By the end of 1980, more than 3,000 firms had become experienced with assessment centers.[2,3,4]

Over the past 50 years, assessment centers have evolved from a military personnel selection technique to a set of procedures that can be applied to a variety of industrial personnel problems. Today, assessment centers are commonly used to measure and assess managerial skills in planning, communicating, delegating, leadership, decision making, sensitivity, judgment, organizing and controlling. Assessment centers are also being used to train and upgrade supervisory personnel skills, to encourage creativity among research and engineering personnel, to resolve interpersonal and interdepartmental conflicts, to assist personnel in career planning, to select candidates for promotion, to train supervisors in performance appraisal and to provide information for manpower planning and organization designs.[10,11,12]

MODERN FORM

Assessment centers can have many variations in form and purpose. However, modern assessment centers have the following five characteristics, which distinguish them from other approaches.

- Assessment in groups. There is a fixed size of the participant group, usually six or 12 persons, who go through the exercises together.
- Peer interaction and feedback. The participants interact, sharing their experiences and feelings, and provide some critiques and evaluations of each other.
- Assessment by experienced teams. The assessor team consists of six to 12 persons who have gone through the assessment center, and who have received additional training in hu-

man relations. Assessor teams are specifically designed and matched to the participant group. For example, if the assessment center is being used to train middle managers for higher-level responsibilities, the assessor team should consist exclusively of higher-level managers. But if the objective is to resolve interdepartmental conflicts, then peers from both departments should be represented in the participant group and on the assessor team.

- The use of multiple methods that simulate several real work environments. A major strength of the assessment center approach is that it uses a combination of objective tests, projective tests, interviewing, face-to-face exercises, problem-solving situations, peer evaluations and trained professional evaluations. The use of multiple methods provides a very broad coverage and many checks and balances that lead to relatively high validity in the results.[13,14]
- Two-way, detailed feedback. Participants and assessors can share and exchange perceptions in a controlled and focused fashion that provides enlightenment for everyone. Users of assessment centers report many indirect benefits, i.e., positive effects on morale, more realistic job expectations and improved interpersonal understandings.[3,7,15]

Eight steps are required to design an effective assessment center, as listed in Table 1. The first step is for top management to carefully decide on the purpose and role of the assessment center. What problems are you seeking to solve? What specific accomplishments or outcomes are you seeking from the center? How will you judge and evaluate the outcome or accomplishments of the center?

The answers to these questions will lead directly into the second step: the identification of the particular human skills of concern to the center. For example, if the center's objective is to aid in selecting candidates for promotions to vice president, the slate of required skills for that job must be carefully identified. Or, if the center's objective is supervisory training, the particular supervisory skills to be enhanced must be carefully specified.

Table 1
Eight Essential Steps in Designing an Assessment Center

1. Objective-setting
2. Skill identification
3. Exercise selection and design
4. Assessor training
5. Center design
6. Definition of observation and evaluation procedures
7. Development of feedback procedures
8. Validation

EXERCISE SELECTION

The specification of the center objectives and the identification of required skills will influence the selection and design of the exercises. Four basic types of exercises may be used: objective, projective, situational and sociometric.

Objective exercises are often referred to as paper-and-pencil tests. The tests are purchased from test publishers and administered according to publisher's directions. Some frequently used tests are the School and College Ability Tests; The Miller Analogies Test, the Gordon Personal Inventory, and the Edwards Personal Preference Schedule.[16] These exercises attempt to measure basic skills and abilities.

By contrast, projective exercises and tests attempt to measure values, attitudes, impulses and motives. Word association tests, the Rorschach test, the Thematic Apperception test, sentence completion exercises and role-playing exercises are common examples.[16] Unlike objective tests, projective tests must be administered and interpreted under the guidance of industrial or clinical psychologists.

Situational exercises are usually developed by the coordinators of the assessment center, or are borrowed from an existing center and modified to meet the new center's needs. Several standardized situational exercises are available. In a standardized exercise, all the known outcomes are listed and interpreted for the assessors in an accompanying key.

One such exercise is the in-basket technique. In this exercise, the participant must sort through an accumulation of mail, memos, reports and other information that might come across a manager's desk. The participant is required to deal with each item and give instructions as to its proper handling. The ways in which the respondent deals with the items provides clues to self-confidence, organizational and planning abilities, decision-making, risk-taking and administrative abilities. Another standard exercise is the irate customer phone call. Here the participant must deal with an assessor posing as a customer with a problem. This exercise tests the candidate's reactions to pressure and threats.

A commonly used situational exercise is the leaderless group discussion. In this exercise, the group is given a problem and each candidate is given a position or viewpoint that they must take in solving the problem. The group is given a limited time in which to solve the problem.

In a sociometric exercise, each participant ranks every other participant on a scale of 1 to 10, with 10 being the most preferred co-worker and 1 being the least preferred co-worker. Rankings are taken before and after each of several interactive problem solving exercises. Using sociograms and other psychometric scaling devices, the changes in rankings are tracked over time.[2,17] The result can be analyzed to reveal some very rich information about the leadership traits, risk-taking propensities, interpersonal abilities, communication and persuasion skills and aggressiveness of individuals within a group setting. However, a sociometric exercise requires the skills of an industrial or clinical psychologist who specializes in psychometric methods. Moreover, a sociometric exercise can be very confrontational, threatening and ego-deflating. It is wise to have a psychologist on hand who can intervene if the session becomes emotionally traumatic for some participants.

ASSESSOR TRAINING

Effective assessor training is the key to an effective assessment center. In concert with top management and the consulting psychologists, the assessors must define or develop the exercises, set the standards for judging performance and evaluate the participant's performance. Typically, the first group of assessors is trained by consulting psychologists, and the assessors then train their successors under the guidance of the psychologists.

The amount of time and expense required for assessor training varies proportionately with the nature of the center, the ratio of assessors to participants, the organization, the center's objectives, the total number of participants, and the types of exercises used. Some programs devote two or three weeks to training, making use of films, lectures, discussions, and practice sessions on interviewing and report preparation. Other programs allow only a few hours for training.[2] When the center focuses on the improvement of skills in human judgment or interpersonal relationships, the ratio of assessors to participants may be one-to-one and the assessor training may be more intense.[18]

The center's physical design and layout should be pleasant, well-lighted, well-appointed and appropriate to the tasks and the participants. A large room with one large round table and two or three smaller tables, each flanked by several stuffed swivel chairs, is an ideal configuration. Adequate space should be left for the participants to move about freely and to break into smaller groups when necessary. Easels and chalkboards should be provided. A fully equipped center will have video-taping and audio-visual equipment.[18,19]

FEEDBACK PROCEDURES

The success of a center will be deeply influenced by its credibility in the eyes of the participants. If the participants find their center experiences helpful in coping with real-world problems, then the center will have achieved a major modicum of success. Thus, the meaningfulness of the assessor's observations, evaluations and feedback is an essential factor. The choice of what to observe and evaluate, how to take the observations and make the evaluations, and how to feed back these observations must be settled as part of the objective-setting and the design of the center.

Basically, the observation and evaluation procedures must be kept consistent with the organization's established policies, climate and general personality. For instance, suppose the prevailing organizational climate is non-innovative, non-confrontational and low-key, and top management desires to change this culture to a faster-paced and more innovative one. The sudden establishment of a center based on sociometric exercises and confrontational personal evaluation may be devastatingly shocking to the personnel. It would be better to start with a much less radical type of center and then to intensify it gradually. Assessment centers can be used as highly effective change agents. But they will not be effective change agents if their immediate impact is to throw the whole organization into cultural shock.

Another basic rule is that the evaluations must be defensible. When the participants ask questions like "What do you mean I did not demonstrate leadership?", the assessors must have a ready answer. Similarly, suppose a participant asks: "How can you infer from this experience that I wouldn't be able to handle that job?" Some credible evidence of such a relationship must be provided by the assessor.

The question of how much feedback to provide for the participant presents an unresolved dilemma. Individuals differ widely in the amount of feedback desired and needed, and in their capacities to handle good and bad news. Current practices range from sharing virtually nothing to presenting the participant with a formal written report containing all the detailed test scores.[20,21] Some feedback is necessary, both out of fairness to the participant and for the center to have any impact. Thus, flexibility to individual needs and wants seems to be the most effective approach: some individuals should receive more details than others, some should get one-to-one feedback with counseling, etc.

VALIDATION

Equal employment opportunity laws have provided additional impetus for validating an assessment center. Two types of validity are of concern: content validity and construct validity. Content validity refers to the degree to which the center exercises resemble the actual job contents and job requirements. Construct validity refers to the degree to which the rating and evaluation criteria are relevant to actual job performance.[22,23] Both types of validity can be checked statistically, through a correlational analysis of center scores and actual job performances.[24] In general, if the assessment center exercises and ratings do not correlate with each other and with the actual job performances and experiences, then the center is not a valid device and it is of questionable merit.

A highly valid assessment center can be empirically designed as follows: select a set of exercises and evaluation procedures that appear to be appropriate, based on the experiences of other centers and results described in the literature. Then put a sample of participants through the center, and correlate their exercise scores and evaluation scores with their actual on-the-job performances. If high correlations are not obtained, alter the exercises or evaluation procedures on the basis of the correlation data. That is, change either the exercises or the evaluation procedures or both, depending on which one does not correlate well. Put another sample of participants through the center and re-check the correlations. Repeat the above procedures until high correlations are obtained.

SYSTEMS DESIGN

In general, the objectives of the center, the skills to be measured or enhanced by the center, the exercises used, the observations taken, the evaluations made and the feedbacks given are all closely interrelated. They must be considered as a total system. Each is dependent on the other. The specification of one influences the other. Moreover, the entire assessment center system must be in harmony with the prevailing organizational goals, policies, procedures and cultures, and with the existing human resource system. These ideas are depicted in Figure 1.

One approach to the systematic design of an assessment center would start with the organization's charter and top management's statements of their expectations from the center. Based on the charter and the statements, and drawing on the experiences of other centers, a taskforce should be appointed to develop a list of criteria for judg-

Figure 1
Systems Design Perspective of an Assessment Center

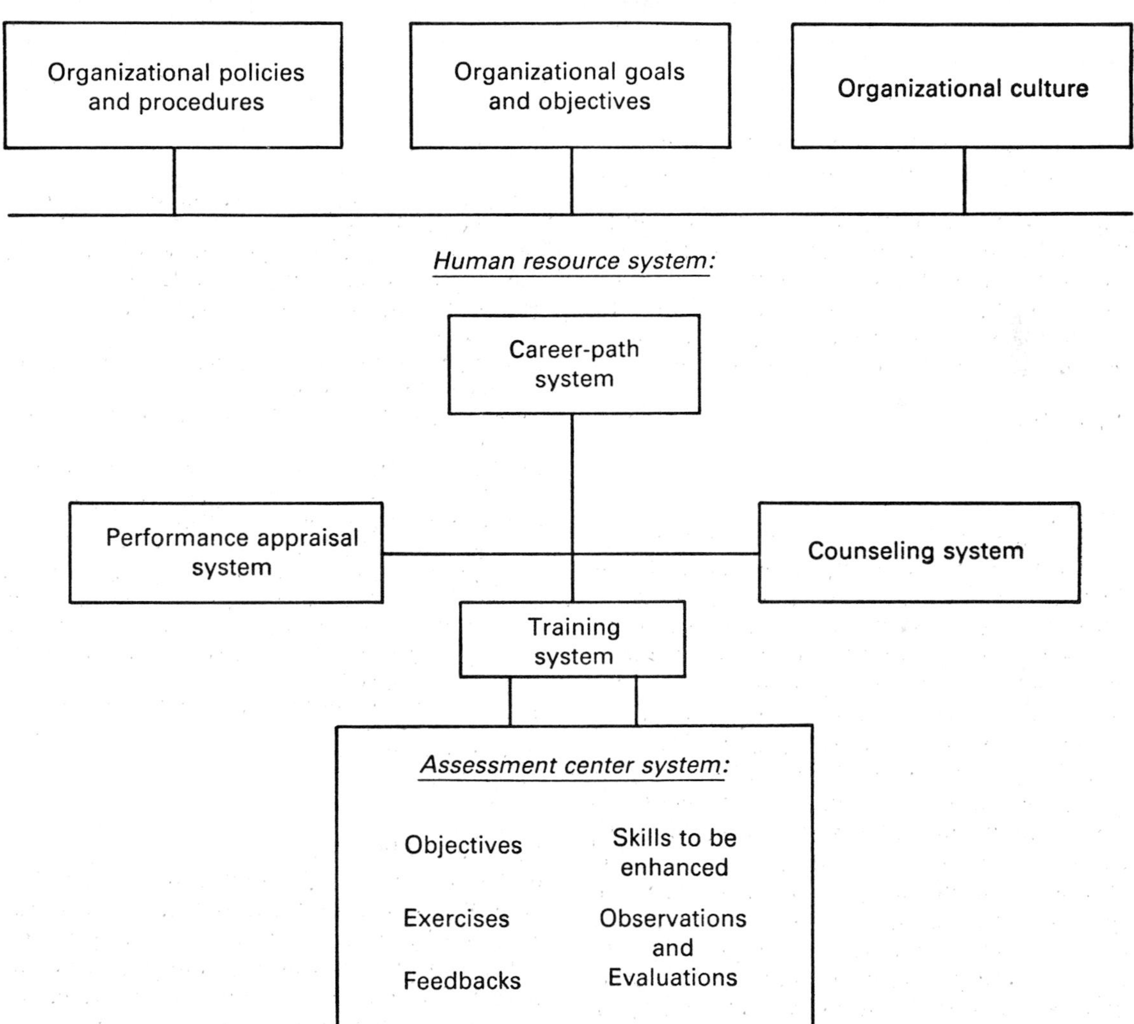

ing the outputs from the center. These criteria should be reviewed for consistency and approved by top management.

At this point, a center director should be selected from the task force members, and the organization of the center should be formulated. The center director should be chosen primarily for his managerial abilities and secondarily for his technical knowledge of human resource systems. The center should report to the vice president of human resources, or some equivalent top management level.

A team consisting of a consulting psychologist, the center director and several managers from various organizational levels should select the exercises and tests. This same team should set the evaluation standards and the feedback procedures, and define the criteria to be used in nominating candidates and selecting participants to go through the center. The validity of the selected exercises and tests should be carefully studied and the exercises should be checked for adequacy and consistency against the top management statements, the charter and the criteria for judging the center. This is the point at which the team must judge the appropriateness of the exercises, the evaluation standards and the feedback procedures vis-a-vis the organization's climate and culture. Assessors can then be chosen and carefully trained through a combination of in-house and outside courses.

The first team of assessors should be drawn from the task force and team members who were involved in the design of the center. This first team of assessors should be retained as the founders of the center, and should serve as a steering committee for the center. As more assessors are trained, the membership of the steering committee can turn over. The steering committee should play an active role in evaluating the center, judging its adequacy and listening to any complaints or frustrations from participants.

CURRENT TRENDS

In the past, if an organization wanted an assessment center it developed its own. Today, contractor-operated, pre-packaged and community assessment centers are available.[5,6,10,25]

In a contractor-operated center, an outside contractor comes into the organization and designs and operates a center on the premises. Many contractor-operated centers are pre-packaged. These approaches generally offer lower costs than developing and operating your own center. They are feasible alternatives for organizations that do not have adequate in-house capabilities. On the other hand, these approaches may not meet particular needs or fit particular cultures, as discussed in connection with Figure 1.

A pre-packaged center consists of standard videotapes, cassettes, tests, exercises, evaluation forms and all the directions for setting up and running a center.

A community center is a jointly owned or leased facility that is shared by several organizations.

Various customizing services have arisen. These services take a pre-packaged center and customize it for particular organizations. The result is a compromise center—somewhere between a pre-packaged and a uniquely designed center. A customized center is sometimes an improvement over a pre-packaged center. On the other hand, the customizing may be so extensive that it would have been preferable to build a unique center.

Second-generation assessment centers are now appearing. This is a highly automated variant of the pre-packaged center, in which the participants follow video taped instructions and dialogue with a computer. For example, in a second-generation center the participants would perform the in-basket exercise at a computer keyboard and the computer would score their performance and feedback the results. It is possible for participants to interact with fictitious players, to dialogue one-on-one with the computer, and to engage in many of the group exercises used in any other type of assessment center. However, the effects of the absence of real human contact in second-generation centers have yet to be determined. The second-generation concept is so new that it has hardly been explored.

Though over 50 years old, assessment center concepts still have not been fully explored and tested. Proponents argue that assessment centers are a cure-all for many organizational ailments. Critics argue that the benefits and predictive qualities of most assessment centers are unproven.

In spite of this, assessment centers have become increasingly popular. In the past 20 years, the number of assessment centers has grown exponentially.

Experience suggests[26,27,28] that three major benefits can come from an assessment center. One is the improved interpersonal understandings and abilities in those who go through the center. Another comes from the assessor training that sharpens the thinking and general perceptiveness of those who receive the training. A third major benefit is the stimulation of more effective performance appraisals and career path efforts.

However, to achieve these benefits, the following five requirements must be met:

- A system perspective must be taken in designing the assessment center. The center must be an integral part of the organization's performance appraisal, training, career path and counseling systems. And the center must be consistent with the organization's established policies, goals and culture.
- The center must have top management support and involvement. Top management must provide the guiding objectives and the criteria for judging the effectiveness of the center. And top management must provide feedback on how well the center is meeting these objectives and criteria.
- The participants should be selected carefully, according to some pre-specified selection criteria that relate to the center's objectives. Not everyone should attend the assessment center, and supervisors should be instructed carefully on the types and categories of candidates desired. In that regard, it is important that some superior performers and a variety of "problem children" be included in the participants. This provides both a healthy variety and a validity check on the center's procedures.
- The credibility of the center must be maximized by maintaining valid exercises, competent assessors and honest feedbacks to the participants. Validity checks should be run constantly on the exercises, since they can become outdated. The participants should be polled as a means of gathering information on the credibility of the center.
- The center should be viewed and managed as an agency of change. Tomorrow's managers, tomorrow's culture and tomorrow's values can come from the center. But in order to achieve this, the center must be properly focused and administered. If the center is too pedantic, it will simply reinforce the existing organizational values and climates. But if the center is too radical, it won't be accepted.

The future of assessment centers is relatively bright. The state-of-art in center design, exercise design, evaluation methods and assessor training is progressing very rapidly. It seems safe to predict that within the next 10 to 15 years nearly every organization will either have its own assessment center or be participating jointly in some "community" center.

REFERENCES

1. "How to spot the hotshots," *Business Week,* October 8, 1979, p. 62.

2. Finkle, R. B., *Handbook of Industrial and Organizational Psychology,* New York: McGraw-Hill, 1976, pp. 861–888.

3. Byham, W. C., "Assessment centers for spotting future managers," *Harvard Business Review,* July–August 1970, pp. 150–167.

4. Cohen, Barry M., Moses, Joseph L., and Byham, William Co., "The validity of assessment centers: a literature review," *Monograph II,* Development Dimensions Inc., Pittsburgh, PA, 1974.

5. Cohen, Steven L., "Pre-packaged vs. tailor-made: the assessment center debate," *Personnel Journal,* December 1980, pp. 989–991.

6. Cohen, Steven L., "The bottom line on assessment center technology," *The Personnel Administrator,* February 1980, pp. 50–55.

7. Rice, Berkeley, "Measuring executive muscle," *Psychology Today,* December 1978, pp. 95–96+.

8. Bray, D. B., "The management progress study," The American Telephone and Telegraph Co., New York, 1956.

9. Howard, Ann, and Bray, D. W., "Today's young managers: they can do it, but will they?" *The Wharton Magazine,* Summer 1981, pp. 23–28.

10. Adler, Seymour, "Using assessment centers in smaller organizations," *Personnel Journal,* September 1978, pp. 484–487+.

11. Hart, Gary L., and Thompson, Paul H., "Assessment centers: for selection or development," *Organizational Dynamics,* Spring 1979, pp. 63–77.

12. Jaffee, Cabot L., and Sefcik, Joseph T., Jr., "What is an assessment center?" *The Personnel Administrator,* February 1978, pp. 40–43+.

13. Cohen, Stephen L., "How well standardized is your organization's assessment center?" *The Personnel Administrator,* December 1978, pp. 41–51.

14. Klimoski, Richard J., and Strickland, William J., "Assessment center—valid or merely prescient," *Personnel Psychology*, Vol. 30, 1977, pp. 353–360.

15. Millard, C. W., and Pinsky, Sheldon, "Assessing the assessment center," *Personnel Administrator*, May 1980, pp. 85–88.

16. Miller, D. C., *Handbook of Research Design and Social Measurement*, McKay: New York, pp. 161–392.

17. Kerlinger, F. N., *Foundations of Behavioral Research;* Holt, Reinhart and Winston: New York, 1980, pp. 467–602.

18. Fitz-enz, Joc, Hards, Kathryn E., and Savage, G. E., "Total development: selection, assessment, growth," *Personnel Administrator*, February 1980, pp. 58–62.

19. Haynes, Marion, "Streamlining an assessment center," *Personnel Journal*, February, 1976, pp. 80–83.

20. Kraut, Allen I., "A hard look at management assessment centers and their future," *Personnel Journal*, May 1972, pp. 317–326.

21. London, Manual, "What every personnel director should know about management promotion decisions," *Personnel Journal*, October 1978, pp. 550–555.

22. Gatewood, Robert D., and Schoenfeldt, Lyle F., "Content validity and EEOC: a useful alternative for selection," *Personnel Journal*, October 1977, pp. 520–522+.

23. "Validity of EEOC testing guidelines approach to content validation," *Labor Relations Reporter*, Vol. 105, No. 3, September 8, 1980.

24. Kerlinger, F. N., *op. cit.*, pp. 301–365.

25. Nichols, Leland C., and Hudson, Joseph, "Dual-roll assessment center: selection and development," *Personnel Journal*, May 1981, pp. 380–386.

26. Hendricks, John R., "An eight-year follow-up of a management assessment center," *Journal of Applied Psychology*, Vol. 63, No. 15, 1978, pp. 596–601.

27. Turner, T. S., and Utley, J. A., "Foremen selection: one company's approach," *Personnel*, May–June 1979, pp. 47–55.

28. Wollowick, Herber B., and McNamara, W. J., "Relationship of the components of an assessment center to management success," *Journal of Applied Psychology*, Vol. 53, No. 5, 1969, pp. 348–352.

Strategic Selection: Matching Executives to Business Conditions

Marc Gerstein and Heather Reisman

Our first contact with selecting executives on the basis of strategic requirements occurred fourteen years ago while we were working on a consulting assignment for a major consumer products company. Part of the assignment involved briefing a new plant manager on the study we were doing. He was replacing the individual who had built the 1,300 man plant from scratch over an eighteen-month period. Through the course of this study, we, however, began to raise questions: Why was senior management making such a change, considering the incumbent had achieved one of the most trouble-free start-ups as well as the highest overall productivity in the division's history?

In preparing the briefing, we had an opportunity to put this question to a divisional senior manager. His answer was very simple: "Some people are better at starting things up, some are better at squeezing the most out of them once they are running, and some are better at fixing them when

Reprinted from "Strategic Selection: Matching Executives to Business Conditions" by M. Gerstein and H. Reisman, *Sloan Management Review*, Winter 1983, pp. 33–49, by permission of the publisher.

they go wrong. Right now, the start-up is completed, and it's time for a new man."

Of course, the concept of matching individuals with specific positional requirements has been around for many years for those manual or technical jobs where both the skills required for the job and the appropriate testing procedures for selecting the candidate are more or less straightforward. The application of this concept to managerial jobs has been slow, however, and slower still to executive positions. Our analysis suggests the following reasons for this lengthy delay:

Management Considered a "Mysterious Act." An untold number of executives feel that management, especially at senior levels, is mysterious and defies objective analysis. Certain critical elements, such as a manager's "style" and the degree to which he "fits in" with his colleagues, are too abstract to be measured and too sensitive to be identified explicitly. Rather, a manager just gets a *sense* of all these factors and makes decisions accordingly.

Promotion Considered a "Just Reward." Although there is little question today that the nature of jobs changes as one moves up the ladder—"the best salesman does not necessarily make the best sales manager"—the pressure is, nevertheless, to reward performance with promotion. In most organizations, objective rewards are still largely hierarchically based, and many managers feel that they have very little choice but to promote their best performers, or they risk demoralizing them or losing them to competition.

Compatibility with People, Not Jobs. There seems to be a pervasive desire for people to surround themselves with individuals of similar kind. Consequently, the selection process is often less one of matching candidates with job requirements, and more of matching candidates with selectors.

Lack of Skill. Hiring subordinates is a skill an executive is expected to possess by virtue of his or her position. Consequently, executives are rarely trained in selection, and only a few executives are naturally gifted in this area. Furthermore, since selection is always time-consuming and often tedious, it may get short shrift, despite the knowledge of its importance.

Belief in the "Universal Manager." For many years, executives believed that a good manager can handle any situation, irrespective of its idiosyncratic demands. Growth businesses and those that are more mature are seen as minor variations of a common theme, rather than specialized business problems that create particular demands on the management in place. Consequently, senior executives have often tended to search for "universal managers" rather than those who are more specialized.[1] Furthermore, executives have not typically replaced managers as business conditions evolve, but they have waited until performance erodes markedly before acting in the belief that "good managers should be able to adapt."

Despite these forces, a number of firms have endeavored to bring increased order to executive selection and to explicitly tie selection decisions to the job requirements created by their firm's strategy. *Business Week* listed Chase Manhatten Bank, Heublein, Texas Instruments, Corning Glass, and General Electric among those companies engaged in linking executive selection with strategic requirements.[2]

Thus the purpose of this article is to elaborate the selection process and tools we have developed to help a number of firms that are committed to strategic selection. The reader will find that the concepts and procedures described here do not make the executive staffing process easier. In fact, they may make it more difficult. However, we believe that they do produce effective results. Our intended audience is, therefore, the senior executive or human resource manager who seeks to improve his or her corporation's executive selection processes and who is willing, if necessary, to devote considerable resources toward this end.[3]

WEAKNESSES OF CURRENT PRACTICES

During recent studies, we have identified several weaknesses in the current practices of staffing at the executive level.[4]

1. *Use of Unclear Language.* As participants in a large number of executive staffing assignments, we have found that the language used to discuss job requirements and individual capabilities is extremely vague. While there is an abundant vocabulary, the words used are not precise. For example, a "simple" term such as *delegation* does not mean the same thing to everyone. Likewise, a "complex" concept such as *interpersonal influence* is even less universally defined.

Consequently, the specification of job requirements and the evaluation of personnel are hampered by a tremendous inefficiency in communication. Most of the time, however, vague and unclear language is not apparent or dismissed as mere "semantics" because the discussions tend to stay at a general level. However, if one probes for concrete illustrations of required on-the-job behavior, one often finds that executives do not necessarily have the same ideas in mind about what the job entails or which skills are critical for success.

2. *Inadequate Job Description.* The job description is one of contemporary business' most common pieces of paper work. Yet, we have found that managers consider job descriptions a "necessary evil," mostly useful for establishing salary levels. However, the reason that job descriptions are generally inadequate is that not enough time and resources are put into writing them, and results show it.[5] Consequently, the selection committee often lacks a clear written focus for its deliberations and, in combination with imprecise language, is heavily hampered in its task.

3. *Enduring Belief in Universal Managers.* As already mentioned, many executives believe that there is an "ideal" managerial profile that is largely independent of the organizational role or business circumstance—the idea that "a manager is a manager," and a good one will do well in any situation. The belief is most significantly manifested in the unqualified use of results in previous positions as a predictor of a manager's future performance.[6]

4. *No Access to Relevant Behavioral Data.* In evaluating candidates, executives generally have access only to the managerial behavior they observe firsthand. Many critical areas, such as the ability to delegate work and relate to one's peers, are not readily observable by superiors, and they must be assessed by specific assessment techniques. In addition, certain skills required for a senior job may not be required in a more junior position, thus making data collection in these areas difficult. For example, strategy formulation may not be required in positions below the general management level, and the only "human resource management" required in many jobs is the occasional replacement of subordinates.

In combination, these four weaknesses lead to ineffectiveness in the executive staffing process, both in terms of hiring the wrong person or not using the existing personnel optimally. In contrast, the strategic selection system we have developed overcomes these weaknesses by providing: (1) a set of starting points to understand job demands in the context of generalized strategic requirements, thereby focusing clearly on job requirements under the actual conditions anticipated; (2) a concise format for documenting these job requirements in order to provide a vehicle for communication; (3) a carefully constructed "common language" for discussing and documenting the managerial aspects of jobs and individual capabilities; (4) the means to collect valid, behavioral data; and (5) a step-by-step guide to help organize the executive selection process.

COMPONENTS OF THE STRATEGIC SELECTION SYSTEM

In its current form, the strategic selection system contains four components. These components are strategy-related job requirements, a role description format, the dimensions of senior management effectiveness, and a set of assessment techniques.

Strategy-related job requirements consist of a set of "educated guesses" as to the business demands that various strategic situations create and the managerial requirements that these situations place on incumbent management (see Tables 1 and 2).[7] The role description format presents a logic or structure for job descriptions that is oriented toward the facilitation of staffing and objective setting rather than of compensation decisions.

The dimensions of senior management effectiveness comprise nineteen performance areas (with explicit definitions) that are used to characterize job requirements with individual capabilities or performances (see Appendix 1). Finally, the assessment techniques comprise various data collection methods, particularly "behavioral interviewing," which shed maximum light on a candidate's capabilities vis-à-vis the dimensions of senior management effectiveness (see Appendix 2).

Each of the components and the manner in which they fit together are derived from a series of consulting projects and field studies of a number of existing executive selection systems. Together, these components enable the individual (or group) charged with an executive staffing assignment to identify specific job requirements based on strategic needs, to document these requirements in an efficient fashion, and to collect data on each candidate that are specifically related to the key managerial requirements of the job.

Strategy-Related Job Requirements

The characteristics required of candidates in specific positions were derived by means of the logic displayed in Tables 1 and 2. First, a set of seven "pure" strategic situations were identified on the basis of discussions with operating executives, case examples, and the strategy literature. These strategic situations are: start-up; turnaround; ex-

Table 1
Characteristics of Various Strategic Situations

I. Start-up	—High Financial Risk; —Limited Management Team Cohesiveness; —No Organization, Systems, or Procedures in Place; —No Operational Experience Base; —Endless Workload: Multiple Priorities; —Generally Insufficient Resources to Satisfy All Demands; —Limited Relationship with Suppliers, Customers, & Environment.
II. Turnaround	—Time Pressure for "Results": Need for Rapid Situational Assessment and Decision Making; —Poor Results, but Business is Worth Saving; —Weak Competitive Position; —Eroded Morale: Low-esteem/Cohesion; —Inadequate Systems: Possible Weak or Bureaucratic Organizational Infrastructure; —Strained and Eroded Relationships with Suppliers, Customers, & Environment; —Lack of Appropriate Leadership: Period of Neglect; —Limited Resources: Skills Shortages: Some Incompetent Personnel.
III. Extract Profit/Rationalize Existing Business	—"Controlled" Financial Risk; —Unattractive Industry in Long Term: Possible Need to Invest Selectively, but Major New Investments Not Likely to Be Worthwhile; —Internal Organizational Stability; —Moderate-to-High Managerial/Technical Competence; —Adequate Systems and Administrative Infrastructure; —Acceptable to Excellent Relationships with Suppliers, Customers, & Environment.

continued

Table 1 *continued*

IV. Dynamic Growth in Existing Business	—Moderate-to-High Financial Risk; —New Markets, Products, Technology; —Multiple Demands and Conflicting Priorities; —Rapidly Expanding Organization in Certain Sectors; —Inadequate Managerial/Technical/Financial Resources to Meet All Demands; —Unequal Growth across Sectors of Organization; —Likely Shifting Power Bases as Growth Occurs; —Constant Dilemma between Doing Current Work & Building Support Systems for the Future.
V. Redeployment of Efforts in Existing Business	—Low-Moderate, Short-Term Risk/High Long-Term Risk; —Resistance to Change: Likely Bureaucracy in Some Sections; —High Mismatch between Some Organization Skill Sets, Technology, People vs. Needs Created by Redefined Strategy; —Likelihood of Lack of Strategic Planning for Some Historical Period—Highly Operational Orientation to Executive Team.
VI. Liquidation/Divestiture of Poorly Performing Business	—Weak Competitive Position, Unattractive Industry, or Both; —Likely Continuance of Poor Returns; —Possible Morale Problems and Skills Shortages; —Little Opportunity for Turnaround or Redeployment Due to Unsatisfactory "Payback"; —Need to Cut Losses and Make Tough Decisions.
VII. New Acquisitions	Acquisitions may be classified into one of the above situations. In addition, the following conditions characterize a recent acquisition situation: —Pressure on New Management to "Prove Themselves"; —Existing Management Ambivalent/Defensive about Change; —Fundamental Need to Integrate Acquired Company with Parent at Some Levels.

Table 2
General Management Requirements for Various Strategic Situations

Situation	*Major Job Thrusts*	*Specific Characteristics of Ideal Candidates*
I. Start-up	—Creating Vision of Business; —Establishing Core Technical & Marketing Expertise; —Building Management Team.	—Vision of Finished Business; —Hands-on Orientation: A "Doer"; —In-depth Knowledge in Critical Technical Areas; —Organizing Ability; —Staffing Skills; —Team-Building Capabilities; —High-Energy Level and Stamina; —Personal Magnetism: Charisma; —Broad Knowledge of All Key Functions.

continued

Table 2 *continued*

Situation	*Major Job Thrusts*	*Specific Characteristics of Ideal Candidates*
II. Turnaround	—Rapid, Accurate Problem Diagnosis; —Fixing Short-Term and, Ultimately, Long-Term Problems.	—"Take Charge" Orientation: Strong Leader; —Strong Analytical and Diagnostic Skills, Especially Financial; —Excellent Business Strategist; —High-Energy Level; —Risk Taker; —Handles Pressure Well; —Good Crisis Management Skills; —Good Negotiator.
III. Extract Profit/Rationalize Existing Business	—Efficiency; —Stability; —Succession; —Sensing Signs of Change.	—Technically Knowledgeable: "Knows the Business"; —Sensitive to Changes: "Ear-to-the-Ground"; —Anticipates Problems: "Problem Finder"; —Strong Administrative Skills; —Oriented to "Systems"; —Strong "Relationship Orientation"; —Recognizes Need for Management Succession & Development; —Oriented to Getting Out the Most: Efficiency, Not Growth.
IV. Dynamic Growth in Existing Business	—Increasing Market Share in Key Sectors; —Managing Rapid Change; —Building Long-Term Health toward Clear Vision of the Future.	—Excellent Strategic & Financial Planning Skills; —Clear Vision of the Future; —Ability to Balance Priorities, i.e., Stability vs. Growth; —Organizational & Team-Building Skills; —Good Crisis Management Skills; —Moderate-High Risk Taker; —High-Energy Level; —Excellent Staffing Skills.
V. Redeployment of Efforts in Existing Business	—Establishing Effectiveness in Limited Business Sphere; —Managing Change; —Supporting the "Dispossessed."	—Good Politician/Manager of Change; —Highly Persuasive: High "Interpersonal Influence"; —Moderate Risk Taker; —Highly Supportive, Sensitive to People: Not "Bull in a China Shop"; —Excellent "Systems Thinker": Understands How Complex Systems Work; —Good Organizing & Executive Staffing Skills.

continued

Table 2 *continued*

Situation	*Major Job Thrusts*	*Specific Characteristics of Ideal Candidates*
VI. Liquidation/ Divestiture of Poorly Performing Business	—Cutting Losses; —Making Tough Decisions; —Making Best Deal.	—"Callousness": Tough-minded, Determined—Willing to Be the Bad Guy; —Highly Analytical re: Costs/Benefits—Does Not Easily Accept Current Ways of Doing Things; —Risk Taker; —Low-Glory Seeking: Willing to Do Dirty Jobs—Does Not Want Glamour; —Wants to be Respected, Not Necessarily Liked.
VII. New Acquisitions	—Integration; —Establishing Sources of Information & Control.	—Analytical Ability; —Relationship Building Skills; —Interpersonal Influence; —Good Communication Skills; —Personal Magnetism—Some Basis to Establish "Instant Credibility."

tract profit/rationalize an existing business; dynamic growth in an existing business; redeployment of efforts in an existing business; liquidation/divestiture; new acquisitions.[8] Second, a set of characteristics associated with each strategic situation was developed, again based on the literature, case examples, and discussions with senior executives.

Logically stemming from the strategic situations and their associated characteristics are sets of *major job thrusts* and ultimately, the *specific characteristics of ideal candidates* (see Table 2). These characteristics were developed on the basis of a large number of executive selections with the help of Personnel Decisions, Inc., a firm specializing in management assessment. General management requirements for various strategic situations are presented in Table 2.[9]

It should be noted, however that actual situations rarely fit precisely with the generalized strategic situations. Often, some combination or modification of strategic situations will exist. For example, a senior executive of a Mexican holding company described one of his operating divisions as "pre-turnaround"—in other words, an operating division that is still functioning but is on the verge of rapid deterioration. This situation combined elements of *redeployment of efforts* and *turnaround.* Likewise, the condition demanded that the incumbent manager have a combination of *specific characteristics* required by each of these strategic situations (see Table 2).

In practice, these managerial characteristics must be augmented by specifying the required industry knowledge, political skills, and personality characteristics that the particular organizational circumstances demand of an incumbent manager. Once these characteristics have been identified, a proper role description can be prepared.

Role Description

A role description is an expanded job description containing the following four elements:

1. A *basic function* statement summarizing the job's overall purpose and thrust, which are conceived in the context of the strategic situation clarified above;

2. A description of the position's technical and managerial responsibilities (a description of the key activities which the incumbent is expected to perform in order to fulfill the elements in the basic function);

3. A description of the key organizational and outside relationships that are necessary to support the above; and

4. Candidate requirements: a synthesis of the characteristics identified under strategy-related job requirements.

In addition to its value as a selection tool, the role description is extremely valuable to brief the new incumbent of his or her responsibilities and to establish job objectives for later performance appraisal.[10]

Dimensions of Senior Management Effectiveness

The dimensions of senior management effectiveness provide a vehicle through which the managerial requirements of various jobs and candidate capabilities may be delineated (see Appendix 1). These dimensions were developed with the aid of Personnel Decisions, Inc., on the basis of a large number of management assessments, the management assessment literature, and many discussions with senior executives.[11]

Subsequently, the dimensions were refined and tested through the creation, validation, and rating of hundreds of "behavioral incidents."[12] (A behavioral incident is a description of a real life story that is written by a manager, then professionally edited, and finally rated by a large number of executives to determine its "fit" with a specific dimension and the performance level portrayed by its main character.)

The development of the dimensions and their associated behavior scales took two years and considerable management time and energy.[13] However, these tools provide an extremely reliable and concrete system for evaluating and comparing managerial behavior, even when the managers who are contrasted are not known equally well by all evaluators.

Assessment Techniques: Behavioral Interviewing and Assessment Center Testing

Two data collection/assessment techniques are employed in the context of our selection system to furnish valid data on identified job requirements. The first, behavioral interviewing, is a method to extract highly specific information on the candidate's past behavior from the candidate himself or herself and from those individuals with whom he or she has worked.[14]

Specifically, behavioral interviewing elicits descriptions of past experiences (of much the same nature as the behavioral incidents mentioned above) from those individuals interviewed. These "story-telling" interviews produce detailed, richly textured information concerning specific skill areas required on the job. This information can then be easily evaluated by a trained interviewer and the selection committee. Unlike more conventional interviews, information furnished during behavioral interviews is very difficult to exaggerate or fake. The only drawbacks to this technique are: (1) considerable interviewing time is required, usually three to four hours at a minimum; and (2) as in any interview, articulate interviewees have some advantage over similarly capable but less self-expressive individuals.

To provide a sense of the methodology, a set of sample questions from our behavioral interviewing primer, a companion document to the dimensions of senior management effectiveness, is presented in Appendix 2. In practice, these questions serve as a jumping-off point for a series of "probes," which is a way of obtaining a complete description of the candidate's behavior that can be identified under circumstances as similar to those he or she will be facing. The basic premise of this assessment technique is that "the best predictor of future behavior is past behavior under similar circumstances."

The second data collection technique we employ is the assessment center testing, a version of which has been developed (again with Personnel Decisions, Inc.) to specifically illuminate performance in senior management skill areas.[15] A full-length center runs for four days and consists of a series of integrated simulation exercises and ability tests.[16] Unlike many other assessment centers, this particular center focuses on the circumstances and prospects of a single company, General Cosmetics, Inc., which forms the backdrop for all of the exercises. The single-company context provides a vehicle to assess the candidate's information processing and associative skills over four days.

The advantage of assessment centers, of course, is that they provide a consistent setting for comparisons across candidates: assessors are able to observe how a large number of candidates handle a standardized set of situations and stimuli. Thus, they are able to develop (1) a clearer picture of the range of typical responses, and (2) a better sense of the unacceptable, acceptable, or outstanding behaviors than is otherwise possible when evaluating an actual working environment.

In combination, behavioral interviewing and assessment center testing provide the selection committee with valid, highly reliable information concerning identified job requirements, When integrated with an assessment of key technical capabilities and personality characteristics, the assessment committee can make a secure prediction of the likely "fit" between the candidate and the job for which he or she is being considered.

THE SYSTEM IN GENERAL USE

It should be noted that we do not imply, through the tools and procedures presented in this article, that the executive staffing process is to be a mechanical one. On the contrary, executive selection always requires considerable knowledge and judgment on the part of the parties involved. The tools and procedures we offer merely structure the thought and decision process in order to leave the members of the selection team free to focus on that which only they can provide: business strategy and candidate evaluation. In this light, our overall process for matching executive requirements to strategic needs progresses straightforwardly, although somewhat more slowly than conventional staffing processes.

Step 1: Specification of Business Condition and Strategic Direction

This step requires a "good sense" of both the current business and its desired future, although not necessarily a detailed strategic plan. Management's objective in this step is to broadly outline the current situation and the business' "strategic posture" over an appropriate planning horizon. (Toward this end, the categories in Table 1 may prove a helpful starting point.)

Two related examples illustrate contrasting strategic situations. A financial services company contains two operating divisions, a consumer finance company and a medium-sized insurance company. The consumer finance division, one of the best run companies in the industry, was faced with the need to consolidate its operations, trim operating costs, and generally adapt to the changing character of the marketplace and the "interest rate squeeze."

The insurance division, on the other hand, faced enormous growth opportunities as a result of the changing character of the consumer, new delivery systems, changing regulations, and a set of constraints encumbering the industry giants, which delayed their adaptation to these conditions.

Clearly, the requirements placed on the chief executives of these two divisions were very different. In simplest terms, the CEO of the consumer finance division needed to "extract profit/rationalize" his business, while the CEO of the other division was clearly mandated to achieve "dynamic growth."

Step 2: Confirmation or Modification of Organization Structure

The notion that structure is a vehicle for strategy implementation is gaining wide support. Consequently, our strategic selection process examines the appropriateness of the current structure and the need for its modification *prior* to the specification of job requirements. Obviously, major reorganizations have direct impact on the nature of the jobs within them.[17] However, equally important are the "minor" modifications that contemporary organizations make to their structures through the creation of various "overlays" to facilitate integration and communication.

For example, as part of a strategy formulation process undertaken by the insurance division mentioned above, a large number of data processing and administrative projects were created within its operations department. As a result, the job of the vice president of operations changed dramatically from routine day-to-day responsibilities to project-oriented responsibilities. This, in turn, required greater group management, interpersonal influence, and large systems skills—in short, a very different capability mix than it did in the past.

It is easy to overlook the impact of job requirements of such changes, and doing so may underemphasize the importance of particular management skills (such as those mentioned), which are far more significant in these organizational arrangements than in the classical functional form.

As structures are changed or important task forces or committees are created to implement required work, it is important that the impact of these changes be reflected in a job's definition and in its skills requirements. In the forthcoming Step 3, these changes are documented so that they become a formal aspect of the job itself.

Step 3: Development of Role Descriptions for Each Key Job in the Structure

While the staffing of positions in stable circumstances focuses almost exclusively on vacant positions, staffing in the context of a change in business strategy involves an examination of the fit between *all* members of the executive team (and perhaps others as well) and the situational requirements of their jobs.

For example, in another financial services company, a change in strategy from a "me-too" marketer to an aggressive developer of new products totally changed every role on the senior management team. The vice president of marketing needed to behave more innovatively and aggressively; the vice president of operations needed to create a more flexible department by upgrading his technology and reorganizing the work; the investment function required much sharper management to produce the yields required for more aggressive pricing; and personnel, previously merely an administrative activity, became a critical component in the facilitation of the many changes required to support the new strategy.

Unfortunately, the notion that strategy may dramatically redefine existing jobs is often inconsistent with the de facto job tenure that exists inside many firms, a problem exacerbated by the retention of many of the same titles after a reorganization, despite altered strategy, structure, and positional requirements.

Our approach suggests the articulation of full role descriptions for each key position in the structure, with an emphasis on analyzing the *differences* between required managerial behavior in the context of the new strategy/structure and that of the old.[18] As a first-pass for this task, we suggest preparing descriptions for ideal candidates, rather than basing the descriptions on the incumbents (or readily available personnel). Adjustments, if appropriate, should be made later in the process when the tradeoffs can be seen in a fuller context.

Step 4: Assessment of Key Personnel

In the context of a change in strategy, structure, or both, the traditional matches between individuals and positions may no longer be appropriate. Our suggestion is to assess the management skills of each member of the management team but delay overlaying this information onto the job requirements that are created in Step 3. Rather, we ask senior management to compare managers' capabilities to one another on a dimension-by-dimension basis, so that the *relative* strengths and weaknesses of the members of the management team become clear.[19] The steps we suggest in the assessment process are as follows:

- Use the role description as a foundation, specify the knowledge, ability, and attitude areas that require assessment.
- Develop a plan to collect this information, based both on the individual being assessed and the organizational circumstances. Clearly, inside versus outside candidates, or better known candidates versus lesser known ones, will require different data collection approaches.

- Collect the required information using interviews, observations, and discussions with third parties; examination of tangible outputs, such as records, reports, and other documentation; assessment centers; and psychological tests, if appropriate.
- Synthesize this information into a narrative report covering each of the required areas.
- Reflect this information in dimension-by-dimension ratings on standardized dimensions for comparison purposes.

The output of this process is a set of comparative ratings among individuals for the entire set of critical areas. This output contrasts with that produced during the traditional selection process, which is typically a set of person-job comparisons. Comparative data are of considerably greater utility in optimizing the use of available staff in the matching process described below in Step 5.

Step 5: Matching Individuals with Positions

The objectives of the job/person matching processes are two-fold. First, we must try to match positional requirements with the skills and aspirations of individuals. This is known as traditional selection logic. Second, we must try to assess the quality of the *over-all team* produced by this one-at-a-time selection process. Often, it is some combination of job/person matching and "team balancing" that produces the most viable working organization.[20] The steps are as follows:

Identify the *feasible* positions for each candidate.

Evaluate each candidate's current capabilities against the job requirements of each feasible position. (This will create a matrix of candidates against jobs.)

Produce two sets of ranks: (1) a list of best candidates for each job; (2) a list of "best-fit" jobs for each candidate. Synthesize this information with any relevant data on individual preferences, organizational constraints, and career plans into a set of optimum matches (or matches and unfillable positions, if the assessment process identifies some major weaknesses).[21]

Step 6: Implementation

The complexity of implementing a change in strategy, structure, and staff obviously depends on the extent of the changes involved. It is important to recognize that the staffing decisions deriving from changes in strategy and structure are not routine replacements. Rather, they tend to induce a ripple effect—a wave of change stemming from the new orientation. Consequently, implementation may be a highly complex undertaking involving the orchestration of multiple structural changes, staffing replacements, and follow-up actions.

In this light, the following outline is offered as a simplified logic for the personnel and structural aspects of these changes. However, it is not intended to be a detailed road map, since each case is likely to be different and all cases are somewhat complex. The steps are:

Itemize the proposed staffing changes.

Develop a logical sequence of structural and staffing changes into an implementation timetable.

Formulate a plan to announce these changes in the most functional manner. Typically, individuals are informed before groups are, but all announcements should take place rapidly to avoid miscommunications and the "rumor mill."[22]

Formulate training/development plans and line-up consulting support for those areas in which individuals are weak relative to the requirements of their job. (Clearly, even the best matches will rarely fully meet all important criteria.)

Provide outplacement resources for any individuals relieved of responsibilities.

Communicate new responsibilities to individuals, possibly as part of a larger reorganization or planning exercise.

Develop a process for establishing "job contracts," performance objectives, and development plans between individuals and their supervisors.

Facilitate the provision of all needed educational and consulting resources to individuals and groups associated with new strategy/structure. (Identifying the need for resources at the time of a staffing change or confirmation usually produces less defensiveness than delaying this information until the first performance review.)

Identify specific steps to help build cohesion and clarify interdependencies within work groups that have had changes in roles or membership.

COMMENTS FROM THE FIELD

When strategies change and structures are modified, especially after a period of relative organizational stability, it is likely that it will be impossible to use all the pieces from the old puzzle to construct the new one, or to easily find all the pieces one needs. Let us discuss two areas of difficulty.

First, managers inevitably ask what trade-offs should be made, since it is unusual to find individuals with all the required skills for each job. Unfortunately, the only answer is: "It depends." Overall, linking staffing to strategy requires a good sense of which requirements are essential and which requirements are peripheral to performance in each role. Furthermore, one must know how important each role is to the functioning of the total structure. This "systems perspective" on the staffing question is in sharp contrast to traditional approaches, which often view the importance of a job solely as a function of its level and managerial skills as largely undifferentiated.

In dealing with essential skills and key roles, we feel that training the manager who has potential to grow is better than trying to compensate for his or her weaknesses.[23] However, strategies often fail and structures collapse because of inadequate skills. Thus, we feel that management should be acutely sensitive to the need for individuals with the proper skills in critical positions, and they should make careful assessments of development potential and training requirements prior to final staffing decisions.

Second, despite their participation in extensive discussions of strategy, organization, design, and staffing, we have found that a number of executives are still unprepared for the *human consequences* of major organization change. Our suggestion, drawn from some very unfortunate incidents, is that it is usually safer to assume that strategic change will involve a certain measure of human suffering than to assume that it will be a painless, purely rational exercise. With this assumption, it is less likely that one will "undermanage" the human side of a strategic reorganization or the staffing changes that inevitably accompany it.[24]

CONCLUSION

The major shift in management thinking underlying the selection system described in this article is not in the specifics of the selection methodology, per se, but in the increased attention paid to the *link* between strategy, organization design, and selection. As business strategy becomes explicit, and as the organizational structures and managerial behaviors necessary to support this strategy become better clarified, the need to align the staffing process with these parameters becomes almost obvious.

On the other hand, a selection decision, like any other business decision, should primarily be guided by an assessment of the risks and rewards. In the general case we have been discussing, the rewards obviously stem from the ability of selected personnel to successfully implement the chosen strategy. Unfortunately, the risks are somewhat harder to assess: Will the strategy fail without the right person in this particular job? What are the strategic costs of a suboptimal candidate? What are the "disruptions costs" resulting from the removal of an incumbent? If one takes three days instead of one making a staffing decision, invests $50,000 in a new selection system, or removes a questionable candidate instead of leaving him in place, what difference will it make to the company's overall results?

Unfortunately, at this time there is very little basis on which to answer these questions. However, we do know that most executives believe that the business conditions of the '80s demand that their companies be both lean and highly effective.

It follows, therefore, that increased attention paid to the link between strategy and selection will be well worthwhile.

APPENDIX 1: THE DIMENSIONS OF SENIOR MANAGEMENT EFFECTIVENESS

Problem Solving

Problem Identification and Analysis (Diagnosis). Recognizing the existence of significant problems—both inside and outside the enterprise—through one's perceptual, analytical, and conceptual abilities; always looking beyond the symptoms to uncover root causes; collecting and analyzing all relevant data to ensure accurate, comprehensive problem diagnoses; developing explicit alternative solutions to problems; examining the implications of each solution.

Solution Implementation. Making, or ensuring the making of, effective and timely decisions to deal with problems; making wise choices even when data are limited; willingness to make decisions on "tough" problems, i.e., problems whose solutions may produce unpleasant personal, interpersonal, or organizational consequences.

Developing practical plans to implement alternatives chosen in the problem-solving process, including the involvement of people and units affected, the delegation of specific assignments, the setting of target dates, the establishment of follow-up mechanisms, and the evaluation of results.

Administration

Execution and Control. Keeping routine activities focused on relevant objectives; directing, monitoring, and redirecting specific work assignments to accomplish objectives.

Communication with Peers, Subordinates, Superiors, and Others. Having the ability to communicate effectively through the use of written material, formal presentations, and verbal interchange, including "listening skills"; possessing a familiarity with all commonly used industrial communications media; choosing the optimum media mix to communicate the desired message within acceptable time and cost constraints; organizing the communication's content to deliver the intended message; keeping relevant persons informed in a timely manner using the appropriate communications vehicles.

Delegation. Allocating sufficient authority and resources to subordinates to enable them to make significant decisions within their areas of responsibility, considering the limits of the subordinates' abilities and the requirements of the work to be done; structuring specific work assignments in a clear, concise manner, while maintaining sufficient room for individual initiative; providing mechanisms to ensure cooperation in delegated assignments of necessary individuals and functions outside one's own; establishing follow-up and control processes that facilitate task accomplishment and the initiation of timely corrective action; having the ability to work with subordinates who are clearly expert in their fields without being either overly deferential or directive.

Crisis Management

Correctly recognizing a crisis situation at the earliest indication of a clear and present danger; identifying the need for specific information/expertise and obtaining these resources within demanding time constraints; making wise decisions under conditions of limited information and significant stress; having the ability to perform competent technical/analytical work under time constraints and emotional pressure; supporting others for extended time periods in a crisis environment.

Negotiation Skills

Demonstrating good judgment in identifying situations requiring negotiation, in contrast to circumstances requiring problem solving; accurately perceiving one's "opponents" fundamental bargaining demands; persuading the other party to relinquish secondary demands or, in the extreme, to accept much less than they wanted, while maintaining positive relationships; having the ability to satisfy one's own interests while considering the needs of the other negotiating party (i.e., "always leaving something on the table").

Human Resource Management

Integrated Approach. Recognizing human resource management as an integrated process involving multiple activities (organization design, job specification, manpower, planning, recruitment, selection, joining-up, performance feedback, transfer and promotion, management development, and reward/compensation practices); committing one's own time and appropriate resources to the achievement of professional human resource practices within one's own area of responsibility.

Staffing. Accurately projecting one's department's requirements for all critical types of manpower over relevant time horizons; articulating the job requirements of subordinates' positions in explicit, concrete terms; possessing a sensitivity to the personality types and management styles that are compatible with the dominant organizational and work group cultures; being able to recruit, select, and integrate subordinates who are technically, managerially, and interpersonally competent; removing nonperforming individuals from positions in a timely and humane manner.

Development of Subordinates. Ensuring the identification of subordinates' development needs in the context of current and potential future jobs; ensuring the formulation of realistic development plans and timetables; monitoring the implementation of development activities within the department; assessing the impact of development programs on departmental results and relationships; demonstrating the importance of subordinate development by devoting one's own time, departmental personnel, and financial resources to development activities in face of competing pressures.

Strategy Formulation

Accurately identifying the aspects of the external and internal environments that will exert significant impact on the business unit's future effectiveness and efficiency; establishing mechanisms to monitor the critical indicators within each identified area; formulating strategies and contingency plans to effectively deal with significant opportunities and critical anticipated problems; establishing mechanisms to ensure the timely implementation of formulated strategies and plans; creating a climate that encourages identification between individual managers and the business unit's strategy.

Openness to Innovation and Change

Desire and willingness to learn; willingness to change established strategies, policies, and practices in order to improve the effectiveness and efficiency of the enterprise; willingness to experiment, coupled with creativity in both the technical and managerial aspects of the business.

Organizational Leadership

Interpersonal Empathy and Influence. Recognizing the impact of one's own behavior on others; being sensitive to the moods, feelings, and motivations of others; having the ability to project to subordinates and outsiders an image of company and departmental goals in a way that evokes understanding and commitment; encouraging effective behavior in others through the use of feedback, clarification, logic, and persuasion; possessing a sufficient "behavioral repertoire" to achieve desired results with relevant people in varied situations.

Group Management Skills. Understanding the appropriate circumstances for the use of groups in contrast to individual work assignments; clearly establishing the agenda and objectives to be accomplished in groups; displaying good judgment in the selection of participants, time allocation, and settings; identifying required pre-work and ensuring its completion; conducting group discussions to maintain both participation and task focus; demonstrating good judgment in dealing with non-agenda items; bringing closure to meetings in a manner that reviews the results achieved and identifies any next steps to be undertaken; ensuring the documentation of outcomes in a managerially useful form.

Large System "Savoir-faire." Building a robust, informal network to augment formal communication channels; recognizing where to go to get things done outside one's own department; recognizing the need to involve persons, functions, and units outside one's own to achieve departmental objectives; recognizing complex functional and temporal interdependencies; having the ability to effectively deal with political realities; having the ability to see the total organization with an integrated perspective (i.e., to "see the big picture from a helicopter").

Self-motivation. Working hard to achieve excellence in one's own and departmental work; being comfortable with the use of power in the accomplishment of legitimate organizational purposes; choosing accomplishment-oriented goals over affiliate ones in the face of goal conflict; possessing a strong survival instinct.

Emotional Strength and Maturity. Resisting short-term and sustained stress; tolerating adversity with a realistic but optimistic outlook for the future; being able to live with the personal consequences of difficult decisions.

Personal Integrity. Evoking trust in others by being appropriately open about contentious issues and one's own feelings; making decisions that are effective rather than politically expedient; being trustworthy with sensitive information; being consistent in one's behavior toward others in the organization as well as being consistent between what one says and what one does; selectively violating a commitment, if conditions necessitate, to maintain the highest internalized values and standards.

General Management Knowledge

Knowing those areas of content knowledge that a top executive should know, such as economics, financial management, marketing, corporate law, labor relations, information systems, behavioral science and organizational development, governmental dynamics affecting the business, and the technical specifics most salient to one's own business.

APPENDIX 2: EXAMPLE INTERVIEW QUESTIONS TO ASSESS SENIOR MANAGEMENT EFFECTIVENESS

I. Problem Identification and Analysis

Scenario: Tell me what has been the most perplexing problem for you over the last two years.

1. When did you first become aware of the problem?
2. What were the origins of the situation?
3. What were the most visible manifestations of the problem? What attracted your attention?
4. How did your understanding of the problem evolve as you dug into it?
5. At what point did you feel you really understood the problem and its causes?
6. At what point were you most perplexed about what to do?
7. What was the dilemma?

Scenario: Sometimes things don't work out as we planned, or the information isn't available, or we just plain blew it. Tell me about the most serious error you've made in sizing up a situation in the past two years.

1. What was the reason for the error?
2. When did you realize you had made a mistake?
3. What did you do to cope with that situation?
4. What could you have done differently?

Scenario: Tell me about the best problem solving you have done, taking me step by step through the entire process from the initial "felt need" through the final result.

II. Solution Implementation

Scenario: Some problems are difficult to analyze, but once you know the causes of the problem, it is easy to do something about it; others are vice versa. Give me an example of a problem which you knew the causes and solution for, but for which it was still very difficult to implement the solution.

1. What did you do?

2. How did you plan to implement the solution?

3. How did you try to get support?

4. What obstacles did you encounter, and how did you deal with them?

Scenario: Tell me about the time when your timing in a decision or action was far from optimal.

1. What led to the poor timing? Why?

2. What were the consequences to you?

Scenario: Tell me about the decision you've been most ambivalent about in the past two years.

1. Why were you uncertain? What were the tradeoffs?

2. How did you go about deciding what to do?

3. What did you say to the affected parties?

4. From which party did you get the most anger, resistance, and withdrawal?

Scenario: Tell me about the last high-risk, high-judgment decision you have made that had implications for several areas of the business and how you went about implementing it.

1. Did you call a meeting? With whom?

2. Did you issue a memo?

3. How did you specify the involvement of people and units involved?

4. How did you assure follow-up?

5. What was the process you established for evaluating the results of your decision?

REFERENCES

1. See T. Levitt, "The Managerial Merry-Go-Round," *Harvard Business Review*, July–August 1974.

2. See *Business Week*, 25 February 1980.

3. It should be noted that the selection system is but one component of an overall executive human resource management system. For an overview of a total system, see E. H. Schein, *Career Dynamics: Matching Individual and Organizational Needs* (Reading, MA: Addison-Wesley, 1978), pp. 189–199.

4. A small number of corporations employ selection methods that are as comprehensive as the one presented here. However, these systems were not found to be the norm in our investigations.

5. We estimate that it takes a skilled professional approximately one day to interview an executive and to document his or her job. If the responsibilities are unclear or undergoing change, the documentation process will take longer.

6. The alternative view that performance in a position stems from the degree of "fit" between a job's requirements and an incumbent's abilities logically suggests that jobs be evaluated as well as people in making assessment decisions. Without job analysis and comparison, results, either positive or negative, cannot be placed in proper context.

7. The perspective that the selection process focuses on the filling of a job at a given point in time is taken here. For a view of job evolution over a longer time frame, see Schein (1978), pp. 203–206.

8. See, for example, C. Hofer and D. Schendel, *Strategy Formulation: Analytical Concepts* (St. Paul, MN: West Publishing, 1978).

9. We have developed similar requirements for other key roles, such as vice president of operations, vice president of marketing, and vice president of human resources.

10. Job documentation and job contracting serve as linkages between the selection and performance appraisal processes in the larger human resource system.

11. PDI assesses approximately 1,000 managers annually for selection purposes. See, for example, J. P. Campbell et al., *Managerial Behavior, Performance, and Effectiveness* (New York: McGraw-Hill, 1970); J. P. Kotter, *The General Managers* (New York: Free Press, 1982). The executives interviewed were drawn from a number of industries, including financial services, manufacturing, retailing, and chemicals.

12. For a description of behavior observation scaling methodology, see M. D. Dunnette, "Aptitudes, Abilities, and Skills," in *Handbook of Industrial and Organizational Psychology* (New York: Rand McNally, 1976), pp. 490–514.

13. The authors would like to thank Henri Tremblay and the senior executives of Steinberg, Inc., Montreal, Canada, for their support of our work on executive selection.

14. Behavioral interviewing is described in J. L. Janz, "Effective Interviewing via the Behavioral Route: The Behavior Description Interview" (Simon Fraser University, School of Business Administration and Economics Discussion Series 81-05-02, 1981).

15. For a thorough review of the assessment center approach, see: R. B. Finkle, "Managerial Assessment Centers," in *Handbook of Industrial and Organizational Psychology,* M. D. Dunnette (New York: Rand McNally, 1976), pp. 861–888; D. W. Bray and D. E. Grant, "The Assessment Center in the Measurement of Potential Business Management," *Psychological Monographs,* 1966.

16. Shorter simulation sessions can be designed to deal with specific assessment requirements, but these shorter sessions may lack the multiexercise and multiassessor evaluations that contribute to the assessment center's high validity.

17. For example, the movement from a functional to a matrix or a product organization, or the replacement of an international division by a worldwide business structure creates tremendous changes in the jobs of most of the key positions in the top several levels of management.

18. In selecting the CEO or general manager, or in replacing a single individual on the management team, it may not be necessary to analyze the entire management team. This is a matter of judgment. In general, however, when the strategy changes markedly, we prefer to review the whole management group.

19. There are psychometric reasons for this process. Dimension-by-dimension comparisons will tend to highlight skills differences among members of the management team, while rating a single candidate for all dimensions tends to obscure them.

20. We have developed a number of tools to facilitate this process. Fundamentally, the purpose of these tools is to help senior management handle the large amount of information generated in the staffing process. Unfortunately, such tools cannot eliminate the hard judgments that must still be made.

21. The selection process must dovetail the organization's manpower/career planning activities. The concrete point of integration, of course, is the actual selection decision.

22. Circumstances often necessitate the implementation of structural and staffing changes on a phased basis. Unfortunately, protracted changes almost always create difficulties and suboptimal organizational performance as individuals "wait for the other shoe to drop."

23. The process outlined in this article will provide a clear picture of the "development gap" between an individual's current capabilities and those required in particular positions. This can provide vital input to a short-term development planning activity, thus linking the selection and development processes within the human resource system. Compensation for a manager's weaknesses may take a variety of forms including hiring assistants or subordinates, contracting for outside consultants, or "filling in" by the boss. Most important for success, however, is recognition by the incumbent that something important is lacking and must be provided by some means.

24. One tendency, often couched as "consideration," is to delay staffing changes until an incumbent's inability to handle the new circumstances has resulted in a substantial deterioration in performance. While the other extreme (making snap judgments) is an equally serious mistake, a third option is preferable. One can negotiate fairly explicit expectations, often called a "psychological contract," with incumbents so that they know in concrete terms what is expected. In addition, one can provide them with some additional resources during the early days of the transition to the new strategy, so that they need not "go it alone."

CHAPTER 4

Performance Appraisal

After recruiting and hiring employees, the organization needs to evaluate their performance and give them feedback about how well they are doing. Concerns about productivity have heightened interest in performance appraisal as a control mechanism that can, if properly used, constructively influence future work performance. Furthermore, recent legislation has forced a more careful examination of performance appraisal and the feedback that is given in support of internal administrative or termination decisions.

Historically, approaches to solving problems in performance appraisal focused on issues of instrumentation or scale development and procedures. It was hoped that these techniques would lead to better results. More recently there has been a shift away from the technical issues to an emphasis on process issues or the dynamics of the supervisor-subordinate relationship in the work setting. The focus on process, as well as concerns with ensuring procedural justice, have encouraged the incorporation of self-appraisals along with supervisor appraisals of the subordinate's performance. This additional information frequently serves to enhance perceptions of fairness on the part of the subordinate and to increase the validity of the resulting evaluations. Such shared feedback on past performance also helps with the establishment of shared goals for the future.

In the first article, Rice focuses on several problems that have plagued performance appraisals and then presents ways to overcome them as well as circumvent them in later encounters. One problem with performance appraisals—managers who do not consider them a legitimate part of their jobs—is the theme of the next article by Schneier, Beatty, and Baird, who offer suggestions for getting managers to accept their appraisal responsibilities. The authors discuss the important role that performance appraisals play in human resources development (HRD).

Next, Fedor takes a look at feedback in the appraisal process. He explains that there is no simple formula for providing feedback because it is open to many inappropriate interpretations by both the sender and the receiver. Many of its benefits and pitfalls are reviewed.

A fair performance appraisal system is the subject of the next article, by Ferris and Gilmore. To have a fair appraisal system, the authors suggest that care must be taken to identify the true causes of fluctuating performance as well as ways to fashion a fair performance appraisal system.

Bernardin and Klatt compare the current appraisal procedures used by companies to what researchers in the field have found valuable. Few managers include the latest research characteristics in their appraisal systems, even though they may view them as important. Small firms are even less likely to do so than larger firms.

Klasson, Thompson, and Luben highlight the legal aspects of performance appraisal in the last article. They discuss how the courts' broadened interpretation of Title VII of the Civil Rights Act of 1964 has brought performance appraisal systems under closer scrutiny. The authors then provide a useful review of representative legislation and make recommendations for ensuring the defensibility of a performance appraisal system.

Suggestions for Further Reading

Bateman, T. S., Ferris, G. R., & Strasser, S. (1984). The "why" behind individual work performance. *Management Review, 73,* 69–72.

Beer, M. (1981). Performance appraisal: Dilemmas and possibilities. *Organizational Dynamics, 9,* 24–36.

Cascio, W. F., & Bernardin, H. J. (1981). Implications of performance appraisal litigation for personnel decisions. *Personnel Psychology, 34,* 211–226.

Cederblom, D. (1982). The performance appraisal interview: A review, implications, and suggestions. *Academy of Management Review, 7,* 219–227.

Fombrun, C. J., & Laud, R. L. (1983). Strategic issues in performance appraisal: Theory and practice. *Personnel, 60,* 23–31.

Harper, S. C. (1986). Adding purpose to performance reviews. *Training and Development Journal, 40,* 53–55.

Kirkpatrick, D. L. (1986). Performance appraisal: When two jobs are too many. *Training, 23,* 67–69.

Latham, G. P. (1984). The appraisal system as a strategic control. In C. J. Fombrun, N. M. Tichy, & M. A. Devanna (Eds.), *Strategic human resource management* (pp. 11–126). New York: Wiley.

Sashkin, M. (1981). Appraising appraisal: Ten lessons from research to practice. *Organizational Dynamics, 9,* 37–50.

Walther, F., & Taylor, S. (1983). An active feedback program can spark performance. *Personnel Administrator, 28,* 107–111, 147–149.

Performance Review: The Job Nobody Likes

Berkeley Rice

A common criticism is that it creates a kind of parent-child relationship between boss and employee. *Industry Week* calls it "a periodic agony thrust on both bosses and subordinates." A personnel administration expert laments, "Probably fewer than 10 percent of the nation's companies have systems that are reasonably good."

The focus of all this concern is the methods used to assess how well workers do their jobs. Personnel experts aren't the only ones dissatisfied with such procedures, known as performance review, evaluation, appraisal or rating. Supervisors and workers are unhappy too.

One reason for the general dissatisfaction with such systems is a lack of agreement on their purpose. Should they merely evaluate performance, or critique and improve it as well? Should they be used primarily to determine salaries and prospects for promotion, or as a means of training and career development? Should they focus on how an employee does the job or the results achieved? Just who are they supposed to help, the employee or the supervisor? No performance-review system can accomplish all these goals, but confusion about conflicting purposes often undermines attempts at effective evaluation.

Many employees complain that the forms and procedures used invite unfair evaluations. They are often based on personality traits or vague qualities such as reliability, initiative or leadership—factors difficult to measure objectively. Many standardized appraisal forms also use criteria that are not relevant to the job under review. Others provide a quick and superficial checklist that leaves no room for individual evaluation. Too often, one-sided performance reviews put employees on the defensive, particularly when they turn into lectures or harangues that end with the boss commenting on "how great it's been to have this open exchange of views."

It might surprise employees who feel threatened by performance reviews to learn that many bosses find them equally burdensome. They, too, grumble about the irrelevance of standardized review forms and the vague criteria. They complain that reviews require piles of paperwork, don't leave room for individual judgment and don't lead to improved performance.

Many managers feel they need more training in how to conduct reviews, but few companies offer any help. Robert Lefton, president of Psychological Associates, a firm that conducts such training sessions, describes performance review as a tough job, "the equivalent of walking up to a person and saying, 'Here's what I think of your baby.' It requires knowing how to handle fear and anger and a gamut of other emotions which a lot of managers aren't comfortable with."

If you wonder why evaluating an employee's performance can be so difficult, consider a simpler appraisal: one made by the barroom fan who concludes that his team's quarterback is a bum because several of his passes have been intercepted. An objective appraisal would raise the following questions: Were the passes really that bad or did the receivers run the wrong patterns? Did the offensive line give the quarterback adequate protection? Did he call those plays himself, or were they sent in by the coach? Was the quarterback recovering from an injury?

And what about the fan? Has he ever played football himself? How good is his vision? Did he have a good view of the TV set through the barroom's smoky haze? Was he talking to his friends at the bar during the game? How many beers did he down during the game?

Compared with barroom appraisals, evaluating performance at work is far more complex. Because evaluation is both difficult and important, it has grown into one of the busiest fields in industrial psychology. Since 1950, more than 300 studies have appeared in academic and management journals. Most of them, until quite recently, focused on the rating format used and on the biasing effect of various nonperformance factors such as race and sex. These latter concerns were spurred by the federal government's Equal Employment Opportunity guidelines, issued in 1969 and 1970.

No consistent pattern of sexual bias has emerged from the research. For example, Michigan State University psychologist Kenneth N. Wexley and a colleague studied nearly 300 manager-subordinate pairs in several companies and uncovered no evidence of sexual bias in the ratings. Research by psychologist Laurence H. Peters of Southern Illinois University found a similar lack of sexual bias in supervisors' reviews of retail-store managers. When psychologist William H. Mobley studied more than 1,000 employees at another company, he found that women generally received higher ratings than did men, regardless of the supervisors' sex.

Occupational sex stereotypes are a different story. Laboratory studies of women working at traditionally masculine jobs show that they usually receive lower ratings than do men of comparable ability in the same jobs. (This effect may lessen as more women enter managerial and other "male" domains.) On the other hand, women in traditionally feminine occupations, such as clerical work, don't seem to benefit from a compensating bias in their favor.

Studies of racial bias have revealed a consistent pattern: White supervisors tend to give higher ratings to white subordinates, while black supervisors favor blacks. A study by psychologist W. C. Hamner and three colleagues found evidence of another, more subtle form of discrimination: White supervisors were more likely to differentiate between high and low levels of performance among individual whites than they did among individual blacks, whom they generally rated close to average on a performance scale.

Some critics of performance reviews suggest that ratings by supervisors may be less accurate than those by fellow workers or subordinates or even self-appraisals by the employees themselves. Several studies have shown that supervisors tend to give tougher evaluations than do fellow workers, while the fellow workers' ratings generally show greater consistency among several raters.

In a study of self-evaluation among job applicants, psychologist Cathy D. Anderson and others at the Colorado State Department of Personnel asked 350 men and women to rate their ability on a variety of job-related tasks. The list included several bogus skills, such as "matrixing solvency files," "planning basic entropy programs" and "resolving disputes by isometric analysis." Nearly half the applicants for what were mostly clerical jobs claimed they had experience with one or more of the nonexistent tasks. Among those who took a typing test, few achieved the speed they claimed, leading researchers to conclude that "inflation bias" in the self-appraisals was "prevalent and pervasive."

Several studies of actual and simulated work conditions have indicated that an employee's attitude and experience can affect the validity of a supervisor's ratings. In a field study, psychologists Ronald Grey and David Kipnis found that supervisors gave "compliant" workers higher ratings when the workers were surrounded by "noncompliant" peers and lower ratings when coworkers were more amenable. An early review by psychologists Rutledge Jay and James Copes of 47 studies showed that employees who had held their jobs longer, particularly in managerial jobs, usually got higher ratings than did peers of equal ability.

The appraisal method itself has received considerable attention from researchers. By far the most widely used format is still the traditional numerical or graphic rating scale. For each trait or skill being evaluated, the scale may be marked simply by numbers, say from 1 to 10, or by such vague adjectives as "unsatisfactory, below average, average, above average, outstanding."

In an attempt to improve the reliability of ratings, several researchers have experimented with varying the number of rating categories. The results indicate that consistency among raters drops significantly when there are less than 4 or more than 10 categories. Five to nine categories seem to produce the most consistent ratings.

Whether these ratings represent accurate measures of performance is another matter. According to industrial psychologist Robert Guion, editor of the *Journal of Applied Psychology,* "You get fairly valid ratings when you look mainly for the extremes of outstanding or very poor performance. But when you look closely at the middle or average range, distinctions among people are less accurate and valid."

That middle range, of course, is where most ratings fall, for several reasons. One is a manager's natural reluctance to cause pain by giving low ratings to poor performers. When supervisors know their subordinates will see the ratings, as they do in most systems, or that they will have to confront them with the ratings in a feedback session, they tend to be more lenient. This is perfectly human, but it doesn't lead to valid appraisals. Another factor may be what psychologists call "central tendency error," the fact that we tend to avoid the extremes when we rate almost anything. Then there's the problem of personal standards that lead tenderhearted managers to give consistently high ratings while "tough guys" rate consistently low. Both tendencies cause inequities when the reviews determine salary increases or promotions.

Some companies try to head off these errors with forced distribution systems that set minimums or maximums for the percentage of ratings in each category; for example, no more than 10 percent of one's subordinates can be rated outstanding, no more than 50 percent rated average. Many supervisors and psychologists object to such arbitrary limits, arguing that no one really knows what the distribution curve for such ratings should be.

Another common source of rating error is the "halo effect" whereby people who are generally well liked get favorable ratings on all categories. Bad chemistry between a subordinate and supervisor can have the opposite effect and produce unfairly low ratings. In both cases, ratings end up based on general impressions of the employee as a person rather than on specific aspects of performance.

Because of growing dissatisfaction with traditional ratings scales, and the search for more objective appraisal methods, many companies have adopted some form of "behaviorally anchored" rating scales (BARS). This development is based on the work of psychologists Patricia Cain Smith and Lorne Kendall, using John Flanagan's theory of critical incidents.

To create a BARS scale, companies first conduct a formal job analysis to determine what kinds of behavior constitute degrees of adequate performance for specific tasks in each job. They then use these behavioral descriptions to define or "anchor" the ratings on the scale. For example, for an item such as "perseverance," a BARS scale might offer choices ranging from "Keeps working on difficult tasks until job is completed" to "Likely to stop work on a hard job at the first sign of difficulty."

While the job analyses used to develop BARS scales are often conducted by outside consultants, many industrial psychologists feel that participation by the employees and their supervisors leads to more realistic performance expectations. Their involvement in the process should increase their awareness of what good work behavior is and thereby improve their performance.

While advocates of BARS, particularly the consultants who do a thriving business with it, claim it's a great leap forward, critics point to several drawbacks. The lengthy job analyses and complex scale construction require a major investment of a company's time and money. A scale designed for use in one department may not apply in another. In fact, separate scales may be necessary for each job category within the same department, since the requirements for good performance may differ markedly.

Comparative studies have found that the BARS method, because of its behavioral specificity, results in greater reliability than do traditional rating scales, and that it may reduce leniency, halo effects and central tendency error. But the improvements may be too slight to justify the time and money required. In addition, while BARS scales are suitable for jobs such as production or clerical work, they are harder to devise for managerial positions in which performance cannot easily be reduced to specific kinds of observable behavior. In such jobs, complex judgment, not easily reduced to a 6-point scale, may be more important than measurable behavior.

For managerial and supervisory jobs, many companies have adopted another form of evaluation, "management by objectives" (MBO), which focuses on results rather than behavior. MBO was proposed in the 1950s by psychologist Douglas McGregor. As customarily practiced today, supervisors and their subordinates sit down at the beginning of each year, or every six months, and agree (often in writing) on specific goals to be accomplished. At the end of the period, the supervisors evaluate their subordinates in terms of how well they have met those objectives.

MBO became popular because, in theory, it can be tailored to each individual job and because it lets subordinates know how their performance will be measured and gives them specific, mutually-agreed-on goals.

In practice, however, MBO appraisals are just as open to claims of unfairness as other systems of performance review are. One major weakness is the difficulty of setting reasonable goals well in advance, when they may be vulnerable to factors outside the employee's control, such as economic conditions, labor problems and price increases. Beyond that, the method's very individuality makes it difficult to compare one subordinate's performance with another's—one ostensible purpose of performance review. For these reasons, use of MBO has declined in recent years.

Frank J. Landy, a psychologist at Pennsylvania State University, reviews performance appraisal studies for the *Journal of Applied Psychology.* He has grown discouraged by the numerous attempts to build a better mousetrap by experimenting with rating scales or sources of bias. Even when those attempts reduce error, he says, the improvements are often so small that they're merely cosmetic.

"After more than 30 years of serious research," Landy wrote, "it seems that little progress has been made in developing an efficient and psychometrically sound alternative to the traditional graphic rating scale. . . . One major conclusion to be drawn from this research is that there is no 'easy way' to get accurate and informative performance data. Methods that aim toward easing the pain for managers who are busy will pay a price in terms of accuracy and value of the information obtained."

Faced with generally meager results from earlier studies, some researchers are turning to cognitive psychology in the hope of better understanding the processes of observation, information storage, retrieval, classification and communication that supervisors use, or should use, in performance evaluation. They suspect that perceptual and cognitive differences among raters may affect their ratings as much as or more than the nature of the rating scale itself and may be impervious to any changes in the evaluation system or the structure of the rating scale.

Many cognitive researchers point to the work of University of Washington psychologist Elizabeth Loftus and others who have demonstrated the fallibility of human observation and memory in studies of eyewitness testimony. Using videotapes of accidents and other incidents, those studies reveal the unconscious tendency of witnesses to "reconstruct" events based on cognitive biases, stereotypes and other unrelated information. If witnesses make all these mistakes on the comparatively simple task of recalling a few details about something that might have happened only a few hours or days before, imagine how difficult it is for a manager to evaluate the work of many subordinates over a period of six months or a year. Like witnesses at a busy intersection, managers often must base their judgments on only fragmentary evidence. It's understandable that unconscious mental habits play a vital part in their evaluations.

In his review of research on the cognitive processes involved in performance appraisal, Jack Feldman, a professor of management at the University of Texas at Arlington, showed that once a rater puts someone in a category, the category filters and colors the rater's observation and recall of that person's behavior. Supervisors thus attend chiefly to behavior that confirms the stereotype they have developed and ignore or forget behavior that conflicts with it. An admired employee whose performance declines may still receive excellent evaluations while another employee, who makes a serious effort to improve, may be condemned by a previous reputation.

When the time comes for evaluation, if the supervisor cannot recall any specific information relevant to a category on the rating form, he or she may unconsciously invent imaginary examples of "appropriate" behavior based on the stereotype.

Advice for Managers

However imperfect, performance reviews will continue to be required of most managers. Fortunately, along with all the criticism and research, there is also plenty of advice around on how to conduct them. The current edition of *Books in Print* lists more than 50 titles devoted to performance review or appraisal, and journals frequently publish articles on the subject. While not all of the advice is useful for every manager, much of it can be adapted to individual needs:

- Know precisely what you want to achieve (and what company policy says you should achieve) with your performance reviews, such as determining raises, evaluation, criticism, training or morale-building.
- Don't wait until the review itself to let your staff know what you expect. Let them know early on exactly what the job requires, what specific goals, standards and deadlines you expect them to meet and how you plan to evaluate and reward their performance.
- Keep a record of subordinates' performance so that you can cite specific examples to back up any criticisms or comments.
- Listen. Numerous surveys of employee attitudes reveal the feeling that "management doesn't care what we think." The review is your chance to get valuable feedback from your own subordinates about their jobs or company policy.
- Ask fact-finding questions to get employees to recall instances in which they performed well or poorly. See if they have a realistic estimate of their abilities.
- Go over your written evaluation with each employee. Find out if they feel your ratings are fair. They don't have to agree with you completely, but strong disagreements will lessen their motivation to improve.
- Focus steadily on each individual's performance. Show that you care about that person's career. Otherwise it looks like you're just going through the motions, and employees will get the message that the review, and perhaps their performance, doesn't really matter.
- When critiquing an employee's performance, do some stroking: Reinforce the good habits with praise.
- Be specific and constructive in your criticism. Don't just tell employees they're not "aggressive enough." Point out how they can improve, with specific examples.
- Critique the behavior, not the employee. Keep the discussion on a professional level.
- Be fair, but don't be afraid to give honest criticism when necessary. Most employees don't want a meaningless pat on the back. They want to know where they stand and how they can improve.
- Don't play the role of therapist. If personal problems are affecting an employee's performance, be supportive, but be careful about getting involved. Suggest outside professional help if necessary.
- Explain how the employee's performance in meeting goals contributes to department or corporate objectives. In this way, the review can help build morale and loyalty.
- Don't wait till the next performance review to follow up. Use informal progress reports or mini-reviews to help spot problems before they become serious.
- Use the occasion to get an informal review of your own performance. Encourage your staff to tell you about any of your habits that make their work difficult or to suggest changes you could make that would help them to do their jobs better.

According to Feldman, these false memories are particularly likely when a supervisor has many subordinates to evaluate and little time or opportunity to observe them on the job.

This kind of categorical information processing is influenced not only by such obvious factors as age, sex, race and attractiveness but also by stereotypes about jobs. Thus some managers may evaluate the performance of all salespeople by how well they fit the traditional image of the fast-talking, aggressive go-getter and all bookkeepers by the image of the cautious, meticulous grind, whether or not these qualities apply to the particular job.

Personality or cultural conflicts can also create problems. Feldman cites the example of employees who act in what they feel is a friendly manner toward their boss, only to find that the boss considers it disrespectful. When review time rolls around, such employees may be shocked to find they have been labeled "insubordinate."

According to H. John Bernardin, professor of management at Florida Atlantic University, another type of error in performance reviews can be explained by attribution theory, which deals with the inferences people make as to why they and others act as they do. Bernardin has found that workers doing poorly on a job will attempt to justify their performance by attributing it to such situational factors as lack of supplies, unpredictable or excessive work load, difficult coworkers and ambiguous assignments. A worker's supervisor, however, is likely to blame personal factors such as lack of ability or motivation.

In one study of middle-level managers, Bernardin found that most of them cited low ability or motivation for their employees' unsatisfactory performance. But when asked to explain poor reviews of their own work, only 20 percent saw such personal factors as the cause. Most cited factors "beyond their control."

While many cognitive researchers are excited about the prospect of applying their findings to performance review, others remain dubious, particularly about using the work to improve rater training. In a recent research review, Bernardin points out that of the 34 rater-training studies he examined, only three involved data from real evaluations of real work. "It is a sad commentary on our discipline," he writes, "that an obvious applied area like rater training should be studied almost exclusively with student raters in an experimental context. . . . There appears to be an increasing emphasis on methodologically sound, internally valid laboratory research, the results of which have added little to our understanding of performance appraisal beyond what we already know."

According to a survey Bernardin did of personnel administrators and supervisors, inaccuracy in performance ratings stems more from intentional distortion than from rating error. Inflated ratings are one example. In tough times, managers may inflate ratings to make sure their subordinates qualify for raises, to keep their departments from being cut or to keep valuable employees from seeking transfers. Central tendency error is another example. It may make good administrative sense to lump most of one's subordinates in the middle range, thereby avoiding invidious comparisons and perhaps heading off arguments with or between employees.

Kevin Murphy, a psychologist at Colorado State University who has done considerable cognitive research on performance evaluation, also questions its relevance in training managers to be better raters. "The real problem is not how well managers can evaluate performance, but how willing they are," he says. "The problem is one of motivation, not ability."

In addition, he says, companies should stop trying vainly to improve rating forms and instead train managers in skills that would make them better observers: gathering and recording supporting evidence; discriminating between relevant and irrelevant information; doing selective work sampling when direct observation is infrequent; and deciding which aspects of performance are really measurable.

The discovery of how cognitive processes affect performance review, Landy says, has shaken the world of management psychology. "Eight years ago we would have given plenty of prescriptive advice about how to do an accurate review," he says, "but most of it would have been wrong. The bad news is that there's simply no easy way to do performance review. As appealing as the notion of a precise method of appraisal is, it's never going to be possible to measure such complex behavior in any absolute way.

"The good news," Landy adds, "is that we've discovered that a lot of that stuff about rating scales and evaluation formats is really trivial. The particular format doesn't make much difference. There is no one 'right' way to do it. There are dozens of ways. You just use whichever method feels right for your company. It may not be very accurate, but the degree of error won't make much difference."

"There's no one system that works," says management psychologist David DeVries, who conducts research and teaches courses on performance appraisal to corporate executives at the Center for Creative Leadership in Greensboro, North Carolina. "What we try to do here," he explains, "is show what the options are and how the companies' own managers can generally design a system most appropriate for them."

DeVries believes strongly that most managers "are much more sophisticated than the researchers realize. I think they understand the appraisal process pretty well because they are the ones who have to live with the results.

"Take traits like integrity, initiative, optimism, energy and intelligence. Researchers today feel such traits shouldn't be used in performance reviews because they're highly subjective, and therefore psychometrically suspect. But in business, those traits are very important, subjective or not. Executives make personnel decisions based on them all the time. If they do, then those traits should be evaluated, and we researchers can't afford to ignore them."

DeVries argues that companies can try to control the level of subjectivity in an appraisal system even though they can't make it go away. Despite the drawbacks of performance appraisal, he insists, "it's important to reward your top performers, and to make it clear to the others why they're being rewarded. . . . A good performance-appraisal system can help managers do this. It must be taken seriously by the managers, by the employees and by the company. It must be the basis for deciding who gets ahead and who doesn't."

Creating a Performance Management System

Craig Eric Schneier
Richard W. Beatty
Lloyd S. Baird

In "Why Performance Appraisal Fails," part one of this two-part series (*Journal,* April 1986), the real problems in performance appraisal systems were linked to the following: little agreement on what aspects of performance to measure; the unrealistic expectation that measures be objective and quantifiable; standards that ignore those personal characteristics and individual behaviors that de-

Reprinted from *Training and Development Journal, 40,* pp. 74–79 by permission of Craig Eric Schneier.

termine success; and the failure to use the results of appraisals as a basis of training, compensation, promotion, and other key HRD decisions.

Perhaps the most glaring performance appraisal system fault, however, is that most systems simply do not recognize the realities of managerial work and of organizational culture. Thus, performance appraisal systems are viewed as external to managers' legitimate tasks and responsibilities.

However, HRD specialists do not ignore such problems. User understanding, ownership, and commitment are understood, and performance appraisal systems are designed with an eye toward simplicity and practicality. Review panels comprising line managers are formed to demonstrate that the system belongs to the users. Senior management is persuaded to write memoranda and state publicly that performance appraisal is vital to the organization's success. While these are reasonable, useful strategies, they do not ensure that performance appraisal systems are fully integrated with managerial work.

Managers complain about the time and effort required to write performance objectives, complete appraisal forms, document performance problems, and hold formal performance feedback sessions. Why shouldn't they complain? After all, do managers get promoted because they complete subordinates' appraisal forms on time? They realize they get promoted because they manage subordinates' performance effectively and achieve desired results. Few managers disagree with this basic notion—their job is to manage the performance of their subordinates. They admit that they hold performance expectations for their subordinates, monitor performance, let subordinates know when they have erred, form overall evaluations of each subordinate, and recommend that various actions be taken as a result of their evaluations. In short, they, with varying degrees of skill, perform key performance appraisal tasks and activities routinely as they carry out their responsibilities.

It is the view that performance appraisal lies outside of these activities that renders it less than useful to managers. Those activities managers already see as legitimate can be termed performance management. By providing managers with a performance management perspective, by detailing a set of sequential performance management activities, and by building their performance management skills, we have been able to show that performance appraisal is integral to their jobs. This has paved the way for successful performance appraisal systems.

Rather than attempt to design and implement an appraisal system (merely a form and the policies governing its use), we implement systems by helping managers effectively manage performance. We have emphasized the performance management skills and related knowledge required of managers (see Figure 1). Training programs can be designed efficiently to teach skills once a needs assessment has been conducted. Since several skills overlap, and the cycle is seen as a legitimate part of their job by most managers, performance management training usually is received well. Activities such as video-based behavior modeling, cases, role-plays, questionnaires, lectures, and group projects all help. Most importantly, the skills easily transfer to job performance because they are essentially general managerial skills. The eight-step performance management cycle follows.

CHOOSE PERFORMANCE APPRAISAL MEASURES AND STANDARDS

Those aspects of job performance that have an impact on success, differentiate between successful and unsuccessful performers, and are at least partially within the control of the person being rated should be identified as performance measures. Since most jobs are multi-dimensional, multiple measures will be chosen. Certainly, measures may be weighted differentially, depending on contribution to overall performance. A thorough, systematic job analysis and an accurate, concise position description are an excellent basis for determining performance measures.[1]

Job analyses and position descriptions provide a view of the job by detailing duties, responsibilities, and tasks. The appraisal measures may include all or some of these. The crucial question asks what is important to evaluate from the descriptive set of duties. If each task a job incumbent performs is to be evaluated, there must be a

Figure 1
Sample Skills and Related Knowledge Required for Performance Management

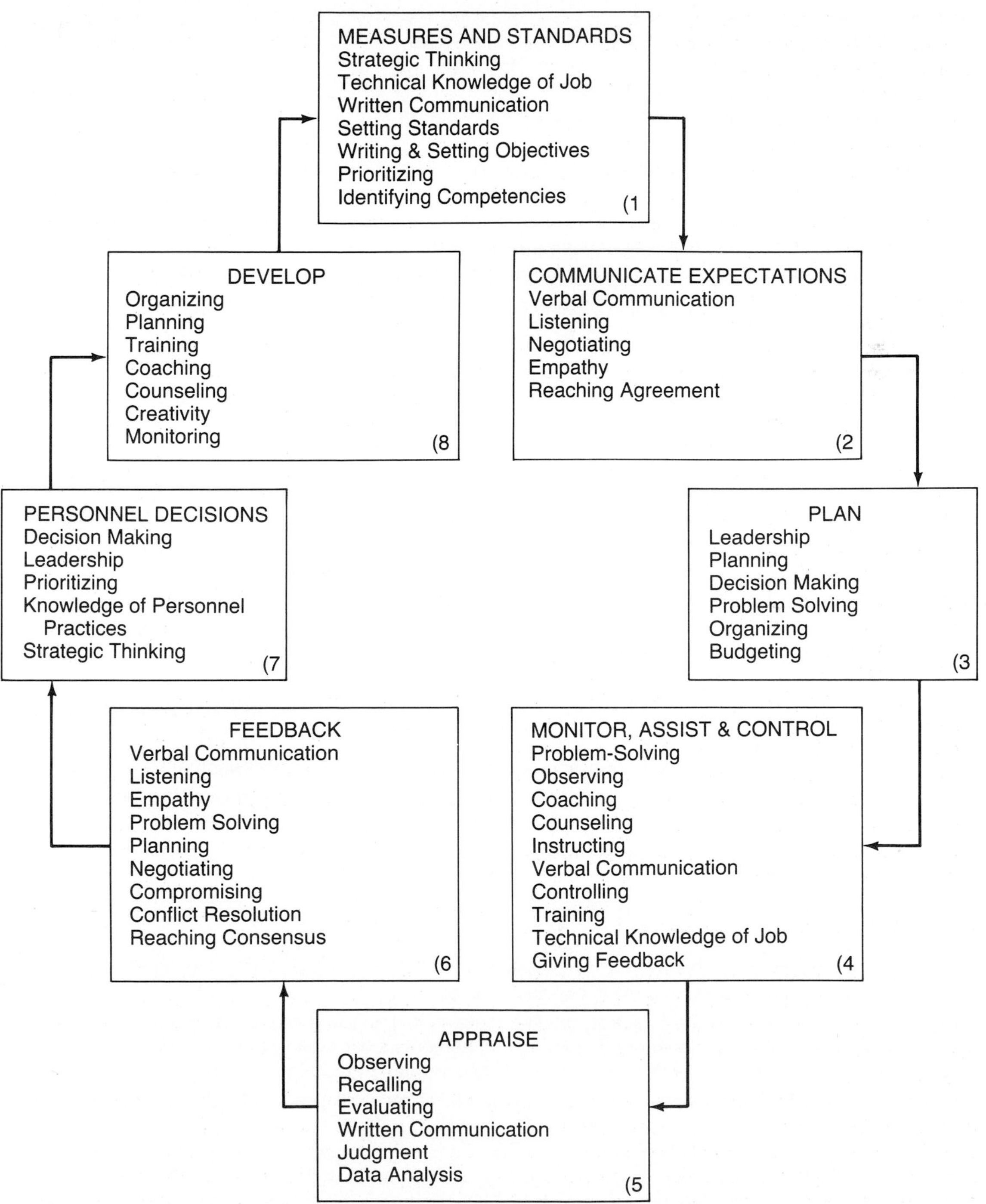

MEASURES AND STANDARDS
Strategic Thinking
Technical Knowledge of Job
Written Communication
Setting Standards
Writing & Setting Objectives
Prioritizing
Identifying Competencies
(1
COMMUNICATE EXPECTATIONS
Verbal Communication
Listening
Negotiating
Empathy
Reaching Agreement
(2
PLAN
Leadership
Planning
Decision Making
Problem Solving
Organizing
Budgeting
(3
MONITOR, ASSIST & CONTROL
Problem-Solving
Observing
Coaching
Counseling
Instructing
Verbal Communication
Controlling
Training
Technical Knowledge of Job
Giving Feedback
(4
APPRAISE
Observing
Recalling
Evaluating
Written Communication
Judgment
Data Analysis
(5
FEEDBACK
Verbal Communication
Listening
Empathy
Problem Solving
Planning
Negotiating
Compromising
Conflict Resolution
Reaching Consensus
(6
PERSONNEL DECISIONS
Decision Making
Leadership
Prioritizing
Knowledge of Personnel Practices
Strategic Thinking
(7
DEVELOP
Organizing
Planning
Training
Coaching
Counseling
Creativity
Monitoring
(8

Figure 2
A Behaviorally-Anchored Rating Scale (BARS)

JOB TITLE: Division Audit Manager
JOB DIMENSION: Conducting Meetings and Briefings

Unacceptable	• Fails to prepare for briefings or meetings and to recognize the status and needs of the audience. • Fails to convey that Division made reasonable efforts to investigate or resolve an issue by not being able to link audit scope and methodology to objective. • Has extreme difficulty in responding to basic questions on status of audit assignment. • Creates hostile environment by being critical of corporate participants during meetings.
Borderline	• Displays limited preparedness for meetings with Corporate staffs. • Generally has difficulty in determining when and what visual aids would be beneficial for a meeting. • Has difficulty discussing audit assignment scope, methodology, objectives and expected results in a clear, concise manner. Responses to questions in briefings are verbose and on some occasions inaccurate.
Fully Successful	• Can conduct entire briefing or meeting with Corporate staffs. Adequately prepared and presents information in a clear, concise manner, devoid of ambiguity. • Responses to questions are direct. Displays some awareness of Corporate participants' understanding of the information and more often than not adjusts the detail of information presented accordingly.
Superior	• Controls the tempo of meetings by awareness of time constraints and level of understanding by the Corporate audience. • Rarely is nonresponsive to questions concerning the audit/project assignment. • Concludes meetings with summary of information presented and agreements reached. • Uses concise visual aids. • Always has written agenda and manages time to end when planned.
Exceptional	• Visual aids are conducive to effective presentation of information and are creative, as well as accurate and concise. • Anticipates questions which may be asked on the subject topic of the meeting or on related topics and responds in a clear, concise manner. • Shows unusual ability to sense how the meeting is going and adjusts tempo and sequence accordingly. Always ensures that mutual agreements exist among the participants on any additional or future work to be done prior to concluding meeting. • Receives letters of appreciation and praise and/or receives positive feedback in briefing or meeting.

method for measuring performance on each. Typically, only a subset of tasks, or a series of tasks grouped together, warrant inclusion in the appraisal system.

The development of performance standards—methods for making judgments about performance—becomes far less complex and problematic when viewed from the manager's perspective. A manager is concerned with three possible measures: what people achieve, what people do, and what people "are." They translate, respectively, into assessing results, assessing behaviors, and assessing personal characteristics. Each dictates a specific type of appraisal format, discussed briefly below:

Behavior-based Systems. Appraisal measures can be defined by specific, job-related behaviors, as in behaviorally anchored rating scales (see Figure 2). These performance appraisal formats present specific behavioral examples for each performance level.[2] They and related behaviorally based systems are useful because they detail what is required to perform effectively and reduce bias in ratings. Just as important, they help communicate a manager's performance expectations to subordinates. Competencies can be defined behaviorally, as can specific job duties.

Competency-based Systems. Measures can also be built around competencies—knowledge, skills, abilities, motivation and other personal characteristics that lead to high performance. These must be characteristics (e.g., cooperation, setting priorities, risk-taking) that distinguish between effective and ineffective performers.[3] They must also be well defined in behavioral terms in order to reduce subjectivity in their application. Competency-based performance appraisal systems recognize the importance of how an individual's characteristics influence results obtained. They capture the organization culture by describing "what it takes to make it" and thus should be developed in each specific organization in which they will be used. (A sample set of competencies that we developed for organizations to enhance the realism and utility of their performance appraisal systems appear in Figure 3.)

Figure 3
Sample Managerial Competencies*

Concern for Cost-Effectiveness
Advocate of Organization Mission
Sense of Priorities
Cooperates as a Member of the Management Team
Understanding of Groups
Creative Thinking Skill
Knowledge of Organization Business Strategies
Knowledge of Customer Base
Expressive Communication Skill
Risk Taker
Concern with Impact
Strategic Thinking
Tolerance for Ambiguity
Supportive Managerial Style

**Definitions and behavioral illustrations are omitted.*

The choice of measures, as well as the methods of measuring chosen and the resulting performance appraisal format, depend on the nature and level of the job in question, the uses intended for the system, and various unique job context characteristics. No one technique applies universally and combination systems often are useful. For example, managers could be evaluated by using a set of objectives to measure outputs or results achieved and with competencies, containing behavioral examples for different performance levels, to measure the process of managing.

COMMUNICATE PERFORMANCE EXPECTATIONS

Once appraisal measures have been determined and performance expectations defined for each level of performance, these expectations must be communicated to those being rated. Negotiation and participation are crucial. Superiors must follow up to be sure expectations are understood.

PLAN FOR PERFORMANCE

Here, the manager helps subordinates develop strategies and plans to meet performance expectations and secure required resources. Action plans are necessary, as are budgets and time schedules. The impact of goal attainment on other units must be considered. Critical relationships between activities must be specified and alternative strategies developed before an effective plan can be implemented. The manager secures necessary resources (information, money, people, technology) to facilitate high performance by clearing a path to goal attainment.

MONITOR, ASSIST, AND CONTROL PERFORMANCE

A crucial distinction between performance appraisal and performance management is that the latter is often seen by managers merely as a once- or twice-a-year activity. While designers of performance appraisal systems admonish managers to view them as a continual process, a specific set of ongoing activities is not well articulated for managers. Managers do agree that they *manage* performance each day, all year long, but perhaps only *appraise* performance annually. Hence, this step is a key part of performance management. Here, the manager monitors performance and provides ongoing feedback, both positive and negative. One popular method is "Management by wandering around," which recognizes that managers need to be away from their desks, observing performance, comparing it to expectations, and intervening in the ongoing process using behavior-based language to improve performance. Problem-solving, coaching, counseling, developing, and removing obstacles to success may all be required during a formal interim review. Performance must also be controlled and corrective action taken, as necessary. Managers must be skilled at diagnosing causes of performance problems and at improving performance.

APPRAISE PERFORMANCE

This is the step typically thought of as performance appraisal. Performance observations are recalled and judgments are made, comparing what is recalled to the rater's interpretation of the standards set in the first step. Complexities of processing information and making judgments are particularly relevant in this step of the performance management cycle. Several strategies are helpful for assisting raters in their job. First, concrete, perhaps behaviorally based performance measures are useful. Second, expectations should be communicated to ratees, thus reducing the potential for subsequent disagreements. Third, raters should document performance, both positive and negative, to assist them in recall and in basing their judgments on a representative sample of performance. Finally, rater training, building both sensitivity to judgment problems and skill in overcoming them through practice, can be very useful.

Many rater training programs emphasize how to complete forms or address possible rating errors such as "leniency" or "halo." Sensitization to such problems is not sufficient. Effective programs should build raters' skills in communication, coaching, planning, listening, negotiating, observing, problem solving, and in those skills related to various phases of the performance management cycle. Rather than merely disseminating information to raters, workshops utilizing modeling and practice can facilitate skill-building.[4,5]

PROVIDE PERFORMANCE FEEDBACK

While the performance management cycle calls for continuous feedback, a formal feedback session should be held subsequent to the appraisal. Here, superiors provide a rationale for their evaluation and allow ratees to participate in the discussion. In providing feedback, raters must distinguish between inferences or conclusions about behavior and behavior itself. The most useful feedback contains facts about behavior, not conclusions or inferences (see Figure 4). Relying on inference leads to defensiveness. Energy is wasted on denying allegations and arguing about judgments, as opposed to solving performance problems. Feedback also should be specific and should not overemphasize the negative.

In order to increase the probability that problems will be addressed, managers must listen

Figure 4
Inferential and Behavioral Performance Feedback[6]

Inferential Feedback	*Behavioral Feedback*
Tells about how other person feels; makes "you" statements Cannot be observed or verified Agreement is difficult Uses the verbs "to be," "to know" Uses absolutes General/abstract Value judgment Attributes causes or motives	Tells about the event Can be observed and verified Makes agreement easier Uses action verbs Differentiates clearly Concrete/specific; doesn't use adverbs Free of values Not locked into attributing causes or motives
Examples	*Examples*
You don't care. . . . You don't know. . . . You don't take into consideration. . . . You need to be more conscientious You should know these things Good work You are never here when I need you You always come late when we have meetings	The report contained a very concise, useful conclusion Your language with the client was vague Six absences in two months is not acceptable The contract omitted a vital section The data analysis was inaccurate according to my figures I observed you interrupting that subordinate
Don't say . . .	*Say . . .*
"You're rude and tactless with other employees." "The work you turn in contains too many stupid errors." "You really botched the semiconductor contract."	"You left Rosena very hurt and angry when you told her that she was not dressed well enough to attend the luncheon meeting and not bright enough to participate." "The computer programmers are having difficulty in processing your work because of coding mistakes." "We had a lot of trouble processing the semiconductor contract because forms were incomplete."

without evaluating. They must help set a positive, open tone. A time and place free of interruptions are required. A detailed plan should be developed indicating specific actions to be taken by the individual, the superior, and the organization, as well as dates for each action.

The performance review discussion is also an opportunity to use results of previous steps in the performance management cycle and to demonstrate the ongoing nature of its activities. Documenting past performance, identifying specific measures, communicating performance expectations, and using results of both the interim review and the final appraisal are relevant at this step.

USING PERFORMANCE RESULTS FOR DECISION MAKING

Subsequent to a final rating and performance review session, various decisions can be made, based on the appraisal results. Decisions related to promotion, demotion, or termination; to allocation of monetary and other types of incentives and awards; and to job assignment are examples. In an integrated, interdependent set of HRD activities and programs, outputs of the performance management system become inputs for other systems.

For example, the rating itself becomes the rationale for awarding merit increases. The control and monitoring process indentifies performance problems that influence training program design efforts. Developmental discussions are used to make human resource plans and forecasts, and are the data base for career development programs and activities. Appraisal measures—detailing performance expectations of a position—are naturally used as selection and promotion criteria.

To ensure success, the results of the appraisal process must be used to affect people's jobs, careers, and rewards. In addition, basing such decisions on performance management results allows the process to become integrated into overall management of the organization and for the results to appear.

DEVELOPING PERFORMANCE

The last step in the ongoing performance management cycle is development of performance. The supervisor, individual, and organization each have responsibilities to develop and improve performance. Here HRD professionals and specialists have a critical role. The organization might provide funds for furthering formal education or offer in-house training and self-assessment. The supervisor might agree to coach a subordinate more frequently or provide an opportunity to enhance job responsibilities. The individual might plan to read current technical information, attend professional society meetings, or learn a new skill. Subsequent to the performance feedback session, a structured individual development plan is useful. It can pinpoint what is required in order to assure that performance develops over time.

The essentials of implementing a performance management system include: setting clear project objectives, obtaining commitment from top management and users, overcoming resistance to change, allowing for participation of users in design phases, conducting pilot testing, building early successes, and continually redesigning and revising. But the system begins with the premise that performance management is not an additional function or responsibility of managers designed by HRD or personnel staff, but a more systematic and effective system for managing performance. This system views management and recognizes the organizational culture in the following ways:

As a Solution to Managerial Problems. Implementation of performance management begins with an analysis of managers' performance management problems and their performance management skill levels. Among these problems might be dealing with poor performance; communicating realistic performance expectations; defending promotion decisions; or planning, scheduling, and delegating work. Performance management does not begin with the HRD staff's problems, which might include an "invalid" appraisal system, appraisal forms not completed, or lack of data on organization-wide deficiencies required to defend a training program. Addressing managers' problems leads to implementing a viable managerial tool (as well as a solution to the HRD staff problems).

As a Tool to Capture and Influence an Organization's Culture. Much has been written lately about the importance of organization culture in improving performance and productivity. The performance management system can help to identify and define salient aspects of the culture by specifying behaviors required for success and competencies necessary to succeed in a given organization, unit, group, or position. Managers especially appreciate a system that has the ring of truth and recognizes valued characteristics. When an appraisal form contains terms like "work quality" or "work quantity," but promotion decisions really hinge on such terms as "is a team player," "can take the heat," and "is tactful," the formal system loses credibility.

System implementation must be preceded by a dialogue about organization strategy, mission, and objectives. Strategic-level decisions include what personal characteristics are required for long-term survival, how excellent performance will be recognized, how potential will be identified, how the system will be used in key decisions, and how the HRD function will be organized to facilitate performance management.[7,8]

Putting Staff Specialists in the Role of Facilitator, Consultant, and Technical Expert. Ownership lies with the users, not staff. Staff does not play an "enforcer" role, ultimately leading to conflict with line managers, but gains visibility, legitimacy, and power from its ability to help managers solve real problems with tools that recognize realities of managers' work styles and work environments.

To implement performance management, a group of managers with performance-related problems is shown the basic model and its rationale. They develop, with HRD staff assistance, performance measures, expectations or standards, action plans, and documentation devices. Supporting programs for orientation and training (skill-building) are designed. Policies governing administration, timing, and use of data are set in advance and are enforced. Relationships of data to other human resource systems and programs are made explicit. Managers begin to use performance management with staff assistance, if required. Revisions are made to enhance utility and relevance for various job settings, but certain overall standards are maintained.

Implementing, Complying Legally, and Validating the System. While performance management is a system of managerial activities—not a set of forms to complete—any documentation of performance, any evaluations, and any decisions made using appraisal data must be assessed as to legal compliance. Guidelines have been offered to designers of appraisal systems which assist in meeting legal requirements.[9] Among these are the following:

- Written instructions on forms;
- Appraisal measures derived through job analysis;
- Performance standards based on work actually performed;
- An absence of "adverse impact" on "protected groups" as a result of decisions based on appraisals;
- User orientation and training programs;
- Appeal and review provisions;
- No exclusive reliance on "subjective" evaluations of supervisors;
- Ample opportunity for raters to observe ratees.

While methods for assessing various validity strategies are available, the system generates valid personnel decisions. It relies on job-related criteria and standards based on job analyses. It emphasizes training of users and communication of performance expectations. And, it allows for review and appeal of rating, forces actual rater observation, and recommends use of performance-contingent rewards.

REFERENCES

1. Beatty, R. W., & Schneier, C. E. (1981). *Personnel administration: An experiential/skill-building approach.* 2nd ed. Addison-Wesley.
2. Schneier, C. E., & Beatty, R. W. (August 1979). Developing behaviorally-anchored rating scales. *The Personnel Administrator, 24*(8), 65–78.
3. Boyatziz, R. E. (1982). *The competent manager.* Wiley.
4. Sashkin, M. (1981). *Assessing performance appraisal.* University Associates.
5. Baird, L., Schneier, C. E., and Laird, D., *The training and development sourcebook* (1984). Human Resource Development Press.
6. O'Connell, S. (1981). *Manager as communicator.* Harper & Row.

7. Fombrun, C. J., et al. (1984). *Strategic human resource management.* Wiley.

8. Baird, L. S. (1985). *Performance management.* Wiley.

9. Schneier, C. E., & Beatty, R. W. (1984). Designing a legally defensible performance appraisal system. In M. Cohen and R. Golembiewski (eds.), *Public personnel update.* Marcell Deckker.

The Many Faces of Feedback in the Performance Appraisal Process

Donald B. Fedor

Managers are more fully realizing that how employees are managed is a critical component in achieving organizational effectiveness. One extremely important dimension of management is finding ways to influence employee job-related attributes, behaviors, and outcomes. Although managers have many methods at their disposal for directing and assisting employees, such as administering rewards and punishment, or providing training and resources, one of the best tools can be the judicious application of performance-related feedback. This article explores the many facets of feedback and discusses the benefits and some of the possible pitfalls associated with the use of feedback.

FEEDBACK'S POSITIVE ATTRIBUTES

Feedback is usually discussed in favorable terms. Employees often use information about their performance to correct inappropriate behaviors. Feedback is relatively inexpensive to administer, it can be given immediately and frequently, and it is not a scarce resource that must be rationed. Along with its positive effects on performance, feedback can alleviate stress that results from feelings of uncertainty. In the longer term, feedback helps employees establish a realistic idea of what is expected of them and how well they will be rewarded. With all these positive qualities attributed to feedback, it is surprising that supervisors are often reluctant to give it, and employees often feel "in the dark" about what and how they are doing.

The answer to this dilemma lies in the fact that feedback is a complex phenomenon and is not simply a resource that we measure like raw materials or capital. Instead, the utility of feedback is created within the context of an interaction between the source of feedback (e.g., supervisor) and the feedback recipient (e.g., employee). An example will help illustrate this statement. An employee is working in his or her office when the supervisor stops by for a short chat. The supervisor mentions that the employee did a very good or bad job on a recent assignment. These two then proceed to talk about the project and soon thereafter the supervisor leaves to attend to other business. Despite the fact that the employee just received some feedback about a particular aspect of his or her performance, it is not clear what the feedback really means and whether its effects will be positive or negative. As is often the case, the answer is—it depends. Let's explore some of the factors that influence the effects of feedback.

FEEDBACK COMPLEXITY

Feedback is not simply a resource (i.e., some piece of objective information) given by the supervisor to the employee, but is an event that takes place between them within the context of their relationship and the broader organizational environment. To determine the outcome(s) of this event we need to look at the qualities of the feedback and the context in which it takes place.

Let's initially tackle the easier parts of this puzzle. Research has indicated that there are some aspects about feedback that can greatly affect its impact. First, whether the feedback is positive or negative is a key issue. It may not come as any big surprise that employees tend to respond more favorably to positive feedback, perceive it to be a more accurate reflection of their performance, remember it better and, overall, find it preferable to negative feedback. Second, how specific the feedback is makes a real difference. For instance, telling someone that he or she is a poor worker is quite different than telling this person that he or she failed to complete two of the last three assignments, or that the rejection rate for his or her product has been running 12 percent above the standard set for the department. Providing very general feedback does not supply useful information to the recipient. The more specific the feedback in relation to goals, standards, or actual outcomes, the less recipients will tend to take the feedback as a statement about them and more as useful, performance-related input.

Third, the timing and frequency of the feedback also have an impact on its effectiveness. For example, if a supervisor lets two weeks pass before evaluating an employee's performance on a particular project, some of the impact will be lost. The employee will then have to try to remember all the pertinent details. For jobs that continue to change, this can be difficult. If the employee did not perform well, the time lag may unfairly obstruct efforts to improve.

The appropriate frequency for feedback is a more difficult issue because feedback has a bit of a dual personality. On one hand, there is useful information in feedback. On the other hand, the feedback can represent a form of control. To illustrate, put yourself in the place of an employee who has just been given a new assignment. Your supervisor first shows you how to do the task and then stops by frequently to point out any mistakes you are making. Within a couple of days you begin to feel comfortable with what you are expected to do. But how would you feel if your supervisor continued to come around and criticize? If you are like most people, the initial feedback would be welcomed, especially if the new assignment was relatively challenging. However, after a while, the value of the information decreases, while the feeling of intrusion (i.e., exertion of unnecessary control) increases. As a result, the proper frequency really depends on the employee's desire for information, how often a product is completed or service provided, and the point at which evaluation or adjustment is appropriate or necessary.

To summarize, whether the feedback is positive or negative will have the greatest impact on how one responds to it. People respond much more favorably to positive feedback. In addition, feedback that is specific and provided relatively soon after the behavior or performance will be most useful. Finally, feedback should be frequent enough to supply relevant information without exerting undue control over the recipient.

FEEDBACK SOURCES

Although this discussion has focused so far on supervisors as the source for feedback, employees can receive or seek feedback from a number of different sources. In organizational settings, we can identify seven. These include the employee's job supervisor, subordinates, co-workers, clients or customers, representatives of the organization (e.g., the personnel department), the job itself, and even the employee him- or herself. Consequently, the supervisor is only one possibility.

Some sources have direct contact with the recipient; no one else is needed to pass along the performance information. This is called *unmediated* feedback because it is not channeled through any other source that could interpret or evaluate it. In other words, unmediated feedback is received directly, either from the job, oneself, or a customer or client.

In contrast, feedback about job performance received from other sources, such as the supervisor or co-workers, is considered *mediated* feedback. For example, a customer telling an employee directly that there is a problem (i.e., unmediated feedback) is quite different than the customer telling the supervisor there is a problem, and the supervisor, in turn, talking to the employee (i.e., mediated feedback). In the first case the employee can try to correct the problem to satisfy the customer, whereas in the second case the employee must try to determine from the supervisor's feedback what will satisfy the customer and worry about the supervisor's evaluation (i.e., possible blame placing).

Before we look at the differences between these sources and why they might have different effects on an employee (besides being mediated or unmediated), we should note that these sources of information are not as independent as they might appear. A supervisor may decide that the employee should chart his or her own progress on a project or keep track of the number of products returned as rejects. In this way, the supervisor is influencing what information the employee uses from an unmediated source. Therefore, the supervisor may be able to affect results without direct involvement in the feedback process.

Now we need to tackle the question of how feedback sources differ. The key distinction between these potential sources and their impact on the employee can be understood through the concept of credibility. The recipient of the feedback will use a number of factors to determine the credibility of the source. The first factor is the source's perceived level of expertise. In other words, how much does this source know about the issue. The second factor is more of a historical judgment and deals with how reliable the feedback has been in the past. The third factor is the extent to which the recipient is attracted to the source. This aspect of credibility is used extensively in advertising. One only needs to turn on the television to see a famous sports figure selling a product to realize how this works. Finally, the fourth factor is the source's intentions toward the recipient. The recipient may ask, "Why is this person giving me this information? Is it to provide me with useful information and support my efforts or simply to put me in my place?" Recipients of feedback use these four factors to determine the credibility of the source, which, in turn, has an effect on their acceptance of it. This is especially true for negative feedback. If from a highly credible source, people tend to accept it more easily.

As a general rule, the greater the distance between the recipient and the source, the less credible that source appears. In other words, feedback from one's co-workers would seem more credible than information from the personnel department. Moreover, the unmediated sources of feedback, such as the job or oneself, tend to be perceived as more credible than the mediated ones. Therefore, falling behind on one's job is a direct signal that something is wrong since the job does not have malicious intent and its expertise and reliability are not really at issue.

In reading this, you may have noticed a problem that faces organizations in providing feedback about performance. The agent usually responsible for this task is the immediate supervisor. However, this source is often viewed as having less credibility than the job, oneself, and co-workers. As a result, the organization relies on a source with only moderate credibility to influence behavior. Now you can see why a supervisor might be more effective influencing the sources that the employee uses, such as specific, organizationally important aspects of the job, rather than providing the feedback directly. This method of providing feedback is used by organizations to improve the quality of employee work life and as a mechanism for allowing employees more involvement in decision making.

THE INTERPRETATION OF FEEDBACK

Now that we have touched on the more straightforward pieces to the feedback puzzle, we need to tackle some of the aspects that make its impact so unpredictable. As noted earlier, feedback is not an object that originates from a source and has certain fixed qualities. Although the source and its characteristics are important, they are not the entire story. Feedback must be interpreted by the recipient. When supervisors tell their employees that they have performed at 2 percent above the standard or that they are very good employees, what does this really mean? Employees must often look for additional information to understand whether they have done well or not. Let's take a common example. Your boss walks into your office and informs you that your last report was poorly done. How seriously would you take this information and how would you respond? If your boss had just spent the last two hours going over your report and did not give adverse criticism lightly, you might be very concerned and pursue the topic in greater detail. However, if your boss tended to be volatile, inconsistent in offering feedback, and had just had a fight with his or her spouse, you might wait to see what happened next.

Feedback is an event that the source and recipient will usually perceive differently. The source might feel comfortable that clear, helpful information was transmitted and thus expect the recipient to respond in a certain "reasonable" fashion. In contrast, the recipient might have heard rumors that the source had been ordered to provide more feedback or increase the level of communication, and used these cues to make sense of the feedback and to formulate a response. Unfortunately, when the recipient does not respond as the source had expected, other problems may follow.

RECIPIENT RESPONSES

So far this discussion of feedback has mainly focused on what factors influence recipients' responses. To complete the picture, we need to turn our attention once again to the feedback source. Supervisors (as one specific source) are often reluctant to give feedback to their employees. If they do so, what kind will it be? For instance, a supervisor is considering telling an employee that his or her work is not up to the departmental standard. (This is not unlike the problem we each face when we try to determine whether we should give a friend feedback about a sensitive issue.) In most cases, it would be the supervisor's duty to supply this information and, presumably, attempt to improve the employee's level of productivity. Talking to this employee seems the perfectly logical thing to do until we investigate a key consideration. Supervisors will often rationalize that the employees "should know what is expected of them" or "don't need their hands held." Why is it that the feedback portion of the supervisor's job can be the most bothersome in spite of the potential benefits? The answer to this question is multifaceted.

When the use of feedback is discussed, we should not overlook the source's perceptions of how the recipient will feel and respond. In other words, what are the source's beliefs about the likely outcomes? Whether these beliefs are valid or not is not as important as the fact that they will have an impact on the source's willingness to give feedback.

In the case of employees receiving negative feedback from their supervisors, expected employee responses can range from constructive (i.e., take steps to correct the problems) or nonconstructive. In the latter case, employees can be emotionally hurt, place some or all of the blame on the supervisor, complain to others, such as coworkers or personnel representatives, or file grievances. Unfortunately, by criticizing employee performance in the form of negative feedback, the supervisor may be vulnerable to counterattack, or this feedback may negatively affect the relationship with that employee or the entire work group.

Sources can also be just as concerned about the harm of giving positive feedback. In the process of helping to install a performance appraisal system in a manufacturing facility, the supervisors I was working with believed that praise would lessen the employees' motivation to perform well. Based on this belief, they were reluctant to use positive feedback to influence employee performance. At the same time, they did not like dealing with the anger and repercussions that could result from negative feedback. Essentially, their philosophy was to "let sleeping dogs lie" and only use feedback when it was absolutely necessary.

Another problem facing the feedback giver is the uncertainty associated with the way the recipient may respond. Responses, as noted earlier, are based only partially on what the source does and says. Even good news can generate a negative reaction when it is not "good enough." Based upon the potential of undesirable or unexpected reactions and responses, it is not difficult to understand why supervisors, in particular, might find it easier to withhold feedback than to offer it.

To summarize, sources will use the recipients'

responses to past feedback and their own beliefs and expectations about the feedback's probable impact when deciding whether to give it. Over time this will result in a certain feedback style. In turn, this style will affect how the recipient interprets the feedback that is received. For example, if a supervisor rarely provides feedback and then suddenly begins to lavish praise on the employees, they are going to wonder what it really means, because such behavior appears out of character. Instead of focusing on the content, they are going to look for reasons behind the change in behavior. If there are causes for the supervisor's new style, such as a recent mandate for more feedback, then the employees may dismiss it as irrelevant to their own performance.

IMPLICATIONS

The intent of this paper is not to discourage organizations or managers from using feedback. It is an extremely important management tool. Instead, the point is that feedback must be used wisely to reap the possible benefits. A supervisor can give feedback with all the right qualities (e.g., constructive, specific, and immediate) and not have the desired effects. The recipient interprets the feedback and combines it with other information. It may be discounted due to contextual factors (e.g., organizational rumors pertaining to why the feedback is given) or because it is discrepant with other sources. Therefore, simply giving feedback may not be enough. The source may have to explore with the recipient his or her perceptions of the intentions behind the feedback and how it fits with other performance information. Some of the most effective feedback directs the recipient to other sources, such as the important characteristics of the job. Performance feedback that one generates for oneself (i.e., unmediated feedback) will have greater credibility than feedback that is mediated through other sources. Moreover, we cannot forget that sources may be reluctant to give feedback due to the negative responses they anticipate. Supervisors can be helped to understand that there are sources other than themselves that can provide feedback on how well employees are performing.

The implication for management training is that there is no simple formula for providing feedback to employees. Simply telling managers to give specific and timely feedback is not appropriate. Managers must learn to analyze employee feedback environments, determine the credibility of different feedback sources available to employees, and check employee perceptions of the feedback. Only then can managers make effective decisions concerning how to intervene in the feedback process.

SELECTED BIBLIOGRAPHY

Ashford, S. J., & Cummings, L. L. (1983). Feedback as an individual resource: Personal strategies of creating information. *Organizational Behavior and Human Performance, 32,* 370–398.

Herold, D., & Greller, M. M. The definition of a construct. *Academy of Management Journal, 20,* 142–147.

Ilgen, D. R., Fisher, C. D., & Taylor, M. S. (1979). Consequences of individual feedback on behavior in organizations. *Journal of Applied Psychology, 64,* 349–371.

Jablin, F. M. (1979). Supervisor-subordinate communication: The state of the art. *Psychological Bulletin, 86,* 1201–1222.

Larson, J. R. (1984). The performance feedback process: A preliminary model. *Organizational Behavior and Human Performance, 33,* 42–76.

Larson, J. R. (1986). *The impact of subordinate behavior on supervisors' delivery of performance feedback.* Paper presented at the Annual Meeting of the Academy of Management, Chicago, IL.

Taylor, M. S., Fisher, C. D., & Ilgen, D. R. (1984). Individuals reactions to performance feedback in organizations: A control theory perspective. In K. M. Rowland & G. R. Ferris (Eds.) *Research in personnel and human resources management.* Greenwich, Conn.: JAI Press, pp. 81–124.

Appraisals Everyone Can Agree On

Gerald R. Ferris and David C. Gilmore

Diane is furious. She's been pounding the keys on her data entry terminal as hard and as fast as she can all year, but her manager has just given her a below-average performance-appraisal rating because her production has barely met the company's standard minimum requirements. In addition, Diane's manager has attributed this performance to lack of effort—something that further mystifies and infuriates Diane.

Her manager, of course, sees the situation differently. Her manager's primary source of performance-appraisal information regarding employees is objective, measurable quality and quantity production data recorded each month on computer printouts. Because Diane's manager has nearly 50 people reporting to her and has other work occupying her time, she often bases each operator's performance-appraisal rating—including Diane's—solely on the computer-printout information. In Diane's case, this information indicated a trend of reduced production, which her manager attributed to a lack of effort.

The problem with this performance-appraisal system is that it doesn't address the causes of performance; it assumes that the employee has complete control over his or her performance. In fact, Diane's performance was adversely affected by malfunctioning equipment which had been interrupting her work throughout the year, frequently cutting into her output.

Performance appraisal has been around for years, but—as the above example shows—it has often been poorly executed. In many cases, employees are not as productive as they could be possibly because we do not measure performance well, or if we do, the performance data is not used constructively to increase productivity.

Enactment of laws in the personnel field may signal the beginning of new concerns about how well a particular practice has been managed in an unregulated environment. The Civil Service Reform Act of 1978 has generated specific directives concerning the establishment of performance-appraisal systems for all Federal agencies. This will likely be extended to the private sector in the near future. In the next decade, Title VII litigation will probably focus less on personnel-selection decisions and more on employee challenges to internal employment decisions regarding pay increases, promotions, and issues typically handled within the context of performance appraisal.

Performance appraisals should be conducted in a fair and unbiased manner, and should be accurate reflections of actual work performance. Thus, to ensure fair and accurate appraisals, there must be assurance that real causes of performance be identified.

For example, consider an employee who receives a poor performance appraisal and a written reprimand from her supervisor because the supervisor believed the low performance resulted from a lack of effort. This employee would not likely view the appraisal session as a fair and accurate representation of her performance if, unknown to the supervisor, the poor performance resulted from faulty equipment, inadequate training, or inadequate supervision.

Uncovering the underlying causes of poor performance is an important and often overlooked function of the performance-appraisal process. If individual performance is to be improved, employees must be given feedback about their performance, causes of performance must be identified, and specific steps must be agreed upon to help the employee show improvement.

BREAKING TRADITION

Unfortunately, many organizations take a very traditional approach to performance appraisal. The manager takes control of the session, provides feedback (often quite general) on the subordinate's performance over the past year, and concludes the session with a directive to sign the performance-appraisal form. This represents a one-way communication process. There's virtually no interaction and sharing of information, and the final evaluation reflects only the supervisor's perspective.

There has been a trend toward more subordinate involvement in the appraisal process. More than half the employees surveyed in a recent Yankelovich poll felt they had a right to be involved in decisions that influence them and their jobs. Based on these results, some experts argue that employees will probably demand a more active role in the performance-appraisal process.

Making self-appraisal a component of the performance-appraisal process is one way of increasing employee involvement. In a study of performance appraisal, conducted at nine different divisions of the General Electric Corp., about 90 percent of the managers and 86 percent of the subordinates surveyed believed that subordinate self-appraisal should be included as an important part of the performance-appraisal process.

Apparently, the inclusion of self-appraisal will increase the effectiveness of performance appraisals. It can give the subordinate greater involvement and participation in the appraisal process and incorporate more than just the manager's perspective.

Of course, for many years, the common belief was that if you give employees a chance to rate themselves, they will always inflate their ratings. Research findings support this belief. However, further research shows that, when given the opportunity, employees will evaluate themselves conscientiously and even be overly self-critical.

At the very least, including both perspectives should expose issues which might not have been detected otherwise. Furthermore, discrepancies in ratings between the two perspectives should stimulate discussion concerning the "why" of performance.

STAYING LEGAL

With the increased legal scrutiny of the performance-appraisal process, organizations must be able to support and substantiate performance evaluations. Data on pay increases (or lack thereof), denials for promotion, or termination decisions is increasingly being considered insufficient, particularly in light of the subjective nature of most performance evaluations. While subjective performance ratings by themselves are not necessarily violations of the law *(Rogers v. International Paper)*, lack of additional documentation may foster charges of capricious or unfair decision making. Therefore, efforts to substantiate or even re-examine performance ratings by searching for and identifying the causes of performance make good sense. This will contribute to enhanced perceptions of fairness in the appraisal process and serve as the basis for more specific feedback to subordinates about their performance.

If you attempt to determine why an employee's performance is less than desirable, and the only reasonable explanation is lack of effort, you can both agree on ways to stimulate improvement. Without this understanding of the underlying causes of performance, a manager may incorrectly attribute certain characteristics to the subordinate.

The types of attributions made by a manager about an employee's performance influence attitudes and behavior toward the employee. For example, a manager who concludes that someone is performing poorly due to lack of effort may take punitive action against him or her. On the other hand, if poor performance was attributed to lack of ability or skill, the manager might recommend some type of training program for skill enhancement.

Since the attributed cause of the employee's performance can seriously affect the subordinate's treatment, the actual causes of poor performance must be accurately identified. In addition, the manager must not form an impression based upon limited information.

CORRALLING THE CAUSES

The performance-appraisal session should not only be an effort to exchange information concerning the employee's performance. It should also serve as an opportunity to pursue the causes of the performance and take appropriate action. A session that establishes an atmosphere of open information exchange, two-way communication, and incorporates both a manager's evaluation as well as a self-evaluation is most conducive to a fair and accurate performance appraisal.

Information provided by the subordinate is useful and may shed light on issues and concerns unknown to the manager, but which might have a substantial effect on the evaluation.

Also, incorporating the perspectives of both manager and employee in the performance-evaluation session will help give both a common view about the causes of good or poor performance and encourage more two-way communication to work out problems when incongruencies exist. This approach to discussing causes can help you keep more informed about the entire work context. It also should result in a better working relationship between you and your employee.

In addition, performance goals that are set jointly between you and your employee during the performance-appraisal session will probably be more realistically based when a common view is shared about his or her current job performance level and causes of effective or ineffective performance.

Studies show that productivity suffers when employees and managers do not share a common view concerning goals and standards of performance. In their extensive studies of supervisor-subordinate communication, experts reported that performance evaluations cannot be accurate or effective when the manager and the employee see things differently. People frequently have different perspectives on job-related factors. If this is recognized, brought out in the open, and discussed, an ineffective and deteriorating situation can be turned into a productive situation.

Another benefit of causal information in performance evaluation concerns Federal regulations regarding fair employment practices. The *Uniform Guidelines on Employee Selection Procedures* can be applied to internal employment decisions typically associated with performance evaluation. Just as selection decisions need to be job-related and not conducted arbitrarily, promotion or dismissal decisions must be specific and based on job-relevant considerations. If they are not, charges of unfair practices can result.

Including causal information in performance-evaluation sessions has several purposes. It provides greater detail and specificity concerning the subordinate's performance. This documented information can prove very useful if the Equal Employment Opportunity Commission (EEOC) files a "desk audit" and requests performance records, personnel files, and other related information. Causal data provides added support and a more consistent rationale for certain decisions or actions being investigated.

In addition, the two-way interactions, the open communication that is encouraged, and the discussions of performance and causes for performance portray a "fair" situation to subordinates. This perceived fairness is likely to lead employees to try to work out differences with their supervisors within the work setting, making them not as likely to file formal complaints with external agencies. Most of the lawsuits filed by the EEOC are based on complaints by current employees or applicants for employment who believe they have been treated unfairly. Creating an impression of fairness for employees through mechanisms such as performance-evaluation sessions should help alleviate this problem.

Recent challenges to the common-law doctrine of employment at-will suggest that the unjust termination of employees will more frequently lead these individuals to seek remedies in the courts. These remedies could prove costly to organizations.

An additional issue of importance to managers in this situation is the potential future legislation which could make supervisors and managers accountable—in addition to the organization—for questionable and non-defensible employment decisions.

Performance appraisal can enhance the productivity of workers, but it must be accomplished in a manner that will increase the employee's commitment to be more productive. Accurate performance appraisal requires more than good performance-appraisal rating tools. Employee involvement is needed to ensure that underlying causes of performance are identified. Employee self-appraisal helps identify differences of opinion and can be used to identify underlying causes of performance. Once the causes of performance have been identified, the supervisor and subordinate can jointly decide what needs to be done in the future.

Self-appraisal and uncovering the causes for poor performance increase employee involvement and should result in appraisals that are fair and accurate. Fair and accurate appraisals which the employee understands are much less likely to be challenged and will encourage greater productivity.

Managerial Appraisal Systems: Has Practice Caught Up to the State of the Art?

H. John Bernardin and Lawrence A. Klatt

For several decades the appraisal of employee and managerial job performance has attracted considerable attention in management research and literature. Certainly, the number of comprehensive reviews of performance appraisal suggests the degree of scholarly study devoted to the topic (e.g., Barrett, 1966; DeCotiis and Petit, 1978; Landy and Farr, 1980; Miner, 1977). During the 1970s a number of surveys were conducted to answer such basic questions as: To what extent are formal performance appraisal programs being utilized? What methods or techniques are most common? What performance factors are typically rated? For what purpose(s) is the performance appraisal used? (See Lazer and Wikstrom, 1977; Locher and Teel, 1977; Lacho, Stearns and Villere, 1979; and Feild and Holley, 1975).

Although these surveys have found that performance appraisal is now used widely throughout most organizations, their results have also pointed to deficiencies in most performance appraisal systems that are in use. For example, Locher and Teel (1977) found that of the companies using a performance appraisal system, 57 percent used rating scales and only 13 percent used MBO systems (nine percent of the smaller firms). In general, these surveys have pointed to the need for greater psychometric sophistication in appraisal methods.

There has been a substantial increase in research on the subject in recent years, the results of which have led not only to a sounder theoretical base for performance appraisal systems but also to the introduction of new PA methods such as BARS and mixed standards. Accompanying this wave of sophisticated research has been a number of books that provide the personnel administrator with specific guidelines on how to select and develop a PA system and how to conduct an appraisal method suited for a given work en-

Reprinted from the November 1985 issue of *Personnel Administrator,* copyright 1985, The American Society for Personnel Administration, 606 North Washington Street, Alexandria, Virginia 22314.

vironment (see, for example, Bernardin and Beatty, 1984; Carroll and Schneier, 1982; DeVries, Morrison, Shullman and Gerlach, 1981; Henderson, 1980; and Latham and Wexley, 1980).

The study described in the following [paragraphs] was undertaken to determine if performance appraisal systems, as currently utilized in organizations, have "caught up" to the state of the art. That is, are those individuals who are responsible for administering PA systems using the added knowledge that has been generated within the past several years?

Bernardin and Beatty (1984) have argued for the use of more qualitative measures of PA system effectiveness to augment the research using a psychometric criteria. Although the appropriateness of psychometric criteria tend to be a function of the purposes that the appraisal data are intended to serve, an administrative evaluation can be tailored to the specific context for PA use. One recommendation was to ask administrators of PA systems to evaluate the extent to which their PA systems were achieving their aims. The validity of such self-report measures should be enhanced by an anonymous response format.

Significant correlations between any appraisal characteristic and the overall evaluation will provide external validity for the findings of previous research using other methodological strategies. For example, several studies have found higher predictive validities for multiple rater systems in predicting supervisory success (Bernardin and Beatty, 1984). In addition, litigation has strongly supported the use of multiple rater systems (Bernardin and Cascio, 1984; Feild and Holley, 1982). Despite the support for multiple rater systems in research and case law, past surveys have all indicated that the model PA strategy involved a single supervisor evaluating the subordinate. A significant correlation between the presence of multiple rater systems and the perceived effectiveness of the PA system by administrators would provide a unique and valuable third source of support for multiple rater systems. Similarly, responses to questions having to do with PA training, the use of job analysis, the format/method for appraisal and the presence of a formal appeal process can also be correlated with an administrative evaluation of the PA system.

The critical questions used in our study were selected based on both the litigation in the area of performance measurement and the most recent research on the topic. Several of the recent texts available on the subject (Bernardin and Beatty, 1984; Carroll and Schneier, 1982; DeVries et al., 1981; Latham and Wexley, 1981) and recent reviews on case law related to appraisal (Bernardin and Cascio, 1984; Cascio and Bernardin, 1981; Feild and Holley, 1982) were major factors in justifying the critical questions. In essence, the questions were designed to measure the extent to which seven positive characteristics are present in existing PA systems. These characteristics are:

1. Multiple rater systems for evaluation
2. Opportunity for rated managers to review their PAs
3. Formal appeal process for ratees
4. System based on specific job related behavior or results
5. Training for raters on conducting the PA
6. Specific written instructions for the evaluation
7. PA system based on job analysis.

Although arguments can be made for the inclusion of other critical questions to measure these and other operative characteristics, the seven questions selected were considered to be those in which *all* scholars were in agreement (see Table 1).

It is hypothesized that the effectiveness ratings by the PA administrators will be positively correlated with the presence of these PA characteristics. Furthermore, the greater the number of these seven characteristics for a PA system, the higher the effectiveness rating.

METHOD

Personnel administrators attending two personnel conferences sponsored by the American Society for Personnel Administration completed the questionnaire (N = 140). The types of organizations represented are: Service (N = 65); Industrial (N = 52); Public (12); and Other (11). Participants were directly responsible for administering the

Table 1
Frequency of Response to Critical Questions as a Function of Organizational Size

Evaluation	Less Than 500 (N = 68) $\overline{X}$ = 3.1 SD = 1.4	500 to 5,000 (N = 57) $\overline{X}$ = 3.9 SD = 1.5	Over 5,000 (N = 14) $\overline{X}$ = 4.4 SD = 1.5	All Data $\overline{X}$ = 3.6 SD = 1.5
V1: How many evaluators are involved in the relevant appraisal(s)?				
Only one rater	65	37	36	51
Two raters	19	46	50	33
Three or more	16	18	15	16
V2: Is the employee given an opportunity to review the performance appraisal?				
Yes	66	90	100	79
No	35	11	0	21
V3: Is there a formal appeal process for employees who do not agree with their performance appraisals?				
Yes	28	42	43	36
No	72	58	57	64
V4: Is your managerial appraisal system based on traits (e.g., dependability, motivation, attitudes), specific job-related behaviors, or results such as sales or productivity figures?				
1. Traits	33	9	0	20
2. Behaviors	5	5	0	4
3. Results	10	14	15	13
4. Traits and behaviors	10	5	0	7
5. Traits and results	16	9	15	13
6. Behavior and results	10	34	31	22
7. Traits, behavior and results	15	23	39	20
V5: Are the raters trained on how to conduct performance appraisal?				
Yes	22	47	57	36
No	78	53	43	64
V6: Are specific written instructions for the completion of the appraisals provided to the evaluators?				
Yes	74	91	100	84
No	27	9	0	16
V7: Was the content on the performance appraisal based on a job analysis?				
Yes	27	46	43	37
No	73	54	57	63

managerial appraisal system (MAS) within their organizations.

Prior to describing the characteristics of their MAS, each participant was asked to consider all of the purposes their MAS was to serve and then make an overall evaluation of the extent to which their MAS were effective.

The following scale was used for this evaluation.

To what extent do you consider your managerial appraisal system to be effective?
0—Not at all
1—To a slight extent
2—To some extent
3—To a moderate extent
4—To a fairly large extent
5—To a large extent
6—To a very great extent

After completing their evaluation, each participant was asked to describe the developmental procedures and the characteristics of the MAS based on the seven critical questions. Table 1 presents the seven questions and the frequency of responses as a function of the size of the organization.

RESULTS

Administrators for the smaller firms rated their PA systems as significantly less effective than the administrators for the larger firms ($p < .05$). A relationship was also found between organizational size and six critical questions. For example, for organizations larger than 500 employees, 37 percent of the respondents indicated that only one rater was involved in the evaluation process. For administrators representing organizations of less than 500 people, however, more than 65 percent indicated that only one rater was involved in the evaluation of managerial personnel.

Lower percentages were also found for the smaller organizations in formal appeals (28 percent), formal PA training (22 percent), written instructions to the raters (74 percent) and the use of job analysis to develop the PA system (27 percent) (see Table 1). Similarly, although 100 percent of the very large firms (over 5,000 employees) provided managers an opportunity to review their PA, only two-thirds of the small firms provided this opportunity. Also, although none of the PA systems in the larger firms were based solely on traits, 33 percent of the small firms had trait-based systems exclusively. With the exception of the question on job analysis, chi-square analysis revealed significant differences for all critical questions as a function of organizational size ($p < .01$) with greater frequencies of positive characteristics for the larger organizations.

Table 2 presents the complete correlation matrix involving the seven characteristics and the administrators' evaluation. The highest correlation with the administrator's evaluation was with responses to the format/method question, i.e., higher evaluations were associated with *non-trait*

Table 2
Correlation of Characteristics with Evaluation and Step-wise Results

	PA Characteristic							
Evaluation	*1*	*2*	*3*	*4*	*5*	*6*	*7*	*Beta*
1	.37							.23
2	.40	.30						.24
3	.36	.19	.39					.19
4	.43	.31	.49	.27				.13
5	.26	.23	.31	.35	.29			.12
6	.25	.15	.33	.14	.34	.20		.08
7	.10	.29	.26	.17	.24	.28	.21	.05
								R = .57

formats, ($r(138) = .43, p<.01$). Other significant correlations were the use of an employee review process (.40), the existence of a formal appeal process (.36), the use of multiple raters (.37), the presence of a rater training program (.26) and the use of specific, written instructions for conducting appraisals.

The responses to the seven critical questions were coded "1" for the presence of the positive characteristic or "0" for its absence. For the question having to do with the format for appraisal, a "trait-only" response was coded "0" while all other responses were coded "1". The administrator's evaluation was then regressed onto the responses to the seven PA characteristics using the step-wise method. Table 2 also presents the results of this analysis.

It should be noted that the mean number of positive appraisal characteristics across the 140 organizations was 4.0 ($SD = 1.9$; maximum score = 7). Administrators from 13 organizations indicated that all seven characteristics were a part of their PA system, while administrators from eight organizations indicated that none of the characteristics were part of their PA method. Over 56 percent of the respondents indicated the use of four or less of the positive PA characteristics. The correlation between the number of positive PA characteristics and the evaluation was .48, $p < .01$. Thus, support was also found for the hypothesized relationship between PA characteristics and the effectiveness rating by the administrator.

The regression analysis strongly supported the previous recommendations for the positive appraisal characteristics. Only the use of formal job analysis was not significantly correlated with the administrator's evaluation. With the six significant variables entered into the regression equation, an R of .57 was obtained ($p < .001$). The correlation between the number of positive PA characteristics (0 to 7) and the effectiveness rating was also significant; $r(138) = .48, p < .01$.

DISCUSSION

Despite the proliferation of research and writing on the subject, the state of managerial performance appraisal is still rather primitive based on the results of this survey. For example, although all of the recent texts on appraisal recommend multiple rater systems, the modal procedure of the 140 organizations involved in this study was still a single superordinate appraisal. In a follow-up analysis of the multiple ratings systems, a total of 10 of the respondents indicated that subordinates were formally involved in the appraisal of their managers. The mean effectiveness rating for this group was significantly higher than the mean rating of the other respondents ($p < .05$).

Despite the increasing evidence that rater training programs are effective (e.g., Bernardin and Buckley, 1981; Pulakos, 1984), a majority of organizations do not use any type of rater training program. In fact, the percentage of organizations indicating that rater training is used was *less* than that which was reported in an earlier survey (Locher and Teel, 1977). A formal appeal process for appraisals was also unusual for sampled organizations despite considerable legal evidence that such a practice is related to successful legal defenses (Cascio and Bernardin, 1981; Feild and Holley, 1982).

Another clear pattern to the results was the lower frequency of usage for the positive appraisal characteristics by the smaller organizations. This finding may indicate a less rigorous approach to appraising managerial performance by smaller organizations. One, of course, can only speculate as to the cause of this clear organizational size effect. It may be that individuals who are responsible for the personnel/human resource function in smaller organizations have less formal training in this area or more diverse job responsibilities. For example, a recent study found that only 40 percent of the smaller firms sampled had separate personnel departments (McEvoy, 1984). Because they are called upon to perform many diverse job functions, these people may be less knowledgeable about the state-of-the-art methods in any given personnel area.

One promising survey result was the decrease in the use of only "trait" ratings to evaluate managers. Only 22 percent of all respondents indicated that "trait" ratings were used exclusively. This figure compares favorably to previous survey work (DeVries et al., 1981, p. 43; Lazer and Wikstrom, 1977, p. 21). This trend is supportive of the overwhelming condemnation of trait-oriented appraisal systems both in the courts (Bernardin and Cascio, 1984; Feild and Holley, 1982) and in scholarly work (e.g., Bernardin and Beatty, 1984; Cascio, 1982a; DeVries et al., 1981).

This study has shown that more effective PA systems, as rated by administrators of these programs, have characteristics that are highly recommended by research scholars. These researchers have generally based their conclusions on psychometric criteria such as levels of halo effect, leniency and reliability and outcomes of court cases involving performance assessment (e.g., Bernardin and Beatty, 1984; Feild and Holley, 1982). Thus, further support is garnered for the implementation of these approaches in PA system development and refinement. In terms of potential for improvement, the low mean rating for positive characteristics (viz., 4.0) found in this study indicates that there is much that can be done with regard to increasing the likelihood of a more effective PA system.

The growing behavioral research on utility analysis linking personnel practices to organizational effectiveness (Cascio, 1982b) strongly suggests the need for personnel administrators to take a closer look at how they might implement state-of-the-art methods in their organizations. Our study suggests further that this "catch-up" is even more necessary among smaller firms.

REFERENCES

R. S. Barrett, *Performance Rating.* Chicago: Science Research Associates, 1966.

H. J. Bernardin & R. W. Beatty, *Performance Appraisal: Assessing Human Behavior at Work.* Boston: Kent, 1984.

H. J. Bernardin & M. B. Buckley, "A consideration of strategies in rater training," *Academy of Management Review,* 1981, *6,* pp. 205–212.

H. J. Bernardin & W. F. Cascio, *An Annotated Bibliography of Court Cases Relevant to Employment Decisions (1980–1983).* San Antonio, TX. AFHRL Technical Report, 1984.

S. Carroll & C. Schneier, *Performance Appraisal And Review Systems.* Glenview, IL: Scott Foresman, 1982.

W. F. Cascio, *Applied Psychology in Personnel Management,* Reston, VA: Reston Press, 1982a.

W. F. Cascio, *Costing Human Resources: The Financial Impact of Behavior in Organizations.* Boston: Kent-Wadsworth, 1982b.

W. F. Cascio & H. J. Bernardin, "Implications of performance appraisal litigation for personnel decisions," *Personnel Psychology,* 1981, *34,* pp. 211–226.

T. A. DeCotiis & A. Petit, "The performance appraisal process: A model and some testable prepositions," *Academy of Management Review,* 1978, *3,* pp. 635–645.

D. L. DeVries, A. M. Morrison, S. L. Shullman & M. L. Gerlach, *Performance Appraisal on the Line.* New York: John Wiley, 1981.

H. S. Feild & W. H. Holley, "The relationship of performance appraisal characteristics to verdicts in selected employment discrimination cases," *Academy of Management Journal,* 1982, *2,* pp. 392–406.

H. S. Feild & W. H. Holley, "Performance appraisal—An analysis of state-wide practices," *Public Personnel Management,* 1975, *4,* pp. 145–150.

R. Henderson, *Performance Appraisal: Theory to Practice.* Reston, VA: Reston Press, 1980.

K. J. Lacho, G. K. Stearns & M. F. Villere, "A study of employee appraisal systems of major cities in the U.S." *Public Personnel Management,* March–April 1979, pp. 111–124.

F. J. Landy & J. L. Farr, "Performance rating," *Psychological Bulletin,* 1980, *87,* pp. 72–107.

C. P. Latham & K. N. Wexley, *Increasing Productivity Through Performance Appraisal.* Reading, MA: Addison-Wesley, 1981.

R. I. Lazer & W. S. Wikstrom, *Appraising Managerial Performance: Current Practices and Future Directions.* New York: Conference Board, 1977.

A. H. Locher & K. S. Teel, "Performance appraisal—A survey of current practices," *Personnel Journal,* 1977, *56,* 245–247, 254.

G. M. McEvoy, "Small business personnel practices," *Journal of Small Business Management,* 1984, *22,* pp. 1–8.

J. B. Miner, "Management appraisal: A review of procedures and practices," in W. Hammer & F. Schmidt (Eds.), *Contemporary Problems in Personnel.* Chicago: St. Clair Gress, 1977, pp. 228–238.

E. Pulakos, "A comparison of rater training programs: Error training and accuracy training," *Journal of Applied Psychology,* 1984, *69,* pp. 581–588.

How Defensible Is Your Performance Appraisal System?

Charles R. Klasson
Duane E. Thompson
Gary L. Luben

Since the enactment of the Civil Rights Act of 1964 and specifically Title VII of that Act, the Federal government has increasingly involved itself with personnel policies and practices of employers in both the public and private sectors.[1] The most historic example is the famous and intensely controversial decree invoking "equal employment" practices at American Telephone and Telegraph, the nation's largest private employer.[2]

While Title VII initially was directed toward discriminatory employee selection practices, the development of case law in this area suggests that the courts now are interpreting the Act much more broadly. Various court challenges have sought to clarify which employment practices the Act encompasses. Over time, this definitional process has gradually come to include performance appraisal systems where they operate to discriminate against *any* individual, to be within the legitimate interest of Title VII and its enforcing agency, the Equal Employment Opportunity Commission (EEOC).[3]

SUBJECT TO THE UNIFORM GUIDELINES

Given the courts' interpretation of Title VII to date, sufficient evidence exists to conclude performance appraisals now are viewed as a selection device and hence subject to the *Uniform Guidelines in Employee Selection Procedures.* Consequently, employers soon may have to defend the adequacy of their existing performance appraisal systems in the light of the Act's prohibition against discriminatory employment practices.

This article presents first, a brief review of critical court cases that bear directly upon performance appraisal practices and employment decisions; second, the options employers have for compliance with the law; and third, an audit procedure for ascertaining how defensible a company's performance appraisal practices are given the emergence of the courts' interpretation of the law.

CRITICAL COURT CASES

Typical performance appraisal programs involve assessments about an employee's performance on a particular job and performance potential to hold different jobs. These assessments typically are categorized as administrative decisions (pay, promotion and layoffs) and developmental decisions (job training, transfer and coaching).

The majority of cases involving Title VII litigation have not challenged directly an employer's performance appraisal programs. In fact, to date there has been no case in the Federal courts which has addressed the specific issue of performance appraisal validation. Rather, the courts have addressed issues dealing with significant components of performance appraisal. Specifically, the courts have found Title VII violations in employment practices involving transfer,[4] promotion,[5] compensation,[6] layoffs[7] and training pro-

Reprinted from the December 1980 issue of *Personnel Administrator,* copyright 1980, The American Society for Personnel Administration, 606 North Washington Street, Alexandria, Virginia, 22314.

grams.[8] All of these employment decisions are directly related to performance appraisal practices of an employer.

TRANSFER AND PROMOTION DECISIONS

Perhaps the single most important case bearing on performance appraisal is *Rowe* v. *General Motors Corp.* In this case, the Fifth Circuit Court of Appeals concluded that the lack of blacks who were promoted or transferred resulted from the reliance upon all-white supervisory recommendations which were based on subjective and vague standards.[9] The court listed five aspects of the promotion/transfer system at GM which it found in violation of Title VII:

1. The foreman's recommendation was the indispensable single most important factor in the promotion process.
2. Foremen were given no written instructions pertaining to the qualifications necessary for promotion.
3. Those standards which were determined to be controlling were vague and subjective.
4. Hourly employees were not notified of promotional opportunities.
5. No safeguards existed in the procedure designed to avert discriminatory practices.[10]

Each of these violations addressed very basic aspects of any appraisal program that was performance based and not seniority based. This challenge was dramatic and clear-cut as it related to discriminatory practices. Another case found a professional promotion system to be discriminatory. In *Wade* v. *Mississippi Cooperative Extension Service,*[11] the Fifth Circuit Court of Appeals again addressed the issue of promotion and concluded that the test used by the state agricultural extension service for evaluation of professional employees was insufficiently job related and as a result was in violation of Title VII.

The court concluded that the test, as employed, was discriminatory since the evaluation was largely subjective and vulnerable to discrimination on the part of the evaluating supervisors. In addition, there was sufficient evidence to indicate the test scores were not used consistently as a basis for promoting employees or establishing their salaries. Finally, there was no showing by the defendant that the test was substantially related to the particular jobs of individuals being evaluated.

LAYOFF DECISIONS

The discriminatory use of performance appraisal ratings in decisions regarding the layoff of employees has been addressed by the courts. In *Brito* v. *Zia Co.,* the 10th Circuit Court of Appeals ruled that Zia had violated Title VII when, on the basis of poor performance ratings, it laid off several Spanish surnamed employees.[12] The court concluded that the practice was illegal since:

- The evaluations were based on subjective supervisory observations.
- The test caused a disproportionate reduction in the number of Spanish surnamed employees.
- The evaluations were not administered and scored in a controlled and standardized fashion.
- Two of the three supervisory evaluators did not have daily contact with the employees being evaluated.

The significance of this case cannot be overestimated, for it is in this case the appeals court accepted performance appraisals as tests. As such, the performance appraisal system employed by Zia was required to comply with EEOC guidelines on employee selection procedures.

The court concluded that the assessments were based on the "best judgments and opinions" of the evaluators, but not on any identifiable objective criteria which was supported by some kind of record. As a result, the court determined that Zia had failed to produce sufficient evidence of validity for its performance appraisal system.

In *Flowers* v. *Crouch-Walter Corp.,* a related case, the Fifth Circuit Court of Appeals decided that the plaintiff had established a *prima facie* case of racial discrimination by showing that:

- He was qualified for the job.
- He met the normal requirements of the job but was discharged.
- The employer assigned white employees to perform the work after his discharge.[13]

The same court stated that the normal procedure required the plaintiff to demonstrate that he had performed the job satisfactorily in order to raise the inference of racial discrimination. In this case, however, the plaintiff was not required to do so, since the employer did not express displeasure regarding the plaintiff's work performance, thereby proving that the employee's performance was satisfactory.

COMPENSATION AND TRAINING

The courts also have supported charges of discrimination in the areas of employee compensation and training. In *Wade* v. *Mississippi Cooperative Extension Service,* the Fifth Circuit Court also determined that aside from discrimination in promotional opportunities, ample evidence existed to indicate discrimination existed in salary determination.[14]

In *James* v. *Stockham Valves and Fittings Co.,* the court concluded the practice of determining which individuals were eligible for the apprenticeship program was discriminatory since the selections were made by predominantly white supervisors without any formal written guidelines and because the practice resulted in a disproportionately low number of blacks selected for the program.[15] Here both skill requirements of the job and performance capabilities of the employees were ignored.

FORMAL JOB ANALYSES

As mandated by the EEOC guidelines, formal job analyses must be undertaken as a prerequisite to any validation study.[16] The courts have interpreted this requirement very strictly. As a result, validation of many selection procedures has been found to be in violation of Title VII for lack of these job analyses.[17]

As discussed earlier, the court rejected the validation as performed in *Wade* v. *Mississippi Cooperative Extension Service,* concluding that the defendant had not shown company tests were based on a formal job analysis.[18] The U.S. Supreme Court in *Albemarle Paper Company* v. *Moody* also rejected that validation on similar grounds.[19]

USE OF SUBJECTIVE CRITERIA

Over the years, the courts apparently have developed a deep suspicion of any form of subjective criteria used in performance appraisal. As mentioned earlier, the U.S. Supreme Court disapproved use of subjective criteria in *Albemarle Paper Company* v. *Moody.*[20] Although this case dealt with the use of subjective criteria in the validation process of pre-employment tests, the intent of the court was to address the issue of subjective criteria and they have consistently disavowed the use of this form of criteria.[21] In *Baxter* v. *Savannah Sugar Refining Corp.,*[22] the Fifth Circuit Court of Appeals dealt with a case factually similar to that of *Rowe* v. *General Motors.* Taking the earlier decision in *Rowe* v. *General Motors* as its primary guidance, the court concluded that the promotion and transfer programs at Savannah Sugar Refining were discriminatory. In reaching its decision the court substantially reaffirmed the five points raised in *Rowe* v. *General Motors.*

The issue of subjective criteria becomes more confused when one considers the extent to which subjective criteria becomes a discriminatory practice. Certain court decisions appear to reject subjective criteria on the grounds that it is not objective. In *United States* v. *Bethlehem Steel Corp.,* the Second Circuit Court of Appeals considered the absence of "fixed or reasonably objective standards and procedures for hiring" to be discriminatory.[23]

This case, however, does not appear to represent the predominant view of the courts. Courts are beginning to realize that not all job performance ratings can be based solely upon objective criteria. As the Eighth Circuit Court of Appeals determined in *Rogers* v. *International Paper Co.:*

> *(Subjective criteria) are not to be condemned as unlawful per se, for in all fairness to applicants and employers alike, decisions about hiring and promotion in supervisory and*

managerial jobs cannot realistically be made using objective standards alone.[24]

The alternatives to this interpretation of subjective criteria appear to be a strict application of the EEOC Uniform Guidelines with the resultant reliance upon more objective appraisals of actual job performance.

In summary, the above Title VII court cases have challenged successfully virtually every aspect of performance appraisal systems (their technology), the usual employment decisions reached based upon use of such systems and the adequacy of such systems in terms of their discriminatory characteristics. The consequences are clear. Employers must decide (1) how they will comply with the Uniform Guidelines, and (2) how they can make their systems defensible to the courts and enforcement agencies and to their employees.

COMPLIANCE OPTIONS

The *Uniform Guidelines on Employee Selection Procedures* focus attention on two areas. First, there is concern when the bottom line does not reflect equity. Second, selection procedures including performance appraisal must be validated (with few exceptions) if there is an adverse impact on protected classes. Two rather simplistic approaches have been suggested to comply with these requirements. One is to use validated selection procedures only. The other is to ensure a clean bottom line through a system of quotas. Neither approach taken to the extreme is plausible.

VALIDATION OPTION

With regard to validation, the courts and the EEOC have shown a decided preference for criterion-related validity. For example, in *Douglas* v. *Hampton,* the District of Columbia Circuit Court of Appeals concluded that content validity is to be employed only in those instances where criterion-related validity is proven to be infeasible.[25]

In addition, Section 6 of the *Uniform Guidelines* requires the sample group used in a criterion-related validation to substantially represent the applicant pool for whom the test is designed. The U.S. Supreme Court rejected the validation in *Albemarle Paper Company* v. *Moody,* partly because the sample was comprised primarily of job-experienced white workers, but tests would be administered to "new job applicants who (were) younger, largely inexperienced and in many instances nonwhite." These and other technical considerations indicate that criterion-related validity studies in many instances are not at all feasible.[26]

Finally, even though the *Uniform Guidelines* assumes equal acceptance of content, criterion-related and construct validity, courts have raised serious questions about content validation efforts of companies. In three recent court cases involving content validity, the "courts relied on the *Uniform Guidelines* either to throw out the employer's content validity study or to disallow ranking from the content valid procedure in the absence of additional empirical evidence." Despite this confusion, the validation of performance appraisal for employment decisions remains a central issue.[27]

If the employer chooses not to validate the challenged employment practice, Section 6 of the *Uniform Guidelines* provides the employer the option of modifying the challenged employment practice so as to eliminate the discriminatory impact. In essence, the *Uniform Guidelines* advocate a quota system to eliminate discriminatory practices. This recommendation is confusing since Title VII specifically precludes employers from discriminating on the basis of race, color, religion, sex, or national origin. The U.S. Supreme Court has addressed the issue of quotas in the landmark case, *Bakke* v. *Regents of the University of California.*[28] Although dealing with educational opportunities, the court's message was clear. The achievement of racial parity through the imposition of quotas is illegal. One can infer from this case that the use of quotas in employment decisions also is illegal.

The U.S. Supreme Court addressed a related issue in *Kaiser Aluminum and Chemical Corp.* v. *Weber.* Here the court ruled that the quota system adopted as a part of a voluntary affirmative action plan by Kaiser Aluminum and the United States Steelworkers was not in violation of Title VII. The court emphasized, however, that its inquiry was concerned only with whether Title VII forbids private employers and unions from voluntarily agreeing upon *bona fide* affirmative action plans that assured racial preference.

Furthermore, the court made no effort to define in detail the lines of demarcation between permissible and impermissible affirmative action plans; hence, its decision must not be interpreted as a blanket endorsement of quotas as a means of avoiding discrimination.[29]

The most recent case which addresses the legality of quotas is *Fullilove* v. *Klutznick.* This U.S. Supreme Court case challenged the requirement that 10 percent of each grant made under the Public Works Employment Act of 1977 be expended for minority business enterprises. While not dealing directly with employment issues, the case has indirect relevance. The court reaffirmed the legality of quotas as a legitimate exercise of congressional power to remedy the effect of past discriminations.[30] Despite the U.S. Supreme Court's acceptance of quotas in certain situations, employers still face the challenge of devising workable systems which provide equity to all employees and remain open to suit if that equity is denied in selection decisions.

CHARACTERISTICS OF A DEFENSIBLE SYSTEM

Despite the rather tenuous nature of the present situation, selection, promotion, transfer, training, retention and compensation decisions continue to be based on employee performance appraisals. The personnel professional, continuously faced with the possibility of charges of illegal discrimination, must find ways of ensuring personnel decisions are made in a way which will satisfy the scrutiny of enforcement agencies and the courts.

Using the above sampling of relevant court cases as guides, it is possible to identify basic characteristics of performance appraisal systems which, if met, would go a long way toward creating an *acceptable and defensible system* falling in mid-range between blind adherence to a set of quotas and frenetic validation studies. All are based on sound personnel practice. Each has been emphasized in at least one significant court case.

A Formalized System. Your chances of defending a formalized system will be enhanced if:

1. The overall appraisal process is formalized (documented completely), standardized and, as much as possible, is objective in nature; this includes statements regarding purposes of appraisals, mandatory use by management, complete disclosure of the program to evaluation and due process procedures.

2. A thorough, formal job analysis procedure has been established for specifying standards of performance for all employment positions being rated.

3. The performance standards (traits, behavior, or results) are based upon relevant job dimensions that are appropriate to the nature of work called for and bear upon the desired job performance.

4. The appraisal involves measures of performance, the proportions which each measure carries with respect to the overall assessment are fixed, and subjective supervisory ratings are considered as only one component of the overall appraisal process.

Companies that fail to meet the above *minimum* requirements are clearly in trouble. But others that appear to satisfy these requirements in terms of long standing and well established personnel policies and procedures may be in trouble too. Failure to utilize a formalized system can be attributed to a variety of causes. But one of the most serious offenders is poor design. Performance appraisal systems must be designed to suit the job structure and appraisal needs of an organization. Dissatisfaction with traditional appraisal systems by line managers can be traced to the utilization of (1) a system which is over-designed for the jobs (for example widespread use of MBO where it is not appropriate), and (2) an inability to make equitable and fair employment decisions based on high quality appraisal information due to limited promotion opportunities and wage guidelines.

To be useful, the system must not only be formalized but tailored to the needs of the organization.

The Process of Appraisal. Your chances of defending actual appraisals and the attending employment decisions will be enhanced if:

1. Your appraisers are adequately trained in the use of appraisal techniques which use written qualification criteria for promotion, transfer and similar decisions.

2. Your appraisers have substantial opportunity to observe a representative sample of an employee's job related performance.

3. Multiple appraisers are used when it enhances the overall quality of assessment.

4. The administration and scoring of performance appraisals are standardized and controlled.

A well designed and documented performance appraisal system can and does produce indefensible appraisals and employment decisions when supervisors are not qualified in its use. Subjective and biased ratings are difficult to minimize and avoid when raters are neither motivated nor qualified to use a system. Poorly designed systems produce poor performance information which is tough to defend. But equally damaging is a good system that is neither understood nor accepted by its users due to lack of training.

An Open Labor Market. The absence of job posting has contributed to charges of discrimination in the area of job promotion and transfer. The last area in which courts' rulings influence an appraisal system involves origination of personnel appraisals. In this regard your system becomes more defensible if:

1. Opportunities for promotion and transfer are posted and this information made available to all interested individuals.

2. An employee initiated promotion/transfer procedure exists which does not require the immediate supervisor's recommendations.

It is important to point out that these characteristics summarize what appear to be the courts' interpretation of what constitutes an acceptable and defensible performance appraisal system. Strict adherence to these system characteristics, however, provides no guarantee that the courts would not find a particular appraisal system to be in violation of Title VII, since one cannot guarantee that the current interpretation of the courts will remain the same in the near future.

Notwithstanding the dynamic nature of the courts' interpretations, however, adherence to these system characteristics represents the employer's best opportunity for complying with the current EEOC guidelines on employee selection procedures.

ENDNOTES

1. 42 U.S.C. §2000e-2(a)(1970) (amended in 1972, codified at 42 U.S.C. §2000e (Supp V 1975).

2. Loomis, C. J. "A.T.&T. In the Throes of Equal Employment," *Fortune*, January 15, 1979, p. 45; Also see L. Smith, "The EEOC's Bold Foray Into Job Evaluation," *Fortune*, September 1978, p. 58.

3. The Equal Employment Opportunity Commission was created with the enactment of the Civil Rights Act of 1964. 42 U.S.C. §2000e-4(a) (1970) (amended in 1972, codified at 42 U.S.C. §2000e-4(a) (Supp. V 1975).

4. See the following cases: *Brito* v. *Zia Co.*, 478 F.2d 1200 (1973); *Alexander* v. *Machinists*, 565 F.2d 1364 (1977); *Rowe* v. *General Motors Corp.*, 457 F.2d 348 (1972); *James* v. *Stockham Valves and Fittings Co.* 559 F.2d 310 (1977); *EEOC* v. *Radiator Specialty Co.*, 16 E. P. D. 8276; and *Abron* v. *Black and Decker Mfg. Co.*, 439 F. Supp. 1095 (1977).

5. See the following cases: *Watkins* v. *Scott Paper Co.*, 530 F.2d 1159 (1976); *Abrams* v. *Johnson*, 534 F.2d 1226 (1976); *Wade* v. *Miss. Coop. Extension Service*, 528 F.2d 508 (1976); *Hill* v. *Western Electric Co.*, 12 F.E.P. 1175; *Rowe* v. *General Motors Corp.*, 457 F.2d 348 (1972); *Robinson* v. *Union Carbide Corp.*, 538 F.2d 652 (1976); *Dickerson* v. *U.S. Steel Corp.*, 15 F.E.P. 752; *James* v. *Stockham Valves and Fittings Co.*, 559 F.2d 310 (1977); *Fisher* v. *Proctor and Gamble Co.*, 14 E.P.D. 7662; *EEOC* v. *Radiator Specialty Co.*, 16 E.P.D. 8276; *Baxter* v. *Savannah Sugar Refining Corp.*, 495 F.2d 437 (1974); and *Abron* v. *Black & Decker Mfg. Co.*, 439 F. Supp. 1095 (1977).

6. See *Wade* v. *Miss. Coop. Extension Service*, 528 F.2d 508 (1976).

7. See the following cases: *Brito* v. *Zia Co.*, 478 F.2d 1200 (1973); *Alexander* v. *Machinists*, 565 F.2d 1364 (1977); and *Flowers* v. *Crouch-Walker Corp.*, 552 F.2d 1277 (1977).

8. See *James* v. *Stockham Valves and Fittings Co.*, 559 F.2d 310 (1977).

9. 457 F.2d 348 (1972).

10. Ibid.

11. 528 F.2d 508 (1976).

12. 478 F.2d 1200 (1973).

13. 552 F.2d 1277 (1977).

14. 528 F.2d 508 (1976).

15. 559 F.2d 310 (1977).

16. C.F.R. §1607.5 (1977).

17. See *Albemarle Paper Co.* v. *Moody,* 95 S. Ct. 2362 (1975) and *Watkins* v. *Scott Paper Co.,* 530 F.2d 1159 (1976).

18. 528 F.2d 508 (1976).

19. 95 S. Ct. 2362 (1975).

20. 95 S. Ct. 2362 (1975).

21. See the following cases: *Albermarle Paper Co.* v. *Moody,* 95 S. Ct. 2362 (1975); *Baxter* v. *Savannah Sugar Refining Corp.,* 495 F.2d 437 (1974); *Rowe* v. *General Motors Corp.,* 457 F.2d 348 (1972); and *James* v. *Stockham Valves and Fittings Co.,* 559 F.2d 310 (1977).

22. 495 F.2d 437 (1974).

23. 446 F.2d 652 (1971).

24. 510 F.2d 1340 (1975).

25. 512 F.2d 976 (1975).

26. Schmidt, F. L., and J. E. Hunter, "The Future Criterion Related Validities in Title VII Employment Discrimination Cases," *Personnel Administrator,* September 1977, pp. 39–42.

27. Sharf, J. C., "Content validity: Whither thou goest?" *Industrial-Organizational Psychologist,* 1980, pp. 8–14.

28. 97 S. Ct. 2733 (1978).

29. 47 L.W. 4851 (June 27, 1979).

30. *Fullilove* v. *Klutznick,* 48 U.S.L.W.4979, U.S. Supreme Court, July 2, 1980.

CHAPTER 5

Compensation

Pay in the form of wages and salaries and a wide range of legally required and agreed upon benefits collectively represent the means by which employees are financially compensated for joining organizations, staying in them, and accomplishing certain levels of work performance. The compensation activity in human resources management, therefore, is a key people-processing activity, which begins with the planning that occurs before people enter organizations and continues until their exit and beyond. For a good many organizations, the compensation provided employees can account for as much as 50 percent of total cash flow. For others, it can account for an even higher percentage, especially if the organization's product or service system is very labor intensive.

In addition to the equal employment opportunity laws—especially Title VII of the Civil Rights Act of 1964 and its amendment, the Pregnancy Discrimination Act of 1978, and the Age Discrimination in Employment Act of 1967—the legal environment in which compensation occurs is bounded by several other major pieces of federal legislation. The most basic is the Fair Labor Standards Act (FLSA) of 1938 and its amendments, including the Equal Pay Act of 1963, which contains minimum wage, overtime, and equal pay provisions. Federal legislation also supports the Old Age, Survivors, Disability, and Health Insurance Program (OASDHI) and a number of legally required benefits associated with that program, such as social security and unemployment insurance. Another major piece of federal legislation is the Employment Retirement Income Security Act (ERISA) of 1974, which regulates the pension programs of employers and includes requirements regarding vesting, accrued benefits, funding, and so forth. Finally, the Revenue Act of 1978, the Economic Recovery Tax Act (ERTA) of 1981, and other tax laws define, as part of the Internal Revenue Code, the taxable or nontaxable status of benefits.

Organizations, in this context, must make their compensation systems both attractive and equitable to current and prospective employees. Information regarding the external labor market, often supplied through industry or area wage surveys, is necessary for determining an appropriate pay structure and making individual wage and salary decisions within that structure. Also necessary is information on the internal labor market. Again, is the compensation system attractive? Is it equitable? A variety of job evaluation methods are available for establishing pay grades and ranges for jobs based on their relative worth to the organization. To match and then maintain a balance between the compensation demands of the marketplace and the compensation demands of employees is not an easy task. The task is further complicated, of course, by the rather subjective nature of the performance appraisal process (discussed in Chapter 4), which should be a primary source of information for making compensation decisions.

In the first article, Mahoney addresses three functions of a compensation system—the attraction, retention, and motivation of employees—and then how compensation can impact each of these areas. Next, Kaye and McKee suggest that companies should begin to rethink their compensation systems, because the current reward structure, which focuses on higher pay and upward movement, is no longer working. They suggest that crowding at the top of the ladder and restless employees waiting below mandate alternative approaches.

Hills, Madigan, Scott, and Markham urge reevaluation of current merit pay programs. The current definition of merit pay is so loose, they feel, that it may be difficult to perform audits. They suggest specific areas that an audit should focus on and outline three audit strategies and guidelines for their implementation.

Mahoney next presents several issues facing managers in charge of company compensation administration, a field with many challenges that so far remain unresolved.

Meyer suggests that executive compensation must promote long-term commitment to long-term goals, a notion still not adequately addressed by the compensation committees of many corporate boards of directors and compensation consultants. Further, changing economic conditions, such as the slowing of inflation, provide opportunities to alter salary expectations and modify short- and long-term incentive programs.

Equal pay for comparable worth has been one of the most controversial issues in the compensation area, and Schnebly addresses it in the final article in this chapter. He examines the legal background of sex-based wage discrimination and how the courts have ruled on such violations under the Equal Pay Act and Title VII of the Civil Rights Act, both before and after the Supreme Court's *Gunther* decision in 1981.

Suggestions for Further Reading

Chakravarthy, B. S., & Zajac, E. J. (1984). Tailoring incentive systems to a strategic context. *Planning Review, 12,* 30–35.

Crystal, G. S., & Hurwich, M. R. (1986). The case for divisional long-term incentives. *California Management Review, 29,* 60–74.

Cummings, L. L. (1984). Compensation, culture, and motivation: A systems perspective. *Organizational Dynamics, 12,* 33–44.

Greene, R. J. (1987). Effective compensation: The how and why. *Personnel Administrator, 32,* 112–116.

Hufnagel, E. M. (1987). Developing strategic compensation plans. *Human Resource Management, 26,* 93–108.

Prokesch, S. E. (1985, May). Executive pay: Who made the most? *Business Week,* pp. 78–88.

Spratt, M. F., & Steele, B. (1985). Rewarding key contributors. *Compensation and Benefits Review, 17,* 24–37.

Stonich, P. J. (1984). The performance measurement and reward system: Critical to strategic management. *Organizational Dynamics, 12,* 45–57.

Velleman, S. J. (1985). Flexible benefits packages that satisfy employees and the IRS. *Personnel, 62,* 33–41.

Von Glinow, M. A. (1985). Reward strategies for attracting, evaluating, and retaining professionals. *Human Resource Management, 24,* 191–206.

Compensation Functions

Thomas A. Mahoney

Typically, the functions of a compensation system are identified as: (1) attraction of persons to seek and accept employment in the organization, (2) retention of employees as members of the organization, and (3) motivation of the behavior or performance desired—acceptance of job assignments, hours worked, and the level of effort expended on the job.

ATTRACTION OF EMPLOYEES

People are attracted to employing organizations for many reasons. In general, they have decided that working offers advantages relative to not working, that one occupation offers advantages relative to others, and that a specific employer offers advantages not offered by others. The supply of applicants for employment varies with the perceived relative attractiveness of employment in an organization and the expectancy of employment. The perceived relative attractiveness varies with the anticipated compensation and with nonpecuniary employment characteristics, such as nature of the job, ease of commuting, and stability of employment. Decisions to make application for employment are influenced also by expectancies of employment; companies that are known to be employing receive more applications than companies known to be not hiring, other things being equal. The role of expectancy in employee job search is illustrated in research findings that indicate that unemployed workers conduct a relatively extensive job search (visit employment agencies, search want ads, and make application at many companies) during periods of high unemployment, and conduct a relatively intensive job search (rely upon friends and relatives for information) during periods of relatively low unemployment (Sheppard and Belitsky, 1966). Extensive job search can be viewed as a search for jobs, an attempt to increase the expectancy of employment, and intensive job search can be viewed as an investigation of specific job characteristics, on the assumption that opportunities for employment are already high. Both expectancy of employment and the attractiveness of employment can be manipulated in the attraction of applicants. When the expectancy of employment with other organizations is low (e.g., during periods of high unemployment), individual employers will be less concerned with making employment attractive through wage comparisons; the relative attractiveness of hiring wage rates is of most concern during periods of relative scarcity of labor supplies.

Establishment of wage rates for entry or hiring jobs requires some comparative standard, but this standard varies with the traditional or intended source of applicants for employment. Often labor market and/or industry wage surveys are cited as the source for these comparative data, but the relevance of these standards may vary from employer to employer, depending upon traditional sources of employees. Candidates for employment compare an employer's wage rates with those of known alternatives, not necessarily the full range of employers in a labor market. Graduating MBA students, for example, tend to compare wage offers with those of other companies recruiting at the school, typically a select sample from a regional or national population of employers. Unemployed, unskilled workers are more likely to compare wage offers with the alternative of continued unemployment and/or with other wage offers encountered in the local labor market. Secondary and/or part-time workers compare employment offers with attractive alternatives such as retirement, school, or housekeeping, and with a

Adapted from *Personnel Management,* © 1982, Allyn and Bacon, Inc.

select sample of alternative employers offering easily available employment that also fits their primary schedules.

Except in instances of employers seeking to hire scarce, high-talent individuals, most candidates for employment are seeking jobs; they are not being pirated from other employers. The pool of relevant employers to consider for comparison in the establishment of hiring wage rates thus will vary with the occupation and the traditional source of employees and may be unique to each employer.

Wage Level Determination

Wage surveys of relevant labor market competitors provide a base for determination of wages an employer ought to offer in order to attract candidates. The establishment of wage rates also is constrained by cost considerations. To remain competitive, every employer seeks to control per unit labor costs to the level of labor costs among competitors in the industry or product market (Mahoney, 1979a). For this reason, there are pressures to standardize wage rates among employers in a single industry, and one finds industry and/or association bargaining between employers and unions in the auto, steel, coal mining, construction, and other industries.

Using average wage of product competitors as a maximum constraint and hiring wage of relevant competitors in the labor market as a minimum constraint, an employer has various options available to satisfy both. An employer with a relatively open internal labor market encounters wage rate minima for every job. The average wage rate paid can be controlled, within the limits of the technology employed, by substituting lower paid jobs and occupations for higher paid jobs. Alternatively, an employer may seek out labor markets with relatively lower wages than the labor markets in which product competitors operate; industry development in the southern sun-belt and along the Mexican border illustrates this strategy. Employers with relatively closed internal labor markets have somewhat greater opportunity to control average wages since they hire into relatively few jobs. Wage rates for entry jobs may be set relative to the relevant labor market alternatives, while wages for nonentry jobs are not as rigorously constrained. Employees in nonentry jobs are relatively less mobile, since they have greater tenure with the employer and typically have developed more company-specific skills and knowledges than employees in entry jobs. The average wage within the organization can be manipulated through control of nonentry wages to compensate for any disadvantages incurred through payment of relatively high entry rates (Bronfenbrenner, 1956). The resulting tendency to raise entry rates while controlling nonentry rates has, in some instances, resulted in wage compression where newly hired employees may receive as much as or more than more tenured employees, a problem which will be considered later.

The rigor of the constraint of product market competitor wages varies considerably, depending upon the degree of competition in the product market. Highly competitive industries, such as soft-goods manufacturing and hosiery and garment manufacturing, seek to pay only the wage rate required to attract employees and change rates in response to changing conditions in the labor market. Less competitive industries, such as hard-goods manufacturing and steel and auto manufacturing, typically pay somewhat more than the minimum required by the labor market and change wages in response to changes in the cost of living more often than in response to labor market conditions (Ross, 1957; Wachter, 1970).

Given the tendencies toward standardization of wage rates among product competitors, competitive advantage must be sought through differentials in employee productivity. To the extent that wage and salary administration succeeds in attracting high potential candidates, encourages long tenure in the organization, and motivates personal development and high performance, it contributes to this competitive advantage. Other elements of the personnel function, such as selection, recruitment, training, and development, also are directed toward achievement of productivity.

LABOR-FORCE RETENTION

Labor-force retention, or the absence of turnover, usually is viewed as a desirable goal for personnel management. Turnover occasions costs of replacement, recruitment, and training, which may in certain instances be considerable. Typically, turnover is viewed as causing a temporary drop in productivity as new, less capable employees are recruited and trained to the level of performance of the terminated employee. The costs occasioned by employee turnover, however, obviously vary with the ease of replacing terminated employees, the availability of candidates for employment, the complexity of the jobs involved, and the amount of training required for new employees.

Employee terminations of employment are rejections of an employment contract previously accepted. For one reason or another, the employment contract is viewed less favorably than previously, and the employee chooses to leave the organization for another specific alternative (job, school, unemployment), or to search for a preferred alternative. Numerous studies of employee turnover suggest that terminations are a direct function of prior intentions to leave, dissatisfaction experienced in current employment, and the availability of attractive alternatives (low unemployment rates) (Ross and Zander, 1957). As in the attraction of individuals to employment, both the attractiveness of outcomes and the expectancy of those outcomes appear to influence decisions to terminate employment.

Labor market research suggests that most people accept employment with the intention of staying, and that once employed in a job do not actively seek out alternative employment opportunities, unless dissatisfied with something in the current employment (Parnes, 1954). There are instances in which people with particularly scarce qualifications are pirated away from what had been a satisfying job, but most terminations probably proceed from a prior dissatisfaction and consequent search for attractive alternatives. Top management recruiters often are employed to seek out particularly qualified individuals and to bring to their attention attractive job alternatives; many of those recruited through this process were not actively seeking alternative employment.

Employees experience dissatisfaction in an employment situation for many reasons, pecuniary and nonpecuniary. Theories of employee satisfaction (dissatisfaction) suggest that satisfaction is an emotional response to the congruence between what one experiences and what one values (expects, desires, or seeks). Dissatisfaction, viewed as the converse of satisfaction, reflects experienced incongruity. Various dimensions or factors of job satisfaction have been proposed by different theories, such as compensation, promotion, nature of work or tasks, recognition, benefits, working conditions, supervision, co-workers, company policy, and management (Locke, 1976).

Compensation figures in one form or another as a dimension of job satisfaction, and, viewed in terms of the overall model of satisfaction, compensation can serve to balance or compensate for dissatisfaction experienced in other dimensions. Compensation elements typically considered in job satisfaction and in the design of compensation programs are: (1) wage level paid by one's employer relative to wage levels paid by other employers, (2) wages for one's job relative to wages for other jobs, and (3) wages paid one relative to wages paid others in the same job. These three dimensions of satisfaction with compensation, although derived empirically in many models of job satisfaction, correspond to what one might expect from consideration of equity comparisons and the attraction, retention, and performance dimensions of labor supply.

Judgments of equity and compensation require comparisons with some "other" compensation referent, and the behavioral relevance of other referents varies with the type of behavior considered. Decisions regarding applications for employment involve comparisons between different employers, and the compensation offered by feasible alternative employers provides a relevant standard. Decisions to seek or reject an alternative job assignment involve comparisons of the compensation and requirements of alternative jobs. And choices among alternative behaviors within a job (exert more effort, work overtime) involve comparisons of the compensation received by people performing differently in the same job. Wage comparisons with other employers, other jobs in the same organization, and other persons in the same job are relevant both in determining the equity of one's payment and in influencing choices of alternative behaviors.

Not surprisingly, employers address these three concerns in the compensation issues of determining wage level, the structure of wages within the organization, and the establishment of schedules of individual compensation. Wage level determination is of most relevance in the attraction of employees and was discussed in the previous section; determination of the structure of wage differentials among jobs probably is most relevant in preventing dissatisfaction, and in maintaining and eliciting the cooperation of the organizational labor force; and individual schedules of payment are most relevant in influencing individual performance on the job.

Wage Structure

Equal pay for equal work is an accepted principle for achieving equity of compensation. Consistent with this principle and with the concept of an employment exchange, people expect to be paid differentially for work in different jobs. A major task in wage and salary administration is the determination of a structure of compensation differentials that both employer and employees can accept as being reflective of differences in the work associated with these jobs. The process of determining the structure of compensation rates is termed *job evaluation.*

Job Evaluation. Job evaluation performs the pricing function in organizations which, for one reason or another, do not rely solely upon wage surveys in the determination of wage rates for all jobs. It is an approach to the determination of equitable pay differentials within a single organization, not the overall labor market, although reference to labor market rates may be considered in the definition of equitable wage rates. Nevertheless, the major focus of job evaluation is upon job and compensation comparisons within the organization rather than upon comparisons between organizations. As an administrative technique for job pricing, it is most relevant for jobs for which no immediate market comparison is available (unique jobs), or jobs for which market comparisons are less relevant than comparisons within the organization (closed internal labor market).

Specific approaches to job evaluation vary from organization to organization, yet all reflect a common model for job pricing. Common steps in the development and application of job evaluation are the following:

1. *Sampling key jobs for development of system.* Job evaluation systems are developed and validated on a sample of jobs and then generalized in application to a larger population of jobs within the organization. A sample of jobs is used in order to reduce the number of different jobs considered at the developmental stage and to make easier the development of an acceptable criterion of validity. This sample of jobs, called *key jobs,* reflects several considerations (Livernash, 1957). Job clusters reflective of social comparison norms can be identified in any organization, that is, clusters of jobs that typically are compared by incumbents in making comparisons of equity of payment. Job clusters are empirical phenomena and may reflect similarities of location, administrative grouping, skills, stage of production process, or anything that makes the jobs visible to one another, and provides a bond suggestive of comparable compensation treatment. Examples of job clusters might include maintenance jobs regardless of skill classification, different jobs within an occupation such as secretary, or all jobs in an oil well drilling team. Each cluster typically has several jobs that serve as benchmarks against which all other jobs are compared, and that serve to make comparisons between job clusters (see Figure 1). These benchmarks or key jobs are representative of other jobs in their respective job clusters, tend to be highly visible both within the cluster and to employees in other job clusters, and tend to be comparable with similar jobs in other organizations. Many of these jobs also will be key in the sense that they represent a relatively large proportion of total wage costs of the organization, since jobs with large numbers of incumbents will more likely meet the criteria for key jobs than will jobs with relatively few incumbents.

Job clusters that commonly are compared with one another often will be grouped into a single population for job evaluation purposes. Production jobs may constitute one such population, office technical and clerical jobs another population, managerial and administrative jobs another population, and engineering and scientific jobs still another population. The assumption underly-

Figure 1
Job Clusters and Key Job Relationships

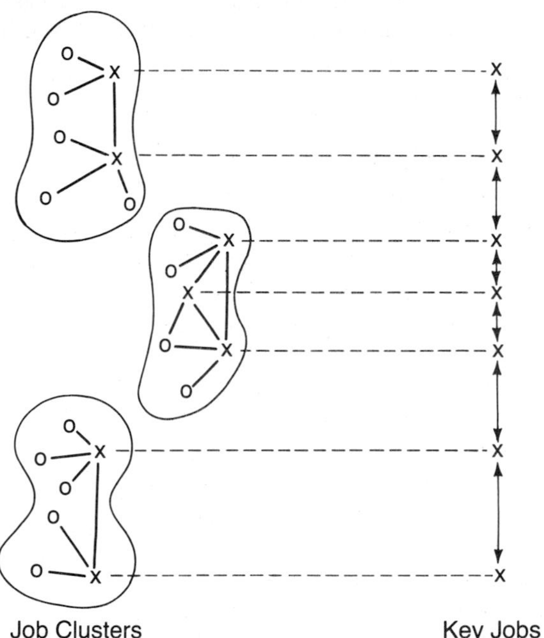

ing this identification of different populations of job clusters is that jobs in one population are rarely compared with jobs in another population in making judgments of equity of compensation. Job evaluation systems designed for more homogeneous populations are assumed to more vividly capture critical dimensions of job variation than a general system designed to cover a wider range of jobs. The different populations of job clusters, in a sense, represent differentiated internal labor markets—employees are recruited from different sources, and careers are constrained within a single population with relatively little movement from one population of job clusters to another. Job evaluation systems designed for, and applied to, different populations of job clusters do, in fact, differ considerably in terms of criteria for differentiation of wages and the degree of compensation differentiation among jobs.

2. *Determination of criterion of equitable relationships.* Since key jobs serve as the benchmarks for evaluation of all other jobs, the criterion for validation of a job evaluation system is a set of compensation relationships among key jobs that can be accepted as equitable. There are various alternative bases for this criterion that may be employed singly or, more commonly, as a joint basis for the criterion. Labor market wage surveys provide one such criterion. Rates of compensation for key jobs ought to be competitive with the labor market if employees are to be recruited into and retained in the organization. Industry wage surveys of key job rates also provide a criterion in the control of wages and labor costs for competitive purposes. Finally, employee attitudes and reactions provide another basis for the criterion of key job relationships. Employees in the workforce must accept these relationships as equitable before they are generalized to other jobs in the organization. Also, criterion rates for key jobs may be negotiated between a union and management. Not uncommonly, existing wage relationships among key jobs will provide the operational criterion, so long as these are accepted by all parties as generally equitable.

3. *Development of measurement and rating system.* Four basic types of systems are traditionally identified in the discussion of job evaluation rating systems (Lytle, 1954). These four types are variants of two underlying dimensions: (1) whether the job is viewed in a holistic fashion or considered as the sum of separate components, and (2) whether jobs are compared directly one with another or compared with some prescribed standard of measurement. These dimensions and the four variants are represented in Figure 2. The

Figure 2
Approaches to Job Evaluation

Unit of Comparison	*Standard for Comparison*	
	Other Jobs	Fixed Criteria
Whole Job	Ranking	Classification
Job Factors	Factor Comparison	Point

simplest approach is the Ranking method, which involves consideration of all jobs and establishing a rank hierarchy among them. All components of each job are considered at once in determining this hierarchy. While specific job components may be identified in structuring job descriptions, the combination of these components in reaching an overall judgment about relative job worth is subjective. Key jobs, once ranked, provide a structure within which other jobs may be ranked on the basis of comparison with the key job ranks. Application of the ranking approach is limited to situations in which there are relatively few jobs, such that rankers can be reasonably familiar with all and make comparisons. This, however, would not be feasible within a large organization with hundreds of different jobs.

The Classification approach involves development of a standard of comparison in the form of differentiated job categories, with definitions of job elements necessary for classification in each category, and then a sorting of jobs into different categories, with the categories ranked in terms of job worth. The Classification approach can be viewed as an extension of the Ranking approach. Key jobs are ranked and then differentiated into groups judged to be significantly different in terms of worth. Job characteristics descriptive of each category are determined from the descriptions of key jobs and used in the specification of requirements for classification into each category. Nonkey jobs are then evaluated by assignment to categories on the basis of job descriptions and the category classification requirements. The Classification approach was commonly used in governmental organizations with a wide range of jobs to be covered, but jobs that tended to be relatively stable in terms of content. It has given way in many instances to the Point approach, which is somewhat more flexible and appears to be less arbitrary than the Classification approach.

The Point approach to job evaluation requires specification of a number of factors or dimensions of job content to be evaluated, design of measurement and weighting scales for each factor, application of the scales to job descriptions, and summing of the points assigned the different scales for each job. Jobs are evaluated, factor by factor, through comparison of job content with the different factor scales. Overall evaluation reflects the sum of the factor evaluations. The Point approach highlights the different dimensions of factors responsible for the relative worth of jobs and thus provides a clear rationale for evaluation. The approach is somewhat more limited in application than the Ranking or Classification approaches, however, since the factors employed must be common to most of the jobs being evaluated; job cluster populations that are significantly different in job content call for different sets of factors and weights for evaluation. The Point system is the most commonly used approach to job evaluation and is used here to illustrate other stages in job evaluation.

The Factor Comparison approach also focuses upon job factors one at a time, but involves direct comparison among jobs rather than with a standard set of degrees and weights as in the Point system. Factor Comparison involves a reasonably sophisticated and complex system of determining relative job worth and is not as commonly employed. Because of its complexity, it is more difficult to develop and to explain to employees.

The development of measurement and rating systems, whatever the specific approach taken, involves a process analogous to multiple regression analysis. Measures of job characteristics are sought which, when weighted appropriately, will reproduce the criterion measures of relative worth. Validation of the approach is demonstrated when the approach, applied to key jobs, reproduces the criterion of relative worth previously discussed. In a purely statistical sense, it is immaterial what job factors are employed and how they are weighted so long as the criterion is reproduced. However, acceptability of an approach also involves questions of face validity. An acceptable approach must consider and weigh job characteristics in a manner that appears reasonable to those affected. The job factors considered in the evaluation system, the scales for measurement of each, and the weights assigned different degrees of each must appear relevant to the determination of job worth. Examples of commonly employed job factors include responsibility, skill, working conditions, physical demands, and required education and training. Since the factors relevant to differentiation among jobs in one population of job clusters may be different from those relevant in another population of job clusters, quite different systems of job evaluation often result for the different populations. Factors such as responsibility and decision making would appear in evaluation systems for managerial jobs, physical demands and skill might appear in systems for factory jobs, and accuracy and amount of supervision received might appear as factors in clerical and technical evaluation systems. As noted later, difficulties in describing and evaluating engineering and scientific jobs have led to the development of maturity curves based upon discipline and years since graduation as the characteristics accepted as relevant in those populations of job clusters.

Job evaluation dimensions or factors in the Point system are operationalized into measurement scales, which identify different degrees or levels of each dimension, and weights are assigned to the different degrees of the various dimensions. Weights often are prescribed initially on the basis of subjective judgments of relative worth. Key jobs are described and evaluated using the weighted scales, and a total score is developed for each job. The validity of the system is then assessed through comparison of the evaluation measures assigned the jobs and the criterion of relative worth specified earlier. The weights assigned factor degrees are adjusted until the system produces a set of job evaluations reasonably aligned with the criterion. It should be noted that empirical analysis employing multiple regression or linear programming is an alternative to subjective judgments in development of job evaluation factors and weights, and has been employed in selected situations. Recently developed approaches that rely increasingly upon statistical analysis and policy capturing analysis may be employed in combination with subjective judgment (Robinson, Wahlstrom, and Mecham, 1974). More commonly, subjective judgment is employed, probably because the process is more easily understood and thus accepted as equitable by the employer and employees concerned. Analogous approaches are applied in the development of the Classification and Factor Comparison systems.

4. *Implementation.* Once a system is judged valid, several steps are required in implementation. The first step, conceptually simple but often costly and involved, requires generalization of the system to all nonkey jobs. This involves development of job descriptions for all other jobs and evaluation of the jobs using the system developed and validated on key jobs.

Another element in implementation involves specification of a structuring of compensation reflective of job evaluations, the determination of pay grades or groupings of jobs to be paid comparably, and the structuring of rate ranges for these pay grades. Jobs are automatically structured into pay grades in the Classification system, all jobs in a class being paid comparably. But the Point and Factor Comparison approaches produce evaluation points unique to each job; 1,000 different jobs might be assigned 1,000 different point evaluations. Pay grade structuring breaks the total range of evaluation points into some smaller number of classes, and all jobs with evaluation points in a single pay grade are compensated in comparable manner. Various considerations enter into the structuring of pay grades; one of these relates to hierarchical authority and promotional relationships among jobs. Two jobs related by a hierarchical reporting relationship, one job reporting to the other, should not be classed in the same pay grade. The same principle would apply to two jobs linked in a promotional career sequence. A noticeable difference between jobs in a career or authority relationship must be confirmed by a noticeable difference in compensation. At the same time, pay grades should be broad enough to permit some change in job duties without requiring reevaluation and assignment to a new pay grade. Tradition also influences pay grade structuring, some organizations recognizing relatively few pay grades with wide ranges of job differences, and other organizations recognizing many pay grades with narrow ranges of job differences. The former permits greater administrative flexibility, but may not satisfy traditional equity considerations within the affected workforce. Typically, something like ten to sixteen pay grades may be recognized for a population of job clusters, but more would be required as the range of job clusters covered increases.

While promotion from one job to another calls for movement from one pay grade to another, jobs within a single pay grade may be linked in the sense of learning and advancement. Learner, operator, and senior operator positions relative to a single job often are distinguished within the same pay grade. These distinctions among performance expectations within a single job call for some equitable distinctions in compensation, which are accommodated through structuring of compensation ranges for the different pay grades. A range of compensation for a single pay grade permits distinction between different positions in the grade, as well as the distinction between performance of different employees in the same job. A common rule of thumb for establishing rate ranges suggests that the range be ±5 to ±20 percent of the range midpoint, but the appropriate range will vary with several considerations (Henderson, 1979). The pay range probably will vary with the breadth of the pay grade, possible differentiation among rates of compensation varying directly with the variability among jobs in the grade. In similar fashion, the rate range will vary directly with the variability of performance recognized within a job in the pay grade, relatively little variation in compensation being necessary if a job is so standardized that there is little opportunity for variation in performance. Finally, it is common to structure overlap in the rate ranges for adjacent pay grades in recognition of the fact that top performers in a job in one pay grade ought at times to be compensated more than low performers in a job in the next higher pay grade.

Pay grade and compensation range structuring typically is illustrated, as in Figure 3, in charts. Relationships between pay grades and compensated worth may be linear or, as in Figure 3, curvilinear, depending upon the rationale employed. Many argue for a curvilinear relationship, particularly among managerial pay grades. There is evidence to suggest that compensation differentials of about 33 percent are necessary between adjacent levels in a managerial authority relationship to be judged equitable (Mahoney, 1979b). Assuming that jobs in adjacent ranks are classified in adjacent pay grades, this would imply a curvilinear relationship with compensation. The exact nature of the relationship will vary, however, depending upon the fineness of distinction between pay grades and empirical observations of relationships accepted as equitable.

A final aspect of implementation involves pricing the structure, assigning exact rates of compensation to the preceding rate structure. Pricing typically is accomplished through consultation of wage survey information, which also provides another test of validity of the evaluation system. The general structure of job evauations should correspond generally with the structure of compensation observed in the relevant labor market(s) if employees are to be recruited and retained in the

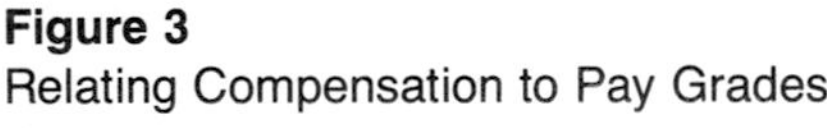
Figure 3
Relating Compensation to Pay Grades

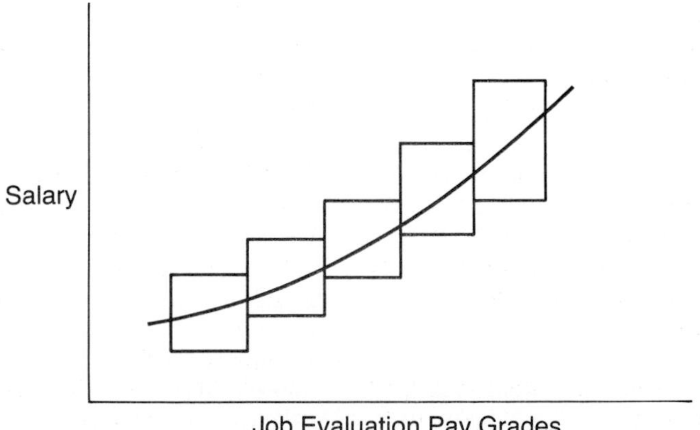

organization. Assuming correspondence between job evaluations and surveys of compensation paid in the labor market, particularly for the key job structure, the entire job structure is priced by anchoring key jobs to these market data. Anomalies between job evaluations and market survey data may reflect significant differences between the job evaluated and that job in other organizations, temporary market imbalances distorting traditional compensation differentials, or lack of validity in the job evaluation system. The latter explanation calls for revision of the evaluation system, while the other explanations can be accommodated through assignment of temporary rates within the appropriate wage ranges. The pricing element of job evaluation is repeated periodically, usually annually, as a continuing check on the validity of the system and as a guide to necessary compensation adjustments.

PERFORMANCE MOTIVATION

The behaviors sought in job performance are much more specific and related to output than are the behaviors sought in the attraction of employees. Similarly, the acceptance of initial employment is more easily conceived as a result of choice and decision making than is hour-to-hour variation in effort expended on the job. This section will consider the motivation of specific job performances and the characteristics of a compensation system most likely to elicit those performances.

One should first distinguish between job performance and behavior. Performance is usually conceptualized in terms of output-related dimensions such as quantity and quality of production, level of productivity, scrap and wastage measures, and the meetings of deadlines and schedules. However, behavior relates to the actions of individuals on the job, actions such as computing estimates of costs, typing manuscripts, negotiating a sale, and operating a machine. Output types of performance are a function of behavior, but they also are a function of the machines used, the nature and quality of raw materials, and the skill level of the individual in the job. What is termed *motivation to perform* refers to the behavior of the individual on the job and, while important in achieving output, it is only a partial determinant of output.

Compensation systems attempt to direct performance behavior by providing rewards that are contingent upon achievement of specific behavior outcomes. Contingent compensation is intended to direct individual choices of behavior and to reinforce desired behavioral patterns. Certain relevant behaviors can be viewed clearly as choices (e.g., decision to skip a day of work for deer hunting), while others are less conscious and reflect habits or patterns of behavior developed over time (e.g., cleaning up the work station or taking a coffee break). Contingency compensation is designed to influence choices in the first instance and to reinforce desired habitual behaviors in the second.

Contingency compensation can be viewed either in terms of incentives to behavior or as rewards for behavior. An incentive is something that is anticipated, a potential reward, whereas a reward is experienced. An incentive is intended to influence choice, while a reward is intended to reinforce past behavior. Insofar as experienced rewards are associated with past patterns of behavior, anticipations of behavior-reward associations are established and serve as incentives. Incentives are not restricted to experienced rewards, however. Behavior-reward contingencies may be inferred from observations of others' experiences or from policy statements, and thus serve as incentives prior to the experiencing of specific reward contingencies. Contingency compensation programs are designed to provide incentives through the announcement of behavior-reward contingencies and to provide reinforcement of behavior through experience of behavior-reward associations.

The distinction between incentive and reward is particularly relevant if one distinguishes between behaviors that are a clear function of choice, and behaviors that are more obviously a function of an established habit pattern. Decisions to accept or terminate employment, to accept or refuse transfer, or to be absent from work on the opening day of deer hunting season illustrate choice behaviors. Work pace maintained throughout the day, cooperation with co-workers, and responsiveness to supervisory requests are more illustrative of habit behaviors. What is here called *choice behaviors* would appear to result from conscious decision making in which the individual weighs the consequences of alternative actions and selects the most attractive action. Expectancy theory and the concept of incentive as anticipated reward would appear most relevant in understanding this behavior. What is here called *habit behaviors* are less clearly the result of conscious decision making and more clearly resemble habitual responses to some stimuli. Reinforcement theory and the concept of reward would appear most relevant in understanding these behaviors. While the implications of expectancy theory and reinforcement theory for the design of performance contingent compensation are often congruent, they occasionally differ in relevant ways and the distinction between choice and habit behaviors can be important.

Compensation contingencies should satisfy several conditions if they are to affect choice, and the establishment and maintenance of habit behaviors. The first and most obvious condition is that the compensation reward associated with behavior ought to be perceived as desirable or as possessing positive valence. In hedonistic terms, individuals seek outcomes that are perceived as pleasurable and avoid outcomes that are perceived as painful. Monetary compensation is one outcome for which most people would agree that "more is better" and thus figures importantly in most contingency reward systems. Other elements of compensation, such as time off, dental insurance, pension rights, and sick leave, hold differing appeal for different individuals. One cannot as confidently assume that all employees will value these forms of compensation in a similar manner. What is termed a "cafeteria" approach to compensation has been proposed as a means of capitalizing upon differing utility assessments of nonmonetary compensation; employees are permitted at least limited choice among amount and form of nonmonetary compensation.

A second, closely related condition concerns the amount of compensation extended as an incentive. While monetary compensation is viewed as generally appealing to most people, it is not clear how much appeal is associated with a given amount of money. Economists assume that money has diminishing marginal utility, that equal increments of money are less appealing as the base for the increment increases. Similarly, psychologists often refer to Weber-Fechner relationships in determination of "just noticeable differences" of stimuli including money; a barely noticeable difference in money might require a constant ratio of the increment to the base of comparison. Relatively little is known about the utilitarian appeal of additional compensation, although, in practice, it often is assumed that equal percentage increments possess equal valence or utility. Clearly, however, the incentive effect of contingent compensation will vary with the amount of the incentive offered (Krefting and Mahoney, 1977). The incentive effects of differing contingency relationships clearly require more study, however, before one can specify the motivational power of different relationships.

A third condition for an effective contingency compensation program is that the employee must be aware of contingency associations, the outcomes associated with different behaviors and the expectancy of these outcomes, given a behavioral choice. Knowledge about these associations may be gained through experience (as assumed in the reinforcement model), through observed experience of others, or through probabilistic analysis of information obtained in other ways (as permitted in the expectancy model). Contingency compensation programs designed to serve as incentives to direct choices are clearly dependent upon prior knowledge of the association between behavior and reward. Piece-rate and commission formulas are designed for communication in advance of performance in order to direct behavior, and performance contracting through some form of management by objectives also is intended to communicate in advance this association between specific performances and reward levels. Performance-reward associations learned through experience, such as learning that a supervisor is more responsive to time off requests for medical reasons, are no less effective in the direction of behavior, but time is often required before the individual learns and responds to the association.

REFERENCES

Bronfenbrenner, M. (1956). Potential monopsony in labor markets. *Industrial and Labor Relations Review, 9,* 577–588.

Krefting, L. A., & Mahoney, T. A. (1977). Determining the size of a meaningful pay increase. *Industrial Relations, 16,* 83–93.

Livernash, E. R. (1957). The internal wage structure. In G. W. Taylor & F. W. Pierson (Eds.), *New concepts in wage determination.* New York: McGraw-Hill.

Locke, E. A. (1976). The nature and causes of job satisfaction. In M. D. Dunnette (Ed.), *Handbook of industrial and organizational psychology.* Chicago: Rand McNally.

Lytle, C. W. (1954). *Job evaluation methods.* New York: Ronald Press.

Mahoney, T. A. (1979a). Economic constraints and the ability to pay. In T. A. Mahoney (Ed.), *Compensation and reward perspectives.* Homewood, IL: Irwin.

Mahoney, T. A. (1979b). Organizational hierarchy and position worth. *Academy of Management Journal,* 22, 726–737.

Parnes, H. (1954). *Research on labor mobility.* New York: Social Science Research Council.

Robinson, D. D., Wahlstrom, O. W., & Mecham, R. C. (1974). Comparison of job evaluation methods: A "policy capturing" approach using the Position Analysis Questionnaire (PAQ). *Journal of Applied Psychology, 59,* 633–637.

Ross, A. M. (1957). The external wage structure. In G. W. Taylor & F. C. Pierson (Eds.), *New concepts in wage determination.* New York: McGraw-Hill.

Ross, I. C., & Zander, A. (1957). Need satisfactions and employee turnover. *Personnel Psychology, 10,* 327–338.

Sheppard, H. L., & Belitsky, A. H. (1966). *The job hunt.* Baltimore: Johns Hopkins.

Wachter, M. L. (1970). Cyclical variation in the interindustry wage structure. *American Economic Review, 60,* 75–84.

New Compensation Strategies for New Career Patterns

Beverly Kaye and Kathryn McKee

Personal attitudes about work and aspirations about careers have been changing substantially for many years. American businesses now accept—even expect—that employees' desires and motivations may be far more complex than the notion of continuing upward advancement. Although the cases are rare enough to be astounding, we have begun to take note of the high-ranking executive who leaves his job to sell real estate at a ski resort or teach management courses at a junior college. Likewise, there is the fast-track manager who spends 12 years in one department but passes up another promotion to make a lateral move to a division of the company that is totally unfamiliar to her. Although these instances do not signal a collective desire to "take this job and shove it," they do indicate serious questioning of standard work values.

More recently, dramatic change has been occurring in corporate structures themselves, especially in the ways in which work is organized. The technological revolution has ushered in a reliance

Reprinted from the March 1986 issue of *Personnel Administrator,* copyright 1986, The American Society for Personnel Administrator, 606 North Washington Street, Alexandria, Virginia 22314 not only on electronic hardware, but also on specialists who can apply their technical knowledge to a variety of situations—sometimes in shifting project teams. The bureaucratic model of hierarchy is adjusting to the trend by shrinking in the middle. No longer does industry need the large, fixed middle management staffs of planners, analysts and interpreters of data; that work can be done by less permanent teams of specialists who manipulate computer output and report to a managerial hierarchy. Further, industries have found themselves in need of "downsizing" to remain competitive, which has disrupted middle management careers.

In addition, certain demographic factors have had tremendous impact on the labor market; the baby-boomers are moving into the managerial ranks and competing with older workers, who are no longer compelled to retire.

The concurrent shifts in employee attitudes and organizational needs present a convincing case for a work future where "upward climb" can no longer be synonymous with "successful career." Employees seem increasingly ready to consider alternatives to the traditional American dream of continually moving up the organizational ladder. Organizations need to establish operating and personnel patterns that do not necessarily rely on vertical arrangements to indicate the management and importance of work.

"Readiness," however, is where the trend seems to stop. Corporate cultures and individual values are exceedingly slow to change, and, for the most part, traditional hierarchical and promotional patterns remain intact. Although the time is ripe for reexamining and redefining career "success," the vast majority of organizations still reward by emphasizing pay-for-promotion and supporting only upward career values. Yet, if organizations are to maximize their use of human resources in the face of change, they need to find ways to modify those traditional values. Otherwise, morale and motivation problems (as well as recruitment and retention difficulties) will stymie the fullest and most beneficial utilization of worker competence.

Perhaps no other organizational tool is as powerful in changing collective values as a firm's reward system. This area deserves serious consideration because of its influence in aligning career patterns and aspirations with changing corporate needs. Fortunately, the repertoire of compensation and reward choices has expanded significantly in recent years, as organizations have attempted to respond to varying employee needs and to search out less costly options than pay raises alone. Unfortunately, however, the options are still geared toward incentives and rewards for upward movement, with little support for employees who might prefer alternate career routes from their organizations, peers or families.

There is no constant cause-and-effect relationship that can prescribe the most appropriate compensation or incentive for every employee in every organizational situation. However, it is essential that managers stand ready to design and deploy any of a number of reward systems to match various potential career movements.

PUTTING THE MONEY WHERE THE MOVE IS

It is quite obvious that upward or vertical career moves are compatible with traditional patterns of pay-for-promotion. They even adapt well to increases in non-cash rewards, such as more impressive titles and working conditions that are generally reserved for the management elite ensconced on the upper floors. But can compensation strategies be designed for other career move options? The answer is a resounding "yes." After all, individuals who prefer nontraditional moves may be valuable contributors who are continuing to expand the abilities and knowledge they bring to the job. They also may be some of the most satisfied and productive workers when they have the option to make a personal choice that their purposes are best served by abandoning the career ladder. And, they can fulfill a growing organizational need to emphasize skill acquisition while deemphasizing management layers.

In considering the compensation aspects of multidirectional career movement, it is useful to think in terms of what might motivate employees to move in any given career direction. Drawing from Abraham Maslow's hierarchy of human needs, various moves can be examined for their relationship to needs and their potential as incentives. This can provide a sense of employees' receptivity to different career moves.

MULTIPLE MOBILITY OPTIONS IN THE ORGANIZATION

In order to fully appreciate the relationship among various compensation options, individual values and organizational cultures, it is useful to view them in the context of a full range of career directions. Although past compensation choices were concerned mainly with supporting vertical mobility along a promotional hierarchy, current realities are beginning to require changes in those patterns.

How to best compensate these alternative career moves and signal their value to the organization is a complex issue that creates yet another barrier to accomplishing a change toward a full range of career options. But, with sensitivity and creativity on the part of top management and human resource development administrators, the question can be addressed.

The typical organizational pyramid structure does not necessarily accommodate the need for increasing technical expertise and flexible "project" arrangements. These factors, combined with deemphasis on middle management, make the issue of compensation far more complex than longstanding pay-for-promotion systems.

HORIZONTAL MOVES, OR "OVER IN THE ORGANIZATION"

Horizontal (or lateral) moves demonstrate the concept of the transferability of skills, abilities and knowledge. They involve changes in function and/or title, without necessarily altering status or salary. At the same time, these moves enable employees to demonstrate adaptive abilities and develop new talents. For example, an employee with data analysis skills in new product development may be qualified to make a lateral move into a position requiring the ability to analyze marketing data.

Lateral moves often provide intensive rewards such as opportunities for new learning and the challenge of a new work environment. By encouraging such movement through a lump-sum payment or "transfer" bonus, organizations can continue to challenge employees. Skill-based pay systems can be particularly valuable in supporting these moves, as employees generally begin to add skills—through training and new experiences—shortly after the move. A compensation program which is designed to reward the acquisition and continued use of new skills can be a powerful incentive for employees to move across or "over" in the organization. Additionally, career path information derived from lateral moves may indicate that such assignments provide the option of an eventual move into positions in higher management. By developing career paths in this area, the organization is planning for future compensation of lateral career movers. Positive recognition, from personal feedback to widespread publicity, is another potentially effective reward that can be provided for horizontal movement.

JOB ENRICHMENT OR STAYING PUT, BUT BETTER

Enrichment on the current job—staying but not stagnating—is another career development option that is often overlooked by organizations and employees. This option suggests that opportunity begins at home and involves increasing the challenge or meaning of the job by changing either the job itself or the employee's concept of it. According to Richard Hackman of Yale, jobs can be enriched through: (1) increasing the variety of skills and talents used; (2) having the opportunity to work on a job from beginning to end; (3) determining and understanding the type and degree of impact the particular job has on the lives of other people in the organization and on the organization as a whole; (4) increasing responsibility, independence and discretion in determining one's work procedures; and (5) establishing opportunities for feedback from the job, co-workers and/or supervisors. The organization which utilizes enrichment as a legitimate career development option can benefit from employee growth and learning on the job, improved attitudes about the current work and reduced pressures for promotion (with an accompanying pay hike) as the only meaningful career move.

Utilizing a skill-based pay system wholly or partially allows organizations to reward employees for further acquisition of additional skills. Such a system adapts best to situations where job opportunities are flexible enough to utilize a variety of skills, rather than fairly routine situations that do not accommodate personal growth and learning. Additionally, skill-based systems are most likely to succeed in organizations that are willing to support career development programs and commit resources to training.

Enrichment of the current job—as with lateral moves—has the advantage of personal challenge and growth. Such an approach also may provide personal compensation through opportunities to delegate lower-level tasks while taking on higher-level ones. As such, these actions also fit well with a skill-based compensation system. The employee is likely to be adding new skills as different tasks and projects are undertaken.

When enrichment involves serving on special committees, undertaking one-time research, joining a project team or assuming new tasks, a one-time cash bonus compensation can be considered. Short-term noncash rewards also can be utilized, such as providing for attendance at out-of-town conferences, greater autonomy in performing the work and public recognition. Organizations also should consider the possibility of relating mentor systems linked to enrichment. The opportunity to acquire a mentor, or to be a mentor, can be a powerful reward tool that leads to better organizational information, professional guidance and personal growth and development.

EXPLORING NEW TERRITORY

Exploratory career development options encourage employees to consider other areas of the organization without committing prematurely to an actual move in another direction. Exploring involves the process of researching, interviewing and testing out ideas and opportunities so that a decision about another field of interest can eventually be made. From this effort, enough information should be gathered by both employee and employer to provide the basis for a sound joint decision as to whether a move into a specific area is feasible.

Exploratory career development often provides an essential first step by helping individuals determine interests and paths to follow. It can provide learning in various fields for the employee, while helping the organization to create an accurate fit between jobs and employee interests and abilities.

At the very least, exploratory career development should carry no "punitive" effect, such as losing ground by spending time off the traditional career track. Employees who are pursuing exploration should be assured that they have the "freedom to fail" and can return to their original assignments if exploration isn't fruitful.

Rewards also can be structured for exploration in areas that support learning—such as attendance at conferences, enrollment in seminars or tuition reimbursement. One-time bonuses and public recognition also are highly appropriate for employees who are willing to explore a number of options in order to discover their own niche in the firm. Organizational compensation systems can accommodate exploring by holding the employee's salary constant during the period of exploration.

Several innovative approaches can be used to encourage managers to reward employees whose positions are successfully enriched, who accept a lateral move or who explore new career avenues:

1. A discretionary pool of dollars to be awarded to employees to compensate for enrichment tasks, based on the degree of contribution to the organization and to the individual's development.

2. Peer review teams that receive a sum of dollars to share based on their contributions to the team.

3. Employees who feel that they have "enriched" the organization report to a special board

about their new skills. Dollars can be awarded based on a point system and the level of performance that is achieved.

4. Managers who encourage development, enrichment or exploration are rewarded for being "people-areas developers" on their performance appraisals and in their variable compensation.

5. The awarding of stock options to work teams at any level in the organization (professional and nonprofessional) for extraordinary or innovative work.

6. Awarding discretionary time that allows employees to pursue outside interests that complement their work and interests.

7. The awarding of a sabbatical for exploratory or special research in a particular area.

DOWN, BUT NOT OUT!

Realignment and downward moves have long carried the stigma of failure. However, our rapidly changing value system and limited promotional opportunities are likely to make them more feasible as legitimate career development options. Many people are looking toward outside interests for self-fulfillment, and see the opportunity to move downward as a chance to free themselves from time-consuming positions. For instance, an employee may be unhappy in a position, and realize that the solution may be to move back to a former job where he or she performed successfully. After all, most people will agree that it is better to do what they do well than to struggle along in a job for which they are not well suited.

Some workers may look to downward movement for health reasons or to relieve tension and stress, or may view it as the only route toward opportunities for switching to more satisfying work or work conditions. In this case, it is possible that they may learn quickly and "blossom" in a new area of work, setting the stage to advance even further than they might have on their former career path.

Realignment has been viewed only negatively in the past, with its only reward being the elimination of a job that may not have suited the employee at all. Generally, downward moves have meant "demotion"—in pay, status, authority and esteem. Compensation in this area is likely to be designed on a case-by-case basis, but the design should at least consider ways to alleviate punitive and demeaning possibilities. Positive practices might include no cut in pay for a period of time, a gradual lowering of the salary, retention of perquisites, continuing education or recognition as a special contributor. In addition, the realigned employee with significant experience may be tapped as a mentor to others or a member of temporary task groups, or assigned to special research that entails long-term calls for long-term organizational knowledge.

RELOCATION WITHIN OR OUTSIDE

Relocation moves to other companies may not warrant compensation from the former company. However, at least they should be encouraged where necessary, and treated as something other than failure. When these moves involve relocating within the same company—to a different department that may be in a different geographic area—appropriate compensation might include "transfer" bonuses, relocation expenses, support network, and perquisites that match the level of the former job.

Relocation moves also should be viewed by organizations and employees as viable career development options. After serious introspection, some individuals may find that their present occupation, industry, profession or firm does not meet their needs, and may opt to move out. A final career alternative is moving to a position outside the organization. This option can be suggested when layoffs are frequent, when the organization cannot continue to facilitate an individual's efforts to meet personal goals or when personal and organizational goals conflict.

Firms which recognize this career option and are willing to provide counseling and support as necessary often alleviate serious mismatching, which can produce motivational problems in even the most promising employees. Those organiztions also find their credibility greatly enhanced among employees who appreciate willingness to encourage exploration of all career options, not

Table 1
Incentives for Career Moves

Career Moves	*Needs*				
	Physiological	*Security*	*Social*	*Esteem*	*Self-Actualization*
Lateral	Base salary to cover the cost of satisfying basic survival needs	Base salary to cover costs of a home; a secure workplace	Attention; relationship with peers.	Recognition of mastery of skill; transfer bonus to recognize achievement	Able to reach full potential pay over the market rate for mastery
Enrichment		Base salary pay for acquisition of additional skills	Respect for achievement of higher skills; attention from peers	Recognition; higher pay for mastery of skills	Able to reach full potential pay over the market rate for mastery
Vertical		Promotional increase	Attention; public recognition	Recognized as an achiever; a sense of mastery	Can mentor lower level colleagues
Exploratory		Pay stays intact	Not working with new colleagues, peer groups	An honor to be allowed to explore, i.e., spend time in a job rotation	Opportunity to strive for achieving full potential
Relocation		Base pay should not be disrupted if employee is a successful contributor and actually opts for this type of move	Will have opportunity to develop new colleagues and new opportunities	Change is an issue—can be positive or negative; will need to adapt to a new environment	A chance over time to strive for full potential in a new area
Realignment			Will have opportunity to develop new relationships in less stressful environment	Self-esteem may be difficult; may need help to feel strong in a new environment	A chance to redevelop a strong sense of self-worth in a new area

just those which are most expedient for the organization.

TAKE IT TO THE TOP

It is probably an understatement to mention that organizational norms change very slowly, if at all. Moreover, when change is in the wind, those who are accustomed to a comfortable set of norms will go down fighting. Compensation practices which only support the concept of "up the hierarchical ladder" have formed a strong promotion norm throughout American industry. Change can only begin to happen when total commitment—and patience—exist at the highest levels. The chief executive officer must be the first to signal support for new compensation patterns, and other top

Table 2
Options for Career Compensation

Lateral	*Vertical*	*Enrichment*	*Relocation*	*Realignment*	*Exploratory*
• Recognition • Skill-based pay • Training opportunities • Transfer bonuses	• Promotions/ pay • Work conditions • Fringe benefits • Perquisites • Recognition • Status	• Responsibility • Learning • Recognition • Bonuses • Perquisites	• Transfer bonuses • Relocation expenses • Retain perquisites	• Retain pay • Retain perquisites • Special assignments • Mentoring	• Bonuses • Training • Recognition • Freedom to "fail"

managers must join in this commitment to alternative plans that consider individual needs.

THE NEW COMPENSATION STRATEGY: MAKING IT HAPPEN

Some guidelines for considering a system that compensates career competence are:

- Get involvement and commitment from compensation executives and human resource development managers early—drawing from them to form a planning team.
- Initiate a career development program that introduces employees to the idea that "up is not the only way" and demonstrates senior management's organizational support for other moves.
- Review current compensation practices, candidly examining them for outmoded tendencies to motivate upward movement only.
- Consider additional rewards and compensation that could be used to motivate a variety of career options.
- Institute a program to favorably publicize those employees who have already made successful career moves in directions other than upward.
- Assign human resource staff to identify and develop career ladders that include *all* options for movement.
- Where possible, link this concept to the organization's human resource utilization plans and strategic plan.
- Review current training and development practices to assure that they support career and compensation options.
- Stay open: from the beginning, communicate widely what is being done and why. Use staff meetings, employee bulletins, special seminars and even payroll stuffers to get the point across. Entertain questions and suggestions for refinements from those who will be affected by the changes.

These guidelines constitute merely a starting point for change. They are meant to ease the way in an effort to stop the traditional use of promotions as the only mark of career development. Follow-through will be different in each organization, and the results will not be immediately apparent. Thus, these concepts challenge those managers who believe that today's organization is different from yesterday's and that new compensation strategies are indeed essential to ensure the highest potential utilization of human resources.

Tracking the Merit of Merit Pay

Frederick S. Hills
Robert M. Madigan
K. Dow Scott
Steven E. Markham

Merit pay, or pay for performance, is well established in corporate America. Surveys of pay practices indicate that the overwhelming majority of U.S. companies have merit pay programs. Moreover, interest in merit pay is surging, despite the voluminous literature pointing out the difficulty of linking pay to performance in practice. Executives see merit pay as a prescription for improving productivity to meet competitive pressures. Similarly, government officials are promoting increased use of merit pay to enhance individual employee performance and organization effectiveness. The idea that pay increases should reflect differences in performance level apparently seems so logical, the need for such programs is usually accepted as self-evident. Unfortunately, once installed, merit pay programs are seldom audited to determine whether they are achieving the goals for which they were designed. Such unquestioning commitment to merit pay programs could be costly in monetary and/or employee relations terms.

It is surprising that little serious attention has been given to auditing merit pay programs. Salary increase budgets have averaged over 6.5 percent of base payroll the past three years, and in recent years of high inflation the percentage often has reached double digits. Expenditures of this magnitude need to be closely scrutinized, particularly in labor intensive organizations where the return on salary dollars can be vital.

MERIT PAY

If you ask salary administrators from 10 companies with merit pay programs to define it, you are likely to get 10 different definitions. Merit plans differ in the definition and measurement of "merit," the strength of the link between pay and performance, the timing of merit increases, and the relationship of merit to seniority, inflation, or other pay criteria. The term "merit pay program" here is used generically to refer to programs in which increases in base pay for specific individuals (excluding increases associated with promotions) are geared to the performance assessment of those individuals for a specified time period. We are not talking about general, across-the-board increases, or any monetary incentive that does not permanently increase the employee's base pay, such as a one-time bonus.

Merit pay plans seldom establish pay increase decisions solely on performance. For example, salary structures are generally not open-ended. A maximum pay level is specified for each position, and progression upward through the pay range is linked to performance until the ceiling is reached. In practice, most organizations pare the size of increases as pay rates move through the top half of the salary range. Thus, both performance level and position in the salary range influence "merit" decisions. In effect, merit increases become a function of both performance and job tenure.

Furthermore, many organizations implicitly recognize seniority or inflationary pressures by granting minimum increases to all employees out of their merit budget. Obviously, this practice affects an organization's ability to reflect performance differences in pay increases. The link between pay and performance is weakened, hence the probability of influencing individual performance through merit increases is reduced. This is

Reprinted from *Personnel Administrator, 32* (1987), pp. 50–57 by permission of K. Dow Scott.

not to suggest that audits of this type of merit programs are inappropriate or unnecessary. On the contrary, the probability of an ineffective program is higher in such situations, making it even more important for management to evaluate the program.

MERIT PAY GOALS

What's the point of merit pay?

The initial answer to this question is straightforward—to motivate high levels of performance. Merit pay functions as a "carrot" to shape the job performance of employees. The assumption is that employees respond to monetary rewards. A primary purpose of any merit pay audit is to test this assumption.

Pay actions send a powerful message to employees. Among other things, they convey displeasure with an employee's performance or signal promotion potential. Hence, merit pay plans provide a means to influence employees' decisions to stay or leave as well as to put forth future effort. By communicating desired messages to valued employees, merit pay can improve the organization's ability to retain top performers. As a result, a second goal of most merit pay programs is to reduce dysfunctional turnover. The extent to which the merit pay program helps achieve this goal should be periodically investigated.

A third goal of pay administration systems is to achieve broad-based acceptance of the merit pay system by employees. If there is widespread disaffection with the pay system, the goals of retaining and motivating employees are not likely to be achieved. Hence, maintaining a reasonable level of satisfaction is the most fundamental goal of merit pay programs. For this reason the extent of employee satisfaction with the system also must be periodically audited.

The goals of influencing employee performance, retaining good employees and providing job satisfaction must be accomplished within legal constraints. Therefore, a fourth goal—legal compliance—applies to all merit pay plans. The merit principle is explicitly recognized in law, but the subjectivity normally involved in appraising individual performance opens merit systems to problems of illegal discrimination under Title VII of the Civil Rights Act. The pattern of performance appraisals and/or merit increases over a period of time could reflect different treatment of women or minority employees. For example, the average increase received by men should not be different from that of women, unless there are legitimate, business-related reasons for the differences. Routine audits of pay patterns provide a tool for identifying possible violations.

AUDIT STRATEGIES

Since the desired outcomes from merit pay plans are both individual (employee behaviors and attitudes) and institutional (retention, compliance, efficiency), a number of different auditing strategies are necessary. Three basic approaches are described here; procedures for their implementation are outlined in the next section.

The starting point for merit pay audits is an analysis of the actual distribution of merit pay increases. Evidence pertaining to the goals of legal compliance, employee retention, and linkage of pay to performance can be developed by analyzing past pay increases. In general, the size of merit increases should be positively related to measures of individual "merit" or performance, negatively related to turnover and unrelated to race, gender and age. Data for these analyses come from organizational records. If personnel information is maintained on computer, this component of the audit is relatively simple and inexpensive.

However, analysis of organizational records reveals nothing about how employees feel about the merit pay program. Hence, the second basic auditing strategy is to track employee attitudes. This can be done most easily via group feedback sessions and/or employee questionnaires. Each method has its advantages. Questionnaires can encourage employee candor, reduce subjectivity in scoring and interpretation, and provide a statistical basis for tracking attitude/opinion changes over time. However, carefully structured group sessions can provide rich detail and intensity not possible in a written survey. For most organizations, a combination of both methods will probably be the most cost effective.

The third component of an auditing strategy focuses on merit pay program characteristics and constraints, rather than outcomes. Numerous factors determine how employees respond to a merit plan. Since this is one topic on which a near consensus exists among practitioners and academics, these "requisites for success" can serve as criteria for assessing merit pay programs.[1] For example, the degree to which merit/performance criteria are specific on the job and accurately measured can be assessed. Deficiencies on either score reduce the likelihood of successful administration. This type of audit complements the first two strategies. By focusing on the program per se, potential determinants of problems evidenced by attitude or merit distributions are more likely to be identified and resolved.

AUDIT PROCEDURES

Merit Increase Analysis

Analysis of actual merit pay increases can range from simple graphic presentations through sophisticated statistical tests. In all cases, the purpose is to determine whether higher performers actually receive larger merit increases (percentage).

However, the relationship between pay and performance is seldom this simple. Seniority or position in the range could legitimately influence the size of pay increases. Additionally, pay actions could be affected by factors, not included in policy, that are actually illegal (e.g., race, age, gender). The task facing the evaluator(s) is to determine to what degree pay actions are affected by these other factors. The quality of any audit of merit pay distributions depends upon how well this problem is handled.

The problem of multiple criteria for pay increases can be addressed singly or in combination. First, the employee population can be subdivided into categories that are similar with respect to one or more of the factors. For example, if the size of merit increases is also affected by the employee's position in the salary range, the overall distribution of pay increases should be broken down into salary-range categories, (i.e. upper 25 percent, 25 percent above midpoint, 25 percent just below midpoint and the bottom 25 percent of a salary range). A separate analysis can then be conducted for each category. This procedure isolates the effect of performance differences on pay increases. It should be noted here that the relationship between performance level and percent of merit increase can also be described statistically by the correlation coefficient which provides an index of the strength of relationships. In a "pure" merit plan, the coefficient theoretically should approach 1.0. To the degree it is lower, factors other than merit are entering into wage determination decisions.

Second, the effects of various factors can be controlled and estimated statistically using multiple regression. In this approach, the unique effect of various determinants of merit pay can be estimated.[2] For example, the auditor could simultaneously assess the effect of performance, seniority and job tenure on the size of pay increases. Use of regression analysis has been greatly facilitated by the development of numerous applications programs for wage and salary analysis on microcomputers. However, unless the auditors are well-grounded in regression analysis, experts should be consulted regarding preparation and interpretation of the analysis.

The specific analysis of merit pay increases that can or should be conducted in an audit of merit pay practices will depend upon factors such as the goals of the program, the size and diversity of the employee groups, the number of administrative units and the availability of data. In most cases, audits of merit pay increases should include analyses of the following types:

1. The distribution of pay increase percentages within each performance level, i.e. high performers, moderate performers and low performers. If job tenure or position in the salary range also influences the size of increases, subgroup analysis (or multiple regression) will be necessary as noted above.

2. The average pay increase percentage by race and gender within each performance rating category. If seniority or other factors also influence the relative size of pay increases, they must also be included. Multiple regression is particularly useful for this type of check for discrimination.

3. The average pay increase by supervisor within each performance category. This analysis should compare increases given by supervisors within and between organizational units. Inconsistency among supervisors in their interpretation and application of merit program guidelines and procedures is a common problem in merit systems. For example, a performance rating score of 4 might result in a 5 percent raise in one department but only 3 percent in another department. If consistency between supervisors in performance ratings is also a problem, the performance rating within departments may need to be standardized before polling them across managers. This may be done manually or with sophisticated statistical techniques, such as Within and Between Analysis of Variance.[3]

4. The distribution of performance levels by range-position. This analysis provides a snapshot of the relationship between salary level and performance level. In general, one would expect to find higher performance levels in the upper reaches of the salary range. The analysis can be further refined by considering seniority, education or any other factor likely to affect the relative level of an employee's pay.

5. The performance rating and merit increase history of promoted employees. If "merit" signals promotability, the ratings of promoted employees should reflect that fact. Promoted employees should be predominantly from the higher performance rating categories.

6. The relationship between merit increases and turnover. The goal of turnover control is being achieved if the leavers are predominantly from the lower end of the performance distribution.

7. The relationship of the current to the previous year's merit increases. Supervisors sometimes operate under a "share the wealth" philosophy and equalize merit increases for their subordinates over a multiple year cycle. Where this is happening the correlation between the increases for any two years will be near zero or negative.

Performance Evaluation

The measure of individual "merit" or performance is *the* critical component of any merit system. Merit must be defined in a way that is understood and accepted by the employee, and its measurement must be accurate. First, the ratings often reveal evidence of errors or other deficiencies of raters. For example, a common weakness of merit plans is the unwillingness of supervisors to differentiate among their employees in their appraisals and/or merit pay decisions. The ratings of such supervisors will typically be clustered near the center or top of the rating scale. Furthermore, analysis of merit ratings often reveals rater biases toward various occupations, job levels or types of employees. These problems with individual supervisors' ratings are compounded by the inconsistencies between raters mentioned above. Analyses of the rating distributions of individual raters and breakdowns of ratings to allow comparisons by unit, job level, and occupation are a basic tool for identifying and rectifying these types of errors.

Second, evidence of the ratings' accuracy can often be obtained by field checks of the rating process. A field check is an actual review of performance appraisal forms and discussion with supervisors to determine the ratings' accuracy of selected employees. The purpose of a field check is to determine whether (a) performance criteria are relevant and complete; (b) employees and supervisors have a common understanding of the criteria and their relative importance; (c) the information available to raters provides a sound basis for judgments of performance; and (d) whether performance reviews are complete and constructive. This audit involves conversations with employees and supervisors and reviews of appraisal documentation relative to other evidence of performance (attendance records, output quantity/quality indicators, etc.). Admittedly this is a judgmental process, but such field audits have the additional advantage of communicating the seriousness of the merit assessment process to all raters.

Employee Attitudes

Whether a merit pay system influences motivation or retention depends upon employees' perceptions of the system. At a minimum, monetary recognition must be important to the employee, and he/she must believe that individual performance determines such rewards. Therefore, information about these beliefs, values and feelings is a necessary part of any merit pay audit.

Some of the advantages of using anonymous questionnaires and group feedback methods were noted. Regardless of the method used to collect information, employees' attitudes toward the following aspects of the merit pay program should be obtained:

1. *The concept of merit pay.* Do employees believe merit pay is a fair way to award pay increases? Do they believe it can be fairly implemented for their occupation or unit?

2. *The definition of performance.* Do employees believe the performance standards for their job are relevant and complete? Are supervisory expectations clear?

3. *The performance measurement procedure.* Do employees believe the process used to assess their performance is adequate? Do they trust their supervisor to be fair?

4. *The size of merit increases.* Is the size of merit pay increases large enough to be motivational? Is the difference in the size of increases between performance levels significant?

5. *Linkage to performance.* Do employees believe that the size of their pay increase is determined predominantly by their performance? Do they believe that the merit criterion is distinct from seniority and cost of living?

6. *The equity of the total system.* Is the base rate or pay range for the job viewed as fair relative to that of other jobs in the organization and to market rates?

If questionnaires are used to obtain data on employee attitudes, they should also request personal and organizational data to allow analysis of responses by employee category. For example, employee attitudes toward the pay system could vary by occupation, job level, size of most recent merit increase, performance level, functional unit and tenure on the job. A breakdown of responses into categories of this type provides a basis for more meaningful interpretation of the responses. Information of this type can be requested without compromising the anonymity of employees' responses.

Program Characteristics

A successful formula for implementing of merit pay has not yet been developed. However, a number of preconditions and program requirements have been identified and generally accepted.

1. *Trust in management.* This applies both to management philosophies and goals and to employee perceptions of their particular supervisor. If employee relations environments are shaky, employers are likely to be skeptical of merit programs.

2. *Absence of performance constraints.* Organizations often have jobs that are externally controlled, highly interdependent or present other barriers to individual performance. Since merit pay programs are based on individual ability and effort, such constraints prevent effective implementation of the merit principle.

3. *Trained supervisors and managers.* The quality of performance planning, monitoring, review and feedback is crucial to merit pay programs. Few managers are born with these skills.

4. *Good measurement systems.* Pay-for-performance systems should be based as much as possible on criteria that are specific to the job and focus on results achieved. Hence, the need for accuracy in measuring performance goes beyond performance appraisals to the information systems providing the data upon which they are based.

5. *Ability to pay.* The merit portion of the salary increase budget must be large enough to provide significant merit pay increments.

6. *Valid job evaluation and externally competitive pay levels.* Merit pay plans are an attempt to introduce interpersonal equity (based on performance) into pay systems. The effect will be negligible at best if internal job relationships are perceived to be inequitable or rates are not competitive with the market.

7. *Distinction between cost of living, seniority and merit.* Employees will assume a pay increase is an economic or longevity increase in the absence of strong evidence to the contrary.

8. *Open pay policy.* A well-conceived and administered merit pay plan is worthless unless the

employees clearly understand how the total pay system works.

9. *Flexible reward schedule.* Perceptions of the linkage between performance and rewards are influenced by the timing as well as the amount of merit increases. It will be more difficult to establish a credible merit pay plan if all employees have the same merit date.

10. *Consistent with the prevailing culture.* Some employee groups regard performance differentials with suspicion. For example, there are situations where cooperative rather than individual effort might be stressed, or a norm of "taking care of our own" might have developed. In such situations, merit pay could be effective as part of a package of interventions designed to modify the culture, but in the absence of a strategy for change, a merit pay program will be rejected or subverted.

CONCLUSIONS

In this paper we have suggested a framework which can be used to evaluate a merit pay program. The recommendations capture some of the technical and analytical capabilities required to conduct such an audit. To the extent that merit pay programs represent both a significant cost factor and a powerful motivational tool, it makes sense to ensure that merit pay is being used effectively and conscientiously.

REFERENCES

1. See, for example, N. B. Winstanley, "Are Merit Increases Really Effective?" *Personnel Administrator,* April, 1982, 37–41.

2. An explanation of multiple regression is beyond the scope of this paper, but examples of its application to pay systems can be found in B. B. Burkhalter et al., "Auditing the Compensation Function for Race and Sex-Based Salary Differences: Further Needed Refinements," *Compensation and Benefits Review,* July–August, 1986, 35–42, and J. F. Sullivan, "Comparable Worth and the Statistical Audit of Pay Programs for Illegal Systemic Discrimination," *Personnel Administrator,* March, 1985, 102–111.

3. See, for example, Dansereau, F., Alutto, J. A., and Yammarionh, F. J., *Theory Testing in Organizational Behavior: The Variant Approach.* New Jersey: Prentice–Hall, 1984.

Unresolved Issues and Challenges in Compensation Administration

Thomas A. Mahoney

Compensation administration faces a number of very real practical issues and challenges. Solutions for certain of these issues are by no means obvious, and the issues are presented here without recommended solutions.

COST OF SUPPLEMENTARY BENEFITS

The compensation cost of supplementary benefits is a very pressing issue of compensation administration and one that is growing annually. Monetary

Adapted from *Personnel Management,* © 1982, Allyn and Bacon, Inc.

compensation has been used (see Mahoney, pp. 202–212) to illustrate various principles and hypotheses, yet, 40 percent of total compensation paid to employees is in the form of supplementary compensation. What was once termed a fringe benefit is now a significant component of the total compensation package. These supplementary benefits take many forms: social insurances (unemployment compensation), vacations, medical, hospital, dental and disability insurances, holidays, pensions, overtime and shift premiums, tuition refunds for education, and subsidization of employee social clubs and eating facilities. Some organizations now provide paid holidays for employee birthdays, the first day of deer hunting season, and "go to hell" days when an employee may arbitrarily be absent from work.

While limited supplementary benefits were provided prior to the 1940s, the real growth in benefits can be traced to the negotiation of pensions during World War II. Pensions were negotiated then as alternatives to wage increases that were limited by wage controls. Since that time, fringe benefits have evolved to the point where their provision is at times regarded as a right of employees and not as a supplement to wages.

Any cost-benefit analysis of supplementary benefits is difficult; each benefit must be analyzed individually and it is difficult to generalize findings. Costs, for example, vary with corporate and individual tax codes, and the size and demographic characteristics of the employee group covered. Costs also vary over time as tax codes and employee demographic characteristics change. Long-run costs of various benefits are particularly difficult to estimate in advance. Often, what appears to be relatively inexpensive in the short run develops into significant long-run obligations.

The benefit of supplementary benefits is also difficult to measure in any form other than current employee preferences. While supplementary benefits are presumed to reduce employee turnover or to discourage absenteeism, research evidence concerning performance and behavioral effects is very meager. Despite the few studies concerning employee perceptions of benefits, relatively little is known about employee assessments of supplementary benefits or perceptions of contingency relationships with behavior.

Meanwhile, the cost of supplementary benefits continues to grow both absolutely and relative to direct wage payments. In fact, since certain benefit levels are related directly to wage payments, the cost implications of a wage increase often are underestimated. Benefit relationships to wage rates often multiply the cost implications of wage changes, rather than serving as alternatives to direct wage payments.

Both the economic and social implications of an increasing portion of the compensation bill being paid in the form of supplementary benefits, as well as the implications of alternative benefits for employee mobility, retirement, and performance, are relatively unknown. Considerable imaginative research into these issues is warranted for both individual employers as well as society.

CAFETERIA COMPENSATION

Evidence concerning the obvious has been collecting for some years—evidence that people differ in the assignment of value to various forms of nonmonetary compensation and that the values assigned often differ from the monetary cost of compensation. Various authors have proposed that employees be permitted at least limited choice in the forms of compensation received, thus, presumably, maximizing the individual utility of a fixed sum of monetary expenditures (Lawler, 1971). Objections raised to the cafeteria plan relate largely to administrative problems—effects of a changing population base on charges, tax treatment of different forms of compensation, and coping with preferences that change over time. However, these administrative problems obviously can be overcome, if desired.

Perhaps more important than the administrative issues is understanding the potential benefits of a cafeteria plan for compensation and the likely effects upon employee behavior. Put more simply, a cafeteria plan for compensation permits achievement of greater individual utility from a fixed sum expended for nonmonetary compensation. Opportunity to participate in a cafeteria plan would truly be a "fringe" benefit and might, other things being equal, affect the attraction of candidates. Since other considerations are not often equal, it is unlikely to impact noticeably upon the attraction of candidates. Since most nonmonetary forms of compensation are contingent solely upon membership and are not related to performance, a cafeteria plan cannot be expected to significantly influence employee job performance. Being contingent upon continued membership, a cafeteria plan might influence decisions to remain with the organization, and in the same fashion increase satisfaction of employees. Main effects of a cafeteria form of compensation are likely to be observed in turnover/retention rates rather than in other forms of employee behavior. Even so, it is difficult to assess the likely relationship between cafeteria compensation and turnover rates. Despite the simple logic of a form of cafeteria compensation plan, the anticipated benefits of such a plan relative to costs of implementation are problematic. They likely will vary considerably from one organization to another. One potential benefit of cafeteria approaches might be the control of benefit costs while permitting realization of individual desires for different benefits. These cost-control implications are worthy of serious study.

VALIDITY OF JOB EVALUATION

Although the process of job evaluation has become reasonably well accepted within employing organizations as a method of developing wage structures, the validity of the approach is challenged by social pressures external to the organization. One such concern relates to inflation and wage spirals as employers rely upon wage surveys to price job evaluation structures. Surveys of wage rates paid by other employers are only that and need not reflect rates dictated by supply and demand considerations. The findings of wage surveys, particularly during periods of high unemployment, ought not to be interpreted as economic market rates, it is argued. Wage increases may be initiated by firms protected from product market competition for reasons other than difficulties in the recruitment of labor; reasons such as maintaining real wages or employee satisfaction. Yet these increases are incorporated into wage survey results and trigger adjustments by other employers. Thus wage rates may increase during periods of high unemployment in response to collective bargaining or social comparison and not because of any need in the attraction of labor supplies.

Job evaluation also is challenged as being biased toward predominantly male jobs and as perpetuating male-female wage differentials (Smith, 1978a, 1978b; Thompsen, 1978). It is noted that different systems of job evaluation typically are employed for managerial jobs (predominantly male) and for clerical jobs (predominantly female) and that these jobs are rarely compared directly in terms of job factors or relative worth. It also is noted that factors more common in traditionally male jobs (physical effort) often are weighted more heavily than factors more common in traditionally female jobs (dexterity), resulting in higher evaluations for the traditionally male jobs. More equitable systems of job evaluation, it can be argued, would employ a common set of factors for the evaluation of all jobs and would avoid assignment of higher evaluations based solely upon characteristics of traditionally male jobs. Current job evaluation systems merely perpetuate past traditions of wage discrimination for women (National Academy of Sciences, 1970).

These criticisms of job evaluation argue, in effect, that while job evaluation ensures "equal pay for identical work," it fails to achieve a goal of "equal pay for work of equal worth," and they challenge the market criterion of worth used in the validation of job evaluation. Market rates, it is argued, reflect past discrimination in the form of channeling occupational choices of women, education and selection, job assignment, and promotion within organizations. A socially justifiable norm of worth is sought to replace the more traditional norm of market rate as measured in wage surveys. An alternative criterion of acceptability already is employed in certain organizations. Thus, for example, many breweries often pay a single rate to all plant jobs, while manufacturing firms more often differentiate among jobs with small, but apparently meaningful, differentials in wages. Where applied, these practices have become traditional and are accepted as just and equitable by the affected employees, although it could be difficult to find validating measures in the surrounding labor markets. Whether or not acceptance of analogous social norms can be achieved within a national society remains to be seen. (See Oettinger, 1964, for an account of national job evaluation in the Netherlands.)

WAGE COMPRESSION

Wage compression, in simple terms, relates to the compression of some previously established differential in wages that may have been based upon tenure, skill level, or performance. Any erosion of wage differentials reduces the relative reward associated with the higher paid status, with consequent perceptions of inequity by persons in that higher paid status, and of reduced incentive associated with movement into the higher paid status. One form of compression that has been experienced periodically is occasioned by an escalation of hiring rates in particular occupations. Hiring rates for engineers, for example, may escalate by 15 percent in a single year because of competition for engineering graduates, while the compensation for employed engineers increases by a smaller proportion. Wage compression of this form has its most serious equity implications for occupations without clearly differentiable jobs in a promotional or career sequence. Salary progression and not job progression is the only clear reward associated with experience and performance in these occupations. The obvious solution to compression, advancement of all related salaries proportional to increases in hiring rates, often is not feasible. Further, hiring rates often vary in response to short-run market influences and should not be the criterion for overall adjustment of the entire salary structure. Some means for recognizing the worth of experience, other than proportional adjustment of salaries as recruiting rates vary, must be sought in order to maintain perceptions of equity of treatment.

A related form of wage compression is occasioned by inflationary price increases and wage level increases associated with cost of living changes. Whether so-called cost of living adjustments are occasioned by a collective bargaining agreement, employer policy, or adaptation to other employers' wage increases observed in wage surveys, across-the-board increases erode any wage differentials associated with employee performance levels. Wage differentiation according to performance level is common in many organizations, particularly for clerical, technical, and managerial employees. Periodic performance reviews serve as the basis for recommending appropriate wage and salary adjustments within the salary grade for the job. Performance or merit increases lose meaning, however, if they do not significantly exceed cost of living increases. A wage increase of 15 percent provides little recognition for performance if cost of living increases average 12 to 13 percent for the same period. Maintenance of a performance increase and recognition policy becomes difficult with inflationary rates and cost of living increases above 10 percent annually. A merit increase program combined with cost of living adjustments also becomes quite expensive to maintain if, as is common, a merit increase for one year is factored into the base from which increases are determined for the following year. One proposal that has been advanced, but is not yet widely practiced except for executives, is to view performance rewards as bonuses or revertible increases. Increases are granted for a year, but are not factored into any base pay and need not be renewed the following year. This proposal would permit annual recognition of performance at less cost over a period of time. Other innovative proposals are necessary if performance differentials are to be maintained as meaningful during periods of rapid price inflation.

EXECUTIVE COMPENSATION

Issues in the motivation and compensation of executives, while similar in concept to issues in motivating and compensating other employees, appear in somewhat exaggerated form and attract considerable interest. Executive salaries and other compensation are published annually for public information. Forms of executive compensation and contingency relationships to performance vary considerably over time, giving the impression of fads that come into and go out of style. Performance shares, stock options, performance bonuses, deferred compensation, and perquisites such as automobiles, club memberships, and personal services are among the forms of compensation often provided executives. One might well question the rationale for these various forms of compensation and their changing contingency relationships with performance.

While the amount spent for executive compensation in any organization is relatively small compared with total employee compensation, the performance of executive functions may be critical to organizational performance. The supply of individuals capable of performing executive jobs is relatively limited, and organizations face somewhat more competition in the attraction and retention of executives than is associated with other jobs. Executive jobs also are relatively free of constraints of technology and procedures, thus allowing greater scope for variation in individual performance. Finally, executives' incomes are subject to relatively higher rates of taxation than the incomes of other employees. Executive compensation provisions differ from other employee compensation provisions in terms of a performance contingency relationship and a concern for finding forms of compensation that maximize the after-tax compensation. Because of the potential for variation in individual performance, contingency forms of compensation are common for executives and may amount at times to more than the individual's base salary. Also, because of tax implications, such compensation may take the form of deferred compensation bonuses or capital gains associated with stock options. Nontaxable perquisites, where available, also are utilized more extensively in compensating executives than in compensating other employees.

What may appear as faddism in changing styles of executive compensation may be explained by the ever-changing provisions in the Internal Revenue Code and the inventing of new forms of compensation as older forms are subjected to income taxation. These changing styles may be explained in terms of the diminishing motivational impact of contingency compensation over time and the need for constant renewal of contingency compensation with alternative rewards. Given the relatively limited market for executives, it is likely that social comparison is a major factor in the attribution of valence to different forms of compensation, and that compensation in the form of relatively new compensation provisions possesses more valence than warranted solely by monetary value. Since executives perform a key role in an organization, it is likely that experimentation with alternative forms and contingency schedules of compensation will continue and that each successive change will elicit positive responses from the affected individuals.

COMPENSATION FOR CHANGING ORGANIZATIONAL FORMS

Traditional compensation programs and practices such as job evaluation and wage surveys were designed for organizations with a reasonably stable technology and structure of jobs. Traditional practices are based upon job descriptions that assume a relatively fixed structuring of tasks and operations in individual jobs. Rates of compensation are based first upon the job and second upon the individual within the job. The assumption that jobs rather than individuals provide the more stable and enduring framework for compensation is being challenged by new forms of work organization. The concept of jobs performed by individuals is giving way to a concept of jobs performed by teams, individual assignments within teams varying considerably among individuals and over time. Matrix and project organizations also challenge the traditional assumptions about jobs insofar as matrix and project assignments are shared among individuals. It was noted earlier how maturity curve compensation was developed for engineers and scientists to replace traditional job-oriented compensation. Similarly, alternative approaches to compensation must be developed for team, matrix, and project organizations.

Compensation criteria for matrix and project organizations tend to reflect both functional competence of the individual and assignment performance measures. An engineer in a project organization, for example, might be compensated on the basis of maturity curve relationships and on the results of specific project assignments. Conceivably some analogous approaches to compensation might be developed for other occupations in a matrix organization, with accountants, personnel representatives, computer programmers, and draftsmen being compensated within the grade structure. Somewhat similar shifts have been proposed for the compensation of workers on team assignments, teams being compensated on the basis of team performance and individuals on the basis of flexibility within the full range of team assignments.

Perhaps the greatest challenge occasioned by newer developing forms of organizations is the challenge to the concept of the job as the primary basis for compensation. This chapter began with an examination of the relationships between work and compensation, noting that employing organizations seek the outcome of work behavior, not the work behavior itself. For reasons developed earlier, the tendency is to compensate work behavior specified in the form of a job description. As it becomes more difficult to specify work behavior with stable job descriptions, compensation will likely increasingly reflect worker inputs in work behavior, that is, the competencies and skills brought to the employing organization by the worker. The employment contract will refer to worker characteristics, and the behavioral implications of the contract will develop only through employment experience in the organization. As the formal employment contract becomes still more general, greater reliance will be placed upon the process of supervision and management to elicit the specific work behaviors desired over time. Employee compensation will continue as a significant element in the employment contract, but it will serve increasingly to reinforce the overall management process and ought not to be viewed as the primary or dominant element of the employment contract. The wage nexus, while important in an employment relationship, will not be sufficient to attain the desired labor outputs in developing organizations.

REFERENCES

Lawler, E. E., III (1971). *Pay and organizational effectiveness.* New York: McGraw-Hill.

National Academy of Sciences (1970). *Job evaluation: An analytic review.* Washington: National Academy of Sciences.

Oettinger, M. P. (1964). Nation-wide job evaluation in the Netherlands. *Industrial Relations, 4,* 45–59.

Smith, L. (1978a). "Equality Opportunity" rules are getting tougher. *Fortune, 97,* 152–156.

Smith, L. (1978b). The EEOC's bold foray into job evaluation. *Fortune, 98,* 58–64.

Thompsen, D. J. (1978). Eliminating pay discrimination caused by job evaluation. *Personnel, 55,* 11–22.

Executive Compensation Must Promote Long-Term Commitment

Pearl Meyer

Looking out across our nation today, we find corporate America in a considerably weakened state—the empty smokestacks of our midwestern industrial machine and a 10 percent unemployment rate. The many explanations offered for this decline in business health—in vigor and confidence—range from unfair foreign competition to high domestic interest rates. But such reasoning ignores the critical ingredient that often separates successful organizations from those that fail—the executives in charge.

Recent studies that matched companies in the same industries (beer, transportation, farm machinery), facing the same stresses, the same busi-

Reprinted from *Personnel Administrator, 28* (1983), by permission of the author.

ness conditions and the same challenges, found that the quality of management and its decisions spelled the difference between success and failure.

Those companies with a history of outperforming their rivals, regardless of industry or economic climate, are noted by two characteristics, by the long-term strategic view of their executives and by the stability of their executive groups.

At the heart of corporate performance and productivity in America, then, is the retention and the consistent motivation of high-quality management, reversing the trend of the last 25 years, during which we have witnessed the growing professionalism of the American executive. He has become a skilled mercenary, loyal to himself alone—a gunslinger who can be hired for pay to run any company, in any industry, and under any conditions.

Our challenge is to turn away from this professionalism, which concentrates on immediate results and rewards, and create the environment in which the professional manager again becomes a career employee who has a long-term stake in building his business.

EXECUTIVE REWARD SYSTEMS

Implicit in this challenge to create a career environment is a shift in the focus of executive compensation, from passive or facilitative, treating today's symptoms of yesterday's ills, to positive or pro-active at the policy level, evolving tomorrow's reward systems in support of our corporations' long-term strategic goals.

In designing such systems, we must understand their impact on how our businesses are run:

- Annual incentive systems encourage the efficient use of existing assets. This demands determination, toughness and attention to detail.
- Medium-term plans of three to four years encourage labor and plant productivity—replacing insufficient or scarce resources with new equipment. This requires capital and the willingness to take moderate financial risks.
- Truly long-term plans—career plans—encourage the development of new processes, plants and products that open new markets and restore old ones. This requires imagination and technology. The American executive's failure of vision and leadership—lack of entrepreneurship and of willingness to take sizeable long-term risks—has eroded our ability to win.

The most significant and successful assignments that we have completed over the last five years were integrated plans for total compensation based on pay for strategic results. This often involved re-balancing each element in the reward matrix: salary, annual incentives, long-term performance awards, stock incentives, benefits and perquisites—shifting the mix as well as the range of opportunity and performance criteria. It's hard work, but well worth it in terms of yield. You can revitalize an entire organization by new focus and commitment to its business mission.

GOVERNMENT INTERVENTION

Today and for the foreseeable future, we will be functioning in a climate that is unfriendly and somewhat critical of executive performance as well as pay.

Recent legislation and regulations that opened doors—to a maximum tax rate of 50 percent on ordinary income and of 20 percent on capital gains, to favorable SEC and IRS rulings on stock swaps, and to the creation of ISOs by ERTA in 1981—have been followed rapidly in 1982 by severe limitations on qualified pensions and on the tax deductibility of individual medical expenses. In addition to a new alternative minimum tax, which can significantly affect the rate paid on ISO profits, withholding requirements have been imposed on pension, interest and dividend income.

While it seems sensible for us to optimize executive tax shelter and corporate tax effectiveness—and indeed, significant further shifts in tax laws or securities regulations that may mandate the introduction of new compensation forms—it may ultimately prove unsound to continuously alter effective compensation strategies and programs solely in reaction to, or in anticipation of, what may prove to be annual tax legislation. There have been five tax bills in the six years since 1976, and we can look forward to a Technical Corrections Act in 1983 and perhaps another shift in direction by 1985 should control of Congress or the White House change.

While adjustments are, of course, necessary to ameliorate the impact of government intervention, remuneration and benefits programs must be designed in light of each corporation's philosophy and strategy.

Examples of excellent response to government edict are: Excess-ERISA pension plans (which henceforth should be called Excess-TEFRA benefits), the gross-up of certain types of moving expense reimbursements that became taxable several years ago, the introduction of insured executive medical reimbursement plans, and the other supplementary wrap-around executive benefits offered by most major corporations. We shall, and indeed we must, continue to do what is right for our businesses and for our employees despite the latest fad on Capitol Hill.

BOARDROOM POWER

Unfortunately, I believe that we are better equipped to deal with government intervention than with an unfriendly business press and critical outside directors.

Skepticism of both executive performance and executive pay is growing in the boardroom, where compensation committees have emerged as real power centers in corporate governance. This derives from their role in setting goals and in assessing corporate and executive performance. Executive compensation has emerged in the 1980s as a major tool of the board in directing and controlling corporate activity.

In prior years, our role as executive compensation consultants involved advising both a corporation's management and its board. I now serve a number of board committees as their own outside counsel in the review of management proposals.

The issue raised in both these closed sessions and in regular presentations is the same: Is the total reward level reasonable relative to the results to be achieved and to amounts paid by similar companies for comparable performance? There is little concern with seven-figure incomes based on stock price appreciation, while similar yields on performance that has not yet benefited the stockholder give rise to real board concern and discomfort.

DIRECTORS' COMPENSATION

Since we are talking about directors, let me digress and address the subject of board remuneration. As significant changes have occurred in the quality, composition and role of boards whose responsibilities have grown more time consuming and hazardous, it is not surprising to find that board remuneration has grown at a faster rate over the past three years than that of any other corporate group. My best estimate is a compound annual growth rate in total remuneration of close to 13 percent. In addition, the director's compensation package is coming to resemble that of an employee, with payment by some companies in stock as well as cash, and the extension of benefits including life travel and medical insurance and deferred compensation.

The fastest growing fringe is retirement income which, based on our recent study, is currently offered by over 10 to 15 percent of the Fortune top 200 industrials whose plans mirror the characteristics of their regular employee pension programs. We anticipate that usage will grow to at least 15 percent up to 25 percent within two years.

Prior to 1973, pensions for outside board members were virtually non-existent. Insurance companies along with the diversified financials were innovators in this area, beginning with Massachusetts Mutual in 1973. During the 10 intervening years, retirement compensation for outside directors has gained widespread acceptance as a leading-edge benefit.

The initial purpose was to gracefully facilitate the retirement of elderly directors, and often its inception coincided with the introduction of mandatory retirement and the use of honorary designations. Since its introduction, however, the reason for the subsequent popularity of this benefit is not dissimilar to the basic philosophy underlying properly structured executive compensation plans—to attract high-quality talent and to retain, motivate and reward those outside directors who are the key long-term contributors to the corporation.

In addition, there is a perceived need for income replacement among "professional" directors who are in occupations (non-profit, government, academia) that are traditionally low-paying, and among retired executives whose incomes and capital have been eroded by inflation. The provision of additional compensation on a deferred basis through a retirement benefit can effectively address this need.

"GOLDEN PARACHUTES"

One of the issues in which boards are most deeply involved is employment contracts and, more recently, change-of-control agreements—often called "golden parachutes." Our best estimate is that at least 25 to 30 percent of the major corporations have such agreements with one or more of their top executives. This trend is growing very rapidly, since such protection is being added as a matter of course to regular employment contracts as well as to termination agreements, with coverage ranging from these few top officers who would represent the company in its takeover negotiations, down to include the entire officer group plus division heads.

There is some backlash building in the wake of the extraordinary sums recently provided by a number of companies.

In any case, financial umbrellas of two to three years' compensation and benefits plus pension credits have grown commonplace. Indeed, all of the new compensation plans developed for our clients over the past few years have included automatic vesting or payout and other provisions appropiate in the event of a takeover, so that most, if not all, management employees will soon have some type of change-of-control protection built into their compensation.

CHANGING CONDITIONS

Inflation is slowing, and economists predict a maximum rate of five to six percent over the next few years. This shift down from double-digit, runaway inflation, coupled with an optimistic stock market and recessionary business conditions, will tax our planning and implementation skills in 1983. Our most pressing task is to critically assess current programs and ensure their continued effectiveness and flexibility in light of a changing economic climate. The implications of deflation are far reaching—in how we deploy our assets, finance our capital requirements, run our businesses and pay our people.

First, with respect to salaries, last September and October we polled our tracking group of representative major companies, which we use to determine current practices and to test trends. Results indicate that 1983 merit budgets will be down 20 percent from the beginning of 1982 and run at the rate of 7.8 percent or less. With respect to top officer salaries, we project that approximately 20 percent of our chief executives will forego increases in 1983. Those that do receive salary hikes will average 9.6 percent, with a range from seven percent up to a high of 15 percent.

With some of the air coming out of salaries, we must lower employee expectations and once again assume control of the administration of our companies' salary dollars.

To those of us designing executive compensation programs, the slowdown in salary increases is a double-edged sword. It represents an opportunity to reduce fixed compensation costs and direct more attention and dollars toward incentive pay based on performance. More importantly, we will again be able to use salary administration to significantly differentiate between good and poor performers at all levels.

On the other hand, of course, tighter control means smaller margin for error in ascertaining fair market values and ensuring equitable salary levels. Performance evaluations tied to merit increases must now operate within a tighter framework.

INCENTIVES AND APPRAISALS

Secondly, with regard to annual incentives, we are finding that they are not truly variable in whole. Despite lip service to "pay for performance," a significant portion of annual bonuses—perhaps as much as one-half—are really year-end salary supplements on which people rely to maintain their living standard and below which companies are loathe to cut, despite poor individual results or indifferent corporate profits.

An underlying reason for this gap between policy and practice is that executives are unwilling to face the hostility of poor performers and therefore shun the appraisal process, which is regarded as a confrontation in which they are forced to brand another person "bad" or label him as "good."

The problem lies not so much in human nature, but rather in the design of appraisal systems that produce one label or one numeric rating for each employee. This one label generally determines every aspect of an individual's compensation and future prospects. But performance is multi-faceted, and each element of our compensation program should be utilized in evaluating and responding to each aspect of performance.

For example, an individual with generally good performance over time and high future potential may have a rotten business year in terms of failing sales or profit or cost goals, while improving market share or productivity over the long term. A well-balanced executive compensation program and performance assessment could result in no annual bonus that year due to poor annual results v. plan, but yet allow for a salary increase based on a sound record as well as a stock option grant based on the individual's high future potential and impact on corporate results.

LONG-TERM PLANS

With respect to long-term incentives, prevalence among the majors is up to about 65 percent. Some 35 percent of our corporations still utilize only stock options, while 50 percent grant stock options in conjunction with long-term performance awards. The remaining 15 percent disdain options and use only performance incentives in the form of units, restricted stock or similar awards.

Regardless of vehicle, most long-term plans are based on one predetermined absolute numeric financial standard, such as earnings per share. Experience teaches that this approach is unrealistic and unrelated to strategic results. We have realized, somewhat belatedly, that long-term performance encompasses qualitative progress as well as quantitative accomplishments, which may often be assessed only on a relative basis. Therefore, entering the third-generation design of long-term plans, results achieved are still to be measured quantitatively—but on a relative basis—relative to competitive performance and/or relative to economic conditions such as real growth v. the GNP deflator, CPI or Producer Price Index. Results achieved are also being measured qualitatively by the board relative to the organization's strategic progress, with attention to key interim milestones as well as the desired end results.

We have also learned over the past 10 years that corporate measures should be retained only for the top corporate echelon. Break down the rest of your company in accordance with long-term business direction—perhaps by strategic business segments, operating groups or other units—and develop long-term plans with criteria for their performance over time periods dictated by their individual business cycles.

The most fruitful use of long-term incentives is at the lowest level definable profit center so that people in the operations are rewarded for building rather than milking their businesses.

STOCK INCENTIVES

With regard to career motivation under the corporate umbrella and to provide for significant executive capital accumulation, it is apparent that we need to go back to basics and reconstruct the executive's mutuality of interest with the owner of his business, the stockholder, by refocusing on shareholder welfare—or stock price—on dividends and on book value. Such strategy goes hand in hand with opportunities available under recent tax laws and rulings favorable to capital gains treatment. Several fine long-term incentive designs such as career shares have been developed, and these plans are both highly motivational and tax efficient when compared to vehicles like restricted stock or options.

Such career share ownership programs combined with long-term incentives are the basic tools by which we can motivate our executives to build their careers and businesses with our companies.

We now know the results of what we have understandably taken great pride in over the past 15 years—the professionalism of our corporate management with its increasing emphasis on short-term results and rewards. It comes as no surprise to learn that during this period, U.S. productivity, R&D expenditures and capital investment—at their peak in the 1960s—have been declining ever since, in both absolute and relative terms.

If we indeed wish to motivate and reward superior performance and drive our companies to success in the marketplace here and abroad, we must return our executives to career employment with stakes in building their businesses for the long term. There must be a completely perceived mutuality of interest between a company's management group and its stockholders.

In stimulating a career environment through properly designed executive compensation programs, we can assist in recommitting America's executives to entrepreneurship.

Comparable Worth: A Legal Overview

John R. Schnebly

In its study for the Equal Employment Opportunity Commission (EEOC), the National Academy of Sciences (NAS) described the theory of comparable worth as the concept that "jobs that are equal in their value to the organization ought to be equally compensated, whether or not the work content of those jobs is similar."[1] Stated another way, by assuming that all jobs have an intrinsic value to each employer, comparable worth advocates seek equal pay for unequal jobs of equal value. The facial fairness of this notion, however, masks significant practical and economic problems in its implementation. These are complex issues beyond the parameters of this article.

There are also significant legal questions about the validity of the comparable worth concept. As a recognized theory of actionable wage discrimination, comparable worth is in the early stages of evolution. While the recent decision in *County of Washington* v. *Gunther*[2] has given impetus to its proponents, the contours and ultimate acceptance of comparable worth will be determined through future litigation.

In order to appreciate the context within which this theory will develop, it is important to understand how wage discrimination claims have fared under existing law. This article will highlight the various statutory and regulatory bases for wage discrimination claims in general with particular focus on comparable worth actions.

Reprinted from *Personnel Administrator, 27* (1982), by permission of the author.

1942 ORIGINS

Preliminarily, it should be noted that comparable worth is not a new idea. In 1942, the National War Labor Board issued General Order No. 16 which allowed employers to make pay adjustments which "equalize the wage or salary rates paid to females with the rates paid to males for comparable quality and quantity of work on the same or similar operations. . . ."[3] While this has been viewed as sanctioning a comparable worth standard, a close review of the actual experiences of the Board reveals that in practice an equal pay for equal work principle was applied.[4]

LEGAL BACKGROUND—WAGE DISCRIMINATION

The Equal Pay Act. The Equal Pay Act[5] passed in 1963, was the first federal law to address the concerns and claims of unfair wage practices in employment. Limited to claims of sex-based wage discrimination, the Equal Pay Act requires employers to provide equal pay for equal work. This familiar standard was an amendment to the Fair Labor Standards Act[6] (federal wage and hour law) and applies to employers and employees subject to that law. Initially enforced by the Wage and Hour Administrator of the Department of Labor, the Equal Pay Act has been administered by the EEOC since 1979.[7]

The legislative history of the Equal Pay Act makes it clear that Congress intended the equal work standard of comparison. In extensive consideration of what obligation should be imposed on employers, Congress expressly rejected the comparable worth theory in favor of the stricter equal work requirement.[8] Thus under the Equal Pay Act, courts and administrative agencies are not permitted "to substitute their judgment for the judgment of the employer . . . who [has] established and employed a *bona fide* job rating system," so long as it does not discriminate on the basis of sex.[9]

The equal pay for equal work standard prohibits an employer from paying its male and female employees differently for doing the same thing within the same establishment. Equal work is defined by the statute as that "which requires equal skill, effort and responsibility . . . performed under similar working conditions. . . ."[10] A plaintiff must establish that the jobs being compared meet each of these conditions before a possible violation may be found.[11]

Moreover, even where the equal work standard is satisfied, an employer may differentiate in its compensation of males and females in four specific situations. These affirmative defenses authorize pay differentials, where such are the result of a seniority system, a merit system, a system which measures earnings by quantity and quality of production, or where based on any other factor other than sex.[12] The employer has the burden of showing the existence of any of these exceptions.

WHAT DO THE COURTS SAY?

Although the standard is equal work, courts have generally held that it is sufficient if the jobs being compared are "substantially equal" rather than identical.[13] Since courts will look at actual job content rather than job titles, an employer will not avoid liability by creating insignificant differences in job classifications.[14]

A violation of the Equal Pay Act subjects an employer to the remedial provisions of the Fair Labor Standards Act.[15] An employer is not permitted to equalize wages by reducing the compensation of the higher-paid employee. The wages of the lower-paid employee must be raised to the higher level.[16] There is a two-year statute of limitations period for the recovery of back pay. However, a three-year period applies where the violation is willful,[17] in which case liquidated damages in an amount equal to the lost wages may also be awarded.[18] The EEOC is empowered to obtain injunctive relief where appropriate.[19] Finally, reasonable attorney's fees and costs may be obtained by a prevailing party.[20]

Recapping, in a wage discrimination action under the Equal Pay Act, the plaintiff must first establish that an employer pays its male and female employees differently for doing substantially equal jobs. The employer may defend by showing that the jobs in question are unequal or, where the jobs are equal, one of the four statutory exceptions is applicable. A comparable worth claim is not actionable under the Equal Pay Act.

TITLE VII OF THE CIVIL RIGHTS ACT OF 1964

Key in the comparable worth controversy is Title VII,[21] the most prominent anti-discrimination law administered by the EEOC. Considerably broader in scope than the Equal Pay Act, Title VII prohibits employment discrimination on the basis of an individual's race, color, religion, sex or national origin. Affecting the full range of employment decisions, including recruiting, hiring, transfers and discharges, Title VII also specifically forbids discrimination in compensation practices.[22] The scope and intent of this wage discrimination proscription underlies the comparable worth dispute.

Title VII affords protection not only against overt discrimination but also against employment practices which, although fair in form and administration, have discriminatory consequences.[23] The former is commonly referred to as disparate treatment and results where an employer intentionally bases a decision on a person's protected status.[24] The latter, known as disparate impact, involves challenges to neutral policies or practices which, in their implementation, fall more harshly on a particular protected group.[25]

The distinction is important because of the differing burdens and orders of proof necessary to establish a violation of Title VII.

In cases raising disparate treatment claims, proof of an employer's discriminatory motive is essential.[26] This discriminatory intent may be inferred in some cases from the differences in treatment itself, often on the basis of statistical evidence of disparities.[27] The general requirements and burdens of proof necessary for a disparate treatment case were set out in *McDonnell Douglas Corp.* v. *Green.*[28] There, the United States Supreme Court held that a plaintiff must first establish a *prima facie* case of discrimination by showing that he or she is a member of a protected class who, although qualified, was rejected for an available employment opportunity while the employer continued to seek other candidates. Once the plaintiff has demonstrated a *prima facie* case, the burden then shifts to the employer to articulate a legitimate nondiscriminatory reason, such as business necessity, for its decision. At this point the plaintiff has a final opportunity to show that the employer's reason is pretextual.[29] The plaintiff has the ultimate burden of persuading the trier of fact that the defendant intentionally discriminated.[30]

In rebutting a *prima facie* case, the defendant must produce evidence of a legitimate business reason for the action taken.[31] This burden is satisfied once the employer produces admissible evidence of the non-discriminatory reason; it is not necessary that the defendant convince the court that its reason was, in fact, lawful.[32]

Moreover, in its rebuttal of a *prima facie* case, an employer is not required to show that its practices maximize the opportunities of minorities and females.[33] As long as its employment system is reasonably related to a legitimate business purpose, an employer does not have to adopt practices which prefer protected class members.[34]

THE BURDEN OF PROOF

Under the disparate impact theory of discrimination, plaintiffs must show that some employment standard that appears neutral has significantly harsher consequences for protected class members.[35] This adverse effect of a particular policy or practice is generally shown through the use of statistical analysis. Once this impact is established, the defendant bears the burden of demonstrating that the practice is required by business necessity. Intent to discriminate is not required.[36] There is one other method of establishing a violation of Title VII—a "pattern or practice" of discriminatory conduct. In such an action, the plaintiff has the initial burden of demonstrating that the employer's policies and practices are routinely discriminatory. In *Wilkins* v. *University of Houston,* the Fifth Circuit framed the issue as "whether (plaintiff's statistical evidence) established that sex discrimination was the University's 'standard operating procedure—the regular rather than the unusual practice,' (citing *Teamsters*)."[37] In applying this standard to a class challenge to the University's compensation practices, the Court found, on the basis of significant pay disparities and on admission that the pay plan was designed to remedy previous sexually discriminatory wage practices, that the University discriminated against its female academic staff members.

Recognizing that it was intended to assure equality of employment opportunities to remove barriers that have operated to favor nonminorities,[38] a violation of Title VII subjects an employer to wide-ranging remedial obligations in an effort to make victims of discrimination "whole."[39] Depending on the nature of the discriminatory conduct, preliminary injunctive relief may be sought to prevent irreparable harm to the plaintiff while the action is pending. Permanent injunctions, the modification of employment practice and the imposition of affirmative action efforts may be imposed on the employer. In addition, victims of discrimination could be ordered reinstated or promoted and granted retroactive seniority and back pay. Front pay—compensating individuals deprived of future wages because there is no current vacancy or where reinstatement is impractical—may be available. Finally, attorney's fees and costs may be awarded to a prevailing party.[40]

As far as compensation practices are concerned, it should be noted that Title VII proscribes discrimination not only on the basis of sex but also race, color, religion and national origin. An employer is specifically permitted to apply different standards of compensation where the differences are part of a bona fide seniority system, a merit system or a system which measures earnings by quantity or quality of production or which apply to employees who work in different locations, provided the differences are not the result of an intent to discriminate.[41]

In connection with sex-based wage discrimination, Title VII contains a further specific exception: "It shall not be an unlawful employment practice . . . for any employer to differentiate upon the basis of sex in determining the amount of wages or compensation paid . . . if such differentiation is authorized by the provisions of [the Equal Pay Act].[42]

The interpretation of this language, the so-called Bennett Amendment, generated the controversy leading to the *Gunther* decision. While it is clear that unequal pay for equal work could violate both the Equal Pay Act and Title VII,[43] *Gunther* interpreted the Bennett Amendment as incorporating into Title VII only the four exceptions of the Equal Pay Act and not the Act's equal work standard. Thus, under Title VII, sex-based wage discrimination claims are not limited by the equal work requirement.

What remains unclear, even after *Gunther,* is the nature of these other wage claims, including comparable worth actions, that may now be recognized under Title VII.

AGE DISCRIMINATION IN EMPLOYMENT ACT

Enacted in 1967 and now administered by the EEOC, the Age Discrimination in Employment Act (ADEA) forbids employers from discriminating against individuals between 40 and 70 years of age.[44] In language similar to Title VII, the ADEA makes it unlawful for an employer to discriminate on the basis of an individual's age with respect to compensation, terms, conditions or privileges of employment.[45] An employer, who unlawfully pays a younger employee more than an older employee, may not reduce the wage rate of the higher-paid employee to achieve equality.[46]

Like Title VII, courts are granted broad remedial powers under the ADEA including compelling employment, reinstatement, promotion and back pay.[47] Liquidated damages in an amount equal to lost wages are recoverable,[48] as are attorney's fees and costs.[49]

EXECUTIVE ORDER 11246

This Presidential Order, issued in 1965, now prohibits employment discrimination based on race, color, religion, sex or national origin by federal contractors.[50] Administered by the Office of Federal Contract Compliance Programs (OFCCP) of the Department of Labor, Executive Order 11246 also imposes affirmative action requirements on contractors. Pursuant to the equal opportunity clause required in federal contracts, the contractor agrees not to discriminate with respect to employment, upgrading, demotion, transfer and rates of pay.[51]

In the context of comparable worth, in 1977, the OFCCP brought an administrative action against Kerr Glass Manufacturing Corp. alleging that Kerr used a job evaluation system which, because of its discriminatory origin and application, resulted in unfair pay rates for traditional female jobs.[52] The action remains pending. Under current regulations, a contractor's wage schedule must not be related to or based on the sex of the employees.[53] The OFCCP will also closely scrutinize jobs where males or females are concentrated to assure that sex has played no role in the setting of the pay levels.[54]

Executive Order 11246 sets forth a number of sanctions and penalties for violations of its provisions.[55] Among these are recommending to the Department of Justice to institute proceedings to enforce the contractual provisions required by the Executive Order and the cancellation, termination or suspension of the contract.[56]

STATE LAWS AND WAGE DISCRIMINATION

Most states have enacted wage and hour laws requiring equal pay for equal work.[57] As under the federal Equal Pay Act, this standard requires plaintiffs to show that the jobs being compared are the "same or similar." [See, *e.g., States of Human Rights* v. *Eastman Kodak Co.*, 55 A.D.2d 842, 390 N.Y.S.2d 332 (App. Div.) 1976.]

A number of states have statutes which are phrased in terms of equal pay for "comparable work." Typical of such laws is Kentucky's statute: "No employee shall discriminate between employees in the same establishment on the basis of sex, by paying wages to any employee in any occupation in this state at a rate less than the rate he pays any employee of the opposite sex for comparable work on jobs which have comparable requirements relating to skill, effort and responsibility."[58]

There is a dearth of cases under these "comparable worth" laws and it is not clear whether comparable worth was truly intended to be the standard of wage comparisons in these states. However, depending on the success of comparable worth at the federal level, it is likely that these statutes might be used as a basis for comparable worth claims.

In addition, the fair employment practices laws of the various states, which often mirror the provisions of Title VII, also broadly prohibit discrimination and could also be used as a means of advancing the theory of comparable worth.

Finally, perhaps indicative of the interest being generated at the state level, in September, 1981, California enacted a statute which establishes a policy of setting salaries for any state jobs which are female-dominated on the basis of "comparability of the value of the work."[59]

THE GUNTHER DECISION

This Title VII case involved the claims of female jail matrons that they were unlawfully underpaid by the county in relation to the compensation of male jail guards. It had been established by the lower court that the matrons and guards performed different jobs. The sole issue before the Supreme Court was whether this unequal work precluded a sex-based wage discrimination claim under Title VII in light of the Bennett Amendment. The Court made it clear that it was only addressing this very narrow question. "We are not called upon in this case to decide whether respondents have stated a *prima facie* case of sex discrimination under Title VII (citation omitted), or to lay down standards for the further conduct of this litigation. The sole issue we decide is whether respondent's failure to satisfy the equal work standard of the Equal Pay Act in itself precludes their proceeding under Title VII."[60]

In a five-to-four decision, the Court held that Title VII wage claims are not limited by the equal work standard. Instead, the Bennett Amendment was interpreted as incorporating into Title VII only the four exemptions or affirmative defenses of the Equal Pay Act. In reaching its decision, the Court emphasized that the matrons' claim was "not based on the controversial concept of 'comparable worth', . . . rather . . . (plaintiffs) seek to prove by direct evidence, that their wages were depressed because of *intentional sex discrimination,* consisting of setting the wage scale for female guards, but not for male guards, at a level lower than its own survey of outside markets and the worth of the jobs warranted."[61]

The Court paid particular attention to the fact that the county had conducted a market survey of the worth of the jobs in question and that while evaluating the matrons' jobs at 95 percent of the guards' jobs, proceeded to pay the matrons only 70 percent of their evaluated rate. Coupled with the plaintiffs' assertion that they would show unlawful sex discrimination as the reason for the differential treatment, the Court returned the case for a trial on the merits of Plaintiffs' charges.

Finally, noteworthy for its possible guidance on the appropriate burdens and order of proofs in future Title VII wage actions is the Court's discussion of the Equal Pay Act's fourth affirmative defense, "any other factor other than sex": "More importantly, incorporation of the fourth affirmative defense could have significant consequences for Title VII litigation. Title VII's prohibition of discriminatory employment practices was intended to be broadly inclusive, proscribing 'not only overt discrimination but also practices that are fair in form, but discriminatory in operation.' [*Griggs*] The structure of Title VII litigation, including presumptions, burdens of proof and defenses, has been designed to reflect this approach. The fourth affirmative defense of the Equal Pay Act, however, was designed differently, to confine the application of the Act to wage differentials attributable to sex discrimination. H. R. Rep. No. 309, 88th Cong. 1st Sess., 3 (1963). Equal Pay Act litigation, therefore, has been structured to permit employers to defend against charges of discrimination where their pay differentials are based on a *bona fide* use of 'other factors other than sex.' Under the Equal Pay Act, the courts and administrative agencies are not permitted 'to substitute their judgment for the judgment of the employer . . . who [has] established and employed a *bona fide* job rating system,' so long as it does not discriminate on the basis of sex. 109 Cong. Rec. 9209 (statement of Rep. Goodell, principal exponent of the Act). Although we do not decide in this case how sex-based wage discrimination litigation under Title VII should be structured to accommodate the fourth affirmative defense of the Equal Pay Act, see *supra,* n. 8, we consider it clear that the Bennett Amendment, under this interpretation, is not rendered superfluous."[62]

BEFORE AND AFTER GUNTHER

After *Gunther,* as before, an employer must pay its employees the same for doing substantially the same work under both Title VII and the Equal Pay Act. *Gunther* held that Title VII further prohibits an employer from intentionally paying women less because of their sex.[63] The evidence necessary to establish this intentional discrimination is unclear although where an employer evaluates jobs and then deviates from the evaluated rates in setting wages, such practice will be closely scrutinized for possible sex bias. Moreover, it would be illegal for an employer to use a "transparently sex-biased system for wage determination."[64]

With respect to comparable worth claims, as noted above, *Gunther* did not endorse the concept. Nevertheless, litigation of those types of wage claims actionable under Title VII can be expected to increase. A quick review of the few cases which have addressed the issue may provide some insight into how other courts may treat the issue.

In two pre-*Gunther* cases, the issue of an employer's reliance on market factors in developing and implementing its wage structure was raised. In *Christensen* v. *State of Iowa,*[65] female clerical workers claimed that they were discriminated against because they were paid less for jobs which, based on the employer's job evaluation, were comparable to that of male plant workers, a violation of Title VII. The employer, in addition to its evaluation, relied on the local labor market in deciding that the plant jobs should be paid at a higher rate. The Eighth Circuit held that plaintiffs failed to establish a *prima facie* case in that they had "failed to demonstrate that the difference in wages paid to clerical and plant employees rested upon sex discrimination and not on some other legitimate reason."[66] The Court further noted:

"The value of the job to the employer represents but one factor affecting wages. Other factors may include the supply of workers willing to do the job and the ability of the workers to band together to bargain collectively for higher wages. We found nothing in the text and history of Title VII suggesting the Congress intended to abrogate the laws of supply and demand or other economic principles that determine wage rates for various kinds of work. We do not interpret Title VII as requiring an employer to ignore the market in setting wage rates for genuinely different work classifications."[67]

In *Lemons* v. *City and County of Denver,*[68] female nurses made a similar claim that in following the market rate for nurses pay, which it was alleged reflected traditional discrimination against this predominantly female woman's job, the employer violated Title VII. The City had set the pay for its jobs strictly on the basis of local surveys for comparable jobs in the community. No job evaluation system was used to rate its jobs. The plaintiffs argued that this practice perpetuated the historical underpayment of nurses, typically females, and urged that their pay be compared with other different jobs in the community which were of equal worth to the City.

The Tenth Circuit rejected this claim stating that "(t)his type of disparity was not sought to be adjusted by the Civil Rights Act. . . ." The court further noted that "plaintiffs are not seeking equality of opportunity in their skills as contemplated by Title VII and described in *McDonnell Douglas* (citation omitted), but instead would cross job description lines into areas of entirely different skills."[69]

Another case that may soon shed some light onto the post-*Gunther* era of wage discrimination claim is *IUE* v. *Westinghouse Electric.*[70] Plaintiffs there alleged that more than 40 years ago, defendant had male jobs and female jobs, and contended also that Westinghouse intentionally paid the female jobs less than the comparably evaluated male jobs. The Third Circuit held, as in *Gunther,* that a Title VII claim could be broader than an equal work claim under the Equal Pay Act. The case presently is back under the jurisdiction of the trial court.

Finally, the recent decision in *Kouba* v. *Allstate*[71] signals the extreme to which one court is willing to go in imposing a very onerous burden on employers. In this Title VII *unequal pay for equal work claim,* the Court accepted a disparate impact analysis of the starting wages paid to new male and female sales agents. Moreover, in construing the employer's reliance on an agent's previous earnings as a "factor other than sex" in setting starting wages, the Court placed on Allstate the burden of showing that each agent's previous earnings itself was based on nondiscriminatory considerations:

"As a matter of law, an employer may not set a salary schedule which differentiates between its male and female employees doing the exact same job, based upon immediate past salaries . . . unless it can demonstrate that it has assessed the previous salaries and determined that they were themselves set on 'other factors other than sex.' . . . A resort to a so-called 'market rate' where the market rate is itself a reflection of the historical discrimination against women will not be considered as a sufficient justification under the Equal Pay Act."[72]

The Court's acceptance of a traditional "market rate discrimination" against females is very troublesome. The resulting burden placed on employers to prove that there was no discrimination in the market is nearly impossible to satisfy, particularly when the judge heard no evidence on this issue. This significant case is on appeal to the Ninth Circuit.

In response to *Gunther,* the EEOC issued a 90-day memorandum to its field offices advising that the Equal Pay Act is not applicable to wage claims where equal work is not provable. It goes on to advise that charges of wage discrimination should be filed under both Title VII and the Equal Pay Act with individual charges used to investigate, on a broad basis, an employer's compensation system. The guidance memorandum specifically asks investigators to review an employer's work force sexual profile, job analyses, wage schedules and job descriptions, documentation of the history of past pay practices and factors used to establish the market wage rate. Obviously, the EEOC will closely scrutinize an employer's job evaluation system for evidence of intentional sex discrimination.

CONCLUSION

As indicated at the outset, the legal standards for comparable worth claims are just developing. While *Gunther* addressed the threshold question of whether Title VII's wage discrimination proscription is identical with that of the Equal Pay Act, there remain serious evidentiary and procedural questions for the litigation of these compensation claims. Among other issues that need to be addressed are:

1. Is the theory of comparable worth feasible? The NAS Study itself was inconclusive in specifying how job evaluation systems could be used to fairly compliment a comparable worth approach. The Study, it should be pointed out, did not establish any standards for job compensation nor did it find any particular wage system as being discriminatory.

2. What are the elements necessary to establish a *prima facie* case of wage discrimination? What are the burdens and order of proof in these types of litigation? Are both disparate treatment and impact analysis applicable? Is an intent to discriminate necessary for finding a violation?

3. What are the employer's authorized defenses? What are the "other factors other than sex" that an employer may rely on in setting its compensation system? Is reference to the "market rate" acceptable?

While those questions are significant and will invite more litigation, it is also likely that major inroads will come from non-legal areas, including legislation and the collective bargaining arena.

REFERENCES

1. "Women, work, and wages; equal pay for jobs of equal value," National Academy of Sciences Committee on Occupational Classification and Analysis, 1981.
2. 452 U.S. 68 L.Ed.2d 751, 25 FEP Cases 1521 (No. 80–429, decided June 8, 1981).
3. National War Labor Board, Termination Report (1945).
4. See discussion of the National War Labor Board experience in E. Livernash, *Comparable Worth: Issues and Alternatives* (1980) at pp. 205–212 and pp. 111–118.
5. 29 U.S.C. §206(d).
6. 29 U.S.C. §§201–219. The Fair Labor Standards Act includes provisions concerning minimum wage rates, maximum hours of work and child labor restrictions.
7. Reorganization Plan No. 1 of 1978.
8. See the Supreme Court's discussion of the legislative history in *Corning Glass Works* v. *Brennan,* 417 U.S. 188, 198–201; 9 FEP Cases 919, 922 (1974).
9. 109 Cong. Rec. 9209 (1963) (statement of Rep. Goodell).
10. 29 U.S.C. §206(d)(1).
11. *Corning Glass,* 417 U.S. at 195.
12. 29 U.S.C. §206(d)(1).
13. *Shultz* v. *Wheaton Glass Co.,* 421 F.2d 259, 9 FEP Cases 502 (3d Cir. 1970) *cert. denied,* 398 U.S. 905 (1970).
14. 421 F.2d at 265.
15. 29 U.S.C. §206(d).
16. *Id.*
17. 29 U.S.C. §§216(c), 255(a), 29 C.F.R. §1620.22.
18. 29 U.S.C. §216(b)(c).
19. 29 C.F.R. §1620.22.
20. *Id.*
21. 42 U.S.C. §§2000e–2000e–17. An employer is subject to Title VII if it employs at least 15 workers during each working day in each of 20 or more calendar weeks in the current or preceding year. §2000e(b).
22. 42 U.S.C. §2000e–2(a)(1).
23. *Griggs* v. *Duke Power Co.,* 401 U.S. 424, 3 FEP Cases 175 (1971).
24. *International Brotherhood of Teamsters* v. *United States,* 431 U.S. 324, 14 FEP Cases 1514 (1977).
25. *Griggs,* 401 U.S. at 431.
26. *Teamsters,* 431 U.S. at 355 n. 15.
27. *Id.*
28. 411 U.S. 792, 5 FEP Cases 965 (1973).
29. *McDonnell Douglas,* 411 U.S. at 804–05; 5 FEP Cases at 969–970.
30. *Board of Trustees of Keene State College* v. *Sweeney,* 439 U.S. 24, 18 FEP Cases 520 (1979).
31. *Texas Dept. of Community Affairs* v. *Burdine,* 450 U.S. 248, 25 FEP Cases 113 (1981).
32. *Id.*
33. *Furnco Construction Co.* v. *Waters,* 438 U.S. 562, 17 FEP Cases 1514 (1977).
34. *Id.*
35. *Griggs,* 401 U.S. at 431.
36. *Teamsters,* 431 U.S. at 335 n.15.
37. 654 F.2d 388, 26 FEP Cases 1230 (5th Cir. 1981).
38. *Griggs,* 401 U.S. at 430–431.
39. *Albemarle Paper Co.* v. *Moody,* 422 U.S. 707, 10 FEP 1181 (1975).
40. 42 U.S.C. §2000e–5(k).

41. 42 U.S.C. §2000e–3(h).

42. *Id.*

43. *Laffey* v. *Northwestern Airlines, Inc.*, 567 F.2d 429, 13 FEP Cases 1068 (D.C. Cir. 197), *cert. denied,* 434 U.S. 1086 (1976).

44. 29 U.S.C. §§621 *et. seq.* Employers are subject to the ADEA if they are engaged "in an industry affecting commerce" and have at least 20 employees for each working day in each of 20 or more calendar weeks during the current or preceding years. §630(b).

45. 29 U.S.C. §623(a)(1).

46. 29 U.S.C. §§623(a)(3).

47. 29 U.S.C. §626(b).

48. 29 U.S.C. §216(b).

49. 29 U.S.C. §626(b).

50. E.O. 11246, §202.

51. *Id.*

52. *Department of Labor* v. *Kerr Glass Manufacturing Corp.*, 77—OFCCP—4.

53. 41 C.F.R. §60-20.5.

54. *Id.*

55. Executive Order 11246, §209(a).

56. *Id.*

57. See generally, 3 Employers Practice Guide (CCH) ¶20,080.

58. KRS §337.423.

59. See Gov. C §19827.2, L. 1981 Ch. 722. The new statute defines "comparability of the value of work" as meaning "the value of the work performed by an employee, or group of employees within a class or salary range, in relation to the value of the work of another employee, or group of employees, to any class or salary range within state service."

60. 25 FEP Cases at 1523 n. 8.

61. 25 FEP Cases at 1522–23.

62. 25 FEP Cases at 1524.

63. 25 FEP Cases at 1528.

64. *Id.*

65. 563 F.2d 353, 16 FEP Cases 232, (8th Cir. 1977).

66. 563 F.2d at 355.

67. 563 F.2d at 356.

68. 620 F.2d 228, 22 FEP Cases 959 (10th Cir. 1980) *cert. denied* 449 U.S. 888 (1980).

69. 22 FEP Cases at 959–960.

70. 631 F.2d 1094, 23 FEP Cases 588, (3d Cir. 1980). *cert. denied,* 449 U.S. 1009 (1981).

71. 523 F. Supp. 148, 26 FEP Cases 1273 (E.D. Cal. 1981).

72. 26 FEP Cases at 1284.

CHAPTER 6

Training and Development

The training and development of human resources is an important activity in organizations. The outcomes of any of the previous activities (e.g., recruitment and selection, performance appraisal) may indicate the need for certain improvements in work performance, updates in job knowledge, modifications in existing skills and abilities, or a new awareness and response to changing environmental conditions. Training and development, in its many aspects, is used by organizations and employees for their own individual and collective self-interests.

Estimates suggest that U.S. organizations spend over $150 billion a year on the planning and implementation of all types of training and development programs, ranging from technical skill training to management development. With an investment of this magnitude, one would expect organizations to have a good deal of evidence about the benefits of those programs. On the contrary, however, the evaluation component of the training and development activity in most organizations has been seriously neglected. Organizations are fairly conscientious in their efforts to determine training and development needs and to design the content, structure, and techniques of programs to meet those needs, but few, if any, exert systematic efforts to evaluate them. Most analysis today is limited to collecting the subjective reactions of program participants, rather than evaluating the longer-term, more objective measures of changes in behavior. But, with an increasing focus on accountability and strategic human resources management, we will likely see more careful program evaluation in the future.

In this chapter, Lacey, Lee, and Wallace discuss the adult manager as learner and offer a four-step process for developing an effective management training program. The next two articles deal with human resources development (HRD). Harvey presents a quiz with which managers may judge the state of their HRD programs and explains some general principles for creating a HRD system to fit each company's needs. Winer illustrates the usefulness of multi-strategic planning to HRD objectives.

The last two articles examine how specific companies' training programs are run. In the first, Eastburn explains why most current training programs are failing—not enough attention paid to application, organizational needs not adequately addressed, and responsibilities of the participants unclear—and how TRW's educational programs have worked to overcome these problems. Finally, Urban, Ferris, Crowe, and Miller address the difficult problem of evaluating a training program for a large U.S. oil company. They used several methods to record the participants' reactions to the program's content and context, to subsequent promotions, pay grade increases, and attrition. Their cost/benefit analysis showed that the cost of the training program was low in comparison to the benefits the company received, in terms of both money and human resources.

Suggestions for Further Reading

Abelson, M. A., Ferris, G. R., & Urban, T. F. (1988). Human resource development and employee mobility. In R. S. Schuler, S. A. Youngblood, & V. Huber (Eds.), *Readings in personnel and human resource management* (3rd. ed.). St. Paul, MN: West.

Bove, R. (1987). Retraining the older worker. *Training and Development Journal, 40,* 49–52.

Digman, L. A. (1980). Management development: Needs and practices. *Personnel, 57,* 45–57.

Kearney, W. J. (1975). Management development programs can pay off. *Business Horizons, 18,* 81–88.

Krayer, K. J. (1986). Using training to reduce conflict and ambiguity. *Training and Development Journal, 40,* 49–52.

Linkow, P. (1985). HRD at the roots of corporate strategy. *Training and Development Journal, 39,* 85–87.

Nielsen, R. P. (1983). Training programs: Pulling them into sync with your company's strategic planning. *Personnel, 60,* 19–25.

Salinger, R. D., & Deming, B. S. (1982). Practical strategies for evaluating training. *Training and Development Journal, 36,* 70–76.

Schwade, S. (1985). Is it time to consider computer-based training? *Personnel Administrator, 30,* 25–38.

Sweet, J. (1981). How manpower development can support your strategic plan. *Journal of Business Strategy, 2,* 77–81.

Training and Development

David W. Lacey
Robert J. Lee
Lawrence J. Wallace

Any discussion of training—whether it be in the large business organization, or in settings ranging from the military to human services agencies—begins with a discussion of how people learn. The personnel professional responsible for training is, above all else, an educator. For this reason, his or her work must be solidly grounded in a theory of adult learning.

All trainers operate either implicitly or explicitly with a theory of learning. For many people, the theory is based on their earliest educational experiences. As students, most individuals were passive participants in an educational process that centered around an all-powerful teacher. This structure, and its underlying learning theory, gave the teacher almost complete authority to determine the substance and form of classroom instruction. It assumed that learners could best benefit from a prescribed curriculum, rather than one that was designed to address individual needs. It also assumed that learners were motivated mostly by rewards inherent in the curriculum or the way it was taught. For this reason, grades and reinforcements from the teacher became extremely important. With this as the model, people carry into their adult lives expectations of what teaching and learning should be. Even though the subjects and settings have varied throughout formal education, all of this experience has taught individuals much about how to be a student: to be dependent and deferential in the classroom and to expect the teacher to be responsible for the planning, design, implementation, and evaluation of the learning.

Malcolm Knowles, a leading theorist of adult education, points out that these assumptions based on childhood experiences are not a valid basis for designing training for adults. He uses the word *andragogy* to describe the unique ways adults learn. The word *pedagogy* has come to be used as a synonym for education. In fact, the root, *peda-*, stems from the Greek *pais,* meaning child, and pedagogy literally means youth learning. Andragogy, from the Greek *andros,* for man, more appropriately describes adult education and is needed if one is to consider the important ways in which adults differ from children as learners. Knowles summarizes these differences:

> Adults see themselves as self-directed and independent; children are dependent on parents, teachers and others.
>
> Because they simply have not acquired much of it, experience may be of little value to children in the classroom. With adults, experience is an important resource for learning. In training, we must recognize that adults have significant experience. Indeed, they often define themselves as the sum of their experiences. Good training draws from this experience and builds on it.
>
> Children must postpone the application of much of their formal learning. Adults need to see immediate application of the learning if it is to be meaningful.
>
> Children's readiness to learn is determined by biological development and social pressure. For adults, readiness is based on the developmental tasks that result from social roles.

> Children's orientation to learning is subject-centered; adults' orientation to learning is problem-centered (Knowles, 1978, p. 110).

All of these differences impact on the trainer's work. Knowles points out that the andragogical learning climate needs to be informal, collaborative, and mutually respectful, as opposed to the formal, authority-oriented, and competitive pedagogical climate. In a pedagogical model, planning, diagnosis of needs, the formulation of objectives, and evaluation are all the responsibility of the teacher. The andragogical approach involves learners in mutual planning, self-diagnosis, negotiation, and, as far as evaluation is concerned, mutual rediagnosis of needs. Teaching techniques become more experiential and move away from the pedagogue's transmittal techniques that rely on an all-knowing teacher and a passive learner (Knowles, 1978).

THE ADULT MANAGER AS LEARNER

With Knowles's theory providing a context for how adults learn, one can turn to the special case of how managers learn. In discussing leadership, Harry Levinson, the noted organization psychologist, says, "By and large, executives are a serious lot, as much concerned as professionals in medicine or teaching with learning how to do their jobs better" (Levinson, 1970, p. 127). In as much as this motivation to learn stems from a need to foster organizational productivity, the manager's learning dilemma is at least twofold: he or she needs to keep abreast of technological innovations in one's field, but the manager also needs to learn how to deal with the complex "people problems" that arise in the organization. Management development and training programs become an essential tool for managers who seek to upgrade their skills in both these areas. The extent to which a manager can learn, through these programs and other means, to solve unanticipated people and technological problems is often directly linked to the productivity and profitability of his or her unit of the organization.

Experience suggests that managers have particularly unique qualities as learners. An Adult/Manager as Learner (A/ML) model is proposed because it relates directly to how the present authors feel personnel development should occur, and because it helps explain why some management training and development efforts have traditionally encountered problems.

It is useful to look first at the implicit model underlying many organizations' training programs. The model includes the following elements:

> The trainer (and training program) has the right answers and will give them to the trainees.
>
> Optimum success is achieved when all of the trainees learn the same points (ideas) and the same materials.
>
> The trainees do the same prework and participate equally in the same exercises.
>
> Learning is intended to happen in the classroom, while on-the-job time is for application.

Implied in this model are important pedagogical principles. The prediction is that such goals and methods will not be effective for adult learners generally, and for managers particularly. The A/ML model attempts to deal with the reality that students are in fact adult people, not children. It is an andragogical model. Breaking away from the assumptions that equate student with "child" and trainer with "teacher" is difficult, but it must be done if training efforts are to have meaning for adults.

Managers are not typical of all adults. Managers have greater responsibilities, control, demands, and resources than many other adults. In most cases, they have received a string of recent rewards for being successful and competent. They are important people—or at least they're told they are.

The Adult/Manager model builds on these features and integrates them with what is known about learning in general. It is consistent with the assumptions underlying a successful personnel development effort. The A/ML model has five key elements.

1. Style
2. Needs

3. Authority
4. Self-Image
5. Studying

The model is illustrated in Figure 1.

TRAINING PROGRAM DESIGN

Organizations are frequently more concerned about the training and development of managers than of other employees. This is understandable. Questions of "What makes a good manager?" are harder to answer than "What makes a good drill-press operator?" or "What makes a good bookkeeper?" Although training professionals may at times concern themselves with all of these questions, their most complicated task is to develop effective managers. These are the people who are empowered to make the key decisions and to solve the complex problems that determine how productive an organization is and will be. A good manager is an invaluable resource for an organization, and it is the training department's job to assist with or, in the case of high potentials, accelerate the development of managerial talent.

The A/ML model begins to describe how training that is more likely to fit the manager's unique characteristics and responsibilities can be designed. Next, a framework that translates these points into a step-by-step process will be provided for putting a training program together. While this process is faithful to the principles of the A/ML model, it is much broader. It is essentially an andragogical system that can be applied to the training of any adult.

Two comprehensive reviews of the training literature have appeared in recent years. Both Goldstein (1980) and Hinrichs (1976) presented analyses of topics related to individual learning and the impact of the training intervention on the organization as a whole. The attempt here is to give the reader a less ambitious overview of the training process, yet one that will provide both a fundamental structure for training and a sampling of real issues that surround the problem of implementing such a structure.

Many discussions of training use a systems model as a context for explaining the training process. This is valuable in as much as it relates the instructional system to other organizational systems that interact with training in a variety of complex ways. Most of the work in this area includes the following: (1) setting instructional goals and objectives based on a needs analysis, (2) determining suitable learning experiences to

Figure 1
The Adult Manager as Learner: An Andragogical Model

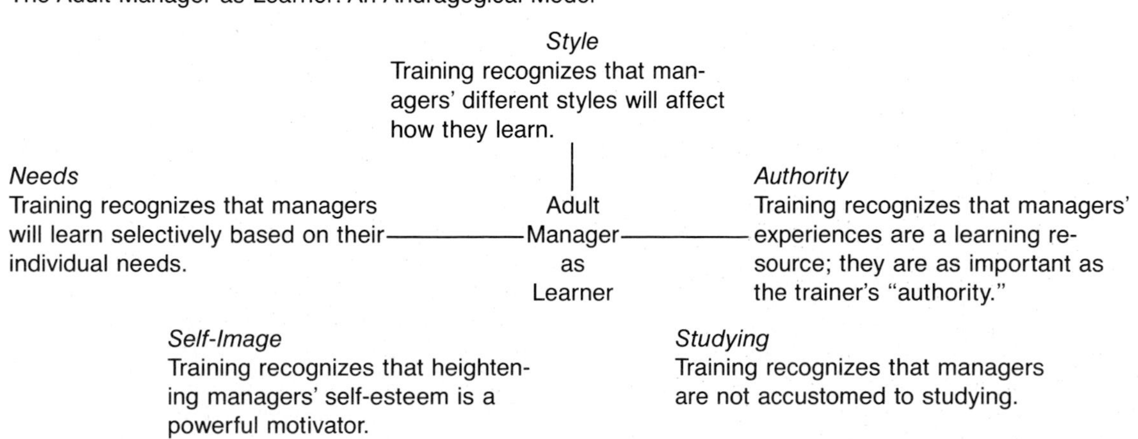

Style
Training recognizes that managers' different styles will affect how they learn.
Needs
Training recognizes that managers will learn selectively based on their individual needs.
Adult Manager as Learner
Authority
Training recognizes that managers' experiences are a learning resource; they are as important as the trainer's "authority."
Self-Image
Training recognizes that heightening managers' self-esteem is a powerful motivator.
Studying
Training recognizes that managers are not accustomed to studying.

Source: From The Adult Learner: A Neglected Species, *3rd ed., by Malcolm Knowles. Copyright ©1984 by Gulf Publishing Co., Houston, TX. Used with permission.*

achieve those goals and objectives, and (3) designing an evaluation of the learning that measures the trainee's improved performance. This suggests a basic, four-step process for the training program design presented in Figure 2.

1. *Needs analysis.* A determination of the skills, knowledge, and attitudes an employee must learn in order to better perform a job-related task.

2. *Training objectives.* Based on the needs analysis, a series of statements describing the out-

Figure 2
Four-Step Process for Training Program Design

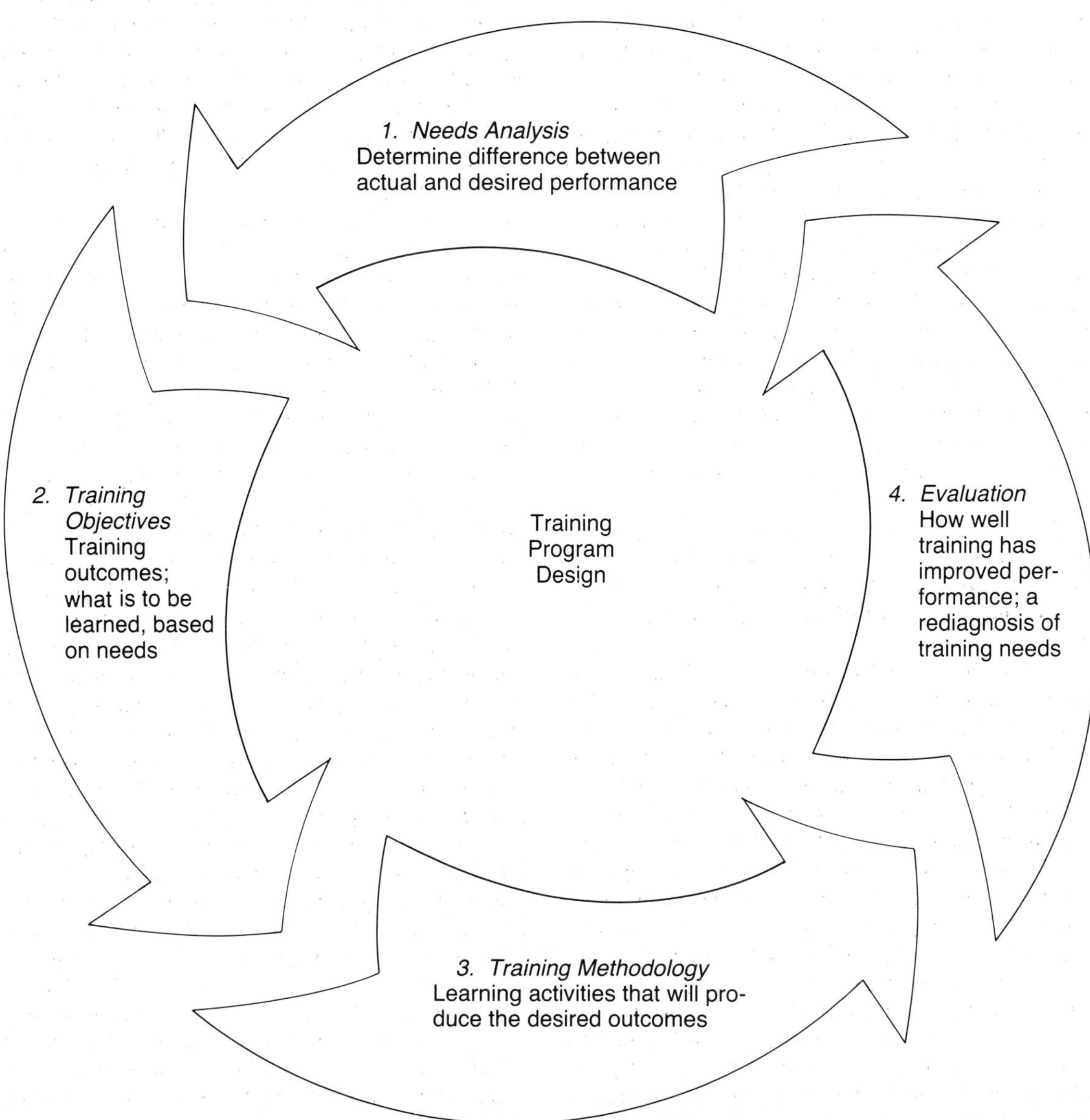

comes of training; that is, what is to be learned—usually written in behavioral terms.

3. *Training methodology.* Learning activities that will produce the desired outcomes as stated in the training objectives.

4. *Evaluation.* A measurement of how well the training methods actually improved the employee's ability to perform the prescribed task.

Needs Analysis

Needs analysis is a process through which skills required of employees for successful job performance are uncovered. Today, it is axiomatic to say that any training within an organization should be based on the assessed needs of individuals or groups. For an organization to function at a required level, workers need to perform at a given standard. When they fall short of that standard, they *may* need training, which, if effective, will enhance their performance. In turn, this increased individual or group productivity results in desired organizational outcomes. Comprehensive diagnosis is more likely to reveal the *range* of factors that inhibit effective employee performance. If discrepancies (differences between actual and desired performance) exist because of skill deficiency, then training is an appropriate intervention (Moore and Dutton, 1978). However, the discrepancy may be rooted in a different problem, that of worker motivation, for instance. Training cannot be expected to address such a problem. A thorough needs analysis should, above all, determine whether the problem is a "training problem."

Training units compete with other organizational units for limited resources. In order to justify their function, they must supply an answer to the question, "Why train?" Showing a relationship between their efforts and improved employee performance is a way to do so. An important element in this relationship is the assurance that training is based on real needs.

Methods of needs assessment vary. McGehee and Thayer's (1961) important work on the subject presents organizational analysis, operational analysis, and individual analysis as the three essential aspects of training needs analysis. Organizational analysis is a procedure that shows where training can be utilized within an organization; operational analysis attempts to break down a given job into a series of specific tasks and standards of performance for each task; individual analysis determines how satisfactorily an individual is performing the tasks required to do his or her job, and, subsequently, areas where one's performances needs to be improved.

In their review of the needs analysis literature, Moore and Dutton (1978) outlined several methods of collecting data in each of these three areas. Using organizational analysis as a means of determining needs, one can look at organizational goals; manpower inventories, which pinpoint areas where training can cover losses caused by retirement, turnover, and age; skills inventories, which look at number of employees in various skill groups and the scope of particular training needs; organizational climate indices, such as labor-management data, grievances, turnover, absenteeism, suggestions, accidents, attitude surveys, customer complaints, quality of products, costs of distribution, waste, down time, and late deliveries; repairs, changes in systems or subsystems; management requests (one of the most frequent determinants of needs), exit interviews; and MBO systems.

Operation analysis relies on the following techniques: job descriptions; job specification or task analysis (more specific and detailed than job descriptions); performance standards; review of literature concerning the job, including research in other industries, professional journals, government sources, and Ph.D. theses; asking questions about the job of the jobholder, the supervisor, or of management; and training committees or task forces.

Personal or individual analysis includes performance appraisals, observation, interviews, questionnaires, tests, devised situations such as role plays or case studies, assessment centers, and coaching.

Despite these extensive lists of methods for determining training needs, Moore and Dutton (1978) concluded that needs analyses are conducted as relatively isolated activities within organizations. They are either geared to single programs, used as a means to avert a crisis, or conducted in some mechanical fashion on a periodic basis. Instead, needs analysis should be able to generate a continuous source of information and should be interrelated with all other aspects of the organization's functioning.

Experience tends to confirm this view of how organizations use needs assessments. If it can be described as a "top down" process—one in which training or personnel administrators call for formal needs assessment to support a particular program or to achieve some other perfunctory purpose—then a more "bottom up" approach would be advocated.

Each individual is ultimately responsible for meeting his or her own personal and competency needs, however those are understood. Each immediate supervisor is responsible for influencing the individual subordinate's definition of his or her needs so that they are clear, realistic, and integrated with foreseeable organizational needs. It is this partnership between supervisor and employee that is the key element in establishing an ongoing needs assessment process. The professional training staff is responsible for helping all employees implement their developmental strategies effectively. Training's efforts are wisely placed in fostering the individual supervisor-employee relationship by offering courses in performance appraisal, counseling, coaching, and career planning. Through this process, employees are more likely to take the initiative to inform training departments of their real needs. As this happens, organizations will find alternatives to general training programs aimed at nonspecific needs.

Training Objectives

Training objectives are the link between needs analysis and the actual content of an instructional program. If needs analysis describes a discrepancy in performance, then the training objective is the statement of posttraining behavior that the employee will display to indicate that the discrepancy either no longer exists or has been decreased. Training objectives tell what the *outcome* of a training program will be, and should specify predicted change in the trainee's skill-level, knowledge, or attitudes. As such, objectives suggest the selection of appropriate training techniques and resources for learning.

Although most trainers agree that objectives are a necessary programmatic component, controversy exists over the proper form objectives should take to be most useful to those who design training and to those who participate in it. Knowles (1978) distinguished between terminal-behavior-oriented procedures and inquiry-process-oriented procedures. The former are precise, measurable, observable statements. Terminal behaviors refer to the observable actions ("describing," "identifying," and "performing," as opposed to nonobservables like "knowing," "understanding," and "realizing") that the trainee is expected to demonstrate at the end of training. The latter sees learning as a much more fluid, less predictable, process. Goals emerge out of the learning process, changing often and varying in degree of clarity. An inquiry-oriented approach leaves no room for prescribed objectives.

Gagne (1972) sees an important function of behavioral objectives to be their role in communicating the expected outcomes of a program to its various organizational constituencies. Instructional designers must communicate clearly to course planners if planners are to choose the proper materials to achieve desired outcomes. The trainer's notion of outcomes needs to be consistent with planners, so that proper instruction and assessment occur. Objectives are a key communication tool between trainer and trainee. They can reassure trainees that the training is geared to their needs, or serve as a basis of negotiation if disputes arise in this area. Finally, objectives help participants' supervisors, top management, and others to form realistic expectations of training.

Some authors, however, feel behavioral objectives used by themselves have little purpose. Kneller (1972) noted that "the use of behavioral objectives is characteristic of a culture which sets a high value on efficiency and productivity, [one that] seeks to measure accomplishment in standard units" (p. 397). He is critical of a strict, behavioral approach to learning. Learning that is thought of as a series of measurable responses to prearranged stimuli leaves little room for individual differences or idiosyncratic learning. He supports an educational process in which objectives play a less controlling role. Scandura (1977), on the other hand, believes that behavioral objectives do not go far enough. In stating only what the learner will be able to do after training, they ignore the underlying competence required to perform the task. Nor do behavioral objectives tell what the teacher must teach. Used by themselves, behavioral objectives do not get at these fundamental aspects of the learning process.

The present view is that the importance of behavioral objectives should not be ignored. Not only do they serve the communications functions that Gagne speaks of, but they are key to the process of training program evaluation. It is necessary to point out here that the essence of evaluation is measuring the extent to which a person's behavior was changed during training, and determining the impact of that change once the person has returned to his or her job. Measuring the relationship between training and behavior change is a fairly straightforward activity when behavioral objectives have been used as a basis for the design and implementation of training. When they have not, determining whether this relationship exists is an exercise in guess work and inference.

If behavioral objectives are useful, they must remain practical. Training departments ordinarily do not have resources to fine-tune the objective-setting process to the point where objectives reflect all possible learnings from a program, or all the varied learning needs of the participants. Although strict behavioralists might say this is possible and desirable, it is impractical. We are convinced that such compulsive attention to objectives tends to overshadow other important aspects of the training process. Behavioral objectives are best used as a guide for designing learning activities and a mechanism for ensuring that people's expectations of training are adequately met.

Training Techniques

The choice of an appropriate training technique to accomplish certain training objectives is perhaps more of an art than a science. The literature in this area is limited (Carroll, Paine, and Ivancevich, 1972). Much of it is nonempirical and nontheoretical, and it has not convincingly demonstrated the usefulness of particular kinds of techniques to accomplish given objectives in respective knowledge, skill, or attitude domains (Goldstein, 1980). Indeed, a trainer's ability to select effective techniques is sometimes more a function of one's intuition and experience than of one's reliance on sound, scientific writing.

Noting the inadequacies of the literature, Carroll, Paine, and Ivancevich (1972) surveyed 200 training directors from *Fortune* 500 companies in order to identify the relative effectiveness of training techniques. Training directors were asked to rate the methods of case study, conference/discussion, lecture, business games, movies, programmed instruction, role playing, sensitivity training, and television lecture according to their effectiveness in achieving objectives in the following six areas: (1) knowledge acquisition, (2) changing attitudes, (3) problem-solving skills, (4) interpersonal skills, (5) participant acceptance, and (6) knowledge retention. Their ratings are shown in Table 1.

The authors suggest that the current popularity of experiential learning may account for the negative reactions to the lecture technique. Also, the lecture is the most adaptable technique for the nonprofessional and this may have biased the training directors against it. For whatever reason, this survey confirms the widespread feeling that lecture-type training is the most primitive and the least likely to produce lasting behavior change. Andragogists point to the need to involve adults by asking them to assume responsibility for their learning, helping them to become self-directed, and recognizing and building on their experience. A didactic technique that allows for little interaction between trainer and trainee makes this difficult.

Keys (1977) categorized alternatives to the lecture in his "Management of Learning Grid." He considers both the trainer's style and his or her choice of technique to be the most important elements influencing the accomplishment of objectives. Included in the styles he describes are the "Experiential Teacher," who advocates learning-by-doing; the "Socratic Teacher," who uses questions and feedback; and the "Academician," who relies on content and testing. The synthesis of these different styles is one called "Manager of Learning," who simultaneously focuses on content, experience, and feedback, thereby integrating

Table 1
Ratings of Training Directors on the Most and Least Effective Training Techniques for Various Training Objectives

Objective	*Most Effective Technique*	*Least Effective Technique*
Acquisition of knowledge	Programmed instruction	Lecture
Changing of attitudes	Sensitivity training	Television lecture
Problem–solving	Case study method	Lecture
Interpersonal skills	Sensitivity training	Television lecture
Participant acceptance	Conference/discussion	Television lecture
Knowledge retention	Programmed instruction	Television lecture

Source: Adapted from S. J. Carroll, Jr., F. T. Paine, and J. J. Ivancevich, "The Relative Effectiveness of Training Methods—Expert Opinion and Research." Personnel Psychology *25 (1972): 498.*

features of all the styles. The purpose of this is to demonstrate the suitability of experiential techniques to accomplish cognitive objectives. Traditionally, experiential techniques have been used to address objectives in the attitudinal domain; Keys' work provides a provocative argument that their use can be more far reaching.

In recent years, computer-assisted and programmed instruction methods have been seen as devices for training departments to cut costs, individualize learning, and generally streamline the work they do. Nash, Muczyk, and Vettori (1971) concluded that although programmed instruction techniques nearly always reduced training time, they do not necessarily improve retention. Seltzer (1971) talked of the unique contribution computer-assisted instruction has made in the areas of simulations, gaming, and problem solving. Even though computer-assisted instruction cannot automatically be expected to reduce costs, Seltzer argues that costs should be a secondary consideration in those cases in which computers offer more creative and efficient solutions to instructional problems.

Aside from choosing training techniques based on their ability to foster particular types of learning, McGehee and Thayer (1961) suggested additional considerations: number of employees to be trained, their skill level, their individual differences, and the relative costs.

Evaluation

Conducting meaningful evaluations is probably the most difficult aspect of a training professional's job. Although writing on the topic has proliferated in recent years, researchers have yet to propose models that can be easily or efficiently integrated into existing organizational systems. Extensive evaluations, though infrequently conducted, depend almost always on the use of outside consultants. Most evaluation of training done within organizations consists only of trainees reporting their level of satisfaction with a particular training program at its conclusion. Such evaluations are called "smile sheets" because of their obvious positive bias.

As has been suggested, precise, measurable training objectives can be a basis for evaluating the extent to which training has had an impact on an employee's ability to perform one's job. Because objectives focus on outcomes, they force planners of training to think about evaluation from the initial phases of a program's design.

Measuring objectives are only one component of the evaluation process, however. Donaldson and Scannell (1978) proposed a four-step procedure for comprehensive evaluation: (1) reaction, (2) learning, (3) behavior, and (4) results. The first step, reaction, involves using a questionnaire or other device to solicit the trainee's feedback about the program. To find out what was actually learned (step two), it is necessary to conduct pretests and posttests. The authors suggest written tests, demonstrations, problem discussions, and role play as techniques to test learning. The third step involves asking the trainee's supervisors and peers to report posttraining behavior change on the job. Finally, results can be evaluated by looking at direct cost reduction, grievance reductions, improved work quality, lowered absenteeism, increased sales volume, greater worker efficiency, and fewer customer complaints.

Blumenfeld and Holland (1971) advocated an empirical approach to training evaluation. According to them, criterion measurement is the single-most important facet of any serious evaluation study. A criterion is a *pre*specified goal of training; it needs to be relevant, reliable, free from bias, and acceptable to management. A basic model is proposed as the minimally acceptable design to generate evidence of behavior change that is caused by training. The design involves pre- and posttests and the use of control groups. Experimental and control groups are tested on the criterion variables prior to training and again following the experimental group's exposure to training. Statistical measures of the training effect are derived.

Perhaps only an empirical process such as Blumenfeld and Holland's (1971) can be called a true evaluation. Pre- and posttests measure behavior change and the use of control groups determines whether the change has been caused by training. Anything less cannot make these claims. This, however, is a much more sophisticated approach to evaluation than most organizations take or, for that matter, would consider taking. Many practitioners feel that such exhaustive evaluation is not necessary to prove that training is making a difference in their organization.

Practitioners recognize a need to do more thorough evaluation. Most training professionals do some evaluation of their programs, but few progress beyond the reaction phase previously mentioned. This probably indicates that not enough attention is being paid to evaluation.

A missing element for many organizations is the close relationship between managers and training departments that can support a more extensive evaluation of training impact. In order to fully assess training outcomes, managers must first make an effort to help a subordinate integrate his or her learning into the day-to-day operation of a department, and then evaluate how effectively this has been done. Baumgartel and Jeanpierre (1972) have done some interesting work in illustrating the importance of the back-home organizational climate for facilitating the application of new knowledge. They found that such factors as the degree higher management is considerate of the feelings of lower management, the degree the organization stimulates and approves innovation, and the degree of free and open communication contribute significantly to how well new knowledge and concepts from training were applied.

Knowles (1978) sees an important part of the evaluation process to be the rediagnosis of needs. Having completed a learning program, the employee first assesses how well he or she has acquired the competencies he or she set out to learn, and then looks for what remains to be done. Perhaps the employee's projection for future learning will not be immediate, but, rather, will anticipate needs that might arise once new skills have been tested on the job. This process is meant to lead to the employee's ongoing self-assessment of learning needs.

The A/ML model began with needs assessments, and, in as much as the evaluation process can inform training departments of new or unmet learning needs, returns to that starting point. There is something of a cyclical nature to the model. Training units are involved at all points. To be most effective, however, they also need to involve their clients at all points. Much, if not most, of training's impact is determined by how receptive the work setting is to new learning. Supervisors and managers need to be responsible for creating climates in which employees' learning and development is not only supported, but stimulated.

Personnel development is an intrinsic, ongoing aspect of everyday organizational life, not an event "put on" by the training staff. The appropriate measure of the training staff's effectiveness is how much value they add to this ongoing process in terms of

Helping others identify the "people" issues likely to affect the company

Helping others to recognize their proper roles and responsibilities in dealing with these issues.

Helping others to implement their responsibilities by giving them tools and supports.

Delivering certain programs of instruction to augment the learning that is happening every day in each job

The ultimate goal is to help the company achieve its business strategy. Some of the factors affecting this goal have little to do with the human side of the business. On the other hand, it seems fair to ask that the personnel development function be evaluated for its contribution to the company's overall ability to have enough of the right people at the right time and place, and adequately trained to do their jobs—all at a reasonable cost.

REFERENCES

Baumgartel, H., & Jeanpierre, F. (1972). Applying new knowledge in the backhome setting: A study of Indian managers' adaptive efforts. *Journal of Applied Behavioral Science, 8,* 675–694.

Blumenfeld, W. S., & Holland, M. G. (1971). A model for the empirical evaluation of training effectiveness. *Personnel Journal, 50,* 637–640.

Carroll, S. J., Paine, F. T., & Ivancevich, J. (1972). The relative effectiveness of training methods—Expert opinion and research. *Personnel Psychology, 25,* 495–509.

Donaldson, L., and & Scannell, E. E. (1978). *Human resource development—The new trainer's guide.* Reading, MA: Addison-Wesley.

Gagne, R. M. (1972). Behavioral objectives? Yes! *Educational Leadership, 29,* 394–396.

Goldstein, I. L. (1980). Training in work organizations. *Annual Review of Psychology, 31,* 229–272.

Hinrichs, J. R. (1976). Personnel training. In M. D. Dunnette (Ed.), *Handbook of industrial and organizational psychology* (pp. 829–860). Chicago: Rand McNally.

Keys, B. (1977). The management of learning grid for management development. *Academy of Management Review, 2,* 289–297.

Kneller, G. A. (1972). Behavioral objectives? No! *Educational Leadership, 29,* 397–400.

Knowles, M. (1978). *The adult learner: A neglected species.* Houston: Gulf.

Levinson, H. (1970). *Executive stress.* New York: Harper and Row.

McGehee, W., & Thayer, P. W. (1961). *Training in business and industry.* New York: Wiley.

Moore, M. L., & Dutton, P. (1978). Training needs analysis: Review and critique. *Academy of Management Review, 3,* 532–545.

Nash, A. W., Muczyk, J. P., & Vettori, F. L. (1971). The relative practical effectiveness of programmed instruction. *Personnel Psychology, 24,* 397–418.

Scandura, J. M. (1977). Structural approach to instructional problems. *American Psychologist, 32,* 33–53.

Seltzer, R. A. (1971). Computer-assisted instruction—What it can and cannot do. *American Psychologist, 26,* 373–377.

Effective Planning for Human Resource Development

L. James Harvey

Planning is a little bit like the weather—everyone talks about it but no one does much about it. This has not been altogether true in recent years, however. I have seen a major effort among corporations to do effective strategic planning. Still, many of these efforts leave much to be desired.

While some corporations such as IBM have effective and systematic planning, many corporations limp along without planning or with planning that fails to affect the direction of the corporation.

It is not my intent to explore the reasons why corporate planning succeeds or fails. I agree with Ebenstein and Krauss that "impressive company performance is often tied to substantial efforts those firms put into developing general business strategies and plans." I am concerned here, however, with planning in the human resource development (HRD) area and what can and should be done about it.

Before proceeding further, you may wish to complete the rating form presented in Figure 1. The survey contains some basic principles for HRD planning that are important and which will be covered later in the article. If you score 80 or above, your HRD planning system is in good shape.

A discussion of corporate HRD planning should begin with a look at some basic management principles. Figure 2 depicts those principles that need to be followed to carry out the systematic operation of any company, subunit, organization or enterprise. Note that I am talking about cycles of activity, as represented by the circle and the arrows showing movement and linkage. Corporations need systematic planning, management and evaluation as depicted here if they are to succeed in an increasingly complex and changing marketplace.

Note some additional items in Figure 2. First, effective planning establishes the framework for evaluation, and the evaluation process feeds the next cycle of the planning process. In addition, note that "developing people" is in the center of the circle.

This, plus the other four items listed there, are the grease and oil that permit a smooth movement of the whole process. Lastly, note that planning leads to the setting of objectives (specific, measurable, outcome-oriented statements) which in essence become the linchpins between the planning, management and evaluation (PME) functions. It is easy to diagram the PME process, but very difficult to carry it out in a complex organization, as there are many points at which it can break down.

The best possible situation for an HRD program is to have a systematic strategic planning process tied tightly to an effective, systematic strategic planning process in the corporation. In this circumstance, the corporation is saying that this is the specific direction it is heading over the next one to five or one to seven years, and here is what it needs to get there. A human resource plan can be developed that will accomplish specific human resource growth and development objectives which will be linked to and help accomplish corporate objectives.

For example, if a corporation decides to add a new division in three years to meet certain pro-

Figure 1
Rate Your Corporate HRD Planning

		No. of Points
1.	Does your HRD plan link directly to the corporate planning process? Are HRD plans clearly assisting the corporation to achieve specific objectives? If yes, strongly—10 pts. If somewhat—5 pts. If very loosely—2 pts. If not at all—0 pts.	______
2.	Is HRD planning systematic and routinely done? Do you have a formal timetable for planning and are plans for specific periods? If yes, very much—10 pts. If somewhat—5 pts. If not—0 pts.	______
3.	Does your HRD plan have both short-range (1 year or less) and long-range (3 years or longer) elements? If both—10 pts. If just short-range—5 pts. If just long-range—2 pts. If neither—0 pts.	______
4.	Does your HRD planning process have provisions for routinely modifying the plan at fixed points? Does the plan allow for flexibility, emergencies and routine changes? If yes—10 pts. If somewhat—5 pts. If very little—2 pts. If not at all—0 pts.	______
5.	Does your HRD plan tie to the budget in a specific and direct way? Are resources estimated and tied specifically to the plan so that costs are clear and tied to outcomes? If yes, strongly—10 pts. If somewhat—6 pts. If very loosely—3 pts. If not at all—0 pts.	______
6.	To what extent is your planning process routinely tied to specific data? Do you have sufficient data upon which to make HRD program decisions? Do you have an HRD Management Information System (MIS)? If yes, very much—10 pts. If yes, somewhat—6 pts. If yes, but not very much—3 pts. If no, it's entirely subjective judgment—0 pts.	______
7.	Does your HRD plan make provisions for a close linkage to management activity to carry it out? Does it lead to assigning work and/or objectives to the staff? To setting timetables and schedules for activity? Is it the reference point for all major activity in the HRD program? If yes—10 pts. If somewhat—5 pts. If little—0 pts.	______
8.	Is your planning process autocratic or participative? Are staff members involved? Are their suggestions used? Is the process truly a group effort? If yes—10 pts. If somewhat—5 pts. If no, it's a one-person operation—0 pts.	______
9.	To what extent is your plan evaluated and used in the next planning cycle? Is the plan reviewed at the end of the planning period? Are outcomes reviewed? Is the data from the evaluation of this plan recycled into the next plan? If yes—10 pts. If somewhat—5 pts. If only informally—2 pts. If not at all—0 pts.	______
10.	If you have read every word in this survey and have faithfully scored your program, give yourself 10 pts. If you have skimmed this survey but have not scored it—5 pts. If this is the first question you have read, you get 0 pts.	______

continued

Figure 1 *continued*

Scoring

100–99 Points	Excellent—You have a sound planning system.
89–90 Points	Good—But there are some basic points that can be improved upon in your planning system.
79–70 Points	Weak—But with some changes you could have a good planning system.
69 and Below	Poor—It's a question of whether any planning you are doing is worth the effort.

Figure 2

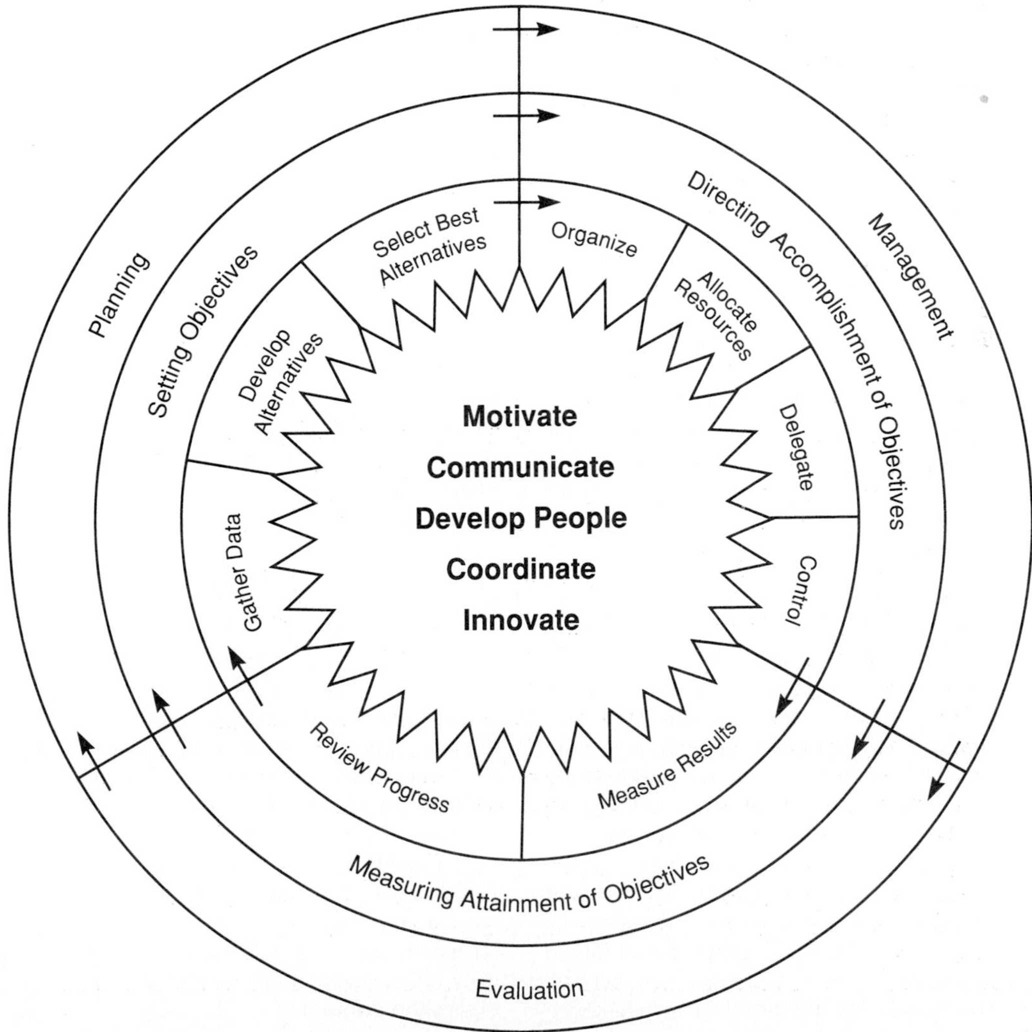

duction and profit objectives, it should develop a detailed plan specifying how this decision will be implemented.

This plan should be specific enough that an HRD plan can be developed that will determine where the corporation can best obtain or train the human resources needed to accomplish corporate objectives. In this case, the objectives are clear and measurable, and the HRD plan is clearly related to and visibly assisting corporate progress.

Unfortunately, this example is probably rare in corporate America. Either corporations do not plan, plan inadequately, or they leave HRD planning on the sidelines when corporate planning is done. If this is the case, what should HRD professionals do? There are several things that can and should be done:

1. *Develop HRD plans.* Even if there is no corporate plan or if the plan is so global it does not permit HRD plans to be effectively linked to it, you can still plan for HRD. While the plan will key off different elements and will not be as focused on corporate outcomes as it could be, it can still be carried out. The HRD plan can, in effect, set an example for the corporation on how to plan. The details of how this can be accomplished will be discussed later.

2. *Encourage effective corporate planning.* There are a number of steps the HRD area can take to encourage effective corporate planning if it does not presently exist, ranging from setting an example in the HRD area of how to plan both in process and format to trying to educate the executive management on how to plan effectively.

The HRD professional can stimulate in-house workshops or seminars in planning; suggest outside programs for key executives in planning; educate their immediate supervisor, who may be in the executive council, to carry the planning banner; encourage an OD effort that could identify this as a need; or institute a reconnaissance study of the HRD area in the hope that an objective, outside expert can point out to the executive management the need to plan more effectively on the corporate level so the HRD area can be of greater help to the corporation. Every corporation has its own dynamics and there are other possibilities, but much can be done even though you may be one or two levels below the top decision makers.

3. *Ask planning questions.* This overlaps the first two suggestions to some extent, but it deserves separate treatment. When doing your annual or long-range planning you can ask some questions of top decision makers that are essential to your planning activities. While you may not get the answers you wish, you could plant some seeds and nudge the corporation toward better planning.

How many managers at each level will the corporation need over the next five years to reach its objectives? What new knowledge and skills will current managers or other employers need to have over the next five years to facilitate corporate development? What major problems does top management feel must be overcome in the near future to meet corporate objectives? (These may not all be subject to HRD solutions, but some are.) How do the top executives feel you can best assist in meeting corporate objectives? These and similar questions, if tactfully presented to top management, can stimulate discussion and lead to effective planning if they are honestly and carefully answered.

One thing is certain: unless the corporation is doing effective strategic planning and the HRD planning is tied to it, and unless the HRD program is carefully aligned with corporate goals and objectives, the HRD effort cannot fulfill its maximum potential. In times of retrenchment, it is at risk in many corporations.

But how do we do effective HRD planning? No one can give a pat, detailed system that will work in all corporate situations. Corporations are like people—each is different and each should have a planning system that accommodates and builds on its own unique qualities and fits into its own corporate culture. We can, however, talk about some basic principles that should be followed if the planning process is to succeed. Within these principles there is plenty of room for designing specific systems which fit each unique situation.

The numbers of the principles listed below are directly related to questions on the survey in Figure 1. If you completed the survey you may wish to pay particular attention to the questions for which you received less than 10 points. In any truly effective planning system the following principles should apply:

1. *Unit plans must tie to organizational plans.* Each corporate unit, including HRD, should base its plan on corporate plans. Every unit needs to plan with the aim of accomplishing corporate objectives. In this way, all units focus their activity and help ensure that corporate goals and objectives are met. This keeps them aligned, productive and accountable, and requires that a corporate plan be prepared in sufficient detail before the HRD or other unit plans are completed.

2. *Planning needs to be conducted systematically and routinely.* Each planning process must be performed in a routine, systematic manner according to a specific timetable and cycle. This cycle and timetable usually tie to the corporate budget and fiscal year (see Item 5). Planning must be given a priority and be seen as an important function that is done on a timely basis. To fail to plan is to invite crises and problems.

3. *Long- and short-range components are needed.* Good planning requires a look at the future, but how far ahead we look depends on many factors. Most experts agree that the 10- and 20-year plans of the past are outdated because of rapid change and the difficulty in predicting that far in advance. Instead, it is the general consensus that detailed operating plans should be done on a six- to twelve-month basis and be tied to the fiscal year. Beyond that, the most common long-range planning period is five years. Some do not go beyond the current year to ensure that the plans and activities are consistent with the overall direction of the organization.

4. *Provisions for the review and modification of the plan are necessary.* Because change comes with increased frequency and because planning data and assumptions can change on us, we need to routinely review and revise plans if necessary. A recession, a new federal regulation, a corporate merger, or a reorganization can sometimes occur quickly, requiring changes in plans. Many planning systems build in quarterly reviews for annual plans and annual reviews of long-range plans. In any event, a routine and systemic review should be made on a scheduled basis or a plan could become meaningless.

5. *The plan must tie to the budget.* In a sense, a budget is a plan; at the very least, it determines whether a plan can be carried out, by allocating funds to the necessary activities. Unless the plan is completed before the budget, there is a good chance that the budget will change the plan rather than the reverse, as it should be. Each corporation and HRD unit should have a planning timetable which provides for completing the plan before the budget is locked in concrete. This will ensure that the plan is realistic and that the resources needed to fund the plan are appropriate and available.

6. *Planning must be data based.* While every planning process involves making subjective and expert judgments, the more relevant the facts and information used, the greater the chances are that the plan will be appropriate, realistic and effective.

There needs to be a solid base of data behind planning deliberations. Computerized data can be a mixed blessing, for while the potential is there for getting information we never had before, there is also a potential for information overload and for obscuring relevant facts with irrelevant facts. Figure 3 indicates the type of data that should go into the HRD planning process, with the corporate objectives being the most important.

More and more corporations are developing HRD management information systems (MIS) which routinely provide the needed data. Every HRD program should work toward this end, because it is only when all relevant data is plugged into the planning process that effective decisions are likely to result.

7. *The plan must tie to management activity.* Unless the plan leads to specific management activity, it will be of little value. There should be provisions for assigning responsibilities and/or objectives in a clear, accountable fashion, or the plan is apt to be only a list of good intentions. A good plan will lead to the assigning of tasks, the development of activity timetables, regular activity reviews, etc. This links the plan to action, which is essential if the plan is to be implemented.

8. *The plan should be participative in development and execution.* If a corporate or HRD plan is to be effectively developed and executed, it will need to be a group effort. When people are involved in developing a plan and have a vested interest in the results, it is likely to be both a good plan and one that will be enthusiastically carried

Figure 3
Inputs to HRD Planning Process

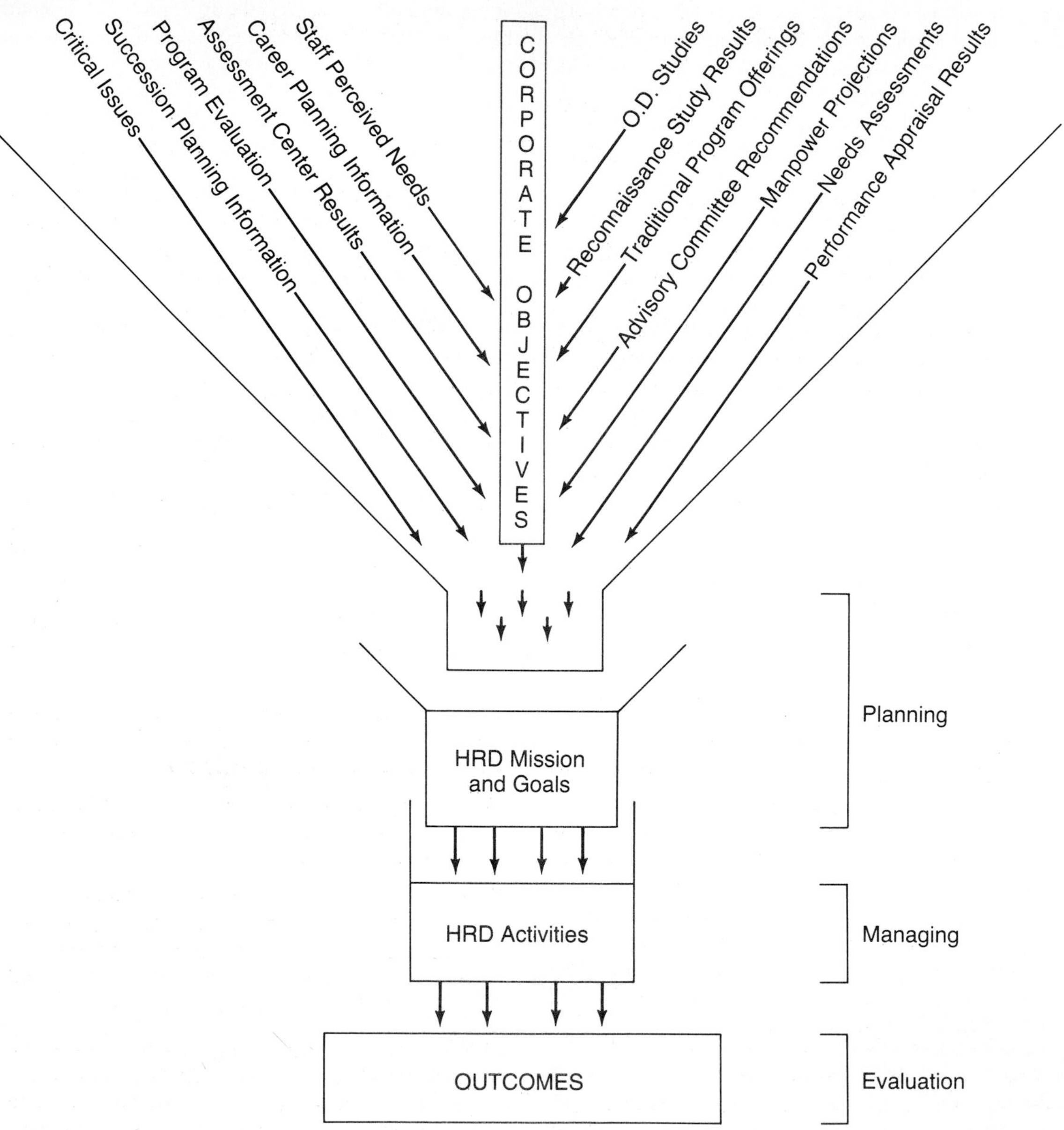

out. This need not mean the plan is the typical "camel" a committee put together; rather, it means that staff has clear and well defined participation in the planning process. The top decision makers in the corporation or HRD area still have the final decision making responsibility, but they will be better decision makers if they listen to everyone who has the relevant data and perspective.

Applying Strategic Planning in Human Resource Development

Leon Winer

Virtually all annual reports claim that the companies engage in strategic planning. However, a survey of chief executive officers in 1,000 of the largest companies in the United States reveals that their primary concern is the lack of strategic planning in their management. As the need to respond to internal and environmental change grows, strategic planning becomes more than a good idea—it becomes vital.

Multi strategic planning is a system that provides for the creation of multiple goal-oriented strategies. It has been applied successfully in different types of businesses and industries ranging in size from 75 to 200,000 employees, on local/regional and worldwide scales. Beginning with a real-world example, this article presents an application of multi strategic planning (MSP) that is tailored to human resource development objectives.

The training and development manager of the Universal Company (real company, disguised name), a worldwide diversified financial services organization, has received the following objective from his immediate supervisor, the vice president for human resources: "To contribute to the profitability and growth of the Universal Company through effective training and development of all employees by initiating, recommending, monitoring and evaluating training and development policies and programs and providing required programs and services which enable line management to train and develop qualified people cost effectively."

A meeting was convened of the 15 supervisors and professionals of the training and development department, and MSP was applied. At this meeting, the group discussed the given objective and its component parts with the aim of establishing one clear, top-ranking objective. Influenced by the training and development manager's concern that, in a declining economy, training and development might be viewed as partially expendable by executive management, the objective that emerged as top ranking was, "To demonstrate to top management the long-term, unquestioned and essential contribution of the training and development department to the Universal Company's profits."

At a second MSP meeting, 41 strengths, weaknesses, opportunities and threats that had bearing on the top-ranking objective were listed. Some of these were:

- Strengths—courses have well-defined objectives, have high participant input, are cost effective;
- Weaknesses—course evaluations are mostly "popularity," not enough planning is done, we don't know who we are;
- Opportunities—we have an image of competence and responsiveness to needs, needs of lower level clients are met;
- Threats—needs of higher management are not met, other groups are doing training and development work, the mission of the training and development department is not well understood throughout the company.

After reviewing the strengths, weaknesses, opportunities and threats facing the training and development department, the strategic planning team was able to confirm that their top-ranking objective was appropriate and attainable. Moreover, the objective was absolutely essential. Possible strategies, such as expanding the client base, relating training and development activities to organizational objectives and discovering the values of higher management, were developed, and a hierarchy of objectives, strategies and tactics was diagrammed.

Using the information from the diagram, participants developed and evaluated action programs for implementation. Throughout the implementation phase, two types of monitoring were required to ensure validity of the plan and to compare actual with expected results.

THE MSP PROCESS

Multi strategic planning should be applied to the planning of activities within the HRD department and taught, as part of the curricula, to executives, managers and professionals throughout the organization. The planning is done by a team of managers, and the meetings are conducted under the leadership of a facilitator or session leader.

There are eight steps to the MSP process. In the first step, all current objectives of the organization are listed. In the second step, top-rank objectives are identified by using a system of objectives, as shown in Figure 1. A top-rank objective is defined as an objective that is *not* a means for achieving another objective. If the question "Why do we pursue this objective?" can be answered without using other objectives, then it is a top-rank objective. Despite all efforts, it may not be possible to fit all of the listed objectives into one system of objectives. If more than one objective emerges as top rank, or if top-rank objectives conflict with one another, the following process will have to be applied with respect to each top-rank objective.

Figure 1
Structure of a System of Objectives

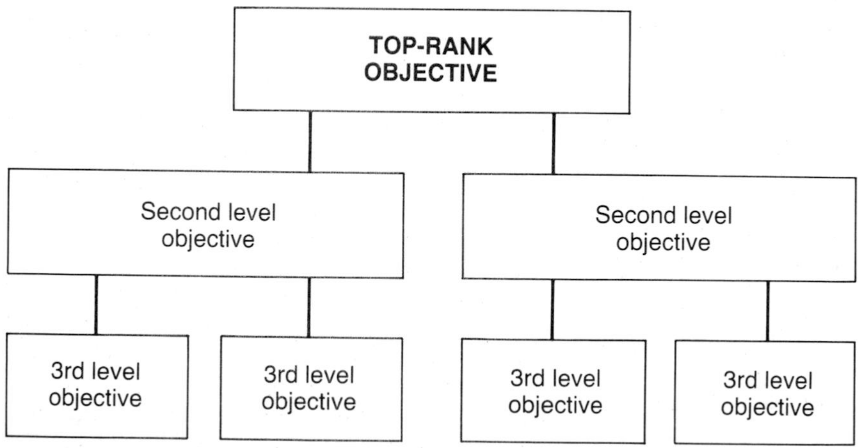

Purpose:
To identify the top rank objective(s).

Questions to help extend the System of Objectives diagram:

- *Downward:* "How do we achieve this objective?"
- *Sideways:* "How else do we achieve the objective above?"
- *Upward:* "Why do we pursue this objective?"

A top-rank objective has been identified when the question "Why do we pursue this objective?" cannot be answered with any of the other objectives listed.

Step three is identifying strengths, weaknesses, opportunities and threats (SWOTs). This serves three purposes: key issues are surfaced; a basis for reviewing top-rank objectives is formed; and a basis for creating possible strategies is established. Strengths must be defined as attributes of the organization that are aids to achieving the top-rank objective. Weaknesses are defined as attributes of the organization that are obstacles to achieving the top-rank objective. Opportunities are outside conditions that are aids to achieving the top-rank objective, and threats are outside conditions that are obstacles to achieving the top-rank objective. Disputed SWOTs must have consensus support to be retained, and all items must be numbered as they are listed to aid in subsequent referencing.

An HRD-oriented checklist is helpful in discovering SWOT items. The following list may serve as a starting point:

- *Strength and weakness items*—quality of courses, education and experience of professional staff, understanding of company culture, ratings received, cost effectiveness, strength of client base, planning ability, availability of resources, relevance of evaluation criteria, coordination within the HRD department, linkages with company strategic plan, utilization of non-classroom time and self-concept.
- *Opportunity and threat items*—client perceptions regarding quality, variety and value of courses and seminars, management attitudes regarding low employee attendance, existence of training and development activities in other departments and skills of top management in using training and development.

The fourth step in the MSP process is reviewing and, if necessary, adjusting the top-rank objective. In reviewing the top-rank objective, this question should be considered: In view of the SWOTs, is the objective suitable and appropriate? From a qualitative point of view, is the objective too ambitious, just right or too modest? If the answer is "yes" to the first question, the analysis can continue. A "no" answer would require changing the top-rank objective. If there are two or more top-rank objectives, it is necessary to consider whether the organization is capable of pursuing all of them. The top-rank objective(s) that survive this critical analysis form the basis of the remaining work.

The SWOT table is used as a source for deriving possible strategies. During this fifth phase, the session leader asks the following questions to stimulate creativity: How can we use these strengths? How can we stop these weaknesses? How can we exploit these opportunities? How can we defend against these threats? Participants engage in structured brainstorming, making sure that each strategy is supported by at least one SWOT item and labeling each strategy with its SWOT source.

By diagramming a hierarchy of objectives, strategies and tactics—step six—new strategies are created and all possible strategies are matched with objectives. The diagram helps to: create additional strategies; match strategies with objectives; develop action plans to implement strategies; evaluate strategies; and detect interactions among strategies. (See Figure 2.) The question "What must be done to implement this strategy?" is answered in detail for each new strategy added to the diagram. As the hierarchies of possible strategies are developed, interactions may be identified. For example, a second or third level tactic or action may support two or more strategies. Such tactics are good candidates for implementation.

The most useful and feasible strategies are selected from the diagram for further development in the seventh step—developing action programs for implementation. This requires naming the strategy and listing specific benefits of implementation, actions required, person(s) responsible, time frame, location, required resources, checkpoints or milestones, rewards or recognition and contingency plans. If resources are available, the risks involved are acceptable and the action plans are mutually reinforcing, the action plans can be implemented.

The eighth and last step of the MSP process is monitoring. Strengths, weaknesses, opportunities and threats are monitored to ensure that the assumptions of the plan are valid. Actual and expected results are also compared, as major

Figure 2
Structure of a Hierarchy of Objectives, Strategies and Tactics (HOST) Diagram

Purpose:
- Generate additional, new strategies;
- Match strategies with objectives;
- Develop tactics and actions to implement strategies;
- Evaluate strategies;
- Detect interactions among strategies.

Questions to help extend the HOST diagram:
- *Downward:* "What can we do to achieve this objective?"
- *Sideways:* "What else can we do to achieve the objective above?"

variances would suggest a need to activate contingency plans or to reevaluate the entire plan.

In addition to stimulating creative problem-solving, multi strategic planning is a process for logical analysis and ranking of objectives. The systematic approach to matching objectives and strategies ensures that effort and resources will not be expended on action programs that do not support the top-rank objectives of the training and development function.

BIBLIOGRAPHY

Abell, D. F. & Hammond, J. S. *Strategic market planning,* Englewood Cliffs, N.J.: Prentice-Hall, 1979.

Allen, L. A. *Making managerial planning more effective.* New York: McGraw-Hill, 1982.

Glueck, W. F. *Strategic management and business policy.* New York: McGraw-Hill, 1980.

HBS Case Services. *Norton company, strategic planning.* (Case 9–377–044) Boston, Mass.: Harvard Business School, 1976.

Naylor, T. H. *Corporate planning models.* Reading, Mass.: Addison Wesley, 1979.

Shaeffer, R. G. CEOs describe their top management staffing needs. Presented at the Conference Board Meeting *Developing Managerial Effectiveness,* New York City, January 20–21, 1982.

Steiner, G. A. *Strategic managerial planning.* Planning Executives Institute, Oxford, Ohio 1977.

Developing Tomorrow's Managers

Richard A. Eastburn

The velocity of change in America has increased dramatically in the last few years. The products on the shelf in the local computer store are different this month from last. Cars now talk to you. Dizzying changes in technology and social values are creating a chasm between what managers do and what they need to do to manage people effectively.

All this is rendering ordinary approaches to developing and educating managers obsolete. Even the most unenlightened companies know that waiting for the cream to rise to the top is a haphazard approach. As a result, some people involved in management development are rethinking their role. They realize that most education and training doesn't work—that it doesn't substantially change management behavior. And even when managers *want* to use what they have learned, they find it difficult to apply the concept to their work.

Is there an answer to this dilemma? Like many things, there is no guarantee. But there *are* people who are willing to break with tradition—to create, experiment and innovate.

THE RIGHT EDUCATION AND TRAINING

The Right Objectives

Being effective at management development starts with deciding which objectives are essential. Are we trying to convey new information, develop a new skill, change some attitudes or values in the management ranks, or change management behavior? For each of these objectives, some educational methodologies are more effective than others. Some of these methodologies are outlined in Figure 1. It lists four kinds of objectives that may be appropriate for management development activity. The right-hand column lists some suggested approaches to achieving the four objectives that are identified in the left-hand column. It's not an exhaustive list of approaches; the intent is to suggest the kinds of activity that help to achieve the objectives in the left-hand column.

To the extent that behavior is an objective of a learning experience, classroom work is only part of the task. The behavior which is expected and taught must conform to the environment in which it will occur. This assumes a model of motivation that is fairly common and familiar to most of us: That a person's behavior reflects what's inside the person as well as that person's environment. People seldom do what the environment does not support. The trouble is that many of our educational

Figure 1
What Are We Teaching/Changing?

Objective	Approach
Information	Lecture Video
Skills	Demonstration Practice
Attitude	Group Discussion Peer Pressure
Behavior	Dilemma Feedback Experience

and developmental activities contradict that principle. Classroom learning requires environmental support for it to justify the time and investment spent on it. Conceptual education alone is inadequate to produce the desired behavior. It needs environmental support and opportunities to take risks with the new behavior.

The standard of excellence for business education and training is not set by Stanford, Harvard, or other business schools. The question is not one of excellence, but of relevance. Academic approaches focus on *conceptual learning;* business education within the organization must focus on *applications learning.* In my experience, I've found consultants from business schools to be notoriously indifferent to actually applying the concepts. As one noted Harvard Business School professor once put it, "Application is your business. My business is teaching the concepts."

With the pace of change increasing, managers don't have a great deal of time to learn a concept, experiment with it for a few months or years, and finally get it down. Educational experiences must permit managers to do some of that experimentation and to acquire an applied capability quickly.

What I have discussed so far is determining the right application for management development and education. A second aspect of that is to focus on the right developmental issue. There are several sources for determining the right issue, including the business strategy, the identified capability needs of an organization and the various roles and responsibilities within it.

The strategy of a business can be written or behavioral. The business may not, in fact, have a well-formulated written strategy. Nonetheless, the business must clearly understand how to develop a set of coordinated actions in the marketplace to achieve and maintain a competitive advantage. To do that, a business must understand its competition, industry structure, customer base, technology and a lot more. Those who attempt to develop managers must understand the strategy and its implications for their functions and roles within the organization.

Organization Capabilities

A second major area of determining the right development issue concerns understanding the capabilities of the organization. Those capabilities exist at three levels: The organization as a whole, various functions within the organization and the individual capabilities of people who perform within those functions.

Individual capabilities have to do with all management responsibilities—technical, administrative and managerial; the ability to think, to resolve problems and make decisions.

Functional capabilities have to do with the actual functions that the organization uses to conduct its business—functions such as manufacturing, engineering, finance, human relations, law and the like.

Organizational capabilities involve the ability of an organization to make decisions that, in time, provide a competitive advantage at a macro level. For instance, IBM recognized that Tandy, Apple and some other small computer companies had developed a new market with the personal computer. To capitalize on that new market, IBM realized that a new structure would have to be established within its organization. Thus, a personal computer organization was cut loose from the rest of IBM to go its own way.

Focus on Roles

A third area of importance in addressing the right education and training has to do with roles and responsibilities. Every organization has six to eight different roles within it. There's executive management, senior management and others. The responsibilities and roles of a plant manager differ from those of a group vice president or a first-line manager. Effective management development can shorten the learning curve of a manager assuming a new role. In fact, if done well, it can cut that learning time in half.

A MODEL OF EDUCATION AND TRAINING

Within TRW, educational programs are customized and focused around a particular role and/or function of the organization. Such customized programs have been conducted in manufacturing, and are now being launched in finance and human relations, among other functions. In manufacturing, we developed four learning experiences. The first is called the "Executive Role in Manufacturing Strategy." The second is the "Plant Management Seminar," the third is the "First-Line Management Seminar," and the fourth is titled "Manufacturing Strategy: The Role of Support Staff." Table 1 illustrates these programs.

The left-hand side identifies the four roles on which we focus at TRW. Across the top are the various functions. There is one more dimension to this diagram: What we call "general mangement skills," or skills which are needed at any level of management. For example, interviewing—managers at every level of the organization interview. The skills of interviewing are the same regardless of the level of the organization, but are applied differently. This completes the model of management development and education used at TRW.

Focus is the critical issue here. So, now we have two key words that identify critical differences in approaches to education and training—"discrimination" is one, and "focus" is the other.

FIT AND SYSTEM

A third key word is "fit." Previously I described a model of motivation that assumes that people do what the environment supports, as well as what they are capable of doing. Put another way, effective behavior within organizations not only needs the capability of the person, but the support of the organizational environment. To design an effective learning experience, management must take into account the norms of the organization, how things really happen and their readiness to make changes in an organization. It would be futile for an organization to attempt to change management's focus to a strategic one when all of the reward systems support an operational short-term approach. Generally, people in organizations do what management rewards. We all seek to avoid pain and acquire pleasure. As a result, the systems in which we live and work determine a great deal of our behavior. But how often does management in its wisdom want something to be taught, yet fails to recognize that the systems, norms and organizational values must be changed for the learning to be applied?

APPLICATION LEARNING

The final word that I would like to introduce is "application." Although the concept of market segmentation is an important one to any business, the ability to use that concept and actually seg-

Table 1
Roles and Responsibilities

	Gen. Mgt.	*Mfg.*	*Finance*	*Human Relations*	*Generic Mgt. Skills*
Executive Management	SMS	ERMS	Competitive innovation in finance	Strategic HR planning	Performance Evaluation
Senior Management	SMS	ERMS			Presentations
Middle Management	SMS	Plant mgmt.	Contemporary issues in finance	Business skills for HR	Interviewing Interpersonal Relationships
First-Level Management		FLM			

Note: *SMS = Strategic Management Seminar*
ERMS = Executive's Role in Manufacturing Strategy
FLM = First-Level Management

ment a market correctly is quite another thing. Our managers in TRW struggle with that concept. They know what it is, they can define it and they can get it right on a test; yet it's remarkable how often managers select a market segment that is inappropriate. In training programs, which are designed to resolve a certain problem, teach a new skill or help managers acquire a new behavior, our managers can talk about it—they just can't do it.

In the end, application results from selecting the right methodology to achieve a specific objective. It also comes from focusing on specific roles and functional areas, and having only those people attend the program that fit within the matrix illustrated in Table 1. It comes from providing a learning experience that is highly involving and participatory; where methodology fits the objectives. It comes from making sure that the systems of the organization are congruent with the objectives of the learning. In short, application comes from doing all the things I've talked about well.

People remember about 15 percent of what they hear and about 35 to 40 percent of what they see and hear; but most of us remember more than 80 percent of what we do. However, all that really has nothing to do with a manager's ability to apply what is retained in the memory. To translate a concept into an ability is the highest cost of education and training—yet we invest little time, energy or dollars to support this translation to application.

If management education and training are going to be effective, they need to be highly involving. Although simulations, discussion, testing of ideas, peer reviews, case studies are all part of a methodology that supports success, even these elements don't go far enough. First, the participatory methodology must be tied to the objectives. Second, the learning environment of the classroom must be extended into the workplace. In other words, management needs to support learning as well as work and accomplishment, so that subordinates can learn new things and accommodate change.

The major difference between this approach to management development and more traditional approaches lies in the discrimination between types of objectives and the linkage of those objectives to the system within which managers work. Thus, the approach described can be called *systems learning*, because there's a built-in compatibility between what managers are expected to learn and what they are expected to do on the job. That kind of learning expects, encourages and supports change, and realizes that if change doesn't occur, the business may be jeopardized, and certainly the learning has not been effective.

To say it another way, these four things—discrimination, focus, fit and application—are absolutely critical for education in today's fast-paced business world. All four must be linked together in an effective system. Up to now, education and training have focused primarily on the classroom and the participatory methodology, in the belief that managers would retain more of what they did. As far as it went, this was true, but memory is not to be equated with performance. Memory and retention aren't the issue; *application* is the issue.

Teaching manufacturing strategy to plant managers is one thing; teaching manufacturing strategy to company executives is quite another. All too often we use the same training program to teach both managers and executives. And both walk away recognizing that there was some value to the training but that it did not quite fit their needs.

TRW'S STRATEGIC MANAGEMENT SEMINAR

One example of systems learning is the Strategic Management Seminar at TRW. This seminar was designed following a major investment of money in a seminar on competitive strategy. Managers reported a great deal of interest and enthusiasm for the concept; however, their enthusiasm wasn't matched by an ability to apply the concepts to their work. So the Strategic Management Seminar was started. It was carefully designed to ensure application of the learning.

The seminar has three phases. First, the concepts are taught. A very detailed assignment is provided to the participants, who attend in teams. The teams apply the concepts to their business, and develop an action strategy—they are asked to plan no more than six actions that they will take over the next 18 months and to determine who will be responsible for those actions.

The people who attend the seminar are natural business teams—for example, a division vice president and staff, who might develop and implement the division's product or market strategy. The teams then "go home" and work on their strategy for about eight weeks.

The second phase of the seminar is called the midterm review. A seminar faculty member visits the team to review their progress on the assignment. While there, the faculty member provides feedback on how well the team is applying the concepts. Major changes in strategy occur at this point as the teams recognize, for example, that their competitive analysis is not thorough enough. This phase builds in the no-risk experimentation discussed earlier.

Then, for another eight weeks, the teams develop their final strategic presentation for a dress rehearsal—the third phase. The dress rehearsal is held with two or three other teams. After one of the teams presents its strategy, the other teams ask questions and raise their concerns about the strategy. Next, the other teams vote on whether to approve the strategy. In addition, they indicate on their ballots what they like and dislike about the strategy. The votes and comments are then collected and offered to the presenting team. Finally, the faculty member raises questions and summarizes his thoughts and concerns about the strategy. Frequently, more than 80 percent of the issues which the faculty member recognizes as problems have already been raised by the other teams. The basic methodology operating here is a powerful peer review process.

It was recognized from the beginning that the seminar's strong emphasis on application would require some organizational modifications. Some of these included changing the process of developing strategic plans, modifying the compensation system so that long-term management is rewarded and changing the review process to emphasize long-term thinking, planning and action. As a result, a number of TRW group vice presidents are reviewing the strategies that have been developed. They, too, went through their own training program on reviewing strategic plans. The training was designed to be appropriate for *their* particular role in the organization. In some cases, the stategy has been revised so radically that it has demanded subsequent review by the CEO. The results of those reviews have been favorable.

One other concern regarding system fit which managers raised in the seminar was whether senior management would encourage or even permit the kind of risk-taking that is required to implement some of the strategies. Happily, from the beginning senior management has demonstrated a willingness to support such risk-taking when it is justified.

LEADERSHIP

Something which we have yet to do is to prepare our managers to lead others in achieving their determined strategies. This is viewed not in terms of obsolete ideas of leadership, but rather in terms of today's *opportunity* leadership. Managers in our environment tend to manage and control. Although these are important capabilities, the needs and capabilities of those who are led have changed, as have the conditions of the business environment. Leadership—as distinguished from managing—must be a far greater part of today's and tomorrow's managers than it is. The competitive battle in today's market can no longer tolerate the low energy level which is created by management that emphasizes control.

CONCLUSION

Business education within organizations must change. We must move beyond the classroom and recognize the importance of the environmental fit and the appropriate organizational changes that must occur to ensure that fit. Not only must the learning reach outside the classroom, but what goes on within the classroom has to change, too. The discrimination among objectives and the choice of classroom methodology go hand-in-hand. These two things—discrimination of objectives and classroom methodology—complement a focus on the roles played by the learners in the organization, and on the fit of the learning objectives to the roles and organizational systems. Applied learning of this nature is essential for managers in a world that is immersed in rapid change.

Management Training: Justify Costs or Say Goodbye

Thomas F. Urban
Gerald R. Ferris
Daniel F. Crowe
Robert L. Miller

During the 1970s, management training delivered developmental skills to a rapidly growing managerial cadre. The attitude was that if training is good, more is better. During the 1980s, however, the survival of the training and development function depends on the answer to the question, "How do we *know* training is good?"

Rigorous, systematic efforts to demonstrate effectiveness generally have been neglected. A recent study of 20 corporations regarded as leaders in corporate training concluded that, "To the degree that evaluation efforts have been undertaken, they seem to have focused on technical training. . . ."[1] Even when evaluation took place, there was no consensus on the best type of evaluation criteria. More top management is agreeing with Odiorne's contention that if management development programs do not show quantifiable economic gains, the programs should be discontinued.

Recent discussions of management development recommend a multi-method approach to assessing its effectiveness. Campbell recommends that subjective evaluations by participants (internal criteria) be combined with measures assessing behavioral change on the job (external criteria) in order to evaluate fully the effectiveness of management development programs.[2]

Our research outlines a multi-criterion approach to evaluating a large-scale supervisory training program in a major U.S. oil company. In addition to the internal criteria of participants' reactions to the program, longitudinal measures were taken in regard to subsequent attrition and career progressions of participants or external criteria. We also developed measures of participants' organizational investment and conducted a cost/benefit analysis. While some evaluation approaches build on existing notions, comprehensive multi-evaluation criteria go beyond these in scope, permitting the convergence of both internal and external criteria to be examined.

THE SUPERVISORY TRAINING PROGRAM

The supervisory training program (STP) was designed for employees newly promoted into first-level supervisory positions and supervisors who had not attended a supervisory training program in the last five years. Progam participants were nominated by their managers for a specific program based on the manager's assessment and discussions of the supervisor's training needs.

The content of the programs included communication, group dynamics, problem solving, decision making and other supervisory skills. Conducted six to ten times per year, each program contained the same generic content and was conducted by three in-house members of the training staff at an off-site location. Participants were selected from diverse functional areas and geographic locations.

This training evaluation effort focuses on STP programs offered between September 1979 and July 1981. The average age of the 533 participants was 36 years, approximately 90 percent earned between \$25,000 and \$63,000, and approximately 22 percent were female and minority group members. The majority of participants came from Texas, Alaska and Louisiana.

CONCEPTUAL MODEL

An understanding and cost justification of the STP effectiveness was developed through use of multiple methods and criteria. Evaluation criteria were developed from a conceptual model outlining the multi-criterion approach to evaluation. The STP project was evaluated relative to participant reactions concerning content and context as well as promotions, grade increases and attrition (performance effects). At the end of each program, participants evaluated their interest in the program, perceived relevance of the program content, the trainers and the overall course.

Participant interest in the course material was determined to be a necessary, but not sufficient condition for implementation on the job. For the 15 programs, overall interest received an average of 5.04 on a 6-point Likert scale, and perceived applicability of the course material an average of 5.02 on a similar scale. The overall course rating average was 3.46 on a 4-point scale with the trainers' ratings averaging 3.63. Participant reactions suggested that the STP rated high in terms of interest, perceived applicability, course and trainers. Participants' narrative comments, which were content analyzed, were also favorable.

While participant reactions are useful, additional criteria were used to determine program effectiveness and to provide a basis for comparison across methods.

ATTRITION

Training programs may not change observable behavior on the job, but they may have value in reducing attrition. Perhaps the most important effect of a development activity is the positive feelings resulting from participants' perceptions of corporate interest in their personal and career development. Participants selected for organizational rewards, such as developmental experiences, may reciprocate through increased loyalty, and commitment, and longer tenure with an organization. Not only is training costly, but so is turnover. Yeager notes that replacement costs for managers is equal approximately to their annual salary.[3] Therefore, a central question in measuring training effectiveness is whether the participants remain with the organization providing the training.

During 1980–1981, the attrition of experienced personnel was of vital importance to the energy industry. Smaller independent oil firms were raiding the major firms to secure experienced engineers, geologists, geophysicists, landmen and managers. Retaining these professionals was of paramount importance for the exploration and production of energy resources by the major oil companies. Of the 533 supervisors participating in the 15 STP programs between 1979 and 1981, 20 subsequently left the organization. This is an annualized average attrition rate of 2.2 percent compared to an overall 6.4 percent for all employees in this category.

Table 1 provides a more specific analysis of the turnover rate among program participants, showing the annual average attrition rates for critical-skills employees in the STP program compared with the overall turnover rates for specific categories of professionals.

The attrition rate for all critical-skill categories, except geologists, was significantly lower for STP participants. The low or nonexistent availability of experienced critical-skills employees magnified the significance of the low attrition rate.

CAREER PROGRESSION

Enhancing performance on the job is a central focus of any developmental activity. Since observing performance changes was not possible, the outcomes of the organizations reward process served as a surrogate measure. Participants' grade increases and title changes gauged organizational rewards. A longitudinal analysis determined organizational reward and career progression of participants in the three programs offered in 1979. Table 2 shows the comparison of pre- and post-

Table 1
Comparison of Annualized Average Attrition Rate for Critical-Skills Personnel

Skill Category	*STP Participants*	*Overall*	*Z*
Reservoir engineers	2.6%	8.1%	3.44**
Drilling engineers	3.2%	8.5%	1.71[a]
Production engineers	0.0%	5.1%	2.55*
Geologists	12.8%	11.8%	.38
Geophysicists	2.9%	6.5%	2.02*
Landmen	0.0%	13.9%	4.63***

[a]*While this value did not reach statistical significance at conventional levels, it was marginally significant ($p < .08$).*

$^{*}p < .05$

$^{**}p < .01$

$^{***}p < .001$

Table 2
Comparison of Pay Increases and Title Changes for STP Participants and Nonparticipants

	Participants (N = 105)	*Nonparticipants (N = 105)*	*z*[a]
Percentage receiving at least one pay grade increase	70.1%	49.5%	4.39**
Percentage receiving position title changes	66.0%	37.1%	6.16**
Total pay grade increases	104 (ratio = .99)	50 (ratio = .48)	14.57**

[a]*This z-test examines the significance of the difference between two proportions.*[4]

$^{**}p < .001$

positional and grade data for the 1979 participants and for employees who did not participate in STP.

The analysis in Table 2 indicates that STP participants received more grade increases and title changes than those in the non-participant sample. The 105 participants received a total of 104 grade increases—more than twice as many as the non-participants. Statistically significant differences existed between participants and nonparticipants on all measures.

COST/BENEFIT ANALYSIS

A systematic and informed evaluation effort should provide an indication of program investment or costs to use a benchmark against which to evaluate benefits. In this study, the costs of a single program appear in Table 3. A single STP program costs approximately $65,000, or nearly 4.0 percent of the participants' annual average salary. If training and development efforts are viewed

Table 3
STP Program Cost Calculation (July 1981 Session)

Participant salaries (1 week at average salary):	$21,500
Trainers salaries (3 trainers for 1 week at average salary)	2,200
Transportation, lodging and meals (participants and trainers):	36,000
Program expenses (materials, conference rooms, etc.):	5,000
Approximate total cost:	$64,700

Table 4
Comparison of Total Resources Under Participants' Control with Total STP Expenses

Resource	*Amount*
Direct Labor	$ 47,737,800
Overhead expenses	254,123,400
Company equipment	806,902,000
Contract allocations	80,849,000
Total resources	$1,189,612,200
Total cost of STP (9/79–10/81)	$1,200,000

as investments in human resources, then a long-range investment perspective seems desirable. Comparing the $65,000 program cost with the total tenure of the STP program participants, the investment per year was $218.86. If the cost of the program was amortized over the projected organizational tenure of the participants, the amortization per year would be $77.20. This expense is minimal relative to projected returns from a supervisor's career.

Another analysis, conducted on October 1981 participants, is analogous to a break-even calculation for cost-benefit justification. Information on the resources that they had under their control was collected from participants. Table 4 shows a comparison between these resources and the total amount expended for the 15 programs conducted between September 1979 and October 1981. The total expenses for STP programs would be covered if participants in one program subsequently increased their resource utilization (e.g., through better management skills) by only 0.1 percent.

In addition, if the supervisors could get their 253 direct reports to increase resources an average of $256.92 per direct report, the program expense would be covered.

SUMMARY AND CONCLUSIONS

This study reports a program evaluation effort of a large-scale management training and development program in a major oil company. The evaluation approach employs multiple criteria, rather than relying on a single dimension which typically is of questionable validity. Using several different methods allows the examination of convergence in the results from the different criteria, thus permitting more confident conclusions concerning the program's effectiveness. In our study, positive participant reactions, post-program promotion and pay grade increases, reduced turnover rates and effective cost measures converged in supporting the effectiveness of the STP program.

In the current uncertain economic climate, fewer resources will be allocated to support training programs without evaluation. Human resource professionals contend that development is an important organizational activity, and managers and other professional employees view development as important to their careers. However, the training and development function must be able to justify, with sound evidence, that programs are actually effective. Multi-evaluation methods that provide accurate measures of program effectiveness assist in the cost justification of training efforts. As training professionals, we are challenged to evaluate corporate development activities before evaluation is forced upon us.

REFERENCES

1. Lupton, A. H. (1983). An overview of the NIE study of corporate education training. *Academy for Educational Development.* Washington, D.C.

2. Campbell, J. P., Dunnette, M. D., Lawler, E. E. & Weick, K. E. (1970). *Managerial behavior, performance, and effectiveness.* New York: McGraw-Hill.

3. Yeager, J. (1982). Coaching the executive: Can you teach an old dog new tricks? *Personnel Administrator, 27,* 37–42.

4. McNemar, Q. (1969). *Psychological Statistics.* New York: Wiley.

CHAPTER 7

Union-Management Relations

A general consensus prevails that labor management relations in this country are changing—and changing, some believe, rather dramatically. For example, the percentage of unionized employees in the non-farm work force dropped from a high of nearly 33 percent in 1950 to 19 percent in 1985 and is predicted to decline further by the year 2000. But this still means that approximately one out of every five employees today is a union worker, with a much higher ratio of unionized to nonunionized employees in such industries as autos, mining, steel, construction, retail food, airlines, and trucking. Those who have responsibilities for the personnel function in unionized organizations, therefore, whether they are directly or indirectly involved with labor management-relations, should become familiar with current trends in the labor movement, why employees want unions, how union campaigns are conducted, the implications of concession bargaining on the employee-employer relationship, and strategies that organizations might follow in the labor relations area.

Although the size and strength of the labor movement is in a period of decline, it appears that unions and the underlying philosophies of unionization will continue to affect the field of personnel and human resources management. Unions and the threats of unionization have played a significant role in the development and elaboration of several human resources activities, especially compensation and safety and health. Nonunionized organizations, in many instances, have modified their personnel policies and practices to discourage unionization.

Labor-management relations are affected by many federal laws and court decisions. The most important federal laws are the National Labor Relations (Wagner) Act of 1935 and its two amendments, the Labor-Management Relations (Taft-Hartley) Act of 1947 and the Labor-Management Reporting and Disclosure (Landrum-Griffin) Act of 1959. Each of these has a somewhat different focus. The Wagner Act encourages unionization, specifies a number of employer unfair labor practices, and establishes the National Labor Relations Board to enforce its provisions. In response to union growth and a series of major strikes and boycotts during the years following enactment of the Wagner Act, Congress, in 1947, enacted the Taft-Hartley Act. This act seeks to achieve a better balance of power for employers in union-management relations by incorporating a number of union unfair labor practices on such topics as union membership, bargaining requirements, strikes, and boycotts. The primary purpose of the Landrum-Griffin Act is to avoid corruption and abuses of power by union leaders.

Strauss, in the first article in this chapter, presents a brief history of industrial relations. He closely reviews the two sides, management and union, to see where the current negotiation power lies and why. The author also explains why concession bargaining began and how it has changed the negotiation relationship.

In the second article, Mitchell suggests that the main reasons cited for concessions in contracts, deregulation, and foreign trade do not always fully explain the situation. Instead wage developments may be pivotal.

There has been a decline in the power and number of unions over the past few years. However, according to Stone, in the next article, unions hope to put an end to this trend with new recruitment strategies, capitalizing on the corporate culture's lack of basic consideration for employee self-esteem, on new "minorities" in the work force, and on the issue of comparable worth. The author also discusses some recruitment methods currently used by the unions and ways management can counteract them. Finally, Fossum outlines the complete unionization procedure from the campaign to allow a vote for union representation through the negotiation of a contract and what can happen later if a dispute arises.

Suggestions for Further Reading

Christiansen, E. T. (1983). Strategy, structure, and labor relations performance. *Human Resource Management, 22,* 155–168.

Fulmer, W. E. (1984). Labor-management relations in the 80s: Revolution or evolution? *Business Horizons, 27,* 26–31.

Fulmer, W. E. (1981). Step by step through a union campaign. *Harvard Business Review, 59,* 94–102.

Goodman, J. P., & Sandberg, W. R. (1981). A contingency approach to labor relations strategies. *Academy of Management Review, 6,* 145–154.

Kochan, T. A., McKersie, R. B., & Cappelli, P. (1984). Strategic choice and industrial relations theory. *Industrial Relations, 23,* 16–39.

Lewin, D. (1981). Collective bargaining and the quality of work life. *Organizational Dynamics, 10,* 37–53.

Mills, D. Q. (1983). When employees make concessions. *Harvard Business Review, 61,* 103–113.

Mitchell, D. J. B. (1987). The share economy and industrial relations. *Industrial Relations, 26,* 1–17.

Schrank, R. (1979). Are unions an anachronism? *Harvard Business Review, 57,* 107–115.

Schuster, M. (1984). Cooperation and change in union settings: Problems and opportunities. *Human Resource Management, 23,* 145–160.

Industrial Relations: Time of Change

George Strauss

For industrial relations scholars these are exciting times. More seems to be happening in our field than at any time since the thirties and forties. For almost 30 years industrial relations was an area of relative stability, certainly compared with other developments such as the civil rights and women's movements, the youth revolt of the sixties, the growing impact of foreign (especially Japanese) competition, the deregulation of many industries, and the rapid spread of computers. Today the cumulative effect of these and other developments is rapidly changing the nature of industrial relations. Perhaps the most newsworthy events occurred during 1982 when three of the country's largest unions, the Autoworkers, Steelworkers, and Teamsters, each agreed to substantial concessions. Concession bargaining occurred in an immediate context of widespread unemployment, deregulation, and foreign competition, and in a larger context of declining union membership and strength and of increasing management determination to operate with minimal union interference.

In the rest of this paper, I will review contemporary developments in U.S. industrial relations from several vantage points. I will also hazard a few predictions about what may lie ahead and suggest some areas of needed research.[1]

MANAGEMENT INITIATIVES

I begin with management since it, rather than the union, is now the prime mover. After 40 years (1935–1975) during which most of the innovations in industrial relations came from unions, companies have stopped merely reacting and have been taking the initiative on many fronts. First, they began introducing "human resources" policies for dealing with their employees, particularly in nonunion plants. Secondly, they fought determinedly and with great success to prevent the spread of unions to unorganized plants. Finally, and most recently, they began demanding give-backs in bargaining. Although the extent to which these developments have occurred has varied considerably among companies and industries, most observers concede that management is now the militant party.

Industrial Relations as a Strategic Contingency

Strategic contingency theory in organizational behavior argues that power goes to the organizational function which deals with critical uncertainties. Labor relations was a critical uncertainty during the thirties and forties, consequently, the industrial relations function flourished. But out of the turbulence of that period came a variety of accommodations, all designed to reduce uncertainty. These included industry-wide and pattern bargaining, long-term contracts, automatic wage adjustments through cost-of-living allowances (COLAs) and productivity increases, mutually accepted work rules, and a quasi-bureaucratic, quasi-legal mechanism for handling workplace differences through grievance procedures and arbitration. All this went with the style of labor relations, called "mature collective bargaining," which involved considerable trust and shared ideology between top negotiators on both sides. The process reached its peak with the 1971 Steel Expedited Negotiations Agreement.

Thus, management bought peace and predictable labor costs. Wages, fringe benefits, and even work practices were taken "out of competition," thus spreading the Webbs' common rule through many industries. As a consequence, industrial relations became a less significant strategic contingency.

By the seventies many managements began asking whether the price of peace and stability was too high. Increased foreign competition and later deregulation meant that wages were no longer "out of competition," while some work rules that inhibited adjustments to technological change and inflation sent COLA costs skyrocketing. Some companies' very survival depended on lowering labor costs. Thus, industrial relations considerations began once again to drive company policy. Long before the current recession management was showing greater determination in resisting unions. Even companies with long histories of good relations with unions in established plants began using hard-ball tactics to prevent unions from spreading to their newer "greenfields" plants, many deliberately built in areas difficult to unionize. By 1981, many firms began to give higher priority to cutting costs in their unionized plants than to the maintenance of industrial peace. So far, however, few companies have taken the final step of seeking to eliminate already existing unions.[2]

Recently, industrial relations have played a critical role in decisions whether to shutdown or move plants and even whether to enter or leave lines of activity or to hive off whole divisions (as at TWA and Greyhound). In some companies the new hard line has meant top management's direct intervention into negotiations as well as the wholesale replacement of oldtime industrial relations experts who had been identified with the old policy of accommodation.[3] By contrast with their immediate predecessors, some of the new decision makers were as ideologically motivated against unions as were their nineteenth century forebears.

Management's renewed concern for industrial relations has been shown also by the growing importance accorded the human resources function and by the introduction of human resources policies.

The Rise of the Human Resources Function

Personnel administration, for many years a stepchild, has been rechristened human resources management (HRM) and is enjoying a renaissance in both academia[4] and the real world.[5] Even at the depth of the 1982 recession, some companies expanded the size of their human resources departments, and salaries in this area have risen more rapidly than managerial salaries generally.[6] HRM's rise has to some extent been at the cost of the traditional industrial relations function. Thus, when General Motors' Vice President of Labor Relations retired, he was replaced by the former director of the company's quality of working life program, not by someone whose career had been in industrial relations (Kochan and Cappelli, forthcoming).

Aside from an anti-union bias, there are a number of reasons for this new concern for the human factor among a significant minority of companies:

. . . Equal employment laws and the erosion of the employment-at-will doctrine have forced major revisions in company selection, personnel, performance appraisal and dismissal policies. Management has learned that losing an equal employment or unjust dismissal suit can be very expensive. The comparable worth issue threatens an equally painful revision in compensation practices.

. . . Women (and some younger men) are demanding flextime as well as the right to change careers and drop in and out of the labor force.

. . . The major thrust of new technology is to permit and require greater flexibility in how the job is done. (White-collar factories—such as those handling credit card accounts—are a major exception to this statement.) Older work rules, adapted to older, mass production technologies and based on rigid job classifications and promotional hierarchies, are often badly out of date.

. . . Japanese management and "corporate culture" are two current top management interests. Whether these interests are more than fads is still in doubt. Nevertheless, the wholesale managerial shakeups occurring in many companies have been partially legitimated by the need to reduce organizational inertia. Human resources staffs are playing a major role in seeking to develop new, "open," participative managerial systems (thus putting into practice the teaching of many business school professors).

. . . Another current management interest—probably more than a fad— is long-run "strategic planning." Strategic human resources planning—which typically involves a hard, cost-oriented evaluation of available alternatives—is viewed as a top management (not just staff) function. Symptomatic of this interest is the presence of corporate controllers at professional courses dealing with human resources planning.

Human Resources Policies

Whether motivated by ideology or fad, by economic necessity or by a desire to keep out unions, companies are increasingly experimenting with what have become known as human resources policies which are designed to increase employee motivation and job commitment (Foulkes, 1980). These new policies have been most widely introduced in nonunion plants and especially in high technology industries. They have been talked about more than they have actually been adopted. Nevertheless, they seem to represent the wave of the future.

. . . Some efforts have been made to provide relatively stable employment for regular employees. (On the other hand, other firms have slashed away at their payrolls, laying off both white-collar workers and managers.) In some cases, hourly pay arrangements have been replaced by salaries. Meanwhile, just as in Japan, use of temporary, contract employees has also increased.

. . . Flextime has become common and greater opportunities have been provided for employees to switch careers.

. . . Training programs have been expanded and career ladders widened and lengthened, thus providing greater job flexibility and greater opportunities for advancement. More and more white-collar and managerial jobs are filled by bidding.

. . . Broad-banded job classifications (also known as job enlargement), autonomous work groups, quality circles, and other "Quality of Work Life" reforms have been introduced.

. . . In setting pay, less emphasis is being placed on job classification and more on individual performance (through performance appraisals) and skill acquisition (through what has been called the merit badge system of compensation).

. . . Appeals procedures, ombudsmen, and other forms of protection against arbitrary management action (especially unjust dismissal) have been introduced into nonunion firms.[7] Some of these policies (e.g., greater job security and protection against unjustified dismissal) are consistent with traditional union demands. Others (e.g., flextime and broad banding) may do a better job of meeting the felt needs of younger professional and technical employees than does the typical union contract. But, as we shall see, among the effects of concession bargaining has been the spread of these policies to the unionized sector.

Taken together, these new company human resources policies, plus new legal regulations (EEO, ERISA, OSHA, and the erosion of the employment-at-will doctrine) have given many workers most of the benefits and protections commonly provided by unionization. At least they do so in principle. To be sure, some of these protections rest on management's good will, many of them are but window dressing, and all of them might be more energetically enforced were a union present. Nevertheless, their net impact has been to make union organizing more difficult.

UNION DECLINE

Union density—the percent of eligible employees organized—has declined from roughly 35 per cent of nonagricultural employees in 1950 to perhaps under 20 per cent today. What are the causes of the decline? How far will it go? Under what circumstances is it likely to be reversed?

Recent research calls into question the conventional view that the primary causes of this fall-off are changes in the distribution of the labor force among industries and occupations. True, nonunion, primarily white-collar occupations and industries have grown faster than have heavily unionized, primarily blue-collar occupations and industries. Union membership has been concentrated in segments of industry that are unusually prone to economic adversity. Nevertheless, impressive evidence has been mobilized that demonstrates that these structural, economic changes explain well under half the union decline (Farber, 1983; Mitchell, 1983).

The main difference between 1950 and the present is the precipitous drop in the rate of union membership gain through NLRB elections (Freeman, 1983; Dickens and Leonard, 1983). During 1950–1954, national unions won elections involving an annual average of 1.52 per cent of nonunion private, nonagricultural employees. By 1975–1979, this figure had dropped to 0.35 (Dickens and Leonard, 1983). Statistically, this falloff can be disaggregated into three parts (Dickens and Leonard, 1983; Freeman, 1983): (1) The total number of elections has increased less rapidly than the increase in the nonunion labor force generally. Meanwhile, (2) the average number of workers per election unit went down, as did (3) the percentage of elections which unions won.[8] (Indeed, unions fared worse in large election units, thus accentuating the impact of the decline.)

A variety of explanations have been given for this drop. Union organizing expenditures have kept pace with the increase in the cost of living, but not with the number of unorganized workers (Voos, 1982). Public support for unions is at an all-time low (Lipsett and Schneider, 1983). But most important, management opposition, particularly illegal opposition (as measured by NLRB charges and backpay awards) is up many fold. Freeman (1983) concludes that "from one quarter to a half . . . of the decline in union electoral success can be attributed to rising management opposition."

Labor's weakness has been further accentuated by its inability to convert into contracts the elections it does win and by its loss of political power, relative to other interest groups.

What can we predict for the future? A cautious scenario is that union density will continue to decline, perhaps to 15 per cent by 1999 (Dickens and Leonard, 1983).[9] But recent events may accelerate all the trends discussed above. The decline in unionism, so far a fairly smooth curve, may kink sharply downward. Employment in the unionized sector has been declining more rapidly than it did prior to 1978—and this may continue.[10] Organizing efforts may become even less successful. Union membership loss through decertification is now merely a trickle, costing unions only one-tenth of 1 per cent of their membership annually (Dickens and Leonard, 1983); the collapse of unions in segments of meatpacking and other industries may convert this trickle to a torrent. The early nineteen twenties—when many unions fell apart in the face of management opposition—may repeat themselves. There is at least a chance we may become the western world's only largely "union free" country.

An alternate scenario is that the union movement will resume its growth. This scenario rests on several assumptions: First, as women become increasingly committed to the labor force they become less and less satisfied with their traditional jobs, and so more prone to the argument of comparable worth and to unionism. This may be the case especially in white-collar factories, such as banks and insurance companies, where heavy layoffs occurred in the recent recession. Secondly, as the South becomes increasingly industrialized, both racial tensions and anti-union sentiments may decline. Third, unions may win converts among college-trained members of the "baby boom generation." Only a fraction of this group can be accommodated in professional and managerial jobs; tremendous frustrations may develop as their occupational aspirations become thwarted. Conceivably, unions could take advantage of these frustrations, although doing so may require substantial changes in organizing strategies and bargaining goals.

Of course, union decline could be self-containing. To date, the threat of being unionized has prevented management from taking full advantage of its economic strength. Once the threat is removed managements may overreach themselves. The primitive tyrannies which laid the grounds for unionism in the nineteen thirties may return, thus setting off a new cycle of union growth. Although plausible, this alternative rests on the questionable assumption that management's primary motivation for human resources policies has been to keep out unions.

In an effort to refurbish their images, a number of unions have been experimenting with innovative new organizing strategies and tactics—from "corporate campaigns" (such as used against J. P. Stevens) to the use of questionnaire survey techniques to pinpoint groups of workers susceptible to being unionized. To date none of these has shown great success. One reason is that aside from nonwhites, union support is so evenly distributed among industries and occupations that there is no obvious target group of nonunion workers, a majority of whom have expressed an interest in supporting unions (Farber, 1983). Nevertheless, a younger generation of union organizers is being trained to use these newer techniques, and they will be in a position to take advantage of any breaks that come their way.

New techniques may not be enough. If Freeman's (1983) analysis is correct, a change in the law and its enforcement is required. Until this happens labor will be fighting an uphill battle. Further, management's human resources strategy which, at its best, combines elements of lifetime employment with enhanced opportunities for individual self-expression and career advancement, may be more appealing to many workers than the unions' "common rule" policy of treating everyone alike.

Were a Mondale administration to adopt a combined incomes and industrial policy, things might look better for unions. An industrial policy might help save members' jobs, while an income policy would presumably make unions equal partners to management in setting national policy.

CONCESSION BARGAINING

Recent concession bargaining has involved some dramatic man-bites-dog behavior. The question is whether we are seeing permanent or merely temporary changes in U.S. industrial relations. Are we moving to a "new state" or is this merely a "rerun," as Derber (1983) puts it? Has Humpty Dumpty fallen off the wall, never to be put together again—or is he just repositioning himself (Mitchell, 1983)? Will previous relationships be restored, once aggregative demand improves, or are we going through a profound structural change?

Here I am with the structuralist. My own imperfect analogy is with an earthquake. By 1980, our collective bargaining system was essentially 30 years old. To be sure, some shifts had occurred over the years, but factors previously discussed—exclusive bargaining rights, no-raid agreements, long-term contracts, wage adjustment by formula, and grievance arbitration—combined to make the system resistant to minor, short-term, or localized pressures. Meanwhile, though masked by the system's seeming stability, pressures of all sorts were building up. Finally, when subjected to the additional strain of the economic recession, the system suffered an earthquake: many relationships changed quite quickly.

How about the future? The final results are far from in, but it seems likely that some structures will be faithfully restored to their pre-earthquake form, while other features of the landscape will be altered for good. Humpty Dumpty may reascend his wall, but he may look more like a carrot than an egg.

Wages and Wage Relationships

By the seventies wages in the unionized sectors had reached something of an equilibrium. In any given major, organized national industry most employers paid roughly the same wages, and there was a fairly stable wage hierarchy among industries. True, these relationships were not cast in concrete, but by current standards the changes which did occur seem trivial.

Concession bargaining hit various industries, companies, and plants unequally, thus knocking old wage relationships helter-skelter. Some workers did much better than others. In 1982, wage increases at GE and Westinghouse were at close to "normal" levels. In 1983, 32 per cent of the workers covered by new contracts in manufacturing took pay cuts and another 24 per cent received no wage increase. On the other hand, the 44 per cent who did receive increases averaged 5.8 per cent, somewhat above the 3.8 price increase. Chrysler workers accepted earlier and bigger cuts than did those at GM and Ford. The new Master Freight agreement proved to be quite flexible, as many companies were given even bigger breaks than the contract provided. Bargaining in the airlines industry became totally disorganized; the packages negotiated with the various companies showed little common pattern. In the auto and steel industries, even relationships among plants were dislocated, as one plant and its union bid against their counterparts for limited available work. Two-tier wages, with lower pay for new workers, introduced another element of instability.

Not only have wage relationships been disturbed, but bargaining itself has become more decentralized. Industry-wide bargaining is but a shell in trucking, while in the auto industry and elsewhere many key wage decisions are made at the plant level.

How permanent will these changes be? The auto and steel contracts provide that most wage give backs will be restored automatically at the end of the contract. Chrysler workers have already gained back much of what they lost. "Restore and more" will likely be the story in the 1984 Ford and GM negotiations. On the other hand, it is hard to imagine that wages in airlines, meatpacking, and trucking will be restored to their pre-1980 relationships in the near or intermediate future. Company ability to pay is partially replacing coercive comparisons as the basis for setting wages. "Putting together the broken pieces of pattern bargaining" in these industries "will be an enormous and possibly impossible task" (Kassalow, 1983, p. 372).

Historically, the Auto and Steel Workers were the innovators in American industrial relations, especially regarding fringe benefits (Kassalow, 1983). It is difficult to predict what union will take the lead, now that these giants are sorely wounded.

Fringes and Job Security

Concession bargaining has cut back some fringes, especially paid time off. Coinciding with federal efforts to curb run-away health costs in governmental programs, a few pioneering contracts provide for joint union-management medical cost containment efforts. In some instances, two-and even three-tier pension systems have been negotiated, with newly hired employees receiving less liberal benefits than oldtimers.

As a quid pro quo for reduced wages and fringes, unions have sought guarantees of job security, in effect to negotiate the number of jobs as well as their pay rate. These efforts have been only moderately successful, however. Unions have won some expanded job protection measures—direct measures, such as expanded SUB's and the Auto Workers' Guaranteed Income Stream—and indirect measures, such as restrictions on subcontracting and outsourcing.

On balance, the long run effect of concession bargaining may be to provide slightly more certain jobs and slightly less certain earnings (especially as some of these are now tied to profit sharing). It is still somewhat dubious whether much Japanese-style lifetime employment can be provided in industries traditionally subject to cyclical and seasonal unemployment.

Work Rules and Quality of Work Life

Relaxation of work rules has been a major management objective. Work-rule bargaining has occurred largely on a plant-by-plant basis, with management success differing from plant to plant. Union resistance has often been fierce, since such rules constitute an important source of job control, protecting workers from the arbitrary exercise of management's power. Where management has been successful, it has won broader job classifications, shorter rest breaks, and greater freedom to move workers from one job to another. There is reason to believe that changes of this sort will be more permanent than changes in wages. After all, wages get changed in almost every negotiation; the same is not true for work rules.

In exchange for job control via work rules, some companies have offered job control via quality-of-worklife (QWL) programs. Such programs were introduced into the automobile industry on an experimental basis in the mid-seventies. Under concession bargaining they have expanded considerably and have taken a variety of forms: quality circles, joint productivity committees, and autonomous work groups, among others. Regardless of their form, they are open-ended in nature and controversial. In principle, they are designed to elicit joint decision making in matters of joint interest to workers and management. Some observers expect them to liberate workers' untapped abilities and restore dignity to work; others see them as means for increasing productivity and thus restoring the company's competitive edge; finally, certain cynics argue that they are merely instruments for orchestrating shop-floor give backs and speedups. Certainly, by permitting flexible work arrangements, QWL may further erode the common rule.

Research is needed which attempts to link the conditions under which QWL is conducted to the outcomes that are realized. It is already reasonably clear that QWL has gone beyond the talking shops (what the British call "tea and toilet committees") prevalent in World Wars I and II. There are union and management leaders who are seriously committed to making QWL work. In some instances a highly participative shop-floor relationship has developed that is considerably less autocratic than the management system and less rule-oriented and adversarial than the collective bargaining model. To the extent that QWL has developed a constituency among shop-floor leaders who enjoy the added power that effective QWL provides, the new committees are likely to be more lasting than their predecessors. As frequently occurs in the Scanlon Plan and other workers' participation plans (Strauss, 1982), rivalry may develop between QWL activists and the traditional union leadership.

Worker Participation in Management and Profit Sharing

Ten years ago U.S. union leaders dismissed out of hand the possibility of being involved in anything like German codetermination. Today they are more ambivalent. While QWL in principle offers the opportunity for workers to participate in making shop-floor decisions, similar (but probably weaker) opportunities have opened up for the union at the company level. Union representatives already sit on the boards of a small number of companies, such as Chrysler, Eastern Airlines, and the Oakland *Tribune* (California). Numerous contracts give the union access to previously secret company data. A variety of agreements provide that the union will be consulted or at least informed before key investment and employment decisions are made. Unions which once sought to slow down the pace of technological change have come to demand (but rarely win) promises of increased investment in return for their own givebacks.

Many of management's concessions were intended merely as symbolic gestures to make union concessions politically palatable to the membership. Particularly for a company facing bankruptcy, symbolic power was the cheapest, if not the only, quid pro quo available. In principle, these management concessions have increased union influence and blurred the dividing line between management prerogatives and the union's scope of bargaining. In practice it is too soon to say how significant they will be. Experiences will doubtless differ from one company to another. For example, the role of the union members on the company board of directors remains to be worked out. Union leaders are divided and uncertain over the extent to which they should take responsibility for making difficult production and investment decisions, some of which may involve layoffs.

Profit sharing and worker stock ownership plans are on the increase, with some firms being 100 per cent employee owned. Often, such stock is held in trust, preventing workers from voting their ownership. Overall, few workers have the skill or interest to take on managerial responsibilities anyway.

Of course, there are exceptions. Many pilots are small businessmen in their spare time. It is not impossible that at Eastern Airlines, where employees will soon own 25 per cent of the stock, the pilots may wish to take over the company. In any event, these entanglements may place conventional relationships under severe strain. Witness the worker-owned Rath Packing Company, where the former local president of the union local, now company president, asked the bankruptcy court to void the union contract.

On balance, few unions have shown much desire to share management's responsibilities. There has been little interest in trading economic gains for institutional power. On the other hand, increased institutional power, once attained, is unlikely to be returned. For example, once unions obtain access to a stream of company financial information, it may be hard to turn off the spigot.

A Weakening of Adversarial Relationships?

Some observers predict the end of adversarial relationships and the beginning of a new era in which labor and management will work together for common goals. Generalization is difficult. Concession bargaining occurred after 30 years of "mature collective bargaining." In some instances management's demands have worsened relationships; in others they have improved.[11]

What of the future? For cooperation to survive, three conditions are required. First, both sides must expect it to lead to a payoff. Secondly, effective mechanisms must be developed for consultation. Third, there must be a measure of trust. (Trust, of course, influences the expectation of future payoff.) As long as survival is at stake, the payoff is clear. Once the immediate emergency passes—as it has in autos—this motivation for cooperation may become less pressing. As for consultative mechanisms, we know very little as to what works best. However, it is clear that much of the trust that existed was quickly squandered.

Aside from the tangible agreement represented by concession bargaining, there was often an unwritten and even unspoken agreement that both parties would turn over a new leaf, i.e., that they would start trusting each other. As Ford's director of industrial relations put it, attitudes began changing "from *we* vs. *they* to *us*; from adversarial to converging; from rigidity to flexibility; and from partisan to common interest" (Slaughter, 1983, p. 54). Indeed, for a while in some companies a spirit prevailed akin to that in Britain after the Dunkirk disaster of 1940. According to reports, when Chrysler's fortunes were their lowest, President Lee Iacocca was cheered by workers as he toured the assembly lines. Unfortunately, a Dunkirk spirit is pretty fragile. Management frequently blew its chances. An implicit understanding in most concession bargaining was that there would be "equality of sacrifice." In numerous cases, however, management violated this expectation by such acts as raising managerial salaries shortly after workers accepted substantial pay cuts or by breaking implicit understandings not to shut down plants. Too often management insensitivity to workers' feelings (and good public relations) did much to dissipate early goodwill. Expectations were too high, and some workers felt betrayed.

Management's goal was usually clear—to lower costs and increase flexibility. If it could win this through cooperation, fine. If not, it was prepared to be tough. Recognizing both management's plight and the weakness of their strike weapon, most unions opted for cooperation. From this experience only a few parties learned how to get along better. Thus, the earthquake brought major and probably fairly permanent changes in power relationships; changes in attitudinal relationships may be less lasting.

CONCLUSION

Unions and collective bargaining are not likely to fade away, but for the intermediate-run management is likely to be the prime mover. Among the major questions for the future will be the extent to which management will seek to implement the various versions of human resources policies, not just in the 80 per cent of the workforce that is nonunion, but in the less-than-20 per cent that is union.

During the post-earthquake period some familiar landmark's may appear quite different. Just as the St. Helen's eruption provided a bonanza for biologists studying plant succession, so the next few years should provide numerous opportunities for scholars interested in how collective bargaining adapts to and facilitates change.

Barring the emergence of incomes and industrial policies, collective bargaining is likely to be somewhat more decentralized than it was until recently. Wage patterns may become weaker and much of the action may shift to the plant and shop-floor levels. Hopefully, there will be a resurgence of plant and shop-level research, at least some of it involving case studies which seek to capture the full complexity of the interacting developments.

Many questions present themselves. How have contract concessions affected the general environment in the plant? Under what circumstances have recent developments led to higher productivity, better understanding, and generally improved morale—and under what circumstances have they led to smoldering resentment and a desire to get back at management as soon as possible? What differences do QWL programs make in the day-to-day interactions on the shop floor? How are workers reacting to broad-banded job classifications and the general loosening of work rules? Have any unions or managements been successful in taking advantage of the Dunkirk spirit which some negotiations engendered? What will be the impact, if any, of greater union access to hitherto secret management information?

On a broader level, other questions loom. In their efforts to win concessions, management tried a variety of persuasive techniques. These ranged from the fairly participative and educational, as perhaps at Ford and some airlines, to the extremely hard-ball, as at Greyhound and Continental. Each approach worked well in some circumstances and poorly in others. Which? Where? How? (A study confined to airlines would be fascinating.) Quantitative scholars may wish to develop equations predicting the extent to which concessions were made in various industries, companies, and plants. My guess is that such equations will explain only a small part of the variance, especially at the plant level, unless some allowance is made for such factors as the personalities on both sides, the history of their relationships, the bargaining techniques that they used, and the long-run philosophy of the particular companies and unions involved. A local in one spot may quickly ratify concessions that another local, ten miles away, may overwhelmingly reject, even though the two locals may deal with the same company and be subject to roughly equal economic pressures.

Research on union impact has become a major industry. Will pre-1980 equations still predict post-1983 impacts? Will it be enough to add a pre- and post-concession variable or will totally new equations be required? Will union impact decline and by how much? And for the intrepid researcher let me suggest a project examining whether, from a union point of view, concessions were really necessary.

There is much to study. This time of change in U.S. industrial relations is as much a challenge for scholars as it is for practitioners.

ENDNOTES

1. This paper came out of a conference on "The Future of Industrial Relations," convened by the Institute of Industrial Relations at Berkeley, October 8–9, 1982. My paper also draws heavily on unpublished papers by members of the MIT research project on "U.S. Industrial Relations in Transition." Let me thank Ralph Bergman, David Bowen, and Lloyd Ulman for helpful comments.

2. Management could have been tougher yet. Even Greyhound allowed its bus drivers' union to survive (though it sold its Armour division to a company which is seeking to operate it nonunion). I suspect that were management so inclined it could eliminate unionism in public utilities and telephones. Under present circumstances, a six-month strike might well crush both the Steel and Auto Workers. Management would be hurt but at least GM would survive.

3. Katz (1983, p. 11) reports that "in the airline industry five out of twenty-three vice presidents of industrial relations were fired in 1982 alone."

4. As of this writing, practically every major business school in the country is seeking to strengthen its offerings and to recruit new faculty for this area. Harvard is attempting to integrate Human Resources Management and Industrial Relations into a single course.

5. The field's increased status can be plotted by the change in typical titles over the years: from welfare secretary to employment manager to personnel director to industrial relations vice president to human resources vice president (and even senior vice president). According to one study (Wall Street Journal, 1983, p. 1), personnel workers receive "at least 30% higher pay . . . if a company uses the trendy 'human resources' title."

6. Personnel administrators received the highest salary increases of 13 professional, administrative, and technical support occupations surveyed during three of the five years, 1977–1982. (U.S. Bureau of Labor Statistics, 1983).

7. To some extent this means the introduction into private business of the "civil service" IR model postulated by Garbarino.

8. Dickens and Leonard estimate that, had these factors continued at their 1955 rates, private-sector union density would still be about 35 per cent, as it was in 1950.

9. Their estimate is based on the assumption that employment will increase by an average of 2.5 per cent annually. Freeman (1983) postulates that "If unions continue to win just 0.3% of the workforce in NLRB elections . . . the steady-state share of the workforce that will be organized will fall to a bare 10% of the nonagricultural workforce."

10. On the other hand, the relative decline in well unionized industries may bottom out. According to a recent prediction (Personik, 1983), the percentage of employed workers in the highly organized mining, manufacturing, construction, transportation, and public utility industries which fell steadily, from 38 in 1959 to 30.3 in 1982, may increase slightly, to 30.5 in 1995.

11. Concession bargaining will likely make union political life more turbulent. Concessions hit various groups within the union unequally, even though most agreements were carefully crafted to win a majority vote. Regardless, since union officers make an easy scapegoat for member frustration, we are likely to see considerable officer turnover.

REFERENCES

Derber, Milton. "Are We in a New Stage?" *Proceedings* of the Thirty-Fifth Annual Meeting of the Industrial Relations Research Association. Madison, WI: 1983, pp. 1–10.

Dickens, William and Jonathan Leonard. "Accounting for the Decline in the Union Movement," unpublished manuscript, Berkeley, 1983.

Farber, Henry. "The Extent of Unionization in the United States: Historical Trends and Prospects for the Future." Paper prepared for the M.I.T. Conference on Industrial Relations in Transition, 1983.

Freeman, Richard. "Why are Unions Fairing Poorly in NLRB Representation Elections?" Paper prepared for the M.I.T. Conference on Industrial Relations in Transition, 1983.

Foulkes, Fred K. *Personnel Policies in Large Nonunion Companies.* Englewood Cliffs, NJ: Prentice-Hall, 1980.

Kassalow, Everett M. "Concession Bargaining—Something Old, But Also Something Quite New," *Proceedings* of the Thirty-Fifth Annual Meeting of the Industrial Relations Research Association, Madison, WI: 1983, pp. 372–382.

Katz, Harry. "Collective Bargaining in the 1982 Bargaining Rounds." Paper prepared for the M.I.T. Conference on Industrial Relations in Transition, 1983.

Kochan, Thomas and Peter Cappelli. "The Transformation of the Industrial Relations and Personnel Function." In Paul Osterman, ed., *Employment Policies in Large Firms.* Cambridge, MA: MIT Press, forthcoming.

Lipsett, Seymour Martin and William Schneider. *The Confidence Gap.* New York: Free Press, 1983.

Mitchell, Daniel J. B. "Is Union Wage Determination at a Turning Point?" *Proceedings* of the Thirty-Fifth Annual Meeting of the Industrial Relations Research Association. Madison, WI: 1983, pp. 354–361.

Personik, Valerie. "The Job Outlook Through 1995," *Monthly Labor Review*, CVI (November, 1983), 25–29.

Slaughter, Jane. *Concessions and How to Best Them.* Detroit, MI: Labor Notes, 1983.

U.S. Bureau of Labor Statistics. *National Survey of Professional, Administrative, Technical, and Clerical Pay,* March 1982, Bulletin 2145. Washington, DC: GPO, 1982.

Voos, Paula. *Labor Unions Organizing Programs, 1954–77.* Unpublished Ph.D. thesis, Harvard University, 1982.

Wall Street Journal, April 27, 1983.

Alternative Explanations of Union Wage Concessions

Daniel J. B. Mitchell

Union pay concessions in the 1980s were sufficiently widespread to influence the aggregate indexes of wage change, even though union workers are a minority of the labor force. Pay concessions required unions to make a painful readjustment after a long period in the 1960s and 1970s in which a new contract typically meant improved pay and benefits. For management, concessions reflected a shift from a defensive to an offensive stance in collective bargaining.

What explains the concessions and their timing? Much has been written on this question.[1] But a clear consensus has not emerged. There has been a tendency to look to specific conditions affecting certain industrial sectors, rather than to search for a unifying theme which crosses sector lines. In particular, it is often argued that two forces—deregulation and foreign competition—have been the key determinants of the concession movement. Superficially, at least, these two forces seem to fit the facts in terms of timing as well as causality.

Accompanying the wage concessions was a decline in the number of workers represented by unions. Again the tendency has been to turn toward deregulation and foreign trade (especially the latter) as an explanation for this loss. Perhaps—so the argument goes—the decline is the result of a corresponding decline in the employment levels of unionized industries brought about by these exogenous changes in the economic climate.

Deregulation was a legislative and judicial event which opened up competition in previously insulated sectors in the late 1970s and early 1980s. Foreign trade competition intensified in the early 1980s when the U.S. dollar appreciated substantially relative to currencies of other countries. Obviously, for certain industries—airlines in the case of deregulation, steel in the case of foreign trade—the story of wage concessions and union employment trends could not be told without reference to these influences. But in many other cases, the explanation is more general.

Examination of data on concession contracts presented below reveals that many such agreements do not fit the deregulation/foreign trade story. Data on the number of unionized workers by industry also do not support a simple deregulation/foreign trade explanation. Of the two forces, deregulation will be seen to have had the greater impact—although for a limited number of industries. A third factor, namely, wage developments in the union sector in the decade and a half preceding the concession movement, is a better candidate for a unifying theme. These earlier wage developments are essential to an understanding of both the concession movement and the union membership losses.

DEREGULATION AND FOREIGN TRADE

Deregulation is primarily a phenomenon of transportation and communications. Airlines, trucking firms, and railroads had long operated in an environment of government regulation of price setting and entry.[2] Legislative changes in the late 1970s opened up transportation to price cutting and new entry. Similar developments occurred in communications, although the mechanism was principally a court decision breaking up the Bell system.[3] With a shift to a competitive environment, wage increases could no longer be passed along to consumers without severe product market consequences. Indeed, cost control (including labor costs) became a key element of success in holding on to, or expanding, market share.

Foreign competition has always been present for much of the manufacturing and mining sectors of the U.S. economy on the import and/or export side. During the late 1970s, however, dollar depreciation—combined with a long-term trend toward higher real wages in other industrialized countries—made U.S. goods especially competitive on international markets. Indeed, measured in dollars, foreign wage costs in several European countries substantially exceeded U.S. levels by the late 1970s.[4] In this advantageous environment, U.S. wage levels could be increased without loss of market share to foreign competitors.

But in the early 1980s, a substantial appreciation of the dollar reversed the U.S. competitive situation.[5] Foreign wage levels, when translated into American dollars, fell dramatically for many key currencies. The U.S. labor cost advantage quickly became a competitive disadvantage on world markets.

THE DISTRIBUTION OF CONCESSIONS

A data file of union wage settlements is maintained on a biweekly basis by the Bureau of National Affairs, Inc. This file began to pick up significant union wage concessions—defined from this point on as settlements providing for a basic wage freeze or cut in the first year of the contract—in 1981, when 3% of the contracts reported fell into the concession category.[6] Thereafter, the proportion rose to 12% in 1982, 28% in 1983, and then began to taper off to 27% in 1984 and 25% in 1985. The BNA data can be classified by industry and assigned to the deregulated, foreign trade, and

Table 1
Union Contracts and Concession Characteristics by Sector

	Sector			
	Deregulated	*Foreign Trade*	*Other*	*Total*
Union Contract Distribution, 1981–85:				
All contracts	4%	43%	53%	100%
Concession contracts	5%	37%	58%	100%
Concession Severity Measures, 1981–85:				
Wage decreases as percent of concessions	32%	11%	26%	21%
Concession severity index	3.2	2.5	3.1	2.9
Incidence of 2-tier wage plans*	10%	10%	19%	13%
Incidence of fixed bonus plans*	7%	23%	16%	16%
Wage Flexibility Indicators in Concession Contracts, 1981–85:				
Mean contract duration (months)	27	33	27 (32*)	29
Incidence of profit sharing*	23%	5%	7%	7%

**Excludes the construction industry.*

"other" sectors.[7] Table 1 shows the summary results of this classification for the period 1981–1985.

The deregulation sector accounted for only 4% of the union contracts negotiated 1981–85. But about 5% of the concession agreements fell into this sector. Thus, there was some overrepresentation of concession contracts in the deregulated sector, although the absolute number of such contracts was small. Forty-three percent of all union contracts in the BNA survey fell into the foreign trade sector. By that standard, the foreign trade sector was *under*represented among union wage concessions. More than half of all union contracts and union wage concessions fell into the "other" sector which was not subject to the direct impact of deregulation and foreign trade.

Concession Severity

Union wage concessions can be classified by their degree of severity. The most severe concessions were those which resulted in absolute cuts in the nominal wage. If deregulation and foreign trade were the main causes of concessions, it might be expected that wage cuts would be most common in those sectors. As shown on Table 1, for the deregulated sector, this prediction "works"; almost a third of concessions in that sector involved wage cuts. But in the much larger foreign trade sector, only 11% of the concessions made were cuts. Wage cuts in the "other" sector fell into an intermediate range of about one-fourth of all concessions.

There are other aspects of wage concession severity which are not captured by looking only at wage cuts. Some union concession contracts contained cost-of-living adjustment clauses (COLAs) which provided for wage increases if the Consumer Price Index rose. Concession agreements sometimes limited the operation of these clauses to permit less money for a given price increase than the unchecked COLA formula would otherwise have provided. Thus, there were really levels of concessions. By increasing severity these levels are:

- wage freezes but with unlimited COLA,
- wages freezes but with limited COLA,
- wages freezes with no COLA, and
- wage cuts.

Table 1 provides an index of concession severity based on these levels of severity, weighting each type of concession respectively, on a scale of 1 to 4.

As can be readily seen, the foreign trade sector again emerges as featuring the mildest average level of concession severity. The index reported on Table 1 suggests that the deregulated sector and the "other" sector had about the same level of concession severity. As before, these data do not neatly fit into an across-the-board deregulation/foreign trade explanation of the concession movement. The explanation works for deregulation, but not for foreign trade.

Two-Tier Pay Plans

Two-tier pay plans have become a prominent feature of collective bargaining. In 1985, for example, 11% of all nonconstruction contracts included a two-tier pay feature. Two-tier plans were especially common in concession agreements; 45% of all two-tier plans (excluding construction) involved basic wage settlements of zero or less in 1985.[8] Under a two-tier plan, the wage schedule is lowered for new hires, while existing workers remain on the standard scale. In effect, two-tier plans represent a compromise wage cut, since the average wage will fall as new workers are hired, even though existing workers avoid a pay reduction.[9]

The incidence of two-tier plans in concession contracts in the deregulated sector is somewhat below the all-sector average. However, since wage cuts were more frequent in the deregulated sector than elsewhere, the lower incidence of two-tier arrangements is not surprising. If the basic wage is cut for all workers, there is no need for a compromise wage cut affecting only new hires. The severity of the basic wage concession lessens pressure for two tiers.

In the case of the foreign trade sector, however—where basic wage cuts were rare—this explanation does not apply. Despite what might seem to be *stronger* pressure for a compromise two-tier pay cut in the foreign trade sector, their incidence is no greater than in the deregulated industries. Part of the reason for the reduced incidence of two-tier pay plans in the foreign trade sector is employment stagnation or shrinkage; a wage cut applicable to new hires has no effect if there are no new hires. Nevertheless, the lower than average frequency of two-tier plans in the foreign trade sector reinforces the impression from the data presented earlier: the overall level of concession severity is consistently lower in that sector than elsewhere.

Two-tier pay plans were most frequently negotiated in the "other" sector, where the deregulation/foreign trade story does not apply. Within that sector, they were common in retail foodstores, an industry characterized by relatively high employee turnover. This turnover ensures that with a two-tier plan, average wages will quickly be reduced as workers hired after the plan is adopted become a larger and larger fraction of the workforce. In the "other" sector, not only was concession severity—as measured above—high, but adoption of two-tier plans reinforced that severity.

Fixed-Bonus Plans

By the mid-1980s, fixed-bonus pay plans came to be even more commonplace for union workers than two-tier plans. Such plans substitute a specified, lump-sum annual bonus, say $1000, for some or all of a basic wage increase. In 1985, for example, over a third of all workers under major union settlements in the private nonconstruction sector were covered by a fixed-bonus pay plan.[10]

Although fixed bonuses substitute for wage increases, they do provide added income to workers. This feature is important to workers who would otherwise be subject to a basic wage freeze. Indeed, in the first year of the contract, there is little difference between a bonus and a pay increase; a worker receiving a 3% bonus in the first year in lieu of a 3% wage hike will receive the dollar equivalent of the wage hike. It is only in subsequent years that the lack of wage compounding produces reduced income.[11]

Viewed in this way, fixed-bonus plans can be seen to be "sweeteners" which lessen the impact of a given wage concession. And as Table 1 shows, these sweeteners have been most commonly included in the foreign trade sector where the concession severity is least, and where concession frequency is lowest. The data on bonus plans suggest that the foreign trade sector has shown the least reaction on the wage side to the forces creating pressure for concessions. Those concessions which did occur were partially "offset" by fixed bonus payments.

Wage Flexibility Arrangements

Since the late 1940s, collective bargaining agreements have typically been of multiyear duration. During the life of the contract, wage increases are periodically provided, either specifically or under a COLA clause. Employers usually preferred the multiyear feature, since it reduced the frequency of negotiations and, hence, the frequency of exposure to potential strikes.[12] But multiyear contracts had a downside; they locked in a series of guaranteed wage adjustments which might prove difficult for the employer to provide if business conditions unexpectedly deteriorated. In effect, workers (at least those senior enough to be insulated from layoffs) were given income security while the employer assumed added risk.

Employers might have been able to shift some of this risk back to employees, had multiyear contracts provided for wage increases which were contingent on business conditions. There are such contingent compensation arrangements, with profit sharing being the most common. Under profit sharing, a deterioration in business conditions (and, therefore, profits) results in a reduced profit-sharing bonus to workers, thus lowering the employer's labor cost outlay.[13] But until the 1980s, profit sharing was extremely rare in the union sector. Unions and their members did not want to assume the risk of a variable income contingent on employer circumstance.

Contract duration and the incidence of profit sharing can thus be used as an index of the degree to which a potential for wage flexibility was introduced into concession agreements. In a period of changing product market conditions—and particularly during an era such as the first half of the 1980s when the risk of a strike was very low—having a short duration contract avoided locking the employer into a long-term commitment to compensation improvements. Similarly, introducing profit sharing into concession agreements allowed variations in employer "ability to pay" to be reflected directly in labor costs.

In keeping with earlier findings that unions in the deregulated sector were prone to make large sacrifices during the concession movement, Table 1 shows that deregulated concessions were accompanied by shorter-than-average contract durations. Concession contracts in the deregulated sector were considerably shorter than those in the foreign trade sector. In the "other" sector, mean duration fell to the level of the deregulated sector, but only because of a sharp drop in the average length of construction concession contracts (to an average of 24 months). Excluding construction, contract duration in the "other" sector showed little impact on the concession movement.

With regard to profit sharing, it is necessary to exclude construction from the comparisons, since the casual nature of the worker-employer attachment in that industry precludes such a pay system. Again, the deregulated sector shows the greatest impact of the concession movement by exhibiting the highest propensity of the three sectors to adopt profit sharing. It is true that the largest number of union workers (as opposed to contracts) with profit sharing is in the foreign trade sector, due to two concessions negotiated in 1982 at General Motors and Ford. But profit sharing has not spread widely to other unionized firms in that sector.

Conclusions on Concessions and Severity

Available data suggest that the deregulation/foreign trade explanation for concessions is, at best, half right (on the deregulation side) and incomplete. Unions in the deregulated sector (chiefly in airlines) made the most far-reaching concessions according to the various indicators reviewed above. In contrast, unions in the foreign trade sector had a lower propensity to make concessions and made the least severe concessions of the three sectors considered. Finally, many concessions occurred in industries outside the deregulation and foreign trade sectors, such as construction and retail foodstores.

THE EROSION OF UNION REPRESENTATION

During the 1980s, the number of union-represented workers declined substantially. In the private, major union sector, union employment declined by 2.4 million from 1979 to 1985, according to the U.S. Bureau of Labor Statistics.[14] Yet, for the economy as a whole, employment of production and nonsupervisory workers rose by over 5 million during the same period. Thus, unionization of the workforce was eroding in both a relative and absolute sense.

As in the case of wage concessions, an obvious—but superficial—explanation of the erosion of unionization is that deregulation and foreign trade adversely affected employment in those industries in which unionized workers were most numerous. But again, a straightforward sectoral story is not supported by the empirical evidence. If unions had simply retained the proportion of production and nonsupervisory workers they represented in 1979 on a detailed industry basis, during the period of erosion (1979-85) they would have lost only about one sixth of the 2.4 million workers who actually disappeared from coverage by major union agreements.[15] Employment shifts in particular industries do not come close to explaining the union erosion phenomenon.

Erosion occurs when either (a) nonunion firms take a growing share of the product market or (b) previously unionized firms open nonunion facilities, convert to nonunion status, or subcontract work to nonunion enterprises. It is easy to cite anecdotal examples of both types of erosion.[16] But the critical factor in both cases is a competitive edge accruing to, or at least perceived to accrue to, nonunion firms and facilities.

Many studies indicate that the union wage premium rose during the general inflation which afflicted the U.S. economy from the late 1960s until the early 1980s.[17] Precise explanations for this tendency vary. COLA clauses (which are rare among nonunion employers) geared union wage increases to increases in the Consumer Price Index during a period when, for a variety of reasons, the index overstated both actual inflation and the nominal increase of employer "ability to pay." Also, a slowdown in the rate of U.S. productivity growth invalidated the assumption of a 3% annual improvement factor in real wages that had characterized union bargaining for many years. Whatever its cause, the widening union/nonunion wage premium created an incentive to substitute nonunion for union workers.

But the wage story of concessions is more complex than a simple widening of the union/nonunion pay premium. Although it is not possible to be precise, it appears that union wages for private sector production and nonsupervisory workers rose at about 8% per annum during the 1970s, and that nonunion wages for that group rose about 7% per year.[19] Some of this differential—not all—is explained by relative slippage of the union wage premium in the mid-1960s, when unanticipated price inflation caught union negotiators by surprise. However, the subsequent wage catch-up period produced a relative increase in union-related costs, since it was characterized by a wave of strikes and other forms of industrial unrest.

From the employer perspective, then, there was first a marked deterioration in the labor relations climate (compared with the tranquil early 1960s) and later a direct increase in relative union wages. Existing employers, if they could, initiated policies which expanded their nonunion operations relative to their (usually older) union plants. New entrants undertook union avoidance policies.

In the deregulated sector, the nonunion alternative was not readily available until deregulation became effective. The shock of deregulation was obvious and irreversible. Table 1 suggests that unions in that sector recognized the inevitable and made sweeping concessions to preserve jobs. As a result, the erosion rate for union jobs in the deregulated sector is the lowest of the three sectors shown. In airlines, in particular, major union employment did not decline during 1979–85, although some erosion was reported due to nonunion employment expansion.

For the foreign trade sector, the shock of dollar appreciation was obvious. But it was not clearly irreversible. Indeed, as the dollar rose, there were steady predictions—including repeated hints from the President's Council of Economic Advisors—that it would eventually decline. Uncertainty over the course of the U.S. dollar, and the tendency of the dollar issue to obscure the domestic union/nonunion wage problem, may have contributed to the relatively low concession propensity and low concession severity in the foreign trade sector. On the other hand, the fact that competitors from abroad were taking market share would have held down the rate of unexplained domestic erosion of union jobs, since the loss of jobs was to foreigners more than to American nonunion sources.

Finally, in the "other" sector, there was no obvious shock to trigger concessions, other than the general economic slump of 1979–82 and its aftermath. Concessions were made, as Table 1 shows. But the potential for erosion was greater than in the foreign trade sector since there were no foreign suppliers to compete with domestic, nonunion sources. Thus, the erosion rate was highest in the "other" sector, with the loss concentrated in construction and retail foodstores.

Table 2 divides industries into those with above-average and below-average concession rates.[20] The table clearly shows that the distribution of union wage concessions among the deregulated, foreign trade, and "other" sectors is about the same for industries most prone, and least prone, to concessions. Examining industries by concession propensity, therefore, rather than dividing them among the three sectors, is more likely to provide evidence of underlying cause.

It is, unfortunately, not possible to obtain data on union versus nonunion wage adjustments prior to the concession movement for industries with high and low concession propensities. However, Table 2 indicates that the concession-prone sector

Table 2
Characteristics of Industries by Concession Propensity

	Most Concession Prone	*Least Concession Prone*	*All Industries*
Distribution of Concession Contracts, 1981–85:			
Deregulated	5%	6%	5%
Foreign trade	36%	40%	37%
Other	59%	55%	58%
Total	100%	100%	100%
Distribution of Union Employment, 1979:			
Workers covered by major union agreements	72%	28%	100%
Major unionization rate*	20%	10%	15%
Percentage Loss of Unionized Workers, 1979–85:			
"Explained" by change in industry employment pattern†	6%	4%	5%
"Unexplained" erosion rate	26%	6%	21%
Total	32%	11%	26%

**Workers covered by major union agreements as percent of production and nonsupervisory workers.*

†Based on production and nonsupervisory employment.

Note: Details need not sum to totals due to rounding.

had the larger concentration of union workers and higher rates of unionization. This tendency suggests the possibility that union/nonunion wage differentials were more likely to have risen in the concession-prone sector (or have risen more) than in other industries, during the pre-concession period.[21]

Concession-prone industries experienced a sharper decline in major union employment during 1979–85 than others (−32% versus −11%). But this employment shrinkage by itself does not explain their greater concession propensity. Table 2 shows that had unions merely hung on to their 1979 unionization rates on a detailed industry basis during 1979–85, union job loss rates would have been about the same in two sectors (−6% versus −4%). The bulk of the difference is in the "unexplained" erosion factor (−26% versus −6%).

The most reasonable interpretation of these data is that industries which were most prone to exhibit high rates of concession behavior in the 1980s were those whose wages had become most out of line with the nonunion alternative during the 1970s and before. Unions made concessions when faced with heavy job losses. But those losses themselves were largely reflections of prior movements of relative wage levels (and related industrial relations developments). The losses reflected deregulation, foreign trade, and general economic trends to a lesser degree.

CONCLUSIONS

Two lessons emerge from the preceding examination of the union wage concession movement. First, although each industry—indeed, each company and union—has a unique tale to tell, it is easy to become lost in details and miss the most general casual factor behind the concessions. That factor is relative labor costs. Deregulation, foreign trade, the economic slump of the early 1980s, and changes in the political and legal climate certainly played a role in the timing of the concessions. But even before the 1980s, union job erosion was in evidence. At some point, pressures would have developed to stop the widening of the union/nonunion wage gap, even if the special conditions of the 1980s had not arrived when they did.

Second, there are important lessons for unions and firms in the union sector, and especially for unions. Collective bargaining is a complex process. At the time of negotiations, short-term interests of both parties focus on avoiding or minimizing short-run costs, namely the costs of a strike. Until the 1980s, it was easy to lose sight of what impact a given settlement—or a string of such settlements—would eventually have on job security, and, as a result, on the fate of the union as an institution.

After World War II, a sharp distinction developed between the appropriate roles for unions and management. Firms were to worry about such matters as market shares, product development, and investments. The union role was simply to demand improved compensation and conditions, and leave it to management to deal with the resulting costs. But when faced with concessions and declining membership in the 1980s, unions began to take on a more "managerial" perspective with regard to such matters. Despite charges from dissident members that such an approach is a "sell out" of the rank and file, this shift in emphasis is a healthy sign, and—in fact—the only path to union survival as a significant voice at the workplace and in society.

REFERENCES

1. The airline wage concessions have become the topic of recent articles. See Peter Cappelli, "Competitive Pressures and Labor Relations in the Airline Industry," *Industrial Relations*, Vol. 24 (Fall 1985): 316–338; and Herbert R. Northrup, "The New Employee-Relations Climate in Airlines," *Industrial and Labor Relations Review*, Vol. 36 (January 1983): 167–181, See also Peter Cappelli, "Plant-Level Concession Bargaining," *Industrial and Labor Relations Review*, Vol. 39 (October 1985): 90–104 on tires and meatpacking. For general studies of concession bargaining, see Robert J. Flanagan, "Wage Concessions and Long-Term Union Wage Flexibility," *Brookings Papers on Economic Activity* 1 (1984): 183–216; Audrey Freeman, "A Fundamental Change in Wage Bargaining," *Challenge*, Vol. 25 (July/August 1982): 14–17; Audrey Freedman and William E. Fulmer, "Last Rites for Pattern Bargaining," *Harvard Business Review*, Vol. 60 (March/April 1982): 30–48; Robert S. Gay, "Union Contract Concessions and Their Implications for Union Wage Determination," working paper series, Board of Governors of the Federal Reserve

System, August 1984; Daniel J. B. Mitchell, "Recent Union Wage Concessions," *Brookings Papers on Economic Activity* 1 (1982): 165–201; Daniel J. B. Mitchell, "The 1982 Union Wage Concessions: A Turning Point for Collective Bargaining?" *California Management Review*, Vol. 25 (Summer 1983): 78–92; Daniel J. B. Mitchell, "Shifting Norms in Wage Determination," *Brookings Papers on Economic Activity* 2 (1985): 575–599. Two symposia on concession bargaining appear in Barbara D. Dennis, ed., *Proceedings of the Thirty-Fifth Annual Meeting*, Industrial Relations Research Association, December 28–30, 1982 (Madison, WI: IRRA, 1983). An early review of concession developments appears in Bureau of National Affairs, Inc., *Labor Relations in an Economic Recession: Job Losses and Concession Bargaining*, special report supplement to the Daily Labor Report of July 16, 1982 (Washington, D.C.: BNA, 1982). The concession movement has provoked opposition in the labor movement. See Jane Slaughter, *Concessions and How to Beat Them* (Detroit, MI: Labor Education and Research Project, 1983).

2. Airlines were deregulated by the Airline Deregulation Act of 1978, trucking firms by the Motor Carrier Act of 1980, and railroads by the Staggers Rail Act of 1980.

3. Under a consent decree in 1982, settling an antitrust suit against AT&T, the company divested its local operating companies, which remain heavily unionized in their core telephone service. However, they have been able to enter new fields of communications, often using nonunion personnel. Various regulatory relaxations have permitted new entry into the long distance field. While AT&T's long distance service is unionized, most of the new entrants (Western Union is an exception) are nonunion.

4. For data, see Daniel J. B. Mitchell, "International Convergence with U.S. Wage Levels," in Barbara D. Dennis, ed., *Proceedings of the Thirty-Sixth Annual Meeting*, Industrial Relations Research Association, December 28–30, 1983 (Madison, WI: IRRA, 1984), pp. 247–255.

5. For example, the trade-weighted U.S. dollar exchange rate index prepared by the Federal Reserve peaked at 177% of its 1979 value (173% in "real" terms, i.e., adjusted for changes in international consumer prices) during the first quarter of 1985. After the first quarter, the dollar declined rapidly. See *Economic Report of the President* (Washington, D.C.: GPO, 1986), p. 373.

6. Data and listings of settlements appear regularly in the *Daily Labor Report*. There is no precise and rigorous definition of a wage concession that can be given. However, settlements of zero or less are easy to identify and seem to capture most settlements that can be reasonably termed concessions. Obviously, settlements where the concession element involved nonwage items such as workrules will be omitted from such a classification if wage concessions were not also included. There is also a problem of using the zero or less criterion in a period of varying price inflation. A wage freeze during a period when consumer prices (CPI-U) were rising at a rate of 8.9% (as in 1981) meant a larger real wage loss than a freeze during 1985 when the price inflation rate was only 3.8%. Note, however, that the vast bulk of concession settlements in the survey discussed occurred during 1982–85, when the price inflation rate was quite steady, falling in a range of 3.8% to 4.0%, on a December to December basis.

7. Settlements were grouped by industry using the employer and union names as a guide. In some cases, where industry determination could not be made from the information provided in the *Daily Labor Report* listings, the employer was telephoned and asked for industry information. The following sectoral definitions were applied:

The deregulated sector was defined as airlines, trucking and warehousing, railroads, and communications.

The foreign trade sector was defined as metals, motor vehicles (and parts), rubber, machinery (electrical and nonelectrical), aerospace, paper and lumber, textiles, food manufacturing (except meatpacking), instruments, chemicals, furniture, cement, mining, transportation equipment (except motor vehicles and aerospace), brick-stone-clay (except cement), glass, leather, petroleum, ordnance, apparel, tobacco, and shipping.

The "other" sector was defined as construction, retail foodstores (including associated wholesale operations), meatpacking, printing and publishing, health care, business services, unions (as employers), entertainment, hotels and restaurants, education, finance-insurance-real estate, retail trade (except foodstore), utilities, and public transit.

Obviously, these definitions cannot be precisely drawn since some settlements cross industry lines and since the influence of forces such as foreign trade can also cross industry designations. However, the results presented below would not be sensitive to reasonable redefinitions.

8. See Bureau of National Affairs, Inc., *1986 Briefing Sessions on Employee Relations: Workbook* (Washington, D.C.: BNA, 1986), pp. 49–51.

9. Discussion of two-tier plans can be found in Sanford M. Jacoby and Daniel J. B. Mitchell, "Management Attitudes Toward Two-Tier Pay Plans: An Analysis," *Journal of Labor Research*, Vol. 7 (Summer 1986): 221–237. The data on Table 1 with regard to two-tier plans, fixed-bonus plans, and profit-sharing plans exclude the construction industry where such plans are not generally feasible due to the casual nature of the worker-employer attachment.

10. This estimate assumes that the fixed-bonus plans were not found in the construction industry for reasons cited in footnote 9. See Bureau of National Affairs (1986), op. cit., p. 20.

11. A worker earning $10 per hour prior to negotiations and receiving three 3% annual bonuses in a 3-year contract will receive the equivalent of $10.30 per hour each year. The same worker receiving three annual 3% wage hikes would receive $10.30 the first year, $10.61 the second year, and $10.93 the third year.

12. See Sanford M. Jacoby and Daniel J. B. Mitchell, "Employer Preferences for Long-Term Contracts," *Journal of Labor Research*, Vol. 5 (Summer 1984): 215–228.

13. Other arguments have recently been put forward for profit sharing. Weitzman argues that employers with profit sharing have an incentive to hire more workers and to hold on to them during recessions. Martin L. Weitzman, *The Share Economy: Conquering Stagflation* (Cambridge, MA: Harvard University Press, 1984).

14. The data on major union coverage were drawn from David J. Schlein, Phyllis I. Brown, and Fehmida Sleemi, "Collective Bargaining During 1986: Pressures to Curb Costs Remain," *Monthly Labor Review*, Vol. 109 (January 1986): 16–3; and from Edward Wasilewski, "Scheduled Wage Increases and Escalator Provisions in 1980," *Monthly Labor Review*, Vol. 103 (January 1980): 9–13.

15. The following industry classifications were used for the calculation: meatpacking, airlines, construction, metals, trucking, transportation equipment, retail and wholesale trade, paper and lumber, machinery, apparel, rubber, maritime, leather, miscellaneous manufacturing, tobacco, transit, food except meatpacking, mining, furniture, instruments, finance-insurance-real estate, communications, services, textiles, railroads, printing and publishing, stone-clay-glass, petroleum, chemicals, and utilities.

16. The entry of the nonunion Michelin firm into the U.S. tire market is an example of type (a) erosion. The conversion of Continental Airlines to effective nonunion status in 1983 after declaration of bankruptcy is an example of type (b).

17. Richard B. Freeman and James L. Medoff, *What Do Unions Do?* (New York, NY: Basic Books, 1984), pp. 52–54; Mitchell (1982), op. cit., pp. 166–167.

18. The housing component of the index included current mortgage interest rates which were generally rising during the 1970s. In addition, "imported" inflation from oil price hikes tended to reduce the ability to pay of U.S. employers (other than energy producers) rather than increase it.

19. The average rate of wage increase under private, major union contracts during the 1970s was 8.2%. Average hourly earnings rose at a 7.4% annual rate. The union weight in average hourly earnings is not known, but a reasonable estimate of the union payroll as a percentage of the total payroll included in the average hourly earnings estimates would probably fall in the 30% range. (Recall that average hourly earnings exclude groups of workers with low unionization rates such as supervisors). If the union wage increase is discounted to 8% (since union settlements for smaller units may not have kept pace with those for larger units), the nonunion rate of wage would have been 6.8% to 7.1%, depending on the weights assumed.

20. The simple average of industry concession rates for the period 1981–85 was about 14%. Industries with concession rates above 14% were designated as most concession prone on Table 2, and others as least concession prone. The industries used were those listed in footnote 7. In addition, two industries—transportation services and pipelines—which were not used for the sectoral classifications, but which appear in some tables in the *Daily Labor Report*, were placed in the least concession prone group.

21. Unfortunately, there are no detailed time series for union wage rates by industry. It is well known that in the pre-concession period, the overall union/nonunion wage differential was rising. This tendency can also be confirmed within such broad classifications as manufacturing and construction. Presumably, unions are stronger in industries in which they represent a higher fraction of the workforce. There is a correlation between the proportion of the workforce organized and the rate of average (union plus nonunion) wage increase across industries. For example, if the industries listed in footnote 15 are ranked by unionization rates (of the type shown on Table 2), those with above average unionization exhibited a simple average rate of increase of compensation per full-time equivalent employee of 8.2% per annum during 1965–80. Those with below-average unionization (including transportation services and pipelines, for which unionization data were not available) exhibited a 7.2% increase. However, it is impossible from these data to separate out the impact of higher unionization on the rate of union wage increase from the impact of the higher weight union wages have in average wage increases in highly unionized industries.

Can Unions Pick Up the Pieces?

Daniel C. Stone, Jr.

Put yourself in the shoes of a typical union president in 1986. You are facing high turnover costs, reduced cash flow, threats to a lifestyle that you have become accustomed to and no real room for growth in the "traditional companies." Meantime, a larger number of unorganized people are now questioning their traditional values. You must organize to survive—and you know it.

It doesn't matter that the union is the Teamsters and the potential members are global funds transfer administrators, or that the union is the meatcutters and the workers are nurses, or that the union is the United Steelworkers and the employees are computer programmers. When you are hungry, you don't discriminate between food sources.

Now put yourself back in the position of the human resources executive. You are running a real risk if your company has been lulled into complacency by "signs" of waning union power. Unions may be down, but they are not out. It is time to face that risk and respond to it. How? By recognizing that all too often corporate culture lacks basic consideration for employee self-esteem, and that organizers seize on that lack to raise interest in unions.

ORGANIZERS FOCUS ON ISSUES OF SELF-ESTEEM

The target groups of union organizers should be obvious; they are white collar and professional workers, especially in health care, financial planning, and insurance positions. These are employees who, by the very nature of their responsibilities, education and training, are likely to value more than a paycheck.

The issues, all tied to employee self-esteem, are also clear: dignity and respect, participation or a voice in management, comparable worth, and a grievance procedure that works. These certainly aren't new issues, but they have taken on new significance in an age in which big business is perceived as swallowing individuals.

What, specifically, are the deficiencies that unions look for? They are best considered broadly.

Respect

Respect is crucial for many of today's professionals. Whether or not they feel they have management's respect can affect every aspect of their productivity and relations because it influences what they hear, say, and, in some cases, see. Such perceptions also affect interpersonal communication. Is it open and honest or defensive?

Unions look for situations in which authority figures—such as supervisors—frequently treat employees in a manner that undermines their self-esteem and sense of respect. Overly and unnecessarily critical managers are one example.

Situations in which employees are not really listened to are also noted by unions. Today's employees need to feel that their concerns are taken seriously, that their ideas are considered carefully and that managers make an effort to solve problems.

A Voice in Management

These issues are also part of the need to be included in the management process, to have a voice in the company. Union organizers look for situations in which employees feel they have no control over the issues that concern them. Obviously, promises of union strength and the potential of overriding management decisions can be very appealing in such situations.

Comparable Worth

Since the majority of jobs in the most frequently targeted industries are usually occupied by females, the issue of comparable worth has recently become an issue for union organizers. For this discussion, comparable worth is defined as equal pay for men and women in jobs that are either of equal worth to an employing organization or intrinsically of equal worth to society. The difficulties arise, however, when attempting to identify jobs of equal worth or to quantify the difference between jobs of unequal worth. The method used most frequently, if not totally, is job evaluation.

The four elements identified in the Equal Pay Act for job evaluation are skill, responsibility, effort, and working conditions. Note that there is no objective, mathematical way to compare the skills, the responsibility, the effort, or the working conditions of two different jobs. In actual wage and salary administration, this problem is "solved" by deferring to the supply and demand laws of the marketplace.

Unions have been arguing that wages paid for job classifications heavily populated by women are the product of sex discrimination and have suggested that there is an objective way of determining how much a job is worth to an employee institution. Whether equity is really the issue, however, has been the topic of some debate. The American Federation of State, County, and Municipal Employees union, perhaps the prime supporter of comparable worth, for example, has never suggested that any wages be adjusted downward.

Grievance Procedures

Finally, unions look for organizations in which there is no actual grievance or concern procedure. Unions have focused upon the fact that although many organizations have a published "open door" policy, in reality, they do not have an effective system that permits an employee to discuss a grievance or concern.

UNION ORGANIZERS HAVE TESTED EFFECTIVE TECHNIQUES

Union organizers employ a wide range of tactics when acting on these four areas of concern, but four of the most effective methods include: 1) concerted activity; 2) sales parties; 3) the disgruntled worker interview; and 4) telephone polling.

Concerted Activity

Section 7 of the National Labor Relations Act protects concerted activity, defined as any *group action* by employees designed to advance legitimate common interests dealing with wage hours and working conditions. Therefore, consider an activity protected if, from any of the circumstances, a reasonable inference can be drawn that the persons involved believe they have a grievance and decided among themselves to discuss it with management.

Two employees or several can act "in concert" for purposes of "mutual aid or protection." Examples of issues protected by concerted activity are: dissatisfaction with the system of job evaluation, desire for a pay raise, wanting to transfer to another shift, crowded working space, inadequate staffing, unsafe working conditions, unsanitary restrooms, and other employees smoking in the work area.

Employees can reduce their work pace, refuse to work or walk away from the job; however, they must explain the reasons for such behavior.

Unions, recognizing that few first-line supervisors have ever heard of concerted activity, let alone how to deal with it, are directing employees to slow down or walk off the job in order to force supervisors into a direct confrontation. The supervisor will generally order the employee to come to his or her office to discuss the problem in private. When the employee refuses, the supervisor will then order him or her back to work. The employee rejects this as well, saying he or she will return to work only when the grievance is adjusted. The supervisor, totally exasperated at this point, suspends or discharges the employee for insubordination—exactly as planned by the union organizer.

The union then files an 8(a)(3) and 8(a)(1) charge—interference with the employee's Section

7 rights—that serves as the springboard for the union's campaign. The National Labor Relations Board will conduct a hearing and, in such cases, order the employer to reinstate the employee with full back-pay plus interest. In addition, the employer will have to post a notice for 60 days admitting it violated the employee's rights and stating it will not do so in the future.

The union takes full credit for saving the employee's job and then campaigns by saying all employees should be represented to make certain the employer does not violate any of the employees' rights. The employer is then hard-pressed to counter such campaign philosophy.

Once you determine the employees are engaging in protected concerted activity, you should do the following:

- Direct the employees to go home and return at a specific time to personally discuss the matter with you.
- If they refuse to go home, explain they have a legal right to do so.

However, you have the legal right to replace them, which means: 1) they will not be paid; 2) they will not participate in the facility's benefit programs; 3) they may not draw unemployment benefits; 4) they may not be entitled to return to work until their job or a similar job opening occurs; 5) they will be noted on all records as replaced employees.

Sales Parties

Another approach currently being used by unions is the retail sales party, at which the union organizer helps one or two employees sponsor a party at home, ostensibly to sell cosmetics, kitchen plastics or other merchandise. These employees are given points, which can be redeemed for valuable prizes, for getting their fellow employees to attend the meeting. Sometime during the evening the talk turns to "problems at work," and the host employee then introduces a "friend" who just happens to be visiting and who can help everyone with their frustrations. Literature and authorization cards are distributed. The organizer, assisted by the host employee, encourages people to sign the cards in order to be put on a mailing list to receive supplemental information, including their rights under the law. The host is awarded additional points for each signed authorization card turned in.

During the evening, certain informal, credible peer group leaders are quietly encouraged to stay after the general meeting for a private meeting. After the others leave, the union organizer establishes them as in-house organizing team leaders and sets up a competitive spirit by offering points to the team leaders who get the most employees to attend future sales parties and sign authorization cards.

Informal Interviews

Still another approach is for a professional union organizer to frequent the happy hour establishments near an office or facility in order to eavesdrop on the discussions about what goes on in a particular organization. The organizer then attempts to identify and befriend a disgruntled employee. At the right moment, the union organizer makes the pitch about what the employee can do to protect his or her rights, as well as make it a better place to work for other employees.

Through clever and thoughtful questioning, the organizer learns a great deal about the organization, such as the names of employees most likely to support a union, employees who feel they have been "stabbed" by the organization for whatever reason, supervisors who play favorites, and supervisors who have a low boiling point and who are apt to make a mistake that can be capitalized upon (concerted activity); pay and benefit structures; organizational structure; policies and procedures; and property line demarcations. This information is collated and forms the foundation of a union organizing drive.

Telephone Polling

Finally, unions employ the telephone polling method. In this approach, people receive a telephone call at home, usually between six and nine in the evening. The caller purports to be from a national polling organization and asks such questions as:

- How do you feel about your job?
- Does your supervisor play favorites in making work assignments?
- Does your supervisor make changes without informing you ahead of time?
- Does your supervisor treat you with respect and dignity while on the job?
- Is your supervisor the kind of person who will sit down with you to discuss any particular problems?
- Can you go over your supervisor's head to file a grievance?
- Does your supervisor seem to enjoy criticizing or disciplining?
- Does your supervisor reprimand people in front of others?
- Do you trust your supervisor?
- Does your supervisor forget to get back to you with information that you brought up?
- Is your supervisor unfair in evaluating you and tactless in telling you about it?

In another variation on this theme, the caller identifies him- or herself as a university graduate student who is gathering information for a thesis. Each person called is told that if he or she supplies the caller with his or her full name and home address, the survey results and a copy of the thesis will be sent. The person called later receives union literature and an authorization card by mail.

MANAGEMENT FREEDOM INVOLVES TWO SOLUTIONS

Once familiar with the issues and approaches unions are using to organize in a tight economic environment, and with some responses to those tactics, there are still two methods that supervisors should use to maintain management freedom. Remember, however, that these methods must be carefully designed to meet the needs and be compatible with your own organization. Canned programs seldom work and are rarely in the best interest of the organization.

Opinion Surveys

The first method is to establish a system to regularly and formally assess employee opinions. There are opinion surveys available that yield a profile in an easy-to-read categorized printout. Only if these surveys are well planned and conducted periodically do employees perceive that management is concerned about them. The survey process must also include a system of feedback (management response to complaints) and resolution of the problem or problems. If these two phases are missing from the process, the results will do more harm than good.

Training Programs

Freedom to manage can also be pursued by establishing a training and development program for all supervisory and management personnel. Such programs are necessary because the majority of supervisors were promoted to their positions on the basis of their technical abilities, rather than on their skill in managing others. There are, of course, few absolutes in supervision. Accordingly, the approach to supervisor development and team-building should encourage the participants to understand some basic principles, rather than memorize a list of what may be arbitrary dos and don'ts of supervision. Finally, any training and development program must be successful in transferring the lessons of the workshop or classroom to the job.

Many of these tactics seem obvious—and are. They are obvious to both management and the unions, and it is just as obvious to union organizers that all too often they are not used. Failing to consider the basics of human relations in establishing management styles often leaves organizations vulnerable to outside interests.

Employees, remember, never vote *for* a union; they vote *against* management.

Selected Issues in Union-Management Relations

John A. Fossum

THE UNION-ORGANIZING CAMPAIGN

The union-organizing campaign is one of the most bitter and volatile situations in union-managment relations. Employers face a situation in which they have the potential to lose substantial amounts of discretion in their management activities. Coupled with this loss is the realization that substantial proportions of their employees are expressing the belief that they would be better off represented by an outside organization in the formulation of personnel policies and practices. Within the employee group in which union representation is sought, substantial proportions of fellow employees may oppose organization. Because of these difficulties, substantial bodies of rules for organizing campaigns have emerged from statutory law and court and NLRB interpretations.

The right to organize or to refrain from union activity is guaranteed by law in Section 7 of the Labor Management Relations Act, which delineates these guarantees as follows:

> *Employees shall have the right to self-organization, to form, join, or assist labor organizations, to bargain collectively through representatives of their own choosing, and to engage in other concerted activities for the purpose of collective bargaining or their mutual aid or protection, and shall also have the right to refrain from any or all of such activities except to the extent that such right may be affected by an agreement requiring membership in a labor organization as a condition of employment as authorized in Section 8(a)(3).*

The organizing campaign can begin within the organization through the efforts of present employees or as the result of a union deciding it would like to organize a group of employees. If it is an internal organizing campaign, the leaders usually try to obtain outside assistance from a union experienced in organizing similar employees. Union-sponsored organizing campaigns seek employees favoring unions since a majority must ultimately favor the union for recognition to be gained. Further, substantial efficiencies of access to employees accrue for employee organizers as compared to union organizers. Union organizers can be barred from the target organization's property (*NLRB* v. *Babcock and Wilcox, Inc.*, 351 U.S. 105 (1956)), while employee organizers can solicit workers in nonwork areas during nonworking time (*Republic Aviation Corp.* v. *NLRB*, 324 U.S. 793 (1945)).

Normally, it is to the union's advantage to conceal organizing activity until a majority of employees desire representation. This blunts management's attempts to convince employees to remain nonunion. However, it may, in some instances, be to the union's advantage to make the company aware of organizing, particularly if it is likely the company would take action against employees based on their membership. This would help to establish the employer's conduct as motivated by an anti-union animus. While laws do protect individuals in their Section 7 rights, the length of time necessary and the small penalties associated with a NLRB unfair labor practice finding are such that they might inspire rather than inhibit unfair practices (Greer and Martin, 1978).

The union will more likely be successful in organizing where the employees have relatively similar goals and perceive management behavior somewhat similarly. There should also be a relatively stable workforce so that employees have a

Adapted from *Personnel Management,* © 1982, Allyn and Bacon, Inc.

likelihood of sharing common experiences and the organizing of newly hired workers does not become a continual overhead burden to the union. A number of procedural issues are important to the union and to the management in the course of organizing. Many of these involve the NLRB. A schematic diagram of the process is contained in Figure 1.

Authorization Card Campaign

As employees are contacted about union organizing, they are asked to sign cards authorizing the union to act as their collective bargaining representative. The union collects these to make a later recognition demand on the employer or to show sufficient interest to obtain a NLRB representation

Figure 1
Sequence of Organizing Events

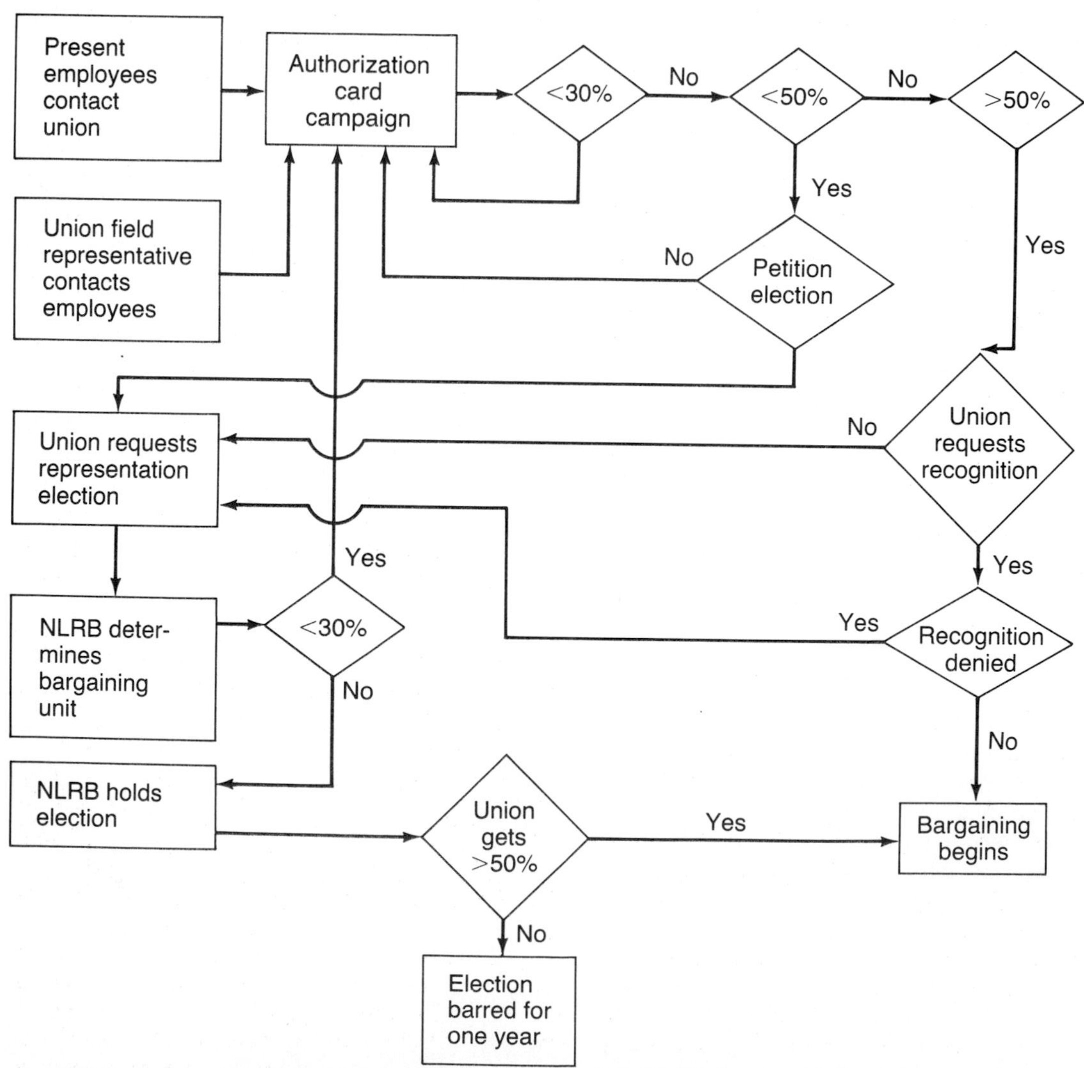

Source: J.A. Fossum, Labor Relations: Development, Structure, Process *(Dallas: Business Publications, 1985), p. 120.*

election. If the union fails to collect at least 30 percent of those it desires to bargain for, the NLRB will not order an election. When the union collects more than 50 percent it can directly demand recognition by showing proof to the organization. Most employers refuse, arguing that employees were coerced to sign or may have changed their minds, so an election is demanded.

Election Petitions

If an employer denies recognition and if more than 30 percent have signed cards, the NLRB will order an election to determine whether or not the employees in the defined unit desire representation. If a majority does, the union is certified as the representative of all employees (whether or not they favored the union individually). This certification bars a further representation election for a one-year period to allow the winner to implement its position and/or negotiate for a collective bargaining agreement.

Bargaining Units

The bargaining unit is initially the group of employees the union seeks to represent. It could consist of all nonmanagerial employees in a single establishment, or a group of employees in a single occupation in one or more establishments of the same organization, or a variety of combinations within these boundaries as long as it is within a single corporate entity. If the employer agrees with the union that this is the appropriate unit for a bargaining election and there are not statutory roadblocks to that unit, the NLRB holds a consent election.

The company might disagree that the union's proposed unit is appropriate. It may recommend a smaller or larger unit. Both desire units where chances of an election victory are greater or where the consequences of the election will be least aversive. For example, a company may urge the NLRB to find a plant-wide unit appropriate where the union has organized in only one occupational area. The union may seek to represent a unit containing employees critical to continued operation to gain more leverage in bargaining. There are a variety of criteria the NLRB uses to determine an appropriate unit (Abodeely, 1971) with the employees' community of interests being a prime criterion. Once the NLRB decides the unit, an election is ordered.

Campaign Strategy and Tactics

One immediate benefit to the union resulting from an order for an election is that the company must furnish it with a list of employees in the proposed bargaining unit and their addresses (*Excelsior Underwear, Inc.*, 156 NLRB 1236 (1966)). The union can then contact employees directly during nonworking hours, where previously it may have had little knowledge about how to reach them. Union campaigns generally stress that the union will establish grievance systems to prevent employer unfairness, improve wage levels, and create an employee voice in wage and working conditions issues; that it is an organization of the employees, not of outsiders; that dues and requirements are reasonable; and that its record for obtaining gains elsewhere is proven (Getman, Goldberg, and Herman, 1976).

Management may attempt to counter union positions by holding meetings on company time to explain its position. Themes stressed by management include the position that improvements do not depend on unionization, present wages are as good as or better than union contracts, unions dues are costly, the union is an outsider in the organization, costly strikes may follow if the union wins, and that the employer has treated employees fairly in the past (Getman, Goldberg, and Herman, 1976).

While both sides devote considerable energy to the post-petition campaign, there is little evidence that the voters are markedly swayed. Getman, Goldberg, and Herman (1976) found that pre-petition intentions predicted voting with a high degree of accuracy. The usual erosion of union strength as the result of a campaign seldom exceeded 5 percent.

The NLRB has imposed several rules and general policy statements for the conduct of representation elections. Elections are to take place under "laboratory conditions" to allow the employee to make a considered, uncoerced choice. To insure this, the employer is forbidden to interrogate employees about their preferences for or against a union and the employer can make no promise of benefit to take place if the union loses. Both unions and employers are forbidden to direct campaign statements to employees within twenty-four hours of the election since the opponent may not have time for a rebuttal (*Peerless Plywood Co.*, 197 NLRB 427 (1953)). Finally, neither the union nor management may make a statement containing a substantial untruth (*Hollywood Ceramics Co.*, 140 NLRB 221 (1962), reversed by *Shopping Kart Food Market, Inc.* 228 NLRB 190 (1977), which was reversed by *General Knit of California, Inc.*, 239 NLRB No. 101 (1978); Truesdale, 1979).

The Getman, Goldberg, and Herman (1976) study raised substantial evidence questioning the necessity of the Hollywood Ceramics rule. They found that voters in representation elections did not pay much attention to the campaign. On the average, about fifty-five issues were raised by contending unions and managements, but electors could remember only about five. Threats involving possible losses of jobs if the union won seemed to have a counter effect since those who remembered this most clearly as an issue were those most often voting for the union. Attendance at campaign meetings increased issue familiarity but had little impact on voting.

Types of Representation Elections

There is a variety of types of NLRB representation elections. A group of employees may seek a representation election (RC), an employer may seek a vote to force an end to union efforts to win recognition by picketing (RM), a group of employees may seek to oust or decertify a presently representing union (RD), or a group of employees may desire to deauthorize a contractual union shop clause (UD). (Union shop clauses are a form of union security to be discussed later.)

Outcomes from Representation Elections

Recent results have generally shown that unions win slightly less than half of representation elections, and generally the larger the unit, the lower the likelihood of a union victory (NLRB, 1980). Besides the fact that many available larger units have already been organized, the sophistication and preparation of larger employees, the innate heterogeneity of employees in larger units, and the number of contacts that must be made to successfully organize inhibits union efforts in large establishments.

In an examination of all NLRB certification elections conducted during the six years beginning in 1973 and ending 1978, Sandver (1980) found that union election success was generally related to smaller unit sizes, consented rather than contested bargaining unit definitions, and less than establishment-sized bargaining units. North-south regional differences in election outcomes were minimal.

While decertification elections are far less common than RC and RM cases, the reasons for decertification have been closely scrutinized recently. A variety of union characteristics has been shown to be related to decertification. The size of the local was inversely related to probability of decertification (Dworkin and Extejt, 1979; Chafetz and Fraser, 1979), and internal local characteristics, such as a lack of leadership, low member involvement, and a change in the member composition within the unit, were related to decertification (Anderson, Busman, and O'Reilly, 1979; Anderson, O'Reilly, and Busman, 1980). The larger the size of the chartering national union, the more likely decertification occurred (Dworkin and Extejt, 1979). This may mean that large nationals are not perceived as adequately servicing small locals. Many craft unions have permanent local union business agents who handle internal servicing, while large industrials more often rely on traveling representatives. The results also suggest a strong interest among members in the union fulfilling its agency function.

Some decertification elections are begun to replace an existing union with another. Anderson, Busman, and O'Reilly (1979) found that this is frequently successful. In very few situations are both contending unions rejected with employees opting for no representation. Overall, the characteristics of unions and their internal affairs appear to be much more important to the outcomes of decertification elections than do the campaign tactics themselves.

Post-Election Aspects

If the company or union has objections to the fairness of the conduct of the campaign, each might file unfair labor practice charges with the NLRB. If the NLRB finds that the conduct disturbed the employees' free choice, then a new election would be ordered. In extreme cases where the NLRB finds that the company's conduct has permanently undermined a union's previously demonstrated authorization card majority, it may order the company to bargain with the union, as if it had won the election (*NLRB* v. *Gissel Packing Co.*, 395 U.S. 575 (1969)).

Where no objections are filed with the NLRB, considerable problems may still be encountered. Both parties have recently completed what is usually an acrimonious campaign. Management has lost its unilateral personnel decision-making power. It has implied to its employees that the union would not gain large concessions and that a strike was likely. The union has made several campaign promises and has suggested that bold, militant action will gain its ends. Neither party has negotiating experience at the local level and may easily misread the other's position.

For organized establishments, either after elections or when existing contracts are expiring, new collective bargaining agreements must be negotiated. The next section covers the bargaining issues, structures, and strategies and tactics used in contract negotiations and their impacts on contract terms.

IMPASSE RESOLUTION

The methods of impasse resolution to be discussed are those that involve more than a simple continuation in bargaining. By definition, an impasse requires something more than bargaining to break it. A variety of procedures can be used. Some are designed to put pressure, such as strikes or lockouts, on one's opponent. Others interject outside assistance at the request of the parties, such as mediation. Still others allow or require third party interventions, such as arbitration to determine and impose a solution.

Laws also have a major impact on the methods of impasse resolution that may be used. In the public sector particularly, certain modes are required or outlawed depending on the jurisdiction or occupation involved. Table 1 gives a general summary of the types of impasse resolutions and their general availability by employment sector.

Mediation

Mediation occurs when an outside neutral attempts to aid the parties in reaching a solution of their own after an impasse has occurred. The mediator usually meets separately with each side to gain an understanding of its position, its settlement range, and its perception of the other side's position. Where the impasse is the result of a breakdown in communications and a misassessment of the real settlement range, the mediator may suggest concession patterns. Where no overlapping settlement range exists, the mediator may inject information about other settlements or problems that will occur to one of the parties if the other insists on a position. Mediators intercede at the invitation of the parties (except in major cases where the President may summon the contenders to Washington for some "mediation"). As such, their roles last only so long as both perceive the activities as fair and effective (Wall, 1980).

Mediators are generally strong proponents of collective bargaining, many having been union or management advocates prior to their present roles (Simkin, 1971). Among mediators, effectiveness is seen as following from the establishment of friendliness and trust between the parties, with lesser emphases related to the apparent benefits of settlements or their own expertise (Berkowitz, Goldstein, and Indik, 1964). The parties ascribe success to the mediator's intellectual competence, the ability to structure the situation, and the abilities necessary to keep them at work (Landsberger, 1960).

Some evidence exists that mediation is more successful when the impasse is caused by a negotiation breakdown rather than an inability to meet demands, the impasse was not highly intense, the parties were motivated to settle, and the mediator was aggressive and experienced (Kochan and Jick, 1978).

From a performance standpoint, mediation is an interesting tripartite situation. Both union and management negotiators must satisfy the demands of their constituents. Mediated solutions may increase the credibility of settlements they had previously proposed, but were rejected by their

Table I
Impasse Resolution Procedures Available by Sector

	Employment Sector		
Procedure	*Private*	*State & Local*	*Federal*
Strike	Yes	No[a]	No
Lockout	Yes[b]	No	No
Mediation	Yes	Yes[c]	Yes[d]
Fact-finding	Yes[e]	Yes[e]	No
Arbitration			
No-constraints	Yes[f]	Yes[g]	No
Final offer	Yes[f]	Yes[g]	No
Closed offer	Yes[f]	No	No
Injunctions	Yes[i]	Yes[j]	Yes[j]

[a]Permitted by a few states for nonuniformed employees. Usually not available unless the employer refuses arbitration.

[b]Only when an impasse has been reached and the contract has expired.

[c]May be required by some states.

[d]Mandatory.

[e]If required by statute. In private sector only if a national emergency dispute has been determined under Taft-Hartley provisions.

[f]Only if mutually agreed to by parties in expiring contract or during negotiations.

[g]Depends on state law, usually for uniformed services.

[i]In national emergency disputes.

[j]Where strike is illegal.

constituents. For their part, mediators are judged by whether they are able to get the parties to agree on a new contract. These three forces, combined with the voluntarism of the process, enhance its utility for impasse resolution.

Federal Mediation and Conciliation Service. The Taft-Hartley Act requires that the FMCS be notified sixty days before contract expiration for those under its jurisdiction if they desire to modify the agreement, and again at thirty days if they have not reached a solution. Thus, the FMCS can keep abreast of potentially problem relationships.

In situations where problems continually recur, a new program has been devised to try to eliminate the cause of recurrent impasses—Relationships by Objectives. This is a program to bring the parties together after contract negotiations. Major parts of the process are to focus on and communicate organizational goals, and to explore methods for achieving consensus in bargaining (Hoyer, 1980; Richardson, 1977). There are components of attitudinal structuring involved both within and between parties. Integrative issues are frequently identified. The atmosphere of trust created in successful programs may stimulate bargaining attention to these issues. If trust is created, a movement from a conflict or containment-aggression mode to a cooperative mode should occur.

Arbitration

Except for the provisions of the Experimental Negotiating Agreement, there have been few uses of interest arbitration (decisions regarding what contract terms should be) in the private sector. In many public sector jurisdictions, particularly the uniformed service, arbitration of bargaining impasses is seen as a *quid pro quo* for agreeing not to strike. Prior to the expansion in interest arbitration, many jurisdictions used fact finding (cf., McKelvey, 1969). Here, an outside neutral examined the situation, cited various "facts" discovered about the dispute, and recommended a settlement. This tended to be helpful only prior to an impasse (Allen, 1968; Stern, 1966) and only where it assisted in intraorganizational bargaining.

The basis for arbitration is for the parties to agree on an outsider to hear their dispute, giving the arbitrator powers to decide the terms of a new contract. The terms decided by the arbitrator are frequently somewhere between those suggested by the bargaining process at impasse. It has been suggested that where parties have tried arbitration, its effect is narcotic (Wheeler, 1975). Several variants have been proposed and implemented to alleviate this situation.

Final-Offer Arbitration. Final-offer arbitration requires that both parties propose a settlement package at, or after, impasse. After hearing both sides, the arbitrator selects, without modification, the position of labor or management. Thus, arbitrators cannot split the differences between the two.

Some evidence exists to suggest that final-offer arbitration has reduced the reliance on third parties where it has been tried (Kochan, et al., 1979; Long and Feuille, 1974). Others have argued that the proposal submitted to the arbitrator after impasse may be a substantial modification of the impasse position in an attempt to get the arbitrator to see the reasonableness of the position (Stern, et al., 1975). Thus, the process is not "final offer" in the sense that it is a "mine or your" position as in impasse.

Some arbitrators also dislike final-offer selection as a method, particularly where the selection is on a package rather than an issue-by-issue basis. They feel the contract may contain a relatively poor settlement because one side's generally better proposal was rejected as a result of an extreme offer in one area that was considered unworkable. If arbitrators are allowed an issue-by-issue determination, final offer may essentially revert to a "split the difference" approach, by balancing numbers of issues rather than positions between issues.

To alleviate this problem, Wheeler (1977) has suggested a "closed-offer" approach, where arbitrators receive information only on what each party's original position was without any information on the bargaining progress to date. The parties thus run the risk that the arbitrator may give one party less than was previously offered, thereby increasing the motivation to bargain their own agreements.

Part of the problem in public sector negotiations relates to the fact that the bargainers are relatively inexperienced compared to the private sector, operate in situations where statutes and managements do not recognize strikes as legitimate bargaining tools regardless of the price of alternatives, and are open to all sorts of elected official intervention (Kochan, 1974).

In the private sector, the FMCS has reported a much higher proportional need for services during first negotiations as compared to subsequent contracts. As the party's bargaining expertise increases, and as legislatures gain increasing evidence that society has not collapsed as the result of *any* public sector strike to date, arbitration and other third party interventions should become less necessary. Unions also will probably use them less frequently, as the replacement of striking public employees is upheld by the courts (*Rockwell* v. *Board of Education*, Michigan Supreme Court, 89 LRRM 2017 (1975); *Certiorari* denied by U. S. Supreme Court, 92 LRRM 2818 (1976)) and their power to influence the public declines.

Regardless of how a contract is settled, there may be disputes during the contract that require resolution as well.

CONTRACT ADMINISTRATION AND RIGHTS ARBITRATION

During the duration of the agreement, disputes may arise regarding the interpretation or implementation of the contract. Virtually all contracts provide a mechanism for handling these disputes without the necessity of reverting to a strike. These grievance procedures usually have several steps available for resolving a problem. First, a union steward may present and negotiate a grievance with a supervisor. If unresolved, the steward or a negotiating committee member meets with an industrial relations department representative. The third step may be between the negotiating committee and the plant manager. A fourth step would involve a national union representative and a corporate industrial relations staff executive. And the fifth, if still unresolved, requires submission to an arbitrator who decides the parties' rights under the contract.

It should be noted that the Taft-Hartley Act also allows union members to directly present grievances to management, but individuals must allow the union to participate in their settlement since the outcome could be contrary to the union's interpretation of the contract or create an undesirable precedent from the union's standpoint.

Contract administration involves intraorganizational bargaining, as the requirements of operations may lead to granting a grievance other management personnel would prefer to avoid. Within the union, certain subgroups may have grievances handled more vigorously by the union because they are politically powerful (Kuhn, 1961).

There have been relatively few reported innovations in contract administration. Those that do exist usually aim to reduce the number of formal grievances filed, by attempting informal settlement at first step levels without writeup or the establishment of precedents (McKersie and Shropshire, 1962). It is difficult to determine whether this reduces the number of grievances, but it does restore the grievance procedure to its contractual base by allowing greater involvement of first-line supervision. It may also reduce the time necessary to process grievances by cutting to a fraction those that reach the formal level.

Expedited Arbitration

If management denies a grievance at the final step, the union may either abandon it or demand arbitration. When the latter occurs, the parties agree on an arbitrator and set a date for a hearing. The arbitrator hears the case with the parties offering evidence, calling witnesses, and cross-examining the opposing party's witnesses. Counsel for both sides may or may not be attorneys. After the hearing, the parties may submit post-hearing briefs and the arbitrator considers these, the evidence, and the contract in arriving at an award. While the process is generally well accepted by the parties and is viewed as a final decision subject to only the most limited court review (cf., Smith and Jones, 1965), critics have argued that the elapsed time necessary to finally receive an award from the filing of the grievance is far too long and the costs are too great. Zalusky (1976) estimated time from filing a grievance to receiving the award averaged 223 days with an average cost, shared equally by company and union, of $4,400 (1976 dollars).

Many cases are routine and may not involve major implications in cost to management or job loss for employees. To reduce costs and time delays, a new variant called *expedited arbitration* has been introduced. Typical cases heard in expedited situations might include discipline amounting to less than discharge, small alleged entitlements to overtime, and so forth. Lawyers are usually not used by the parties and awards are rendered quickly. Table 2 summarizes several currently implemented processes.

Problems in Representation

Two issues of major importance to unions and managements relate to the union's representation of bargaining unit members: *fair representation* and *adequate representation*. Since the union exclusively represents bargaining unit employees, it must scrupulously judge each case on its merits, not on union membership, union activity, or other non-contractual issues. The union may make its own judgment about whether or not to concede the grievance and whether or not to take it to arbitration even if it has merit. But it must do so conscientiously and consistently (cf., *Vaca* v. *Sipes*, 386 U. S. 171 (1967); Summers, 1977).

It is clear that unions have a duty to speedily process and adequately investigate grievances brought by their members (*Hines* v. *Anchor Motor*

Table 2
Expedited Arbitration Procedures

	Steelworkers—Basic Steel Industry	*American Arbitration Association Service*	*AIW Local 562 Rusco, Inc.*	*American Postal Workers—U.S. Postal Service*	*Mini-Arbitration Columbus, Ohio*
Source of arbitrators	Recent law school graduates and other sources	Special panel from AAA roster	FMCS roster	AAA, FMCS rosters	Its own "Joint Selection and Orientation Committee" from FMCS roster
Method of selecting	Preselected regional panels Administrator notifies in rotation	Appointed by AAA regional administrators	Preselected panel by rotating FMCS contacts	Appointed by AAA regional administrators	FMCS regional representative by rotation
Lawyers	No limitation, but understanding that lawyers will not be used	No limitation	No lawyers	No limitation but normally not used	No limitation
Transcript	No	No	No	No	May be used
Briefs	No	Permitted	No	No	May be used
Written description of issue	Last step grievance report	Joint submission permitted	No	Position paper	Grievance record expected
Time from request to hearing date	10 days	Approximately 3 days depending or arbitrator availability	10 days	Approximately 7 days depending or arbitrator availability	Not specified
Time of hearing to award	Bench decision or 48 hours	5 days	48 hours	Bench decision written award 48 hours	48 hours
Fees (plus expenses)	\$100/½ day \$150/day	\$100 filing fee Arbitrator's normal fee	\$100/½ day \$150/day	\$100 filing fee \$100 per case	\$100/½ day, 1 or 2 cases; \$150/full day, 1 or 2 cases; \$200/day, 3 or 4 cases

Source: J. Zalusky. "Arbitration: Updating a Vital Process," November 1976 AFL-CIO Federationist, *the official monthly magazine of the AFL-CIO.*

Freight, 424 U. S. 554 (1976)). But it is not as clear what a union's obligations are where any possible outcome will place one or more of the bargaining unit's members at an advantage relative to others. There was a recent Appeals Court case (*Smith* v. *Hussman Refrigerator Co.*, & *Local 13889, United Steelworkers of America* (1980)) in which the duty of fair representation went unfulfilled because a union took to arbitration a grievance in which senior workers were awarded jobs the company had given to those most qualified. The contract held seniority and ability would govern. The company opted for ability in its promotions, while the union championed rejected senior candidates. The court held that the union must provide advocacy for both groups since it was an exclusive agent for both.

What differences does fair representation make to an employer? It seems, essentially, an internal union problem. But the reason the employee grieved initially is that the management allegedly violated the contract. If the grievant is inadequately or unfairly represented, the relief from the allegedly violative action taken by management cannot be redressed. The employee may go to court and obtain relief against the company there (*Vaca* v. *Sipes*, supra). Thus, it is to the company's benefit to ensure that the union regularly discharge its representation obligations to bargaining unit members.

PERSPECTIVE

Problems in contract administration and arbitration have received considerable attention in the previous sections. Arbitration, in particular, has been one of the most widely incorporated and mutually satisfactory processes in U. S. collective bargaining. Dispute resolution in the public sector has evolved toward the private sector model, with the Civil Service Reform Act, Title VII, making arbitration the statutorily required resolution process where a union represents federal employees.

REFERENCES

Abodeely, J. E. (1971). *The NLRB and the appropriate bargaining unit* (Labor and Public Policy Series Report No. 3). Philadelphia: Industrial Research Unit, Wharton School of Finance and Commerce, University of Pennsylvania.

Allen, R. (1968). 1967 school disputes in Michigan. *Public employee organization and bargaining.* Washington: Bureau of National Affairs.

Anderson, J. C., Busman, G., & O'Reilly, C. A. (1979). What factors influence the outcome of union decertification elections? *Monthly Labor Review, 102,* 32–40.

Anderson, J. C., O'Reilly, C. A., & Busman, G. (1980). Union decertification in the U. S.: 1947–1977. *Industrial Relations, 19,* 100–107.

Berkowitz, M., Goldstein, B., & Indik, B. P. (1964). The state mediator: Background, self-image, and attitudes. *Industrial and Labor Relations Review, 17,* 257–275.

Certiorari denied by U.S. Supreme Court, 92 LRRM 2818 (1976).

Chafetz, I., & Fraser, C. R. P. (1979). Union decertification: An exploratory analysis. *Industrial Relations, 18,* 56–69.

Dworkin, J. B., & Extejt, M. M. (1979). Why workers decertify their unions: A preliminary investigation. *Proceedings of the Academy of Management,* Atlanta, GA.

Excelsior Underwear, Inc., 156 NLRB 1236 (1966).

Fossum, J. A. (1979). *Labor relations: Development, structure, process.* Dallas: Business Publications.

General Knit of California, Inc., 239 NLRB 101 (1978).

Getman, J. G., Goldberg, S. B., & Herman, J. B. (1976). *Union representation elections: Law and reality.* New York: Russell Sage.

Greer, C. R., & Martin, S. A. (1978). Calculative strategy during union organizing campaigns. *Sloan Management Review, 19,* 61–74.

Hines v. *Anchor Motor Freight,* 424 U.S. 554 (1976).

Hollywood Ceramics Co., 140 NLRB 221 (1962).

Hoyer, D. T. (1980). A program for conflict management: An exploratory approach. *Proceedings of the Industrial Relations Research Association.*

Kochan, T. A. (1974). A theory of multilateral collective bargaining in city governments. *Industrial and Labor Relations Review, 27,* 525–542.

Kochan, T. A., & Jick, T. (1978). A theory of the public sector mediation process. *Journal of Conflict Resolution, 23,* 209–240.

Kochan, T. A., Mironi, M., Ehrenberg, R. G., Baderschneider, J., & Jick, T. (1979). *Dispute resolution under factfinding and arbitration: An empirical analysis.* New York: American Arbitrators Association.

Landsberger, H. A. (1960). The behavior and personality of the labor mediator: The parties' perception of mediator behavior. *Personnel Psychology, 13,* 329–347.

Long, G., & Feuille, P. (1974). Final offer arbitration: "Sudden death" in Eugene. *Industrial and Labor Relations Review, 27,* 186–203.

McKelvey, J. T. (1969). Fact-finding in public employment disputes: Promise or illusion. *Industrial and Labor Relations Review, 22,* 528–543.

McKersie, R. B., & Shropshire, W. W. (1962). Avoiding written grievances: A successful program. *Journal of Business, 34,* 135–152.

National Labor Relations Board (1980). *Forty-fifth annual report of the National Labor Relations Board.* Washington: Government Printing Office.

NLRB v. *Babcock & Wilcox, Inc.,* 351 U.S. 105 (1956).

NLRB v. *Gissel Packing Co.,* 395 U.S. 575 (1969).

Peerless Plywood Co., 197 NLRB 247 (1953).

Republic Aviation Corp. v. *NLRB,* 324 U.S. 793 (1945).

Richardson, R. C. (1977). *Collective bargaining by objectives: A positive approach.* Englewood Cliffs, NJ: Prentice-Hall.

Rockwell v. *Board of Education,* Michigan Supreme Court, 89 LRRM 2017 (1975).

Sandver, M. H. (1980). *Regional differentials in outcomes in NLRB certification elections.* Paper presented at the annual meeting of the Academy of Management, Detroit.

Shopping Kart Food Market, Inc., 228 NLRB 190 (1977).

Simkin, W. E. (1971). *Mediation and the dynamics of collective bargaining.* Washington: Bureau of National Affairs.

Smith v. *Hussman Refrigerator Co. & Local 13889, United Steelworkers of America,* 619 F. 2d 1229 (1980).

Smith, R. A., & Jones, D. L. (1965). The Supreme Court and labor arbitration: The emerging federal law. *Michigan Law Review, 63,* 7.

Stern, J. L. (1966). The Wisconsin public employee fact-finding procedure. *Industrial and Labor Relations Review, 20,* 3–29.

Stern, J. L., Rehmus, C. M., Loewenberg, J. J., Kasper, H., & Dennis, B. D. (1975). *Final offer arbitration.* Lexington, MA: Heath.

Summers, C. W. (1977). The individual employee's rights under the collective bargaining agreement: What constitutes fair representation? In J. T. McKelvey (Ed.), *The duty of fair representation.* Ithaca, NY: New York State School of Industrial and Labor Relations, Cornell University.

Vaca v. *Sipes,* 386 U.S. 171 (1967).

Wall, J. A. (1980). *Mediation: A categorical analysis and a proposed framework for future research.* Paper presented at the annual meeting of the Academy of Management, Detroit.

Wheeler, H. N. (1977). Closed offer: Alternative to final offer selection. *Industrial Relations, 16,* 298–305.

Wheeler, H. N. (1975). Compulsory arbitration: A "narcotic" effect? *Industrial Relations, 14,* 117–120.

Zalusky, J. (1976). Arbitration: Updating a vital process. *American Federationist, 83,* 1–8.

CHAPTER 8

Productivity Improvement and Quality of Work Life

Productivity in work organizations became a prominent concern in this country when the annual rate of productivity increases in the United States, which had led the world for many years, fell below those of other industrialized nations, especially Japan and West Germany. In turn, a growing number of organizations in this country became interested in trying to determine what conditions of the work environment might contribute to their overall effectiveness. More recently, interventions or productivity improvement strategies have been examined in the continuing efforts to compare management practices in the United States with those of foreign competitors.

Perhaps this country's strongest response to the productivity problem, at least from a personnel and human resources management perspective, has been the emergence of the quality of work life (QWL) movement. The choice to pursue and create working conditions that are conducive to improved productivity has resulted in positive outcomes for some employees and organizations. Other efforts in this direction have failed. One factor that might help or impede an organization's quality of work life efforts is its corporate culture. The notion that organizations, like people, have different personalities or cultures is not new. But how these cultures might be assessed, strengthened, or changed for the development of the organization represents a fresh area of investigation for personnel management.

Physical and psychological components make up the work environment for employees and may result for some in excessive job stress, poor performance, and the breakdown of work and off-work social relationships. For still others, it may result in even more serious outcomes, such as alcoholism and drug abuse, a permanent handicap, or death. A major piece of federal legislation designed to remove or reduce such physical and psychological hazards is the Occupational Safety and Health Act (OSHA) of 1970. While opinions regarding the effectiveness of OSHA are mixed, it certainly has increased awareness of the importance of protecting employees. Federal legislation also seeks to prevent sexual harassment at the workplace.

While there is general awareness of the decline of U.S. productivity relative to other industrialized countries, some confusion remains as to how we define and measure productivity, the extent of the decline, what caused it, and how it might be reversed. Clearly, a better understanding of the productivity concept is needed, as is an analysis of possible strategies for achieving that goal. In this regard, a variety of interventions, which are grounded in the behavioral sciences and often included under the QWL rubric, have been proposed. A common theme, as in most QWL efforts, is that of employee involvement in the decision-making processes that affect them and the organization.

The first four articles in this chapter all deal with the issue of productivity. First, Hallett questions whether firms can increase productivity while also increasing quality, utilizing current definitions of these concepts, and suggests that by redefining productivity as a state of mind or a work ethic, new techniques, such as rewarding employees for innovation and greater production, will lead to higher quality. Simply by increasing the quality of their products, companies would sell more and productivity would increase. McFillen and Podsakoff, in the next article, focus on motivation as a way to increase productivity, identifying common mistakes managers make, and then present a plan to increase individual performance and overall productivity. Crosby focuses on twelve guidelines for creating a successful employee involvement program and the expected results. Scott, Markham, and Robers suggest financial incentives to motivate American workers and present contests as one way companies might reward productivity. A contest held at the Maid Bess Corporation illustrates their idea.

Among all QWL-type interventions in the United States, perhaps the most popular is quality circles (QCs). Yet, in contrast to the general success of QCs in Japan, those in the U.S. have often floundered or failed. In the next article, Ferris and Wagner give primary emphasis to the apparent assumptions underlying the use of QCs in the United States and Japan. While they question the adequacy of these assumptions, based on a review of the relevant literature, they point out that the societal context in which these assumptions exist and are played out in organizations may make the difference between the essentially positive effects of Japanese QCs and the mixed (positive, negative, unknown) effects of American QCs on organizational productivity goals. Carmel and Dolan address employee-right-to-know laws and what they mean to the employer and employee.

Beehr and Fenlason examine the problem of work-related stress. The authors define work stress, present a model that seeks to better explain it, and discuss approaches for dealing with it and its consequences for the individual and organization. They suggest ways managers can recognize and help manage stress.

Bradshaw analyzes an important concern for many organizations: sexual harassment. Because of the inherent difficulties in defining sexual harassment, the author utilizes a court case to establish background for this issue. He then summarizes the steps an employer can take to guard against sexual harassment claims. In the final article, Ramanathan describes the history of Employee Assistance Programs (EAP), illustrates how varied the services are, and explains the roles of an EAP professional and the costs and benefits a company faces when establishing an EAP. The author concludes by discussing the strengths of contemporary EAPs as well as their limitations.

Suggestions for Further Reading

Bullock, R. J., & Lawler, E. E., III. (1984). Gainsharing: A few questions and fewer answers. *Human Resource Management, 23,* 23–40.

Dickman, F., & Emener, W. G. (1982). Employee assistance programs: Basic concepts, attributes, and an evaluation. *Personnel Administrator, 27,* 55–62.

Faley, R. H. (1982). Sexual harassment: Critical review of legal cases with general principles and preventive measures. *Personnel Psychology, 35,* 583–600.

Gadon, H. (1984). Making sense of quality of work life programs. *Business Horizons, 27,* 42–46.

Goodale, J. A. (1987). Employee involvement sparks diagnostic conferences. *Personnel Journal, 66,* 79–80, 82–87.

Jackson, S. E., & Schuler, R. S. (1983). Preventing employee burnout. *Personnel, 60,* 58–68.

Nadler, D. A. & Lawler, E. E., III. (1983). Quality of work life: Perspectives and directions. *Organizational Dynamics, 11,* 20–30.

Rice, B. (1981). Can companies kill? *Psychology Today, 15,* 78–85.

Tuttle, T. C. (1983). Organizational productivity: A challenge for psychologists. *American Psychologist, 38,* 479–486.

Wiley, J. W., & Campbell, B. H. (1986–87, Winter). Assessing the organization to identify productivity improvement opportunities. *National Productivity Review,* pp. 7–19.

Productivity and Quality: The Never-Ending Quest

Jeffrey J. Hallett

By now, American managers must be getting tired of the call for increased productivity and higher levels of performance. After all, we have been there before—several times. I remember productivity well—in the early '70s I spent six years with what evolved into the National Center for Productivity and Quality of Working Life. During that time, the best of our business, academic and labor minds turned to an examination of American productivity performance and the reasons for its decline after nearly 40 years of sustained high-level improvements.

The results of this attention generated a lot of papers and talks and concern with governmental interference in the mechanisms of business and enterprise. Too many rules, regulations and requirements from the alphabet soup of EPA, OSHA, DOE, FDA, CPSC, DOL, etc. Restrictive work rules within the industrial unions were also pinpointed as barriers to increased productivity, and the work habits of what was then described as "the me generation" didn't help either.

Times have changed. We seem to have come a long way in removing overly burdensome federal regulations; the unions have been losing clout, making both work rule and compensation concessions; and the "me generation" has matured into a more dependable group of employees. Unfortunately, our productivity has not yet made great leaps forward. And without improved productivity in the use of our resources, improvements in our standard of living in an increasingly competitive world will not come. Therefore, the call to productivity is being heard again.

The whole "quality" issue is also here to stay. Higher levels of productivity cannot come at the expense of quality. Not only do we have to find a way of generating more output with fewer resources, that has to be done while improving the overall quality of our products and services. The challenge is clear. The answers, however, are less so.

WHAT ABOUT ENTREPRENEURSHIP AND INNOVATION?

Some managers will justifiably demand a clarification of priorities before proceeding. After all, the last three years have been focused on a totally different thrust: innovation and entrepreneurship. Our managerial and organizational methods have been too rigid. We have been missing the new opportunities and holding on to dying products and markets too long. Entrepreneurs and "intrapreneurs" are the new heroes!

There appears to be some confusion, if not a direct contradiction, in the simultaneous call for more innovation and entrepreneurship and productivity and quality improvements. How can we set people loose from tightly organized and defined systems to stimulate creativity and innovation while generating more output of higher quality at the same time? The total message seems to say: "To effectively compete, the people in this organization have to produce more goods and services with fewer total resources while introducing innovations that allow us to distinguish ourselves in a rapidly changing marketplace. And, in order to ensure that we have loyal and enthusiastic employees, we will honor new needs for educational leave, maternity leave and time off to compete in marathons, while paying above-standard wages plus performance bonuses."

For human resource professionals, the expectations will be high—to say the least.

PRODUCTIVITY REDEFINED

To move ahead with some degree of control over this situation requires that we redefine the key terms. Productivity, for instance, must be carefully reviewed for its real meaning in today's environment. While this may appear unnecessary, it may turn out to be the key to the entire issue.

In its most basic and traditional form, productivity is a measure of output divided by input. Productivity, however, only has value as a relative term; that is, it is the change in productivity that's important. We make progress when the measure of output divided by input improves. So far, this defines a simple enough procedure for obtaining productivity improvements: either increase output or reduce input, and the ratio improves.

The fun begins and the arguments get heated when you attempt to define the correct output and input numbers for the formula. The literature is filled with deep economic, statistical and philosophical arguments presented by engineers, MBAs, economists and others who have tried to solve this measurement problem. All of this work, however, has failed to solve the measurement issue.

To illustrate the problem we will produce the ubiquitous widget, which today is used as a component in automobile engines. Last year we produced 100,000 widgets, which we sold for $1 each. To produce the widgets we spent a total of $90,000. This year we want to improve productivity by 10 percent. Simple enough. We simply make needed adjustments to produce 110,000 widgets while still only spending $90,000. Our productivity ratio goes from 1.11 to 1.22; there is our 10 percent improvement. So far so good. (For those who want only to measure labor productivity, we will assume the labor hours were the same in both years.)

Unfortunately, we then discover that there was a concurrent increase in the productivity of all widget manufacturers and the automobile industry was in a small slump. We could only get $.90 for our widgets. We sold the output, therefore, for $99,000 instead of the $100,000 we received the year before. Now we have a productivity increase of 10 percent and a bottom line loss of 1 percent in the same year.

In the meantime, we discover that in order to get the added 10 percent increase in output with no additional people or equipment, our quality slipped a little. We have received notice that 5 percent of the widgets we shipped were defective. Additionally, another firm has introduced a new widget made of entirely different materials that costs 20 percent less to produce and lasts 5 years longer than our widgets.

This brings us to the numbers in the denominator of the equation (input), since these reflect decisions of resource allocation to salary, research, marketing, etc. What happens to productivity over the long run depends not just on the simple output/input figures, but the components of each. Added dollars in research might pull the productivity figure down this year but keep us happily productive five years from now. Added training expenditures may reduce turnover and improve work force contributions.

The exercise could go on forever, and probably will—unless we really pay attention to what our friends in Japan have been trying to tell us for a long time: Productivity is not a matter of data, statistics and measurement. *Productivity is a state of mind; it is an ethic; it is a purpose.*

All research on productivity at the operational level demonstrates very clearly that what distinguishes one highly productive organization or work group from another—no matter how you measure it—is the sustained, systemic, enthusiastic, unending effort by everyone involved to find ways of doing things a little better. Productivity gains come from thousands of little things over long periods of time throughout the system—not from some super new piece of equipment, job redesign, compensation scheme or mystical insight.

What about robotics, CAD-CAM, the automated factory? The story here is the same. The new technology is going to revolutionize our capacity to produce more output using fewer resources.

However, technology is technology is technology. It is designed, purchased, installed, utilized and maintained within systems that are created, organized, operated and maintained by groups of individuals. The literature again is loaded with examples of how a piece of equipment produces extraordinary productivity gains in one place and is a disaster in another. Today, the Japanese are way ahead of us in the effective installation and use of automated equipment—not because they have equipment or capital that we lack, but because we have yet to attain an overall "state of mind" that is constantly evolving toward whatever will generate higher performance. In the words of an expert in computer-integrated manufacturing, our problem is "human resistance to change. Most CEOs are reluctant to tackle the five to 10 years of gut-wrenching cultural upheaval that the installation of these systems requires."

Remember, productivity improvements are descriptive of change. Continuous improvement comes from continuous change. Our "state of mind," it appears, still is not ready to embrace change and make it our ally.

MEASURING QUALITY

Defining productivity is a difficult task; getting clear about "quality" is even tougher. By definition, quality is a subjective term. It is also a *relative* measure; it positions something as "better" or "worse" than something similar. For all producers of a good or service, quality means what its customers decide is "most desired." The highest quality good or service, therefore, is the one that meets the expectations and desires of the marketplace most fully. It possesses attributes that an ever-changing, complex (and perhaps fickle) market wants.

Measuring quality is most often reflected in things like rejects or defects during production. That, however, is more a measure of productivity than of quality. Quality suggests things that are not reflected in production data, such as design, creativity, style, dependability, etc. In short, quality is a measure of how closely and how carefully the producer has reflected the cares and interests of the customer.

Again, we get high-quality results because of a "state of mind." In this case it comes from the constant effort to make the product or service better—to serve the needs of the customer a little better. There are no quality "standards" in a high-quality system of production because the purpose is *always* to do it a little better. *Quality comes from never believing "that's good enough."*

Our notion of quality is sometimes confused with "cost." We tend to associate a quality item as the most expensive, rare or precious. This probably explains why the overall quality of our products has slipped. Quality is *not* measured by price; it is measured by the level of satisfaction delivered by a product or service, regardless of price.

DOING *MORE* VERSUS DOING *BETTER*

Here is an interesting test which any organization can take to demonstrate the power of the shift of mind set. It is the simplest example of the difference in performance that occurs when the primary emphasis is on quantity as opposed to quality.

Take two work groups with identical or similar tasks. To one group, suggest that they must improve their productivity through increased output. Set a target of 10 percent greater output with no increase in input costs. Further, suggest that they will share in the rewards from the 10 percent increase. With the second group, establish a challenge of improving the *quality* of the product or service with no increase in costs. Let them determine the quality measure and the goal. Then observe the behavior of the groups.

Essentially, the first group will focus its attention *inward.* It will focus on effort. It will try to squeeze 10 percent more out of the existing system, and will work harder. Numbers will be important.

The second group will turn its attention *outward*. It will learn more about the customer. It will learn about the competition, and will make efforts to better meet market needs. In this group the energy level will increase, and new ideas will come out of the woodwork. There will be a new sense of identity with the product and with the consumer. Numbers will be less important than results.

If you succeed in improving the quality of a product or service, eventually you will sell more. If you succeed in producing *more* of a product, you will not necessarily sell more.

THE TROUBLE AT THE TOP

To really make the progress we need to in the area of productivity and quality, the change in our fundamental view of business and economics must change. To compete in the world—indeed, to fulfill our responsibilities as managers and leaders—all of our wit, energy and resources must be focused on productive enterprise. The possibility that our long-term chances for success are dim is reflected very clearly in a recent survey of CEOs around the world by Booz Allen and the *Japan Economic Journal.* When asked what they perceived to be their greatest responsibility, American CEOs replied: "Increase shareholder value" (51 percent). Japanese CEOs, on the other hand, replied: "Increase market share" (54 percent).

As long as we direct our attention to the abstractions of paper value as celebrated by the investment bankers and lawyers on Wall Street, we will continue our current flurry of mergers, acquisitions, divestitures and leveraged buy-outs. With all eyes turned to Wall Street, with our attention focused on the computer printouts and hefty documents of mega-deals, the possibilities of higher levels of productivity and higher orders of performance will continue to move to those whose attention is focused on the market.

For those who are actually toiling in the vineyards of management, you will have to continue to do it while top management struggles to outsmart the other guys' lawyers.

A Coordinated Approach to Motivation Can Increase Productivity

James M. McFillen and Philip M. Podsakoff

For at least 40 years, the attention of academicians and managers in the United States has shifted steadily from employee performance to employee satisfaction. Organizations have developed programs in the areas of compensation, job design and supervisory leadership—all aimed at making employees feel better about their jobs and their employers. And evidence suggests that industry's efforts in behalf of employee satisfaction have been successful.[1]

Although U.S. workers overwhelmingly express satisfaction with their jobs, their productivity improvement has slowed appreciably. Recent reports paint a picture of steady decline of U.S. industrial productivity relative to other industrialized nations.

Reprinted from the July 1983 issue of *Personnel Administrator,* copyright 1983, The American Society for Personnel Administration, 606 North Washington Street, Alexandria, Virginia 22314.

But hourly compensation in the United States has been rising over the same period that productivity has been slipping. The cumulative effect has been a rise in labor costs of over 220 percent during the 20 years from 1957 to 1977. Coupled with the increased costs of energy, government regulation, taxes, etc., this damaged America's economic position at home and abroad.

When the wages for a given year are adjusted by the inflation rate for that year, the results indicate a leveling off of real compensation. The effect of inflation exceeding productivity improvement is that the real economic gains of employees have ceased. All of industry's efforts to improve productivity have gone into offsetting the rapidly rising cost of labor, such that the real unit labor cost has remained relatively stable. Organizations have had to run faster to stay even.

Numerous reasons have been cited for America's poor performance. The finger has been pointed at problems of capital formation due to taxation, savings patterns and a general redistribution of wealth. A second target has been the effects of government regulation and legislation in the areas of safety, pollution, employment and energy. Changes in work force composition and competence have been offered as a third cause.

The examples used to support this conclusion are the lower skills, training and experience brought to the workplace by teen-agers, minorities and women who increased their labor participation rates in the '70s.

The final category of causes is changes in the motivation and work ethic of the American worker. This category is best exemplified by references to the declining role of work in a person's life, coupled with the rising demands for more leisure. For whatever reasons, it has become apparent that American industry is getting less work per dollar of wages than it did just a few years ago.

PLACING BLAME

Most of the causes of lowered productivity appear to be beyond the control of an individual manager, and many seem beyond the influence of an organization's management team. However, productivity is not strictly a function of variables external to the firm, over which management has no control.

A closer examination of the motivational causes of lowered productivity show that many management policies and practices are at least partially to blame for the change in employee attitudes toward work. Many potentially powerful tools lie within management's control if only management chooses to develop an overall strategy for performance improvement. This strategy must utilize the various elements of human resource management in a unified program consistent with enhancing employee motivation to work. Too often, effective management strategy has been sacrificed for ease of administration, standardization and a preference for equality of treatment over equity.

Management has frequently dismissed or diluted some of the most influential practices, while at the same time opting for isolated programs in which performance on the job is to be encouraged by allowing good workers to escape from the workplace through flextime, modified work weeks and other opportunities for increased leisure time. Such programs usually provide a job change designed to improve the quality of work life with the hope that employees will reciprocate with increased performance or reduced personnel-related costs. The results frequently are a set of conflicting incentives and policies. Motivation should be a positive, active concern of management, rather than a negative, passive issue to which management responds only when something goes wrong.

To develop a consistent, unified strategy for increasing employee productivity through motivation, management must develop a framework for motivation that allows the policies and programs in human resource management to be coordinated. Without some underlying framework, the interdependence of the wide variety of policies and programs involved will be difficult to identify and their administration will be confusing and conflicting. Motivation is complex, but its importance and potential contribution are so great that management must attempt to fashion some overall direction for their motivation efforts. Motivation must not be left to chance with the hope that some combination of elements will prove motivating.

MANAGEMENT MISTAKES

To understand the importance of management philosophy and practice in the productivity problem, the context of the human resource side of the issue must be considered. Management has played a major role in developing the conditions of motivation found in business today, and therefore must accept responsibility for the demotivating effects of current management practice. A fundamental problem has been the adoption of a philosophy suggested by the human relations movement that employee satisfaction causes employee performance. Adherence to this philosophy has led to a major change in the way organizations try to motivate their members.

Under this philosophy, providing employees with things they desire is expected to make employees more satisfied with the firm, or more indebted to it, with the hope that they will be more productive. The result of this practice, as most managers can attest, is not improved productivity, but rather increased costs. If providing boosts in wages or other employment benefits prior to increased performance were the key to improving motivation and productivity, then establishing and raising the minimum wage should have been a major boon to worker productivity.

The fact is that negotiated, legislated or management-mandated increases in the general wage do not result in improved worker output. Management has, instead, reduced employment and substituted machines and automation to improve productivity as a way to offset increased labor costs.

A related management practice has been a general movement away from performance-related rewards. This is true with regard to financial and nonfinancial rewards. Some firms have felt compelled to abandon the use of financial incentives in favor of hourly or salary-based compensation, due to management philosophy, policy ease or external pressures. Regardless of the reason, the long-term effects have been the same: The relationship between employee compensation and daily performance has been seriously diminished.

Annual merit increases or across-the-board wage adjustments are not satisfactory substitutes for performance-related compensation. Coupled with the effect of inflation upon the financial resources available for pay raises and the neglect and misuse of performance appraisals by management, the transition to salary and hourly pay has all but eliminated the tie between performance and the earnings, and has eroded employee beliefs that their economic gains are somehow tied to the gains of the firm. If managers wish to test their firm's effectiveness on this issue, they need only ask what advantages or benefits accrue to high-performers that do not accrue to low-performers. If the list is short and of little value, then the organization has seriously reduced the effectiveness of its reward system.

DEMOTIVATING MESSAGE

More and more managers are finding that although their organizations give "lip service" to providing merit raises or other financial incentives, the allocation of such rewards often is quite arbitrary due to the use of poor appraisal practice or to a dependence upon seniority and cost-of-living as the principle criteria for raises. The results are the same.

The only consistent message to employees is that performance does not determine compensation. What does influence compensation is the action taken by unions, government and management independent of any employee efforts toward increased productivity. Increased pressure on management, not increased performance, is the key to earning more. The motivation implications should be obvious, and the focus of employee efforts readily apparent. Management must consider the long-term costs as well as the short-run benefits of such practices.

Non-financial rewards have grown increasingly important with the growth in non-contingent compensation. Hourly pay, salary and fringe benefits basically encourage employees to do only what is necessary to maintain employment. If management expects employees to go beyond this minimum level of acceptable performance, the burden falls upon non-financial means of motivation. Management either must hire only those individuals whose dominant characteristic is intensive self-motivation, or use its own managerial skills to arouse employee motivation. The problem in depending upon either of these two solutions is that neither is very likely. Self-motivation relies essentially upon self-interest and only rarely do jobs and self-interest significantly overlap. As for managerial skills, individuals in management positions frequently lack either the time, inclination or skill to motivate others.

For various reasons, managers are unable or unwilling to invest the degree of involvement and effort required to really encourage subordinates to perform. When advised on using feedback, recognition and participation as motivation tools, managers commonly respond by claiming they do not have the time to become so involved in the interpersonal side of motivation. The organization and its managers, however, find the time and resources to deal after-the-fact with the results of low employee motivation and commitment to performance. Managers are forced to find the time to fight the fires that erupt; it's just the prevention that suffers from such a low priority.

Organizations frequently turn to complex programs, such as job enrichment and MBO, as solutions to motivation problems. Management employs a promising new program only to find that the beneficial effects are short-lived or that the few benefits are buried by an avalanche of forms, meetings and procedures. The disruption and disillusionment that frequently follow dampen enthusiasm and produce a disdain for future efforts to enhance motivation. At the heart of the failure is a fundamental problem: Management has failed to utilize a framework for motivation that facilitates the development and integration of human resource programs and policies.

New programs are planned, but they are not integrated with existing systems. A framework is needed that allows motivation problems to be analyzed logically and systematically, and that permits management to assess in what manner a given program might contribute to or detract from motivation.

DEFINING MOTIVATION

Before a framework can be developed, some common idea of what is meant by motivation must be established. When a manager says an employee is unmotivated, what the manager really means is that the employee is not motivated to do what the manager wishes to be done, but instead is motivated to do something the employee, or the work group, or someone else wants done. This, then, is a matter of direction of motivation and not a matter of being motivated or unmotivated.

All employees exhibit motivated, purposeful behavior. The problem is that the employees' purposes are not always the same as those of management. The question for management then is to create situations that motivate employees in the desired direction.

A manager's concept of motivation appears to have two components. The first involves the effort or attempt to perform: Does the employee try to do what is asked? The second involves the actual performance or results accruing from the employee's efforts: Does the employee actually accomplish what is asked? Although one component might seem to imply the other automatically, the fact is the components may be considered as separate elements. For example, it is easy to see how an employee's efforts might be blocked or misdirected and therefore fail to result in satisfactory performance.

The employee might be willing, but lack the proper skills or have the wrong idea as to what is expected. What is sometimes harder to see is that performance attributed to one employee may have resulted from the efforts of others or from the wrong kind of effort. Like Tom Sawyer's fence painting, an employee's performance could be due to misplaced efforts, as in taking short cuts or getting others to do the employee's work. Performance might also emerge from the natural interdependence of the work as when performance is a function of group rather than individual effort.

Similarly, a lack of effort may be due to a lack of incentives, or to competing incentives, or to past failure. Employees engage in their personal cost-benefit analysis and opt for those bargains they perceive profitable for themselves. Managers must examine the work situation from the employee's perspective. A recent example of this problem was a supervisor for a large appliance manufacturer who could not understand why a college-educated hourly worker would not transfer from a

$7.50 per hour, late-shift janitorial job to the assembly line, where the employee could earn 10 percent more per hour.

As the situation was examined, it became apparent that not only would the job change mean a decline in autonomy—which was important to the college graduate—but it also meant a sizeable increase in the amount of effort required. Management was expecting the employee to voluntarily switch from a job requiring an honest five hours of work per eight-hour shift to one requiring seven and one-half hours on the line. For this 50 percent increase in work, the employee was offered a 10 percent increase in pay. All motivation-related issues must be viewed from the perspective of the one being motivated, not the one trying to do the motivating.

EFFECTIVE FRAMEWORK

Creating a framework for motivation requires a consideration of what encourages effort and what channels that effort toward satisfactory job-related performance. Such a framework must include the specification and description of what is to be done and the elements that contribute to a willingness to perform. This willingness results from an interaction between the incentives for performance and employee knowledge and confidence regarding performance. A simplified version of a model of motivation developed by Vroom[2] and extended and elaborated by Campbell, Dunnette, Lawler and Weick[3] can serve as the origin for a framework of motivation (see Figure 1).

BARRIERS TO PERFORMANCE

The limits to the effort-performance relationship are quite different from those affecting the performance-outcome relationship, but all of the limits share the requirement for viewing motivation from the perspective of the employee. The common effort-performance limits fall into four categories:

- Doubts about ability, skill, or knowledge;
- Physical or practical possibility of the job;
- Interdependence of job with other people or activities;
- Ambiguity surrounding the job requirements.

Employees may be reluctant to try to perform, because they doubt their capacity to do the job, or doubt whether the job can be performed as described. If employees doubt whether they can be successful at their jobs, their expectation of receiving rewards also will be reduced. Assuming no change in the level of promised outcomes, motivation declines as the odds against success become higher. Employees discount the value of

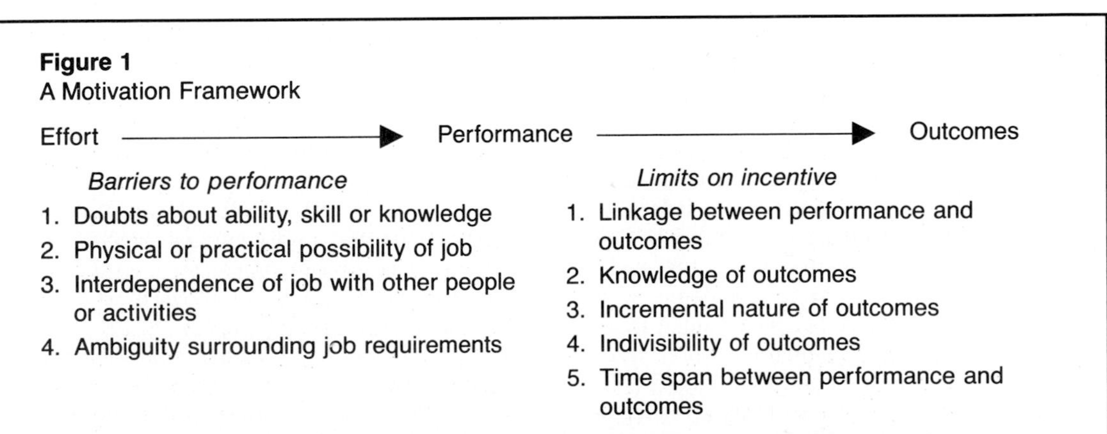
Figure 1
A Motivation Framework

trying as the probability of successful performance diminishes. Past failure in the same or similar work can contribute to doubts about whether successful performance will follow effort.

The barriers due to interdependencies arise when the employee's desired activity is entangled with the activities required of others or with other activities in which the employee is engaged. If an employee's work is dependent upon work done by others prior to or simultaneously with their own work, the employee is less likely to feel that they are able to control the level of performance. The necessity to coordinate with others dampens one's expectation of successful performance unless similar situations in the past have proven satisfactory.

All managers have experienced that initial sense of anguish when a new committee is formed to handle some complicated problem. Similarly, when an employee is faced with several highly interdependent tasks, the problem of coordinating and prioritizing those tasks appears. When some of those tasks are in direct conflict due to time or resource limitations or to conflicting goals, the effect is to lower the employee's expectation of successfully completing all or part of the tasks. Therefore, interdependencies that are not carefully coordinated and controlled by management will result in lowered employee motivation.

The final category of barriers to the effort-performance relationship is ambiguity. Ambiguity can take many forms. It may signify poor communication regarding what is to be done. Confusion over methods or authority can also cause ambiguity. Employees who are unsure what is expected of them may be hesitant to act—or worse, may embark on their own interpretation of what is to be done. In essence, management leaves performance to chance when it allows ambiguity to develop around the task. If the intent is to test an employee's initiative, ambiguity might serve a useful purpose. In daily management practice, however, unnecessary ambiguity about the task is likely to reduce an employee's confidence of successful performance and therefore reduce motivation to perform. Highly ambiguous work coupled with highly important outcomes can also be damaging by inducing high levels of employee stress.

LIMITS ON INCENTIVE

In examining motivation, managers must ask themselves why an employee should desire to do what is asked. The answer lies in whether accomplishing the desired performance will result in outcomes accruing to the employee that otherwise would not have been available. Does performance result in outcomes that non-performance does not? There are five limits that affect the employee's perception of the performance-outcome relationship:

- Linkage between performance and outcomes;
- Knowledge of outcomes;
- Incremental nature of outcomes;
- Indivisibility of outcomes;
- Time span between performance and outcomes.

Much of what management, organized labor, and government have done in the area of employment has driven a wedge between performance and outcomes. Salary, fringe benefits, seniority-based raises and ineffective performance appraisals all contribute to reducing the linkage between pay and performance. The result is that one's earnings are not influenced by what one does on behalf of the organization, but rather by the power or influence employees collectively have over the organization or by the benevolent actions of management. The former defeats management's ability to manage and the latter creates a childlike dependence for the employees. Similarly, managers fail to use feedback, praise and recognition in a manner consistent with encouraging performance.

The performance-outcome linkage also is weakened when the receipt of outcomes is clouded by ambiguity. The confusion may be due to a lack of knowledge of outcomes, to a discounting of the value of outcomes because of their incremental nature, or to an inability to limit the benefits of some outcomes, such as department bonuses only to those employees who deserve them. All three cause employees to doubt that they receive anything significant for their role as a high-performer. Employees may be unaware of benefits that accrue to those who perform well or may perceive each benefit in such a piecemeal fashion that the total value of the benefit goes unappreciated. Employees subject to group-based incentives often feel short-changed because unequal performances are rewarded equally. Since individual motivation is weakened, the best performers tend to drift downward to the level of the mediocre performer.

The final limit to the performance-outcome relationship relates to the problem of the timing of reward allocation once desired performance has occurred. The annual bonus or annual salary increase is an example of the timing problem.

An employee receiving a merit raise in July for performance during the prior year associates that raise less with daily performance than if merit increases were allocated more frequently but covered shorter periods of time. When incentive pay lags two, three or four weeks behind the date of the performance due to the complications of administration, employees tend to lose the immediate association between pay and performance, which in turn weakens the performance-outcome linkage engineered into the compensation system. The key element in this problem is the immediacy of the outcomes accomplished by actually allocating the rewards or by providing employees with tangible evidence of their current performance and upcoming rewards.

INTERDEPENDENCE

The effort-performance barriers are damaging to the level of employee motivation. Since they affect motivation through a different route than the performance-outcome limits, they require different resolution strategies. Although different solutions are required, the effects of the two sources of limits are not totally independent. Management can attempt to heighten an employee's motivation on a difficult task by increasing the value of a performance-contingent reward or by strengthening the contingency between task performance and rewards. This balancing act has its limitations. Attempting to offset very low performance probabilities by making the performance-related outcomes more important can induce high levels of stress and frustration in employees. A manager may not achieve positive results by telling an employee, "I know you don't think you can handle the job, but if you don't try you're fired." Here the payoff for performance is high (keeping one's job), but it does not overcome the limits perceived by the employee. The motivation to try may be higher, but so may be the anxiety.

APPLICATION OF THE FRAMEWORK

The framework of motivation developed here suggests three key areas of management responsibility:

- Performance definition
- Performance facilitation
- Performance encouragement.

Attention to these areas will reduce the limits to motivation, and will serve as a guide to the coordination and integration of human resource policy.

Performance definition involves the initial disclosure of what is expected from employees and a continuous process of orienting employees toward job performance. It involves three elements: goals, measures and assessment. Establishing goals is critical to motivation. Employees might be instructed as to what the work goals are or permitted to participate in the actual goal-setting process. Participation in goal setting tends to increase employee acceptance of the goals. In either case, the goals need to be precise, reasonable and specific as to the what, how and when of performance. Goal setting improves the direction of effort as well as enhancing accountability.

Goals also help employees to understand their relative contributions to the firm. For example, an electronics manufacturer had trouble with performance quality along an assembly line. Management discussed the quality standards and the reasons behind each with the employees. The discussion included a display along one wall of the work area that demonstrated the effects of one operator's error upon subsequent work stages and the final product. The display made it quite evident that the performance goals were not arbitrary.

The presence of goals, however, is not sufficient. Management also must find a means for operationalizing and therefore measuring the goals. Goals such as making the company successful not only lack specificity as to what level of success is desired, but also fall prey to many potentially competing measures of success. A goal that has no direct or surrogate measure is of little use to management beyond window dressing.

The third aspect of performance definition is assessment. Management can identify measureable goals, but if there is no intent to assess individual or organization performance on those goals, the goals will serve no purpose motivationally. In fact, goals that are stated but that go unassessed over time send important messages to employees about management commitment to those goals and raise questions about management commitment in other areas. Sloppy, unprofessional assessment of performance not only tarnishes management's image, but potentially leads to misinformation about the performance of individuals as well as the organization. Misinformation makes the accurate rewarding of performance impossible and therefore reduces the motivating potential of the reward system. Assessment also encourages a continuing orientation toward job performance.

Performance definition aids establishment of effort-performance and performance-outcome relationships. It helps determine the ability and knowledge required for the job, clarifies interdependencies and conflicts, and improves directionality of effort through reduced ambiguity. Performance definition also makes possible the creation of a performance-outcome linkage. The pivotal role of performance definition to motivation should be readily apparent.

The second key area, performance facilitation, involves elimination of roadblocks to performance. Its major contribution to motivation is that it increases the effort-performance relationship. To facilitate employee performance, management must be active in these areas:

- Removing performance obstacles
- Providing means and resources for performance
- Selecting proper personnel.

When designing jobs, management must create highly supportive task environments. Jobs should be free of unnecessary obstacles to performance. These obstacles frequently take the form of poorly maintained equipment, cumbersome management practices and poorly designed work methods. The effect of these is to make it more difficult and frustrating to do the assigned work. Motivation declines as employees develop the opinion that management is apparently unconcerned about getting the job done.

A similar problem develops when management fails to commit the resources necessary for performance. This is typified by organizations that try to do everything on a "shoestring" budget. Assigning minimal financial, human or material resources can be self-defeating and extremely costly in terms of performing the task at hand, as well as in terms of future employee motivation to perform. Such practices cause employees to doubt whether the assigned task can be done well, and signal the relative importance management assigns to the task.

The final element of performance facilitation is the proper selection of personnel. Although selection has been made more complicated by equal employment legislation, management cannot afford to back away from proper selection policy. Selection, training and placement are essential to employee motivation to perform. Poor staffing procedures guarantee reduced motivation by placing employees in jobs that either demand too little from them or require more than their skills and abilities can supply. The result is higher turnover and absenteeism as well as reduced performance. An additional effect is the hiring of more employees than actually required. This means generally higher fringe benefit costs as well as higher wage costs. Productivity is reduced and costs increase simultaneously.

THE FINAL KEY

Performance encouragement is the final key area. In order to encourage employee performance through the performance-outcome linkage, management must be concerned with five issues:

- Value of reward
- Magnitude of reward
- Timing of reward
- Likelihood of reward
- Equity of reward.

Value and magnitude of reward relate to the choice of rewards to be used in an organization. Much has been said in the popular literature about the changing values of American workers. Management must offer outcomes to employees that are attractive in both value and magnitude. Job redesign, cafeteria pay systems and altered work weeks all have been attempts to offer employees outcomes they value.

Sometimes, however, the problem is not one of value, but rather of amount. For example, an organization may offer insufficient inducement to exert more effort. A manager in a government agency complained that the new breed of employees was not as motivated as it should be. Even though the employees were eligible for merit increases, the manager felt that they just did not seem to put much effort into their jobs.

When asked how much of a raise he gave his top performer, the manager proudly stated, "Why, I gave him 8 percent." When asked what his worst performer received for a raise, the manager responded, "Seven percent, but the difference really was based on merit." One may argue whether 7 percent is of sufficient magnitude given 10 percent inflation, but the belief that a 1 percent differential is sufficient to reward high performance is purely wishful thinking.

The issues of timing and likelihood of rewards apply to the linkage between performance and outcomes. As discussed under the framework for motivation, management practices that serve to seriously dilute the relationships between performance and subsequent rewards destroy the reason for employee performance. Whether the rewards are in the form of raises, incentive pay, promotions, or recognition for a job well done, timing and likelihood are fundamental to an effective reward system. Outcomes that are delayed in coming lose their potential for motivation just as outcomes do that accrue independent of performance.

Many production incentive systems require lengthy delays in the allocation of rewards. In the tubing department of a major steel producer, the production bonus was computed daily as a function of the employee's job and production level for the day. The incentive was included on payroll checks distributed two weeks later. Since employees commonly worked on three or more different machines in a given week and their levels of performance varied as a function of both the product and the quality standards involved, employees found it nearly impossible to account for the fluctuations in incentive pay that occurred on their checks each week. Employees either doubted whether performance was related to pay or believed the formula was too complicated for them to understand. The result was a feeling that the production bonus was like dropping coins in a slot machine; the payoff was by chance.

The final issue, equity, affects the magnitude and likelihood variables. Equity is simply a judgment about whether one gets what they deserve, and is made in reference to other employees or acquaintances. Employees who believe they work harder than other people in similar jobs believe they should receive more in return from the organization.

This means they expect greater magnitude of rewards. If they fail to receive those increased rewards they may reduce the quantity or quality of their performance and come to believe that rewards are unrelated to performance. Experience has shown that people have a much greater tolerance for being inequitably overpaid than for being inequitably underpaid. Treating all employees equally invariably results in inequitable treatment, because people rarely perform equally. The high-performers are underpaid and hence reduce their level of performance. Low-performers are overpaid but find numerous ways to justify it rather than increase their performance. Equal treatment, therefore, results in equally low performance for all employees over time or results in the good employees quitting to take jobs with firms that will appreciate their contribution.

Inequity often occurs in well designed but poorly administered reward systems. Employees read management's intentions not from what management professes to do but from what, in fact, occurs. Inattention to the details of the reward system's administration—for example, performance appraisal—guarantees feelings of inequitable treatment.

IMPLICATIONS FOR MANAGEMENT

Many causes of lowered or static levels of employee productivity exist. Employee motivation is only one of the contributors. In fact it is hard to say what percent of the productivity problem is attributable to changed attitudes toward work. Some experts go so far as to say that productivity cannot be improved by employees working harder, but rather that employees must work smarter. However, if recent estimates are accurate and the average employee works only four hours out of every eight-hour shift, there appears to be room for employee-based improvements in productivity. The fundamental point to remember is not whether working smarter or harder is the answer, but that prevailing management practice often fails to reward employees for either working harder or smarter. Management has been racing to get increasing productivity from a declining employee commitment to performance.

The call for performance-contingent rewards is not a request for the return of the sweatshop. However, future personnel practice must renew the relationship between employee performance and employee outcomes. The complexities of human motivation combined with problems of productivity make coordinated human resource policy essential in modern organizations. Failure to apply a logic or framework to management practice produces confusion and conflict in personnel administration. In formulating future human resource policies, management must:

- Quit relying on employee indebtedness to encourage performance and instead consider what the organization owes to good performers.
- Be aware of the context of performance and productivity problems in the organization.
- Examine the motivational properties of the personnel policies and practices in the organization within the context of a motivation framework.

Improved productivity deserves the attention of management and labor. It is worth management's time to design and administer programs that encourage improved employee productivity. Management would do well to add a new slogan to guide future personnel practices: productivity is no waste of effort.

REFERENCES

1. Szilagyi, A. D., and Wallace, M. J. *Organizational Behavior and Performance.* Santa Monica, CA: Goodyear Publishing Co., 1980, p. 90.

2. Vroom, V. *Work and Motivation.* New York: Wiley, 1964, pp. 8–28.

3. Campbell, J. P., Dunnette, M., Lawler, E. E., and Weick, K. E. *Managerial Behavior, Performance and Effectiveness.* New York: McGraw Hill, 1970.

Employee Involvement: Why It Fails, What It Takes to Succeed

Bob Crosby

Just as one was bombarded a few years ago with employee involvement stories—usually popularized through the Japanese quality circles idea—today one is bombarded with stories of their failure. Success stories whet one's appetite. Yet we now hear statements like: "75 percent of all such efforts fail," "We tried small employee groups at our company and they bombed," or "They seemed to work for a while, but they don't even exist in our company anymore."

Paradoxes abound. On the one hand, we know that the resources of each individual must be used to the maximum. On the other hand, American adaptations of Japanese quality circles don't seem to be the answer for most companies.

Recently I heard a corporate executive expound a three-pronged strategy for success for his company, one element of which was employee involvement. "With this strategy we are already waving goodbye to our competition," he said while waving his hand to emphasize the point. So, why do so many employee involvement quality circle programs fail? Even more important, what makes them succeed?

First, "employee involvement" should be defined. At one level, employees have always been involved in companies merely by virtue of being employed, and companies have always hoped to get the most out of their employees, to use their time and talent to the maximum. So what we are talking about is a fundamental shift from viewing employees as workers who need to be prodded, to viewing them as individuals with valued skills who *want* to do excellent work and contribute to the well-being of their companies.

Modern employee involvement is an effort to involve employees in a special way—to utilize their talents and experience for the greatest possible good of the company. The fact that this makes economic sense should be plain to almost everyone; that it also makes for a better work environment is clear as well. That it *can* be done is not at all clear, nor is it obvious how best to make this happen.

At their core, bosses and employees are not adversaries. They have many goals in common. There is ample support for the notion that people have pride of craft; that is, people want to do high-quality work. Work well done leads to a higher sense of self-esteem, and the American work force shares a wish to do a good job. People do not really want to be in conflict. Nobody joins a company in order to purposely screw up; by and large, people join with good intentions.

From direct experience with some 50 organizations and the second-hand reports of more than 200 companies over the last six years—noting both stark failures and striking successes—I have formulated 12 guidelines for employee involvement success.

1. CONTEXT

Context is everything. That's an overstatement, but it's close to the truth. How we speak about employee involvement is critical. Ideally, employee involvement applies to every employee, from the least paid to the highest paid. It is a process of fully utilizing the talents and experience of everyone.

More than anyone, middle managers work in a void. Top management often wonders what it takes to get things operating the way they want. In

Reprinted from *Personnel Administrator, 31* (1986), pp. 95–106 by permission of the author, Robert P. Crosby, of Management Analysis Company (MAC), San Diego, California.

short, top management depends on an effectively functioning "middle" and "bottom." *The basic context is that employee involvement truly means just that, not merely the involvement of hourly employees.*

Also, employee involvement must be implemented in the context of *making it work.* This is a positive and empowering force. In the context of finding fault, griping and blaming, employee involvement is a negative, defeating force. *Making it work* means that anything can be discussed with quick feedback and minimal defensiveness. Finding fault means that underlying causes will be avoided, people will be defensive, feedback will be distorted and employee involvement will fail. Finding fault focuses on the narrow spectrum of what's wrong. *Making it work* encourages a search for new opportunities for productivity and facing up to persistent problems. The fundamental basis for effective employee involvement is in this context. (These are no idle words, ideals or slogans. Companies which do not know how to shift ground need to seek help from resources that can help them make this shift. It is far more than simply talking differently.)

Another crucial context: Economics. Employee involvement is about economic success. "Do-good," love-thy-neighbor motivation does not cause a company to adopt employee involvement. (If so, it doesn't work, because the executives who initiate the program are either naive or are distorting the truth.) Companies have to make money; competition is tough. Employees know that today more than they ever did—they've seen many companies fail.

Employee involvement done well is productive. That it also creates a better and more humane workplace is a happy corollary. The economic sense context is believable. *With* that context, companies are dead serious about employee involvement. *Without* that context being central and visible, it simply won't work.

Without such contexts implemented by people who are skilled in change processes, employee involvement programs tend to be "tinkering" fads. Successful employee involvement requires leadership from skillful "context creators."

2. TOP-DOWN STRATEGY

The complaints about employee involvement are clear: "We tried employee involvement with several employee groups and it didn't work." "It worked for a while, but it died out." "Employees just got together and griped." "Supervisors and middle managers blocked good ideas or were apathetic."

Beginning with successful experience at the top supports the context that it *is* for everybody, that it works and is not simply a new program, but is actually a new way of life for the company.

But even more important, a top-down strategy provides an example of success, and offers an involvement model to top management, middle management and first-line supervisors *before* they are asked to encourage hourly workers to strive for similar successes. The process begins after the people at the top have learned how to deal with the tough issues they face with their bosses and with the people they supervise. Before the program moves to hourly workers, top and middle management have already had successful experiences in making it work.

By itself, philosophizing isn't effective. Simply to have an orientation session with the top people to announce an employee involvement program for hourly employees doesn't work. The importance of employee involvement is measured by how seriously it is integrated into the structure of the company, including the people at the top.

3. MIDDLE-MANAGER TRAINING

Management needs to be clear about the function of middle managers. Except in organized religions and the military, middle management did not exist at the turn of the century. Most industries were home industries, where parents were executives and children were workers. There were no middle managers. But as home industries merged and became larger, someone—perhaps the eldest child—became a supervisor. Those who became supervisors immediately discovered that they were no longer involved mainly with technical issues. Now they had to figure out a way to manage people effectively.

When people become middle managers, they need greater knowledge about policies and procedures. They may continue to provide expertise in technical areas, but by necessity they become more and more dependent on employees for that expertise. Effective middle managers soon discover that their primary function is the utilization of human resources. If this isn't discovered, the middle manager competes with the smartest first-line workers, fearing that those workers' technical expertise will become so well known by the company that they will be promoted, eventually replacing the middle manager.

It is critical that companies train supervisors in the utilization of human resources to help people be clear about their jobs, get the information they need to do a good job and get the authority to do what they are given responsibility to do. These human factors, managed well by middle managers, will lead to greater productivity and will foster collaboration and a spirit of cooperation at all levels of the company. In order for this to happen, not only do middle managers need to be trained, but top management also needs to make it very clear that they are rewarding middle managers and first-line supervisors primarily for their ability to utilize the resources of the people they supervise.

4. EMPOWERMENT WITH CLEAR AUTHORITY

Employee involvement is about empowerment in which people make the distinction between influence and decision-making. When employee involvement is done well, bosses are able to perform better and use their authority quicker and more clearly. They're also free to listen better—many bosses don't listen well because they aren't sure that their authority is accepted. The difference is that in daily decisions maximum effort is made to use the experience and talents of *everyone* in the company who has knowledge about how a particular decision will affect productivity.

Empowerment of all means that bosses have more power to make authoritarian decisions when they need to. It means that employees have more power to truly influence the workplace as it relates to their talents and experience. But it also means that people do not confuse influence with decision-making. That clarity is essential, or top managers will resist employee involvement for fear that they will lose their decision-making authority. Also, employees at lower levels will falsely believe that they are being asked to make decisions rather than offer their opinion. Empowerment means people being clear—clearer than ever before—about *how* they influence and *who* makes decisions.

5. USING DATA

The most common complaint about employee involvement programs is that they degenerate into gripe sessions. Employee involvement programs which work best begin with a database. The most effective database is one that identifies the human factors: How clear are people about roles? Are they getting the information they need to do a good job? What sense do they have about their future in the company? Are they appreciated for what they do? If their work group is unproductive, can they influence it to be productive? Are they clear about the larger picture, or are they expected to function without any sense of direction of the company? When plans are made, do they hear about them in time to implement them? If a decision is being made in an area where they have experience and expertise, are they consulted?

These and many similar questions are about human factors. Presenting data to employees that they have helped to generate is a good starting place for successful employee involvement. This makes it okay to talk about the aspects of work that often aren't even noticed or clearly conceptualized by anyone in the company.

We all know that human resources are important, but who would realize in advance that unless all the questions listed above—and many others like them—are addressed, even a company with outstanding technical expertise won't use those skills well?

A common error is to gather data and keep them at the top management level. In fact, this is detrimental to productivity. Effective employee involvement programs require that data be shared. Although not all data from *all groups need to be known to every* group, if a group that works in shipping, for example, can see the shipping data that they helped to generate they may be able to come up with some recommendations for effective change.

Perhaps no change process is more effective than feeding data back to the work force. Employees then can systematically respond to the data, develop recommendations to which management will respond and share in monitoring the follow-through.

6. STRUCTURING EMPLOYEE INVOLVEMENT

Employee involvement needs to be tailored to each company. The people within each company must be the ones who develop the structure that will make it work. Only in an "indigenous" structure that is monitored constantly will employee involvement become a way of doing business on a daily basis. The organization needs to decide about the birth, death and leadership of groups, the issue of intact work groups versus task forces handling certain issues, the kind of report forms to be developed and the kind of training that will support ongoing employee involvement.

These issues are unique to each company and, although it is useful for management to know what other companies have done, it is most likely to succeed when a company, instead of buying another firm's prescription, develops its own unique ways of making employee involvement work.

Although employee involvement can be started quickly with the survey feedback method mentioned above, the program also moves rather quickly from the generic to the specific. Outside consultants can help start employee involvement, but management must make its own unique adaptation.

7. SYSTEMS ISSUES RESOLVED

Effective data-gathering makes it clear that many issues permeate all groups in an organization. If all groups in an organization have an issue in common, a systems issue exists. Sometimes a group can create its own environment and succeed in addressing systems issues for its own level; however, for maximum overall productivity, systems issues need to be resolved at the top.

8. SKILLS TRAINING

In order for employee involvement to work, a large proportion of people in the organization have to be trained in simple problem-solving. Employees at all levels need to know exactly what they're to do when working on problems. At the very least, it is essential to be able to distinguish between interpretive and concrete statements. Note the difference, for example, between a recommendation that says: "Improve sanitation in Department B" and one that says: "Department B's hoses are leaking from broken connecting joints and the drain is partially clogged." Superiors need skills training in completing the feedback loop; i.e., in getting back to their people in a supportive, intelligent way. One of the major reasons why employee involvement fails is that no response is made to suggestions or recommendations. Clearer recommendations and completing the feedback loop must be part of an effective employee involvement program.

9. CRISIS INTERVENTION

Effective employee involvement programs need people who can quickly handle dysfunctional supervisor/employee situations. For example, if the company has determined that a dysfunctioning supervisor is to be kept on as a supervisor, third-party work must take place between the supervisor and the employees. Third-party work involves a person who knows how to get two individuals together, prepare them for a meeting, deal with the issues directly and quickly, and keep them from dealing with an issue as if it were a personality conflict.

An effective third party can remedy 80 to 90 percent of all perceived unhappy supervisor/employee situations. It is not unusual to see a chronic situation which has been going on for a year or two turned around in a few weeks by a highly skilled third-party negotiator. If these reversals do not occur, employee involvement is imperiled, at least, in any group that is experiencing supervisor/employee difficulties.

10. HANDLING BREAKDOWNS

People must be prepared for breakdowns. They will occur, no matter what. When a breakdown happens, people have two choices: One is to say, "See, it isn't working"; the other is to say, "Let's fix it." People must be reminded repeatedly that of course there will be breakdowns. Breakdowns do not result from a devious plot. They just happen. So, "Let's fix it."

Employee involvement must occur in the context that "not everything will work perfectly." In life people begin by crawling, then walking, and then running. Employee involvement must begin with the clear understanding that it will become a way of life for the company—a long-term involvement—and that we begin by focusing on central, important issues. First, people in the company will take care of the things that are basic. Second, the program will continue, and will be a part of everyday life for the company. And, after a while, it won't even be called a program. It will simply be the way the people in the company work together. Later, people will be walking, and then running, but one step at a time. There will be breakdowns and they will be fixed. Then, the focus will shift from problems to potential and opportunity.

11. CULTURAL TRANSITION

Employee involvement needs to be seen as a gradual transition of the company. Some of the items identified by one company as directions in which it preferred to move are illustrated in Table 1. The critical point is that the company is in transition. Employee involvement is not a three-month program to magically accomplish grandiose goals. Rather, it is a way of life for the company in directions that, over time, will represent a significant cultural shift.

12. THREE-RING ASPECT OF EMPLOYEE INVOLVEMENT

For employee involvement to succeed, it must be seen in the context of three interlocking circles. One circle represents the individual as a contributor to the employee involvement program—as a

Table 1
Preferred Directions

From (The way it once was)	*Toward* (The way we want it to be)
Authority related primarily to status and role	Authority primarily related to knowledge and competence, and yet with clear lines of status and role authority when needed
Low trust	High trust
Engineering design decided at the top without reference to people working with equipment	All employees who will use equipment to influence engineering design
Supervisors feeling attacked, criticized, or threatened by hourly workers' suggestions	Supervisors feeling supported by hourly workers' suggestions
Supervisors holding on to the notion that they have to know the most about technical matters	Supervisors experiencing power from effective management of people who are freed to use their technical knowledge and experience

person who has a commitment to making it work. The second circle represents various groups of employees, both informal and work-assigned. These groups share all kinds of norms favoring or working against employee involvement. An effective employee involvement program deals with these norms and helps people become more sophisticated about how they are shaped and how one keeps from becoming a victim of them.

The third circle is the organizational one—representing cultural transition items. It is the basis for the whole program. All three circles are important, but they work only if the organizational circle truly demonstrates consistent commitment to the utilization of human resources. This quality is demonstrated by statements from the top, by the presence of top people along with hourly people in training programs and in learning how to make employee involvement work. When the top executive joins hourly workers and middle managers in learning how to develop and recognize a recommendation that is specific and concrete, the chances of effecting change increase from very dismal to very likely.

Many organizations approach motivation, stress management or employee involvement by trying to work within just the individual or the group circle. Employee involvement which works is based on the basic principle that these three factors are primarily a matter of how a system manages its people. Therefore, employee involvement needs to be operative in all three circles.

RESULTS

What about results? When all of these issues are addressed, dramatic economic results are produced. All kinds of changes occur. For example, safety improves, even though it may not be addressed directly. People feel free to turn in requests, disagree with their boss, bring up a point that isn't popular and identify safety problems.

Usually, productivity increases strikingly in companies with an effective employee involvement program:

- There were dramatic safety improvements in a nuclear industry with dramatic productivity improvements
- Lost labor was greatly reduced in a printing plant
- A law firm billed 27 percent more clients
- A car dealership reduced the time a car was in for repairs while increasing maintenance results
- Turnover in a fast-food restaurant was reduced from 43 percent to 21 percent
- A light manufacturer with 250 employees increased sales 23 percent and saved $50,000 through accident reductions.

Sometimes such results happen even when the program is haphazard and does not fully take into account the 12 guidelines for success. But for those companies which want to "wave goodbye" to their competitors, employee involvement of the scope described in this article must be a way of life.

Boost Productivity with Employee Contests

K. Dow Scott
Steven E. Markham
Richard W. Robers

The Maid Bess Corporation, an apparel manufacturer in Salem, Virginia, like the rest of the domestic textile and satellite industries, was faced with increasing foreign competition and high production costs. Customer abandonment for cheaper, often better-quality foreign products, skyrocketing prices for resources and relatively high U.S. wages necessitated an upswing in productivity. Subsequently, and after careful analysis, the company realized traditional pay-for-performance measures weren't the solution.

Instead it turned to employee contests, developed to reward employees for attaining specific productivity goals during a specified period, to provide a needed boost. The gravity of the productivity-plus-high-production-cost problem is best understood with wage comparisons among this worldwide industry.

In the United States, the minimum wage is $3.35 an hour, but the majority of imported apparel is from Nationalist China (minimum wage: 20¢ an hour), Sri Lanka (40¢ an hour), and Central America (a little more than $1 per hour).

Although domestic producers can often beat the performance of foreign competitors in terms of delivery time and quality, the major area of cost concern is productivity. Domestic producers must determine how to reduce unit production costs while still making a quality product.

A part of the solution to this problem is state-of-the-art equipment and machinery. Another aspect is the continual development of the most efficient methods of job performance. However, because the apparel industry is labor intensive, the "people factor" must be incorporated into any plans for obtaining substantial increases in productivity.

FINANCIAL INCENTIVES ARE STILL THE MOST EFFECTIVE

Because of productivity gains made by the Japanese, books and seminars about Japanese management have been very popular in this country. However, in the rush to adopt Japanese managerial approaches, a traditional American way to increase productivity has been overlooked: financial incentives.

Financial incentives represent a management program that captures the basic values of the American culture. It is simply not enough to tell many people they are doing a good job. Unless employees are recognized in a special way, such as with pay raises, recognition programs enjoy limited success.

Financial incentives not only provide an opportunity for people to earn more, but also satisfy their needs for recognition, esteem and enriched lifestyles.

Numerous monetary reward programs linking an employee's pay with his or her performance have been tried in American industry. Researchers have found strong evidence that, in situations in which pay is linked to individual performance, employee motivation is high and the tendency for turnover is restricted to poor performers. In fact, they have found financial incentive programs are more often associated with higher levels of performance increases than other management programs, such as goal setting, job enrichment or employee participation.

There are, however, several problems with pay-for-performance programs.

- The complexities of work and the differences between jobs make it difficult to identify performance measures that distinguish between people and their jobs.
- Companies can't always afford to invest large enough sums of money in incentive pay to make such increases meaningful.
- Managers sometimes feel pay increases must be given to average performers to retain those employees who would be difficult to replace in a tight labor market.
- Pay differences between peers can result in unintended conflict, negative feelings and disincentive.
- Union leaders are often unwilling to negotiate incentive pay because major pay differences between employees doing similar work can create competition and conflict between employees.

There are, however, other financial incentive programs that can motivate employee performance without having the undesirable consequences associated with merit pay programs.

Employee contests represent such an alternative. Contests are widely used to motivate consumers to buy, to stimulate sales people to sell, and to encourage the public to donate to worthy causes. Contests, however, have been largely overlooked in terms of their potential for motivating employees who are not in direct sales.

For the Maid Bess Corp., however, an employee productivity contest eased its employee motivation and competitive market problems. The corporation has 370 non-exempt employees, 278 of which are paid on a piece rate. Most employees are women (94%), and their average education is 11th grade.

Job applicants are screened for psychomotor skills and receive as many as 14 weeks of training. The annual turnover rate is 40%—low for the industry.

Most piece-rate workers earn between $4.50 and $5.25 an hour—above the industry average. Their piece-rate system includes a bonus for high levels of performance.

During 1983, the average absenteeism rate at the plant was 6.2%; employees are not paid when they are absent.

A CONTEST'S SUCCESS HINGES ON THE PERCEPTION EVERYONE IS A WINNER

The company's contest took into account employees' varying abilities—even those on similar jobs. One goal was to convey to all employees that just by competing in such a contest they would be winners, even if they did not receive the prize for their category because successfully increasing their output—in an attempt to achieve the contest's goal—would ensure a higher hourly wage. Thus, the contest was structured so employees with similar earnings would only compete against those employees with similar productivity abilities.

The groups were formed on the basis of each individual's average productivity, or hourly rate, based on the previous 13-weeks' performance. For contest purposes, six piecework earnings groups were formed with a 50¢/hour range in each group. Hence, those whose earnings fell within the $4.00/hour to $4.50/hour average earnings would compete with those in the same range. If a $3.50/hour earner were to compete with a $6.50/hour earner, there would be an inequity in required productivity increases, i.e., a 10% increase at $3.50/hour would be only $0.35, while the $6.50/hour earner would have to increase by $0.65.

Three separate contests were conducted during a two-year period and each contest lasted three months. During the contests, employees could not miss more than two days and remain eligible for the prize. The person in each of the six groups who had the highest productivity level during the three-month period won the prize—a cash award or a trip to the World's Fair.

The contest rules were posted in the plant, and employees were informed frequently of their progress. Because the contests were held at three different times, a comparison between productivity during and between contests was facilitated.

Studies indicate the productivity contests for hourly employees had a significant effect on plant productivity. On average, productivity increased 3.79 percentage points during contest periods, which represented a $103,800 increase in profit to the company. Based on the $1,800 spent on prizes, the company obtained more than a 5,700% return on its investment.

While holding seasonal effects constant, productivity during the three contest periods averaged 87.32%; when the contests were not in effect, productivity averaged 83.53%. This is a particularly noteworthy accomplishment because the employees at this company were already being paid for their output—there was a piece-rate and bonus system. Thus, one can only estimate the effect a contest would have on employees who were simply paid by the hour and not by what they produced.

Interestingly, when a contest ended, the plant productivity level never dropped back to its pre-contest level; no changes to the hourly standards were made during post-contest periods. Absenteeism averaged 7.15% when the contests were not in effect, and 5.44% when they were.

When the seasonal effect was held constant, however, there was no significant difference between the absenteeism rates for contest and non-contest periods.

Why did the contest have such a dramatic effect?

- A concrete, identifiable type of performance was specified.
- Rewards were directly linked to performance.
- Employees were recognized for good performance.

Personnel professionals can follow several principles to create a successful contest program:

1. Make the program understandable and spell out the rules in complete detail.
2. Ensure that all contestants perceive a chance to win.
3. Develop realistic, achievable and measurable goals.
4. Run the contest for a relatively short, specific time period.
5. Be sure the prizes or rewards are desired by employees.
6. Ensure rewards and recognitions are given promptly.
7. Actively promote the program and the objectives of the program. Involving employees in the development of the contest makes them more likely to achieve the goals.

By following these straightforward principles, managers can design contests for employees that will contribute significantly to increased productivity. Besides, a contest now and then just might make organizational life a little more fun.

Quality Circles in the United States: A Conceptual Reevaluation

Gerald R. Ferris and John A. Wagner III

Recently, the United States has experienced serious problems in the growth of productivity. While productivity grew about 3% per year during the 1960s and 1.4% in the 1970s, American growth subsequently stalled, with the U.S. falling to the sixth position among several leading industrial nations (cf. Latham, Cummings, & Mitchell, 1981). Much of the historical rise in American productivity stemmed from technological innovation, and to some extent the recent plateau has resulted from the decrease in technological advances in the U.S. relative to those of competitors abroad. While current advances such as robotics and computerized shop floor control are revolutionizing production technologies, trends in American productivity are also influenced by human resources. The American public seems to believe that employees could do more work, since more than 50% of the adult respondents in a recent Gallup poll agreed that American workers are not producing as much as they might. Managers may well share this view, prompting the contemporary focus on the improvement of worker productivity.

Because of this focus, Japanese management practices have attracted increasing interest (e.g., Hatvany & Pucik, 1981; Ouchi, 1981a; Pascale & Athos, 1981; Takeuchi, 1981). Of these Japanese practices, quality circles (QCs) have been targeted as a particularly promising approach to improving the productivity of American workers (e.g., Blocker & Overgaard, 1982; Gryna, 1981). Testimonials in the professional literature promote QCs as a panacea for productivity problems (e.g., Dewar & Beardsley, 1977; Zemke, 1980). Unfortunately, most of the literature appraising the effectiveness of American QCs has consisted of anecdotal case data presentations; little rigorous research exists (e.g., Ramsing & Blair, 1982). This lack of scholarship is especially alarming in light of recently reported failures of American QCs (e.g., Burck, 1981; Metz, 1980; Takeuchi, 1981), and it indicates that social scientists should critically evaluate the use and implementation of QCs in the United States. To this end, this article questions several assumptions underlying the current use of QCs, examines why American QCs might prove less successful in the long run than Japanese experiences appear to suggest, and proposes new implementation strategies aimed at the reduction of long-term QC failure in the U.S.

QUALITY CIRCLES: DESCRIPTION AND ASSUMPTIONS

QCs are small groups of employees, usually ranging in size from 3–15 members, that meet periodically to identify and resolve job-related problems. Membership in American QCs is usually voluntary and the amount of time members spend in QC activities may range from an hour per month to a few hours each week. Most Japanese QCs are institutionalized processes and, as a result, are not truly voluntary (Cole, 1979). Japanese QCs typically meet twice monthly, on company time, for about one hour per session (Takeuchi, 1981). While QCs were originally designed as a shop floor process focused on quality control, they have recently become directed at a wider variety of organizational problems, such as cost reduction, pollution control, and improvement of employee morale (cf. Cole, 1979). Additionally, American QC interventions have recently been included in organization-wide quality of working life (QWL) interventions—

Reprinted from *Journal of Applied Behavioral Science, 21,* pp. 155–167, copyright 1985, JAI Press.

which often include structural changes such as management-worker steering committees, semiautonomous work teams, and the like—patterned after European industrial democracy projects headed by Tavistock researchers (e.g., Emery & Thorsrud, 1964, 1976; Trist & Bamforth, 1951; Trist, Susman, & Brown, 1977). Since production workers usually participate in QC decision making, organizations must often provide training in techniques such as control charts, cause-and-effect diagrams, data gathering, and Pareto analysis, all of which are designed to cultivate quantitative problem-solving skills (e.g., Wood, Hill, & Azumi, 1982).

Although considered a Japanese innovation, two Americans—Edward Deming and J. M. Juran—apparently were involved during QC development in post-World War II Japan. The Lockheed Missile and Space Company reintroduced QCs to America in 1974. By the end of 1975, Lockheed had 15 QCs, and the company doubled that figure by 1977. Researchers estimated in 1980 that more than 3,000 QCs had been initiated in more than 500 U.S. organizations (Ramsing & Blair, 1982), and these numbers appear to be increasing at present. One can attribute this growth to American managers' interest in the benefits—such as savings in production costs, quality improvements, and increased work force satisfaction—expected to occur through QCs. These expectations are based on three major assumptions: that groups outperform individuals in the identification and solution of organizational problems, that participation enhances the productivity of organization members, and that American workers desire work place participation. These assumptions merit close attention, and we examine them below.

Group Performance

A fundamental assumption supporting QCs, both in America and Japan, is that grouping workers together enhances their ability to identify and resolve problems. In Japan, this assumption appears at least partially valid (e.g., Cole, 1979). Examination of American research on group and individual decision making, however, suggests otherwise (Hare, 1976; Hill, 1982; Shaw, 1976; Smith, 1973). Hare (1976) suggests that, in many cases, individuals can solve problems better than groups can. Only when tasks can be divided into independent, individualized jobs do groups demonstrate greater effectiveness. Hare also reported that groups exhibit more efficiency on manual tasks than individuals, but not on intellectual tasks. Furthermore, he noted that while groups typically perform better than the average member, they seldom perform better than the best member. He argued, therefore, that many cases of apparent superiority of the group over individuals result from the presence of one superior individual. Since probability theory implies that highly capable people are not likely to be found in most groups if abilities are normally distributed (Hill, 1982), Hare's research suggests that many groups will likely consist of medium- and low-ability members whose group performance is weak on conjunctive or intellectual tasks.

Additionally, research on "brainstorming" indicates that individuals usually produce more ideas when working alone than when working in brainstorming groups (Bouchard, 1969; Bouchard & Hare, 1970; Campbell, 1968; Dunnette, Campbell, & Jaastad, 1963; Street, 1974). The distraction of other group members possibly decreases each individual's, including the best member's, ability to perform (Lamm & Trommsdorf, 1973). This explanation is compatible with theory and research on social facilitation (e.g., Street, 1974; Zajonc, 1965), which indicates that the presence of others inhibits the performance of novel tasks but facilitates the performance of well-learned tasks. As a whole, American research appears to suggest that intellectual, novel, brainstorming-type tasks, such as the tasks often undertaken by QCs, can be better performed by individuals than by groups.

The assumption that groups outperform individuals receives further contradiction from Steiner's (1972) proposal that member effort tends to decline with increasing group size, presumably because of reduced feelings of personal responsibility. Early research in a variety of settings appeared to support this notion (e.g., Darlay & Latané, 1968; Shaw, 1960). More recent research that has focused directly on "social loafing" (e.g., Latané, 1981; Latané, Williams, & Harkins, 1979) has generally supported Steiner's model, indicating that members who believe that personal performance cannot be accurately measured tend to reduce their levels of performance. Aggregate performance is likely to suffer in direct proportion to the number of members in a group—and the accompanying difficulty of checking others' performance—(cf. Olson, 1971), so the effects of group size on QC performance deserve researchers' attention.

In sum, one cannot unconditionally accept the general assumption that American QCs perform better than their individual members would. Much of the research cited in this section, however, has been performed in experimental laboratory settings and is suspect because of the novelty that experimental conditions often possess—such as tasks of short duration, social isolation, observers and monitoring equipment—and the situational control that laboratory experimenters can exert (Argyris, 1975; Katz, 1980). In contrast, ongoing QCs generally become familiar settings within which participants can exert strong personal or social control. Prior to its acceptance or rejection, therefore, the assumed relationship between QC-type group work and performance merits close investigation by field researchers sensitive to the work setting *in situ*.

Participation and Productivity

Japanese QCs are participative in name but institutionalized obligations in practice (cf. Dore, 1973), while American QCs are considered mechanisms for increasing participation in the workplace. In part, proponents see QC participation as a way of increasing participant commitment to the process and outcomes of decision making, as suggested by various commitment models (e.g., Kiesler, 1971; Salancik, 1977). Additionally, even if the assumed productivity of group work is subject to question, as suggested above, one may still assume that the personal involvement afforded by QC participation might enhance the productivity of workers employed in formerly autocratic organizations.

Although participation contributes to higher employee satisfaction and health than does directive decision making (French & Caplan, 1972; Jackson, 1983), research on participative decision making has provided only mixed support for the participation-productivity assumption (Frohman, Sashkin, & Kavanaugh, 1976; Lowin 1968; Locke & Schweiger, 1979). According to Locke & Schweiger (1979), much of the research that appears to support the participation-performance assumption is so contaminated by other factors—such as goal-setting interventions (Latham, 1983)—that one cannot reach specific conclusions about the effects of participation alone. Sashkin (1982, 1983) suggests, however, that the effects of participation on productivity are strongly influenced by the implementation strategy. When properly implemented—by training in information gathering techniques, open discussion, collaborative problem solving, and consensus decision making, for example (Maier, 1963; Huse, 1980)—and when consistent with the managerial values and climate in the surrounding organization (Walton, 1975), participative group decision making can increase productivity by 15% or more (Frohman & Sashkin, 1983; Marrow, 1972; Marrow, Bowers, & Seashore, 1967; Sashkin, 1982).

Apparently, the validity of the participation-productivity assumption is so dependent on the extent to which participative interventions are carefully implemented—rather than simply "installed" without training (Sashkin, 1982)—that one cannot take for granted the assumption's validity in every QC situation. In American interventions patterned directly after Japanese QCs, attention to quantitative problem solving skills might overshadow the development of participative group process skills, undermining potential QC productivity gains.

Worker Desires for Participation

A third assumption underlying American QCs is that all workers want, seek, and profit from participation. Grounded in the human relations movement (e.g., Argyris, 1964; Likert, 1961; McGregor, 1960), this assumption stands behind the recent use of QCs in American QWL interventions.

Contrary to the assumed universal desire for participation, Hackman and Oldham (1976, 1980) discovered that some American workers resist taking on enriched tasks that involve, among other things, increased job autonomy. Their explanation for this finding suggests that an individual's desire to participate in the control of her or his working life can be conditioned by prior work experiences, and, therefore, the people unaccustomed to participating in workplace decision making may attempt to avoid doing so. Similarly, Hall and Schneider (1973) and Kopelman (1977) found that people's needs for challenge and personal growth become reduced by long periods of deprivation. Katz (1980) identifies this devaluation as an adaptive strategy that immobile employees use to adjust to the realities of routine task situations, suggesting that such workers might be motivated more by clearly defined jobs than by jobs higher in novelty or autonomy. As an aside, we note that managers in Scandinavian QWL projects found it necessary to preserve a set of traditionally managed tasks for employees resistant to shop floor participation, even after extensive training in workplace collaboration and participative management techniques (*Job Reform in Sweden*, 1975). This appears to lend cross-cultural corroboration to the findings of American researchers.

In a different vein, Kanter (1982) suggests that some workers might view participation as inauthentic or lacking any real impact. Such individuals would argue that through QCs management does not provide workers with actual control, but merely with the "illusion of control" by offering them the chance to provide input that the organization subsequently ignores. Employees who believe this would likely avoid participation, portraying it as a subtle form of manipulation.

Overall, researchers question the assumption that workplace participation is universally desired, either in America or abroad. Rather, some workers apparently desire participation while others may not, especially in the absence of the sort of participation training discussed above.

CONCEPTUAL ANALYSIS

Considered together, one cannot accept the above three assumptions in all QC situations without reservation. Therefore, we are not surprised that problems have occurred in the long-term preservation of many American QCs. At Lockheed, for example, QCs have languished since their initial promoters left the firm to consult elsewhere (Burck, 1981). Yet QCs have had long-term success in Japan. Two considerations, often ignored in the anecdotal investigation of QCs, may underlie this difference in QC success. First, typical Japanese and American QCs differ significantly, partly because of differences in the ways organizations are usually structured in the two nations. Second, and more fundamentally, typical Japanese and American QC members have contrasting orientations toward work. We will examine below these differences and their potential effects on QC success.

Organizational Differences

Japanese and American QCs differ most notably in that American QC membership is typically voluntary while Japanese membership is usually institutionalized. Additionally, QC participation in the U.S. apparently does not aim to ratify predetermined outcomes or managerial values to the extent that participation in Japan does. Both of these contrasts stem from modal differences in the typical forms of organization that surround Japanese and American QCs.

The large Japanese work organizations that most often use QCs usually consist of latticeworks of groups developed through intensive initial socialization and sustained through a unique set of managerial practices (Wagner, 1982). Upon entry, blue-collar workers become members of a workgroup whose supervisor fills an *in loco parentis* role (Cole, 1971). The supervisor provides small gifts and favors, organizes social events, inquires at sick workers' homes about their health, and so forth, with such actions aimed at obligating workers to their supervisor in patterns of shared coworker dependence. This dependence holds each work group together in much the same way that parent-child relationships sustain many American families (cf. Abegglen, 1958). QC work is a group task that strengthens the salience of work group membership, a function that is especially important when Japanese workers must perform Western-style, individualized assembly line tasks. The subordinates' dependence on their superior enables the work group supervisor to control apparently participative QC problem solving by selectively offering or withholding support. In turn, the group supervisor—who is also dependent on a superior—ensures that QC performance reflects the directives of upper-level managers. Japanese QCs, which are most often formed among blue-collar workers, therefore constitute an integral part of the control system that sustains organization in large Japanese firms.

In contrast, American organizations conventionally assign individualized tasks (i.e., one worker per job and vice versa), especially at the blue-collar level. Employees are usually organized through inducements-contributions arrangements (March & Simon, 1958; Thompson, 1967) in which each worker formally or implicitly agrees to perform as directed in return for pay, praise, privileges, and so forth. American organizations, therefore, often rely on a form of control based on the utilitarian exchange of acquiescence for self-interested reward. QC voluntarism directly contradicts this exchange pattern to the degree that members are not personally rewarded for their participation. In fact, bonus payments for successful QC participation, which are not distributed in Japanese QCs, constitute one of the latest attempts to sustain American QC viability. Additionally, the participative nature of American QCs effectively reverses the power relations that may exist between blue-collar workers and their superiors during non-QC work. Therefore, while QCs are an integral part of the normal Japanese way of organizing, they can differ markedly from the structure of typical American organizations. This difference in degree of organization-QC "fit," a strong likelihood in American organizations lacking other participative managerial techniques, provides a powerful reason for expecting the long-term success of Japanese and American QCs to differ. Of course, American organizations that incorporate QC interventions in participative QWL programs may enhance the fit between organization and QC. In such instances, differences between American and Japanese employees' work orientations become especially important as a possible explanation for QC failure.

Orientational Differences

Underlying the contrast between Japanese and American organizations is a more fundamental difference in the way workers typically make sense of and react to work experiences. Several researchers (e.g., Hofstede, 1980; Ouchi, 1981b) have noted that most Japanese organization members espouse collectivism, an orientation in which group interests sometimes take precedence over personal interests. As collectivists, the majority of Japanese workers attribute the success or failure of performance to group efforts and abilities. Consequently, they resist personal rewards for exceptional performance (Ouchi, 1981a) and form close-knit, long-term relationships with peers and immediate supervisors (Cole, 1971; Dore, 1973). Additionally, Japanese collectivists are quite likely to adopt values, such as the recently publicized value placed on product quality, that may make their jobs more difficult yet contribute to the success of their organization.[1]

Conversely, most American organization members espouse individualism (e.g., Hofstede, 1980), an orientation that considers self-interest more important than group interests and attributes performance to personal efforts and abilities. The majority of American workers desire personal rewards for a job well done (e.g., Latham & Wexley, 1981), and usually form only transitory, work-oriented relationships with all but a few coworkers. Workers will likely pursue group interests and shared benefits only when they contribute to personal well-being—that is, when personal and group interest are consistent.

Differences between collectivism and individualism suggest an important reason why Japanese QC success has not been duplicated in the U.S. The positive orientation toward group work that exists among Japanese collectivists casts QCs in a favorable light. Long-term relationships among coworkers, together with a positive orientation toward group interests and values that benefit the organization, contribute to the continued viability of Japanese QCs. As collectivists, Japanese QC members do not oppose bearing personal sacrifice to ensure group well-being. Therefore, QCs support and are supported by the work-related orientation of many Japanese workers.

One cannot say the same about most workers in the U.S., however. American workers' positive orientation toward individualized effort can undermine the group-oriented nature of QC work, particularly in situations in which overlapping personal and group interests have not developed through the participative discovery of commonly held personal desires. In such situations, each American worker's pursuit of personal interests can be a major detriment to QC performance—as when, for example, the QC decides on a production method that increases the difficulty of one member's task, but that member refuses to conform to the decision without an increase in pay. The absence of all but a few long-term relationships among many American coworkers further erodes the basis of Japanese-style QC success. To the extent that American organization members possess individualistic orientations, they consider the self-sacrifice sometimes required to sustain QC productivity a burden to be avoided, if possible (cf. Wagner, 1982). In sum, while Japanese collectivism supports QC viability, American individualism may not.

SUGGESTIONS FOR QC IMPLEMENTATION

Besides contributing to the long-run viability of QCs, Japanese work-related collectivism, and the type of organization enacted through its possession, also sidesteps the validity questions associated with American QC assumptions. First, American assumptions about the effects and desirability of participation are unlikely to be possessed, at least in a similar form, by Japanese managers. To the Japanese, the pseudo-participation (Pateman, 1970) that occurs in QCs is a way of ensuring blue-collar subordinates' continued acceptance of the values, if not goals, of upper-level managers (Dore, 1973; Wagner, 1982). Neither performance expectations nor work force demands seem to have stimulated Japanese QC implementation, although American researchers such as Abegglen (1958) appear to have mistakenly inferred otherwise. Second, American research on groups, which apparently invalidates the assumption that QCs perform better than individuals, has been based on laboratory observations of American research subjects. One might expect these subjects, who most often possess individualistic orientations—and therefore a positive orientation toward individualized work—to perform better as individuals than as group members. In contrast, the collectivism typically espoused by Japanese organization members supports the proposition that group performance is both desirable and superior to individualized work. To the extent that Japanese QC members behave according to their vision of the working world, the assumption that groups enhance productivity is likely to be sustained. As a result, American research does not invalidate a major managerial assumption behind Japanese QC success.

In light of the preceding discussion, this observation appears to indicate that QCs in the United States might prove more successful if American organizations and their members were more participative and/or more collectivistic in form and orientation. This suggests that the following three implementation strategies might improve American QC success: carefully cultivated work-place participation, as exemplified in recent American QWL interventions, so as to enhance group commitment and commonalities in personal interests; an intensive individualistic-to-collectivistic reorientation of members and practices in U.S. organizations so as to replicate Japanese organizational practices; and the selection of the minority of American workers who already possess collectivistic orientations for inclusion in QC projects so as to produce Japanese-like work groups. The first strategy—workplace participation—requires organizations to provide workers with access to technical information and performance feedback, both of which are used in decision-making processes characterized by a high degree of political equality between managers and workers (Wagner, 1982). This strategy can require deep structural changes in formerly autocratic firms, as it is well known and documented elsewhere (e.g., French & Bell, 1978; Huse, 1980). Therefore, we will devote the remaining discussion to the second and third collectivistic strategies, both of which are less familiar in the United States.

The option of intensive reorientation appears both difficult and expensive, probably outweighing the gains expected through QC performance; organizations will not, therefore, likely adopt it. To initiate organizational collectivism, a form of group building similar to the process used in American military training might prove successful. Newcomers to the military are isolated from outsiders, housed in barracks, fed in central facilities, and issued uniforms, all of which reduce the salience of the newcomers' formal personal identities. They are indoctrinated in groups and are taught, through repeated demonstration, that each individual is responsible for the well-being of the entire group. This training produces a team of soldiers willing to place collective well-being ahead of personal welfare, whenever the two conflict, in combat situations. We must emphasize that, as an organizational intervention, even a weakened version of the military indoctrination process would go "deeper" (Harrison, 1970) than the team-building programs currently employed by organizational change agents (e.g., Beckhard, 1972; Bell & Rosenzweig, 1978; Dayal & Thomas, 1968). While team-building attempts to foster collaboration through the development of jointly adopted but personally accepted goals or interests, the type of group building necessary to stimulate individualistic-to-collectivistic transition would have to nurture in employees the willingness to occasionally ignore personal interests for the sake of work group—or organizational—well-being. To sustain this willingness, the organization or work group might have to ensure the long-term well-being of the members through such Japanese practices as lifetime employment and subsidized food, clothing, and housing. Without these kinds of practices, personal well-being could remain so problematic that organizational collectivism might lose credibility.

The second alternative, selecting for QC work those collectivists who currently exist in American organizations, appears more immediately plausible. While most members in U.S. organizations are individualists, evidence exists that a sizeable minority are collectivists (Moch & Wagner, 1982). Research does not explain this phenomenon, but one can speculate that American collectivism might arise through religious doctrines or familial relations that stress that "the whole sustains its parts" (cf. Weber, 1958) or through immigration and the consequent possession of work orientations developed elsewhere. Moch and Wagner (1982) have developed a set of questionnaire items that might prove useful in the identification and selection of organizational collectivists for inclusion in QCs. Breer and Locke (1965) and Hofstede (1980) have proposed other scales. American organizations might sustain those collectivist orientations currently held by employees if they bring together the collectivists in work situations, thereby separating them from the influence of individualist peers. Such a strategy could contribute further to the long-term viability of QCs in the U.S.

CONCLUSION

As concerns for productivity have grown in recent years, methods for improving production effectiveness have been sought. Recent attention has focused on Japanese management practices, with a particular interest in the full-scale importation of such practices as QCs. Although QCs have enjoyed considerable success in Japan, U.S. organizations seem to have adopted them on the basis of emotional appeals rather than sound evidence, without critical evaluation of their underlying assumptions. This article does not suggest that QC efforts in the U.S. should be abandoned, but that researchers and managers should reexamine several assumptions about QCs and consider certain issues both before and during implementation. QCs may work well in some situations, but we find it unreasonable to assume that they will be equally effective in all.

ENDNOTES

1. The form of collectivism typical to the Japanese and discussed in this article differs from the communistic self-sacrifice demanded by Leninist organizations in Russia. Current Soviet ideology dictates sacrifice to benefit the interests of a state apparatus directed by privileged officials. In contrast, collectivistic sacrifice benefits a membership group composed of the sacrificing individuals and close associates, all of whom share a psychological sense of safety, security, and community, even in the presence of other, differing personal interests.

REFERENCES

Abegglen, J. C. (1958). *The Japanese factory.* New York: Free Press.

Argyris, C. (1964). *Integrating the individual and the organization.* New York: Wiley.

Argyris, C. (1975, April). Dangers in applying results from experimental social psychology. *American Psychologist, 30,* 469–485.

Beckhard, R. (1972). Optimizing team-building efforts. *Journal of Contemporary Business, 1*(3), 23–32.

Bell, C. H., Jr., & Rosenzweig, J. (1978). Highlights of an organization improvement program in a city government. In W. C. French, C. H. Bell, Jr., & R. A. Zawacki (Eds.), *Organization development: Theory, practice, and research.* Dallas: Business Publications.

Blocker, H., & Overgaard, H. (1982). Japanese quality circles: A managerial response to the productivity problem. *International Management Review, 22,* 13–16.

Bouchard, T. J. (1969). Personality, problem-solving procedure, and performance in small groups. *Journal of Applied Psychology Monograph, 53,* 1, Pt. 1.

Bouchard, T. J., & Hare, M. (1970). Size, performance and potential in brainstorming groups. *Journal of Applied Psychology, 54,* 51–55.

Breer, P. E., & Locke, E. A. (1965). *Task experience as a source of attitudes.* Homewood, IL: Dorsey.

Burck, C. G. (1981). What happens when workers manage themselves? *Fortune, 104*(2), 62–69.

Campbell, J. P. (1968). Individual versus group problem solving in an industrial sample. *Journal of Applied Psychology, 52,* 205–210.

Cole, R. E. (1971). *Japanese blue collar,* Berkeley: University of California Press.

Cole, R. E. (1979). *Work, mobility and participation.* Berkeley: University of California Press.

Darley, J., & Latané, B. (1968). Bystander intervention in emergencies: Diffusion of responsibility. *Journal of Personality and Social Psychology, 8,* 377–383.

Dayal, I., & Thomas, J. M. (1968). Operation KPE: Developing a new organization. *Journal of Applied Behavioral Science, 4,* 473–506.

Dewar, D., & Beardsley, J. P. (1977). *Quality circles.* Menlo, CA: IAQC.

Dore, R. P. (1973). *British factory-Japanese factory.* Berkeley: University of California Press.

Dunnette, M. D., Campbell, J. P., & Jaastad, K. (1963). The effect of group participation on brainstorming effectiveness for two industrial samples. *Journal of Applied Psychology, 47,* 30–37.

Emery, F. E., & Thorsrud, E. (1964). *Form and content in industrial democracy.* London: Tavistock.

Emery, F. E., & Thorsrud, E. (1976). *Democracy at work.* Leiden, The Netherlands: Kroese.

French, J. R. P., Jr., & Caplan, R. J. (1972). Organizational stress and individual strain. In A. J. Marrow (Ed.), *The failure of success.* New York: AMACOM.

French, W. L., & Bell, C. H., Jr. (1978). *Organization development* (2nd ed.). Englewood Cliffs, NJ: Prentice-Hall, 1978.

Frohman, M. A., & Sashkin, M. (1983). *Participative work redesign: A data-based case.* Unpublished manuscript, University of Maryland, College Park, MD.

Frohman, M. A., Sashkin, M., & Kavanaugh, M. J. (1976). Action research applied to organization development. *Organization and Administrative Sciences, 7,* 121–168.

Gryna, F. M. (1981). *Quality circles: A team approach to problem solving.* New York: AMACOM.

Hackman, J. R., & Oldham, G. R. (1976). Motivation through the design of work: Test of a theory. *Organizational Behavior and Human Performance, 16,* 250–279.

Hackman, J. R., & Oldham, G. R. (1980). *Work redesign.* Reading, MA: Addison-Wesley.

Hall, D. T., & Schneider, B. (1973). *Organizational climates and careers.* New York: Seminar Press.

Hare, A. P. (1976). *Handbook of small group research* (2nd ed.). New York: Free Press.

Harrison, R. (1970). Choosing the depth of organizational intervention. *Journal of Applied Behavioral Science, 6,* 181–202.

Hatvany, N., & Pucik, V. (1981). Japanese management practices and productivity. *Organizational Dynamics, 9,* 5–20.

Hill, G. W. (1982). Group versus individual performance: Are N + 1 heads better than one? *Psychological Bulletin, 9,* 517–539.

Hofstede, G. (1980). *Culture's consequences: International differences in work-related values.* Beverly Hills: Sage.

Huse, E. (1980). *Organization development and change* (2nd ed.). St. Paul: West.

Jackson, S. E. (1983). Participation in decision making as a strategy for reducing job-related strain. *Journal of Applied Psychology, 68,* 3–19.

Job Reform in Sweden. (1975). Stockholm: Swedish Employers' Confederation (SAF).

Kanter, R. M. (1982). Dilemmas of managing participation. *Organizational Dynamics, 11,* 5–27.

Katz, R. (1980). Time and work: Toward an integrative perspective. In B. M. Staw and L. L. Cummings (Eds.), *Research in organizational behavior* (Vol. 2) (pp. 81–128). Greenwich, CT: JAI Press.

Kiesler, C. A. (1971). *The psychology of commitment.* New York: Academic Press.

Kopelman, R. E. (1977). Psychological stages of careers in engineering: An expectancy theory taxonomy. *Journal of Vocational Behavior, 10,* 270–286.

Lamm, H., & Trommsdorf, G. (1973). Group versus individual performance on tasks requiring ideational proficiency: A review. *European Journal of Social Psychology, 3,* 361–388.

Latané, B. (1981). The psychology of social impact. *American Psychologist, 36,* 343–385.

Latané, B., Williams, K., & Harkins, S. (1979). Social loafing. *Psychology Today, 13*(4), 104–110.

Latham, G. P. (1983). The role of goal setting in human resources management. In K. M. Rowland and G. R. Ferris (Eds.), *Research in personnel and human resources management* (Vol. 1) (pp. 169–199). Greenwich, CT: JAI Press.

Latham, G. P., Cummings, L. L., & Mitchell, T. R. (1981). Behavioral strategies to improve productivity. *Organizational Dynamics, 9,* 5–23.

Latham, G. P., & Wexley, K. N. (1981). *Increasing productivity through performance appraisal.* Reading, MA: Addison-Wesley.

Likert, R. (1961). *New patterns of management.* New York: McGraw-Hill.

Locke, E. A., & Schweiger, D. M. (1979). Participation in decision-making: One more look. In B. M. Staw (Ed.), *Research in organizational behavior* (Vol. 1) (pp. 265–339). Greenwich, CT: JAI Press.

Lowin, A. (1968). Participative decision-making: A model, literature critique, and prescriptions for research. *Organizational Behavior and Human Performance, 3,* 68–106.

Maier, N. R. F. (1963). *Problem-solving discussions and conferences.* New York: Wiley.

Marrow, A. J. (1972). *The failure of success.* New York: AMACOM.

Marrow, A. J., Bowers, D. G., & Seashore, S. E. (1967). *Management by participation.* New York: Harper & Row.

March, J. G., & Simon, H. A. (1958). *Organizations.* New York: Wiley.

McGregor, D. (1960). *The human side of enterprise.* New York: McGraw-Hill.

Metz, E. J. (1980, August). Caution: Quality circles ahead. *Training and Development Journal,* 71–85.

Moch, M. K., & Wagner, J. A., III. (1982). *The measurement of individual-collectivism.* Working paper, Department of Management, Michigan State University, East Lansing, MI.

Olson, M. (1971). *The logic of collective action.* Cambridge, MA: Harvard University Press.

Ouchi, W. G. (1981a). *Theory Z: How American business can meet the Japanese challenge.* Reading, MA: Addison-Wesley.

Ouchi, W. G. (1981b). Individualism and intimacy in industrial society. *Technology Review, 83*(7), 34–36.

Pascale, R. T., & Athos, A. G. (1981). *The art of Japanese management.* New York: Simon & Schuster.

Pateman, C. (1970). *Participation and democratic theory.* Cambridge, England: Cambridge University Press.

Ramsing, K. D., & Blair, J. D. (1982). An expression of concern about quality circles. In K. H. Chung (Ed.), *Academy of Management Proceedings* (42nd annual meeting). Wichita, KS: Academy of Management.

Salancik, G. R. (1977). Commitment and the control of organizational behavior and belief. In B. M. Staw and G. R. Salancik (Eds.), *New directions in organizational behavior.* Chicago: St. Clair.

Sashkin, M. (1982). *A manager's guide to participative management.* New York: American Management Association.

Sashkin, M. (1983). *The ethics of participative management.* Unpublished manuscript, University of Maryland, College Park, MD.

Shaw, D. M. (1960). Size of share in task and motivation in work groups. *Sociometry, 23,* 203–208.

Shaw, M. E. (1976). *Group dynamics: The psychology of small group behavior.* New York: McGraw-Hill.

Smith, P. B. (1973). *Groups within organizations.* London: Harper & Row.

Steiner, I. D. (1972). *Group process and productivity.* New York: Academic Press.

Street, W. R. (1974). Brainstorming by individual coacting groups and interacting groups. *Journal of Applied Psychology, 59,* 433–436.

Takeuchi, H. (1981). Productivity: Learning from the Japanese. *California Management Review, 23,* 5–19.

Trist, E. L., & Bamforth, K. W. (1951). Social and psychological consequences of the long-wall method of coal-getting. *Human Relations, 4,* 3–38.

Trist, E. L., Susman, G. I., & Brown, G. R. (1977). An experiment in autonomous working in an American underground coal mine. *Human Relations, 30,* 201–236.

Thompson, J. D. (1967). *Organizations in action.* New York: McGraw-Hill.

Wagner, J. A., III. (1982). *Individualism, collectivism, and organizational behavior: A macro comparison of micro processes.* Working paper, Department of Management, Michigan State University, East Lansing, MI.

Walton, R. E. (1975). The diffusion of work structures: Explaining why success didn't take. *Organizational Dynamics, 3*(1), 3–22.

Weber, M. (1958). *The Protestant ethic and the spirit of capitalism.* New York: Scribner's.

Wood, R., Hull, F., & Azumi, K. (1982). *Evaluating quality circles.* Unpublished manuscript.

Zajonc, R. B. (1965). Social facilitation. *Science, 149,* 269–274.

Zemke, R. (1980, January). Quality circles using pooled effort to promote excellence. *Training and Development Journal,* 31–34.

An Introduction to Employee Right-to-Know Laws

Matthew M. Carmel and Michael F. Dolan

On December 29, 1970, Congress promulgated the Occupational Safety and Health Act. Its stated purpose was "to assure safe and healthful working conditions for working men and women and to assure that each employer furnishes to each employee a place of employment free from recognized hazards likely to cause death or serious physical harm."[1]

Although passage of the act established several administrative bodies, such as the National Institute for Occupational Safety and Health (NIOSH) and the Occupational Safety and Health Review Commission, the one agency most personnel administrators are familiar with is the Occupational Safety and Health Administration (OSHA). This agency is primarily responsible for establishing and enforcing safety and health standards in addition to statistical and record-keeping duties.

OSHA standards which apply to general industry are contained in Title 29, Code of Federal Regulations (CRF), Part 1910. Several references to employee rights of access to workplace information are contained here (e.g., those regulations dealing with lead, asbestos and noise) but more pertinent to this discussion, Subpart C, Section 1910.20, titled "Access to Employee Exposure and Medical Records," affords workers or their designated representatives broad access rights to relevant environmental exposure and medical records.

OSHA's preamble to the final rules on this standard states its simple purpose as "enabling workers to play a meaningful role in their own health management." The agency found that "individuals have greater self-interest in maintaining their own well-being and sound public policy dictates employees be afforded an opportunity to identify, correct or prevent health problems since there were no assurances that anyone else would protect them with equal vigor or determination."[2]

In association with the underlying philosophy for and benefit of creating an informed workplace, current OSHA policy has been perceived, rightly or wrongly, as deemphasizing regulatory enforcement of health standards. Thus interpreted, its approach has been to shift this burden to state and local levels or develop more "performance-oriented" standards. Heightened public awareness of environmental health issues, increased union vocalism, advances in toxicological research and the need for more specific criteria not addressed at the federal level have acted in concert to create a demand by various groups for so-called "employee right-to-know" laws.

CURRENT LAWS

As of July 1, 1984, at least 19 states have passed legislation governing employee rights of access to workplace environmental or chemical substance information (see Figure 1). Given the dynamic nature of the legislative environment on this topic, however, personnel administrators should seek appropriate consultation with an expert in the field prior to initiating compliance efforts.

Although most of the current laws vary in detail, all address six common issues: Definition of toxic or hazardous substance, employer duties, manufacturer or supplier duties, employee rights, trade secret protection and enforcement provisions.[3]

Figure 1
States Incorporating Employee Right-to-Know Laws as of July 1, 1984

Alaska	New Hampshire
California	New Jersey
Connecticut	New York
Illinois	Oregon
Maine	Rhode Island
Maryland	Washington
Massachusetts	West Virginia
Michigan	Wisconsin
Minnesota	

Definition of Toxic or Hazardous Substances. Defining, understanding and appropriately applying the words "toxic" and "safe" are possibly the two most difficult tasks facing individuals who communicate such ideas to laymen or the public at large. It is well recognized that several factors must be considered when defining toxicity such as dose, duration of exposure, critical organ, route of entry into the body, predisposition to potential harm (i.e., age, sex, previous exposure) and nature of undesirable effect. Furthermore, every substance is both toxic and nontoxic. For example, water, if ingested in sufficient quantity and speed, can upset the body's electrolyte balance. On the other hand, absorption of small enough quantities of arsenic will not cause death. Determining when exposure to a toxic chemical substance is safe from a social viewpoint can only be based upon subjective evaluation of acceptable inherent risk. Frequently, this comes down to a cost-benefit analysis or assigning a dollar value to human life or health. Certainly, this subject will continue to be a matter of debate and controversy.

Notwithstanding those definitional problems, some states and municipalities have elected to define a toxic chemical substance as any of the nearly 400 recognized by OSHA as an air contaminant (listed at 29 CFR 1910.1000 Subpart Z). This listing was an incorporation by reference of the 1968 American Conference of Governmental Industrial Hygienists Threshold Limit Value booklet of recommended airborne limits for workplace contaminants and represents some of the more common substances present or used in industry. Considering OSHA's limited resources and the time-consuming nature of standard setting processes, permissible levels for significant numbers of additional chemicals are not likely in the near future. This has led to criticism of the list as being too narrow.

A second frequently cited reference used by governmental bodies is the NOISH Registry of Toxic Effects of Chemical Substances. This document is an annual compilation of all known toxic substances by chemical name, synonyms and published biological concentrations at which toxic effects occur in various animal species. More than 45,000 substances are listed, including common items such as sugar and salt, and approximately 6,000 are added each year. It has been argued this list is overly broad and presents an unmanageable burden upon industry.

Additional methods of definition referenced, either singly or in combination, include substances listed as carcinogens by the International Agency for Research on Cancer: substances listed by the federal Environmental Protection Agency as possessing known adverse human health risks, i.e., materials listed within or meeting definition of hazardous waste as promulgated in the Resource Conservation and Recovery Act; substances listed in the federal Department of Transportation Hazardous Materials Table 49 CFR 172.101: substances defined as hazardous or toxic by other state agencies; any "poisonous" chemical; and no definition at all.

Employer Duties. An employer subject to one of these laws has three primary tasks: Informing employees of their rights of access afforded to them under applicable statutes and providing details on chemicals with which they work, maintaining and allowing employee access to appropriate records and providing employee training. Where the law deals with the issue, the universal method of informing employees of their rights is through posting a conspicuously located notice. Some states and municipalities only require that employees be notified and do not specify a method.

The common method of providing detailed information on chemical substances is via Material

Safety Data (MSD) sheets, also known as Form OSHA-20. This format summarizes material identification, ingredients, physical properties, fire and explosion data, health hazard data, reactivity data, spill or leak procedures and other special precautions. Typically, manufacturers or suppliers are in a better position to prepare accurate and up-to-date MSD sheets on their products. However, employers are responsible for forwarding the information to employees as required.

Employers must keep accurate records of environmental conditions, measurement data, employee medical examinations and other information related to chemicals in the workplace. These provisions are closely allied to the federal OSHA standard discussed earlier.

A final employer duty is training workers regarding chemicals used at their jobs. Specified methods range from verbal explanation of MSD sheets to written communications or more formalized instruction for each substance used or present in the workplace. Several states require training initially upon assignment and annually thereafter. One even specifies monthly explanation of the notices including use of an interpreter where necessary.

Manufacturer or Supplier Duties. The most important responsibility assigned to manufacturers is preparation of actual MSD sheets. As indicated earlier, manufacturers should have greater familiarity with physical properties, handling procedures and their products' potential for causing health or safety problems. Most laws seem to acknowledge by this approach that purchasers cannot be expected to possess the depth of knowledge or experience required for relaying pertinent and accurate information on specific chemicals.

In addition to preparation of MSD sheets, the law may also impose requirements upon a manufacturer for labeling, time frames in which information must be provided, periodic information updating and providing MSD sheet copies to state agencies.

Employee Rights. Herein lies the heart of all employee right-to-know laws. Essentially all statutes permit employees to receive copies of MSD sheets or similar information concerning chemicals they work with. Provisions are generally included to prevent discrimination against those exercising their rights, prohibit waiver of rights and establish time frames in which requests for information must be honored (ranging from five days to 72 hours). At least two states provide for employee refusal to work if information is not supplied as requested. Unlike the OSHA Employee Exposure and Medical Records Access rule, most state and local right-to-know laws apply to both private and public sector employees.

Trade Secret Protection. Disclosure of information concerning chemical processes occasionally may compromise a company's competitive advantage if this information is considered a trade secret. This point is particularly important to certain industries, such as flavor and fragrance manufacturers, whose very livelihood is dependent upon maintaining confidentiality regarding product formulas.

Addressing these very real concerns, several jurisdictions have incorporated trade secret provisions in their right-to-know laws. Generally, employers or manufacturers must claim and provide justification for certain information to be protected and request nondisclosure status. The governing agency would then make a final determination. Once protected, all or specific portions of the information would not be released. It is important to realize, however, that several states do not address trade secrets and one state allows disclosure after 30 days' notice to the employer or manufacturer.

Enforcement Provisions. Many employee right-to-know laws have been criticized as being "toothless." In the final analysis, however, enforcement or threat thereof will determine their true effectiveness. Presently, enforcement provisions, where provided, establish civil or criminal penalties ranging from $10 to $10,000 and up to 90 days imprisonment.

CONCLUSION

Many employers are rightfully distraught over the bureaucratic entanglement being created by enactment of right-to-know laws. The seemingly endless conflicts in purpose, definitions, terminology and required actions not only hinder interstate commerce, they work to the detriment of employees by delaying smooth passage of regulations designed for their protection. No one wishes to deny employees their information-access rights and the benefits of an informed workplace are not disputed. However, only through a nationally uniform hazard communication rule which preempts state and local laws, addresses both labor and management concerns, and whose implementation is technically, logistically and economically feasible, will the ultimate goal of effective worker protection be realized.

REFERENCES

1. Public Law 91–596, Occupational Safety and Health Act of 1970.

2. *Federal Register,* Volume 45, Number 102, May 23, 1980.

3. Michael F. Dolan, "Impact of right to know laws upon the industrial hygiene profession," American Industrial Hygiene Association Conference, Philadelphia, PA. May 22, 1983.

The Experience and Management of Work-Related Stress

Terry A. Beehr and Kristofer J. Fenlason

It has become popular in recent years to blame all sorts of unusual and dramatic employee actions on the "stress" of the job. Newspaper articles have appeared describing incidents across the country in which disgruntled employees or former employees shoot or otherwise attack their supervisors or their co-workers, in which specific jobs are labeled stressful because there is occasional danger to life and limb, and in which an employee commits suicide. While these incidents *may* be the outcome of work-related stress, there is usually little strong evidence that this is the case. Such dramatic examples are not the routine or most typical outcome of occupational stress.

The more typical outcomes of occupational stress develop more slowly and result in less dramatic, but still serious consequences for both employees and the organization. Employees have been reported to suffer from peptic ulcers and cardiovascular disease in addition to anxiety, depression, and job dissatisfaction, all results of work-related stress. These outcomes may be harmful to the health of the employee, and they may also affect the productivity or health of the organization. Recent reports indicate that organizations are facing an increasing number of court cases and worker-compensation claims based on charges of work-related stress. It has been estimated that nationally the cost of just two possibly stress-related illnesses, peptic ulcers and cardiovascular disease, may be around forty-five billion dollars, and the cost of job stress for executives alone has been estimated in the billions of dollars. Many of these estimates are based on the *direct costs* of illnesses and so don't include hidden costs, such as the effect of employees who are working at lowered levels of efficiency but who are still on the job. Clearly, job-related stress is an issue that managers must deal with for their own health, the health of their subordinates, and the health of their companies.

A DESCRIPTION OF WORK-RELATED STRESS: THE CASE OF CARL JOHNSON

The following composite description of an employee experiencing the beginning stages of stress is drawn from almost two decades of research on work-related stress.

> Carl Johnson is thirty-two years old, has a wife and two children, an MBA from Central Michigan University, and has been working at General Manufacturing, Inc., for eight years. Carl works in the personnel department, and although he has had adequate pay raises over the years, his basic responsibilities have remained pretty much the same. He travels a good deal at certain times of the year to recruit new employees. The recruiting activity has become increasingly difficult and uncertain because of General's decision to expand and because of pressure to hire large percentages of minorities and women among the new recruits needed to meet the expansion. While in the office, Carl supervises four people; each does a variety of work, including job analysis using a system developed by Carl's supervisor, interviewing applicants, giving orientation sessions to new employees, providing training sessions for supervisors, and so forth.
>
> In the last couple of years, slow but perceptible changes have occurred in Carl's behavior. When he started working at General, he was fresh from college, newly married, and was considered a hard-driving, aggressive, ambitious, outgoing employee. Now Carl often arrives at work late and leaves early. At work, he stays to himself, keeping his door closed most of the day. His supervisor and coworkers do not come around to talk to him the way they used to, and he does not seek them out. Even lunches, which he used to enjoy with others, are taken alone now. He has had trouble sleeping, and finds that a drink or two before bedtime helps. He often feels ill and experiences a sense of dread on Sunday nights and on nights before his recruiting trips. He has been having periodic stomach trouble, and although he has not yet seen a physician, he has taken quite a few sick days off from work in the last six months. He feels that his life is going nowhere and that it makes no real difference how he does his job.
>
> Carl has been wanting to quit his job for several years, but has taken no concrete actions. He has fantasized about making a career change, although he is not certain what direction to take. Lately, he has been thinking that maybe he should return to school to become a psychologist.

Carl Johnson is a typical example of an employee who is just far enough into the stages of job stress that people who know him well notice it, including his supervisor, the manager of personnel at General Manufacturing. As with many issues, employee health becomes important only when something has gone wrong; it is poor health that catches the manager's attention.

It is apparent that Carl Johnson is experiencing stress in his job, but what constitutes it, and what causes it?

WHAT IS JOB STRESS?

The typical use of the word *stress* implies negative effects for the individual, but this broad definition of stress can sometimes be confusing. In the workplace, work-related or job stress can be defined as a topic concerned with the adverse effects of work situations on the health (both psychological and physical) of employees. These same work situations that affect employee health can also have consequences for the organization that employs the people. In the case of the individual employee these consequences (ill health) are referred to as "strains" on the individual worker. The aspects of the work environment that "cause" the individual strains and may lead to organizational consequences are known as *stressors.*

Job stress is a difficult subject to master because of its complexity. Understanding requires a combination of skills from the fields of management, medicine, psychology, and sociology. It also requires long-term studies to discover cause-and-effect sequences in job stress, because some of the most serious consequences are slow to develop. Finally, organizations vary greatly in their composition, orientation toward their employees, and their styles of management, adding further variables.

Because working conditions and organizations differ there is a need to pinpoint which aspects of the job, the person, or organization contribute to job stress. Many different models and theories have been proposed as methods to conceptualize stress in organizational settings. One model, put forward by Beehr, is useful for analyzing stress in organizations.

A Three-Part Model of Job Stress: Uncertainty, Importance, and Duration

This model defines stress as a cognitive (psychological) state in which an individual faces a particular decision-making or problem-solving situation. This situation has a great deal of *uncertainty* associated with obtaining *important* outcomes, and the uncertainty goes on for a long *duration.* If this model is written out mathematically it takes the form:

$$\text{Stress} = (\text{Uncertainty} \times \text{Importance} \times \text{Duration})$$

Because this is a multiplicative model of stress there would be *no stress* if any of the three terms is zero. That is, there would be no stress in a situation when someone has no uncertainty associated with obtaining the expected outcomes, or the outcomes are of no importance, or the situation is very brief (duration close to zero). The total amount of job stress would be the sum of all of the work situations that have some measure of uncertainty, importance, and duration.

It seems obvious that stress is greater when important outcomes are involved and when the stress is of long duration, but what about uncertainty? It is intuitively appealing to think of uncertainty as stressful; certainly it can be uncomfortable and disruptive. The uncertainty in this model is present in two situations that apply to a wide range of circumstances within the work environment. In the first situation the employee (manager or subordinate) is uncertain whether his or her *efforts* will lead to a desired *performance.* For example, Carl Johnson may be uncertain about whether his efforts to recruit minorities and females will result in enough hirings. The less certain he is that his efforts will have the desired effect, the more uncertainty he feels.

The second situation occurs when a person is uncertain if his or her own *performance* (which may or may not be satisfactory) will lead to a desired *outcome.* For example, Carl Johnson may be performing his job adequately from day-to-day, but he may question whether this will lead to a sense of personal satisfaction.

Different instances of uncertainty may be found in any job. The two mentioned above, that is, uncertainty that effort will result in a performance ($E \rightarrow P$) and that performance will lead to a particular outcome ($P \rightarrow O$) are associated with particular stressors.

THREE APPROACHES TO JOB STRESS

The Person-Centered Approach

One of the popular approaches to understanding job stress starts with the assumption that stress is primarily a function of the person. For example, employees exhibiting certain personality traits or behaviors may be identified as those most likely to develop heart disease. Unfortunately, with this approach the chances for change are slim, because the logical treatment would be to alter the employee's basic personality or behavior patterns—a very difficult task.

The Job-Centered Approach

A second approach is to identify stressful jobs. One can isolate a single job, such as air traffic controller, or rank order many jobs in terms of their stressfulness. This method will not eliminate the negative effects of stress, however. For example, if the job of air traffic controller is stressful, the only apparent suggestion would be to do away with it, obviously, an unacceptable solution.

The Job Characteristics Approach

The job characteristics approach entails the identification of the job's stressful *characteristics.* Many jobs can have similar characteristics; for example, an element of time pressure. The job characteristics approach focuses on more specific causes of stress than the job-centered approach does, and is more likely to be useful in remedying the adverse effects of job stress. While it may not be possible to eliminate a job, it may be possible to change some of its stressful characteristics.

In this approach, the causal elements (stressors) are the job characteristics themselves. Role conflict, role ambiguity, role overload and underutilization of skills are four such stressors. *Role conflict* occurs when an employee is expected, as part of the job, to do something that would conflict with other job or non-job demands or with his or her personal values. With *role ambiguity,* an employee is not sure what is expected on the job or how the reward system works. In *role overload,* the employee cannot complete the work that is expected because there is too little time or because he or she does not have the necessary skills. *Underutilization of skills* may occur when an employee has more skills than the job requires.

Carl Johnson may be experiencing some of these stressors. He may be experiencing role conflict if he has not met the expectations that he recruit an increased number of highly qualified employees *and* that many of these employees be females and minorities. While Carl's usual recruiting efforts have led to an adequate number of highly qualified people, they might not simultaneously result in an increased percentage of females and minorities. He, therefore, might feel conflicting expectations (of course, one solution might be to change his usual recruiting tactics). Judging from the case description, Carl is probably not experiencing role ambiguity; his job appears to be well defined. In fact, it may be that he knows all too well what is expected of him and is feeling the third role stressor, role overload—not having enough time to do what is expected of him and a high level of uncertainty about whether his recruiting efforts will succeed. Finally, Carl seems to be underutilizating his skills. His job has not changed in years and, if regular raises are proof, he is performing it adequately. This underutilization may result in uncertainty about job satisfaction and personal fulfillment in his career.

Although there are other stressors in the work environment, those mentioned here seem to occur frequently in many different jobs. Some of the stressors may be present in a job from time to time, but not constantly. Role overload, for example, is worst at times of deadlines, such as the end of a tax year for many accountants. It is assumed that the more pervasive these stressors, the more they influence important outcomes that, in turn, may prove unsettling to employees.

Another job characteristic deserves mention in relation to job stress: the degree of social support. Although some researchers have defined social support as just the presence of others, most see it as a more "active" type of social influence; that is, when something supportive is done by someone for someone else. It appears that there are at least two types of social support, *instrumental* and *emotional.* Instrumental social support involves someone suggesting ways or actually lending a hand to complete the work, or help deal with work stressors. Emotional social support may simply mean caring, listening sympathetically, and a felt intimacy in the work relationship. Employees benefit from caring friends at work as well as off the job, particularly when stressors are especially evident.

The social influence of managers on their subordinates has long been considered important in the area of leadership and organizational dynamics. Similarly, the supportive activities of coworkers in general, and work groups in particular, have been recognized since the days of the Hawthorne studies as important aspects of the work environment. Consequently, it is logical to expect social influences on job stress—whether the social support comes from supervisors or coworkers. There are organization theories that recommend supervisor and co-worker support for the sake of organizational effectiveness, but such support also may help to alleviate occupational stress.

CONSEQUENCES OF JOB STRESS

Consequences for the Employee

Three types of consequences that are especially relevant to the employee are suggested: physical, psychological, and behavioral. Among the potential *physical consequences* are coronary heart disease, peptic ulcer, and other more general effects on the person's physical health. It has been suggested that stress may increase susceptibility to a variety of physical problems. *Psychological consequences* include dissatisfaction with one's life, low self-esteem, psychological fatigue, boredom, emotional exhaustion, resentment toward the job, and generally poor mental health often characterized by depression. The *behavioral consequences* include increased smoking or reduced ability to quit smoking, which may have long-term effects on the employee's physical health, increased drinking, and even marital discord.

Interviews by Beehr for a study of occupational stress in employees netted the following remarks:

> [There is a] "general uptightness"—[I] "cannot relax."
>
> [I drink enough coffee that] "I get pretty wired by 5:00."
>
> "I get pretty soused."
>
> "I fear I'm going to forget to do something important or not be in tune, and something terrible will happen."
>
> "I can't eat, because of all the things that get brought up and nothing gets done."

Consequences for the Organization

Although most of the consequences of job stress are important to both the employee and the organization, several have traditionally been of particular interest as measures of organizational effectiveness. Organizations need to be concerned about very high levels of stress, because it seems most likely that poor job performance (and therefore organizational ineffectiveness) will occur in such situations. In general, the higher the level of stress on the employee, the lower the level of performance. It is possible, however, that job performance may even improve with a limited increase in stress, since the job becomes more challenging under such circumstances. Organizations may also suffer the effects of employee job stress through an increased monetary burden in worker's compensation and court judgments leveled against them by employees who believe their lives have been adversely affected. If the present legal trends continue, companies will not only pay more in compensation judgments and court costs but corporate insurance rates will also rise.

Other consequences for the organization can be classified under the rubric of withdrawal. Employees experiencing too much stress tend to be frequently absent and less involved with their work. This latter form of withdrawal is psychological—employees too long under stress just seem to quit caring. Obviously, this also has implications for their behavior at work. They may also withdraw through turnover, changing jobs within the organization, or going outside. One extreme form of withdrawal is *occupational abandonment.* An employee not only leaves the organization but also the field. This type of withdrawal should be viewed as especially serious when the field is difficult to get into—one requiring years of school or a great deal of sacrifice or dedication to gain entry. The withdrawal, both physical and psychological, represents an attempt to cope with the stress. If work is an aversive experience, employees are behaving rationally by trying to get away and stay away from it. Withdrawal from work may not be an effective coping mechanism, however. In fact, some forms of withdrawal may lead to additional problems for the organization. The following quotes from people experiencing job stress indicate some of these organizational consequences:

> "My goal is to get a new job by September."
>
> "I wouldn't want to do this forever."
>
> "Sometimes I would like to get out of this business."
>
> "Getting no recognition for something leads to an 'I don't care' attitude."
>
> "My needs sometimes get in the way of doing a good job."
>
> "I do not socialize with people I work with."
>
> [Other people here are] "touchy. I don't want to talk with them."
>
> "I don't want to know about decision making here anymore."

Consequences for Society as a Whole

The consequences of job stress are not limited to the employee and the employer. Our society has long cherished an ethic that expects hard work from its citizens. Some forms of withdrawal mentioned here are clearly inconsistent with that ethic, and they, therefore, are in conflict with a dominant society norm. If the incidences of ill health due to job stress are sufficiently widespread, there are also costs to society in terms of an increased burden on already overloaded medical and social welfare resources. In addition, if negative effects on performance were frequent, a reduced gross national product and fewer products and services available for consumption would result. A broad perspective on the problem of job stress shows that it is important to more parties than just employee and employer.

HOW MANAGERS CAN RECOGNIZE STRESS AND WHAT THEY CAN DO ABOUT IT

Because managers are in positions of responsibility, they can influence the organizational situations more directly than lower-level employees.

Stress on the Manager and How to Deal with It

The responsibility, along with ambiguity, conflict, overload, and sometimes underutilization of skills, can make a manager's job very stressful. One obvious way for managers to determine whether they are experiencing job stress is to assess the stress potential of the job by looking for potential effects on themselves or their work. There are several diagnostic questions to ask. For example, "Is the quality of my work deteriorating?" Under conditions of overload, the quality may decline even if the employee is highly productive. "Do I dread coming to work each day? Do I avoid co-workers while I'm at work? Do I dislike answering the telephone because it may mean more work, or questions about the progress I'm making on current projects?" If these questions are answered affirmatively, the manager could be using withdrawal as a technique for avoiding job stress. "Has my health been declining? Do I seem to have more than the usual (for me) number of physical complaints? Am I frequently nervous and jumpy? Do I become tired easily? Am I feeling more depressed than usual?" These questions are aimed at the personal consequences of the job stressors.

Finally, one may ask diagnostic questions directly about potential stressors in the job environment. "Do I have frequent deadlines? Is it clear exactly what I should do on my job? Has it been made clear how my work is evaluated and rewarded in my company? Are there conflicting expectations placed upon me by people in my work situation?" If the answer to these questions is yes, some potentially stressful situations are present, regardless of whether they have yet affected job performance or health. Employees who were beginning to recognize that they were in stressful work situations made these statements to interviewers:

> "This job does not allow me to use my talents."
>
> [My superiors here] "fail to recognize some of my better talents."
>
> [There is] "sometimes a lack of leadership, and some of us move in and take control. Ambiguity results. We are not really in command but feel we must do something."
>
> [There is] "too much work to do to get sick."
>
> [I am] "being told, 'you have to do this. I don't know how the hell you're going to pull if off, but you have to do it.' "

If the answers to the questions indicate that the manager is in a stressful situation, there are three ways to alleviate it. A first set of strategies is aimed at the symptoms of the job stress. One of the most important steps is to see a doctor about one's current physical health. A thorough physical examination will often uncover physical symptoms before they become severe. Without early diagnosis, prevention is difficult.

Similarly, seeking help from psychological counselors is an approach aimed at the psychological symptoms. Other approaches recommended by some psychologists include attempts at controlling physiological symptoms psychologically. The mind and body are interrelated, and some methods by which the mind can control aspects of the physiology are becoming popular in

America today. Some examples are relaxation training, biofeedback, and transcendental meditation. While scientific proof that these techniques can cure or prevent the ill effects of job stress is lacking, it is clear that people can learn to control some of their physiological processes when they engage in these techniques. As with many decisions faced by management, however, it behooves us to take action before waiting for years of research; these techniques represent current possibilities for relieving the effects of job stress.

A second set of approaches for easing job stress is aimed more directly at the causes—the job stressors. If the problem is role conflict, the people sending the conflicting messages can often be told the problem. A joint session, aimed at reducing the conflict, can result in a new definition of the employee's role(s)—one that is more productive and satisfying. If the manager experiencing the conflict does not tell these people that their messages are in conflict, they have no reason to change. If role ambiguity is the job stressor, asking for clarification of company policies, procedures, and job duties should help. If the responses to these questions are also unclear or indicate that nobody knows for sure what the particular manager's job entails, the manager could take the initiative by defining the job himself or herself—defining it clearly so that stress is reduced and defining it so that it is productive for the organization. In most companies, a manager who chooses this approach and performs well in the redefined job is considered highly effective. Approaches aimed at reducing role overload as a job stressor include delegation of authority and seeking additional assistants, either on a temporary or permanent basis. Most managers have at least some minor tasks that can be delegated to competent assistants; in fact, the assistants may find this rewarding. This not only relieves the overload of the manager, but it helps to develop the skills of other employees.

A final approach aimed at the stressor directly, one that could reduce all the stressors, is to seek a job in another company. If no other remedies are possible in a given organization, it may be beyond the ability of a manager to alleviate the situation. A more favorable situation may be necessary for the welfare of an employee. This approach does little to help the organization, however. It often takes many cases of turnover before any large-scale organizational change is attempted to correct the problem.

The third set of strategies consists of approaches aimed at easing the effects of job stressors without changing them directly. If the stressors (for example, overload) in the manager's job cannot be reduced directly, making some other changes can often reduce their ill effects. Some of Beehr's work has shown that employees can withstand the effects of role ambiguity better if they have job autonomy. If the manager can get more autonomy in day-to-day activities, he or she is less likely to suffer ill effects. Similarly, psychological support seems to help, whether it comes from work or from friends and family after work. When overload is the problem, the practice of queuing, or deciding the order in which to tackle one's many tasks, may help alleviate the stress. Obviously, there is still the same amount of work to complete, but this orderly approach ensures that the most important things will get done, and the manager can derive a sense of accomplishment by progressing through the list.

Another strategy for reducing the harmful effects of stress involves off-the-job activities. One straightforward approach is to take time out to eat lunch away from the office. Too often managers feel they need to work every minute of the day, even during lunch. In fact, this may be a symptom of overload; there is probably too much to do in the time available. Taking a break may even improve the quality of the work that gets done. Managers can also try to take nonworking vacations. Overloaded managers tend to skip vacations or to take work with them when they do go. But when there are legitimate opportunities for time out, they should be taken. It is surprising to many people to discover that they can still get their work done.

Finally, exercise is important if people are to withstand some of the physical effects of job stress. Vigorous exercise may be better for reducing coronary heart disease than milder activities such as walking or playing golf. Because vigorous activity can be detrimental to the health of some people, always consult a physician first. Choose an activity that is intrinsically interesting; otherwise, there is a tendency to quit the exercise program.

Stress on the Subordinate and How to Deal with It

The symptoms of stress in a subordinate's job are the same, but they are often difficult for the manager to observe. Withdrawal in the form of absenteeism is a potential sign of stress, but there are many other causes of absenteeism. Ill health is another sign of job stress, but as with absenteeism, the reasons are not always clear. If absenteeism and ill health combine with avoidance of other employees (including the manager) and with low-quality work, however, job stress may be the culprit.

In trying to discern job stress, a manager may also want to ask some of the same diagnostic questions as he or she asked of his or her own behavior. If it is apparent that an employee is experiencing job stress, a manager may want to personally intervene by trying to alleviate stressors (such as role ambiguity) or refer the employee to an appropriate resource, such as a company employee assistance program. It is clear from the rising number of stress-related worker's compensation claims and court cases that the manager who is aware of employee stress should do something.

One important response that a manager can make is to be socially supportive. Because the characteristics of the workplace appear to contribute to job stress and since managers control some of these characteristics, they should consider themselves potential sources of support. For example, a manager may be supportive in responding to a subordinate's requests for help. If it is at all possible, when the subordinate asks for assistants, clerks, or secretaries, the manager can try to supply them, if only on a temporary basis. This can help the subordinate get through especially heavy periods of stress, such as approaching deadlines. If the stressor is in the form of ambiguity or conflict, the manager may be one of the parties sending ambiguous or conflicting messages. A subordinate asking for clarification or resolution of such conflict deserves a manager's serious attention.

Another way social support can affect stress in the workplace is through direct effects on the strains. Researchers have found that social support almost always reduces a number of strains in work-related stress. This finding is especially important if managers are unwilling or unable to change the stressful characteristics of the job itself. Even though the job may remain the same, social support may still help to alleviate the harmful effects of stress. For example, socially supportive co-workers help to relieve boredom or dissatisfaction, or a manager helps to relieve an employee's anxiety about a project by discussing the expectations and making it clear that he or she will be supportive of the employee's efforts.

THREE MANAGEMENT STYLES AND THEIR RELATIONSHIPS TO JOB STRESS

If job stress is a relatively new concept for most managers, it would be helpful to indicate probable relationships between this topic and other topics that are more familiar. Therefore, this section attempts an integration of the concept of job stress with each of three management styles: traditional management, participative management, and contingency management.

By the *traditional* management style, we mean the use of bureaucratic and classical administrative approaches. Some of the key elements of the traditional style are hierarchy of authority, written job descriptions, unity of command, impersonality, and rational-legal authority, usually administered in a relatively authoritarian manner. Role ambiguity is not supposed to occur in such organizations because of the clearly written job descriptions. With one exception, the traditional management style should result in little ambiguity. The exception refers to unexpected situations; written job descriptions cannot cover all possible events. This can result in widespread role ambiguity, especially if the organization's environment is changing so rapidly that new descriptions cannot be written quickly enough to keep up with the changes.

Similarly, if the structure of the organization and all written job descriptions are initially adequate, there should be little role overload, except in unexpected situations, such as those caused by a change in the work environment or a change to a different work environment. In a like manner, conflicting demands from two or more people would not be expected in such organizations because of the unity-of-command principle. Other kinds of conflict may occur, however, if unexpected situations arise requiring the individual to accomplish a task in a manner that would break bureaucratic rules. It is possible for underutilization of skills to occur under the traditional style of management, however. Employees may become "trapped" in a job that is overly routine and not challenging. In summary, while the traditional management style may allow underutilization of skills it is not likely to generate the first three types of job stressors if (1) the organization structure and all job descriptions are initially adequate, and (2) the organization's environment does not change or changes only gradually.

Once job stress occurs in a traditionally managed organization, however, it can be difficult to alleviate. Any change here tends to be slow, and change aimed at alleviating stress would be no exception. Because traditionally managed organizations are supposed to be impersonal, there may be little opportunity for psychological support. Because of the hierarchy of authority and traditional authoritarian use of power, job autonomy would not be delegated to many people. Therefore, these two ways (social support and autonomy) of alleviating the effects of stress are essentially eliminated. The ability of the traditional management style to deal with job stress, therefore, is low.

The *participative* management style emphasizes the sharing of authority with subordinates. Sometimes this is done with groups of subordinates, and at other times it is more a case of delegation of authority to individuals. Participation can occur in many areas—goal setting, scheduling, methods of work, and evaluation. Taken as a whole, these techniques are sometimes labeled the *human resource approach,* because they attempt to use more of the skills and abilities of employees (their resources) than most other management approaches.

The participative management style is likely to result in role clarity rather than ambiguity, because employees in this case have more say in defining their roles. People who define their own roles should understand them more clearly. Similarly, there is likely to be little role conflict fostered by this management style, particularly if it encourages group rather than individual participation in decision making. Group participation results in more interactions with the people who make demands upon the employee, and conflicting and ambiguous expectations are likely to be noticed and changed. It is less clear what impact the participative management style has on the existence of role overload. Ideally, overload would also be addressed in group sessions, but this may not always occur. It is even possible that this style could result in greater rather than less overload, because employees have more responsibility and more meetings to attend.

The amount of psychological support available for alleviating job stress is likely to be high in participatively managed organizations, because of the high degree of interaction with co-workers. Autonomy is also likely to be strong enough to help ease the effects of stress. This is less likely with group participation than with more individually oriented participation, however, because group influence may at times limit the individual's autonomy. Overall, the participative style is more likely to create lower-stress jobs than the traditional management style.

The *contingency* management style dispenses with the notion that there is one best organizational structure and management style for all situations. For example, the traditional management style may be effective when employees have few skills and strong security needs, and when the organization's technology and environment are relatively simple and stable. Participative management style may be more effective when employees are highly skilled and have strong ego needs, and when the organization's technology and environment are complex and rapidly changing.

The contingency management style has the most promise for reducing job stress. Conflict and ambiguity are likely to be low in traditionally managed organizations as long as the environment is stable; if the environment is unpredictable, the recommended style is participative, helping to reduce the ambiguity and conflict caused by environmental change. Role overload is likely to be

low in traditionally managed organizations, but in participatively managed organizations it may be somewhat higher, for the reasons cited earlier. Autonomy and support are likely to be low in traditionally managed organizations, but presumably they would be less necessary in those organizations, because the amount of ambiguity and conflict would be lower, due to the stable environment. Participatively managed organizations, on the other hand, are likely to have high levels of autonomy and support.

INDIVIDUAL WELFARE AND ORGANIZATIONAL WELFARE: CONFLICT OR COMPLEMENT?

By definition, the primary focus of the job stress topic is the welfare of the individual rather than the welfare of the organization. For humanitarian reasons, managers would like to help the employee by reducing aversive stress. If reducing stress would mean harming the organization's effectiveness, however, the employee could be harmed anyway—by employment in a floundering organization. Therefore, it is important to examine the approaches for reducing job stress in light of both the individual's and the organization's welfare.

Approaches aimed at reducing the effects of stress are not likely to harm the organization; in fact, they may even improve organizational effectiveness. Medical treatment of employee illnesses, psychological counseling, and programs of exercise will (1) make employees stronger and therefore more capable, (2) reduce absenteeism due to illness, and, (3) result in employees with higher self-esteem and the desire to perform well to keep that self-esteem high.

Similarly, increasing social support and the degree of job autonomy is likely to benefit the organization as well as the individual. In fact, some organizational theories promote the use of support and autonomy (whether these or other terms are employed) in order to increase organizational effectiveness.

With one possible exception, approaches to reducing job stress by attacking the causes, the job stressors themselves, are also likely to help the organization. Reduction in role ambiguity and role conflict will make the employees more effective by clarifying how they should direct their efforts, and it will reduce absenteeism due to stress. Reduction of role overload may be the exception, however. While improving organizational effectiveness by reducing absenteeism and increasing the effort the employee expends toward high-quality job performance, reducing overload may also result in lower quantity performance. It is not known, however, whether the benefit of increased quantity due to overload is enough to offset the cost of decreased quality of work and decreased attendance.

Another technique for reducing stress on the individual that may hurt the organization is the employee search for a better job (one in which he or she can be productive with less stress) in another firm. It seems especially likely that highly skilled workers will take this approach, because it is easier for them to find new jobs than it is for the less skilled. This type of turnover may be especially costly for the organization, although the individual may benefit from it. One of the implications, of course, is that management should try to reduce stress so that employees will not make this choice.

Finally, it has been suggested that contingency management approaches would result in relatively lower amounts of job stress for organization members. It seems that this technique for helping the individual could only benefit the organization; in fact, contingency management often is proposed primarily for the reason that it makes for more effective organizations.

Overall, it is clear that alleviating job stress is nearly always likely to help rather than hinder the organization's functioning. Giving attention to job stress does not mean that the organization's welfare is being ignored.

Sexual Harassment: Confronting the Troublesome Issues

David S. Bradshaw

Every human resource manager knows that sexual harassment is one of the major employment problems of the 1980s. Surveys show that anywhere from 42 to 88 percent of women feel that they have been victims of sexual harassment on the job. Not surprisingly, employment discrimination agencies report that an increasingly large percentage of their caseloads involves claims of sexual harassment.

Sexual harassment is not expressly prohibited by Title VII of the Civil Rights Act of 1964. However, the Equal Employment Opportunity Commission has contended for years that sexual harassment is a prohibited form of sexual discrimination. This view was recently validated by the United States Supreme Court in its landmark decision in *Meritor Savings Bank v. Vinson* (June 19, 1986). In that case, the Supreme Court declared that both "quid pro quo" sexual harassment (where a term or condition of employment is conditioned on sexual favors) and "hostile environment" sexual harassment (where an employee is subjected to unwelcome sexual advances or other verbal or physical contact of a sexual nature) are prohibited forms of sex discrimination.

On the state level, many state fair employment practice laws expressly prohibit sexual harassment in the workplace. Some states, such as California, even offer victims of sexual discrimination the possibility of compensatory and punitive damages (as well as back pay) and hold employers strictly liable for sexual harassment by their supervisors.

Unfortunately, sexual harassment can be difficult to define and even more difficult to eradicate from the workplace. While it is clearly a form of employment discrimination, it has some unique characteristics. For one thing, it is frequently an individualized form of discrimination, directed at one or several victims rather than a class of people, such as blacks or Hispanics. For another thing, the conduct that constitutes sexual harassment may be conduct that in other contexts or relationships would not be harassment at all.

In the *Meritor* case, the Supreme Court focused on whether conduct of a sexual nature was *unwelcome* in defining whether the conduct constituted sexual harassment. This is an important concept, particularly since the Supreme Court adopted it instead of the concept of "voluntariness" as the litmus test of sexual harassment. The Supreme Court recognized that a woman may be the victim of sexual harassment even though she may have voluntarily participated in acts of a sexual nature, in the sense of not being forced to do so.

How does one know, for example, that a supervisor's conduct toward a female subordinate is "unwelcome"? In fact, how does one know that the conduct in question is occurring at all? There are no easy answers to these questions. Obviously, it is difficult for an employer to know that sexual harassment is occurring. Even when it is clear that some sort of relationship exists between a supervisor and a subordinate, it may be far from clear that the relationship is not completely "welcome."

Fortunately, the Supreme Court in *Meritor* may have given us a partial answer to these questions

in its discussion of grievance procedures that may insulate employers from liability for acts of their supervisors. In *Meritor*, the employer claimed that it was insulated from liability for supervisorial acts because of its general nondiscrimination policy. The Supreme Court rejected this contention, and expressly pointed out that the employer's policy "did not address sexual harassment in particular, and thus did not alert employees to their employer's interest in correcting this form of discrimination." The Supreme Court also faulted the employer's policy, which required an employee to complain first to her supervisor, who could be the very harasser who was victimizing her. According to the Supreme Court, the employer's defense would have been substantially stronger "if its procedures were better calculated to encourage victims of harassment to come forward."

It would seem, therefore, that the way employers will learn about acts of sexual harassment will be for employees to come forward and tell them. The key is to have a policy and a set of procedures that allow victims of sexual harassment to complain to appropriate employer officials about the conduct they have been subjected to in a confidential and supportive environment.

Of course, particularly in dealing with "hostile environment" sexual harassment, employers should put an obligation on their supervisors to ensure that offensive comments, obviously unwelcome advances, inappropriate touching, and other similar forms of conduct, are eliminated from the workplace.

Here is a summary of some of the steps that an employer can take to guard against sexual harassment claims:

1. Publish a policy prohibiting sexual harassment in the workplace. Be sure to clearly prohibit both types of sexual harassment (i.e., "quid pro quo" sexual harassment and "hostile environment" sexual harassment).

2. Develop procedures whereby employees who feel they are victims of sexual harassment can state their complaints in confidence. These procedures must have a mechanism so that employees are not forced to complain to the very person who is harassing them.

3. Educate both employees and supervisors about sexual harassment and about the employer's policy and procedures to combat it.

4. Take swift action against harassers. Get the word out that this conduct will not be tolerated and back up the policy against sexual harassment with firm action.

Of course, even taking these steps will not provide an employer with any guarantees. Few harassers ever admit their conduct or the severity of their conduct. Terminating a harasser without strong evidence can lead to another set of problems. An employer should make sure it is not trading a potential sex harassment claim for a wrongful termination lawsuit by insisting on strong evidence that the harassment actually took place. An employer should not be so zealous in eliminating suspected sexual harassment from the workplace that it treads unfairly on the employment rights of employees who might be the victim of false accusations. At a minimum:

1. The victim must be carefully interviewed. Generally speaking, a careful written statement should be taken from the victim.

2. Other witnesses identified by the victim should be interviewed. Take written statements if possible.

3. The alleged harasser should be confronted with the evidence against him and thoroughly interviewed. Again, a written statement is highly desirable.

4. If additional time is needed for completion of interviews or other steps in the investigation, one possibility is to suspend the alleged harasser "pending investigation." The terms of the suspension should require the alleged harasser to stay away from the victim and not interfere with the investigation by such steps as seeking to influence witnesses.

5. Extreme care should be taken to preserve the confidentiality of the investigation and any statements given by the victim, the alleged harasser and other witnesses. While there may be certain defenses, there is a real danger of defamation claims in cases of this nature.

Sexual harassment cases raise some very tough issues—ones that have no easy answers. About the only thing that is certain is that it is no longer possible to dodge these issues. Sexual harassment is now a major employment problem, with large potential exposure for those employers who refuse to confront the tough issues of what it is and what should be done about it.

Employee Assistance Programs: An Overview

Chathapuram S. Ramanathan

INTRODUCTION

Productivity losses as a result of employee alcoholism, drug abuse, and stress are of increasing concern to American business. In a study completed in 1973, for example, Knox and Burke reported that losses related to employee alcoholism alone in the United States amounted to fifteen billion dollars a year. A decade later this had escalated to forty billion dollars a year (Swegan, 1983). In addition to alcoholism, losses to American business resulting from drug abuse in the form of reduced productivity, absenteeism, medical expenses, disability claims, and theft are currently estimated at sixteen billion dollars a year. From this, one can begin to understand the size of the "troubled employee" problem in this country (Scanlon, 1986).

According to the Association of Labor-Management Administrators and Consultants on Alcoholism (ALMACA), there will be 77.7 million people in the United States between the ages of twenty-five and forty-four in the year 1990. A conservative estimate is that 12 percent of these people will be involved with substances that either harmfully or adversely impact job performance. This 12 percent of the workforce represents 9.3 million employees. Based on an Employee Assistance Program (EAP) participation rate of 12–15 percent, there will be about 1.9 million more employees in the workforce seeking EAP services in 1990 than in 1980 (ALMACA, 1987).

Many businesses have responded to both current and future productivity losses by providing EAP counseling services to their employees and their families, thus taking a rehabilitative approach. The creation and implementation of EAPs has become one of the fastest growing components of the field of human resources management.

This article provides the reader with basic knowledge about EAPs. In doing so the article:

- Defines and describes an EAP
- Traces the historical development of EAPs
- Highlights the various service delivery models
- Explicates the roles of the EAP worker
- Addresses financial gains attributed to the establishment of an EAP
- Discusses the components of contemporary EAPs
- Discusses the limitations of EAPs.

WHAT IS AN EAP?

Employee Assistance Program (EAP) is the commonly accepted term for workplace-centered efforts to provide counseling services to employees. An EAP can be defined as a set of company or union policies and procedures for identifying or responding to personal or emotional problems of employees that directly or indirectly interfere with job performance. The EAP usually provides information or referrals to appropriate counseling and support services for which the company or the union may pay in part or in whole (Walsh, 1982).

HISTORY OF EMPLOYEE ASSISTANCE PROGRAMS

Employer's initiatives to help alcoholic employees are not new. As early as 1940, a few employers started offering treatment to identifiable alcoholic workers (Maxwell, 1981). The real impetus for meaningful action in caring for the alcoholic occurred with the acceptance of alcoholism as a disease, and with passage of the federal Comprehensive Alcohol Abuse and Alcoholism Prevention, Treatment and Rehabilitation Act of 1970. This act established and funded the National Institute of Alcohol Abuse and Alcoholism (NIAAA). Business has recently moved into the forefront in the fight against this disease, both through the initiative of management and union pressure when management has failed to act (Knox & Burke, 1973). In its 1981 report to Congress, the NIAAA described the trend of occupational alcoholism programs. It indicated that between 1940 and 1945 the number of programs had increased from 4 to 6, then to 50 in 1950, to 500 in 1973, to 2,400 in 1977, and to 4,400 in 1979–1980 (U.S. Department of Health and Human Services, 1981).

Some contemporary EAPs evolved first through a focus on alcohol-related programs, while others from the outset defined their mission in broader terms (Trice & Schonbrunn, 1981). According to Walsh (1982), EAPs grew out of a tradition of hand-holding in the personnel department, informal counseling in the medical department (usually by nurses), and trouble-shooting by unions. Organized EAPs, therefore, are not a new endeavor, but a formalization of an old tradition with specially trained personnel.

Emerging in the 1970s with the new view of alcoholism as a disease was the growing concern about substance abuse as a disease; a disease rooted in psychological and community problems and interwoven with pathologies in home and family life (Jenkins, 1971). In this environment, there developed an interest in the observed correlation between social stress and coronary heart disease. These findings complemented the findings on organizational stress in work settings (Wilinksy & Wilinsky, 1951; Kahn, Wolfe, Quin, Snoek, & Rosenthal, 1964). The result for American business was the emergence of various Quality of Work Life programs, including EAPs.

According to Ford and McLaughlin (1981), interest in the theory and practice of EAPs has been growing rapidly. The traditional supporting argument for an organization funding an EAP is based on the notion that it is more desirable both economically and socially to rehabilitate previously proven and trained employees than to discharge them. Gaeta, Lynn, and Grey (1982) also indicated that many companies are becoming increasingly aware that the troubled employee incurs significant financial liabilities. Factors contributing to financial liabilities are absenteeism, increased accidents on and off the job, lowered productivity and morale, and excessive utilization of medical and disability benefits. Most of the EAP literature addresses only alcohol rehabilitation (Ford & McLaughlin, 1981). Despite the wide array of services that EAPs offer, many consider an EAP to be an alcohol referral service.

A 1981 survey indicated that EAPs were provided by 29 percent of health care agencies, 23 percent of manufacturing companies, 13 percent of retail or wholesale businesses, 25 percent of banking and financial institutions, and 12 percent of service organizations (Ford & McLaughlin, 1981). Organizations employing more than five hundred workers have a higher probability of offering an EAP. The foregoing survey mailed questionnaires to one thousand members of the American Society for Personnel Administration (ASPA). The response rate was 51 percent. Twenty-one percent or 210 of the respondents had an EAP. Lanier (1981) cited the NIAAA's third special report on alcohol and health, which states that over 2,400 organizations, most of them companies and unions, have programs for counseling employees about job-related alcohol problems. Lanier also indicated that 60 percent of the Fortune 500 companies have programs for counseling troubled employees or employees who have job performance difficulties related to personal, social, or emotional problems.

SERVICE DELIVERY SYSTEMS

Phillips and Older (1981) indicated that several different models for the delivery of EAP services have evolved in organizations. The diversity in service delivery is attributed to the variation in the size of the organization, the availability of internal resources for EAPs, and the willingness of the organization to expend resources, including both people and dollars. The literature highlights six major service delivery systems. They are:

1. Internal programs (in-house)
2. Service center programs
3. Internal programs with service center support
4. EAPs located in a treatment or social service agency
5. Union-based EAPs
6. Group consortia

Internal Programs (In-House)

This model is not widely practiced. It is usually prevalent in very large corporations that have their own legal departments, medical staffs, benefits managers, and trained EAP personnel with alcohol and drug counseling skills (ALMACA, 1987). Employees of the work organization use the EAP as a referral point to community resources or internal counseling resources. Services provided by internal programs vary. The classification based on services are (1) assessment and referral services; and (2) assessment, referral, and counseling services. Internally-based program services can be offered at an off-site location.

Internal program responsibilities include the coordination of all client activity within the work environment. However, most internal programs focus on problem assessment and referral to treatment facilities outside the company. Follow-up and feedback for most internal programs are coordinated by the treatment facility and the designated EAP professional or professionals (Phillips & Older, 1981).

Service Center Programs

In this model, the work organization contracts with an independent EAP service provider in the community. The service center in the community provides problem assessment and may provide some short-term counseling. It is the responsibility of the service center to provide diagnosis and the necessary referrals to treatment resources in the community. Thus, the service center is the liaison between employees and the treatment network, and coordinates all client-centered activities. This system allows employees to receive treatment off the work site, and may allow for treatment to more employees because the service center staff time is not involved in the provision of long-term treatment.

Internal Programs With Service Center Support

Here the work organization has an internal program, but, in addition, has a contractual relationship with a service center. The internal program with service center support utilizes the same service center approach, but provides one or more professionals in the organization to facilitate and encourage employees to seek appropriate counseling assistance. This arrangement allows options for assistance either on or off the work site. The external service center resources support the internal EAP. Although the treatment typically takes place outside the internal EAP, staff within the internal program may facilitate the treatment process and are available for program coordination.

EAPs in a Treatment or Social Service Agency

EAP services located in a treatment or social service agency can be offered by a company through a contractual agreement between the company and the agency. Thus, EAP services are offered through a community resource because assessment and treatment services are not available in the company. However, the work organization may have an internal coordinator who facilitates the training and referral activity.

Union-Based EAPs

EAP services within this structure are provided by the union at the union office or hiring hall. Motivating union members to seek assistance is done at the work site by union coordinators and followed by a treatment referral. Community treatment resources are usually utilized. Follow-up of treatment provided through the community resources is coordinated by the EAP staff. This modality does not prohibit management or union members from making referrals to the EAP office.

Group Consortia

This system is used by companies that have too few employees to justify their own EAP consulting services. In this case, a number of smaller companies form a consortium by joining their working populations. Then this consortium contracts with an EAP provider for services (ALMACA, 1987).

ROLES OF THE EAP PROFESSIONAL

The roles of the EAP professional vary according to the service modality of the particular EAP. In general, the roles include problem assessment/diagnosis, case consultation, referral, supervisor training, client follow-up, marketing of EAP services, generating EAP contracts, and so forth. A recent new role for EAP workers is the development and design of corporate-wide substance abuse policies. As companies engage in cost-savings activities to reduce accident rates and workers' compensation claims, they are likely to focus on drug testing and involve EAP professionals as consultants. This is because EAP specialists are experts in the field of substance abuse. This consultative role for EAP workers seems to originate more from companies that do not have an EAP. Depending upon the philosophical orientation of the company, the interventions are usually focused on substance abusers. The company can either adopt a punitive policy and terminate substance abusers or take a more rehabilitative approach so as not to lose those employees. In the latter instance, it is more meaningful to offer EAP services. The ultimate objective of an EAP is to prevent drug abuse through educational activities.

Other emerging roles for EAP professionals may arise in response to the special needs of employees. For instance, if a large number of single parents are facing day care issues, then that can be addressed. Because there are more Americans who are nearing retirement age, some EAPs focus on retirement counseling. Further, the roles vary if the EAP provider is a national or a local provider. For example, national-provider roles include, besides the classic EAP roles, the recruiting of and contracting with local providers, trouble shooting and mediating between local providers and local management, and setting performance standards for counselors.

FINANCIAL GAINS

A study by Illinois Bell of 306 employees with medical-behavioral problems demonstrated an estimated savings of $459,000 in reduced absence, accidents, medical and disability benefits following rehabilitation (Gaeta, Lynn, & Grey, 1982). The authors also indicated that companies such as the New York Transit Authority reported yearly savings of over two million dollars since the beginning of their rehabilitation program.

Ohio Bell, with 24,000 employees, saves four million dollars annually with a recovery rate of 60 percent from its alcoholism treatment recovery program (Lanier, 1981).

According to Lanier (1981), for every dollar General Motors invests in its EAP it gets three dollars back. This three for one return includes only sickness and accident payments and reduced hospitalization costs. Lanier also documents another cost-savings benefit for General Motors, which indicates that in 1980 General Motors saved $3,700 per employee successfully enrolled in its EAP, or a total of nearly $37,000 million for the ten thousand employees who made use of the company's EAP that year (Lanier, 1981). Insurance and health organizations estimate that most EAPs will have a five dollar return for every dollar invested

(ALMACA, 1987). Some airline companies are claiming that they recover as much as eighteen dollars for every dollar invested in their EAPs (ALMACA, 1987). Besides saving dollars, EAPs are pro-human dignity programs and they are an investment in human lives.

FACTORS AFFECTING EAPS AND THE ROLE OF THE PROFESSIONAL

Overall Organizational Philosophy

1. The organization recognizes that personal problems can be successfully dealt with and have a greater likelihood of being resolved if they are identified early and prompt action is subsequently taken. This is in reference to physical illness, mental or emotional illness, alcoholism, drug abuse, marital or family distress, financial or legal difficulty, and so forth.

2. The organization recognizes the need for personal problems to be resolved. Hence, it provides EAP services for its employees, and encourages employees to take advantage of the professional services available through the EAP. Thus, employees may refer themselves to the program for help before deterioration of job performance.

3. It is the responsibility of the employee to seek assistance through, or accept referral to the EAP, and to comply with the recommended action plan when personal problems are affecting work performance.

4. The decision to seek or accept assistance through the EAP will in no way be detrimental to the employee's job security or advancement opportunities.

5. Participation in the EAP in no way relieves the employee of the responsibility to meet acceptable work performance standards.

The nature and composition of the EAP varies depending upon the EAP model utilized by the organization. Based on the model used, the roles played by EAP professionals will vary. However, there are some basic features that are common to most contemporary EAPs.

EAP Philosophy

The overall EAP philosophy reflects a rehabilitative philosophy (Hollmann, 1981). The belief that the workplace can be kept separate from the other aspects of an employee's life is a myth (Kanter, 1977). Such a philosophy recognizes that on-the-job activities affect an employee's off-the-job life, and vice-versa. It is imperative, therefore, that the employee be viewed from a holistic perspective, and that EAP interventions are undertaken through appropriate professional means.

Performance/Productivity Emphasized

EAP services are provided to address problems that affect an employee's job performance/productivity. Though supervisors may refer employees to an EAP, their referrals are to be based on performance deterioration and not on any clinical speculation, since supervisors do not have the clinical expertise to make a clinical diagnosis.

Referral Sources

Employees may obtain professional assistance through an EAP by self-referral, supervisor referral, supervisor recommendation, and medical referral.

Self-Referral. An employee or a member of an employee's family can obtain confidential services for personal problems through the EAP. The EAP counselor will assess the client's situation and either directly refer by telephone, or will arrange to see the individual or the family for further confidential services.

Supervisor Referral. The basis of a referral to the EAP by a supervisor must be a request by the employee for assistance with a personal problem that threatens to further affect work performance, or a particular on-the-job incident that indicates the possible presence of a personal problem.

When an employee's performance is the basis for a supervisor's referral to the EAP, the supervisor is to prepare a written account of the performance problem that has been observed.

Supervisor Recommendation. Supervisor recommends to the employee that he/she seek help through the EAP, but this is not based on any documented decline in performance.

Medical Referral. This referral is made by a physician, nurse practitioner, or social worker. The basis of the referral should be either the identification of a medical symptom or disorder that is commonly associated with a personal problem, such as alcoholism, or a request from the employee for assistance.

The physician or other professional as a referring agent should advise the employee that the appointment with the EAP counselor is being viewed as part of the required treatment plan, and that the situation will be noted in the employee's medical record. The decision to accept assistance through the EAP will be left to the employee.

Duration of EAP Sessions

Contemporary EAPs primarily provide assessment and referral services. Under special clinical circumstances, long-term therapy may be provided, though this is rare. In general, EAP interventions are brief encounters of two to three sessions.

Turf Issue

Primary responsibility for the administration of an EAP usually rests with the human resources department or the medical department. Immediate supervisors have the responsibility of identifying employees whose performances have deteriorated and offering EAP services to them. Employees have a responsibility to use the EAP as a means to resolve personal problems and improve their job performance/productivity.

Comparative Analysis

In addition to the United States, EAPs or EAP-like efforts exist in Canada, India, Western Europe, and Australia. Canadian programs are similar in structure to the U.S. programs and emphasize alcohol abuse. However, in Canada there is a strong involvement with organized labor. There is a large percentage of self-referrals in the United States and Canada, while in Australia little emphasis is placed on self-referral. Australians view alcohol and drug abuse as a national threat and, hence, have a tough federal policy in this area. In the Australian system (called the Industrial Program), the coordinator's primary responsibility is to target substance abusers for counseling services. The Australian model also has strong union backing (Roman, 1983).

Limitations of EAP

EAPs represent a positive approach to dealing with troubled employees. Despite the amount of time, effort, expertise, and dollars that are spent on these programs, EAPs still have fundamental limitations (Hollmann, 1981). These limitations should be systematically addressed by EAPs; that is, to become more proactive rather than maintain the current reactive posture.

In an effort to define and specify their functions, many EAPs have adopted a "specific problem" approach. That is, they organize their practice around a particular problem or group of problems such as alcohol and drug abuse (Ramanathan & Kagle, 1986).

Though there are EAPs that adopt a "broad brush" approach in intervening with troubled employees, they tend to be treatment oriented. A broad brush approach will address any personal problem that an employee may be experiencing, including substance abuse. Often the focus is on the individual rather than on the environmental circumstances as the source of the problem. In doing so, the role of the environment in creating, sustaining, or even alleviating problems is seldom addressed (Ramanathan & Kagle, 1986). Contemporary EAPs then are designed to improve employee's performance. While there is nothing wrong in improving performance, this treatment-oriented approach tends to neglect factors in the work environment that cause or contribute to the problem presented (Hollman, 1981).

EAP services emphasize confidentiality, and this is critical. However, because of that emphasis and the short-term nature of EAP services, practitioners tend to undertake more individual assessments rather than family or other sub-system assessments. A significant number of referrals for long-term therapy for EAP clients are made to private practitioners, who, in general, tend to have more of an individual intervention bias. Nearly one third of EAPs are housed in health care facilities, and they tend to adopt the "disease-based" medical model, which targets individual change instead of also bringing about organizational changes in relevant situations.

There limitations do not imply that EAPs should be eliminated. Rather they can serve as the needed stimuli for EAP growth and development. EAP counselors can work closely with human resources professionals in bringing about organizational changes via job redesign, job enrichment, team building, facilitating quality circles, and so forth. This will ensure that the organization remains sensitive and alert to solving its structural problems, and to building internal resources among its labor pool.

REFERENCES

The Association of Labor-Management Administrators and Consultants on Alcoholism, Inc. (1987, January). *EAPs value and impact.*

Dupont, R. L., & Basen, M. M. (1980, March-April). Control of alcohol and drug abuse in industry: A literature review. *Public Health Reports,* pp. 137–148.

Ford, R. C., & McLaughlin, F. D. (1981). Employee assistance programs: A descriptive survey of APSA members. *Personnel Administrator, 26,* 29–35.

Gaeta, E., Lynn R., & Grey, L. (1982, May-June). AT&T looks at program evaluation, *EAP Digest,* pp. 22–31.

Hollman, R. W. (1981). Beyond contemporary employee assistance programs. *Personnel Administrator, 26,* 37–41.

Jenkins, C. D. (1971). Psychologic and social precursors of coronary heart disease. *New England Journal of Medicine, 284,* 412–427.

Kahn, R., Wolfe, D., Quin, R., Snoek, J., & Rosenthal, R. (1964). *Organizational stress: Studies in role conflict and ambiguity.* New York: Wiley.

Kanter, R. M. (1977). *Work and family in the United States: A critical review and agenda for research and policy.* New York: Russell Sage Foundation.

Knox, A. E. H., & Burke, W. E. (1973). The insurance industry and occupational alcoholism. *Labor Law Journal, 24,* 491–495.

Lanier, D. (1981, January-February). Industrial social work in the computer age. *EAP Digest,* pp. 18–33.

Maxwell, R. (1981). *The booze battle.* New York: Ballantine.

Phillips, D., & Older, H. (1981, May-June). Models of service delivery. *EAP Digest,* pp. 12–15.

Ramanathan, C. S., & Kagle, J. D. (1986). *Coping with stress through social support: A framework for EAP practice.* Paper presented at the annual program meeting of the Council on Social Work Education, Miami, FL.

Roman, P. M. (1983). Employee assistance programs in Australia and the U.S.: Comparisons of origin, structure, and the role of behavioral science research. *Journal of Applied Behavioral Science Research, 19*(3), 367–369.

Scanlon, W. F. (1986). *Alcoholism and drug abuse in the workplace.* New York: Praeger.

Swegan, E. E. (1983, May-June). Industry's biggest headache, alcoholism. *EAP Digest,* pp. 13–16.

Trice, H. M., & Schonbrunn (1981). A history of job-based alcoholism programs: 1900–1955. *Journal of Drug Issues, 21,* 171–198.

U.S. Department of Health and Human Services. (1981). *Fourth special report to the U.S. Congress on alcohol and health.* Washington, D.C.: U.S. Government Printing Office.

Walsh, D. C. (1982). Employee assistance programs. *Health and Society, 60*(3), 492–517.

Wilinsky, J. L., & Wilinsky, H. L. (1951). Personnel counseling: The Hawthorne case. *American Journal of Sociology, 57,* 265–280.

CHAPTER 9

Organizational Exit

The final people-processing activity in personnel and human resources management is organizational exit, or the ways in which people voluntarily or involuntarily move out of organizations. The two most commonly discussed forms of exit are absenteeism and turnover. They are among the most persistent problems in personnel management and represent major costs to many companies; However, a basic difference exists between the costs associated with these two forms. The costs and causes of absenteeism, whether personally or situationally determined, tend to remain with the organization. On the other hand, the costs and causes of turnover sometimes disappear when employees leave the organization. This can be a positive outcome, especially if those who leave are poor performers and replacements bring new perspectives and talents. Decisions about absenteeism and turnover are ultimately made by employees and are, therefore, considered voluntary rather than involuntary in nature.

Other forms of organizational exit, in which representatives of the organization often directly initiate and control exit decisions and policies, are termination for cause (e.g., disobedience, insubordination), redundancy or incompatibility, and retirement. For the last two, outplacement services are sometimes provided. An increase in the number of successful challenges to the common law doctrine of employment-at-will—the need from time to time to terminate employees with loyal and productive service to the organization—and a realization of the difficulties inherent in the transition from work life to retirement have promoted additional interest in these forms of exit.

The first article in this chapter addresses both absenteeism and turnover. Steers and Stone explain reasons and ways for measuring absenteeism and present a model that looks at factors impacting employee attendance, the opposite of absenteeism. They offer suggestions for reducing absenteeism and for areas future research should pursue. A similar approach is taken with the subject of turnover. The authors analyze ways to measure turnover, discuss its consequences, and conclude with recommendations for managing turnover and topics for further inquiry. In the next article, Kuzmits focuses on the notion of long-term absenteeism, the costs involved, and the actions one company took to deal with its long-term absenteeism problem. He discusses what should be included in a long-term absenteeism control plan and how to prevent long-term absenteeism.

Martin and Bartol present a performance-replacement strategy matrix, which they suggest can be utilized to control turnover. They describe the type of individuals who would fall into each category of the matrix, explain which ones the company should attempt to keep, the difficulty with replacing them, or some combination of both, and which the company can let go, thus addressing the functional versus dysfunctional turnover issue.

Youngblood and Bierman introduce the employment-at-will (EAW) doctrine, which protects the employer's right to discharge workers for no reason. The authors outline the history of EAW and then focus on how court cases have begun to change some of the freedoms employers have had under the EAW doctrine.

Turk addresses issues related to the need at times for a reduction in force. The "golden handshake" is discussed relative to efforts to ease the transition of employees out of the organization.

In the next article, Edson focuses on outplacement. Why has there been an increased interest in outplacement, how has it changed the organization (i.e., reduction in the need to fire employees), and what can it do for the employee?

Another type of exit, retirement, is the topic of the last two articles. In the first, Seibert and Seibert examine several factors that influence retirement. Then, they stress the need for a pre-retirement program—what it should include, when it should be offered, and what benefits it will have for both the company and the employee. In the final article, Morrison takes a comprehensive approach to retirement planning for an aging U.S. work force. Following a discussion of population, work force, and retirement trends, he presents convincing arguments for more comprehensive retirement planning in personnel and human resources management.

Suggestions for Further Reading

Abbasi, S. M., Hollman, K. W., & Murrey, J. H. (1987). Employment at will: An eroding concept in employment relationships. *Labor Law Journal, 38,* 21–32.

Bearak, J. A. (1982). Termination made easier: Is outplacement really the answer? *Personnel Administrator, 27,* 63–71.

Drost, D. A., O'Brien, F. P., & Marsh, S. (1987). Exit interviews: Master the possibilities. *Personnel Administrator, 32,* 104–110.

Ewing, D. (1982). Due process: Will business default? *Harvard Business Review, 60,* 114–122.

Fottler, M. D., & Shuler, D. W. (1984). Reducing the economic and human costs of layoffs. *Business Horizons, 27,* 9–16.

Leonard, M. (1983). Challenges to the termination-at-will doctrine. *Personnel Administrator, 28,* 49–52, 55–56.

Mowday, R. T. (1984). Strategies for adapting to high rates of employee turnover. *Human Resource Management, 23,* 365–380.

Ropp, K. (1987). Downsizing strategies. *Personnel Administrator, 32,* 61–64.

Scott, D., & Markham, S. (1982). Absenteeism control methods: A survey of practices and results. *Personnel Administrator, 27,* 63–71.

Absenteeism and Turnover

Richard M. Steers and Thomas H. Stone

MEASURING AND MANAGING EMPLOYEE ABSENTEEISM

There are a variety of ways to approach the study of employee absenteeism. Many managers approach the subject by using various rules of thumb derived from their years of experience and personal assessments concerning the major causes of absenteeism. For instance, one sometimes hears that "When it is harder to stay off the job than it is to come to work, employees will have regular attendance." Such rules of thumb, while interesting, typically fail to get at the heart of the problem.

A second approach to understanding absenteeism is to consider various isolated facts that are made known about it. For example, one hears that females in general have higher absence rates than males. In a recent book on the subject (Yolles, Carone, and Krinsky, 1975), the following such (isolated) facts were presented:

1. Absenteeism is far more severe in major cities than in smaller towns and rural areas.
2. Absenteeism among females tends to decline during their career, while absenteeism among males tends to increase.
3. Cigarette smokers experience 45 percent more days lost because of illness and injury than nonsmokers.
4. In Belgium, which has very little absenteeism, the law requires that there be a bar in every factory where wine, beer, brandy, and vermouth are served.

Here again, the manager is faced with a problem of integrating these various pieces of information and determining the relative importance of each. A more useful approach than either of the first two is to view absence behavior systematically, and to attempt to gain a clear picture of the various major influences on such behavior and the way in which they are interrelated. Toward this end, a model of employee absenteeism aimed at highlighting many of the more important determinants will be presented. While no model can be all-inclusive, it is felt that such an effort can serve to provide a relatively clear portrait of the general process.

Before considering this model, however, it is useful to examine for a moment how serious a problem absenteeism can be for an organization. One way to answer this question is to look at nationwide absenteeism statistics. In the United States each year, approximately 400 million work days are lost as a result of absenteeism. This amounts to about 5.1 days lost per year per employee (Yolles, Carone, and Krinsky, 1975). In many industries, daily absence rates approach 15 to 20 percent per day! If one takes a commonly accepted estimate of the average daily cost per employee per absence of $66, including wages, fringe benefits, and so forth (Mirvis and Lawler, 1977), the estimated annual cost of absenteeism in the United States is about $26.4 billion. Using similar techniques, the estimated cost to industry in Canada would be about $10 billion. Clearly for managers, absenteeism represents a major problem that must be understood and dealt with.

In considering the costs associated with absenteeism, it is important to note that absenteeism does not always lead to reduced operating efficiency. For instance, Staw and Oldham (1978) have pointed out that some absenteeism may actually facilitate performance instead of inhibiting it. That is, absenteeism relieves dissatisfied workers of job-related stress and, in some cases, may allow them to be more productive when they return to work. Furthermore, Moch and Fitzgibbons (1980) have identified at least three conditions or situations that might serve to mitigate the effects of absenteeism on operating efficiency. These situations are the following:

1. Jobs that have been "people proofed" by automating production and reducing the role of employees to machine monitors.

2. Work environments that anticipate and adjust for expected ("legitimate") absenteeism. For instance, some companies use "floater pools" where people are employed primarily to replace absent employees throughout a plant.

3. Instances in which employees have little direct effect on plant-level efficiency.

Based on a study among blue-collar workers, Moch and Fitzgibbons (1980) found that absenteeism influences plant efficiency primarily in situations in which (1) production processes are not highly automated, and (2) the absences cannot be anticipated in advance. Hence, managers can have a significant impact on improving operating efficiency in certain types of work environments if they can succeed in reducing absenteeism.

Perhaps because of the lack of systematic attention concerning absenteeism, several misconceptions exist about the topic. To begin with, it is often assumed that the major cause of absenteeism is job dissatisfaction. As shall be seen, while job attitudes clearly play a part in determining absence behavior, many other factors are equally important. Second, it is often assumed that employees are generally free to choose whether or not to come to work. Again, such is not always the case. There are other events (e.g., illness, family problems, transportation problems) that at times inhibit actual attendance.

Finally, some people assume that absenteeism and turnover share common (if not identical) roots and, hence, can be treated with similar methods. Once again, such is not the case. Absenteeism as a category of behavior differs from turnover in several respects:

1. The negative consequences associated with absenteeism for the employee are typically much less than those associated with turnover.

2. Absenteeism is more likely to be a spontaneous and relatively easy decision, while termination is usually more carefully considered by the employee over time.

3. Absenteeism often represents a substitute for turnover when the employee is not in a position to quit (Porter and Steers, 1973).

Therefore, it would appear that sufficient reason exists to examine absenteeism in its own right as a separate behavior from turnover.

Measuring Absenteeism

Given the fact that absenteeism represents a serious problem for organizations, questions are logically raised concerning what can be done to reduce it. To begin with, in order to reduce absenteeism, managers must first know the extent of the problem in their own particular organization. Surprisingly, available evidence suggests that many organizations do not know the extent of their own problem. A survey of 500 U.S. firms found that fewer than 40 percent kept absenteeism records (Hedges, 1973). Moreover, a similar survey among 1,600 Canadian firms found that only 17 percent kept such records, despite the fact that 36 percent felt absenteeism ranked among their more severe problems (Robertson and Humphreys, 1978). Thus, it would appear that before one can solve a problem one must first understand its extent and severity.

In fact, there are several reasons why organizations should insist on keeping accurate records of attendance and absenteeism (Gandz and Mikalachki, 1979). Among these reasons are: (1) to more accurately and equitably administer the organization's payroll and benefits programs, (2) to aid in manpower planning and production scheduling, (3) to identify absence problems, and (4) to measure and control personnel costs.

Once the decision has been made to keep such records, it is necessary to decide how to classify the various types of absences that are recorded. One such classification scheme is shown in Table 1 (Gandz and Mikalachki, 1979). This classification scheme differentiates between legitimate absences and illegitimate or questionable ones. Based on such information, it is possible to identify the extent of the absence problem, if one exists. That is, a manufacturing firm may experi-

Table 1
A Classification Scheme for Employee Absenteeism

A. Certified medical illness
B. Certified accident
  B-1. Work-related accident
  B-2. Domestic accident
C. Contractual absence
  C-1. Jury duty
  C-2. Bereavement
  C-3. Union activities
  C-4. Other
D. Disciplinary suspensions
E. Other absences
  E-1. No reports
  E-2. Personal or family reasons
  E-3. Uncertified medical illness or accident

Source: J. Gandz, and A. Mikalachki, Measuring Absenteeism, *Working Paper No. 217, School of Business Administration, University of Western Ontario, 1979, p.11.*

ence a 15 percent absence rate, but closer examination may demonstrate that two-thirds of this rate is accounted for by job-related accidents. Such a finding would indicate that absenteeism may be more easily reduced through safety programs than through tightening the absence control policies.

In addition to identifying the reasons behind various absences, it is also useful to differentiate between the *frequency* of absences and the *severity* of absences. Frequency refers to the number of episodes of absence over a given period of time, while severity refers to the duration or length of each episode. Consider the following example: During the past three months (in which he was scheduled to work sixty-two days), an employee was absent nine days. Of these nine days, five were episodes of one-day duration, while the other four days were taken together and were the result of a job-related accident. Based on this information, a manager can calculate the following:

$$\text{Frequency} = \text{5 days in 3 months} = \text{20 days per year}$$

$$\text{Severity} = \frac{\text{No. of days absent}}{\text{No. of days scheduled}} \times 100\%$$

$$= \frac{9}{62} \times 100 = 14.5\%$$

To go one step further, both of these measures can be broken down into categories based on the reasons behind the absences, as shown in Table 1. Hence, using the same example, this employee's absence record would read as follows:

Frequency = B–1 = 1 per 3 months = 4 days per year (because of accident)
Severity = B–1 = 6.5% (because of accident)
E = 8.0% (unexplained)

These data highlight the fact that in terms of instances or frequency of absences, this employee is out more often for unexplained or unverified reasons than for certifiable reasons. Such an approach helps managers to track employee absenteeism and its various causes.

A Model of Employee Attendance

There are many ways one can attempt to model attendance behavior. The approach taken here is to divide the problem into two distinct parts. First, the major causes of attendance motivation (or one's desire or willingness to come to work) will be considered. Next, the major causes of actual attendance can be considered. Throughout this discussion, it is important to remember that the answers to these two questions are quite different.

Attendance Motivation. The absence model to be discussed is shown in Figure 1 (Steers and Rhodes, 1978). This model is based on a review of 104 empirical studies of absenteeism. As can be seen, *attendance motivation* is believed to be influenced by two primary factors: (1) satisfaction with the job situation, and (2) various "pressures" to attend. Hence, if an employee enjoys the work situation and the tasks associated with the job, one would expect him or her to be more likely to want to attend since the work experience would be a rewarding one. Moreover, even if the job is not pleasurable, employees may be motivated to come to work because of a series of external and internal influences that lead the employee to believe it is in his or her best interest to attend. Each of these motivational influences will be looked at separately.

In general, people tend to be more satisfied when the job situation and the surrounding work environment match up with their personal values

Figure 1
Major Influences on Employee Attendance

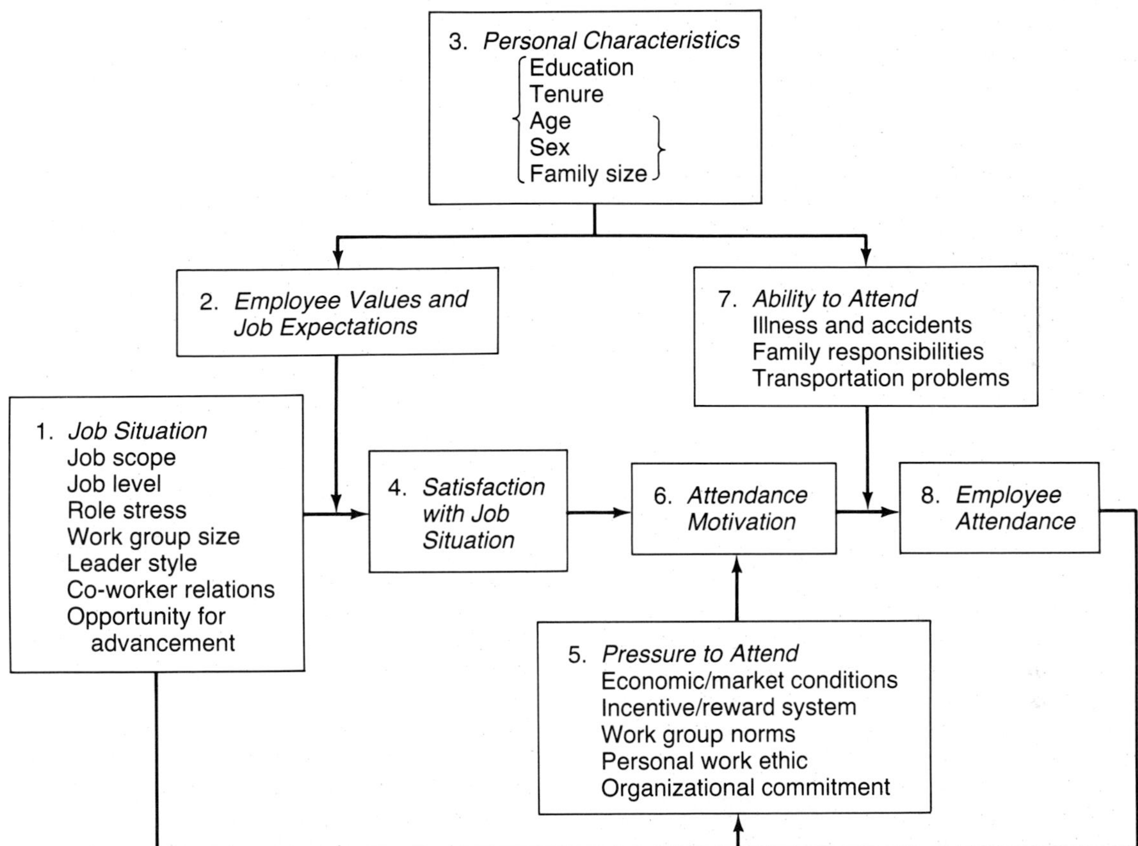

Source: R. M. Steers and S. R. Rhodes. "Major Influences on Employee Attendance: A Process Model." Journal of Applied Psychology, 63 *(1978): 393. Copyright 1978 by the American Psychological Association. Reprinted by permission of the author.*

and job expectations (Locke, 1976). This job situation, as shown in box 1 of Figure 1, can be characterized by many factors, including job scope, job level, role stress, and so forth. These factors are evaluated by employees and compared against their own values and job expectations (box 2) to determine the extent to which employees are satisfied or dissatisfied with work (box 4). These job expectations are, in turn, influenced by several personal characteristics, such as educational level, tenure, and so forth, as shown in box 3.

For example, in a situation in which an employee has considerable seniority (a personal characteristic) and, as a result, comes to expect certain perquisites because of his or her length of service, these expectations may include being first in line for promotion, receiving greater status, or working on higher-grade jobs. Where such expectations surrounding the work situation are met, one would expect the employee to be relatively satisfied and, as a result, increase his or her attendance motivation. Where such expectations are not met, the employee may be less satisfied and, consequently, less desirous of coming to work.

In addition to satisfaction, a second set of factors influencing attendance motivation may be categorized under the rubric of "pressures to attend." Such pressures represent conditions, characteristics, and incentives that make attendance desirable from an employee's viewpoint, even if he or she finds the job dissatisfying. As shown in box 5 of Figure 1, these pressures can include: (1) economic and market conditions, including how easy it is to find an alternative job; (2) the incentive/reward systems of the organization, including the extent to which rewards are contingent upon good attendance; (3) work group norms favoring good attendance; (4) one's personal work ethic, reflecting the belief that one has a moral obligation to attend; and (5) one's level of commitment to helping the organization achieve its goals.

When taken together, these pressures can represent a potent force for attendance or nonattendance, particularly when combined with one's general satisfaction with the job situation. However, as noted, it is important to draw a clear distinction between attendance motivation and actual attendance. The relationship between these two variables can now be considered.

Determinants of Employee Attendance. As shown in Figure 1, actual attendance is jointly determined by attendance motivation and one's ability to attend. It is possible to identify at least three limitations on an individual's ability to attend (see box 7): (1) illness and accidents, (2) family responsibilities, and (3) transportation problems. Clearly the most significant problem here is illness and accidents. It has been estimated that about sixty percent of all absenteeism is health-related. In addition, approximately 40 million work days are lost each year as a result of work-related accidents (Hedges, 1973).

Beyond illness and accidents, family responsibilities can also take their toll. The importance of family responsibilities can be seen when one considers the fact that females, on average, are absent more often than males. When one looks behind such a statistic, it can be discovered, among other things, that some female absenteeism results from the traditional roles and responsibilities ascribed to women (that is, it is usually the wife or mother who remains at home with a sick child). Hence, as family size increases, so too does absenteeism among female employees.

The third ability to attend factor is problems in getting to work. Such problems can include distance from work, weather conditions, and the reliability of one's mode of transportation (e.g., auto, bus, etc.). These factors, while often overlooked, can represent a very real impediment to good attendance.

In essence, then, ability to attend serves a very important "gatekeeper" function in the attendance process. Assuming one has the ability to come to work, one would expect attendance motivation to predict actual attendance fairly accurately. The stronger the motivation, the more likely the person will come to work. On the other hand, when an employee is ill or has car problems, attendance motivation alone will probably not be sufficient to produce actual attendance. Hence, both factors must typically be present for one to expect high levels of attendance.

Finally, it should be noted that the model suggested in Figure 1 contains a feedback loop, highlighting the cyclical nature of the model. Thus, superior attendance is often viewed as an indicator of good performance and readiness for promotion, thereby possibly improving the work situation and the incentive for continued attendance. Poor attendance, on the other hand, may lead to a deteriorating relationship with one's supervisor and co-workers and could lead to a change in the various pressures to attend (e.g., the implementation of a stricter absence control policy). In any event, absenteeism or attendance should not be viewed as an end result. Rather, such behavior causes reactions (both positive and negative) that influence subsequent attendance behavior.

Reducing Absenteeism at Work

Now comes what is perhaps the most difficult part of the study of employee absenteeism. Reasons why absenteeism deserves managerial attention have been examined. A model that attempts to highlight several of the more common causes of absenteeism has been reviewed, and methods by which absenteeism can be measured and tracked over time have been reviewed. Based on this information, what can one tell the manager who hopes to reduce absenteeism in his or her particular department or organization?

Based on the materials presented, several specific methods for reducing absenteeism can be suggested. The first suggestion deals with the approach that managers take to analyzing the problem. Specifically, instead of using rules of thumb, managers can learn more about the causes of absenteeism in their own organization if they take a *systematic* approach to the problem. One can use the model outlined in Figure 1 as a diagnostic tool and work through the process, asking at each juncture whether this aspect of the model may be causing the problem. What is the nature of the job situation (box 1)? Are employees generally satisfied (box 4)? What about the various "pressures" to attend (box 5)? Do employees really have an ability to attend (box 7)? Answers to questions such as these can help managers to pinpoint where the problems are—and where they are not.

Second, if a diagnosis such as the one suggested reveals a problem with the satisfaction component of the model, efforts can be made to improve job attitudes. Several techniques may be employed here, including enriching employees' jobs, reducing job-related stress, building group cohesiveness and co-worker relations, clarifying job expectations, and providing career counseling for employees. Such techniques focus on the job situation and, if successful, should increase the likelihood that job expectations are met and positive attitudes developed.

Third, if the diagnosis suggests that the major problem lies in the area of "pressures" to attend, again several techniques are available for use by managers. These include clarifying rewards for good attendance, reviewing sick leave policies, encouraging an attendance-oriented work group norm, fostering a personal work ethic, and facilitating employee commitment to organizations.

Perhaps the most successful strategy here lies in the use of incentives for good attendance. For instance, in one experiment using operant conditioning, a sample of nurses were made eligible for cash prize drawings of $20 if they had no absenteeism for a three-week period. As a result of this simple attendance-reward contingency, absenteeism declined significantly (Stephens and Burroughs, 1978). In another study, it was shown that allowing employees to participate in the development of a bonus plan for perfect attendance also reduced absenteeism (Lawler and Hackman, 1969).

Fourth, if the diagnosis reveals that the major problems of absenteeism lie with employees' ability to attend, several additional strategies may be useful. For instance, organizations can encourage sound physical health (perhaps through company-sponsored exercise programs, physical examinations, etc.), institute employee counseling programs to foster sound mental health, be sensitive to problems of alcoholism and drug abuse and provide relevant programs where necessary, consider company-sponsored or supported day care facilities for employees with young children, and consider using shuttle buses to clusters of employees living in outlying areas. All of these techniques have been used successfully by organizations concerned about insuring employees' physical health and ability to get to work.

By taking a diagnostic approach to solving problems of absenteeism, managers have a great opportunity to focus their solutions and their limited resources on the major causes of the problem, instead of applying more general solutions that may not get at the heart of the problem. In this way, greater progress should be made toward reducing avoidable absenteeism and facilitating a workforce more committed to the goals of the organization.

New Directions for Research on Absenteeism

Clearly, a great deal has been learned in recent years concerning the causes—and possible solutions—associated with employee absenteeism. Even so, more remains to be learned. In particular, the following topics are suggested in need of further work in the area of employee absenteeism.

1. To begin with, it should be recognized that the conceptual model of absenteeism presented here rests largely on an integration of disparate research findings. Very few comprehensive multivariate studies of absenteeism are to be found. Hence, there is a need for further studies to test such models using longitudinal and experimental methods. Before this is done, the model suggested here must be considered more for its heuristic value than as a definitive statement on the topic.

2. Some potentially important influences on absenteeism have been omitted from the model because of a lack of information concerning their impact on such behavior. For instance, there is the problem of multiple commitments. What effect does a strong commitment to one's family or to a hobby (instead of the organization) have on attendance motivation? Moreover, what effect does psychosomatic illness (perhaps brought on by role pressures) have on actual attendance? Questions such as these are in need of answers before a more complete model of attendance can be suggested.

3. It would be helpful if further study could be done concerning the extent to which changes in absence rates do or do not have adverse consequences for organizational effectiveness. One such effort has been made by Moch and Fitzgibbons (described earlier). If reduced absenteeism is accomplished at the expense of product quality, accident rate, strike activity, or employee mental health, serious questions should be raised about the desirability of improving such attendance. Hence, some effort is needed to examine the potential trade-offs in rigorous as opposed to lax enforcement of attendance policies in organizations.

4. Finally, it should be noted that the vast bulk of research on absenteeism has focused on blue-collar workers. Ignored in these studies are managers, perhaps because researchers feel there is no problem with managerial absenteeism. However, in view of the increased autonomy that managers have (which makes short absences relatively easy), it may be useful to reexamine *de facto* absenteeism among such employees. This reexamination really suggests a need to consider the productivity of managers. That is, when an assembly-line worker is absent or present, but not actually working, it is quite noticeable. However, when a manager is "in conference" or "working privately," questions must be raised concerning the extent of actual work activity. Lenz has pointed out that one of the prerogatives of managers is the right to be absent. "It is the right to sit around the office and talk, the right to take a slightly longer lunch 'hour' than anyone else, the right to run personal errands during the day while blue-collar workers must wait until Saturday" (Lenz, as cited in Yolles et al., 1975, p. 17). In other words, it would be useful to consider more closely the active participation levels of managers as well as other employees, instead of simply determining whether or not they came to work.

MEASURING AND MANAGING EMPLOYEE TURNOVER

Interest in the study of employee turnover dates from the early 1900s when industrial engineers and industrial psychologists attempted to ascertain the major reasons behind employees' level of interest in various jobs. To date, well over 1,000 separate studies of turnover have been carried out (Steers and Mowday, 1981). Many of these studies attempted to determine the relative levels of employee turnover among various occupations. One way to do so is to examine the longevity or tenure rates of employees across industries. One example of this is shown in Table 2, where median years on the job of the employees in various areas are shown. As can be seen, longevity rates differ substantially across occupations and industries.

Other studies have attempted to calculate turnover rates for various organizations or types of work in percentage form. Such studies have found turnover rates ranging from almost zero to a high of 731 percent per year in one factory situation (Price, 1977). Still other studies have attempted to look for primary factors that influence the turnover decision. Several reviews have pointed out that a multitude of factors have been found to be related to turnover (March and Simon, 1958; Mobley, Horner, and Hollingsworth, 1978; Porter and Steers, 1973). These factors range from personal characteristics to job characteristics to economic factors. What is needed here is a conceptual framework to tie these various fragments of information together into a unified whole, so that managers can benefit from the information. Such a model is presented here. First, however, brief consideration will be given to how turnover is measured in organizations.

Table 2
Median Years on the Job for Male Workers in Selected Industries

Industry	*Median Years on Job*
Railroads and railway express	19.6
Agriculture	11.5
Postal service	10.3
Federal public administration	7.6
Automobile manufacturing	7.0
Chemical and allied products manufacturing	6.8
Mining	6.4
Electrical machinery manufacturing	5.7
Communications	5.2
Instrument manufacturing	5.1
Food and kindred products manufacturing	5.1
Finance, insurance, and real estate	4.0
Rubber and plastics manufacturing	4.0
Medical and other health services	2.8
Construction	2.7
Wholesale and retail trade	2.6
Entertainment and recreation services	1.9
All durable goods manufacturing	5.7
All nondurable goods manufacturing	5.3

Source: Bureau of Labor Statistics, 1975.

Measuring Turnover

There are many different ways in which employee turnover can be measured. The most common method is what is called "separation rate." It is calculated as follows:

$$\text{Separation rate} = \frac{\text{No. who left during time period}}{\text{Average no. of employees}}$$

Hence, if ten employees left during the past year and the average number of employees is 100, the organization experienced a 10-percent turnover rate.

For purposes of analysis, it is useful to calculate such rates for each department or subunit as a means of identifying potential trouble spots. If the accounts receivable department in Accounting has a 10-percent turnover rate and the accounts payable department (with similar kinds of jobs) has a 50-percent rate, attention is focused on other nonjob-related factors (e.g., supervisory style) that may account for the turnover. On the other hand, if Accounting in general has a 10-percent rate and the rate is 50 percent among the janitorial staff, perhaps the nature of the work is causing the attrition.

A final point needs to be made concerning the measurement of turnover. If effectiveness of operations is a chief goal of the enterprise, then one could argue that it may be desirable to minimize turnover among good or outstanding performers and *maximize* turnover among poor performers, particularly those poor performers who are inca-

Department	% Turnover Among All Employees	% Turnover Among Good Performers	% Turnover Among Poor Performers
Accounts receivable	10%	20%	5%
Accounts payable	50%	10%	80%

pable of change. Given this, it may be useful to calculate two sets of turnover rates based on performance level. Using this technique, one may discover something like the [above].

In such a situation, one may conclude that the high original turnover rate in the accounts payable department (originally 50 percent) was justified because only poor performers are leaving. In fact, one could further conclude that accounts receivable had the more serious problem since it was losing its better people. While decisions concerning the interpretation of turnover data are seldom so clear cut, this example does highlight many of the nuances of the problem.

A Model of Employee Turnover

As a result of the many studies of employee turnover, several useful efforts have been made to develop models of the processes leading up to the decision to stay or leave (March and Simon, 1958; Mobley, 1977; Price, 1977). While several models could be reviewed here, one of the most current efforts will be presented. This model, developed by William Mobley (1977), is based on a thorough review of existing studies and has been supported in several field tests.

Mobley's model represents a cognitive model of the withdrawal process. It assumes that employees typically make conscious decisions concerning job choices and tenure. It is also a process model in that it makes an effort to describe the processes leading up to actual attrition. The model itself is shown in Figure 2.

As can be seen, the model begins by considering an employee's evaluation of his or her existing job, shown in block A of the figure. This is the same starting point as was noted in the absenteeism model. That is, as employees begin to think about the positive and negative aspects of their jobs, they experience various levels of job satisfaction (block B). When an employee experiences a state of job dissatisfaction, two outcomes are likely to result. First, the employee may begin thinking about leaving (block C) and make alternate plans for employment. In addition, however, the employee may also initiate several alternative forms of withdrawal, including absenteeism, passive job behavior, and so forth (shown in arrow a).

As a result of the employee's thoughts of leaving, the utility and costs associated with searching for and possibly accepting a new job are then considered, as shown in block D. This expected utility of search could include such factors as the probability of finding a new job, the attractiveness of this new job, and the costs of search (e.g., travel costs, time away from the job). The employee's evaluation of the costs associated with quitting could include consideration of one's loss of seniority and status, loss of benefits in the retirement program, and so on. In sum, the employee at this phase asks whether the search for a possible new job is worth the effort.

If it is determined by the employee that the costs of search or the costs of leaving are too high, one would expect the employee to remain. Under such circumstances, the employee may proceed to reevaluate his or her job and begin to see it in a more positive light. The employee may come to believe that the job is actually better than was previously thought. If, on the other hand, the employee concludes that the costs of searching for a new position are reasonable and the expected utility of such a search is high, then one would expect that the employee would establish a behavioral intention to search for alternative jobs (block E). This intention to search could also be influenced by various nonwork factors such as a spouse's employment situation, geographic preferences, etc. (arrow b). Once decided, intention to search generally leads to actual search behavior (box F).

Figure 2
The Employee Turnover Decision Process

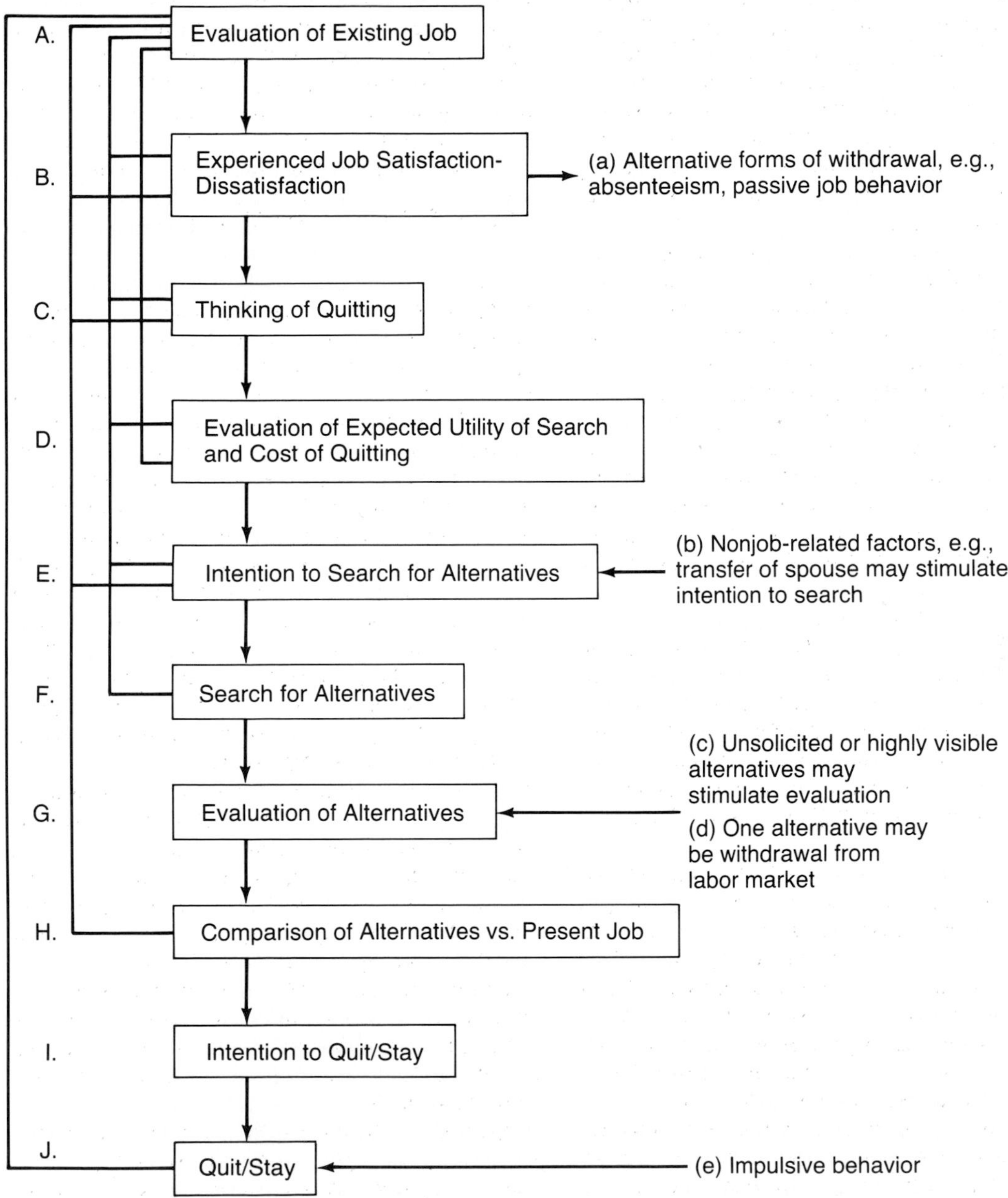

Source: W. H. Mobley, "Intermediate Linkages in the Relationship between Job Satisfaction and Employee Turnover." Journal of Applied Psychology, 62 *(1977): 238. Copyright 1977 by the American Psychological Association. Reprinted by permission of the author.*

When search yields a suitable alternative job or jobs, or where a unique job opportunity suddenly presents itself (arrow c), the employee proceeds to evaluate the alternatives (block G). In this process, the alternatives are compared against one's current position (block H) to determine the relative merits of staying or leaving. As a result of this comparison, the employee makes a decision to stay or leave (box I), followed by actual behavior (box J). In this final process, it must be recognized that some individuals bypass the rational decision process just described and act more out of impulse (arrow e). That is, they simply decide to leave because of an argument with a co-worker, disagreement over a performance rating or pay raise, and so forth. Hence, whatever the reason, it is important to note that the turnover decision is not entirely a rational one. At times, impulsive behavior takes over and guides the employee very quickly to a decision to leave.

While recognizing that this model does not describe every case of turnover, it is useful in providing a rather general description of the process that many employees go through in their decision to stay or leave. As such, the model can be quite useful for managers interested in learning more about managing employee turnover, as shall be seen next. First, however, a few words should be said about the effects of such turnover on individuals and organizations.

Consequences of Turnover

Research on employee turnover has been concerned almost exclusively with the factors leading up to the decision to stay or leave. Managers often assume that once this decision has been made, their concerns are over. Such is not the case, however. Managers have a responsibility to be concerned not only with the causes of turnover, but also with the *consequences* of turnover.

The consequences of turnover can be viewed from at least four perspectives (Steers and Mowday, 1981). First, the decision to stay or leave an organization clearly has important consequences for the person making the decision. The decision to leave carries with it a certain amount of disruption for the employee and his or her family. Existing work relationships are often broken, children are often relocated, and adjustments to a new job situation must be made. Hence, considerable adjustment is often required on the part of the leaver.

In addition, turnover by employees can have repercussions among other employees who choose to (or must) remain. Turnover can be interpreted by co-workers as a rejection of the job and a recognition that better job opportunities exist elsewhere. For those who remain, ways must be found to reconcile their decision to stay in the light of evidence from others that the job may not be good. As a result, those who remain may reevaluate their present position in the organization and, as a result, may develop more negative job attitudes.

Third, employee turnover may also create problems for supervisors, since it is the supervisor who must initiate actions aimed at reducing such behavior. High turnover rates may reflect adversely on the effectiveness of the supervisor, particularly when the best performers are those who choose to leave. As a result, supervisors may attribute the causes of turnover to factors other than themselves in order to defend their own behavior. When this happens, top management fails to receive sufficient valid information with which to recommend strategies for change.

Finally, employee turnover can have fairly serious consequences for the organization as a whole. From the organization's standpoint, several negative consequences can be identified, including increased selection and recruitment costs, increased training and development costs, continued disruption of organizational processes, and the demoralization of the remaining members of the organization (Staw, 1980). Such factors represent real costs in terms of time, money, and effort. On the other hand, several positive consequences of turnover can also be noted for organizations. These include the possibility of increased performance brought about by recently trained and enthusiastic new employees, the possibility that long-running conflicts between people will be reduced or eliminated through attrition, increased chances for promotion and transfer for those who remain, and the possibility for increased innovation and adaptation brought about by the introduction of fresh ideas.

Hence, turnover appears to have both good and bad side effects for work organizations. As a result, it is not easy to categorically condemn high turnover rates in an organization. More information is first required concerning who is leaving, why they are leaving, and what will result from their departure. Only after this information has been secured can managers make reasoned decisions concerning the extent and nature of the turnover problem in their organizations.

Reducing Turnover at Work

An attempt has been made to suggest a general framework concerning how people decide whether or not to leave. As with the absenteeism model, this model clearly does not describe the process that every individual goes through. Rather, it attempts to identify a general process that many individuals go through, recognizing that there are exceptions to the process. Even so, if one uses the model for guidance, several recommendations for managing the turnover process come to mind:

1. It is important to clarify job expectations for new employees. One way to do so is to use "realistic job previews," where both the positive *and negative* aspects of a job are described to job applicants. In this way, people have a clear idea of the nature of the job and what is expected of them and can therefore make a more informed choice. Research has clearly shown that such realistic job previews clarify job expectations and, as a result, reduce subsequent employee turnover (Wanous, 1977).

2. Managers can attempt to insure that expected rewards or outcomes are closely tied to desired behaviors. In this way, the probability is increased that employees' expectations will be met following acceptable job performance.

3. As noted, it is often useful for managers to differentiate between good performers and poor performers when considering turnover rates. While most managers believe that reducing turnover among good performers is desirable, they may actually wish to increase it among poor performers. Hence, managers may want to pay particular attention to the reasons for termination among these good or superior employees.

4. It is important for managers to recognize the importance of job attitudes as one major factor capable of influencing subsequent behavior. While no direct relationship exists, turnover is at least moderately related to job dissatisfaction. Hence, efforts can be made to improve job attitudes at work through such techniques as job redesign.

5. Managers should recognize individual differences among employees and make an effort, where possible, to match employees to jobs. They should insure that employees have the necessary skills and abilities to successfully complete the required task assignments.

6. Managers should recognize that a series of nonwork factors can influence turnover. In many cases, employees do not leave by choice but because of outside factors (e.g., a lack of day care facilities, transfer of a spouse). Special attention by management may produce solutions to some of these problems, thereby enabling the valued employee to remain.

7. It is desirable in many cases to monitor employee attitudes on a fairly regular basis (perhaps once a year or once every two years). If attitudes serve as an early warning system with respect to turnover, such monitoring through attitude surveys may tell managers in advance when a possible problem is developing. With this advance notice, managers can attempt to intervene and remove the problem in the hope of reducing subsequent turnover.

8. Managers should be sensitive to "off-quadrant" employees (that is, satisfied leavers and dissatisfied stayers). In many instances, actions can be taken to help such individuals accommodate their dilemma and find workable solutions to the problem.

In summary, it can be seen from this discussion that there are several specific actions that managers can take in an attempt to reduce employee turnover. While not perfect, such activities should help the organization in its attempt to maintain a stable and productive workforce.

New Directions in Research on Turnover

Despite the considerable amount of research carried out to date on turnover, several questions remain. Among the more important research questions outstanding are the following:

1. Little is known about the role of job performance in the turnover process. Specifically, do high performers leave for reasons different from those of poor performers? What is the effect of poor performance on subsequent job attitudes and desire to stay? Do high performers raise their level of job expectations, thereby making it more difficult for the organization to satisfy (and perhaps retain) them?

2. It was noted long ago that dissatisfied employees may make efforts to change the work situation or eliminate the more distasteful aspects of it (March and Simon, 1958). However, to date no systematic study of this phenomenon has taken place. If employees do undertake systematic efforts to change the work situation, what are some of the more common change mechanisms? Moreover, when such efforts are unsuccessful, are negative attitudes strengthened or do they remain unchanged?

3. Also ignored in most work on turnover is a host of nonwork factors that can influence staying or leaving. How, for example, do family considerations (e.g., a dual career family) affect turnover decisions?

4. Most turnover models, including the one described here, include the notion of search behaviors for more preferable job alternatives. However, surprisingly little is known about how people initiate search behavior, the quality of information they receive, or the way they process such information in arriving at a decision to stay or leave.

5. When an employee is unable to leave an undesirable job, how likely is he or she to find alternative modes of accommodation? What are these various accommodation mechanisms and which are used most often? Is there a generalizable sequencing of substitute behaviors, perhaps beginning with increased absenteeism and then proceeding to alcoholism and drug abuse, or do different employees simply select different accommodation mechanisms?

6. Finally, how do employees respond when their co-workers are seen as leaving on a fairly regular basis? How do they explain such "abandonment" to themselves and each other? In other words, how do employees interpret the causes of turnover by others and how do they cope with such interpretations? (see Steers and Mowday, 1981).

REFERENCES

Bureau of Labor Statistics. (1976). *Directory of national unions and employee associations 1975.* Washington, D.C.: U.S. Government Printing Office.

Gandz, J., & Mikalachki, A. (1979). *Measuring absenteeism* (Working Paper No. 217). London, Ontario. University of Western Ontario, School of Business Administration.

Hedges, J. N. (1973). Absence from work—A look at some national data. *Monthly Labor Review, 96,* 24–31.

Lawler, E. E., & Hackman, J. R. (1969). Impact of employee participation in the development of pay incentive plans: A field experiment. *Journal of Applied Psychology, 53,* 467–471.

Locke, E. A. (1976). The nature and causes of job satisfaction. In M. D. Dunnette (Ed.), *Handbook of industrial and organizational psychology.* Chicago: Rand McNally.

March, J. G., & Simon, H. A. (1958). *Organizations.* New York: Wiley.

Mirvis, P. H., & Lawler, E. E. (1977). Measuring the financial impact of employee attitudes. *Journal of Applied Psychology, 62,* 1–8.

Mobley, W. H. (1977). Intermediate linkages in the relationship between job satisfaction and employee turnover. *Journal of Applied Psychology, 62,* 237–240.

Mobley, W. H., Horner, S. O., & Hollingsworth, A. T. (1978). An evaluation of precursors of hospital employee turnover. *Journal of Applied Psychology, 63,* 408–414.

Moch, M. K., & Fitzgibbons, D. E. (1980). *Absenteeism and efficiency: An empirical assessment.* Working paper, University of Illinois, Champaign.

Porter, L. W., & Steers, R. M. (1973). Organizational, work, and personal factors in employee turnover and absenteeism. *Psychological Bulletin, 80,* 151–176.

Price, J. L. (1977). *The study of turnover.* Ames: Iowa State University Press.

Robertson, G., & Humphreys, J. (1978). *Labour turnover and absenteeism in selected industries.* Northwestern Manpower Adjustment Study (Component Study No. 10), Toronto.

Staw, B. M. (1980). The consequences of turnover. *Journal of Occupational Behavior, 1,* 253–273.

Staw, B. M., & Oldham, G. R. (1978). Reconsidering our dependent variables: A critique and empirical study. *Academy of Management Journal, 21,* 539–559.

Steers, R. M., & Mowday, R. T. (1981). Employee turnover and post-decision accommodation process. In L. L. Cummings & B. M. Staw (Eds.), *Research in organizational behavior* (Vol. 3, pp. 235–281). Greenwich, CT: JAI Press.

Steers, R. M., & Rhodes, S. R. (1978). Major influences on employee attendance: A process model. *Journal of Applied Psychology, 63,* 391–407.

Stephens, T. A., & Burroughs, W. A. (1978). An application of operant conditioning to absenteeism in a hospital setting. *Journal of Applied Psychology, 63,* 518–521.

Wanous, J. P. (1977). Organizational entry: Newcomers moving from outside to inside. *Psychological Bulletin, 84,* 601–618.

Yolles, S. F., Carone, P. A., & Krinsky, L. W. (1975). *Absenteeism in industry.* Springfield, IL: Charles C. Thomas.

What to Do about Long-Term Absenteeism

Frank E. Kuzmits

John Bradley, a press operator for a large metropolitan newspaper, was absent from work last Friday. Over the past four months, he has been absent a total of 11 times; each absence was a single-day episode on either a Friday or a Monday.

Mary Green, a claims adjustor for a large insurance company, was absent 83 days last year and 129 days the previous year. Her absenteeism stems from a work-related injury suffered in a fall from a ladder at work. She is scheduled for surgery in three days, and is expected to be recuperating at home for several weeks.

These hypothetical cases demonstrate that most organizations have two kinds of absenteeism problems. One kind is the frequent offender, the employee whose numerous one-day absences often fall on a Friday or Monday. This kind of employee collects a high number of so-called "attitudinal" absences, temporary respites from work which generally reflect a preference to do something other than spend eight hours in the office or plant. The absence is deliberate, planned and surreptitious. The employee may feign illness or claim an emergency in order to avoid disciplinary action for unexcused absenteeism.

The second form of absenteeism—long-term absenteeism—is very different. First, it is not deliberate or planned. Long-term absenteeism results from a work or nonwork injury which generally has nothing to do with the employee's work ethic or personal value system. Second, the chronic single-day offender may hold a different set of values and attitudes about work. The behavioral practices of high-frequency absentees places their work ethic in question—in that they deliberately avoid going to work on a regular basis. Third, the organizational consequences of the two forms of absenteeism are much different. Single-day absences may cause supervisors to shift employees around in order to fill vacant positions, often requiring immediate on-the-job training followed by close supervision to ensure that productivity and

Reprinted from the April 1986 issue of *Personnel Administrator,* copyright 1986, The American Society for Personnel Administration, 606 North Washington Street, Alexandria, Virginia 22314.

quality standards are met. Single-day offenders may also be subjected to frequent counseling and discipline, and therefore further consume supervisors' time.

It is precisely for these reasons that management may not believe that long-term absenteeism is really that much of a problem and that absenteeism control efforts should be directed primarily at the chronic high-frequency absentee. Unfortunately, this belief fails to recognize that long-term absenteeism can be very costly indeed.

THE HIGH COST OF LONG-TERM ABSENTEEISM

What are the costs of long-term absenteeism? Elements of labor overhead which are affected by long-term absenteeism include:

1. *Benefits*. Most organizations continue to provide benefits for employees who are absent on a long-term basis, for a stipulated number of days. It is common for a firm to provide benefits up to 120 or 180 days or more for employees on long-term leave. With the average cost of benefits estimated at $3.65 per hour, an employee who is absent for a 60-day period (480 hours) costs the firm $1,752.00 in benefits alone.[1] (In addition, the firm also may be required to absorb the cost of replacing the employee's benefits, in effect doubling the cost of benefits for a single position).

2. *Workers' compensation premiums*. Employers who use a private carrier for workers' compensation are likely to face a premium increase as a result of work-related long-term absenteeism. With a private insurer, a firm's premiums are usually determined in part by comparing their three-year loss record to a three-year industry standard. Premiums increase for a firm whose loss experience is above the industry standard.

3. *Lost productivity*. As is the case with short-term absenteeism, the time and effort associated with recruiting, orienting and training replacement employees also exists for the long-term absentee. The productivity of the new or transferred employee will suffer until a standard level of competence is achieved—perhaps days or weeks after assignment.

Long-term absenteeism is expensive and often disrupts the normal functioning of an organization. For these reasons, firms must take long-term absenteeism seriously and create mechanisms to minimize and control the problem.

ONE COMPANY'S EXPERIENCE

One company which has successfully managed the problem of long-term absenteeism is the H. J. Scheirich Co., a medium-sized cabinet manufacturer located in Louisville, Kentucky. The firm employs approximately 400 skilled and semiskilled employees who are represented by an AFL-CIO union.

Several years ago, the firm's management realized that frequent one-day absences and long-term absenteeism were both having a negative impact on labor costs and worker productivity, due primarily to the factors cited above. To combat these problems, the company formulated absenteeism policies in 1979 to control both incidental and long-term absenteeism. The policies were negotiated between Scheirich and the union, and were included in the firm's labor agreement. To combat the problem of incidental absenteeism, the firm enacted a no-fault absenteeism policy that places conservative limits on the number of occasions an employee may be absent without disciplinary action being taken.[2]

To control the long-term absenteeism problem, the absenteeism policy included a statement that enabled the firm to take action when excessive long-term absenteeism occurred. The statement read: "Action may be taken when cumulative time lost from work for any reason substantially reduces the employee's services to the company." This statement was included in the absenteeism policy to enable management to take necessary action when an employee's long-term absenteeism becomes detrimental to the operation of the business. As a rule of thumb, Scheirich industrial relations personnel determined that any employee whose absenteeism record was three percentage points above the plant average was excessive, and their absenteeism record would be closely monitored. Because of the need for a flexible policy, management stressed that this was only a guide and not a hard and fast rule.

Although the union asked management for a specific percentage that would result in an automatic discharge for unavailability for work, management had several reasons for believing that this would create undue hardships in administering the policy. First, establishing a set percentage of absenteeism would not permit evaluation on a case-by-case basis. A defined percentage might be disastrous for employees who may have had excellent attendance records but, due to one serious illness, may miss a considerable amount of time over a period of a year or two. Second, should a set percentage of absenteeism subject an employee to discharge, an employee may be tempted to return to work too soon, and perhaps aggravate an injury or illness. Third, a defined percentage may serve as an open invitation to be absent for that amount of time. Nonetheless, several arbitrators have held that the company does not have to establish a set of percentage of absenteeism.

Between 1979 and 1985, the company terminated 11 employees for "unavailability for work." In each case, the employee's absence record was far in excess of Scheirich's rule of thumb, and it was determined that the services of the employee to the company were reduced to the point where termination was the only reasonable option for the company. Of the 11 employees, three employees did not grieve the termination; three employees (with the union) grieved the termination through the third step of the grievance procedure; and five employees grieved the termination through arbitration. Although minor differences among the five arbitrated cases existed, the positions of the company, the union and the arbitrators were very similar. Their positions are summarized below.

The Company's Position

The text of the arbitration records shows that the company offered the following evidence to support the discharges.[3]

1. "The company's absenteeism policy has two parts. The more frequently utilized provision is aimed at discouraging frequent absenteeism. It deals with employees who are chronically absent. However, arbitrators unanimously recognize an employer's right to release employees who, in the judgment of the employer are unable for work to such an extent and over such a time that their value as an employee ceases to justify retaining them. This view is consistently applied even when the excessive absenteeism is for legitimate reasons. This is particularly valid when there is no evidence that the employee's attendance can ever become acceptable. The last paragraph of the company's attendance control rules explicitly states the company's intent to utilize this doctrine when the need arises.

2. "The basis for the employee's termination was 'unavailability for work.' The terminations were not processed under the progressive disciplinary procedure for excessive short-term absenteeism. The company did not question the legitimacy of the absences. The employees were discharged because the company believed that their unavailability for work was such that their value to the company was reduced to the point where their continued employment could not be justified.

3. "The employee's absence over a period of five years averaged well over twice the plant average (the plant average was five to seven percent a year with little fluctuation from year to year). Unavailability for work becomes a factor only after it extends over a two to three year period.

4. "In each case, the company determined that it was unreasonable to expect the physical condition of the employees to improve. Therefore, the company also believed it to be unreasonable to expect their attendance to improve."

The Union's Position

In each arbitration hearing, the union argued that the employee was improperly discharged. The union's reasons for requesting that the discharges be overturned included:

1. "The grievant was improperly terminated without contractual just cause. Just cause does not exist when an employee's absences are a result of genuine occupational injury. The grievant's disabilities were not incurred in an intentional manner, and without proof of intentional or reckless misconduct on the part of the grievant, no discipline whatsoever could appropriately be imposed.

2. "The company has promised that it would not take disciplinary action against any worker

who is absent because of hospital confinement and work-incurred injury. The labor agreement specifically states that these forms of absenteeism will not be recorded as occurrences of absence for purposes of disciplinary action; therefore, the company has imposed discipline for excused absences.

3. "Other employees have accumulated worse records than the discharged employees and have not been discharged.

4. "The company has not established a fixed percentage of attendance which must be maintained by employees even though the union has asked for this."

The Arbitrators' Positions

As in the case of both management and labor, the position and opinions of the arbitrators in all five cases were very similar. The following opinions are included in the discussions of the arbitrators:

1. "The employer has the right to determine that it is going to operate its business with full-time employees and if an employee is hired to be a full-time employee he or she has no right to expect an arbitrator to grant part-time status. If the employee can not remain a full-time employee, then it is not unreasonable that the employment relationship cease.

2. "It would be unreasonable to expect the company to set a percentage cut-off point as the benchmark for determining whether an employee has become a part-time employee. The case-by-case method currently used by the company is a reasonable method for making a difficult determination required in cases of this sort.

3. "The company has a legitimate need to maintain its right to terminate employees for non-disciplinary reasons because it has a substantial interest in maintaining a reliable and efficient workforce. Chronic absenteeism is an obstacle to an efficient operation.

4. "It is well established that a company may terminate an employee who is excessively absent for legitimate reasons without any indication that the condition giving rise to the absence will improve. Where an employee cannot produce some evidence that he will eventually be able to return to full-time work or where the evidence indicates no realistic hope that the employee will be able to resume his job on a regular basis, the arbitrator has held that management is entitled to release the individual and reassign the work.

5. "If an employee is off for medical reasons often and for lengthy periods of time, the individual in reality becomes a part-time employee. No company can compete when it cannot count on the regular and continued attendance of its employees . . . when over a period of several years the employee is out for lengths of time for one or more medical reasons, the company cannot nor should be required to continue such an individual as an employee."

Interestingly, two arbitrators quoted Frank and Edna Elkouri's widely read *How Arbitration Works* (Washington, D.C.: Bureau of National Affairs, 1981) in regard to the issue of long-term absence as a legitimate reason for discharge. The following quote is included in the discussion of two arbitration proceedings: "The right to terminate employees for excessive absences even when they are due to illness is generally recognized by arbitrators."[4]

Arbitrators' Awards

The arbitrators supported the company's position and upheld the discharges in four of five cases. In one case, the award was given to the employee only because management failed to notify her before discharge. The arbitrator stated, "If there had been sufficient warnings to the grievant, I would have had no hesitancy in sustaining the termination but under the circumstances it is my intention to return the grievant to work."[5] The employee declined to return to work.

CAVEATS FOR MANAGEMENT

A review of the arbitration cases discussed above underscores the fact that something can be done to control long-term absenteeism. However, management must be prepared to carefully plan and enact a strategy to ensure that long-term absenteeism is kept at minimum levels. Elements of a plan to control long-term absenteeism should include:

1. *Dual-purpose absenteeism policies*. One of the primary elements in the strategy to control long-term absenteeism is an absenteeism control policy that focuses on both short-term and long-term absenteeism. Each form of absenteeism represents a unique form of employee behavior and therefore must be addressed with individual and specific policy statements.

2. *Guidelines for "excessive" absenteeism*. A second issue deals with the problems of determining when long-term absenteeism becomes "excessive." Although the definition of "excessive" is management's responsibility, it must be perceived as fair by employees, unions and—should a grievance reach arbitration in the union firm—arbitrators. If the policy is not fairly written and enforced, employees will reject and grieve the policy and arbitrators may invalidate it. It is important to develop a rule of thumb for defining excessive absenteeism such as the guidelines of the firm discussed in this study; it's also important to recognize that the guidelines must be flexible to enable management to consider each case on its individual merits.[6]

3. *Likelihood of improvement*. Evidence must strongly suggest that the employee's long-term absenteeism is not likely to abate. In particular, arbitrators will seek medical evidence from health care professionals that pertains to the employee's ability to return to full-time work. If the employee cannot produce evidence of an ability to resume the job on a full-time basis, an arbitrator is likely to support management's right to release the employee and reassign the work.

4. *Documentation*. Employees whose absenteeism labels them as potential candidates for dismissal should be notified in writing that their behavior is being monitored and that their attendance must improve to avoid further action. (The importance of this procedure is underscored by one arbitrator's decision to give the award to the employee solely because of management's failure to properly warn the employee.)

5. *Communication*. It is important that management's attitudes, policies, practices and procedures concerning long-term absenteeism be communicated and explained to employees. Although the events which lead to long-term absenteeism—accidents, injuries and serious illnesses—are not the deliberate choice of the employee, knowing that management takes the issue of long-term absenteeism seriously may motivate employees to return to work as soon as possible.

PREVENTIVE MEASURES

The focus of the discussion so far has been directed towards solving a problem once it has occurred. In closing, it seems appropriate to note that organizations should also take specific measure to *prevent* long-term absenteeism from taking place. Some important measures include:

1. *Thorough physical examinations*. Medical examinations by health care professionals will uncover many existing health problems, such as back and other musculo-skeletal problems. Some firms require applicants applying for heavy-labor jobs to undergo two independent examinations.

2. *Pre-employment checks*. The investigation of applicants' work histories should include inquiries into their accident and injury records in addition to their absenteeism behavior.[7]

3. *Safety program*. Although job-related illness accounts for only a portion of long-term absenteeism, a successful safety program in industrial settings will no doubt keep on-the-job accidents and injuries—and thus long-term absenteeism—at a minimum.

Reducing and controlling long-term absenteeism is a formidable challenge to human resource managers. It may require new systems and procedures to define, monitor and control absenteeism; and in the unionized firm, certain policy and procedural decisions will likely be subject to negotiation. However, the investment in time and effort in developing a strategy to control long-term absenteeism will help maintain a productive labor force and minimize labor overhead.

REFERENCES

1. J. R. Morris, "Benefits Growth: Back to the Days of Yore," *Nation's Business*, February 1985, p. 22.

2. See F. E. Kuzmits, "Is Your Organization Ready for No-Fault Absenteeism?" *Personnel Administrator*, December 1984, pp. 119–127.

3. The quotes reflecting the opinions of the company, union, and arbitrators are taken from the following arbitration proceedings: H. J. Scheirich Co. (S. E. Alexander, November 9, 1981); H. J. Scheirich Co. (W. G. Seinsheimer, November 17, 1981); H. J. Scheirich Co. (E. R. Render, July 9, 1982); H. J. Scheirich Co. (E. R. Render, November 6, 1984); H. J. Scheirich Co. (W. G. Seinsheimer, November 20, 1985). Information concerning the arbitration proceedings may be obtained from the author, School of Business, University of Louisville, Louisville, KY 40292.

4. F. Elkouri and E. Elkouri. *How Arbitration Works*, Washington, D.C.: Bureau of National Affairs, 1981, p. 545. Arbitrators are in general agreement that management may discharge employees for excessive absenteeism even where the absences are caused by legitimate illness. See *Kimberly-Clark Corp.*, 62 LA 1119 (1974); *Pennsylvania Tire and Rubber Company* 59 LA 1078 (1972); *Westinghouse Air Brake Company* 53 LA 762 (1969); *Husky Oil Co.*, 65 LA 47 (1975); *General Electric Company*, 39 LA 979 (1962); *Celanese Corporation*, 9 LA 143 (1947); *Coca-Cola Bottling Co.*, 65 LA 357 (1975); and *Hawaii Transfer Company*, LTD, 74 LA 531 (1980).

5. H. J. Scheirich Co. (W. G. Seinsheimer, November 17, 1981, p. 13)

6. One arbitration case not included in this article dealt with chronic absenteeism that was not related to long-term disability, but to a high degree of occasional absences which put the employee's absence percentage over twice the plant average, (H. J. Scheirich Co., D. L. Beckman, September 24, 1984). The employee was terminated for unavailability for work and, with the union, grieved the termination to arbitration. The arbitrator gave the award to the company, primarily because the employee's absence exceeded the long-term absence guidelines created by the company. Thus, this case points out that guidelines for excessive absenteeism pertain not only to sickness and disability but a large accumulation of occasional absenteeism as well.

7. Pre-employment checks which include medical history inquiries or physical examinations should be based on an applicant's current ability to do the job for which he or she is applying. Check your state employment statutes if you have any question regarding your legal rights and responsibilities regarding your screening procedures.

Managing Turnover Strategically

David C. Martin and Kathryn M. Bartol

In today's workplace, turnover rates are frequently used as a measure of organizational health.[1] Although they *are* helpful as a gauge of the general outflow of employees for employment planning purposes, turnover rates actually provide only limited information regarding the status of human resources in an organization. One reason for this limitation is that turnover can have both negative and positive consequences. Therefore, in order to assess the implications of turnover, it is necessary to monitor and evaluate its organizational consequences.

The negative consequences of turnover have been documented in human resource management literature.[2] For example, turnover can necessitate costly expenditures for recruitment and selection of replacements. According to one estimate, it can cost more than $400 just to process one resignation—a figure that mushrooms to more than $40,000 if 100 employees leave in a year.[3]

Turnover can cause major disruptions in work projects and patterns. Even if newcomers possess necessary skills, initial costs can involve not only formal orientation training, but also the lost productivity of others who help orient the new employee. Individuals who leave may represent the loss of sizeable investments in training and experience. In addition, departing employees frequently cause morale problems, particularly if it is perceived that they are leaving due to poor working conditions.[4]

Although it is possible to point to the many negative consequences of turnover, there is greater recognition today that turnover can have many positive consequences as well.[5] One such possibility is that the relatively poor performers who leave are replaced by better performers, resulting in a net gain in productivity in the long run. Higher levels of turnover normally produce a work force with lower overall longevity, which can translate into lower salary levels.[6] In some cases, due to more recent training, new recruits may have greater knowledge and skill levels than those who left. New employees frequently bring with them experience gained elsewhere, an infusion of new knowledge and ideas that can help an organization remain innovative. Turnover also can open up promotion possibilities for high-performing lower-level staff. In addition, when poor performers and individuals who tend to create disruptive conflict leave an organization, the result can be better morale.

Because turnover can have both positive and negative consequences, one crucial issue is the extent to which it is possible to influence turnover in such a way that the positive effects are maximized and the negative effects are minimized. As this article points out, maximizing the positive effects of turnover requires consciously monitoring and managing the turnover process within the parameters of an organization's strategic plan.

PERFORMANCE-REPLACEABILITY STRATEGY MATRIX

In any discussion of turnover, it must be recognized that some turnover is unavoidable. Obvious examples of unavoidable turnover are retirements, promotions and the loss of seasonal help. Employees also leave for a number of personal reasons that are largely beyond the control of the organization, such as the job transfer of a spouse or relocation necessitated by an illness in the family. Successfully maximizing the positive effects of turnover requires concentrating on the kinds of turnover that the organization has a high probability of influencing.

In managing turnover, the goal should be to retain those individuals who are valuable to the organization in terms of two factors: overall performance and replacement.[7] Performance refers to the productivity of the individual as measured by supervisory ratings and objective indicators such as production, sales or services rendered. Related issues such as an individual's ability to work with others and potential to take on greater responsibilities can be considered here too. Under normal circumstances, organizations would rather lose low performers and retain high performers.

Replaceability derives mainly from the characteristics of the position, and is related to the ability to fill a position with a replacement having the required skills, abilities, work experience and rapport to perform the job at the proper level. Positions in which replacement is difficult are typically of two types: (1) positions where specific knowledge about some aspect of the organization and/or its environment is both difficult to acquire and crucial to effective operation in the positions; and (2) positions which require skills that are in relatively short supply.

Operating in conjunction, both performance and replaceability have an important bearing on the consequences of turnover for an organization. The organizational implications of these two factors related to turnover can be seen in the performance-replaceability strategy matrix shown in Figure 1. (In discussing Figure 1, we will use examples from a large metropolitan commercial bank, which we call United Interstate Bank, although the matrix can be applied to virtually any type of organization.)

As suggested by Figure 1, individuals in Category A are high-performing individuals who are either particularly knowledgeable about the organization and are operating in positions where such knowledge is important (if not crucial), or possess skills that are in relatively short supply. A corporate lending officer with a solid credit background and a familiarity with the industries and organizations in which the bank has a particular

Figure 1
The Performance-Replaceability Strategy Matrix

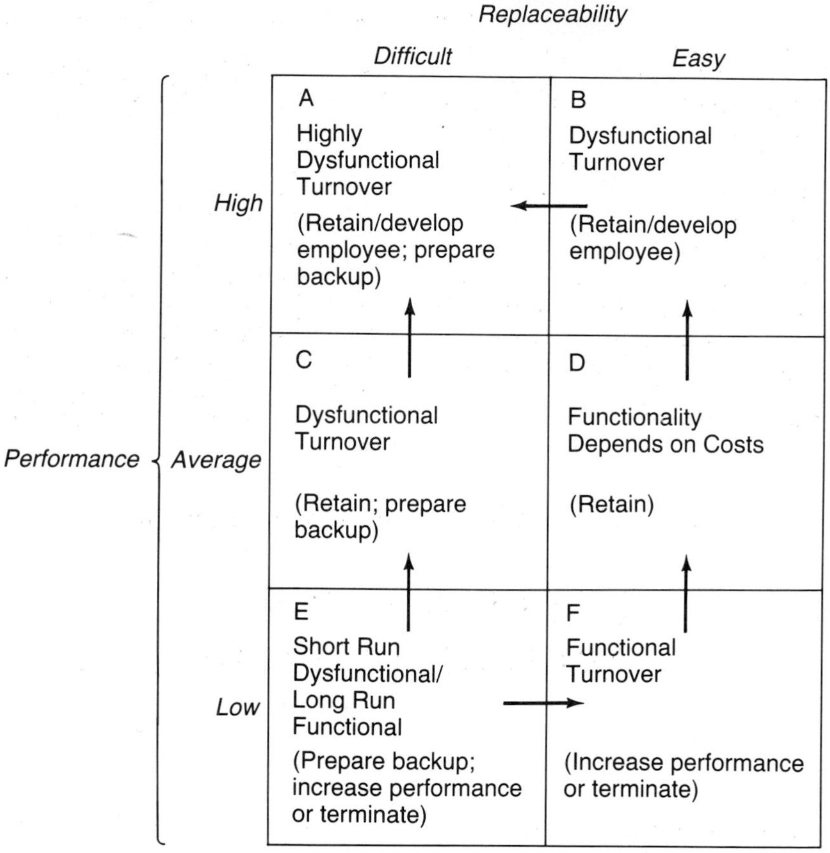

interest is an example of an individual who would fall into Category A. Another example would be a head of operations who possesses both the technical skills to interact with various bank units and strong people management skills, a combination that is in short supply. If either of these two individuals left, it is likely that finding comparable replacements would be difficult and costly. As a result, turnover in this category is considered to be highly dysfunctional.

On the other hand, individuals who fit into Category B are high performers who possess skills that are in relatively great supply and who work in areas where the required knowledge about the organization is either not crucial or is relatively easy to acquire. An example would be a high-performing teller who is both technically competent and effective with customers. Another would be a branch manager who runs a cost-effective operation and shows good account/deposit growth. Although the potential consequences normally are not as great as in Category A, individuals in Category B also constitute dysfunctional turnovers for the organization. The main reason is that when a high-performing individual leaves there is some risk that the replacement will not be as productive, despite organizational efforts at judicious selection.

In contrast to Categories A and B, individuals in Categories C and D are average performers. By "average" we mean that the individuals at least meet the minimum standards of effective performance in their positions but do not perform at a level that would cause them to be identified as high performers. These individuals form the backbone of an organization in the sense that they constitute the largest percentage of employees in a reasonably well-run operation.

Individuals in Category C are average performers who are difficult to replace. Examples might be an average-performing loan officer with specialized skills in an area like commercial construction or an auditor with extensive knowledge of the bank's data processing systems. Individuals in this category are valuable to the bank because they do perform to at least minimum standards in positions where their departure is likely to have negative consequences due to replacement difficulties. As a result, turnover in this category is generally dysfunctional.

Individuals in Category D, however, are average performers in positions where replacements are relatively easy to obtain. Here the functionality or dysfunctionality is more likely to depend on relative costs associated with turnover. For example, suppose an individual in Category D is an average-performing data entry clerk doing relatively routine bank work. Under some circumstances, turnover in this category actually may be beneficial from a cost point of view. This could occur, for example, if the clerk is replaced by a less highly paid individual or if the new employee is a high performer and/or has skills using new software the bank has just acquired.

In other instances, costs associated with the turnover of an individual in Category D may be high, even though replacements are available. This may be the case when an expensive recruiting process must be initiated to hire a financial officer even though appropriate individuals can be found. Thus turnover in Category D can be costly, and may be considered to be dysfunctional under some circumstances. However, there is always the possibility that a replacement will be a high performer.

In contrast to the groups of employees in Categories A through D, those who are regarded as low performers (Categories E and F) represent particular difficulties to their organizations. Employees in Category E are similar to those in Categories A and C in that they are also difficult to replace. An example of an individual in Category E might be a programmer whose job is to make changes in one of the complex financial data processing systems of the bank, but who makes frequent errors before finally completing the required alterations. Because the programmer knows the particular system very well, it will be difficult to replace the individual in the short run. However, if the programmer is allowed to continue this low-performing behavior over a significant period of time, the long-run effects on bank productivity can be quite negative.

On the other hand, Category F includes low-performing employees who would be relatively easy to replace. An example here would be a personal trust officer who has not kept up technically and who achieves relatively poor returns for bank clients. Assuming that a better substitute can be found, the departure of these individuals will improve the efficiency and overall health of the organization. This is functional turnover. It is normally good for both the organization and the individual, as least in the long run.

From this discussion, it should be clear that merely monitoring turnover rates may mask a condition in which an organization is retaining individuals in Categories E and F and losing individuals in Categories A and B. If it is allowed to continue, such a situation would have a long-run disastrous effect on productivity. Thus the crucial issue is not how many are leaving, but the performance and replaceability of those who are leaving versus those who are staying.

MANAGING TURNOVER

Organizations wishing to be staffed adequately to carry out their strategic plans must devote considerable attention to retaining most employees in Categories A and B and a large number of those in Categories C and D, while reducing as much as possible the number of individuals in Categories E and F. This can be accomplished by setting up a monitoring system and gearing human resource programs to achieve positive turnover consequences.

Monitoring the System

The strategic plan of the organization forms the basis for the monitoring system because it ultimately determines which positions are critical to reaching organizational goals. For example, due particularly to deregulation and interstate banking trends, banks face accelerating competition and difficult choices about where they will direct their efforts. The risks inherent in engaging in new business activities are increased when banks do not have employees who are adequately qualified to handle these new lines of endeavor. At the same time, existing business areas often are damaged by resignations of experienced officers in key slots.[8] In essence, making determinations of ease of replaceability for organizational positions is a necessary outgrowth of strategic planning and a part of effective human resource planning.[7] Positions where the work is important and replacement is difficult are key jobs whose major strategic value must be recognized. Failure to acknowledge the importance of these jobs and plan accordingly increases the chances of the strategic plan being derailed. Yet, identification of these key positions can be accomplished relatively easily through collaboration of human resource professionals and managers in the various units of the organization.

Once positions have been classified according to ease of replaceability, the performance-replaceability strategy matrix can be completed using performance appraisal information for position incumbents. The result will be an assessment of the performance and replaceability associated with each incumbent/position in the organization. This information can be used for two purposes. First, it can be used to monitor turnover in terms of who is leaving which positions and to obtain unit and overall organizational patterns. Second, it facilitates the planning of appropriate human resource programs (e.g., career development, training, succession planning and recruiting).

HUMAN RESOURCE PROGRAMMING

Each of the cells in the performance-replaceability strategy matrix calls for a different strategy, although the strategies are related and can be part of an overall human resource programming approach. The basic strategies are shown in parentheses within the categories outlined in Figure 1, and are discussed below in turn. The arrows in Figure 1 depict the generally desirable movements of personnel across segments or cells. (Again, we use United Interstate Bank to illustrate how this approach can work in practice.)

Category A. These are an organization's most valued employees. They are high performers, and possess skills and/or organizational knowledge that are difficult to replace. The human resource strategy should be to retain and develop individuals in this group. They should be trained to the maximum extent possible—not only in technical areas, but also in the broader aspects of managing the organization. According to a recent survey of the banking industry, for example, attracting and retaining competent people and long-term staff development are two of the five most critical human resource issues facing the industry.[9]

At United Interstate, then, individuals in Category A become prime candidates for career development programs and management development, as well as specialized training. In essence, the performance-replaceability strategy matrix determines priorities for delivery of human resource programs. Due to the high probability of these individuals receiving attractive offers from competitors, more frequent salary surveys are done on these positions and greater attention is given to reviewing salary increases for these individuals in order to ensure that the bank remains competitive.

At the same time there remains the significant issue of replaceability, should any of these individuals decide to leave despite efforts to encourage them to stay. Also, due to the development efforts described above, some of these individuals may be promoted to other positions. As a result, substantial efforts are made to plan for and develop backup individuals who can become replacements for members of this group. Such efforts fall in the category of succession planning, which should be a part of every organization's human resources plan.[10] By developing successors, the bank reduces the prospects of sudden, difficult and costly replacement problems, while at the same time providing for the development and motivation of employees with high potential. Where successors cannot be developed, recruitment planning is done and contingency funding is maintained so that replacements can be obtained as quickly as possible.

Category B. This group includes some of the best-performing individuals in the organization. However, they are in positions where it is relatively easy to locate replacements when compared to Category A. As a result, succession planning for these positions is less important. Nevertheless, individuals in this category are valuable because of their high performance levels, and efforts should be made to retain and develop them. At United Interstate such efforts include skills training, job rotation, participation in making decisions that concern their work and projects that include a high degree of personal identity. Because of their high performance, individuals in this category are potential candidates for positions in Category A that involve significant organizational knowledge.

Through specialized training, some individuals in this category may also be developed to fill critical specialist positions in Category A. For example, high-performing junior financial officers at United Interstate may follow career and training paths that lead to more critical positions in commercial lending. At some banks, opportunities for high-performing tellers are provided through innovative branch specialist career paths.[11] Therefore, a primary orientation of the career development actions for this group should be to increase the value of these individuals through opportunities to acquire greater organizational and technical knowledge using mechanisms such as job rotation, special assignments and training. Compensation systems which recognize high performance also are useful in helping to retain these individuals.

Category C. This group of individuals includes some of the most dependable employees in the organization. Although they do not rank among the highest-performing individuals, they have demonstrated that they can perform satisfactorily in areas requiring important organizational knowledge or where skills are in short supply. Because they are difficult to replace despite their average performance, the appropriate human resource strategy should be to attempt to retain these individuals and also to provide backups, where possible, through succession planning. Because the organization is dependent on their continued satisfactory performance, efforts at United Interstate are made to maintain and reinforce performance by setting standards through the performance appraisal process and by providing appropriate rewards in the forms of recognition, pay, flexible hours and job enrichment opportunities. Efforts also are made to encourage those who have the capacity to perform at a high level to do so. Thus Category C is considered to be another potential pool of individuals who could possibly function in Category A positions if they have the capabilities and can be motivated to improve their performance.

Category D. Like Category C, this group contains some of the organization's most dependable employees, and efforts should be made to retain them even though they are replaceable. However, turnover in this category is less likely to have dysfunctional consequences for the organization, depending on replacement costs. As a result, the human resource strategy should be to place an emphasis on maintaining or improving performance through performance appraisal and rewards systems. For example, developing incentive reward systems for tellers has been shown to have a positive effect on both performance and retention.[12] At United Interstate emphasis is placed on good training, performance feedback systems and promotional programs aimed at maintaining necessary levels of performance. However, somewhat less effort is expended in career development efforts for individuals in this group unless they show some willingness to become high performers (e.g., move into Category B) or the costs of replacement are calculated to be undesirably high.

Category E. These employees create a dilemma. They are characterized as generally unreliable, undependable, requiring an unusual amount of supervision and marginally efficient. Yet their output contributes to overall production; they are difficult to replace because of their skills or organizational knowledge. Normally there would be at least a short-term decrease in the organization's ability to meet its obligations if a person from this group left. As a result, low performance is often tolerated in members of this group. Unfortunately, if it is allowed to continue, the situation not only results in a loss of productivity in the position in question, but may demoralize the rest of the work force.[13] At United Interstate considerable emphasis is placed on training managers to properly handle low-performing employees. This is done primarily through performance appraisal training, which includes dealing with poor performers through setting standards, providing feedback and encouraging these individuals to become at least average performers.[14] If such efforts fail, the manager involved works with human resource advisors to decide whether to begin procedures to terminate the individual or to reassign the employee to a position in Category F where the organization is less dependent and where further efforts can be made to encourage the individual to high levels of performance. For Category E, efforts also are made to provide some means of backup to the position in order to reduce dependence on individuals who are essentially unreliable. This is often done through cross-training and gradual shifts in work assignments.

Category F. These individuals do not fit the norms of the organization in that they perform below standards. Furthermore, they are in positions where they are relatively easy to replace. Whenever possible, the aim should be to encourage the members of this group to achieve standard levels of performance (Category D).

At United Interstate, the degree of effort expended in training, counseling, placement in another type of job and other remedial actions depends on the longevity of the individual with the organization, the quality of performance during prior periods, the stress of the job, an assessment of the probable salvageability of the situation and organizational policies regarding terminations. Standard-setting and coaching through the organization's performance appraisal system are crucial here. For individuals with lengths-of-service of five years or more, strong efforts are made to resolve the performance problem without having to resort to termination. If efforts to raise the level of performance are not successful, steps are then taken to terminate the individual. Toleration of serious performance problems sets the stage for feelings of inequity among the employees who do perform their assigned functions reliably.[13] Tolerating poor performance can also encourage some individuals in Categories C and D to lower their performance. Thus a spiral begins which has the effect of shifting performance and organizational productivity levels downward, and ultimately encouraging high performers to leave. Such a scenario is the exact opposite of what is desired.

CONDUCTING PERIODIC REVIEWS

Both organizations and individuals change. The replaceability ratings of various positions can be altered by new directions in strategic plans. At the same time, individual performance levels can shift in an upward direction (one hopes) as a result of effective human resource programming. Thus the necessity for a periodic re-evaluation is clear if the system is to be responsive to organizational needs. The timing of the re-evaluations depends on the character of the work environment and demands on individuals. The most practical approach for most organizations is to review both position replaceability and performance in conjunction with the annual performance appraisal cycle. Such a review must take into consideration shifts in strategic plans and related staffing implications. The re-evaluation process then becomes the mechanism through which turnover patterns are continually monitored and human resource programs are modified to meet the emerging needs of an organization's strategic plan. It is only through these active monitoring and human resource planning processes that organizations can maximize the positive consequences and minimize the negative consequences of turnover.

REFERENCES

1. James L. Price, *The Study of Turnover.* Ames, IA: The Iowa State University Press, 1977.

2. William H. Mobley, *Employee Turnover: Causes, Consequences, and Control.* Reading, MA: Addison-Wesley Publishing Co., 1982.

3. Wayne F. Cascio, *Costing Human Resources: The Financial Impact of Behavior in Organizations*. Boston, MA: Kent Publishing Co., 1982.

4. Barry M. Staw, "The consequences of turnover," *Journal of Occupational Behavior*, 1980, *1*, pp. 253–273.

5. Michael A. Abelson and Barry D. Baysinger, "Optimal and dysfunctional turnover: Toward an organizational level model," *Academy of Management Review*, 1984, *9*, pp. 331–341.

6. Dan R. Dalton and William D. Todor, "Turnover: A lucrative hard dollar phenomenon," *Academy of Management Review*, 1982, *7*, pp. 212–218.

7. Dan R. Dalton, William D. Todor and David M. Krackhardt, "Turnover overstated: The functional taxonomy," *Academy of Management Review*, 1982, *7*, pp. 117–123.

8. David B. Dyche, Jr., "1985: A time to revisit the strategic plan," *The Bankers Magazine*, 1982, *168*(2), pp. 39–66.

9. Ron Zemke, "American banking: Industry in an HRD crunch," *Training*, 1983, *20*, pp. 165–170.

10. John W. Walker, *Human Resource Planning*. New York: McGraw-Hill Book Co., 1980.

11. Steve Cocheo, "Ignore personnel in mergers at your peril," *ABA Banking Journal*, 1983, *75*(9), pp. 55–58.

12. "A banker's advice: Try incentive pay," *ABA Banking Journal*, 1985, *77*(2), p. 20.

13. John E. Dittrich and Michael R. Carrell, "Organizational equity perceptions, employee job satisfaction, and departmental absence and turnover rate," *Organizational Behavior and Human Performance*, 1979, *24*, pp. 29–40.

14. David C. Martin and Kathryn M. Bartol, "Training the raters: A key to effective performance appraisal," *Public Personnel Management*, in press.

An Introduction to Employment-at-Will

Stuart A. Youngblood and Leonard Bierman

INTRODUCTION

Employment-at-will (EAW), the U.S. common law doctrine that protects the employer's right to discharge workers for good, bad, or no reason at all promises to be one of the most controversial personnel and human resources issues for the decade of the 80s. In many ways, the evolutionary nature of this doctrine represents the paradox of freedoms available in the U.S. workplace. The freedom afforded the American worker is one of being able to voluntarily choose employers, and to change employers in the pursuit of his or her own self-interest. Similarly, employers in a capitalistic, market-oriented economy are afforded the freedom to mix capital and labor in whatever combination they deem efficient for the production of goods and services. Therein, however, lies the crux of the problem: What is the appropriate balance of freedom between the employer's right to discharge workers in the pursuit of organizational goals versus the individual worker's due process right to fair and secure employment treatment and some degree of control over his or her employment?

A SHORT HISTORY OF EMPLOYMENT-AT-WILL IN THE U.S.

The uniqueness of the employment-at-will doctrine to the United States today is surprising in

Excerpted from "Due Process and Employment-At-Will" by S. A. Youngblood and L. Bierman in *Research in Personnel and Human Resources Management,* Volume 3. © 1985, JAI Press Inc.

light of the early reliance by the American judiciary on British common law doctrines governing employer-employee relations. Until the late 19th century, there was some evidence that the Americans might follow the British common law doctrine (Blades, 1967; Committee on Labor and Employment Law, 1981; Feinman, 1976). The British common law was linked to domestic or master-servant relationships and to rules developed from early labor statutes (Hill, 1982). Under the British common law, in the absence of a contract, an indefinite hiring was presumed to be for *one year* and reasonable notice was required by either party prior to terminating the employment relationship. What constituted "reasonable notice" varied by trade and custom as the rule was applied to employment other than domestic and agricultural work. The common law rule, based in master and servant law, did contain a certain symmetry in terms of a balancing of rights. A master could do injustice to servants by supporting them during planting and harvest seasons and then releasing them to avoid support over the winter months. Similarly, servants could harm their masters by leaving when their services were most needed. As the rule was applied to other types of employment, British courts tended to place less emphasis on the duration of the hiring and more emphasis on what constituted "reasonable notice" for discharge.

During the 19th century, the U.S. rule governing a hiring for an indefinite term was somewhat less settled. Early American treatise writers on master and servant law (Reeve, 1846; Smith, 1852) noted in the British rule that a general hiring was presumed to be yearly and terminable upon reasonable notice where customary. But, the courts did not always apply this standard. However, the confusion as to whether master-servant law was applicable to employer-employee relationships was clarified by H. G. Wood in his 1877 *Master and Servant* treatise. Wood, to whom the current U.S. employment-at-will rule is attributed, stated in no uncertain terms:

> *[w]ith us the rule is inflexible, that a general or indefinite hiring is prima facie a hiring at will, and if the servant seeks to make it out a yearly hiring the burden is upon him to establish it by proof. . . . (I)t is an indefinite hiring and is terminable at the will of either party, and in this respect there is no distinction between domestic and other servants (Wood, 1877, p. 134).*

As Feinman (1976) has noted, the rapid and uniform spread of Wood's employment-at-will rule is both remarkable and puzzling; it caught on very quickly and developed uniformly across the United States during the 20th century despite being based on seemingly flawed legal analysis. First, the cases Wood relied on to document his interpretation of the rule did not precisely support his analysis (see Note, Implied Contract Rights to Job Security, 1974). Moreover, Wood incorrectly reported that no American court had approved the British rule, that the rule was entirely inflexible, and failed to adequately discuss notice requirements.

A number of observers (e.g., Committee on the Development of the Law of Individual Rights and Responsibilities, 1982; Committee on Labor and Employment Law, 1981; Feinman, 1976; Werhane; 1983) have suggested that several historically rooted legal, political, social, and economic factors were the primary contributors to the evolutionary acceptance of Wood's at-will rule in the United States during the early 20th century. The political and social climate of the nation at the beginning of the 20th century was characterized by industrialization and a transformation away from traditional master-servant to employer-employee relationships. Themes of self-reliance, self-sufficiency, and protection of the individual were prevalent; thus, judicial action protecting employers' freedom to manage the workplace was congruent with the times.

Further, individual workers desiring greater job security could, in the tradition of self-sufficiency and individualism, legally negotiate service or employment contracts to protect their interests. If at the time of hiring the employee failed to negotiate a contract, then the hiring was considered for an indefinite period and terminable at the will of either party. The U.S. Supreme Court upheld the absolute right of employers to discharge at will employees, absent the existence of an extant contract, in the cases of *Adair* v. *United States* (1908) and *Coppage* v. *Kansas* (1915). Indeed, it was not until the passage of the National Labor Relations Act of 1935 and the U.S. Supreme Court decision upholding the act in *NLRB* v. *Jones & Laughlin Steel Corp.* (1937) that complete employer freedom, absent an extant contract, to discharge workers for whatever reasons they wished was at all constrained. Moreover, even under the National Labor Relations Act, employers still retain generally broad rights to discharge "for cause."

The legal, political, and social climate of the early 20th century was also matched by a prevailing economic philosophy of "laissez-faire" designed to promote growth and economic efficiency. Feinman (1976) has argued that perhaps the strongest rationale for the employment-at-will rule is the protection and flexibility it affords employers. The practical implications of this flexibility were perhaps best expressed by the Tennessee Supreme Court in the case of *Payne* v. *Western & Atlantic Railroad* (1884), which noted an at-will employee could be terminated for good cause, for no cause, or even cause morally wrong without the employer being thereby guilty of legal wrong. Under the "at-will" doctrine, owners of capital can purchase the labor of employees but nonetheless retain authority and control over the workplace. From a Lockean perspective of private property (Locke, 1983), the employer creates and owns the jobs needed for the production of products and services; therefore, the employer's freedom to combine labor and capital in whatever manner deemed necessary must be protected by the at-will rule. Although Feinman's analysis is only cursory, he noted that many of the at-will cases in the late 19th and 20th centuries involved educated, middle managers who posed the greatest threat to the authority of owners of capital. Given the turbulence of seasonal and cyclical swings in business activity, owners of capital arguably needed the at-will rule for flexible expansion and contraction of their work force to survive.

In summary, the development of the American employment-at-will rule is rooted in master and servant law that originally developed in Great Britain. The American rule, however, diverged from the British rule which considered both the period of employment intended and the mutual obligation of reasonable notice. The American evolution of the Wood "at-will" rule was influenced by the mechanistic and formal application of developing contract law theory, as well as a political, social, and economic climate that emphasized individualism and a laissez-faire approach to employer-employee relations. Until passage of the National Labor Relations Act (NLRA) in 1935, employers enjoyed essentially unfettered discretion to fire workers "at will" in the United States. Although this and subsequent legislation has eroded the at-will rule somewhat (exceptions to employment-at-will are discussed in greater detail in a subsequent section), the majority of American workers are still today generally subject to the rule of employment-at-will. We turn first to a discussion of the magnitude of the problem in terms of the actual number of American workers currently subject to the at-will rule.

Magnitude of the Problem

Critics and proponents alike have attempted to estimate how extensive the EAW rule is in terms of its impact on the U.S. labor force. One problem with such estimation is that no direct evidence is available on the number of workers who are discharged without just cause and without recourse to appeal. A number of scholars, however, have used bits and pieces of data from a variety of sources, together with a few assumptions, to arrive at estimates of the number of workers unjustly discharged. By examining these data and assumptions, one can gain an appreciation for the scope of the problem and obtain reasonable upper and lower estimates of the number of workers affected by EAW.

From a macro perspective, one could exclude from the U.S. labor force those workers who currently enjoy some form of "due process" protection from arbitrary discharge. Two primary groups in this regard are (1) government workers (federal, state, and local) who are protected both by civil service legislation and the U.S. Constitution and (2) union workers who typically are covered by collective bargaining agreements with explicit discipline and discharge provisions. A recent BNA (Bureau of National Affairs, 1979) report revealed that provisions for just cause discipline and discharge existed in 96 percent of the union contracts examined, and even where a labor contract is silent, arbitrators will often infer "just cause" protection on the basis of contractual language governing employee promotion, transfer, and layoff rights based on seniority. In 1984, according to Census information, approximately 25 percent of the nonagricultural labor force belonged to a union and approximately 18 percent were employees of federal, state, or local governments (U.S. Bureau of the Census, 1984). If we assumed that roughly 50 percent of all government workers belonged to a union, this means that approximately 65 percent of all U.S. workers in 1984 were at-will employees.

In terms of the actual number of employees who are unjustly discharged annually without recourse to any meaningful appeal, a number of different approaches to estimation have been taken. Peck (1979), generalizing from the experience of the American Arbitration Association and the Federal Mediation and Conciliation Service, has estimated upwards to 300,000 employees are discharged annually without recourse to appeal. Stieber and Murray (1983), using 1981 labor force data, estimated that of nearly 48 million nonprobationary U.S. employees, 1.4 million were separated annually (assuming a 4 percent quit rate) and that two of every ten quits would be a contested discharge. Assuming a successful appeal rate of 50 percent (based on published arbitration cases), then 140,000 U.S. workers were discharged in 1981 who might have been reinstated with or without back pay under collective bargaining protection from unjust discharge.

Summers (1982, 1983), drawing on both American and Canadian experience, estimated a lower figure for the total number of possible discharge appeals. The Canadian experience, according to Summers, is one appeal per one thousand workers. Using 1981 data from contested unemployment compensation claims in Pennsylvania, Summers reported that approximately 12,750 employee-initiated cases were heard from a total state labor force of 5.4 million, which would yield an appeal rate of approximately two cases per one thousand employees. Bierman and Youngblood (1985) examined the 1983 case load of the South Carolina Labor Management Service and estimated that approximately 2700 workers brought claims of unjust discharge to the agency for adjudication. Based on a nonunion labor force of approximately 1.5 million, the appeal rate in South Carolina is also approximately two cases per one thousand employees. If one were to apply an appeal rate of one case per thousand to the 65 percent of the U.S. labor force subject to at-will employment in 1980, then approximately 58,000 at-will employees were that year unjustly discharged without recourse to appeal.

Whether these numbers are too high or too low depends to some degree on whether they are examined in a relative or absolute sense. Perhaps a more compelling argument for the magnitude of the problem is the cost of settlement of at-will cases that go to court. In a recent study of California EAW cases of over 40 employment-at-will cases settled in favor of the employee, the median award exceeded $500,000 (Lublin, 1983). In sum, in a relative sense, the number of employees discharged annually may represent a very small percentage of the entire U.S. labor force (e.g., less than one-tenth of 1 percent). But, given the heightened awareness by employees of individual rights in the workplace and an increasingly active judiciary, this small segment of the labor force may account for significant money expenditures by firms. In the context of recent judicial and legislative activism in this area, we now turn to the legal framework that governs employment-at-will in the United States.

A LEGAL ANALYSIS OF EMPLOYMENT-AT-WILL

Legal scholars have often attacked the EAW rule because of the incongruity of the rule with other sources of rules that protect specific groups of workers from unjust discharge (Blades, 1967; Peck, 1979; Summers, 1976). Basically, five general sources of rules place restrictions on an employer's freedom to discharge: statutory, arbitral, contractual, constitutional, and judicial limitations. In the following sections, we will review briefly these sources of restrictions and consider in more detail the judicial source in light of the recent application of common law doctrines to remedy individual claims of unjust discharge.

Statutory Protection

Two major federal statutes, the Railway Labor Act (1926) and the National Labor Relations Act (1935), have provided a significant number of workers with protection from discharge related to unionization attempts and collective bargaining activity. In addition, these enabling statutes have further led to negotiated agreements that typically provide for arbitration of unjust discharge disputes in the final step of the grievance procedure. The National Labor Relations Act created the National Labor Relations Board (NLRB) which has the power to investigate employer unfair labor practices related to discharging a worker for union activity or for filing an unfair labor practice charge with the NLRB. In 1937, the constitutionality of the NLRA was upheld in *NLRB* v. *Jones & Laughlin Steel Corp.* (1937). This development was significant in light of earlier U.S. Supreme Court rulings (*Adair* v. *United States*, 1908; *Coppage* v. *Kansas*, 1915) that prevented federal or state statutes from modifying the EAW rule because regulation of the employment relationship was believed to be a violation of employer and employee freedom of contract.

Title VII of the Civil Rights Act (1964, 1972) similarly provides protection to private and public sector employees from unjust discharge based on race, color, religion, sex, or national origin. Although the focus of Title VII is on hiring, promotion, and seniority practices, nearly 70 percent of all charges involve discharge complaints, failure to hire, or refusal to promote (Blumrosen, 1983b). Based on the 1981 annual report of the Equal Employment Opportunity Commission (EEOC), which enforces Title VII, charges of discriminatory discharge accounted for over 30 percent of all Title VII charges in that year (EEOC, 1983b). Peck (1979), however, noted the peculiar irony of Title VII protection that presumably encourages the "color-blindness" and "job-relatedness" of employment practices which effectively benefit majority and minority workers alike (see, for example *McDonald* v. *Sante Fe Trail Transportation*, 1976), and the apparent one-sidedness of federal labor legislation which has led to protection from unjust discharge for unionized workers only. If the courts were to extend this logic, then Title VII could be generalized to protect all employees from unjust discharge, although this is an extremely unlikely outcome.

Other significant federal legislation includes the Civil Service Reform Act (1978), which provides just cause protection from discharge, grievance procedures, and appeal machinery (e.g., Merit Systems Protection Board) independent of what workers may additionally negotiate through collective bargaining. States may also pass legislation similar to federal labor and EEO legislation that provides grievance procedures and appeal mechanisms designed to protect workers' due process rights.

Other federal statutes that provide employees with potential, albeit somewhat more narrow, protection from unjust discharge include: the Fair Labor Standards Act (1938), which prohibits dismissal of employees filing a complaint or exercising a right under the statute; the Age Discrimination in Employment Act (1967, 1978), which prohibits age-based discharge by private and public employers of persons between the ages of 40 to 70; the Rehabilitation Act of 1973, which prohibits federal contractors of federally supported programs from discriminating against handicapped individuals; the Vietnam Era Veterans Readjustment Assistance Act (1979, 1982), which provides veterans protection from discharge from civilian service; the Occupational Safety and Health Act (1970) and the Railway Safety Act (1982), which prohibit dismissal of employees in reprisal for exercising their rights under these acts; the Energy Reorganization Act (1974), the Clean Air Act (1981), and the Federal Water Pollution Control Act (1978), which protect employees from discharge who institute or testify at a proceeding against the employer in relation to the substance of these acts; the Employee Retirement Income Security Act (1974), which prohibits discharge of employees to avoid the attainment of vested pension rights; the Consumer Credit Protection Act (1982), which prohibits discharge of employees for garnishment of wages for an indebtedness; and the Judiciary and Judicial Procedure Act (1982), which prohibits discharge of employees who serve on juries in federal courts.

In addition to these federal statutes that place some restrictions on employee discharge, state statutes, which mirror federal statutes, have also been passed that prohibit discrimination because of employee acceptance of jury duty, political activities, refusal to take a lie detector test, filing a workers' compensation claim, reporting state safety code violations, and physical handicaps. Nevertheless, despite this potpourri of legislation, the majority of the U.S. work force still remains subject to the general EAW rule.

Arbitral Protection

A unique feature of the U.S. industrial relations system, in contrast to European systems, is the growth and development of arbitration procedures for workers covered by collective bargaining agreements. Arbitration has created a substantive body of common law that governs employer discharge decisions. Typically, this protection is invoked where the collective bargaining agreement contains language that prohibits discipline and discharge without "just cause." Even where the contract is silent, arbitrators will often infer just cause protection from other contract provisions, such as seniority clauses or generalized grievance procedures (Hill & Sinicropi, 1981; Platt, 1956).

Arbitration of discharge claims under collective agreements has produced a considerable body of common law (Elkouri & Elkouri, 1973), yet a small number of principles related to just cause discharge can be distilled from the numerous cases heard. According to Summers (1976) and Daughterty (Hill, 1982, p. 140), these principles can be summarized as follows:

a) Employee Right to Know What is Prohibited—did the employer give the employee forewarning or knowledge of the disciplinary consequences of his . . . her conduct?

b) Management's Right to Manage—were company rules reasonably related to orderly, efficient, and safe operation of the enterprise and the performance expected of the employee?

c) Procedural Fairness—did the company make an effort to fairly and objectively investigate the rule violation or disobeyance of a management order?

d) Right to Equal Treatment—have company rules, orders, and penalties been applied consistently to all employees?

e) Corrective Discipline—did management's punishment fit the crime given the seriousness of the offense and the seniority of the employee?

If the answer to one or more of the above questions is "no" when applied to a given discharge case, then it is safe to assume that an arbitrator will rule that just cause did not exist. Despite the volume of arbitration cases heard each year under collective agreements, considerable uniformity and consistency in rulings has emerged. As Summers has so aptly described the process, "[r]esults . . . may well depend on the length of the arbitrator's foot, but that leads to relatively small differences, for there are few peg-legs or abominable snowmen among arbitrators, and no one follows in their footsteps" (Summers, 1976, p. 162). For these reasons, arbitration has been proposed by a number of scholars (e.g., Summers, 1980) as the antidote to the "poisonous" consequences of EAW for nonunion workers.

Constitutional Protection

Two relatively recent U.S. Supreme Court cases, *Board of Regents* v. *Roth* (1972) and *Perry* v. *Sindermann* (1972), have resulted in a constitutional interpretation under the 5th and 14th Amendments that *public* employees are entitled to constitutional procedural and substantive due-process protection. In both the *Roth* and *Sindermann* cases, public university professors were terminated and each argued that a property interest in their job was taken without due process of law (i.e., there was a failure to provide a reason for termination and a failure to provide a hearing). The public universities' actions were interpreted as "state action," hence the question of constitutional protection from "state action." The facts of each case differed, however, and only in the *Sindermann* case was a potential due-process violation recognized; Sindermann was a ten-year employee of the system, the college had no formal tenure system, the faculty guide stated that each faculty member's job was secure as long as the teacher's services were satisfactory and he or she was cooperative, and Sindermann was terminated with the college providing no official statement, no hearing, and no appeal. The Court ruled that Sindermann was entitled to the right to demonstrate a property interest in his job and, thus, at a minimum, to 14th Amendment protection encompassing a hearing and a statement of the reasons for his discharge.

Judicial Protection

Although recent legal analyses of EAW cases are not exhaustive (Bureau of National Affairs, 1982; Lorber, Kirk, Kirschner, & Handorf, 1984; Note, Implied Contract Rights, 1974; Note, Protecting Employees, 1980; Note, Protecting Employees, 1983; Shepard and Moran, 1982), the evidence suggests that the relative dormancy of the EAW issue during the 20th century has been awakened by a spate of judicial rulings within the past decade. Although state-by-state comparisons of court rulings reveal increasing judicial activism, it is fair to say that EAW is still the recognized common law doctrine governing at-will employees in the United States (see, for example, Bureau of National Affairs, 1982, p. 8; Hill, 1982, p. 155; Lorber et al.. 1984, Appendix A; and Shepard & Moran, 1982, pp. 26–29).

The development of common law theories has, however, provided a basis for judicial erosion of the EAW doctrine well beyond the four previously discussed areas of protection. Although different typologies have been used to catalog these new theories, three basic approaches to modifying EAW have been used by the courts: (1) public policy exceptions, (2) duty of good faith and fair dealing, and (3) implied contract terms.

Public Policy Exceptions. The most common limitation to the EAW doctrine is the public policy exception, whereby a wrongful discharge claim can be brought in a contract or a tort action. The basic notion underlying this type of claim is that an employer's discharge decision contravenes a defined and well-established public policy. The question of what constitutes a clearly mandated public policy has been interpreted differently by various courts. One court in *Palmateer* v. *International Harvester, Co.* (1981) has stated that the courts must look to the state's constitution, existing statutes, and, if necessary, other judicial opinions.

Three different types of employee motives are usually involved with public policy contested discharges. Employees may contest discharge decisions where they have been asked to commit an unlawful act. A leading case is *Petermann* v. *International Brotherhood of Teamsters* (1981) where Petermann, a business agent, was instructed by his union (employer) to make false statements before a committee of the California legislature. Similarly, the California Supreme Court found protection to exist for an employee who refused to participate in an illegal price fixing scheme (*Tamney* v. *Atlantic Richfield Co.*, 1980). In *Pierce* v. *Ortho Pharmaceutical* (1980), a physician refused to perform research she considered medically unethical on a controversial drug. Although the New Jersey Supreme Court acknowledged that state public policy could be found in codes of professional responsibility, the court held for the defendant employer. In the court's opinion, Pierce failed to demonstrate that continued work on the project violated a specific state law or professional ethical code or obligation.

A second motive for public policy protection is where an employee is discharged for performing an important public obligation or whistle-blowing. A leading case is *Nees* v. *Hocks* (1975), where Nees's employer fired her for agreeing to serve on jury duty after the employer had warned Nees not to serve. The Oregon Supreme Court held for Nees, citing a duty to perform public functions established by the state legislature, the state's constitution, and common law. In *Palmateer* v. *International Harvester* (1981), the court found a tort of retaliatory discharge on the part of the employer for discharging Palmateer when he supplied information to police about the suspected wrongdoing of a fellow employee. The court reasoned that "public policy which favors citizen crime fighters" is served by ruling for the employee. Two other cases, *Harless* v. *First National Bank of Fairmont* (1978) and *Geary* v. *United States Steel Corp.* (1974), involved instances of employee whistle-blowing on the employer. In *Harless*, a cause of action was found to exist for an employee who sought to require his employer to comply with a state consumer credit and protection statute. Although *Geary* involved concern over a defective product, the court ruled, however, that the employee "made a nuisance of himself" and that no evidence existed to support a claim that the discharge caused harm or was predicated on Geary's refusal to break any law.

A third motive protected by public policy is where an employee exercises a statutory right or privilege. A leading case in this area, involving a discharge for filing a worker's compensation claim, is *Frampton* v. *Central Indiana Gas Co.* (1973), where the Indiana Supreme Court recognized a cause of action for abusive or retaliatory discharge even though the state statute did not explicitly bar the employer from such an action. In *Kelsay* v. *Motorola, Inc.* (1978), the Illinois Supreme Court ruled that punitive damages could be awarded to deter employer retaliation for employee filing of a worker's compensation claim. In *Perks* v. *Firestone Tire & Rubber* (1979), an employee refused to take a lie detector test in a state (Pennsylvania) that statutorily prohibited employers from requiring such tests of employees. Because the state statute embodied public policy, the U.S. Court of Appeals for the Third Circuit found the termination supported an action for tortious discharge.

A major problem with public policy exceptions to EAW is that each court must make a determination of what precisely the public policy is. Inconsistent rulings across court jurisdictions have appeared, especially in discharge decisions involving employees who file worker's compensation claims. Another problem is that although public policy exceptions are the most common exceptions to EAW, this type of exception may not be available to lower-level, less-skilled employees. This argument warrants further attention, given Selznick's finding that workers from different occupations perceive and define fair treatment differently (Selznick, 1969, p. 187). One study (Note, Protecting Employees, 1983) examined 46 public policy cases cited in Shepard and Moran (1982), as well as 92 public policy cases from 1976–1981, and concluded that lower-level, less-skilled, lower-paying occupations were underrepresented. The arm of judicial relief to EAW, therefore, may not reach far enough for a large group of victims of wrongful discharge.

Duty of Good Faith and Fair Dealing. Three cases characterize the general nature of an implied-in-law good faith/fair dealing contract exception to EAW. In *Fortune* v. *National Cash Register Co.* (1977), the discharge of a salesman with 25 years of service the day after the company obtained a $5,000,000 order effectively deprived the salesman of a substantial commission. The Massachusetts Supreme Court upheld a jury finding that the discharge was motivated by a desire to avoid paying the commission and reasoned that even contracts for employment "at will" contain a covenant of good faith and fair dealing. Similarly, in *Cleary* v. *American Airlines* (1980), a California court ruled that termination of a long-service employee without legal cause offends the implied-in-law covenant of good faith and fair dealing, as well as the employer's own policies governing fair, impartial, and objective procedures for reviewing employee discipline and grievances. Finally, a New Hampshire court ruled that an employer's termination of an "at-will" employee was motivated by bad faith and malice, was not in the best interest of the economic system or the public good, and constituted a breach of contract (*Monge* v. *Beebe Rubber Co.*, 1974).

Implied-in-Fact Contract Rights. The Michigan Supreme Court in a landmark ruling in *Toussaint* v. *Blue Cross & Blue Shield* (1980) held that provisions in a personnel manual or handbook unilaterally and voluntarily adopted by the employer, distributed to employees after hire, and stating discharge will only be "for cause," may become a part of the employment contract. In addition, verbal assurances at the time of hire that an employee such as Toussaint would not be discharged if he was doing his job led the court to conclude that these assurances of job security were indeed enforceable. In another case (*Novosel* v. *Sears, Roebuck & Co.*, 1980), however, a federal district court cited an exception to *Toussaint* in applying Michigan law to an employee who signed an application that stated that employment could be terminated by either party with or without cause or notice at any time. In any event, it appears that at least in the short run many employers will be able to avoid legal liability in this regard by requiring new employees to sign job application and other forms that clarify their at-will status.

Other Judicial Approaches. Other common law exceptions to EAW, while infrequently used, illustrate further how the EAW doctrine has been modified by judicial decisions. The legal doctrine of "promissory estoppel" has been applied to unjust discharge, whereby the discharged employee alleges that he or she was induced to work for the employer (e.g., through aggressive recruiting tactics) and relied on this inducement, only to be fired and subsequently suffer detrimental consequences. In *Grouse* v. *Group Health Plan, Inc.* (1981), pharmacist Grouse resigned his employment and declined an offer of employment elsewhere to accept a position at a clinic, only to find the clinic had hired another individual upon failing to obtain needed references for Grouse. The Minnesota Supreme Court ruled that the clinic's job offer to Grouse induced him to quit his present job and that injustice could be avoided only by holding the clinic liable for this breach of promise. Another type of exception to EAW was developed by the Massachusetts Supreme Court in the case of *Agis* v. *Howard Johnson Co.* (1976), where waitresses were fired alphabetically to pressure them into supplying information regarding employee theft. The court held this to be a tort of intentional infliction of emotional distress; the employer's conduct was deemed so extreme and outrageous that it gave rise to a tort claim. Finally, one court has ruled that an employer is tortiously negligent in terminating an employee without providing a performance evaluation indicating to said employee that discharge was imminent, absent an immediate change in behavior (*Chamberlain* v. *Bissell, Inc.* 1982).

SUMMARY

Although a majority of U.S. employees are "terminable-at-will," a patchwork of rules provide some degree of protection for isolated groups of workers. To the extent that EAW is viewed as unduly harsh and inequitable, a number of approaches to modify the doctrine are suggested by the foregoing legal discussion. Federal or state statutes could be passed that effectively eliminate the doctrine by substituting a just cause standard for discharge. In fact at the federal level, the *Corporate Democracy Act*, introduced in 1980, attempted unsuccessfully to amend Title IV of the National Labor Relations Act to provide uniform protection to union and nonunion workers from EAW. At the state level in Michigan and California, bills have been introduced that would eliminate EAW and provide grievance machinery to adjudicate unjust discharge claims.

Some observers have argued that relief from EAW exists through unionization. In light of a declining proportion of workers who belong to unions, and the fundamental shifts in the demographic (more females), industrial (shift from smokestack to high technology firms), and occupational (shift to service and information workers) composition of the labor force, unionization would appear, at best, to be a slowly developing and uncomprehensive approach to modifying EAW.

A third alternative is to rely on continued judicial activism as a means to chip away at the reach of the EAW doctrine. Accordingly, legal scholars have attempted to arm the judiciary with a variety of common law theories to attack EAW; Blades (1967) has argued for tort remedies to abusive discharge, others have suggested an implied contract approach (Blackburn, 1983; Note, Implied Contract Rights, 1974), while still others have argued for public policy (Note, Protecting Employees, 1983) or duty of good faith and fair dealing (Note, Protecting Employees, 1980) doctrines as a means to override EAW.

REFERENCES

Adair v. *United States*, 208 U.S. 161, 172–175, (1908).

Age Discrimination in Employment Act of 1967, 29 U.S.C. sec. 623, 631, 633(a) (1975 & Supp. 1982).

Agis v. *Howard Johnson Co.*, 371 Mass. 140, 355 N.E. 2d 315 (1976).

Bierman, L., & Youngblood, S. A. (1985). Employment-at-will and the South Carolina experiment. *Industrial Relations Law Journal, 7,* 28–59.

Blackburn, J. (1983). Judicial action. In J. Stieber & J. Blackburn (Eds.), *Protecting unionized employees against unjust discharge,* (pp. 31–45). East Lansing, MI: School of Labor and Industrial Relations, Michigan State University.

Blades, E. (1967). Employment at will vs. individual freedom: On limiting the abusive exercise of employer power. *Columbia Law Review, 67,* 1404–1435.

Blumrosen, A. W. (1983a). Exploring voluntary arbitration of individual employment disputes. *University of Michigan Journal of Law Reform. 16,* 249–276.

Blumrosen, A. (1983b). Title VII of the Civil Rights Act of 1964. In J. Stieber & J. Blackburn (Eds.), *Protecting unorganized employees against unjust discharge* (pp. 21–24). East Lansing, MI: School of Labor and Industrial Relations, Michigan State University.

Board of Regents v. *Roth,* 408 U.S. 564 (1972).

Bureau of National Affairs. (1979). *Collective bargaining negotiations and contracts.* Washington, D.C.: Bureau of National Affairs, 51:5.

Bureau of National Affairs. (1982). *The employment at will issue: A BNA special report.* Washington, D.C.: Bureau of National Affairs.

Chamberlain v. *Bissell, Inc.,* 547 F. Supp. 1067 (W.D. Mich. 1982).

Cleary v. *American Airlines,* 111 C. App. 3d443, 168 Cal Rptr. 722 (2d Dist. 1980).

Civil Rights Act of 1964, Title VII, 2 U.S.C. secs. 2000e to 2000e–17 (1976 & Supp. III 1979).

Civil Service Reform Act of 1978 5 U.S.C.A. secs. 303(A), 7513 (a) (1980).

Committee on Labor and Employment Law. (1981). At-will employment and the problem of unjust dismissal, Bar of the City of New York *The Record, 36*(4), 170–216. New York: Committee on Labor and Employment Law.

Committee on the Development of the Law of Individual Rights and Responsibilities in the Workplace. (1982). Labor and employment law committee reports, 14–24, Washington, D.C.: Committee on the Development of the Law of Individual Rights and Responsibilities in the Workplace.

Consumer Credit Protection Act, 15 U.S.C. sec. 1674(a) (1982).

Coppage v. *Kansas,* 236 U.S. 1, 13–14 (1915).

Elkouri, F., & Elkouri, E. A. (1973). *How arbitration works.* Washington, D.C.: Bureau of National Affairs, pp. 610–666.

Employment Retirement Income Security Act of 1974, 29 U.S.C. sec. 1140, 1141 (1975).

Energy Reorganization Act of 1974, 42 U.S.C. sec 5851 (Supp. 1981).

Equal Employment Opportunity Commission Annual Report. (1983). Washington, D.C.: U.S. Government Printing Office.

Fair Labor Standards Act, 29 U.S.C. secs. 215 (a)(3), 216(b) (1975 & Supp. 1982).

Federal Water Pollution Control Act, 33 U.S.C. sec. 1367 (1978).

Feinman, J. M. (1976). The development of the employment at will rule. *American Journal of Legal History, 20,* 118–135.

Fortune v. *National Cash Register Co,* 373 Mass. 96, 346 N.E. 2d 1251 (1977).

Frampton v. *Central Indiana Gas Co.,* 260 Ind. 249, 297 N.E. 2d 425, 428 (1973).

Geary v. *United States Steel Corp.,* 456, pa. 171, 319 A. 2d 174 (1974).

Grouse v. *Group Health Plan, Inc.,* 306 N.W. 2d 114 (Sup. Ct. Minn. 1981).

Harless v. *First National Bank of Fairmont,* 246 S.E. 270 (W. Va. 1978).

Hill, M., Jr., (1982). Arbitration as a means of protecting employees from unjust dismissal: A statutory proposal. *Northern Illinois University Law Review, 3,* 111–185.

Hill, M., Jr. & Sinicropi, A. (1981). *Remedies in arbitration.* Washington, DC: BNA Books.

Judiciary and Judicial Procedure Act, 28 U.S.C. sec. 1975 (Supp. 1982).

Kelsay v. *Motorola, Inc.,* 74 Ill. 2d 172, 384 N.E. 2d 353 (1978).

Kolb, D. (1983). *The mediators.* Cambridge, MA: MIT Press.

Locke, J. (1983). The justification of private property. In T. Donaldson & P. H. Werhane (Eds.), *Ethical issues in business* (pp. 206–211). Englewood Cliffs, NJ: Prentice-Hall.

Lorber, Z., Kirk, J., Kirschner, H., & Handorf, R. (1984). *Fear of firing: A legal analysis of employment-at-will.* Alexandria, VA: ASPA Foundation.

Lublin, J. S. (1983, September 13). Legal challenges force firms to revamp ways they dismiss workers. *The Wall Street Journal.* p. 18.

McDonald v. *Sante Fe Trail Transportation Co.,* 427 U.S. 273 (1976).

Monge v. *Beebe Rubber Co.,* 114 N.H. 130, 316 A. 2d 549 (1974).

National Labor Relations Act, 29 U.S.C.A. secs. 151 *et. seq.* 158 (1976).

Nees v. *Hocks,* 272 Or. 210, 536 P. 2d 512 (1975).

NLRB v. *Jones & Laughlin Steel Corp.,* 301 U.S. I (1973).

Novosel v. *Sears, Roebuck & Co.,* 495 Supp. 344 (E.D. Mich. 1980).

Occupational Safety and Health Act of 1970, 29 U.S.C. sec. 660(c) (1975).

Palmateer v. *International Harvester Co.,* 85 Ill 2d 124, 411 N.E. 2d 876 (1981).

Payne v. *Western & Atlantic Railroad,* 81 Tenn. 507 (1884).

Peck, C. (1979). Unjust discharges from employment: A necessary change in the law. *Ohio State Law Journal, 40,* 1–49.

Perks v. *Firestone Tire & Rubber Co.,* 611 F. 2d 1363 (3rd Cir. 1979).

Perry v. *Sindermann,* 408 U.S. 593 (1972).

Peterman v. *International Brotherhood of Teamsters,* 174 Ca. App. 184, 344, 2d 25 (1981).

Pierce v. *Ortho Pharmaceutical Corp.,* 84 N.J. 58, 417 A2d 505 (1980).

Platt, H. (1956). Arbitral standards in discipline cases. *The Law and Labor Management Relations,* 24–25. University of Michigan.

Railroad Safety Act, 45 U.S.C. secs. 441(a), (b)(1) (Supp. 1982).

Railway Labor Act U.S.C.A. secs. 151 *et. seq.* 152 (Fourth) (1976).

Reeve, T. (1846). *The law of baron and fennue, of parent and child, guardian and ward, master and servant, and of the powers of the Court of Chancery.* 347.

Selznick, P. (1969) *Law, society, and industrial justice.* New York: Russell Sage Foundation.

Shepard, M., & Moran, L. (1982). "Wrongful" discharge litigation. *ILR Report, 10*(1), 26–29.

Smith. C. (1852). *Master and servant.*

Stieber, J., & Murray, M. (1983). Protection against unjust discharge: The need for a federal statute. *University of Michigan Journal of Law Reform, 16*(2), 319–341.

Summers, C. (1976). Arbitration of unjust dismissal: A preliminary proposal. *The Future of Labor Arbitration in America.* New York: American Association of Arbitrators.

Summers, C. (1980, January–February). Protecting all employees against unjust dismissal. *Harvard Business Review,* pp. 132–139.

Summers, C. (1982). The need for a statute. *ILR Report, 10*(1), 8–12.

Summers, C. (1983). General discussion. In J. Stieber & J. Blackburn (Eds.), Protecting unorganized employees against unjust discharge. East Lansing, MI: School of Labor and Industrial Relations, Michigan State University, 2.

Summers, C. (1983). Individual rights in the workplace: The employment at will issue (special issue). *University of Michigan Journal of Law Reform,* 16(2).

Tamney v. *Atlantic Richfield Co.,* 27 Cal. 3d. 167, 164 Cal. Rptr. 839 (1980), 610 p. 2d 1330.

Toussaint v. *Blue Cross & Blue Shield,* 408 Mich. 579, 292 N.W. 2d 880 (1980).

U.S. Bureau of the Census. (1984). *Statistical abstract of the U.S.* Tables No. 489, 727–729, (pp. 303, 440–441).

Vietnam Era Veterans Readjustment Assistance Act, 38 U.S.C. secs. 2021 (b)(1), 2024 (c)(1979 & Supp. 1982).

Werhane, P. H. (1983). A theory of employee rights. In T. Donaldson & P. H. Werhane (Eds.), *Ethical issues in business* (pp. 315–320). Engelwood Cliffs, NJ: Prentice-Hall.

Wood, H. G. (1877). *Master and servant.*

The "Golden Handshake": An Alternative to Reduction in Force

Harry N. Turk

In an earlier article,[1] employers were cautioned that the recession could lead to serious liability risks if reductions in force (RIFs) among salaried employees were not carefully planned and executed to limit claims of race, sex, and most important, age discrimination.

While RIFs were instituted by many companies, some chose to accelerate voluntary early retirements among their salaried, nonunion employees.[2] These accelerated voluntary retirement programs, euphemistically referred to as "golden handshake" programs, offered employees an extra incentive to take their early retirement—either a cash bonus or an unreduced pension.

The companies achieved both cost savings from headcount reductions and, in most instances, minimized their legal exposure from an RIF. As explained in the earlier article, careful attention to advance planning, communications, and existing case law can obviate almost all the legal pitfalls in an RIF and realize significant headcount reductions and savings.

TYPES OF PROGRAMS

Pacific Telephone's managers with thirty years of service or whose age plus length of service equaled or exceeded seventy-five years in "positions deemed to be surplus" were offered the program. Employees selected received full pension eligibility and a bonus of one year's pay over a twenty-four-month period for early retirement. Firestone offered, in addition to the pension itself, two weeks pay for each year of service not to exceed twenty-six weeks of pay; Uniroyal gave a cash bonus to selected employees based on 1 percent of the employee's annual salary times years of service; Chrysler Corporation offered an unreduced pension to those employees who, under normal circumstances, would be entitled to only an actuarially reduced pension.

In addition, the programs were offered either across the board, that is, to all eligible employees, or selectively, based on the company's needs. In one company, the incentive was offered across the board and was so attractive that it created a "brain drain" among management. In another, the offer was so selective and marginally attractive that not enough employees accepted the program and a subsequent RIF was still necessary.

Obviously, a middle ground is preferable: the incentive should be attractive enough to induce employees to accept it and avoid a subsequent RIF, and it should not be offered to everyone. While a company cannot prevent a key employee from retiring early, a company is under no obligation to give him or her cash incentive to do so.

RECENT CASES

A significant decision in this area is *Ackerman v. Diamond Shamrock Corp.*, decided by the U.S. Court of Appeals for the Sixth Circuit.[3] The case did not, however, involve a "golden handshake" program.

Ackerman was the company's fifty-nine-year-old director of corporate communications whose job was eliminated and the duties divided between his two younger subordinates. His superior suggested Ackerman take early retirement since his job was being eliminated. The "package" offered to Ackerman included an additional payment of $100,000 plus outplacement counseling and job search expenses.

Ackerman signed a memorandum that said he and the company "mutually desire" to make this arrangement and his entitlement to the retirement benefits was conditioned on his "decision to elect early retirement." He testified he signed the agreement of his own free will, he understood its provisions, and the company had lived up to the terms of the agreement.

The district court granted summary judgment for the company: Ackerman signed the agreement voluntarily and therefore had not been "discharged" from employment. Since he hadn't been discharged, he could not satisfy the second requirement necessary to prove a prima facie case of age discrimination.[4]

The court of appeals affirmed, noting that the Age Discrimination in Employment Act (ADEA) was not a vehicle for judicial review of business decisions. The company, the court went on, made a legitimate decision to eliminate Ackerman's job and divide his duties, and there was no evidence that age was in any way a factor in the decision. Rather than terminating him or transferring him to a lower paying or less prestigious job, the court noted, the company offered him an opportunity to "retire with dignity."

Chrysler Corporation did not fare as well as Diamond Shamrock, although the *Chrysler* case has not yet gone to trial on the issues noted herein.[5] During the company's 1979 economic crisis, it instituted a Special Early Retirement Program (SER) whereby all qualified employees not yet sixty-five were offered *full* retirement benefits (actuarially unreduced), group life insurance coverage until age sixty-five, paid medical coverage, and could retain income from other sources without diminution of benefits. Approximately 1,600 employees who took SER signed forms that indicated voluntary acceptance of the program. However, many in this group claimed their early retirement was coerced.

In its decision, the court said that, where an employee could show she or he was coerced into retirement and not laid off, retirement would be considered involuntary and thus illegal under ADEA. The court also held that the employees could not be forced into retirement even in the face of job elimination or an RIF. Where an employee with more than ten years of service was involuntarily retired, that retirement was based solely on age and therefore was unlawful.

GUIDELINES FOR EMPLOYERS

There are several principles that can guide a company through the legal "minefield" inherent in an early retirement program.

1. *A cash incentive should be offered to employees in exchange for their acceptance of early retirement.*

2. *The program may either be selective or across the board, in either event it must be strictly voluntary*. Employees must be told there will be no reprisals if they refuse the program. The aim of the program is to eliminate *jobs* that need not be replaced, not weed out unsatisfactory performers.

3. *The company must plan its communication of the programs to employees*. Assuming a program of selective participation:

- The context of talks with individual employees must be prepared in advance. Write out what is to be said, but be prepared to allow the employee an opportunity to comment or ask questions. Also have the numbers with you: the amount of incentive payment, the employee's pension, etc.
- Make the offer in private. Acknowledge that the business situation (specifics) makes it mandatory to reduce staff levels. Make it clear that the offer is being made because the company must reduce its costs and not because of the employee's performance.
- Prepare a list of questions the employee may ask and consider the answer to each one. For example, "How soon do I have to make my decision?" "What advantage is there for me in accepting the payment?" "What if I choose to stay?"
- The earlier you speak with eligible employees you want to keep, the better off you'll be—at least from a morale point of view. Emphasize that since the program is not across the board, they will be key members of a smaller group.
- The entire organization should know what's being done. This can be accomplished, depending on size, either by individual or small group meetings.

4. *Each employee that participates in the early retirement program must execute a written agreement that contains*:

- A statement that both parties mutually agree to enter into the agreement;
- A statement that the employee voluntarily elects early retirement in consideration of the additional sum of money (or benefits, or both);
- A release that discharges the company from all claims arising under Title VII, ADEA, and state fair employment practice law; and
- A statement whereby the employee acknowledges she or he has read the entire agreement, understands it, and has accepted its terms without coercion or duress by the company.

Remember, if employees refuse to sign the document, they cannot avail themselves of the benefits of the early retirement program.

A final note of caution: Regardless of the employee participation in the early retirement program, a subsequent RIF may still be necessary. Employees who refused to take early retirement may not be made scapegoats in the RIF. A corporate policy that gives considerable weight to age and length of service in deciding which employees to retain will be a considerable defense in any subsequent age discrimination suit.

NOTES

1. Harry N. Turk and Gayle A. Gavin, "Reductions in Force: EEO Minefield for the '80s," 7 *EEO Today* 209 (Autumn 1980).

2. Among the companies using these programs were: Xerox, Texaco, Firestone, Chrysler Corp., Dow Chemical, Shell, Uniroyal, Monsanto, Hooker Chemical, and Pacific Telephone.

3. 670 F.2d 66, 27 Fair Empl. Prac. Cas. 1563 (6th Cir. 1982).

4. In order to establish a prima facie case of age discrimination, an individual claimant must establish that he or she:

   1. Was a member of the protected class (40–70 years);
   2. Was discharged;
   3. Was qualified for the position; and
   4. Was replaced by a younger person. [*Marshall v. Goodyear Tire & Rubber Co.*, 554 F.2d 730 (5th Cir. 1977).]

   A prima facie case in an RIF situation is somewhat different. There, the plaintiff must:

   1. Show he or she is within the protected class and was adversely affected—discharged or demoted—by the defendant's employment decision;
   2. Show he or she was qualified to assume another position; and
   3. Produce evidence from which a fact finder might reasonably conclude the employer intended to discriminate in reaching its decision. [*Williams v. General Motors Corp.*, 656 F.2d 120 (5th Cir. 1981).]

5. *EEOC v. Chrysler Corp.*, 29 Fair Empl. Prac. Cas. 284 (E.D. Mich. 1982). The EEOC moved for a preliminary injunction and Chrysler moved to dismiss certain claims and for partial summary judgment.

Outplacement: Is It for You?

Andrew S. Edson

Outplacement programs are well on their way to becoming a standard business practice. A decade ago, most corporate personnel managers—now called human-resource executives—could not define outplacement. It was a new and vaguely understood area of counsulting, which a few corporations provided as a service for a select group of top executives. In fact, there were only three firms specializing in corporate outplacement in the United States.

Today there are more than 100 such firms, and an Association of Outplacement Consulting Firms dedicated to maintaining a code of ethics and high professional standards. Right now it's easy for almost anyone to claim to do outplacement. Precisely why the Outplacement Association was formed, says President Paul W. Lyon. According to one industry observer, many public relations recruiting and executive-search firms purport to provide outplacement services, but most of the work is being done by outplacement consulting organizations.

Outplacement programs have gained importance as companies have had to deal with realities of the current economic and social climate: layoffs in recessionary periods create a corporate responsibility to provide employee benefits, and a need to protect the company's image; career counseling can provide an alternative to firing employees who show the least promise, and helps those who have no opportunity for advancement; helping employees who are fired find employment elsewhere creates mutual benefits.

Public accounting firms were among the first to establish outplacement programs. The "up or out" philosophy is nowhere more evident than in this business. CPA firms are pressure cookers, and the work takes its toll. Annual turnover can be more than 35 percent, according to Edward Witherell, director of personnel for Arthur Andersen & Co., New York, one of the "big eight" firms.

"When our employees leave us," Mr. Witherell says, "they tend to rise in the organizations they go to. If you look at the financial people in *Fortune* 500 companies, you will find a lot of Arthur Andersen alumni." That fact alone caused Mr. Witherell to formalize existing outplacement practices. The program is an effective marketing tool, he reports. "We want the ones who leave to think well of us. That can pay many dividends later on."

Since Arthur Andersen instituted outplacement three years ago, few of the firm's employees have been fired in the usual sense. The vast majority, about 75 percent (after all, everyone cannot become a partner), make the decision to leave on their own, largely because of job pressures or negative performance evaluations.

OPTIONS FOR EMPLOYEES

Firing is probably the most distasteful task a manager must perform. This is where outplacement can be an effective and powerful tool for change, suggests Thomas E. O'Reilly, vice president and director of management resources at the Chase Manhattan Bank, N.A. Outplacement gives the employee options. Mr. O'Reilly maintains, "The employee can choose to stay in the organization and do a particular job for an indefinite period of time, knowing the corporation doesn't see him or her as having the potential to move to a higher level of responsibility. Or the employee can take the opportunity to reassess career interests and direction, and investigate what's available on the outside, before making a decision."

Many corporations, large and small, are starting to offer outplacement as a perquisite under the umbrella of a "cafeteria" benefits plan. General Mills, for example, has been providing in-house outplacement for its employees for two decades, and Chemical Bank has had an internal department since the mid-1970s. "All the people who have gone through the program have been placed," says Karen Rosenbach, Chemical's manager of outplacement. The program offers training, skills assessment, résumé writing, consultation, feedback and salary-negotiation services.

COUNSELING FIRM PROGRAMS

Public relations counseling firms also offer forms of outplacement. Ketchum Public Relations uses outside outplacement firms, and the Rowland Co. has an informal program, according to Executive Vice President Mary Dixon. Burson-Marsteller tailors its outplacement program to the individual. Hill and Knowlton helps outplaced employees with résumé writing and job-hunting leads.

The majority of public relations firms, however, do not maintain an outplacement program or use outside experts. But lost accounts, plant closings, early retirement, recessionary cutbacks—all facts of life in the 1980s—are forcing the growth of the emerging outplacement business.

Outplacement is starting to "feel its oats" maintains the Outplacement Association's Mr. Lyon. And observers predict that outplacement will be a $500-million-a-year business within the next two decades, spurred by new technologies' displacement of workers and a strong trend toward mergers.

Henchey & Co., which annually canvasses outplacement and severance practices, found that 94 percent of the 140 companies queried provide some form of outplacement assistance, compared with 74 percent a year ago. The survey also found that 38 percent of respondents now offer outplacement aid to nonmanagement as well as management personnel.

Not bad for an industry that is just coming of age.

Retirement: Crisis or Opportunity

Eugene H. Seibert and Joanne Seibert

Mixed messages are bombarding the workplace concerning retirement planning decisions. From "golden handcuffs" to "parachute" see-saw offerings, continued confusion has been perpetuated for all age groups—a broad spectrum of employees, from those who do not have vested pension benefits to those with early-out windows or attractive pension sweeteners.[1,2]

Also involved in the "to work or not to work" decision are those contemplating early-out Social Security benefits at age 62, and those who formerly planned an age 65 retirement date. This latter group now finds age 70 or even an open-ended career a viable alternative.

To further complicate the retirement timing decision, additional factors have surfaced that are affecting the length of one's working career, stability of employment and the quality of the retirement promise of tomorrow.[3] Taken singularly, in concert, or in tandem, these factors—which will be examined in this article—are responsible for the confusion that abounds, resulting in retirement decision dilemmas shared mutually by human resource personnel, employees and their families (see Figure 1).

Figure 1
Factors Affecting The Retirement Timing Decision

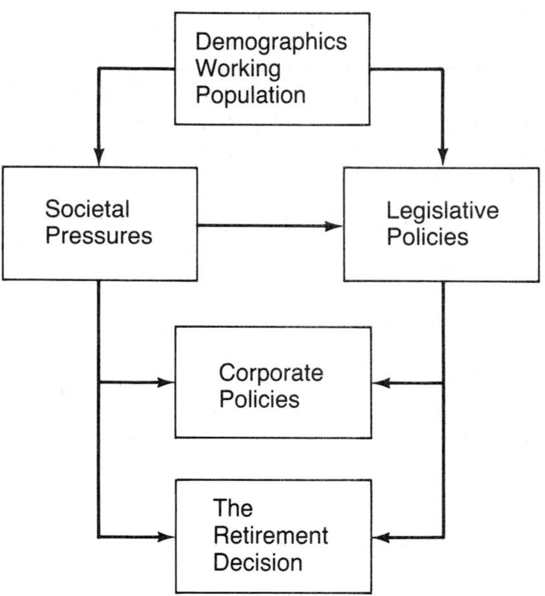

FACTOR ONE: DEMOGRAPHICS OF THE WORKING/RETIREMENT POPULATION

This influence, substantiated through life expectancy tables, early retirement trend studies, and aging work force statistics, confirms that those living beyond age 65 and well into their eighties will increase at a more rapid rate than the work force supporting them. If one then applies the economic law of supply and demand to this population imbalance and equates the number of workers available in the future compared to the potential demand for their services, planning for future work force needs and pension funding for those in retirement is essential.

Presently, however, the planning mandate is not a front-burner issue for many human resource and employee benefit professionals, as immediate concerns take precedent over future contingencies, but certainly they must be dealt with well before the baby boomers approach their retirement period shortly after the year 2000, just 14 years from now.

In defense of the inability to plan for this period of crisis, no one has a crystal ball accurate enough to predict exactly what this work force imbalance might mean. Some futurists say there will be a labor shortage; others say our changing industrial technology, women's entry into the labor market and more efficient management will alter worker demand. It appears certain, however, that sometime, somehow, the issue of ratio imbalance of retirees to supporting workers will have to be addressed.

Malcolm H. Morrison summed up the aging work force dilemma. "In recent years, there has been considerable discussion of the implications of the aging of the U.S. population for the overall economy, the future work force and human resource and employee benefit policies. Most analyses have highlighted the aging work force, and the need to develop more flexible personnel and employee benefit policies for mature employees."[4]

FACTOR TWO: LEGISLATION AND GOVERNMENT POLICIES

In addition to demographic factors, legislation also affects corporate retirement policies—which in turn affect the population as a whole. The positive influence of government, for all practical purposes, is an unknown. Presently, a consistent legislative policy does not exist—Congress frequently passes conflicting laws, and political rhetoric blows hot and cold. The federal government's legislative posture on retirement issues often seems like a yo-yo.

These changes in direction continue to send mixed and confusing messages. We need to examine the basics. Phyllis Z. Borzi, Pension Counsel for the House Subcommittee on Labor Management Relations said, "We need to examine where we are, where we want to be, and how we should get there." This is about as basic as one can get.

President Reagan has supported legislation to underwrite more responsibility in the area of personal financial planning (IRA legislation bears this out). Yet on Capitol Hill his own appointees are sending different signals, such as the assault on private pension plans—which is unprecedented.

One specific law, the Tax Equity and Fiscal Responsibility Act of 1982 (TEFRA), is legislative testimony directed toward the defeat of personal retirement independence. When TEFRA's intent—reducing top executives' pension benefits while raising revenues—took hold, all other workers in some organizations were affected by pension benefits reductions of as much as one third. In other situations, existing plans were discontinued and new plans were postponed.

One example at the opposite end of the seesaw is the amount of government influence thrust upon the business sector to supplement Social Security retirement benefits by providing contributory savings, thrift and profit-sharing plans. Thus were born a potpourri of pension plan supplements, including 401(k)s, Keoghs, SEPS and others. The accompanying tax advantages prepared the launching pad for their success. However, today the message has a somewhat different connotation—these tax incentives are being minimized, contributory ceilings lowered, and some benefit programs scratched altogether—again, another yo-yo message.

On the one hand, government says self-reliance is the name of the game, but then legislative policies remove many of the incentives to make that happen. These ambiguous enunciations from government sources continue to confuse the private sector and undermine public expectations.

FACTOR THREE: SOCIETAL INFLUENCES

America's economy has changed from one that was industrial-based to one that is information- and service-based. The pace of change has been so rapid that despite a head-in-the-sand attitude by many, most of today's workers have been touched in some way by the new high-tech era.

Change and new societal patterns are typified in one community's experience during the last six months of 1985. General Motors announced the construction of a modern plant in Fort Wayne, Indiana. They offered to relocate over 1,200 Janesville, Wisconsin workers who were willing to move to the new facility, most of whom had lived their entire lives a few miles from their employer's door. Now, suddenly, everything changed. They had the choice of moving to a new community, leaving family, friends and their homes for an unknown, or accept the possibility of unemployment.

Simultaneously, The Parker Pen Co., with headquarters located in the same community, was acquired by a British company. Parker's corporate headquarters was moved to England. The new owners substantially reduced the Janesville payroll, causing many in both management and factory labor to seek other employment. Uncertainty and change touched the entire community.

Change is not easy, especially for those who formerly leaned heavily on others to provide for their futures. But the government is communicating to all who wish to listen that Social Security benefits are being tightened, and in some cases eliminated altogether. The influence of unions as protectors of their members has diminished. And employers continue to send underscored messages about cost effectiveness and staying lean in order to compete in today's global marketplace.

If there is to be less dependency on government, unions, and one's employer, then clearly another message must be sent, that of a need for more self-reliance in planning for one's future.

And it *is* beginning to happen. Unpublished studies conducted for the American Council of Life Insurance by Yankelovich, Skelly and White in 1981 indicated that 53 percent of the public thinks that the government or the employer is responsible for furnishing the bulk of retirement income. However, this percentage is down from the 60-percent rating of a similar survey in 1973. It would appear that the trend in public opinion is headed in the direction of more personal self-reliance. Motivation, however, is certainly required to continue this trend.

A survey of 200 benefit managers at *Fortune* 1000 companies conducted by Merrill Lynch in January 1983 resulted in 80 percent of those polled expressing the belief that their organizations' pensions are not designed to be the main source of retirement income, even when combined with Social Security.[6] If the trend seems to be headed in the direction of more personal self-reliance, where and how will the motivation be reinforced?

FACTOR FOUR: CORPORATE INFLUENCES

An analytical blitz by many companies on all forms of employee benefit programs has been occurring in the past several years. Not to be forgotten is the recession of the late '70s and early '80s. The attack centers on cost effectiveness, sharpening communications and the relevance of benefit programs to the needs of employees and their families.

As a result of this analysis, benefit priorities are being redefined and former retirement policies are being changed, which in turn has created financial, physical, and psychological chaos for many.

Although this attention is being given to a wide range of benefit programs, the early retirement trend that started several years ago continues. Presently, it is the American preference. Even though early-out incentive programs have lessened, they are still popular, as management attempts to balance the work force with openings for younger workers while maintaining the same size or smaller work force.

According to the *Wall Street Journal*, a vast majority of the 363 companies polled by The Conference Board continued to encourage retirement before age 65. The article goes on to say that over 60 percent of those polled include early retirement inducements in their pension plans, and only 3 percent offer employee incentives to stay past age 65. Moreover, the Board said that an average retirement age of 65 or older was reported by only 14 percent of the companies, down from 42 percent in 1972. The average retirement age was 62 or less in 51 percent of the companies, up from 23 percent in 1972. According to Shirley H. Rhine, author of the study, "Efforts to discourage older workers from retirement before age 65 or to encourage them to postpone retirement beyond age 65 are exceedingly rare."[7]

Being lean and cost-effective will continue to be major priorities for management. There is a prediction that "1986 may be remembered as 'the year of the cost cutters.' Rarely have so many axes sliced into business at a time of economic growth. And the evidence of that can be seen not only in firms battling to stay alive, but in many corporations whose profits are healthy and whose prospects are good."[8]

Among the priorities is an effective use of the human resources of an organization without adding any additional staff. There is added pressure to find ways to accommodate the desires of valuable workers so that defections or premature retirement losses will not occur. On the other hand, others wish to make early retirement so attractive that it cannot be passed up. Again, more mixed messages.

According to George Heiring of Hewitt Associates, the 1980s are referred to by some as the battleground for human resources. If there can be any credence to this, he believes, "Retirement is a strategic consideration in any organization's battle plans. Helping employees understand their retirement and retirement choices can be one of the critical questions facing human resource practitioners."[9]

FACTOR FIVE: PERSONAL INFLUENCES

Of prime importance is one's attitude about the future and whether the life stage of retirement is perceived as being a positive or negative event. Some translate retirement to mean "over the hill" by confusing it with the aging process, which actually begins during one's teens.

Others feel that if they are no longer a part of the work force they are not contributing their fair share. Self-worth is then diminished. In part, this is a carryover from the deeply ingrained work ethic that still is an integral part of our societal definition of value.

Which personal influences affect the length of working careers and retirement decision timing? According to author Robert C. Atchley, many factors have come into play.[3] Besides national and corporate policies, others include personal readiness ("can I afford to retire?" or "how much monthly income can I count on?") and one's attitude about ending active employment and facing the future. That future has the potential of being more than one-third of one's total lifetime, based on new life expectancy statistics.

Because apprehension can build over future uncertainties and concerns, one is apt to deny decisions that may disturb the status quo. The stage following one's working career is an unknown, and the implication exists that potential changes following retirement can occur in our social and economic status, self-worth, health, morale and interpersonal relationships (see Figure 2).

THE NEED FOR PRE-RETIREMENT INFORMATION PROGRAMS

"When an employee knew he or she had to retire at age 65, plans were made accordingly. However, under the new, open-ended retirement policy there is nothing to trigger one to prepare for retirement," wrote David C. Wineland in 1980.[10] Reinforcing this viewpoint, Richard P. Johnson of the University of Florida stated that the retirement timing decision "is almost entirely on the shoulders of the individual worker. Without clearly defined retirement goals and a commensurate positive outlook toward retirement, the worker may be caused much undue stress as a result of this new decision responsibility and may act inappropriately without preparation."[11] In addition to motivation, what information sources can be made available if self-reliance is to occur? One source is through employer or community-sponsored pre-retirement planning seminars.

Many believe that planning, the key element, should begin as one approaches his or her potential retirement date. Those responsible for pre-retirement planning seminars target eligibility minimums at age 50 or 55. This is certainly the very latest that any effective planning can be realized. According to a 1985 *Wall Street Journal* series, other experts in the field of financial planning believe that pre-retirement planning should not be directed just to those 50 and over.

One survey concluded that more than half of young professionals age 25 through 39 admitted they would rather spend than save for retirement. This figure does not include those who would rather save for retirement than spend but haven't the motivation or knowledge to do so. Also, 61

Figure 2
Personal Influences Affecting the Retirement Timing Decision

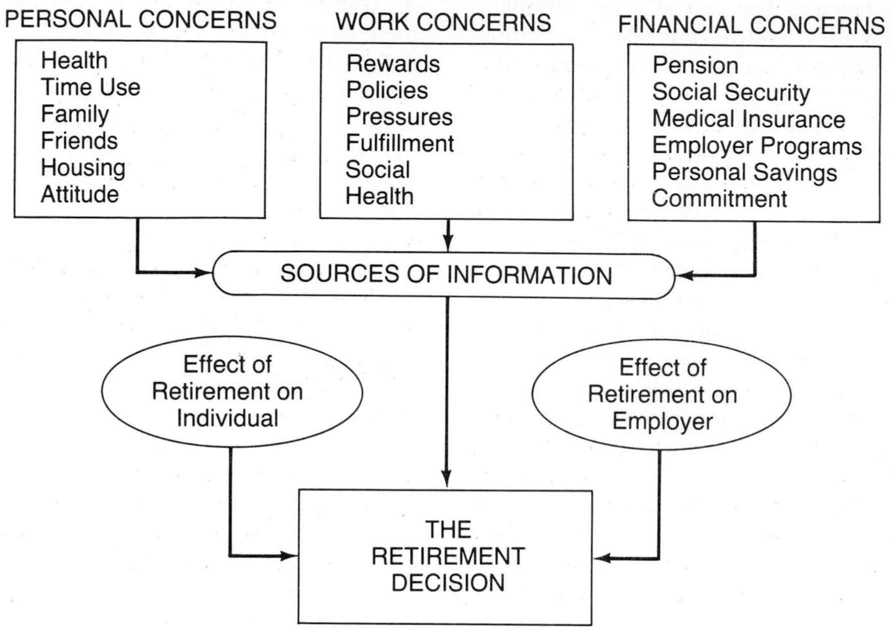

percent admit to worrying about what's in store for them financially when they reach retirement, "whatever or whenever that is." Timing, again a garbled message.

Many would opt out of the Social Security system if they could because they have lost confidence in it. Feeling that at this point in their lives they can't afford to set aside more for the future than the amount contributed to Social Security, they also are feeling pressures aptly stated in one of the subtitles of the series: "Worry, Yes; Plan, No."[12]

Whether it is a crisis or opportunity, the retirement decision affects all age groups, including those who are not even within the vesting periphery of their company's pension plan. Whatever age is considered, a company-sponsored pre-retirement planning program can be valuable. "It offers a solid ledge for employees who feel they're sinking under the trauma of facing a whole new scary world—retirement."[13] The 1985 *Money Guide: Planning Now for Your Successful Retirement* article, "How to Size Up Your Company Plan," provided another perspective. "If the employee benefits department routinely holds retirement planning seminars, that generally shows that the company isn't ashamed of its retirement benefits."[14] Of course, this is not to say that those without seminars are ashamed of their benefit structures. Some may, for various reasons, have postponed the implementation of a pre-retirement program while others are considering the expansion of their programs to include more information than the employer-provided benefits and Social Security.

The framework for a pre-retirement information program lacks precise criteria. Currently it can mean anything from a one- or two-hour meeting for employees covering a company's benefit plans and Social Security to multi-session seminars for employees and spouses/guests that include a wide range of topics and information on pre- and post-retirement issues, with the benefit plans an important segment. Of the current programs that are broader in scope, most are prepackaged and can be purchased with or without in-house facilitator training.

According to author Sidney R. Siegel, "Regardless of whether a particular preretirement program is designed to encourage early retirement or simply to provide a smoother transition for regular retirees, the content of existing programs as well as those 'on the drawing board' needs to be restructured."[15] Programs on the leading edge emphasize social and attitudinal needs of the participants as well as their financial and physical well-being. The customized design, content and format are coordinated by in-house personnel (usually benefit administrators) according to the program goals and objectives. Both professional outside resources and in-house talents can be selected to perform the facilitation responsibilities. Also, specific age and income groups can be targeted by adding to or subtracting from a seminar's agenda only those subjects which are pertinent to the participants.

Information resources are available through publications, library reference services, the International Society of Preretirement Planners, independent consultants and computer programs. Employee focus groups can also be a valuable source of information. A customized approach has the advantage of offering material that pinpoints specific areas of interest and concern rather than following a preconceived agenda with a corresponding schedule.

One such customized program has been offered to employees and spouses four times a year since 1983. In 1985, due to a budget-cutting mandate, consideration was given to skipping two of the four seminars originally planned for 1986. Prior to the final decision, the company's manager of employee benefits quantified in a program analysis the pluses and minuses of the program and what delaying two seminars might mean. There were several items listed on the "plus" side. One specific point was that an early-out program was avoided due to voluntary early retirements traced directly to the pre-retirement program.

The benefits manager wrote that those who had retired said the program removed their fears about the future. This included information on how to project their present income and disbursement patterns into retirement. In addition, they indicated they were stressed, unhappy with the changes taking place in the company, and probably not as productive as they were years ago. They left their life-long working careers with a positive attitude about retirement, "due to the program's influence," and were appreciative of the company's role in providing them with an in-depth preretirement planning experience. The direct annual payroll savings amounted to $179,000, compared to only one minus: an expenditure of $2,000 per seminar. As a result of the benefits manager's analysis, the program commitment for 1986 and beyond has been confirmed.

"We must play an active role in exposing people to the realities of the retirement situation. We also believe pre-retirement programs improve employee motivation. They see not only that we will help them maximize their resources, but that we are concerned about them. That has to help maintain a high level of efficiency and loyalty to the company," according to Ken McKenna, former manager of pensions for Pepsico.

Not only is it necessary to communicate the importance of personal planning, the motivation to plan also requires the support of those who had previously adopted the role of mentor and provider. In short, employers must examine the need for instituting programs that assist in motivating employees to do their own planning for the future.

REFERENCES

1. *The Wall Street Journal*, April 24, 1984, p. 1.

2. Steve Markam, "Once and Future Retirement," *Across the Board*, May 1985, pp. 40–50.

3. R. C. Atchley, "Issues in Retirement Research," *The Gerontologist*, Vol. 19, No. 1, 1979, pp. 44–54.

4. Malcolm Morrison, "Retirement and Human Resource Planning for the Aging Workforce," *Personnel Administrator*, June 1984, pp. 151–159.

5. Paul Craig Roberts, "Treasury's Assault on Middle-Class Pensions," *Business Week*, November 18, 1985, p. 26.

6. D. Underwood, "Toward Self-reliance in Retirement Planning," *Harvard Business Review*, May-June 1984, pp. 18–20.

7. *The Wall Street Journal*, January 23, 1985.

8. *Research Institute Recommendations*, February 21, 1986.

9. G. W. Heiring, "Communicating Preretirement Information," *Benefits News Analysis*, April 1980.

10. David C. Wineland, "Retirement Planning—More Important Than Ever," *Management World*, September 1980.

11. Richard P. Johnson, "A Call for Comprehensive Preretirement Programs," *ISPP*, Winter 1980.

12. *The Wall Street Journal*, "Halfway to Retirement" series, December 8, 1985 through December 15, 1985.

13. Scott Dever, "Planning Your Future May Really Pay Off," *Personnel Administrator*, October 1981.

14. Richard Eisenberg, "How to Size Up Your Company's Plan," *Money Guide Planning Now for Your Successful Retirement*, 1985.

15. Sidney R. Siegel, "Pre-retirement Programs in the '80s," *Personnel Administrator*, February 1986.

Retirement and Human Resource Planning for the Aging Work Force

Malcolm H. Morrison

In recent years there has been considerable discussion of the implications of the aging of the U.S. population for the overall economy, the future work force and human resource and employee benefit policies.[1,2,3,4] Most analyses have highlighted the aging of the work force and the need to develop more flexible personnel and employee benefit policies for "mature" employees. In addition, more than a few commentaries have mentioned the recent increase in age discrimination in employment litigation and have recommended more attention to age-neutral personnel and employee benefit policies by management.[5,6]

Analyses of employer policies regarding aging employees have generally recommended the following approaches: (1) management policies (age audits, sensitivity training, revised performance appraisals, training, job redesign, remotivation, etc.); (2) compensation and fringe benefit policies (salary adjustment, flexible benefits, specialized pension accrual policies, health and insurance benefits); and (3) flexible employment options (full time, part time, reduced hours/reduced pay, flex-time, job rotation, job sharing, phased retirement, etc). Focus on the older employee has produced the general recommendation that management should explore and implement more employment and benefit options for older workers but not attempt to modify current early retirement age patterns. Occasionally, references are made to retirement preparation programs but usually this area is not carefully explored. This article considers the implications of an aging work force for retirement planning and concludes that significant changes in retirement preparation programming will be needed in responding to developing work life trends.

Over the next 20 years, the growth of the middle-aged to older work force will be the most important characteristic of the labor market. This change is already reflected in the views of employers who now generally believe that in the years ahead, early retirement policies will have to be changed and employee benefit policies modified to attract and retain more older employees. At present, management is being confronted with the

Reprinted from the June 1984 issue of *Personnel Administrator*, copyright 1984, The American Society for Personnel Administration, 606 North Washington Street, Alexandria, Virginia 22314.

consequences of structural changes in the economy resulting in increased job mobility and career change. Accompanying these shifts are such patterns as changes in the age structure and composition of the labor force and increased flexibility in work patterns, encouraged by flexible scheduling and job assignment approaches. These developments are leading to a broader view of the work life involving multiple career transitions, continuous training and less rigidity in career stages. In other words, today each employee is considered to have human capital potential which can be developed in a variety of ways during a work life. A career need not be influenced by age barriers or rigid stages of development.

This more balanced developmental view of employees means that retirement no longer automatically means complete loss of labor for participation, but instead becomes a flexible option involving pension receipt and possible employment. While many employees will continue to choose complete retirement, a growing number will opt for part-time work, career changes, training, self-employment, education, etc. Retirement choices will continue to be influenced by availability of pension income and health considerations, but there will be a growing diversity in preferences for post-retirement activity. Responding to this diversity will require familiarity with flexible employment options and facility in using financial planning tools to communicate with employees about their retirement life options. Such communication is well suited to the retirement planning function but will require retirement planners to significantly expand their training repertoires by learning about flexible personnel and employee benefit policies.

Despite some predictions of future labor shortages[7] (as a consequence of declining numbers of youths in the population) it is by no means certain that older workers will desire (or be encouraged) to be the primary labor supply to fill full-time positions. In fact, in the near future, continuing early retirement patterns are virtually assured because of availability of public and private pensions at relatively early ages. Thus, to the extent that older workers exercise employment options, these will mainly involve part-time work, self-employment and education/training.

One response to the continued early retirement pattern is to maintain the status quo in providing conventional retirement preparation programs to employees nearing retirement or, as is the common case, having no such program at all. But, this approach is not responsive to current labor force trends and problems. In addition, in a short time, demographic trends and human resource policy changes will require that organizations alter policies to accommodate the aging work force. Therefore, a better and more practical response is to review the current and projected work force characteristics of the firm, evaluate the extent of the work force aging and begin development of employment and retirement policies that are responsive to organizational and work force needs. In so doing, the importance of *retirement planning* will automatically emerge as a focus or activity and the need to go beyond conventional pre-retirement programs will influence the development of enhanced retirement preparation for the increasingly mature work force.

POPULATION, LABOR FORCE AND RETIREMENT TRENDS

An understanding of population and labor force changes, retirement trends and existing retirement planning programs provides the background and rationale for recommending major changes in the content and format of retirement preparation programs.

In 1982, the U.S. population was estimated at 232 million with a median age of 31 years (compared to 29 years in 1976). Twenty percent of the population—48 million—were age 55 or over and 26 million (11 percent) were 65 or more. By the year 2010, 25 percent of the population—70 million—will be age 55 or more and 35 million (12.5 percent) will be 65 and over. At that time the median age will have reached 37 and median life expectancy will be 73 years for men and 82 for women. In 2010, the average 65-year-old person can expect to live almost 20 additional years. The older population will continue to grow at least until 2030, when 30 percent of the population will be 55 or more and *20 percent age 65 or over.*

It is now well understood that the growth of the older population will result in major social and economic changes in the years ahead, particularly after the year 2000. An important aspect of the aging society will be the changing age structure of the work force. An aging work force will require modifications in personnel and employee benefit policies and possible increased use of older workers. National retirement policies may change to provide more financial incentives for later retirement to reduce pension financing problems and enhance the supply of employees. However, predicting the age composition of the future labor force is difficult since so many factors influence the retirement decisions of workers and since economic conditions (which directly affect labor supply and demand) cannot be predicted with reasonable certainty. Nevertheless, some conclusions can be reached about the future, by analyzing information on population, labor force and retirement trends.

However, between now and the year 2000, there will be a decline of about eight million in younger persons aged 18–29 and an increase of 28 million persons aged 35 to 54. Subsequently, the major change will be the large increase in number and proportion of older persons (as the middle-aged reach the older ages) and a relative stabilization of younger age groups. Thus population aging will take place in two broad phases, the first characterized by the growth of the middle-aged and the second by the burgeoning of those aged 65 and over, with very substantial increases in those over 75.[8]

These population shifts will be reflected in changes in the composition of the labor force. With the continuation of early retirement policies, the most significant labor force changes will occur over the next 20 years. During this time, the younger labor force, persons aged 18 to 34 (now 48 percent of the work force) will decline, representing only 37 percent in the year 2000. However, simultaneously, the middle-aged work force, those age 35 to 54, percent will grow from 35 percent to 49 percent of all workers. Thus in the decades ahead, predominance of middle-to-older age workers in the labor force is assured. Projections indicate that labor force participation of older workers will continue to decline and by the year 2000, only 11 percent of the work force will be over age 55 and just two percent over age 65.[9]

It is uncertain whether the declining younger population and labor force will result in labor shortages. Statistics indicate that a reduced younger age group may participate more heavily in the labor force and that the women's participation rate will continue to increase. With relatively stable participation by the middle-aged, major labor shortages may not materialize. In light of the growth of the middle-aged labor force, increasing participation by women and continuing early retirement policies, it is even more difficult to anticipate major increases in employment of older workers in the near future. Therefore, taking into consideration both population and labor force trends over the next 20 years, it is clear that the numbers of employees approaching and entering retirement will increase considerably and their need for retirement preparation assistance will be commensurately great. Because of changing individual preferences regarding retirement activities and the changing work life conditions mentioned earlier, current preretirement programs which do not emphasize these trends cannot respond to the needs of the growing middle to older aged work force.

The importance of retirement preparation programs is of course fundamentally influenced by the development of the social pattern of retirement in the United States and its broad acceptance over the past 30 years. Even before the introduction of Social Security in 1935, there was an established trend of declining labor force participation for the older population. It is very clear that the maturation of the Social Security system and the increasing availability of private pensions substantially accelerated the retirement trend.

Since 1950, the labor force participation rate for men aged 55 to 64 has dropped from about 86 percent to 72 percent. For men 65 and over, the drop has been even more precipitant, from 45 percent to 17 percent. Today, only 13 percent of *all persons* age 65 or more participate in the work force, and projections indicate further declines in the years ahead. For women, those aged 55 to 64 have participated more frequently in the labor force over the last 20 years, reflecting the national trend. But in recent years participation by this group has leveled off at about 40 percent. Women over age 65 have had low participation rates for more than 30 years and this pattern is continuing.

A substantial amount of research on the determinants of retirement indicates that health and expected pension benefits seem to most significantly influence the retirement decisions of workers. However, other factors including job attitudes, assets, job characteristics, family circumstances, wages and Social Security and private pension earnings limits have also been shown to influence the retirement choice.[10] Despite the large amount of research conducted on this issue, the process by which individuals make decisions to retire is still not well understood. More research will therefore be needed to improve our understanding of retirement decision-making in the years ahead, when options will be increasing.[11] Furthermore, there are some major policy issues concerning employment and retirement that are unresolved. Among these are questions about whether the usual working life should be extended, whether work after retirement should be encouraged and whether the early retirement incentives in public and private pension plans should be modified to promote more balance in employee retirement age choices.

Some recent evidence, including the recently enacted extension of the Social Security eligibility age (to take effect after the year 2000), leads to the view that extension of the work life will become a national policy goal. However, it is still unlikely that major efforts to change current early retirement policies will be undertaken in the near future. This means that most employees approaching retirement will continue to make choices based on the relatively early availability of public and private pension benefits.

Despite the increasing older population and the decline in younger persons, a review of labor force participation and retirement trends demonstrates that the growth of the middle-aged to older work force will be the major characteristic of the labor force in the coming years. The *supply* of older workers is likely to be the major factor influencing their frequency of employment. And, while this supply will increase due to changing work life preferences, a major shift in labor force participation would require alteration of public and private retirement policies to provide more financial incentives to remain in or re-enter the labor force. While such incentives will undoubtedly develop in the future, their implementation to assist in reducing pension financing problems over the next two or three decades is unlikely.

Thus, it is certain that the demand for retirement preparation services will be growing rapidly in the years ahead. In fact, there will be more need for programs than at any time in the past. But future programs will have to include new elements, especially those relating to employment (partial retirement, phased retirement, job sharing, training, second careers, etc.) in order to effectively respond to the post-retirement concerns of upcoming cohorts of retirees.

RETIREMENT PREPARATION PROGRAMS

Today, surveys indicate that the majority of larger and mid-size firms do offer some type of preretirement assistance to employees.[12,13] This is in marked contrast to circumstances just 20 years ago when such assistance was often unavailable. Despite increasing availability, however, the majority of business and nonprofit organizations in the nation still do not provide such programs and therefore most workers do not have the opportunity for any employer-based preretirement counseling.

The most basic and most frequently provided preretirement planning service is making available financial information on pensions, Social Security, profit sharing and other retirement income sources. This appears to be the only type of assistance in more than half of all firms with retirement planning programs. Information about health, life and disability insurance benefits is also often provided by firms having programs. Other forms of assistance, including information on health maintenance, housing, legal matters, second careers, leisure time, psychological adjustment, etc., are provided by no more than 20 percent of organizations having programs. Personal counseling on financial and/or other issues is provided by a very small number of organizations and is not typical.

It is important to note that today, between 15 percent and 20 percent of organizations are providing various forms of gradual retirement and/or extended leaves, vacations or sabbaticals prior to retirement. This is a distinct change from the 1970s when such programs were very unusual. Another recent development is tuition and/or education assistance, also provided by about one-fifth of organizations. Finally, nearly half of all organizations now have policies that permit employees to continue to work beyond the "normal" retirement age with various arrangements for deferring or receiving private pension benefits.

Program designs in retirement preparation are of two major types: *individual interviews* (usually to provide financial information) and *group sessions* covering major topics such as pensions and Social Security, health, housing, insurance, life planning, etc. Some individual counseling is often provided when group sessions are used. Frequently, printed materials on various topics, often purchased from private or nonprofit vendors, are provided to employees attending group sessions. Some organizations also provide their own printed information with specific reference to policies and procedures of the employer. Although some organizations purchase their entire retirement planning program from private vendors or consultants, most design and implement such programs using in-house staff. Thus, many programs are specifically designed to reflect the needs of each organization's employees. Most programs are offered one to five years before retirement and there is a trend toward earlier provision of preretirement planning. This undoubtedly is a response to the continuing early retirement pattern.

A very large number of organizations provide various types of post-retirement assistance to former employees, including employee benefit eligibility (life, health insurance), employee discounts, retiree clubs and retiree employment programs.

Despite the growth of traditional retirement preparation programs, only a small percentage of U.S. employees have access to them; thus the extent to which programs are effective in promoting practical planning by employee participants is difficult to evaluate. Nevertheless, while program growth has been slow, once implemented, programs are usually retained and enhanced due to employee demand. Other than technological innovations such as programs using audio and video taping, computer-assisted financial planning and the very recent development of several life planning programs, the structure and content of retirement planning has remained much the same for many years.

However, current changes in the economy coupled with changing work patterns and preferences and the aging work force require the introduction of additional foci within retirement preparation programs and more dynamic and integrated presentation formats. In other words, retirement planning must be redefined and restructured to address the entire middle-to-later work life. Such a redefinition represents a major change and a challenge to human resource professionals within organizations and retirement planners who serve as consultants and/or vendors of proprietary products.

RETIREMENT PLANNING REDEFINED

The early retirement trend will continue in the future but will be accompanied by changing preferences for middle- to late-life career changes, post-retirement employment, later life education and training and desire for more flexible work schedules and job assignments. The restructuring of U.S. production and service industries will continue, as will accompanying personnel dislocations affecting many older employees.

Because of their relatively limited focus and late presentation, most existing retirement preparation programs do not address these developing work life patterns and preferences. Therefore, while the market for retirement planning services will be expanding, new types of programs must be introduced to meet the needs of corporate human resource planners and their older work forces. First, employment and retirement must come to be viewed as a process rather than as discontinuous events, a more developmental and career-like planning point of view must be adopted that recognizes the likelihood of multiple careers, job changes, flexible work patterns and possible late life employment. Employees must be encouraged to think about their middle-to-later work life in a dynamic framework which may lead to an active rather than passive retirement. Planning for this period must begin far earlier than a few years before retirement and must emphasize various employment, training and retirement options that should be considered by each individual. This human resource development framework involves taking an age-neutral view of employee performance, productivity and utilization. It also implies the need for different management policies and programs in assisting the older work force as it approaches and enters retirement.

Adopting a human resource development approach means that retirement planning is no longer focused solely on the years just before retirement nor directed mainly towards the goal of maintaining activities completely outside of the regular economic mainstream. Instead of advice on adjustment to a life of leisure, a life planning perspective would emphasize preparing for career change, education and alternative work options possible during the middle-to-later years of life. Financial, living-arrangement, self development, family and other forms of planning would be introduced relatively early during an employee's tenure with the organization and developed constructively as individuals approached retirement. Employees could enter the planning program at any time and receive education appropriate to their particular concerns and work life stage. What we now know as preretirement planning would still take place but would be more thoroughly integrated into the broader type of developmental planning just described. Retirement planning would in effect be incorporated within career life planning and therefore would be viewed in a larger, more comprehensive and more relevant context.

Not all retirement planning professionals or corporate retirement specialists are prepared to endorse or support this view of the retirement planning function. However, changes in economic and work life patterns are underway and will result in increasing demands on human resource professionals to provide policies to accommodate the needs of organizations and their older work forces. Retirement planners will be challenged no less than other professionals to develop practical programs to advise employees about their options. The retirement planning professional will therefore be required to develop new knowledge about managing the aging work force in order to be effective in the changing organizational environment.

KNOWLEDGE FOR THE FUTURE RETIREMENT PLANNER

The future retirement planner could be called upon to provide assistance to management in developing policies and programs for the older work force. The extent to which such assistance can be provided will depend on the planner's familiarity with work force planning, work options and employee benefit policies and their application to specific firms' circumstances. Work force planning involves such areas as manpower analysis, recruitment and staffing, career planning, retirement preparation and strategic manpower utilization. Work option policies include scheduling options, phased retirement approaches, part-time employment, job redesign and reassignment, second careers, post-retirement employment and outplacement programs. Employee benefit policies include flexible benefit packages, pension plan options, supplemental insurance, post-retirement benefits and financial planning. Retirement planners will not necessarily be responsible for defining and implementing most of these policies in an organization. However, their effectiveness in assisting both the organization and its employees will be significantly enhanced if they understand the linkages between these policy areas and successfully communicate policies to employees. For this reason, the future retirement planning professional may well have a background as a human resource generalist who has the capability to influence the development of organizational policies and interpret these policies for aging work forces that have far more options than in the past.

REFERENCES

1. Malcolm H. Morrison, "The aging of the U.S. population: Human resource implications." *Monthly Labor Review*, May 1983.

2. Susan R. Rhodes, Michael Schuster and Mildred Doering, "The implications of an aging work force." *Personnel Administrator*, October 1981.

3. Nicholas J. Beutell, "Managing the older worker." *Personnel Administrator*, August, 1983.

4. Malcolm H. Morrison, "Aging and the work force: Focusing on the realities." *Aging and Work*, V. 6., No. 1, 1983.

5. James F. Walker and Harriet Lazer, *The End of Mandatory Retirement*. John Wiley and Sons, 1978.

6. Monte B. Lake, ed. *Age Discrimination in Employment Act, A Compliance Manual for Lawyers and Personnel Practitioners*. Equal Employment Advisory Council, Washington, DC. 1982.

7. Lawrence Olson, *The Elderly and the Future Economy*. Lexington Books, 1981.

8. U.S. Bureau of the Census, True Level Population Projections, 1977.

9. Howard N. Fullerton, Jr. "The 1995 labor force: A first look." *Monthly Labor Review*, December 1980.

10. U.S. Senate Special Committee on Aging. "Emerging Options for Work and Retirement Policy, An Information Paper." June 1980.

11. Malcolm H. Morrison, ed. *Economics of Aging: The Future of Retirement*. Van Nostrand Reinhold, 1982.

12. J. Roger O'Meara, "Retirement: Reward or rejection?" The Conference Board, 1977.

13. Survey of the Transition to Retirement and Older Worker Work Options, Bureau of Social Science Research, Inc., Washington, DC. 1984.

Index